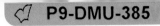
The Good Hotel Guide 2016

GREAT BRITAIN & IRELAND

Editors:
Desmond Balmer
Adam Raphael
Nicola Davies

Editor in chief:
Caroline Raphael

THE GOOD HOTEL GUIDE LTD

The Good Hotel Guide Ltd

This edition first published in 2015 by
The Good Hotel Guide Ltd

Copyright © 2015 Adam and Caroline Raphael
Maps © 2015 David Perrott

Chief executive: Richard Fraiman

Contributing editors:
M. Astella Saw
Emma Grundy Haigh
Rose Shepherd
Claire Baranowski
Kathryn Hearn

Production: Hugh Allan
Managing editor: Alison Wormleighton
Designer: Lizzy Laczynska
Text editor: Daphne Trotter
Computer consultant: Vince Nacey
Website design: HeadChannel
Researcher: Cristina Recio-Corral

A CIP catalogue record for this book may be found in the British Library.

ISBN 978 0 9932484 0 5

Cover photograph: Glenfinnan House, Glenfinnan

Printed and bound in Spain by Graphy Cems

*'A good hotel is where
the guest comes first'*

Hilary Rubinstein, founding editor
(1926–2012)

Hotel Endsleigh, Milton Abbot

CONTENTS

CONTENTS

INTRODUCTION

It might seem old-fashioned to publish a print edition of the Good Hotel Guide when our website has an international flavour with an ever-expanding selection of hotels in Europe, North America and the Caribbean. But the Great Britain and Ireland print edition remains the foundation on which our multi-media activity is based. This is our unbiased choice of the best hotels, inns and B&Bs with personality and character. Hotels do not pay to be included, nor do they provide hospitality to Guide inspectors, who pay their way and remain anonymous throughout their visit. This allows us to make our judgments without fear or favour.

The Good Hotel Guide was founded as a crusade on behalf of the small independent hotel; from the first edition in 1978, readers have played a crucial role by sharing their hotel experiences and discoveries. The editors rely on reports from readers and inspectors to select and update the descriptions of the 419 main entries in the Guide and the 429 hotels on the Shortlist. Unlike many review websites, we filter out both collusive praise and malicious complaints.

The Good Hotel Guide website carries the entries for most, but not all, of our selected hotels. Our UK and Ireland hotels are asked to make a modest payment if they wish their entry to appear on the website in order to recoup our production costs. If they choose not to pay, their listing remains, but without the detail or photographs.

Our internet appeal is growing. As we went to press, visitors to the GHG website were up 25% in the past year. Our Twitter followers now number close to 5,000 (up 260% compared with the previous year) and Facebook fans are up 83%. We have also written numerous articles about our selected hotels on prominent digital third-party sites like MSN.com, CNTraveler, and Huffington Post. We continue to see increasing downloads of our GHG smart phone app (available for iPhone, Android and Windows phones). We are also increasing our selection of European hotels on the website. There are now nearly 200 selected GHG hotels in Europe and around the world.

Desmond Balmer and Adam Raphael
July 2015

CÉSARS 2016

We give our César awards to the ten best hotels of the year. Named after César Ritz, the most celebrated of hoteliers, these are the Oscars of hotel-keeping.

🏆 LONDON HOTEL OF THE YEAR
Artist Residence, Pimlico
Young hoteliers Justin Salisbury and Charlotte Newey have brought their quirky style to the capital in this stylish renovation of a former pub in Pimlico. It is staffed by young hosts who are cheerful and helpful in equal measure.

🏆 COUNTRY HOUSE HOTEL OF THE YEAR
Hotel Endsleigh, Milton Abbot
In a beautiful estate on the bank of the River Tamar, this former hunting lodge has been restored with charm and taste by Olga Polizzi. Managed by Adam Cornish, it is a glorious place, run with a generous spirit.

🏆 INN OF THE YEAR
The Lord Crewe Arms, Blanchland
The Calcot Hotels group has modernised this old inn in the North Pennine moors retaining the character of its 900-year-old history. By employing local staff, they have rooted it firmly in the area; the accent and the friendly mood are very much of the north-east.

🏆 NEWCOMER OF THE YEAR
The Coach House at Middleton Lodge, Richmond
An exciting newcomer in the north, James Allison's restaurant-with-rooms is a sensitive conversion of Georgian buildings on a large estate near Scotch Corner. In the restaurant, chef Gareth Rayner produces fine and interesting dishes.

🏆 WALKING HOTEL OF THE YEAR
Hazel Bank, Rosthwaite
The MacRae family have created a welcoming, relaxed atmosphere at their charming stone house in the beautiful Borrowdale valley. They earn an extra tick for effort at every stage as they continue to make improvements.

❧ ECCENTRIC HOTEL OF THE YEAR
Zanzibar International Hotel, St Leonards-on-Sea
With its exotic name, themed bedrooms and showers
that talk, Max O'Rourke's laid-back hotel has a
splendidly quirky feel and an informal charm.
Delicious, unpretentious meals are served in
Pier Nine restaurant.

❧ FAMILY HOTEL OF THE YEAR
Augill Castle, Kirkby Stephen
Boredom is never a danger for any age group at Wendy
and Simon Bennett's turreted castle in the Eden valley.
Children and adults alike are kept occupied by the
many activities within the castle and the estate.

❧ ROMANTIC HOTEL OF THE YEAR
The Pig on the Beach, Studland
Above Studland Bay, this 18th-century Gothic building,
with turrets, mullioned windows and multiple roof
levels, was a perfect match for the newest addition to
Robin Hutson's litter of Pig hotels. The quirky, shabby-
chic style creates an informal atmosphere.

❧ SCOTTISH HOTEL OF THE YEAR
Kilmichael Country House, Brodick
Excellent service is given in personal style by Geoffrey
Botterill and Antony Butterworth at their period
mansion on the largest island on the Firth of Clyde.
They have created the feel of a private home; meals are
first class and interesting.

❧ WELSH HOTEL OF THE YEAR
The Grove, Narberth
In landscaped grounds facing the Preseli hills, this
striking 18th-century mansion is run as a relaxed small
hotel by Neil Kedward and Zoë Agar. The service is
warm and generous.

REPORT OF THE YEAR COMPETITION

Readers' contributions are the lifeblood of the Good Hotel Guide. Everyone who writes to us is a potential winner of the Report of the Year competition. Each year a dozen correspondents are singled out for the helpfulness of their reports. They win a copy of the Good Hotel Guide and an invitation to our annual launch party in October. This year's winners are:

ROWENA MOORE of Ashurst Wood
IAN MARSHALL of Bournemouth
ANTHONY BRADBURY of Buckhurst Hill
PETER GOVIER of Christchurch
DAVID GRANT of Greenwich
TONY & VIRGINIA AYERS of Hungerford
PHILIP WARLAND of London
DR MIKE CRADDOCK of Painswick
TOM LOMBARDO of Seattle
ROBERT SANGER of Truro
MARY COLES of Wellington
DOROTHY BRINING of West Kirby

JOIN THE GOOD HOTEL GUIDE READERS' CLUB

Send us a review of your favourite hotel.
As a member of the club, you will be entitled to:
1. A pre-publication discount offer
2. Personal advice on hotels
3. Advice if you are in dispute with a hotel
4. Monthly emailed Guide newsletter

The writers of the 12 best reviews will each win a free copy of the Guide and an invitation to our launch party. And the winner of our monthly web competition will win a free night, dinner and breakfast for two at one of the Guide's top hotels.

Send your review via:
our website: www.goodhotelguide.com
or email: editor@goodhotelguide.com
or fax: 020 7602 4182
or write to:

In the UK
Good Hotel Guide
Freepost PAM 2931
London W11 4BR
(no stamp needed)

From abroad
Good Hotel Guide
50 Addison Avenue
London W11 4QP
England

EDITOR'S CHOICE

A visit to a hotel should be a special occasion.
Here are some of our favourite hotels in
various categories. Turn to the full entry
for the bigger picture.

NEWBEGIN HOUSE
BEVERLEY

In a 'fine' East Riding market town this 'unusually large' Georgian house with a walled garden is the home of Walter and Nuala Sweeney and three generations of their family. The three spacious bedrooms, in one part of the building, have 'a very comfortable bed, good lighting enabling easy reading; lots of space for clothes and luggage'. An 'excellent' breakfast has a wide choice. Read more, page 97.

THE SEASIDE BOARDING HOUSE
BURTON BRADSTOCK

A former B&B on a cliff above Chesil Bay has been transformed into a sophisticated restaurant-with-rooms by Mary-Lou Sturridge and Anthony Mackintosh, formerly of the Groucho Club, London. 'Everything has been done in good taste'; the bedrooms are elegant; dinner, taken in a dining room facing the sea, is unfussy and delicious. It is 'laid-back and friendly; everyone is very obliging'.
Read more, page 127.

ECKINGTON MANOR
ECKINGTON

At once a hotel, a cookery school and a popular restaurant. these converted buildings on a working farm have a tranquil, rural setting. The striking bedrooms are in a former milking parlour and cider mill, and the 17th-century Lower End House, where the 'stylish' lounge has an honesty bar. 'Delicious' modern dishes are served in the popular restaurant.
Read more, page 155.

THE CARPENTERS ARMS
FELIXKIRK

In a Domesday village near Thirsk, this pub-with-rooms has striking bedrooms in a new block built around a kitchen garden. These are 'stunning and well thought out'; light streams through large windows. Good bistro-style dishes are served in the two dining areas of the main building: 'the cooking highlighted the freshest of ingredients.'
Read more, page 162.

OLD DOWNTON LODGE
LUDLOW

A cluster of old stone and brick farm buildings (pictured) near Ludlow

has been remodelled into a stylish restaurant-with-rooms by Willem and Pippa Vlok. Ranged around formal parterre gardens, the bedrooms are decorated in an understated style that is rustic and calm. There are quality fittings, interesting lamps. Chef Karl Martin's delicate dishes with 'wonderful' flavours are served in the dining room, which dates to Norman times.
Read more, page 208.

THE BARN AT ROUNDHURST
LURGASHALL
On a 'neat and tidy' organic farm within the South Downs national park, Moya and Richard Connell's 'delightful, friendly' B&B has a 'very impressive' renovated 17th-century threshing barn, 'an enormous, soaring space' with a lounge (modern art, magazines, 'plenty of comfortable seating') and an eating area (a four-course dinner is served here three nights a week). Rustic bedrooms are in converted stables. Breakfast is 'perfect'.
Read more, page 209.

SANDS HOTEL
MARGATE
Yards from the Turner Contemporary gallery on the sea front, this Victorian hotel has been smartly renovated. Some sea-facing bedrooms have a balcony; other rooms face the old town. The focal point is the glass-fronted Bay restaurant where modern dishes are presented. Alfresco meals may be taken on the 'spacious' balcony overlooking Margate Sands. Don't overlook Melt, a gelato bar, which has milkshakes, sundaes and ice cream sodas.
Read more, page 213.

ST MARY'S INN
MORPETH
A 'clever' renovation of the administration building of a disused Victorian hospital has created 'a new type of place to stay and eat'. A modern glass porch and bar 'belie a traditional pub interior; mismatched chairs and tables in booths and separate rooms, some with a wood-burning stove'. Classic pub grub and local specialities with a modern twist are on the menu in the busy dining areas, where service is 'swift and knowledgeable'.
Read more, page 222.

KNOCKENDARROCH HOUSE HOTEL
PITLOCHRY
A 'feeling of friendliness' is found at this small hotel, a Victorian stone mansion with a baronial entrance tower with 'beautiful views across the Tummel valley'. It has been renovated throughout by experienced hoteliers Struan and Louise Lothian, who have created 'a lovely place to stay'. Original Scottish contemporary art is hung throughout. The bedrooms are decorated in 'fresh and tasteful' colours.
Read more, page 378.

THE BRIDGE INN AT RATHO
RATHO
By a bridge over the Union Canal in a village near Edinburgh, this 'lively' restaurant and pub-with-rooms has 'an informal atmosphere'. The 'smart' ground floor has a busy bar on one side; on the other, a bar-cum-parlour. The cooking in a light-filled dining room is imaginative. Breakfast is 'very good; enormous, with two of everything'.
Read more, page 384.

THE PORTOBELLO
LONDON

A discreet hideaway on an elegant street in Notting Hill, this small, quirky hotel has been refreshed by new owners, the small Curious Group of Hotels. They have retained the eccentric features of many of the themed rooms which were much loved by an earlier generation of rock 'n' roll celebrities. You could try the room once favoured by Johnny Depp and Kate Moss which has a Victorian bathing machine and a gilded ceiling.

Read more, page 60.

BURGH ISLAND HOTEL
BIGBURY-ON-SEA

Cut off from the rest of the world at the whim of the tides (it is set on a tidal island at the end of Bigbury beach), this 1930s hotel was once a hideaway for Wallis Simpson and Edward Windsor. It has been restored to its 1930s splendour and remains a 'romantic, delightful' place to stay, with Art Deco decor, a luxury spa, and black tie at dinner.

Read more, page 98.

THE OLD RECTORY
BOSCASTLE

Surrounded by 'the most beautiful and romantic gardens', this tranquil B&B can be found in the winding country lanes of north Cornwall. The 'comfortable, private' bedrooms are named after the blossoming romance between poet Thomas Hardy and his future wife, Emma, for which this Victorian house was the backdrop. With strong green credentials, this is the ideal destination for eco-conscious romancers. Butterflies linger in the cloistered walks and hidden corners of the garden.

Read more, page 104.

LINTHWAITE HOUSE
BOWNESS-ON-WINDERMERE

Sleep under the stars in the loft suite at this creeper-clad hotel overlooking Lake Windermere. A sliding glass panel in the ceiling opens up to allow star-gazing; a telescope is provided. It has its own entrance, an open-plan design; the highlight is the bathroom which has a huge free-standing Italian bath.

Read more, page 108.

TOR COTTAGE
CHILLATON
There are streamside hammocks and a gypsy caravan to hide in at this rustic B&B surrounded by woodland. Romantic retreats begin with the trug containing sparkling wine, home-made truffles and fresh flowers awaiting guests in the bedrooms. The rooms are situated in converted outbuildings, each with its own wood-burner and private garden. Guests might take advantage of the heated outdoor swimming pool for a moonlit swim.
Read more, page 135.

THE OLD RAILWAY STATION
PETWORTH
Eccentric and intimate in equal measure, this B&B on a disused railway recalls the romance of a bygone era. The elegant Edwardian-style bedrooms, with brass fittings and glossy mahogany panelling, occupy four restored Pullman carriages, which sit outside the renovated Victorian station house where there are two other, larger rooms. Breakfast can be taken in the colonial waiting room or in the carriage.
Read more, page 252.

DRIFTWOOD
PORTHSCATHO
The sea seems to stretch out for ever on the approach to this luxury hotel overlooking Gerrans Bay. It is 'a charming place in a charming situation'. There are secrets waiting to be found in the landscaped gardens where seating is hidden in nooks and behind hedges. You can walk down the path to the private sandy beach. The atmosphere is 'relaxed, calm'.
Read more, page 256.

GILPIN HOTEL AND LAKE HOUSE
WINDERMERE
For seclusion, head for the six-room luxury Lake House in the wooded grounds of this luxury hotel in the Lake District. There are rowing boats for guests to drift into the middle of the private lake (picnics can be arranged), should an alternative be needed to the temptations of the spa (a hot tub, sauna and swimming pool). A chauffeur transports guests up to the main hotel for candlelit dinners.
Read more, page 324.

ARDANAISEIG
KILCHRENAN
Possibly the 'most peaceful hotel in Britain', this late Georgian baronial mansion lies in wooded grounds down more than ten miles of winding track. Guests seeking romance need look no further than the split-level converted Boat Shed on the shore of Loch Awe. It has its own boat, allowing couples to explore the tiny islands on the loch.
Read more, page 364.

MOOR OF RANNOCH HOTEL
RANNOCH STATION
For lovers of the great outdoors, this renovated 19th-century hotel will appeal. Close to a station on the West Highland line, it stands on the edge of the moor, one of Europe's last wildernesses. A full breakfast awaits guests who arrive on the overnight sleeper. This is truly away from it all; there is no phone signal or Wi-Fi reception. Not a spa-pampered romance, perhaps, but an away-from-it-all place for those who find their romance in the hills and glens.
Read more, page 383.

HARTWELL HOUSE
AYLESBURY

In the grounds of a hotel in a National Trust stately home, this luxury spa (modelled on an orangery) has a pool lined with blue mosaic tiles, with poolside loungers, plants and statuary. There is a steam room, saunas, spa bath, a hot tub on a sun terrace, and a well-equipped gym.
Read more, page 82.

BARNSLEY HOUSE
BARNSLEY

Plants and natural materials such as Cotswold stone and wooden beams have been used to harmonise the inside of this secluded spa with the surrounding hotel gardens. The softly lit lounge has floor-to-ceiling windows overlooking the heated hydrotherapy pool. In the treatment rooms you can choose music to help you to relax, as you opt for 'Calm Your Mind', perhaps, or 'Inner Strength'.
Read more, page 84.

PARK HOUSE
BEPTON

You pass through a marble shower to immerse yourself in the 15-metre mother-of-pearl indoor pool at the spa of this tranquil country house hotel. There's a swimming lane, four treatment rooms (one a double) and saunas. In summer you have the use of a heated outdoor pool, with loungers on the sun terrace. In the gym and fitness studio a personal trainer will step up on request.
Read more, page 96.

DORMY HOUSE
BROADWAY

'Time to switch off your mobile and come to your senses' reads a sign at this innovative spa. You might choose a lavender-infusion in the thermal suite, the dry heat of the Hot Juniper Finnish cabin – or swelter in the salt steam room before a drench shower and the 'Ice Experience'. There is an infinity pool (pictured) , terrace with hydro pool, double treatment room and mud room, gym and personal-trainer studio, and a lounge.
Read more, page 117.

LIME WOOD
LYNDHURST

From yoga in a rooftop herb garden to a sauna with views of the New

Forest, from a Technogym work-out to Ayurvedic therapies and Bamford massage, the stylish, state-of-the-art Herb House has everything to help you to wind down or to limber up. Two double treatment rooms for couples each have a steam room and private bath – one of them alfresco.

Read more, page 211.

THE SCARLET
MAWGAN PORTH

Overlooking the beach, the spa at this adults-only eco-hotel is a place of escape, with lantern-lit, tented treatment rooms, a cliff-top hot tub and a chemical-free pool filtered by reeds. The emphasis is on holistic well-being, with a meditation room, a hammam for scrubs and wraps, a couple suite with double bath, and rhassoul for a slathering of mineral mud. Should you wish just to cocoon, you can simply curl up in a hanging canvas pod.

Read more, page 217.

CHEWTON GLEN
NEW MILTON

The spa at this luxury hotel has a 17-metre, ozone-treated swimming pool, overlooked by the Pool Bar, where a daily buffet is served, based on an alakaline diet. There is a hydrotherapy pool, male and female aromatherapy saunas, a crystal steam room, cold drench showers, an outdoor whirlpool, a grooming lounge, a dance studio and treatment rooms.

Read more, page 229.

SEAHAM HALL
SEAHAM

An underground walkway leads from the hotel to the Serenity Spa, designed on the principles of feng shui. There is a 20-metre swimming pool with massage stations in the daylight-filled pool room which has floor-to-ceiling windows, a hammam with snail showers and a spa bath, a hydrotherapy pool, a sauna, a samarium with crystal light therapy, outdoor hot tubs, a fitness suite, plunge pools, a fully equipped gym and a roof terrace.

Read more, page 279.

CALCOT MANOR
TETBURY

In the grounds of this Cotswold hotel, the spa occupies converted stone outbuildings, around an open-air hot tub, in a space fragrant with lavender and smoke from an open log fire. Inside, soft lighting creates a relaxed mood. The seven treatment rooms are individually styled. There is a 16-metre indoor pool, steam room, sauna and high-tech gym. A healthy lunch menu is available.

Read more, page 302.

THE LAKE
LLANGAMMARCH WELLS

Visitors (among them Kaiser Wilhelm II) once came from afar to drink the waters of a barium spring in the Pump Room in the gardens of this lakeside hotel. Today the attractions at the Kingfisher Spa, a short stroll from the main building, include an outdoor tub on a balcony overlooking the lake, a 15-metre indoor pool and a fully equipped gym. In four treatment rooms therapists offer a range of health and beauty treatments.

Read more, page 423.

THE CARY ARMS
BABBACOMBE
Hiding in a 'fabulously secluded cove' near Torquay, Peter and Lana de Savary's small nautical hotel has sea views from every bedroom; some have a balcony with table and chairs. There are stripy deckchairs on the sea-facing terrace; dolphins can be watched from the lounge. Seafood is a speciality in the kitchen; meals are served in the conservatory, in the bar (with the feel of a 'fishermen's pub') or on the terrace. Read more, page 83.

THE HENLEY
BIGBURY-ON-SEA
On the tidal Avon estuary, Martyn Scarterfield's unpretentious Edwardian villa is liked for its 'relaxing and comfortable' environment, 'friendly and excellent' service and 'fabulous and inspiring' coastline. The bedrooms, furnished in a simple country style, have a sea view (binoculars are provided). A steep private path leads through the garden and down to the beach. Read more, page 99.

THE WHITE HORSE
BRANCASTER STAITHE
Above the tidal marshes and sandy beaches of north Norfolk, Cliff Nye's small hotel has appropriate nautical furnishings and seaside colours. One bedroom has a viewing terrace and telescope. Walkers and dog owners will appreciate the path at the bottom of the garden which leads straight out on to the coastal countryside. Chef Fran Hartshorne's 'very good' daily-changing menu focuses on fish and shellfish supplied by local fishermen. Read more, page 112.

HELL BAY HOTEL
BRYHER
On a rugged island in the Scilly archipelago, this seaside hotel (owned by Tresco Estates) overlooks the Atlantic Ocean. It is accessible only by boat from the larger islands. A 'wonderful collection' of Cornish artworks occupies the lofty lounge. Individually decorated in a discreet maritime style, most of the bedrooms face the sea; the best have direct access to garden and beach. A rustic crab shack operates in summer months. Read more, page 121.

THE BEACH
BUDE

In a fine position above Summerleaze beach, Susie and Will Daniel's contemporary hotel makes the most of its position. A terrace has lovely views over the sheltered beach, popular with families and surfers alike. In warm weather, cocktails and light meals can be taken here. The best rooms have a private terrace or a Juliet balcony facing the sea. The beach has a seawater swimming pool set in the rocks.
Read more, page 123.

ROMNEY BAY HOUSE
NEW ROMNEY

On a private road between a golf course and the beach on the Kent coast, Clinton and Lisa Lovell's 1920s house was designed by Sir Clough Williams-Ellis for American actress Hedda Hopper. In the 'light, bright' upstairs lounge, you can spot France on a clear day with the help of the telescope provided.
Read more, page 230.

SOAR MILL COVE HOTEL
SOAR MILL COVE

Family-run and child-friendly, Keith Makepeace's 'welcoming' hotel stands on the Devon hillside above its own sandy beach, with 'stunning' views of the coast (pictured). Many of the well-appointed bedrooms look out on to the sea; all have a private patio. An on-site spa includes a heated saltwater spring-fed swimming pool. Sailing and surfing expeditions can be arranged.
Read more, page 283.

DUNVALANREE IN CARRADALE
CARRADALE

Looking out from the Mull of Kintyre across Kilbrannan Sound to the Isle of Arran, Alan and Alyson Milstead's small hotel is flanked by two beaches. The bedrooms are individually decorated; binoculars are available. The food is 'a highlight'. Chef Alyson Milstead is a founder member of the Scottish Seafood Trail; guests can expect much freshly caught seafood and local produce, served in a dining room overlooking the sea.
Read more, page 345.

THE COLONSAY
COLONSAY

On a hillside above the harbour of 'the Jewel of the Hebrides', Jane and Alex Howard's renovated 18th-century inn overlooks the sea to neighbouring Jura. Rooms are 'warm' and 'simply furnished'. The hotel's kitchen garden and oyster farm supply chef David Kinnear's 'relaxed and unpretentious' menu. With over a dozen beaches, the island is ideal terrain for coasteers, birders and anyone with a fondness for seals and otters.
Read more, page 347.

THE WHITE HOUSE
HERM

This is the only hotel on the privately owned, car-free island. Radios are barred from its beaches. Tranquillity also reigns in the hotel – no clock, television or telephone in the bedrooms; no background music. On the approach by boat, visitors see a long stretch of sand that unfolds into three beaches – Bear's, Fisherman's and Harbour. Over the hill is Shell Beach, rich in colour from tiny shells.
Read more, page 440.

FISCHER'S AT BASLOW HALL
BASLOW

Max and Susan Fischer are the welcoming owners of this Peak District Edwardian manor house. Chef Rupert Rowley serves a menu based on local, home-grown and foraged ingredients. His dishes, which have a modern twist on classic favourites, might include pan-fried brill, roast salsify, sea herbs, champagne and oyster sauce; dry-aged sirloin and smoked short rib Derbyshire beef, grilled asparagus, onion purée. There is a tasting bench in the kitchen for four diners to watch the brigade at work.
Read more, page 87.

READ'S
FAVERSHAM

Dinner in the elegant dining room at Rona and David Pitchford's Georgian manor house restaurant-with-rooms is served up with a quotation for each dish on the menu. His seasonal menu might include pan-fried halibut, crushed new potatoes, cep purée, champagne and chive velouté, accompanied by a quote from AA Milne: 'How long does taking thin get, asked Pooh anxiously.'
Read more, page 161.

MR UNDERHILL'S
LUDLOW

Self-taught chef Chris Bradley serves an 'inventive' eight-course, daily-changing 'market menu' at this riverside restaurant-with-rooms below the castle. Praise came this year for 'a delicious almond velouté, outstanding duck-liver custard, wonderfully tender venison accompanied by braised venison cannelloni, rhubarb tart with olive-scented ice cream'.
Read more, page 207.

MORSTON HALL
MORSTON

It was at the urging of Delia Smith that Tracy and Galton Blackiston opened their restaurant-with-rooms in a 17th-century farmhouse in this coastal village. Guests gather at 7.30 pm for aperitifs before a seven-course dinner from a daily-changing menu. The dishes might include Stilton beignets with grape jelly; slow-braised pork belly, apple soup, garlic purée.
Read more, page 223.

THE YORKE ARMS
RAMSGILL-IN-NIDDERDALE

Frances Atkins has many fans for the 'divine' food she cooks at this restaurant-with-rooms in an 18th-century coaching house in the Dales. Husband Bill is the 'friendly' host front-of-house. The dining room (pictured) is rich with dark wood, and has a huge dresser. There is praise for the 'imaginative combination of ingredients' and 'exquisite flavours'. Marinated smoked duck and hazelnut was 'faultless', slow-cooked loin of hare 'fabulous', puddings 'outstanding'. Read more, page 258.

THE ALBANNACH
LOCHINVER

Lesley Crosfield and Colin Craig run their restaurant-with-rooms in a walled garden above the harbour, where wild sea fish and shellfish are landed daily. Their five-course, daily-changing, set menu has seasonal dishes like mousseline of wild halibut, lobster sauce, langoustine, lobster; roast saddle of wild roe deer, candy beetroot, truffled squash, potato galette, croft baby turnip, game port sauce. Read more, page 371.

YNYSHIR HALL
EGLWYSFACH

This former country house retreat for Queen Victoria is run by two hospitable couples, with the aid of 'welcoming' staff. Chef Gareth Ward (former sous-chef at the lauded Sat Bains, Nottingham), is winning plaudits for his 'superlative' modern cooking. His speciality multi-course tasting menus deliver 'wonderful bursts of flavour', with such dishes as duck liver, cox apple, smoked eel, spelt; Jerusalem artichoke, partridge, celeriac. Read more, page 411.

TYDDYN LLAN
LLANDRILLO

Bryan and Susan Webb's 'truly lovely' restaurant-with-rooms, a former shooting lodge, maintains its 'very high standard' of welcome and comfort. Bryan Webb makes the best of seasonal ingredients for his 'imaginative' cooking. For example, Cefnllan Farm duck breast, confit potato, cider, apples; roast turbot, leek risotto, red wine sauce. Read more, page 420.

PLAS BODEGROES
PWLLHELI

In a Georgian house on the remote Lleyn peninsula, Chris and Gunna Chown's restaurant-with-rooms is liked for the 'warmth of the welcome, and the relaxing ambience'. In the dining room, Chris Chown and Hugh Bracegirdle, the chefs, prepare modern interpretations of traditional dishes, perhaps smoked salmon and halibut terrazo, wood sorrel, horseradish cream; roast loin of Welsh mountain lamb, devilled kidneys, onion cake, rosemary sauce. Read more, page 432.

THE WHITEBROOK
WHITEBROOK

In the wooded Wye valley, this 17th-century drovers' inn has been 'rethought, refreshed and redecorated' by the owner/chef, Chris Harrod. He pursues his love of foraging for the ingredients for his 'very special' modern cooking. 'He makes it all taste so fresh and different,' say visitors. This might mean an 'amazing' parsnip croquette with salsify, beer onion and charlock; wild sea bass, rainbow chard, wood blewit, foraged fennel. Read more, page 437.

BLAGDON MANOR
ASHWATER

A welcome is assured from Cassia, Mace and Saffron, chocolate Labradors, at this restaurant-with-rooms close to Dartmoor. (Owners Liz and Steve Morey are hospitable, too.) For £10 a night, your dog gets a fleece blanket, a bowl and treats. Short and long leads, please, in the three acres of gardens in a 20-acre estate.
Read more, page 78.

THE TRADDOCK
AUSTWICK

Dogs with impeccable manners (no bouncing on furniture) can stay here for £5 per dog/night (maximum two dogs in a room), join owners in lounges and bar if kept on a lead, and romp in the gardens. There's a waste bin, poop bags on request, and a hose and towel for a freshen-up. You can embark on the Wainwright walk to Crummackdale from the door.
Read more, page 81.

THE CARY ARMS
BABBACOMBE

'We want our guests to experience the very best during their stay – including your four-legged friends,' say Peter and Lana de Savary, whose secluded hotel has two dog-friendly ground-floor rooms (£20 per dog/night). A welcome pack includes bed, bowl, treats and a book of local walks. Canine connoisseurs can lap up a 'dog's dinner' in the bar after a swim in the sea.
Read more, page 83.

OVERWATER HALL
IREBY

Dogs on leads are 'genuinely welcomed', at no extra charge, in one lounge, the bar and the bedrooms at this Georgian mansion set in 18 acres amid wonderful walking country. 'Not on the chairs, please,' say the owners, who provide a pet-sitting service for days when it's raining cats and dogs and a visit to a museum or gallery is preferable to a Lakeland hike.
Read more, page 187.

CROWN AND CASTLE
ORFORD

Dogs can stay in the five garden rooms at this characterful hotel in a Suffolk coastal village (£6 per dog/night). Co-proprietor and chef Ruth Watson pens welcome notes to four-legged guests, bakes them organic cheese biscuits, and can provide bowls, poop bags, leads, towels and a protective bed cover. There is a bookable doggie table in the restaurant area. No puppies under five months, 'however cute'.
Read more, page 245.

PLUMBER MANOR
STURMINSTER NEWTON

'It is easy to take your dog for a quick walk whenever necessary,' say the Prideaux-Brune family who welcome canines to four courtyard bedrooms at their 17th-century manor house (£10 per visit charge). Dogs are not allowed in the main house, but the courtyard rooms have direct access to the gardens. There are long country walks from the door.
Read more, page 293.

CLIVEDEN
TAPLOW

Your pedigree chum gets the five-star treatment at this stately home in 250 acres of National Trust woodland, with map of walks provided. For £30 a night, dogs aged at least one year are welcome in bedrooms and most public areas. They can eat à la carte from a menu that runs from dry food (£15) to fillet steak and rice with light gravy (£27).
Read more, page 297.

PRINCE HALL
TWO BRIDGES

Dogs arriving at Fi and Chris Daly's small Devon hotel are greeted with treats and have the run of the grounds (one or two dogs stay free; three or more an additional £5 per dog/night). Dog-in-residence Polo has the low-down on great walks and cosy corners for a nap. There's an outside tap for mucky pups, who can join their owners taking a light lunch in one of the lounges.
Read more, page 308.

KILCAMB LODGE
STRONTIAN

'We love our dogs, so let's make them as happy as they make us,' say Sally and David Ruthven-Fox, who lay on bags, treats, towels, toys, mats and bowls for canine guests, and help resident dog Spike with his Facebook page. The four dog-friendly rooms have garden access, with advice on forest and beach walks. No access to main reception areas, but a dog-sitting service is available.
Read more, page 389.

THE FALCONDALE
LAMPETER

There is a big 'croeso' for visiting dogs from residents Pudgeley and Major at Chris and Lisa Hutton's Italianate hotel in 14-acre grounds. For £10 a night they get bowls, treats, blankets, towels, throws, a poop bag and a guidebook to walks in the Cambrian Mountains and around Cardigan Bay. They can even, by arrangement, have breakfast and dinner with their owners in the conservatory.
Read more, page 418.

ROTHAY MANOR
AMBLESIDE

A short walk from Lake Windermere, this Regency mansion (built for a wealthy Liverpool merchant) has been run 'meticulously' by the Nixon family for over 45 years. The spacious bedrooms are 'beautifully furnished'; some have a view to Wansfell Pike. Guests might linger over a 'sparkling afternoon tea' (served with champagne) or explore the landscaped gardens. Chef Jane Binns's seasonal menu is 'dangerous for those of us on a diet'. Read more, page 75.

ASKHAM HALL
ASKHAM

Charlie and Juno Lowther have eschewed tradition to create a 'Bohemian home from home' in this 13th-century, Grade I listed country house, while still retaining its historical charm. With a mix of antique and contemporary modern furnishings, Juno Lowther's original portraits and a kitchen garden café housed in the converted Grade II listed barn, it is a true 'hotel of character'. Read more, page 79.

GRAVETYE MANOR
EAST GRINSTEAD

Surrounded by beautiful countryside, the gardens of Jeremy and Elizabeth Hosking's Elizabethan manor house (pictured) were designed by William Robinson, pioneer of the English natural garden. The Arts and Crafts public rooms have original features and bold floral displays, bringing the garden inside; bedrooms have rich fabrics, hand-crafted beds and modern technology. Read more, page 151.

HAMBLETON HALL
HAMBLETON

'The perfect country house', Tim and Stefa Hart's old-school luxury lakeside hotel has a fascinating history (Noel Coward was once a house guest). Public rooms have 'lush' furnishings, with antiques and spectacular flower arrangements. Bedrooms are 'elegantly arranged'; the best have a 'stunning' view over the meadows and Rutland Water. Michelin-starred chef Aaron Patterson uses chiefly local produce in his 'magnificent' modern cooking. Breakfast has 'divine' bread from Tim Hart's nearby bakery. Read more, page 174.

LIME WOOD
LYNDHURST

A modern take on country house values, this family-friendly Regency manor house hotel in the New Forest (originally a 13th-century hunting lodge) is liked for its relaxed atmosphere. Public rooms are filled with artwork and ceramics. Chefs Angela Hartnett and Luke Holder offer an Italian-infused menu. Wellies can be borrowed for exploring the sheep-smattered orchard in the grounds.
Read more, page 211.

CHEWTON GLEN
NEW MILTON

The 'faultless' service is admired at this 'top drawer' country house hotel and spa on the edge of the New Forest. As well as the luxurious bedrooms in the main house, tree-house suites out in the woods provide a 'luxurious' escape from reality, with wood-burning stoves and 'cosy' blankets. Hampers served through the dumb-waiter hatch mean romancers need never leave the whirlpool tub on the wrap-around terrace.
Read more, page 229.

LORDS OF THE MANOR
UPPER SLAUGHTER

In 'wonderful' gardens on the edge of a Cotswold village, this 'superlative' country house hotel is 'classy without ostentation'. The interiors are 'impeccable'; afternoon tea can be taken in 'grand style' in one of the lounges. In an elegant dining room, Richard Picard-Edwards's Michelin-starred cooking is much admired.
Read more, page 311.

JUDGES
YARM

Visitors to this 'immaculate' Victorian country house, a former residence for judges, enjoy the manicured parkland, the blossoming trees and the scampering squirrels on the lawns. Beyond the grand entrance hall with its coal fires and comfy armchairs, guests will find 'impressively spacious' bedrooms with many nice little touches: a bowl of fruit, a carafe of sherry, home-made biscuits, a resident teddy bear, a goldfish circling its bowl.
Read more, page 330.

GLENAPP CASTLE
BALLANTRAE

Fay and Graham Cowan have restored this 19th-century sandstone castle which they have furnished with fine paintings, Middle Eastern rugs, antiques. The service is 'exemplary', 'no standing on ceremony'. The spacious bedrooms have an open fire; there are wide beds, books, 'everything for your comfort'. In the formal dining room, chef Tyron Ellul looks to local producers to supply his modern British dishes
Read more, page 339.

LLANGOED HALL
LLYSWEN

Standing in large grounds in the 'stunning' Wye valley, this 'splendid' Jacobean mansion was redesigned by Sir Clough Williams-Ellis (of Portmeirion fame) in 1912. Once owned by Sir Bernard Ashley (husband of Laura Ashley), his mainly 20th-century art collection is still displayed in many 'lovely' public rooms, bedrooms and picture gallery. Nick Brodie's modern menu, using garden-fresh and locally sourced ingredients, is admired.
Read more, page 425.

BARNSLEY HOUSE
BARNSLEY

The late Rosemary Verey, doyenne
of country-house gardeners, began
redesigning the grounds of her William
and Mary house in the 1950s. A knot
garden, laburnum walk, statuary and
ornamental fruit and vegetable garden
are typical of the old-fashioned style
she espoused. The 'temple' was brought
here from nearby Fairford Park by
Rosemary's husband, the architectural
historian David Verey.
Read more, page 84.

LINDETH FELL
BOWNESS-ON-WINDERMERE

Seven acres of gardens, laid out in
1907 by landscape designer Thomas
Mawson, surround the Kennedy
family's Edwardian house on Lake
Windermere. People come in spring and
early summer to see the rhododendrons
and azaleas. There is a shaded and
sequestered private tarn, a terrace
with views of the lake and the odd
trespassing deer, mature specimen trees
and lawns laid for bowls, croquet and
pitch-and-putt.
Read more, page 107.

GRAVETYE MANOR
EAST GRINSTEAD

Gardens created by William Robinson,
the great exponent of the natural style,
surround this Elizabethan manor house,
Robinson's home from 1884. Scourge
of the high Victorian formal bedding
system, Robinson planted drifts of
narcissus, cyclamen and scylla, hosts of
daffodils, a wild garden. After his death
the property fell into neglect, before
being renovated by Peter Herbert. The
current owners, Jeremy and Elizabeth
Hosking, have continued restoration.
Read more, page 151.

LIME WOOD
LYNDHURST

Cutting-edge design meets Regency
elegance at this New Forest hotel. The
roof garden of the Herb House Spa has
been planted 'to emphasise the infusing
nature of herbs'. A bay-tree-lined
walkway underplanted with lavender
leads to the 'mintarium', where four
ancient olive trees are surrounded by
mint in 15 varieties. In ground-level
walled gardens, cordon trees such as
cherry, peach and pear, grape and fig
provide fruit for the spa.
Read more, page 211.

HOTEL ENDSLEIGH
MILTON ABBOT

As one of his last commissions, two centuries ago, the landscape gardener (a term he coined) Humphry Repton laid out the grounds of the Duke of Bedford's hunting lodge – now run as a luxury hotel by Olga Polizzi. Formal gardens run down to the River Tamar. There are grottoes, follies, dells, streams, a arose and jasmine walkway, a shell-encrusted summer house and an arboretum.
Read more, page 220.

MILLGATE HOUSE
RICHMOND

The garden of this Georgian house off the main square has won plaudits from Alan Titchmarsh and the RHS, for owners Austin Lynch and Tim Culkin, who have worked on it since 1980. This small town garden, open to the public in summer, is laid with paths amid a profusion of densely planted roses and clematis, hostas, ferns and shrubs (pictured).
Read more, page 262.

STONE HOUSE
RUSHLAKE GREEN

The ancestral Tudor home of Jane and Peter Dunn overlooks an ornamental lake. There is a rose garden, a croquet lawn, a summer house, a 100-foot 'hot' herbaceous border, greenhouses, an orchard, and an 18th-century walled garden where vegetables, herbs and soft fruits (tayberries, wine berries, gooseberries) are grown for the hotel kitchen.
Read more, page 269.

CLIVEDEN HOUSE
TAPLOW

This stately home turned hotel on the River Thames stands in extensive gardens and woodlands, managed by the National Trust. There is a four-acre parterre, created by John Fleming in 1855, while extraordinary themed gardens include an Italianate Long Garden of topiary, laid out in around 1900, and a Japanese-style Water Garden with pagoda. There is a maze, an amphitheatre and an octagonal temple on the edge of chalk cliffs.
Read more, page 297.

GLENAPP CASTLE
BALLANTRAE

A large monkey-puzzle tree stands sentinel at the entrance to the 30-acre grounds of Graham and Fay Cowan's Victorian fantasy castle, resplendent with rhododendrons in late spring. There are bamboos and giant redwoods in the arboretum, a formal garden and a walled kitchen garden with espaliered apple and pear trees. In a 150-foot glass house, head gardener Bobby Cunningham grows apricots, nectarines and kiwi fruit, and tends a 50-year-old dessert grapevine.
Read more, page 339.

BODYSGALLEN HALL AND SPA
LLANDUDNO

Under the stewardship of the National Trust, this 17th-century mansion is surrounded by gardens of delight – a parterre of box hedges planted with aromatic herbs, a rockery with cascade, lily pond, a walled garden and follies. A designated walk leads to a mountaintop Gothic tower and obelisk.
Read more, page 421.

BLAKENEY HOTEL
BLAKENEY

Large windows and a terrace facilitate 'magnificent' views of the estuary and salt marshes that stretch before the Stannard family's quayside hotel. The Lookout Lounge and the best bedrooms (some with a private patio) face the meandering River Glavern, rippling tidal sands and the reedy salt marshes. There are walks from the door; seal-spotting trips out to Blakeney Point can be arranged.
Read more, page 101.

THE COTTAGE IN THE WOOD
BRAITHWAITE

Approached via the chain of tight curves of Whinlatter Pass, this whitewashed converted 17th-century coaching inn sits within England's only mountain forest. Kath and Liam Berney's cottage-style restaurant-with-rooms has sweeping views of the Lakeland peaks from the terrace: a perfect backdrop for summer drinks. The area provides a rich larder for the conservatory restaurant (fresh fish from Whitehaven harbour, wild food from the fells), which overlooks the surrounding forest.
Read more, page 110.

BELLE TOUT LIGHTHOUSE
EASTBOURNE

On the chalk cliffs of Beachy Head sits this decommissioned lighthouse-cum-B&B with, unsurprisingly, 'fantastic views' of the English Channel, countryside and Seven Sisters coastline. The former lantern room has wraparound windows, offering 360-degree panoramas from 'comfy chairs and sofas'. Each bedroom has its own outlook, plus original features; the Keeper's Loft in the tower has a mezzanine loft bed (reached by the original fixed ladder).
Read more, page 154.

BATTLESTEADS
HEXHAM

Look skywards for the most impressive views at Dee and Richard Slade's small hotel and restaurant at the edge of Northumberland national park, the largest 'dark sky park' in Europe. Guests staying in one of the five eco-lodges have full access to an on-site observatory offering unrivalled opportunities for stargazing. Cutting-edge technology allows astronomers to take in the night's star performers.
Read more, page 182.

SWINSIDE LODGE
NEWLANDS

There are 'thrilling' views of Cat
Bells and Causey Pike, or Skiddaw
and Blencathra mountains, from
the bedrooms of this white-painted
Georgian building. Pastoral sights and
sounds greet visitors, from bleating
lambs in nearby fields to the pheasants
and red squirrels roaming the lawns.
The Biltons advise on the best walks
in the area; packed lunches can be
provided.
Read more, page 233.

PEN-Y-DYFFRYN
OSWESTRY

Most of the 'delightful' bedrooms at
Miles and Audrey Hunter's former
Georgian rectory have splendid views
of the Welsh hills. The small country
hotel stands amid beautiful countryside
on the last hill in Shropshire. Rooms
in the coach house have a private
patio opening on to the garden. The
restaurant has south-west-facing sash
windows.
Read more, page 246.

THE THREE CHIMNEYS AND
HOUSE OVER-BY
DUNVEGAN

A gourmet destination in the north-west
of the Isle of Skye, this restaurant-with-
rooms gives a gastronomic experience
combined with a panoramic view of the
island. A telescope, handily set up in
one of the public rooms, allows guests
to take a closer look at Loch Dunvegan;
the menu gives guests a taste of Skye's
shoals and farms. There is a sea view
from each of the six bedrooms.
Read more, page 350.

KYLESKU HOTEL
KYLESKU

By the former ferry slipway on the
shores of Loch Glendhu, this old
coaching inn dates back to 1680. It
is now run as a small hotel by Tanja
Lister and Sonia Virechauveix who
have continued to renovate. Most of the
bedrooms have a view of the lochs; in
the restaurant, the mountains come into
focus (pictured). Seals and birdlife can
be watched from the comfort of the bar,
restaurant and lounge.
Read more, page 369.

SCARISTA HOUSE
SCARISTA

On a windswept stretch of coastline
on the Isle of Harris, Tim and Patricia
Martin's white-painted Georgian manse
looks out to the Atlantic Ocean; behind,
heather-covered mountains stretch
out on the horizon. The bedrooms are
in the main house and in an adjacent
outbuilding; they have 'wonderful'
views of the bay. Guests can explore
the nearby three-mile-long white shell
sand beach.
Read more, page 386.

BRYNIAU GOLAU
BALA

On the eastern edge of Snowdonia
national park, this stone-built Victorian
guest house has 'wonderful' views down
to the narrow-gauge railway that passes
alongside Lake Bala and across to the
Arenig Mountains. Each bedroom,
named after a nearby mountain range,
has a view of the lake; in Aran, this
can be enjoyed from the bathtub. The
terrace is an ideal vantage point to take
in the sunset over evening drinks.
Read more, page 403.

APSLEY HOUSE
BATH
Built by the Duke of Wellington for a mistress, Nicholas and Claire Potts's elegant Georgian house is furnished with fine antiques and paintings. The spacious, light lounge, with an honesty bar, has tall windows facing the garden. Set back from a main road, the house is quiet at night. The welcome is 'impeccable'; breakfast has a large buffet on a dresser; 'enjoyable' cooked plates. The house is a 20-minute walk to the centre.
Read more, page 89.

NUMBER THIRTY EIGHT
CLIFTON
BRISTOL
With 'wonderful views down to Bristol and beyond', Adam and Mike Dorrien-Smith's luxury B&B occupies a refurbished five-storey Georgian merchant's house at the top of Clifton. Its 'stunning contemporary interior' is inspired by Bristol's seafaring history. A 'very good' breakfast 'uses the best and freshest locally sourced ingredients'.
Read more, page 115.

PARFORD WELL
CHAGFORD
Owner Tim Daniel escaped from London to run this 'professional but personal' B&B within Dartmoor national park. There is a supply of books and board games, and a wood-burning stove for wet days, in the elegantly furnished lounge where guests are welcomed with tea and home-made cake. On fine days, visitors can sit in the pretty walled garden and look out across the unspoilt countryside of the River Teign valley. The 'superb' breakfast is cooked to order by Tim Daniel.
Read more, page 133.

TIMBERSTONE
CLEE STANTON
In a remote hamlet in the Clee hills near Ludlow, Alex Read and Tracey Baylis have restored and extended this traditional stone cottage which they run on eco-friendly lines. Two bedrooms in the old house have original beams; two newer rooms, in an extension, have been 'beautifully crafted' with oak fittings. A connecting room, serving as lounge and dining room, has 'comfy' sofas and chairs, books, games.
Read more, page 139.

BLACK ROCK HOUSE
HASTINGS

A 'terrific host', owner/manager
Yuliya Vereshchuk runs this handsome
Victorian villa as a B&B. 'Everything
has been thought of' in the bedrooms:
a carafe of filtered water; home-made
biscuits and a cafetière; fresh milk in a
fridge. Breakfast has a buffet of granola,
muesli, fruit compote, 'a wide variety of
fresh fruit'.

Read more, page 177.

JEAKE'S HOUSE
RYE

On a cobbled street in this former
Cinque Port town rich in literary
associations, this 17th-century wool
store and adjoining Elders House
was once the 'deeply cherished home'
of American writer Conrad Aiken.
Today it is run as a much-loved B&B by
Jenny Hadfield. Bags are carried to the
bedrooms which are reached along a
warren of corridors. Tables are set with
crisp white cloths in a galleried hall
for breakfast.

Read more, page 270.

CHERRY TREES
STRATFORD-UPON-AVON

A short walk across the Avon footbridge
to the town, Tony Godel and Royd
Laidlow's B&B is in 'an ideal position'
for theatre-goers. The 'spacious, well-
equipped, spotlessly clean' bedrooms
have a king-size bed, sitting area,
'proper' fresh milk in the mini-fridge.
A former stage manager, Tony Godel
enjoys talking about productions at the
Royal Shakespeare Company's theatres.

Read more, page 290.

STOBERRY HOUSE
WELLS

The view is 'stunning' from Frances and
Tim Meeres Young's converted five-
room coach house. Set in a landscaped
six-acre sloping park, it looks over
Wells and the Vale of Avalon (pictured).
It has wildlife ponds, water features,
sculptures, a walled garden, a potager
and much else. The 'copious and
delicious' breakfast has home-made
breads, scones and croissants, a vast
choice of organic preserves, full English
cooked to order.

Read more, page 318.

TIGH AN DOCHAIS
BROADFORD

Built by award-winning architects, Neil
Hope and Lesley Unwin's contemporary
house has an uninterrupted sea view.
Entered by a bridge to the upper floor,
it has solid oak flooring throughout;
the guest lounge, dining room and
bedrooms have floor-to-ceiling windows
facing the bay. Guests can sit out on
the decking to enjoy the long summer
evenings.

Read more, page 342.

PENBONTBREN
GLYNARTHEN

Richard Morgan-Price and Huw
Thomas have converted a 19th-century
livestock farm into an 'attractive' B&B
with 'beautiful, spacious' suites. Each
has a sitting room and private terrace;
one, with a separate single bedroom and
a wet room, is suitable for families and
wheelchair-users. 'Varied, generous'
breakfasts have linen table napkins, eggs
from the house's own hens, and smoked
fish from neighbouring Rhydlewis.

Read more, page 415.

THE ABBEY HOUSE
ABBOTSBURY

Beside the ruins of an 11th-century abbey, this traditional B&B has long been run by the 'most welcoming' owners, Jonathan and Maureen Cooke. The bedrooms are 'wonderfully quiet, clean, well equipped and very comfortable'. Breakfast ('good' muesli and grilled haddock, cafetière coffee) is taken in 'an impressively oaky-beamy dining room with huge open fireplace'. The gardens have 'pergolas, arbours, lots of tables and chairs'. Per room B&B £75–£125.

Read more, page 70.

CASTLEMAN
CHETTLE

Visitors appreciate the 'gorgeous, unspoilt and atmospheric' setting, and the 'charming, helpful, laid-back' staff at this informal restaurant-with-rooms, a former dower house in a feudal Dorset village. It is run by Barbara Garnsworthy and her brother, Brendan, 'real personalities'. It reminded visitors this year of a country hotel in rural France. Per room B&B £100–£115. Dinner £30.

Read more, page 134.

THE NOBODY INN
DODDISCOMBSLEIGH

Sue Burdge's 'lovely old pub' is in a village reached down a maze of country lanes near Exeter. In the popular beamed bar, there is an 'enormous' whisky selection ('262 at last count'), 'good' cask ale, an 'excellent' wine list, which can be enjoyed in 'cosy' spots in front of the inglenook fireplace. The bedrooms upstairs are 'incredibly peaceful'. Per room B&B £75–£105, dinner £26.

Read more, page 149.

THE OLD STORE
HALNAKER

Once home of the village bakery and shop, Patrick and Heather Birchenough's B&B, a Grade II listed 17th-century brick-and-flint house, has seven 'immaculate', recently redecorated bedrooms each with an en suite shower room. Arriving guests are greeted with tea and a slice of the hostess's home-made cake – 'such a delight after a long journey'. Per person B&B £35–£50.

Read more, page 173.

THISTLEYHAUGH FARM
LONGHORSLEY

Shielded from the world by a 720-acre organic sheep and cattle farm run by her husband, Henry, Enid Nelless runs her Georgian farmhouse as a good-value guest house. The bedrooms are priced according to size; there are 'excellent' beds; 'masses of towels, all the goodies we needed'. The communal dinner (preceded by a glass of complimentary sherry) is described as 'farmhouse cooking with flair'. Per person B&B £50, D,B&B £75.

Read more, page 202.

THE NAG'S HEAD
PICKHILL

In a pretty Domesday village close to the A1, this old coaching inn is run in personal style by Janet and Edward Boynton. It is liked for the excellent service and inventive cooking. Vegetarians are well catered for in the menus which can be taken in the tap room, the lounge bar or the 'lovely' dining room. The bedrooms are simple but 'perfectly adequate'. Per person B&B £40–£48.50, dinner £25.

Read more, page 254.

THE BLACK SWAN
RAVENSTONEDALE

In a village that lies amid upland pastures at the foot of the Howgill fells, Alan and Louise Dinnes's 'thoroughly dependable' country-pub-with-rooms is 'remarkable value for money'. Bedrooms vary in size and decor: one has an iron bedframe, a log-burning stove; others are decorated in soft colours. 'Delicious' meals are taken in the bar or dining room. Per room B&B from £75, dinner £25.

Read more, page 259.

BEALACH HOUSE
DUROR

The welcome is warm at Jim and Hilary McFadyen's small guest house, a former shepherd's croft in a remote glen with 'fabulous' views. As far as possible, everything on Hilary McFadyen's menus is home made or home grown; from bread and marmalade to petits fours, and fruit and vegetables from the garden. Dinner, taken at a communal table, is a sociable affair. The bedrooms are well equipped. Per room B&B £90–£110, dinner £25–£30.

Read more, page 351.

GRASSHOPPERS
GLASGOW

On the penthouse sixth floor of the former head office of the Caledonian Railway Company, this unusual and relaxed hotel has a Scandinavian styling. The bedrooms, which vary in size, are well designed; bathrooms have a power shower. The kitchen is at the hub, and tea and coffee are always available. Suppers are home cooked, served at wooden tables. Per room D,B&B £115.

Read more, page 357.

AEL Y BRYN
EGLWYSWRW

The owners, Robert Smith and Arwel Hughes, welcome guests 'as friends' to their striking guest house, a former prisoner-of-war camp, which they have restored 'with flair and imagination'. The bedrooms are 'superbly equipped'. A communal dinner ('fresh and innovative' food) is served under 'striking' chandeliers in the baronial-style dining room. Per room B&B £100–£130. Set dinner £24–£28.

Read more, page 412.

THE VICTORIA
LONDON

A short stroll from Richmond Park, this 'cheerful' pub-hotel with a 'family ambience' is owned by Greg Ballamy and TV chef Paul Merrett. There are books, leather sofas and an open fire in the bar. In the conservatory the changing à la carte menu might include spiced lamb leg steak, baba ganoush, roasted sweet potato, tomato chilli jam; Jerusalem artichoke ravioli, buffalo mozzarella, blushed tomato, rocket. Read more, page 59.

THE HORSE AND GROOM
BOURTON-ON-THE-HILL

Brothers Tom and Will Greenstock win praise for the 'consistently high standard' of cooking at their honeyed stone Cotswold inn. Chef Will Greenstock uses local and home-grown produce to create the 'imaginative yet unpretentious' dishes chalked up on the blackboard: perhaps pressed Tamworth pork terrine, celeriac remoulade, crispy toasts; griddled Moroccan spiced lamb burger, hummus, green sauce. There is an open fire in the dining room – alfresco dining when the sun shines. Read more, page 106.

THE SUN INN
DEDHAM

Piers Baker's sensitively restored, beamed and panelled village pub in deepest Constable country is 'highly recommended' for friendly atmosphere and 'really good cooking' con brio, from a daily-changing seasonal menu. Chef Jack Levine prepares such dishes as slow-cooked salt marsh lamb, onion, baby turnips, broad beans, mint. Read more, page 147.

THE RED LION FREEHOUSE
EAST CHISENBURY

Chef/proprietor Guy Manning holds a Michelin star for his 'exciting' cooking at this thatched village pub, which he runs with his American wife, Brittany. 'Excellent' dinner, served at 'nicely set' wooden tables in the restaurant, is prepared from local, home-grown, home-raised and foraged ingredients in 'interesting combinations'. Pan-fried halibut, brown shrimp, mussels, gnocchi, grelot onions, lobster bisque; agnolotti, truffle, hazelnuts, purple sprouting broccoli. Read more, page 150.

THE BROWNLOW ARMS
HOUGH-ON-THE-HILL

A 'winning combination of gastropub, local inn and restaurant-with-rooms', Paul and Lorraine Willoughby's 17th-century inn is in a 'pretty stone village' in East Lincolnshire. In the restaurant, which has an 'informal air', chef Ruaraidh Bealby's 'imaginative' menus have 'a great deal of choice' of modern dishes, perhaps baked goat's cheese, truffled honey; 'perfectly pink' venison, dauphinoise potatoes.
Read more, page 185.

THE FEATHERED NEST
NETHER WESTCOTE

At Tony and Amanda Timmer's converted malthouse turned village pub, chef Kuba Winkowski cooks 'excellent' modern fare, using locally sourced and home-grown ingredients. There are cask ales and an open fire in the flagstoned bar. In the light-filled restaurant, looking on to the terrace, typical dishes include spring white truffle tagliatelle; grilled Ibérico feathered loin, chunky chips, chorizo, garlic mushroom.
Read more, page 227.

STAGG INN
TITLEY

At Steve and Nicola Reynolds's 'most relaxed', 'friendly', unpretentious, whitewashed inn, meals are served in both bar and dining room. While Nicola is 'very much in charge' and takes orders, Steve cooks 'delicious' food that showcases the best of Herefordshire produce. Enjoyed this year: 'Scallops with the tastiest pickled cauliflower; sea bass, leeks and samphire; a trio of crèmes brûlées.'
Read more: page 306.

THE CAT INN
WEST HOATHLY

Andrew Russell's 16th-century inn in a pretty hilltop Wealden village wins praise for the 'warm welcome' and 'friendly atmosphere' in a bar popular with locals. Chef Max Leonard cooks pub standards and classics with modern flourishes. Prime aged Hereford beef burger, emmental, bacon, confit onion, brioche bun, fries; roast breast of guinea fowl, braised Puy lentils, pancetta, fondant potato, chargrilled broccoli, jus.
Read more, page 319.

THE GURNARD'S HEAD
ZENNOR

Next to the Coastal Path in west Cornwall, this 'laid-back, well-run' yellow-painted inn has open fires, wooden floors, a library of paperbacks (pictured). Jack Clayton has stepped up to run the kitchen. He uses local produce for his seasonal menus which can be taken in the bar or in one of two dining rooms. Typical dishes: herb-crusted hake, crushed potatoes, leek, tarragon mustard; Creedy Carver duck, Puy lentils, kale, Madeira sauce.
Read more: page 332.

THE FELIN FACH GRIFFIN
FELIN FACH

As at the Gurnard's Head (above), brothers Charles and Edmund Inkin create a modern-meets-traditional ethos at this 'ridiculously welcoming' roadside inn on the Welsh borders. Chef Max Wilson uses local and home-grown organic produce to create seasonal menus of such dishes as potato gnocchi, butternut squash, cavolo nero; Bwlch venison, honey-glazed parsnip, red cabbage.
Read more: page 413.

WOOLLEY GRANGE
BRADFORD-ON-AVON

Wellington boots flank the entrance of Nigel Chapman's characterful, family-friendly Jacobean stone manor in 'glorious' countryside. Young guests will find much diversion in the house (clubs, dens) and in the rambling grounds (play areas, garden games, a fairy trail). Families can dine together in the Orangery; in the evening, adults can dine alone (with a baby monitor perhaps).

Read more, page 109.

THE EVESHAM HOTEL
EVESHAM

'A great-value family hotel where all ages will have a good time,' was the comment of a Guide inspector whose children had a 'terrific stay' at John and Sue Jenkinson's quirky, informal hotel. Indoors there is a play area, a swimming pool; outdoors there are slides and a trampoline. The 'amazing' Alice in Wonderland-inspired family suite has bunk beds and nooks for children to play in.

Read more, page 159.

MOONFLEET MANOR
FLEET

'Parents needn't feel guilty as their children disappear' to the twice-daily crèche at this 'pretty' Georgian house, part of the child-friendly Luxury Family Hotels group. 'It doesn't feel like a dumping ground; they made papier mâché jewellery trees, and had a ball in the lovely playroom which was full of toys and dressing-up clothes.' The smallest children can take high tea; families can eat together until 7.30 pm, after which 'exhausted' parents can dine alone.

Read more, page 163.

FOWEY HALL
FOWEY

'The staff are totally committed to making sure the guest has a good time' at this Victorian mansion overlooking the Fowey estuary. Family-focused facilities include a crèche, an outdoor play area and a games room; young beachgoers may borrow wellingtons, fishing nets, buckets and spades. Baby-listening and baby-sitting can be arranged.

Read more, page 165.

CONGHAM HALL
KING'S LYNN
In pretty gardens near the Queen's estate at Sandringham, Nicholas Dickinson's ivy-clad Georgian house welcomes families. A list of child-friendly activities in the area is provided: youngsters might fly a kite on Old Hunstanton beach or have a private tennis lesson. Family rooms are available: a suite has a separate sitting room with a sofa-bed.
Read more, page 189.

AUGILL CASTLE
KIRKBY STEPHEN
Boredom is not a danger at Simon and Wendy Bennett's turreted Gothic castle in the Eden valley which is an ideal venue for a multi-generational group. Children will appreciate the tree houses and Little Cooks classes. They can spend an afternoon playing knights and princesses, or sit in the cinema watching a film with popcorn.
Read more, page 191.

SWINTON PARK
MASHAM
'Elegant, even luxurious but never stuffy', Mark and Felicity Cunliffe-Lister's 19th-century Gothic castle offers a particular welcome to families. Children will find a playroom full of toys; kites and bicycles; baby bathtime products and wipes are provided for the youngest; teenagers can enjoy a spa treatment. Downstairs, a playroom converts into a private cinema.
Read more, page 215.

BEDRUTHAN HOTEL AND SPA
MAWGAN PORTH
'The children's activities are a godsend' at this 'fantastic' family-friendly hotel on the north Cornish coast. It has swimming pools and playgrounds; kites and binoculars are available to borrow; there is a fine sandy beach just below. Toddlers have their own supervised club. Light meals can be taken by a family in the Wild Café.
Read more, page 216.

CALCOT MANOR
TETBURY
In 'admirable' gardens in the Cotswold countryside, this converted 14th-century farmhouse allows adults and children to 'coexist happily'. Children have much to occupy their days: nature trails, play areas, indoor and outdoor swimming pools; horse riding can be arranged. Little ones are cared for in the Ofsted-registered Playzone.
Read more, page 302.

LOCH MELFORT HOTEL
ARDUAINE
Children will love the playground at Calum and Rachel Ross's country hotel on Asknish Bay. Toys, books and games are supplied in the family-friendly bedrooms. There are three Highland cattle – Campbell, McDonald and Dougal – to feed. A child-friendly menu is available at the Bistro; well-behaved children can dine in the main restaurant.
Read more, page 335.

PORTH TOCYN HOTEL
ABERSOCH
In a wonderful setting above Cardigan Bay, this 'lovely, wacky' hotel has been run by three generations of the Fletcher-Brewer family since 1948. Families like the unstuffy feel and can take advantage of baby-listening services, a guest fridge and microwave, a games room and a snug with books and television; a children's high tea is served at 5.30 pm.
Read more, page 401.

BIGGIN HALL
BIGGIN-BY-HARTINGTON
After breakfast at this 'not posh but
straightforward' hotel, you can help
yourself to a packed lunch of wholemeal
sandwiches, fresh fruit, chocolate bar
and crisps, before heading out to explore
the Peak District national park. Several
walking routes, to suit varying abilities,
start from or run past the door of the
17th-century house.
Read more, page 100.

THE HORN OF PLENTY
GULWORTHY
A 19th-century house on a 'beautiful'
hillside overlooking the Tamar valley,
this 'very comfortable' hotel stands
within an Area of Outstanding Natural
Beauty. You might head for the summit
of Brentor, follow the 1,000 acres of
paths and forest roads around Burrator
Reservoir, or head for the beauty spot of
Dartmeet and the confluence of the East
and West Dart.
Read more, page 172.

UNDERLEIGH HOUSE
HOPE
A full 'Peak District' breakfast at this
B&B in a Victorian cottage and barn
conversion sets guests up to explore
Hope valley in the Peak District
national park. Whether it's to be a
ramble or a route march, the 'very
helpful' hosts, Philip and Vivienne
Taylor, can advise on where to go and
what to see, will supply a packed lunch,
lay on tea and cakes for returning
walkers, and dry their waterproofs.
Read more, page 184.

PEN-Y-DYFFRYN
OSWESTRY
Miles and Audrey Hunter's former
rectory occupies an 'Arcadian setting in
a beautiful valley' in woodland close to
the Welsh border. Their enthusiasm for
the countryside is expressed in the folder
of walks they have put together, some
just 30 minutes long, others a full-day
trek, pointing out things to look for along
the way. Take a hotel packed lunch.
Read more, page 246.

THE BURGOYNE
REETH

This Georgian country house hotel stands on the green of a village near the midpoint of Alfred Wainwright's coast-to-coast walk, in a landscape of dry-stone walls and sheep-grazed pastures. Owners Mo and Julia Usman can provide a packed lunch and will advise on routes. Follow the road westward on to the Pennines to the highest pub in England, the Tan Hill Inn.

Read more, page 260.

BOSKERRIS HOTEL
ST IVES

For some, the climb from the station to Jonathan and Marianne Bassett's small hotel will be exertion enough. Others may opt for a guided tour of this buzzy, arty town. But serious walkers will want to follow the South West Coast Path, perhaps towards Hayle, picking up the ancient pilgrims' route known as St Michael's Way.

Read more, page 272.

TITCHWELL MANOR
TITCHWELL

With the RSPB nature reserve and the north Norfolk coast almost on the doorstep, Ian and Margaret Snaith's Victorian farmhouse hotel has much to attract walkers. You can follow a marsh path to Brancaster beach. Or ride the Coasthopper bus as it shadows the Norfolk Coast Path, towards the fishing village of Cromer or the resort of Hunstanton.

Read more, page 305.

HOWTOWN HOUSE
ULLSWATER

Walkers are spoilt for choice in the Lake District, but it is a rare hotel where they wake you with a pot of leaf tea and such kindness. This 17th-century farmhouse is run by Jacquie Baldry and her son, David, with few concessions to fashion. They will provide a sustaining packed lunch for a walk along the lakeside to Patterdale or over the more demanding fells, before you are summoned by the dinner gong on your return.

Read more, page 309.

GLENFINNAN HOUSE HOTEL
GLENFINNAN

A Victorian mansion in a 'lovely' situation with lawns stretching down to Loch Shiel and distant views of Ben Nevis, this hotel is ideally placed for guests in search of scenic walks. You might take a short stroll through the Glenfinnan Estate, where red deer graze, to see the historic viaduct familiar from Harry Potter films; or take a National Trust walk for viewpoints of the Glenfinnan Monument, viaduct and loch.

Read more, page 358.

THE MANOR TOWN HOUSE
FISHGUARD

Helen and Chris Sheldon's 'delightful' Georgian house stands right above the Pembrokeshire Coastal Path, where it runs through a wooded valley. The Pembrokeshire Greenways initiative urges you to 'bus it', with public transport covering the entire length, so you can ride and alight for walks along the way. The Poppit Rocket runs to Cardigan, the Strumble Shuttle to St David's. You can relax on your return with tea and cakes on the seaward terrace.

Read more, page 414.

THE ZETTER
LONDON

Ideally placed in the heart of Clerkenwell, overlooking cobbled St John's Square, this 'small hotel with a big personality' is in the former headquarters of Zetter Pools. The bedrooms have been decorated with wit: bold colours, retro fittings and state-of-the-art technology fill the bijou rooms and deluxe rooftop studios (each with a private terrace).
Read more, page 52.

THE ZETTER TOWNHOUSE
LONDON

Across the square from its sister hotel, The Zetter (see above), this small town house hotel has been styled as the home of an eccentric great aunt, Wilhelmina. It is filled with oddities and curios from her collection (ceramics, portraits, a stuffed kangaroo). The bedrooms have reclaimed and vintage furniture, perhaps a headboard from an old fairground ride.
Read more, page 53.

THE LEVIN
LONDON

'Everything is just about perfect' in David Levin's small but sophisticated town house hotel in Knightsbridge. A 'spectacular' light installation (designed by Sarah Marsden) cascades down the spiral staircase in the pistachio-coloured lobby. Bedrooms are individually decorated in contemporary style with Art Nouveau furnishings and designer lighting; each has a champagne minibar and marble bathroom with underfloor heating.
Read more, page 56.

THE GRAZING GOAT
LONDON

Hiding in a 'peaceful little zone' minutes from Marble Arch, this stylish public house hotel has an inviting, rustic atmosphere: iron beams, lots of French oak in the bar and first-floor dining room. The bedrooms, on the top three floors, are 'simple but beautifully furnished'; the 'excellent' bathrooms have 'especially good' toiletries. A seasonal British menu is served in the bright, airy first-floor dining room.
Read more, page 57.

ARTIST RESIDENCE
LONDON

Once a pub, this handsome Pimlico building has been stylishly outfitted with furnishings made from salvaged industrial material, bare brick walls, unusual artwork. In the bedrooms are metal-framed beds and bespoke armchairs; some bathrooms have a cast-iron bathtub and exposed piping. After a day at the nearby Saatchi Gallery, sharing platters can be enjoyed in the 64 Degrees restaurant; or cocktails in the youthful basement bar.
Read more, page 61.

THE QUEENSBERRY
BATH

Occupying four converted Georgian town houses near Bath city centre, Laurence and Helen Beere have given their 'excellent' establishment a sophisticated, modern touch, but it's the 'little things' that appeal. Every room has its own character, 'like the guest room in the house of some stylish friends', maybe a four-poster bed, a transparent plastic armchair or a decorative fireplace. The modern menu in the Olive Tree restaurant is 'a real draw'.
Read more, page 90.

JESMOND DENE HOUSE
NEWCASTLE UPON TYNE

This 'unexpectedly delightful' converted Arts and Crafts mansion sits at the head of a forested valley but is close enough for easy access to the city centre. Original windows, ornate fireplaces and oak panelling are complemented by contemporary art and striking modern design. Bedrooms are decorated in muted shades with bursts of colour; some have a private terrace. Chef Michael Penaluna serves an 'imaginative' dinner menu.
Read more, page 232.

HART'S HOTEL
NOTTINGHAM

Purpose-built on the former ramparts of the city's medieval castle, Tim and Stefa Hart's contemporary boutique hotel (pictured) offers 'stunning' views over the city. The 'very modern, small but well-equipped' rooms (individually designed by Stefa Hart) have specially selected artwork and louvred shutters; some have French doors and a private garden. Weary travellers might enjoy an in-room spa treatment.
Read more, page 241.

OLD BANK
OXFORD

Jeremy Mogford's modern conversion of three old stone buildings retains the spacious, airy feel of its Georgian beginnings. Many of the rooms look out over the city's dreaming spires and cultural landmarks, including the Bodleian Library and All Souls. The owner's extensive collection of original artwork by young British artists decorates the walls throughout. The former banking hall houses the lively Quod brasserie.
Read more, page 247.

THE PIG IN THE WALL
SOUTHAMPTON

Set into the medieval defensive wall in Southampton's historic Old Town, this branch of the Pig chain is on the 'stylish side of shabby chic'. The rooms, designed by owner Judy Hutson, are 'modern and well thought out', retaining original beams, slanted ceilings and decorative fireplaces. Most have a roll-top bath and a 'larder' of snacks and drinks. Guests can enjoy 'piggy bits' and fine wines by the fire in the deli bar.
Read more, page 285.

BRIDGEHOUSE
BEAMINSTER

This 13th-century former priests'
house in a pretty market town mixes
contemporary with traditional in a
way that is sympathetic to its heritage.
Standing by the River Brit, the hotel
has several different spaces licensed
for intimate wedding ceremonies.
The garden brasserie offers an open-
air alternative in warmer weather;
the walled garden is a picture-perfect
backdrop. Exclusive weekend wedding
parties can be arranged.
Read more, page 93.

NORTHCOTE MANOR
BURRINGTON

In extensive grounds in the Taw valley,
this 18th-century manor house caters
for weddings with two to 120 guests.
There are three rooms licensed for
wedding ceremonies: the Oak Room
and Conservatory make full use of the
magnificent public areas; the Sanctuary
in the grounds deploys 'nature's bounty'
to create the mood. Chef/manager
Richie Herkes creates the menu for the
wedding breakfast.
Read more, page 126.

LANGAR HALL
LANGAR

'Enjoyably eccentric', this honey-
stone Georgian mansion specialises
in intimate 'quintessentially English'
weddings for up to 50 guests, in idyllic
grounds. The queen of romance,
Barbara Cartland, was a frequent guest.
Country house weekend weddings
can be arranged (guests can be
accommodated in the 12 bedrooms); a
marquee can be set up on the lawn for
large events. Dramatic entrances are
made possible with the helipad outside
the front door.
Read more, page 192.

HOTEL TERRAVINA
NETLEY MARSH

A bespoke cake, made by the in-house
pastry chef, Moyra, can be part of the
deal for a wedding at Gérard and
Nina Basset's stylish small hotel. The
ceremony and celebration will take
place in the private dining room, the
Rutherford Bench, which opens on to a
terrace and gardens. The host, a world
champion sommelier, is well placed to
advise on the best wines.
Read more, page 228.

BINGHAM
RICHMOND-UPON-THAMES

On the banks of the River Thames, just outside the bustle of London, this Grade II listed Georgian town house has a 'lovely outlook'. Once the home of Katherine Bradley and Edith Cooper (poets and lovers), its opulent interiors are Art Deco inspired; outside, terraces and flowerbeds lead to the towpath and the river. It can seat 90 civil-ceremony guests (150 standing for a dinner/cocktail reception).
Read more, page 263.

ROSE IN VALE
ST AGNES

In a peaceful wooded valley, surrounded by extensive grounds and a winding river, this elegant Georgian house hosts Cornish weddings. Intimate ceremonies can be held in the Valley Room or the Summer House. A marquee on the lawns will allow for more extensive celebrations. Living up to its name, the garden is awash with roses in summer.
Read more, page 271.

WATERSMEET
WOOLACOMBE

This classic seaside hotel above Woolacombe Bay was once an Edwardian gentleman's retreat. Ceremonies take place in the spacious lounge, with 'stunning' views across Combesgate beach to Lundy Island beyond. In fine weather, canapés and cocktails will be served on the lawn. A snug treatment room opened this year, with aromatherapy, massage and reflexology treatment, just right for a bit of pampering – or recovery after the big day.
Read more, page 328.

KNOCKINAAM LODGE
PORTPATRICK

In extensive grounds, with a private beach on the coast of the Rhinns of Galloway, this stylish grey-stone 19th-century former hunting lodge offers rustic luxury, from wedding ceremony to honeymoon. The Michelin-starred restaurant sits up to 70. Wedding planners will help arrange the registrar for a Scottish wedding.
Read more, page 381.

LONGUEVILLE MANOR
ST SAVIOUR (JERSEY)

Sumptuous elegance and excellent service allow wedding parties to relax and enjoy the day at this luxury Channel Islands hotel. The Oak Room is licensed for wedding ceremonies; wedding planners will liaise with Jersey registrars. Wine-lovers take particular note: the cellars contain almost 400 bins. The extensive grounds are picturesque – black swans swim in the private lake.
Read more, page 443.

BALLYMALOE HOUSE
SHANAGARRY

In the idyllic countryside of east Cork, this long-established ivy-covered hotel/restaurant is filled with Irish romance. Part late Georgian country house, part Norman castle, the building is surrounded by well-maintained gardens and woodland. The 'cheerful' dining rooms are intimate and filled with paintings and sculptures. The recently converted grain stores offer a unique alternative for larger parties. Licensed to hold civil ceremonies, Ballymaloe has connections with nearby churches.
Read more, page 475.

Each of these hotels has a tennis court (T) and/or a swimming pool (S)

LONDON
One Aldwych,
  Strand (S)

ENGLAND
Deans Place,
  Alfriston (S)
Askham Hall,
  Askham (S)
Hartwell House,
  Aylesbury (T,S)
Park House,
  Bepton (T,S)
Burgh Island,
  Bigbury-on-Sea (T,S)
Blakeney,
  Blakeney (S)
Woolley Grange,
  Bradford-on-Avon (S)
Dormy House,
  Broadway (S)
Hell Bay,
  Bryher (S)
Tor Cottage,
  Chillaton (S)
Rectory,
  Crudwell (S)
Dart Marina,
  Dartmouth (S)
Fingalls,
  Dittisham (S)

Old Whyly,
  East Hoathly (T,S)
Evesham,
  Evesham (S)
Moonfleet Manor,
  Fleet (S)
Fowey Hall,
  Fowey (S)
Stock Hill House,
  Gillingham (T)
Hambleton Hall,
  Hambleton (T,S)
Congham Hall,
  King's Lynn (S)
Augill Castle,
  Kirkby Stephen (T)
Feathers,
  Ledbury (S)
Lime Wood,
  Lyndhurst (S)
Bedruthan,
  Mawgan Porth (T,S)
Scarlet,
  Mawgan Porth (S)
Budock Vean,
  Mawnan Smith (T,S)
Mullion Cove,
  Mullion Cove (S)
TerraVina,
  Netley Marsh (S)

Chewton Glen,
  New Milton (T,S)
Old Rectory,
  Norwich (S)
St Enodoc,
  Rock (S)
Rose in Vale,
  St Agnes (S)
Star Castle,
  St Mary's (T,S)
Salcombe Harbour,
  Salcombe (S)
Seaham Hall,
  Seaham (S)
Soar Mill Cove,
  Soar Mill Cove (T,S)
Plumber Manor,
  Sturminster Newton (T)
Cliveden House,
  Taplow (T,S)
Calcot Manor,
  Tetbury (T,S)
Nare,
  Veryan-in-Roseland (T,S)
Holbeck Ghyll,
  Windermere (T)
Watersmeet,
  Woolacombe (S)
Middlethorpe Hall,
  York (S)

SCOTLAND
Glenapp Castle,
  Ballantrae (T)
Isle of Eriska,
  Eriska (T,S)

WALES
Trefeddian,
  Aberdyfi (T,S)
Porth Tocyn,
  Abersoch (T,S)
Glangrwyney Court,
  Crickhowell (T)

Gliffaes,
  Crickhowell (T)
Bodysgallen Hall and Spa,
  Llandudno (T,S)
Lake,
  Llangammarch Wells (T,S)
Portmeirion,
  Portmeirion (S)

CHANNEL ISLANDS
White House,
  Herm (T,S)
Atlantic,
  St Brelade (T,S)
Longueville Manor,
  St Saviour (T,S)

IRELAND
Rathsallagh House,
  Dunlavin (T)
Marlfield House,
  Gorey (T)
Rosleague Manor,
  Letterfrack (T)
Currarevagh House,
  Oughterard (T)
Rathmullan House,
  Rathmullan (T,S)
Coopershill,
  Riverstown (T)
Ballymaloe House,
  Shanagarry (T,S)

Each of these hotels has at least one bedroom equipped for a visitor in a wheelchair. You should telephone to discuss individual requirements

LONDON
Zetter,
  Clerkenwell
Rookery,
  Smithfield
Goring,
  Victoria
One Aldwych,
  Strand

ENGLAND
Wentworth,
  Aldeburgh
Deans Place,
  Alfriston
Rothay Manor,
  Ambleside
Hartwell House,
  Aylesbury
Master Builder's,
  Beaulieu
Park House,
  Bepton
Lord Crewe Arms,
  Blanchland
Millstream,
  Bosham
Woolley Grange,
  Bradford-upon-Avon
White Horse,
  Brancaster Staithe

Brooks,
  Bristol
Dormy House,
  Broadway
Hell Bay,
  Bryher
George,
  Buckden
Northcote Manor,
  Burrington
Pendragon Country House,
  Camelford
Captain's Club,
  Christchurch
Kings Head,
  Cirencester
Beech House & Olive Branch,
  Clipsham
Hipping Hall,
  Cowan Bridge
Clow Beck House,
  Croft-on-Tees
Dart Marina,
  Dartmouth
Dedham Hall,
  Dedham
Eckington Manor,
  Eckington

Evesham,
  Evesham
Carpenters Arms,
  Felixkirk
Fowey Hall,
  Fowey
Manoir aux Quat'Saisons,
  Great Milton
Horn of Plenty,
  Gulworthy
Castle House,
  Hereford
Battlesteads,
  Hexham
Byfords,
  Holt
Congham Hall,
  King's Lynn
Lime Wood,
  Lyndhurst
Swinton Park,
  Masham
Bedruthan,
  Mawgan Porth
Scarlet,
  Mawgan Porth
Redesdale Arms,
  Moreton-in-Marsh
St Mary's Inn,
  Morpeth

TerraVina,
  Netley Marsh
Chewton Glen,
  New Milton
Jesmond Dene House,
  Newcastle upon Tyne
Packhorse Inn,
  Newmarket
Beechwood,
  North Walsham
Hart's,
  Nottingham
Grange at Oborne,
  Oborne
Old Bank,
  Oxford
Old Parsonage,
  Oxford
Pig near Bath,
  Pensford
Old Railway Station,
  Petworth
Black Swan,
  Ravenstonedale
Burgoyne,
  Reeth
Coach House at
  Middleton Lodge,
  Richmond
Rose in Vale,
  St Agnes
Idle Rocks,
  St Mawes
Salcombe Harbour,
  Salcombe
Seaham Hall,
  Seaham
St Cuthbert's House,
  Seahouses
Swan,
  Southwold
Arden,
  Stratford-upon-Avon
Titchwell Manor,
  Titchwell

Tuddenham Mill,
  Tuddenham
Nare,
  Veryan-in-Roseland
Holbeck Ghyll,
  Windermere
Watersmeet,
  Woolacombe
Middlethorpe Hall,
  York

SCOTLAND
Summer Isles,
  Achiltibuie
Loch Melfort,
  Arduaine
Boath House,
  Auldearn
Dunvalanree in Carradale,
  Carradale
Three Chimneys and
  House Over-By,
  Dunvegan
Bonham,
  Edinburgh
Langass Lodge,
  Locheport
Craigatin House,
  Pitlochry
Green Park,
  Pitlochry
Viewfield House,
  Portree

WALES
Harbourmaster,
  Aberaeron
Ye Olde Bulls Head,
  Beaumaris
Gliffaes,
  Crickhowell
Ynyshir Hall,
  Eglwysfach
Penbontbren,
  Glynarthen

Tyddyn Llan,
  Llandrillo
Bodysgallen Hall and Spa,
  Llandudno
Lake,
  Llangammarch Wells
Portmeirion,
  Portmeirion
Old Rectory on the Lake,
  Tal-y-llyn

IRELAND
Mustard Seed at Echo
  Lodge,
  Ballingarry
Stella Maris,
  Ballycastle
Seaview House,
  Ballylickey
Quay House,
  Clifden
Rayanne House,
  Holywood
No. 1 Pery Square,
  Limerick
Sheedy's,
  Lisdoonvarna
Rathmullan House,
  Rathmullan

LONDON

St Paul's Cathedral and the Millennium Bridge, London

CHELSEA Map 2:D4

THE DRAYCOTT

The Union flag flies above the entrance of this
'sophisticated, very friendly' luxury hotel, part of
Adrian Gardiner's Mantis Collection, on a quiet
street near Sloane Square. 'It is one my favourite
hotels,' said a visitor this year. 'The impeccable
service lives up to the cost,' said Guide inspectors
on an earlier visit. Occupying three red brick
Edwardian town houses, the hotel has 'a
comfortable country house atmosphere' and
'lots of character'. Each of the original houses
has a 'fine' wooden staircase and 'a warren of
corridors'; the high-ceilinged public rooms have
antiques and paintings. In a 'charming' lounge,
flagging guests are revived by complimentary
refreshments: tea and home-made biscuits at
4 pm, champagne at 6 pm, hot chocolate and
biscuits at 9.30 pm. Decorated with Edwardian
antiques, theatrically themed bedrooms range
in size from a small single room to a 'beautiful'
suite overlooking the private garden square; a
family suite is equipped with toys and Nintendo
Wii. There is no restaurant, but snacks and hot
dishes from the all-day room-service menu may
be taken in the bedroom or the breakfast room.
(Oliver Thomas)

25% DISCOUNT VOUCHERS

26 Cadogan Gardens
London
SW3 2RP

T: 020 7730 6466
F: 020 7730 0236
E: reservations@draycotthotel.com
W: www.draycotthotel.com

BEDROOMS: 35.
OPEN: all year.
FACILITIES: drawing room, library,
breakfast room, free Wi-Fi, 1-acre
garden, unsuitable for disabled.
BACKGROUND MUSIC: none.
LOCATION: Chelsea, underground
Sloane Square.
CHILDREN: all ages welcomed.
DOGS: allowed in 2 bedrooms, not in
public rooms.
CREDIT CARDS: all major cards.
PRICES: [2015] room only from
£342. Continental breakfast £17.50,
cooked breakfast £21.95.

SEE ALSO SHORTLIST

SAN DOMENICO HOUSE

There is 'a most pleasing ambience' at this 'delightful' hotel, on an elegant residential street of red brick Victorian town houses off Sloane Square. It has been run by the Melpignano family, with 'an emphasis on comfort and service', since 2005. 'The charming staff could not have been more helpful.' The hotel has been richly decorated with 'impeccable taste': there are antiques, swagged curtains, Victorian mirrors and 'prints of the famous from previous centuries'. The 'luxurious, inviting' lounge has fresh flowers, sofas, an open fire in a marble fireplace. Each of the high-ceilinged bedrooms has a modern marble bathroom. 'I had a large room filled with beautiful and distinguished antiques – a carved bedhead, a mirror with an extravagant gilded frame, a chaise longue with good-quality cushions.' There is no restaurant, but a room-service menu is available all day; drinks and afternoon tea are taken in the lounge or on the roof terrace in good weather. Served in the bedroom, in the basement breakfast room or on the roof terrace, breakfast has pastries, 'good' coffee, freshly squeezed orange juice. (DH, and others)

29–31 Draycott Place
London
SW3 2SH

T: 020 7581 5757
F: 020 7584 1348
E: info@sandomenicohouse.com
W: www.sandomenicohouse.com

BEDROOMS: 17.
OPEN: all year.
FACILITIES: lounge, breakfast room, roof terrace, free Wi-Fi, unsuitable for disabled.
BACKGROUND MUSIC: classical and jazz in lounge and breakfast room.
LOCATION: Chelsea, underground Sloane Square.
CHILDREN: all ages welcomed.
DOGS: not allowed.
CREDIT CARDS: all major cards.
PRICES: (excluding VAT) room from £255. Breakfast (including VAT) £14.40–£21.60.

SEE ALSO SHORTLIST

CLERKENWELL

THE ZETTER

The service is 'exceptional' at this privately owned, contemporary hotel beside St John's Square. It is managed by Ashley Ely. Guide inspectors in 2015 were impressed: 'Everything was mint fresh (the first-floor corridor was being painted when we checked in). We were warmly greeted every time we went near reception; help was readily available.' A small lounge and bar in a central atrium is 'brightly decorated – lots of well-chosen contemporary art here and in the corridors'. The bedrooms vary considerably in size and price. 'Our pleasing room had dual-aspect large windows; it was decorated in subtle shades of beige, grey and olive; a zingy orange throw on the bed and two multi-coloured armchairs added splashes of colour. The furniture and lighting were modern and stylish; a compact, well-equipped bathroom.' Each suite on the rooftop has a private patio. Picture windows in the restaurant and bar face the square. The style of menu and service was due to change as the Guide went to press. The Zetter Townhouse, Clerkenwell (see next entry), is under the same ownership; a Marylebone branch opened in 2015.

25% DISCOUNT VOUCHERS

St John's Square
86–88 Clerkenwell Road
London
EC1M 5RJ

T: 020 7324 4444
E: reservations@thezetter.com
W: www.thezetter.com

BEDROOMS: 59. 2 suitable for disabled.
OPEN: all year.
FACILITIES: 2 lifts, ramps, cocktail bar/lounge, restaurant, 2 function/meeting rooms, free Wi-Fi.
BACKGROUND MUSIC: none.
LOCATION: Clerkenwell, NCP garage 5 mins' walk, underground Farringdon.
CHILDREN: all ages welcomed.
DOGS: only guide dogs allowed.
CREDIT CARDS: Amex, MasterCard, Visa.
PRICES: [2015] room from £185.

SEE ALSO SHORTLIST

THE ZETTER TOWNHOUSE, CLERKENWELL

♥César award in 2012

A 'friendly, welcoming' place, this 'elegant' Georgian town house on a cobbled square is praised by a visitor this year for its 'informality and excellence'. It is part of the small Zetter group; manager Ashley Ely manages an 'excellent' staff. Decorated with 'wit and (zany) flair', the 'atmospheric' hotel is filled with oil paintings, antique ceramics, old photographs and a stuffed kangaroo; bedrooms have reclaimed and vintage furniture and classic novels. 'Our large, colourful room facing the square was pretty quiet considering the city location; the compact bathroom had one of the best showers – a real cascade.' The 'stylish, spacious' cocktail bar is 'regularly crowded' with locals in the evening ('staff do their best to find good seating for residents'), 'but this gives the lounge much atmosphere'. A room-service menu is available all day; 'small eats' (perhaps 'superb' herring roe on toast) are served in the cocktail lounge. The sister hotel, The Zetter (see previous entry), is across the square. 'Continental breakfast in the bar was a delight.' (Max Lickfold)

49–50 St John's Square
London
EC1V 4JJ

T: 020 7324 4567
E: reservations@thezetter.com
W: www.thezettertownhouse.com

BEDROOMS: 13.
OPEN: all year.
FACILITIES: cocktail lounge, private dining room, games room, free Wi-Fi.
BACKGROUND MUSIC: none.
LOCATION: Clerkenwell, underground Farringdon.
CHILDREN: all ages welcomed, under-18s must be accompanied by an adult.
DOGS: not allowed.
CREDIT CARDS: Amex, MasterCard, Visa.
PRICES: [2015] room from £228.

SEE ALSO SHORTLIST

THE FIELDING

A hop, skip and grand jeté from the Royal Opera House, this small hotel fronted by flowering window boxes is a 'simple, well-located place to stay'. It is managed by Grace Langley, with 'helpful' staff, for private owners. Guide inspectors 'were welcomed by a charming receptionist; before we left the next morning, he looked up the weather for us, and gave us a map and directions'. Reached by narrow corridors, modest bedrooms have an en suite bath or shower room. 'Our first-floor double room was small but had all the necessities: a large bed, a dressing table, one bedside table; excellent lighting. It had a tea and coffee tray with biscuits, a bottle each of sparkling and still water, slippers and an eye mask. The bathroom was clean, with a decent shower.' Some concerns have been expressed about worn fixtures that need refurbishment. The hotel is 'remarkably quiet': 'Our room was on a side street; we were able to sleep undisturbed with the windows wide open.' Breakfast is not served, but there are many eating places nearby. 'Relatively good value for its position.'

4 Broad Court
off Bow Street
London
WC2B 5QZ

T: 020 7836 8305
F: 020 7497 0064
E: reservations@thefieldinghotel.co.uk
W: www.thefieldinghotel.co.uk

BEDROOMS: 25.
OPEN: all year.
FACILITIES: no public rooms, free Wi-Fi, unsuitable for disabled, free access to nearby spa and fitness centre.
BACKGROUND MUSIC: none.
LOCATION: central, underground Covent Garden.
CHILDREN: all ages welcomed.
DOGS: not allowed.
CREDIT CARDS: all major cards.
PRICES: [2015] room only single from £108, double from £168.

SEE ALSO SHORTLIST

THE CAPITAL

♥César award in 2008

On a quiet street in fashionable Knightsbridge, a smiling doorman greets guests at this traditional stone and red brick town house hotel; past the threshold, the small lobby has fresh flowers, paintings and a grand fireplace. The hotel has been owned by David Levin for more than 40 years; his daughter Kate is the manager. Individually decorated with classic English fabrics, antiques and artwork, the elegant bedrooms vary in size and decor; each has a customisable minibar, and a marble bathroom with oversized bathrobes. Some of the smaller rooms, ideal for a single traveller, have been refurbished this year. In the intimate Outlaw's at The Capital restaurant, chef Nathan Outlaw has a Michelin star for his 'outstanding' modern dishes. He specialises in seafood, but well-considered vegetarian options (pickled vegetable and cheddar tart, fennel and apple salad; crispy hen egg, sprouting broccoli, crispy capers) are available as well. 'The staff were very good, even finding out where the butter was sourced.' Whisky tastings with long-serving barman Cesar da Silva, are taken in the bar. David Levin also owns The Levin, next door (see entry).

22–24 Basil Street
London
SW3 1AT

T: 020 7589 5171
F: 020 7225 0011
E: reservations@capitalhotel.co.uk
W: www.capitalhotel.co.uk

BEDROOMS: 49.
OPEN: all year (restaurant closed Sun).
FACILITIES: lift, sitting room, bar, restaurant, brasserie/bar next door, free Wi-Fi, access to nearby health club/spa, only restaurant suitable for disabled.
BACKGROUND MUSIC: 'relaxing', at low volume, in public rooms sometimes.
LOCATION: central, underground Knightsbridge, car park.
CHILDREN: all ages welcomed.
DOGS: small dogs, on request.
CREDIT CARDS: all major cards.
PRICES: [2015] room only £245–£355, B&B (continental) £265–£373. À la carte £55 (plus 12½% discretionary service charge).

SEE ALSO SHORTLIST

THE LEVIN

David Levin 'clearly sets high standards' at his 'immaculate' hotel in a discreet town house steps from Harrods and Hyde Park. 'Everything is just about perfect,' reported a recent guest. 'It is expensive, but it offers peace and quiet,' said another. Harald Duttine is the long-serving manager; 'interested and interesting' staff are 'superb'. Up a staircase with a 'spectacular' light installation, the bedrooms, individually decorated, have 'tasteful' furniture; beds are 'very comfortable'. There are three types of room, which vary in size; all have a champagne minibar and a marble bathroom. 'Our standard room was not large, but was well appointed, and had very good lighting (we could actually read in bed); an excellent bathroom.' In the basement Metro bar and bistro, the menu includes classics such as pork escalope, egg, capers; the wine list has a Sauvignon Blanc from David Levin's Loire valley vineyard. A 'traditional' afternoon tea, with sandwiches and home-made scones, is served here every day. At breakfast, guests help themselves from a buffet of cereals, yogurt, fresh fruit and 'especially good croissants and pastries from the owner's bakery'.

28 Basil Street
London
SW3 1AS

T: 020 7589 6286
F: 020 7823 7826
E: reservations@thelevinhotel.co.uk
W: www.thelevinhotel.co.uk

BEDROOMS: 12.
OPEN: all year, restaurant closed Sun after 5.30 pm.
FACILITIES: lobby, library, honesty bar, bar/brasserie (Le Metro), free Wi-Fi, access to nearby health club/spa, unsuitable for disabled.
BACKGROUND MUSIC: 'calm' in restaurant, live acoustic guitar on Thurs evening.
LOCATION: central, underground Knightsbridge, private car park.
CHILDREN: all ages welcomed.
DOGS: not allowed.
CREDIT CARDS: all major cards.
PRICES: [2015] per room B&B (continental) £204–£515. Set menu £14–£18, à la carte £27.

SEE ALSO SHORTLIST

THE GRAZING GOAT

'Youthful in spirit', this pub-with-rooms lies in a chic enclave behind Marble Arch within the Portman Estate (the name comes from the goats once grazed here by Lady Portman, who was allergic to cow's milk). Rob Jones is the manager for the small Cubitt House group (who also own The Orange, Pimlico, see entry). 'Interesting' cocktails are served in the downstairs bar which has iron beams, a long bar with stools, lots of French oak. In the panelled dining room, a 'light, bright' space on the first floor, the menu has English bistro dishes like home-cured meats, apple and tomato chutney; salmon, haddock and mussel pie, green bean salad. The bedrooms are on the top three floors: 'Our room was beautifully furnished in simple, modern style; a wooden floor with coir mats; a mix of pale wood fittings with some darker wood furniture.' The rooms are well equipped ('good' coffee and a cafetière on the hospitality tray, a 'useful' map of London, a hairdryer and an iron). Breakfast in the bar, charged extra, is 'excellent', says a visitor this year.

6 New Quebec Street
London
W1H 7RQ

T: 020 7724 7243
E: reservations@thegrazinggoat.
co.uk
W: www.thegrazinggoat.co.uk

BEDROOMS: 8.
OPEN: all year.
FACILITIES: bar, dining room, free Wi-Fi, unsuitable for disabled.
BACKGROUND MUSIC: none.
LOCATION: central, underground Marble Arch.
CHILDREN: all ages welcomed.
DOGS: not allowed.
CREDIT CARDS: Amex, MasterCard, Visa.
PRICES: [2015] room only £210–£250. Cooked breakfast from £6.50, à la carte £35.

SEE ALSO SHORTLIST

DURRANTS

♥César award in 2010

In lively Marylebone village, the Miller family's traditional hotel has a 'personal, slightly eccentric' feel. 'We like the ambience, and the staff, particularly the amazing head porter, are delightful,' said guests this year. The hotel occupies a conversion of four terraced houses with a Georgian façade. 'Nicely old-fashioned', it has 'creaking, irregular floorboards' and 'pleasant' sitting rooms filled with antique furniture, engravings, and original paintings and prints. Ian McIntosh is the long-serving manager. Individually designed bedrooms vary in size, shape and aspect; most have air conditioning; all have antiques and prints. Some rooms have been refurbished this year. Visitors should discuss their choices before booking: recalling her 'perfect, silent' room on a previous visit, a returning guest this year found that a room at the front of the hotel suffered from traffic noise. In the wood-panelled restaurant, chef Cara Baird's dishes might include grilled sea trout, runner beans, carrot purée. 'Properly cooked' breakfasts are 'first rate'; less liked is the hotel's manner of charging separately for individual breakfast items.

26–32 George Street
London
W1H 5BJ

T: 020 7935 8131
F: 020 7487 3510
E: enquiries@durrantshotel.co.uk
W: www.durrantshotel.co.uk

BEDROOMS: 92. 7 on ground floor.
OPEN: all year, restaurant closed 25 Dec evening.
FACILITIES: lifts, ramp, bar, restaurant, lounge, 5 function rooms, free Wi-Fi.
BACKGROUND MUSIC: none.
LOCATION: off Oxford Street, underground Bond Street, Baker Street.
CHILDREN: all ages welcomed.
DOGS: only allowed in George Bar.
CREDIT CARDS: Amex, MasterCard, Visa.
PRICES: [2015] room from £195. Set dinner Mon–Fri £19.50–£21.50, Sun £27.50–£32.50, à la carte £55 (excluding 'optional' 12½ % service charge).

SEE ALSO SHORTLIST

THE VICTORIA

In a leafy residential neighbourhood with 'a pleasant village feel', this 'cheerful' pub-with-rooms is owned by restaurateur Greg Bellamy and celebrity chef Paul Merrett. Popular with locals, who like the 'friendly' staff and 'family ambience', the pub has leather armchairs and classic Penguin paperbacks; in cool weather, drinks and snacks are taken by the open fire. Meals are served in the conservatory restaurant and on the garden terrace. Paul Merrett uses much local produce, including foraged nettles, woodland herbs and wild mushrooms, in his modern British menus. Typical dishes: London gin-cured salmon gravadlax, beetroot gel, quail's eggs; spiced leg of lamb steak, baba ganoush, roasted sweet potato, tomato-chilli jam. The drinks list has many wines available by the glass. A light supper is served on Sunday nights in the winter; there are evening barbecues in summer. 'Good-value', modern bedrooms, with a coffee machine and home-baked cookies, are in a separate building reached via a covered walkway. Children are welcomed: they have their own menu; swings and a climbing frame in an outdoor play area. Richmond Park is five minutes' walk away.

10 West Temple Sheen
London
SW14 7RT

T: 020 8876 4238
E: bookings@thevictoria.net
W: www.thevictoria.net

BEDROOMS: 7. 3 on ground floor.
OPEN: all year, except 1 Jan.
FACILITIES: bar, lounge, restaurant, free Wi-Fi, garden, unsuitable for disabled.
BACKGROUND MUSIC: in pub and dining room.
LOCATION: Mortlake (10 mins' walk) from Waterloo/Clapham Jct, car park.
CHILDREN: all ages welcomed.
DOGS: allowed in pub and garden.
CREDIT CARDS: MasterCard, Visa.
PRICES: [2015] per room B&B (continental) single £125, double £135. Full English breakfast £10.50 per person, à la carte £40 (including 12½% discretionary service charge).

SEE ALSO SHORTLIST

THE PORTOBELLO **NEW**

On an 'elegant' residential street in Notting Hill, this quirky little hotel returns to the main section of the Guide under the new ownership of Peter and Jessica Frankopan, whose small Curious Group of Hotels includes the Canal House in Amsterdam (see GHG website). They have repainted throughout, freshening some of the older colour schemes, and providing new carpets, curtains and chair covers. They have retained the eccentric features of many of the themed rooms which were much loved by an earlier generation of rock 'n' roll celebrities. The rooms are now categorised as good, better, great and exceptional. The best rooms have a king-size bed, a view of the gardens at the back (not open to hotel guests), a sitting area. They have flamboyant colours and drapes; Alice Cooper, famously, is said to have kept a boa constrictor in the freestanding Edwardian bathing machine in Room 16. The corridors are narrow and some rooms are small (these have been cheered up this year). A continental breakfast and snacks are served in the large, light drawing room, which has an honesty bar.

22 Stanley Gardens
London
W11 2NG

T: 020 7727 2777
F: 020 7792 9641
E: stay@portobellohotel.com
W: www.portobellohotel.com

BEDROOMS: 21.
OPEN: all year.
FACILITIES: lift, drawing room, free Wi-Fi, unsuitable for disabled.
BACKGROUND MUSIC: 'chilled out' in drawing room.
LOCATION: Notting Hill, underground Notting Hill Gate.
CHILDREN: all ages welcomed.
DOGS: not allowed.
CREDIT CARDS: Amex, MasterCard, Visa.
PRICES: [2015] per room B&B (continental) from £195.

SEE ALSO SHORTLIST

♣ ARTIST RESIDENCE

NEW

César award: London hotel of the year

'The quirky rooms are full of character' and the staff are 'cheerful and helpful in equal measure' at this small hotel within walking distance of Tate Britain, say Guide inspectors in 2015. Owners Justin Salisbury and Charlotte Newey, who run sister hotels in Brighton and Penzance, have stylishly restored the former pub, using salvaged industrial materials for the eclectic fittings and furnishings. 'The entrance sets the style: there are retro touches, quirky artwork.' A 'youthful, modern' basement bar specialises in cocktails; the residents' lounge overlooks a courtyard garden. The bedrooms are on three upper floors. 'Our high-ceilinged first-floor room had well-thought-through details: excellent lighting, good storage, a well-stocked minibar; a small shower room with a fine rain shower. There were good linens on the metal-framed bed; stools were used as bedside tables. A large sash window (which could be opened) overlooked neighbouring houses; there was no noise at night.' Chef Michael Bremner serves 'delicious' sharing plates in the 64 Degrees restaurant. Breakfast, charged extra, has freshly squeezed juice, leaf teas, buttermilk pancakes.

25% DISCOUNT VOUCHERS

52 Cambridge Street
London
SW1V 4QQ

T: 020 7828 6684
E: london@artistresidence.co.uk
W: artistresidencelondon.co.uk

BEDROOMS: 10. 2 suites.
OPEN: all year except 24–26 Dec.
FACILITIES: lounge, bar, restaurant, private dining room, free Wi-Fi, unsuitable for disabled.
BACKGROUND MUSIC: soft jazz in reception and lounge all day.
LOCATION: Pimlico, underground Pimlico.
CHILDREN: all ages welcomed.
DOGS: not allowed.
CREDIT CARDS: Amex, MasterCard, Visa.
PRICES: [2015] room only £160–£380. Cooked breakfast from £6.50, à la carte £25–£35. 1-night bookings sometimes refused.

SEE ALSO SHORTLIST

THE ORANGE `NEW`

In a converted Georgian building in Pimlico, this 'friendly, informal' pub earns an upgrade from the Shortlist after a positive report by Guide inspectors. 'We liked it a lot for the style (lime oak, wooden flooring, high ceilings) and the engaging staff. Although it had a bustling pub atmosphere, we felt that as hotel guests we belonged.' Owned by the small Cubitt House group (see entry for the Grazing Goat, Marble Arch), it is managed by Bethany Young. There are four 'beautifully crafted, comfortable' bedrooms, reached by a narrow staircase, above the first-floor restaurant. 'Our room had large sash windows, a king-size bed, a wardrobe with free-range hangers, and a small writing table; the marble bathroom had a strong shower. Heavy curtains blocked most of the road noise.' In the L-shaped dining room, the seasonal modern menu of 'expected pub classics and well-presented mains' might include 'a lovely citrus prawn salad'; 'just-right' pan-fried salmon with Jerusalem artichokes and charred fennel. Breakfast, for an extra charge, has 'perfect scrambled eggs with delicious smoked bacon; good tea and coffee, freshly squeezed orange juice'.

37 Pimlico Road
London
SW1W 8NE

T: 020 7881 9844
E: reservations@theorange.co.uk
W: www.theorange.co.uk

BEDROOMS: 4.
OPEN: all year.
FACILITIES: restaurant, 2 bars, free Wi-Fi, unsuitable for disabled.
BACKGROUND MUSIC: none.
LOCATION: Pimlico, underground Victoria.
CHILDREN: all ages welcomed.
DOGS: none.
CREDIT CARDS: Amex, MasterCard, Visa.
PRICES: [2015] per room B&B £205–£240. À la carte £35.

SEE ALSO SHORTLIST

SMITHFIELD

THE ROOKERY

On a quiet alley near the historic meat market, Peter McKay and Douglas Blain's small luxury hotel is a 'soothing space' in the middle of a fast-developing area. A conversion of a collection of refurbished Georgian houses, it is decorated in 18th-century colours: public rooms have polished flagstone floors, panelled walls, gilt-framed portraits; there is 'a club-like calm throughout'. 'Friendly, helpful, always available', staff are 'outstanding', Guide inspectors said. Richly styled bedrooms have pictures and antiques; the quirky Rook's Nest suite has a sitting room under the spire. 'Our dark, masculine room had a huge, carved wooden headboard; red velvet curtains; a table and two chairs by a window. Double doors opened on to the immaculate bathroom; double-glazed windows provided solid soundproofing.' There is no restaurant, but a room-service menu and drinks from the honesty bar may be taken in the conservatory or on the small garden terrace. A short breakfast menu, delivered at a pre-arranged time, has freshly squeezed orange juice, bacon sandwiches and a 'generous' basket of 'delicious' pastries. Hazlitt's (Soho, London, see entry) is under the same ownership.

12 Peter's Lane
Cowcross Street
London
EC1M 6DS

T: 020 7336 0931
F: 020 7336 0932
E: reservations@rookery.co.uk
W: www.rookeryhotel.com

BEDROOMS: 33. 1 on ground floor suitable for disabled.
OPEN: all year.
FACILITIES: drawing room, library, conservatory, meeting rooms, free Wi-Fi, small garden terrace.
BACKGROUND MUSIC: none.
LOCATION: Smithfield, underground Farringdon, Barbican.
CHILDREN: all ages welcomed.
DOGS: not allowed.
CREDIT CARDS: all major cards.
PRICES: [2015] per room B&B £282–£750. À la carte (room service only) £22.

SEE ALSO SHORTLIST

HAZLITT'S

♥César award in 2002

Guests ring a bell to enter Peter McKay and Douglas Blain's 'stunningly individual' hotel, which occupies three Georgian houses off Soho Square. Inside, 'every corridor and every room has much to investigate and appreciate'. 'It is an island of civility amongst the stream of maddening hoards that flock into London,' says a regular visitor. Public areas are filled with 'old architectural features, old furniture, old paintings'; the library has a working fireplace, an honesty bar and plenty of books. Quentin Hales is the manager; staff are 'friendly and efficient'. Elaborately furnished bedrooms have original panelled walls, antiques and silk curtains; period bathrooms have restored fixtures and fittings, sometimes a roll-top bath. 'Our room at the back had a wonderfully comfortable bed. We slept with two windows ajar and heard no noise during the night – admirable for central London.' A short breakfast menu, served in the bedroom or the library, has bacon sandwiches, fruit and Greek yogurt, or a baker's basket of freshly baked croissants and pastries. A small room-service menu is available all day. (Peter Reynolds, and others)

6 Frith Street
Soho Square
London
W1D 3JA

T: 020 7434 1771
F: 020 7439 1524
E: reservations@hazlitts.co.uk
W: www.hazlittshotel.com

BEDROOMS: 30. 2 on ground floor.
OPEN: all year.
FACILITIES: lift, 2 sitting rooms, meeting room, free Wi-Fi, unsuitable for disabled.
BACKGROUND MUSIC: none.
LOCATION: Soho (front windows triple glazed, rear rooms quietest), NCP nearby, underground Tottenham Court Road, Leicester Square.
CHILDREN: all ages welcomed.
DOGS: not allowed.
CREDIT CARDS: all major cards.
PRICES: [2015] per room B&B £288–£834.

SEE ALSO SHORTLIST

NUMBER SIXTEEN

♔César award in 2011

Guests like the vibrant colours and stylishly mismatched furnishings at this modern hotel, on a discreet side street of white stucco terrace houses. 'I was blown away,' one visitor said. Another comment: 'No bland corporate anonymity here.' Part of Tim and Kit Kemp's small Firmdale Hotels group, it has 'a personal, home-from-home feeling' throughout; staff are 'helpful' and 'courteous'. The drawing room and library have fresh flowers, books, plenty of seating, floor-to-ceiling windows overlooking the street. They lead to a bright conservatory and a small, lush garden, where guests may take meals and afternoon tea in warm weather. Individually decorated bedrooms have 'a wonderfully comfortable' bed, a writing desk and a 'well-equipped' bathroom. A basement room was less liked. Interconnecting rooms can accommodate a family. Children are welcomed with a book of London activities, their own bathrobe and toiletries; DVDs, books and board games are available to borrow. An all-day room-service menu has light meals and snacks. In-room massages and beauty treatments may be arranged. (AL, and others)

16 Sumner Place
London
SW7 3EG

T: 020 7589 5232
E: sixteen@firmdale.com
w: www.firmdalehotels.com

BEDROOMS: 41. 1 on ground floor.
OPEN: all year.
FACILITIES: ramp, drawing room, library, conservatory, free Wi-Fi, civil wedding licence, garden.
BACKGROUND MUSIC: none.
LOCATION: Kensington, underground South Kensington.
CHILDREN: all ages welcomed.
DOGS: not allowed.
CREDIT CARDS: Amex, MasterCard, Visa.
PRICES: [2015] room from £174. Breakfast £18.50–£24.50 per person (plus 12½% discretionary service charge).

SEE ALSO SHORTLIST

ONE ALDWYCH

♀César award in 2005

A papier mâché dog covered in Beano comic pages greets guests at this contemporary luxury hotel on the edge of the West End's theatre district. Once home to the offices of the Morning Post newspaper, the grand Edwardian building, at the junction of Aldwych and the Strand, has 'elegant' public spaces, 'comfortable', modern bedrooms, and 'superb' food. The 'large and light' double-height lobby has huge flower arrangements; modern sculptures and artworks from the hotel's collection are displayed throughout. Sleek, stylish, air-conditioned bedrooms have lots of thoughtful touches: a minibar is filled with local treats; flowers and fresh fruit are delivered daily; a weather forecast for the following day is placed on the pillow at turn-down. Children are welcomed with their own bathrobe and slippers; games, books and toys are available to borrow. There are two restaurants: relaxed Indigo serves modern European dishes; the more formal Axis has seasonal British menus that might include Rhug Estate pork, sea purslane, crackling, winter truffle. Guests also have access to a residents' lounge, for cocktails and an all-day menu.

1 Aldwych
London
WC2B 4BZ

T: 020 7300 1000
F: 020 7300 0501
E: reservations@onealdwych.com
W: www.onealdwych.com

BEDROOMS: 105. 6 suitable for disabled.
OPEN: all year.
FACILITIES: lifts, bar, 2 restaurants, guest lounge, free Wi-Fi, function facilities, health club (18-metre swimming pool), civil wedding licence.
BACKGROUND MUSIC: 'easy listening' in bar and Indigo restaurant.
LOCATION: Strand, valet parking, underground Covent Garden, Charing Cross, Waterloo.
CHILDREN: all ages welcomed.
DOGS: not allowed.
CREDIT CARDS: Amex, MasterCard, Visa.
PRICES: [2015] rooms and suites £338–£1,545, breakfast from £19 (continental), pre- and post-theatre menu £20–£25, à la carte (Indigo) £30, (Axis) £45 (including 12½% optional service charge).

SEE ALSO SHORTLIST

THE GORING

◊César award in 1994

Founded by Otto Goring, great-grandfather of the present owner, Jeremy Goring, this grand Edwardian institution continues to innovate and renovate. The doors closed for a month for the first time in 105 years early in 2015, to enable work on the front hall, which has been redesigned by Russell Sage: he has created a whimsical scene showing exotic wild animals in an English park setting, with the windows dressed with Gainsborough silk. David Morgan-Hewitt is managing director. Michael Beavan, the 'host', continues to patrol the lobby to assist guests; many of the staff are long serving. The 'attention to detail' (from shoe cleaning to valet parking) is often commented on. Guests in the more expensive suites now have the services of a footman. A croquet lawn has been established in the garden, where afternoon tea can be taken on the veranda (an eclair trolley is new). Shay Cooper, the chef, serves English dishes in the smart restaurant, perhaps Suffolk pork fillet, pickled turnip, suckling pig belly, beetroots, smoked eel fritter. Children are welcomed: new parents receive a basket of essentials to help with the baby.

Beeston Place
London
SW1W 0JW

T: 020 7396 9000
F: 020 7834 4393
E: reception@thegoring.com
W: www.thegoring.com

BEDROOMS: 69. 2 suitable for disabled.
OPEN: all year.
FACILITIES: lifts, ramps, lounge bar, terrace room, restaurant, function facilities, free Wi-Fi, civil wedding licence, private garden (croquet).
BACKGROUND MUSIC: none.
LOCATION: near Victoria station, mews parking, underground Victoria.
CHILDREN: all ages welcomed.
DOGS: not allowed.
CREDIT CARDS: Amex, MasterCard, Visa.
PRICES: [2015] per room B&B from £430. Breakfast £24–£32, set dinner £52.50.

SEE ALSO SHORTLIST

ENGLAND

Boats moored on the River Avon, Bidford-on-Avon

ABBOTSBURY Dorset

THE ABBEY HOUSE

In a 'glorious position' on the fringes of a historic coastal Dorset village, this traditional B&B has long been run by the 'most welcoming' Jonathan and Maureen Cooke. The ruins of the adjacent 11th-century abbey give it its name. The 14th-century house has views of the largest tithe barn in England, a millpond and a 'spacious' garden. The bedrooms are 'wonderfully quiet, clean, well equipped and very comfortable, with fast broadband, a good TV and little chocolates by the bed'. This year the Cookes have given the Benedictine room 'a complete make-over with new carpets'; it has a new bathroom with a bath and separate shower. Monks, the smallest room, has views of the abbey ruins. The gardens have 'pergolas, arbours, and lots of tables and chairs'. The lounge doubles as a tea room. Breakfast ('good' muesli and grilled haddock, cafetière coffee) is taken in 'an impressively oaky-beamy dining room with huge open fireplace'. No evening meals, but restaurant recommendations are given. Walkers and fossil hunters take note: Dorset's Jurassic Coast is within walking distance; so is Abbotsbury's swannery.

Church Street
Abbotsbury
DT3 4JJ

T: 01305 871330
E: info@theabbeyhouse.co.uk
W: www.theabbeyhouse.co.uk

BEDROOMS: 5.
OPEN: all year, tea room open for lunches Apr–Sept, dinners for house parties only.
FACILITIES: reception, lounge, breakfast/tea room, free Wi-Fi, civil wedding licence, 1½-acre garden (stage for opera), sea 15 mins' walk, unsuitable for disabled.
BACKGROUND MUSIC: none.
LOCATION: village centre.
CHILDREN: not under 12.
DOGS: not allowed.
CREDIT CARDS: MasterCard, Visa.
PRICES: [2015] per room B&B £75–£125.

ALDEBURGH Suffolk

Map 2:C6

THE WENTWORTH

Overlooking the fishing boats on the shingle beach, this 'welcoming' hotel has been run by three generations of the same family since 1920; Michael Pritt, the current owner, has been at the helm for 40 years. 'Nothing changes: it is a real treat each time we visit,' a regular visitor says. (The traditional atmosphere may not cater to all tastes: a guest this year thought some overall refurbishment was in order.) Another comment: 'Excellent service.' The hotel is popular with older guests who like the 'comfortable' rooms, 'excellent', long-serving staff and 'continually good food, especially fish from Aldeburgh beach'. Public rooms have a 'well-put-together' mix of antique and modern furniture; afternoon tea, taken in the open-plan lounge, has a cake of the day. Many of the bedrooms in the main hotel have sea views; those in Darfield House, across the road, have access to a garden with outdoor seating. There are fresh flowers on the tables in the restaurant, where chef Jason Shaw's British menus might include grilled East Coast plaice, buttered new potatoes, salsa verde. Breakfast is 'excellent'. (Simon Rodway, and others)

25% DISCOUNT VOUCHERS

Wentworth Road
Aldeburgh
IP15 5BD

T: 01728 452312
F: 01728 454343
E: stay@wentworth-aldeburgh.co.uk
W: www.wentworth-aldeburgh.com

BEDROOMS: 35. 7 in Darfield House opposite, 5 on ground floor, 1 suitable for disabled.
OPEN: all year.
FACILITIES: ramps, 2 lounges, bar, restaurant, private dining room, conference room, free Wi-Fi, 2 terrace gardens, shingle beach 200 yds.
BACKGROUND MUSIC: none.
LOCATION: seafront, 5 mins' walk from centre.
CHILDREN: all ages welcomed.
DOGS: welcomed (£2 per dog per night), not allowed in restaurant.
CREDIT CARDS: all major cards.
PRICES: [2015] per room B&B £160–£285. Set dinner £19.50–£25. 1-night bookings refused Sat.

SEE ALSO SHORTLIST

DEANS PLACE

On the outskirts of a pretty medieval village, this country hotel stands in 'lovely' gardens on the banks of the Cuckmere river. Liked for its 'nice traditional feel', it is owned by Michael Clinch; James Dopson is the manager. 'There is plenty of space for sitting and relaxing'; 'nooks and crannies where you can hide with a good book'. The 'well-decorated' bar area has a log fire and a good selection of gins. Lunch and cream teas may be taken in the Terrace lounge, overlooking the croquet lawn. In the 'attractive' restaurant, chef Stuart Dunley cooks modern British menus with European influences, perhaps rabbit and celeriac terrine, plum purée, cider bread; roasted rump of lamb, basil and goat's cheese bread and butter pudding, braised purple endive. A vegetarian menu has 'varied, unusual choices – not your typical fare'. Many of the 'well-furnished' bedrooms have views of the gardens or the surrounding countryside; family rooms are available. The hotel is on the South Downs Way; Glyndebourne is a 15-minute drive away; the coast is within easy reach. (OH, SR)

Seaford Road
Alfriston
BN26 5TW

T: 01323 870248
F: 01323 870918
E: reception@deansplacehotel.co.uk
W: www.deansplacehotel.co.uk

BEDROOMS: 36. 1 suitable for disabled.
OPEN: all year.
FACILITIES: lounge, bar, restaurant, function rooms, free Wi-Fi, civil wedding licence, terrace, heated outdoor swimming pool (12 by 6 metres, May–Sept), 4-acre garden.
BACKGROUND MUSIC: classical, jazz in restaurant.
LOCATION: edge of village.
CHILDREN: all ages welcomed.
DOGS: allowed in some bedrooms (£5 a night charge).
CREDIT CARDS: all major cards.
PRICES: [2015] per room B&B from £140, D,B&B from £210. Set meals £35, à la carte £38.

SEE ALSO SHORTLIST

AMBLESIDE Cumbria

Map 4: inset C2

NANNY BROW   `NEW`

Surrounded by landscaped gardens and private woodlands, this Arts and Crafts home has views of the River Brathay below and the fells beyond. It has been 'extensively and sympathetically' refurbished by 'friendly owners' Sue and Peter Robinson into a 'very comfortable' guest house. The lounge has sofas, period armchairs, cards, games and magazines; the bar in the renovated rear courtyard serves locally brewed real ales. Bedrooms are individually furnished with antique bed and period pieces; all look over the garden and the surrounding countryside. Three garden suites lead directly to outdoor seating and the lawns. 'Our room was not large, but the bathroom was modern and beautifully fitted out.' Served in a large, light room, 'excellent' breakfasts have home-made muesli, home-baked drop scones, porridge with runny honey and dark sugar; hot dishes are cooked to order. Evening meals are not provided (a light supper may be ordered in advance), but the Robinsons have many recommendations of eating places. Good walks to Loughrigg and Grasmere 'directly from the property'. Guests have access to a swimming pool and spa close by. (John and Kay Patterson)

25% DISCOUNT VOUCHERS

Clappersgate
Ambleside
LA22 9NF

T: 015394 33232
E: unwind@nannybrow.co.uk
W: www.nannybrow.co.uk

BEDROOMS: 14. 2 in annexe, with own lounge.
OPEN: all year.
FACILITIES: lounge, bar, dining room, free Wi-Fi, civil wedding licence, 5½ acres of formal garden (sun terrace, croquet) and woodlands, unsuitable for disabled.
BACKGROUND MUSIC: 'low volume' in breakfast room and bar.
LOCATION: 1½ miles W of Ambleside.
CHILDREN: not under 12.
DOGS: not allowed.
CREDIT CARDS: Amex, MasterCard, Visa.
PRICES: [2015] per room B&B £150–£280.

AMBLESIDE Cumbria

Map 4: inset C2

THE REGENT

'A well-run hotel with a great atmosphere', the Hewitt family's white-fronted building is opposite a slipway and pier on Lake Windermere. The owning family are much in evidence: Andrew Hewitt is the 'hands-on' manager who 'seemed to be everywhere', say visitors. Bedrooms ('tastefully furnished') vary in size and shape. Garden rooms, which are on the first floor, have a king-size bed, a large sitting area and a private terrace. The Sail Loft room has a private wooden terrace with a lake view. Smaller rooms are 'comfortable and well equipped'. The Regent is 'proud' to be dog-friendly; courtyard rooms are ideal for dog owners (£10 a night charge). In the split-level restaurant, chef John Mathers' seasonal menu might include tomato, red pepper and basil soup; stuffed shoulder of Lakeland lamb, baby roast potato, sugar snap peas, port wine jus. A 'late, late' breakfast (served from 8 am until noon) has handmade Cumberland sausage, Manx kippers, oak-smoked salmon, Bury black pudding, home-made muesli, Belgian waffles; vegetarian alternatives to the full cooked. 'An excellent location to explore the Lakes.' (ID)

Waterhead Bay
Ambleside
LA22 0ES

T: 015394 32254
F: 015394 31474
E: info@regentlakes.co.uk
W: www.regentlakes.co.uk

BEDROOMS: 32. 10 in courtyard, 5 in garden, 7 on ground floor.
OPEN: all year except 24–26 Dec.
FACILITIES: ramp, lounge, sun lounge, bar, restaurant, free Wi-Fi, courtyard, ¼-acre garden, on Lake Windermere, unsuitable for disabled.
BACKGROUND MUSIC: relaxing in restaurant.
LOCATION: on A591 at Waterhead Bay.
CHILDREN: all ages welcomed.
DOGS: welcomed, not allowed in restaurant (or bar at busy times).
CREDIT CARDS: Amex, MasterCard, Visa.
PRICES: [2015] per room B&B from £119, D,B&B from £169. Set menu £22–£28, à la carte £30.

AMBLESIDE Cumbria

Map 4: inset C2

ROTHAY MANOR

♥ César award in 1992

'Comfortable, welcoming and very professional', the Nixon family's traditional hotel has many fans. The Regency features of the house, built for a prosperous Liverpool merchant close to the town and Lake Windermere, have been retained. Tables are well spaced in the elegant restaurant (recently redecorated) where long-serving chef Jane Binns serves a daily-changing British menu of seasonal dishes, perhaps Stilton and walnut pâté, apricot-vodka dressing; roast venison, baked red cabbage, baby spinach. The tempting desserts are 'too good for those of us on a diet', is a recent comment. The 'immaculate' bedrooms are 'beautifully furnished'; bedside lighting might be 'muted' but there is 'good storage', a selection of coffee, tea and hot chocolate; 'a flat-screen TV and a good selection of DVDs to borrow'. The best rooms have a balcony and views to Wansfell Pike. Guests can explore the landscaped gardens; take a short walk to the head of Lake Windermere; or look out from the restaurant over afternoon tea, with its 'large selection of cakes'. Breakfast is informal and 'substantial'. (J and MB)

25% DISCOUNT VOUCHERS

Rothay Bridge
Ambleside
LA22 0EH

T: 015394 33605
F: 015397 33607
E: hotel@rothaymanor.co.uk
W: www.rothaymanor.co.uk

BEDROOMS: 19. 2 in annexe, 2 suitable for disabled.
OPEN: all year except 3–22 Jan.
FACILITIES: ramp, 2 lounges, bar, 2 dining rooms, meeting/conference facilities, free Wi-Fi, ½-acre garden (croquet), free access to local leisure centre.
BACKGROUND MUSIC: classical/'easy listening'/acoustic in restaurant, morning and evening.
LOCATION: ¼ mile SW of Ambleside.
CHILDREN: all ages welcomed.
DOGS: not allowed.
CREDIT CARDS: MasterCard, Visa.
PRICES: [2015] per room B&B £100–£220, D,B&B £155–£275. À la carte £32.50. 1-night bookings often refused Sat.

SHALLOWDALE HOUSE

Cesar award in 2005

'On my five-hour drive I wonder if it is too far to go for a weekend; as soon as I enter the front door, the tranquillity and comfort reassure me that the journey is worthwhile.' A frequent visitor explains why he returns to Phillip Gill and Anton van der Horst's 'immaculately' kept hillside guest house which overlooks a designated Area of Outstanding Natural Beauty. Visitors can take in the view over afternoon tea on the terrace, or use the binoculars provided on the bedside table. The food ('always superb') and the warm hospitality are often praised. 'The public rooms are filled with antiques and objets d'art, comfortable chairs and a wide range of books (not a Mills and Boon among them!).' Afternoon tea can be taken outside in the 'well-kept' gardens. The bedrooms are 'spacious and elegant, thoughtfully equipped and well lit'. Phillip Gill's 'excellent' four-course set dinner might have potato and celeriac pancakes, supremes of guineafowl, pancetta, rosemary and mascarpone; 'a pear and blueberry tart that was simply magic'. At breakfast 'the freshly squeezed orange juice deserves a mention'. (Richard Creed)

West End, Ampleforth
nr York
YO62 4DY

T: 01439 788325
E: stay@shallowdalehouse.co.uk
W: www.shallowdalehouse.co.uk

BEDROOMS: 3.
OPEN: all year except Christmas/New Year, occasionally at other times.
FACILITIES: drawing room, sitting room, dining room, free Wi-Fi, 2½-acre grounds, unsuitable for disabled.
BACKGROUND MUSIC: none.
LOCATION: edge of village.
CHILDREN: not under 12.
DOGS: not allowed.
CREDIT CARDS: MasterCard, Visa.
PRICES: [2015] per room B&B single £95–£129, double £115–£150. Set dinner £39.50. 1-night bookings occasionally refused weekends.

ARUNDEL West Sussex

Map 2:E3

THE TOWN HOUSE

'The food and the welcome are superb' at Lee and Katie Williams's 'pleasant' restaurant-with-rooms at the top of the High Street. It is within walking distance of the antique shops and historic sites of a 'busy, handsome Georgian market town'. The owners have added a family suite this year in the top floor of the Grade II listed Regency building. It has two bedrooms and a shared shower room. The other bedrooms are on the first and second floors. 'Rosemary has a large, comfortable bed; white-painted original coving and panelling; plenty of storage space; and a splendid view of Arundel Castle (seat of the dukes of Norfolk) and its battlements.' The dining room has a remarkable gilded 16th-century carved walnut ceiling imported from Florence ('worth a visit in its own right'. Guests are encouraged to 'feel as if they are at a casual dinner party with friends'. Lee Williams cooks a modern menu of 'excellent' dishes, perhaps warm confit salmon, artichoke purée, pea shoots. Breakfast includes 'home-made bread and any permutation of full English. The bacon was very good.' (Richard Crosby)

65 High Street
Arundel
BN18 9AJ

T: 01903 883847
E: enquiries@thetownhouse.co.uk
W: www.thetownhouse.co.uk

BEDROOMS: 6.
OPEN: all year except 25/26 Dec,
1 Jan, 2 weeks Easter, 2 weeks Oct,
restaurant closed Sun/Mon.
FACILITIES: restaurant, free Wi-Fi,
unsuitable for disabled.
BACKGROUND MUSIC: 'easy listening'
in restaurant.
LOCATION: top end of High Street.
CHILDREN: all ages welcomed.
DOGS: not allowed.
CREDIT CARDS: Diners, MasterCard,
Visa.
PRICES: [2015] per room B&B £105–
£140, D,B&B (midweek) £145–£180.
Set dinner £25.50– £29.50. 1-night
bookings refused weekends in
high season.

ASHWATER Devon

Map 1:C3

BLAGDON MANOR

♥ Cesar award in 2006

'In the depths of the Devon countryside', this Grade II listed restaurant-with-rooms has 'beautifully manicured gardens where birds sing and bees buzz'. The owners, Liz and Steve Morey, are 'the best kind of hoteliers – friendly and helpful without being ingratiating'. Guests are likely to be greeted by their three chocolate Labradors. 'Kings of the place, they are friendly, and guests' dogs are received with particular civility.' Bedrooms have a mix of modern and reproduction furniture; 'our room had thoughtful touches: good biscuits, a selection of quality magazines. Though small, it was well appointed; the bathroom had a spectacular shower and a bath with country views.' The large conservatory dining room has 'well-spaced, elegantly laid' tables. Steve Morey's 'excellent' cooking is 'very fresh and pleasant'. 'Tempura of lemon sole melts in the mouth; scallop, confit pork belly, apple and red onion with cinnamon was incredibly tasty.' In season, aperitifs, tea or drinks are served on a large patio. A 'generous full English breakfast' was 'the best ever'. (Francine and Ian Walsh, Steve Hur)

Blagdon Manor
Ashwater
EX21 5DF

T: 01409 211224
E: stay@blagdon.com
W: www.blagdon.com

BEDROOMS: 6.
OPEN: all year Wed–Sun.
FACILITIES: ramps, lounge, library, snug, bar, conservatory, restaurant, private dining room, free Wi-Fi in lounge, 20-acre grounds (3-acre gardens, croquet, giant chess, gazebo, pond), unsuitable for disabled.
BACKGROUND MUSIC: none.
LOCATION: 8 miles NE of Launceston.
CHILDREN: not under 12.
DOGS: welcomed (£10 charge per night).
CREDIT CARDS: MasterCard, Visa.
PRICES: [2015] per room B&B £155–£260. Set dinner £35–£40. 1-night bookings refused Christmas.

ASKHAM Cumbria

Map 4: inset C2

ASKHAM HALL

'A hotel of character', this Grade I listed country house, 13th-century in origin, has been renovated by its owners, Charlie and Juno Lowther. They eschewed the formality of traditional hotels in favour of creating a 'Bohemian home from home', mixing antiques and contemporary furnishings. Three additional bedrooms were being added as the Guide went to press. Inspectors had a 'pretty room with an original stone fireplace, an antique chest of drawers, two upright chairs; traditional fabrics with a design of leaves and flowers on the bedhead and the curtains; a large roll-top bath and a well-stocked bookshelf in the bathroom'. Guests have use of the drawing room ('the epitome of a wealthy family home'); there's a heated outdoor swimming pool, a spa; birdwatching in the colourful terraces of the well-maintained gardens. In the restaurant, chef Richard Swale uses ingredients from the kitchen garden for his modern dishes, perhaps oxtail ravioli, broccoli, onions and Hawkshead beer; poached rhubarb, pistachio cake and rhubarb panna cotta. 'Breakfast included poached eggs from local farms; fruit salad and coffee were both enjoyed.'

Askham Hall
Penrith
Askham
CA10 2PF

T: 01931 712350
E: enquiries@askhamhall.co.uk
W: www.askhamhall.co.uk

BEDROOMS: 12. (3 being added in 2015.)
OPEN: all year Tues–Sat (Sun/Mon groups only), except Christmas, 2 Jan–mid-Feb.
FACILITIES: drawing room, library, billiard room, 3 dining rooms, free Wi-Fi, civil wedding licence, 12-acre gardens, small heated swimming pool (10 by 5 metres), only restaurant suitable for disabled.
BACKGROUND MUSIC: none.
LOCATION: 5 miles S of Penrith.
CHILDREN: all ages welcomed, not under 10 in restaurant.
DOGS: allowed in bedrooms (£15 charge per stay), public rooms except in restaurant.
CREDIT CARDS: all major cards.
PRICES: per room B&B £150–£320. Set dinner £50.

AUSTWICK North Yorkshire

Map 4:D3

AUSTWICK HALL

At the apex of Yorkshire, Lancashire and Cumbria, this 'highly personal' manor house is run as a B&B with 'obvious enthusiasm' by Michael Pearson and Eric Culley. Their 'loving' restoration of the house (originally a 12th-century peel tower with Tudor and Georgian additions) extends to the grounds, which have a snowdrop walk, walled kitchen garden, sculpture trail (with pieces by local artists), 'the occasional pony just outside a gate, busily munching hay'. Inside, 'an eclectic mix of antiques and artefacts is displayed with style'. Guide inspectors in 2015 were welcomed with 'relaxing' tea and home-made fruitcake in front of the fire. 'Our cosy room had a wooden floor with rugs, a very comfortable, beautifully draped four-poster bed, good-sized wardrobe, plenty of seating; small, bright en suite bathroom with walk-in shower, freestanding bath, nice hot water. Tea/coffee facilities, biscuits and TV were provided, but the best entertainment was looking out at the gardens from the two windows.' Breakfast has fresh fruit, cereals, smoked salmon, cooked options; juices were freshly squeezed, wholemeal toast 'sliced thickly' and jam home made.'

Townhead Lane
Austwick
LA2 8BS

T: 01524 251794
E: austwickhall@austwick.org
W: www.austwickhall.co.uk

BEDROOMS: 4.
OPEN: all year.
FACILITIES: hall, sitting room, drawing room, dining room, free Wi-Fi, 13-acre gardens, hot tub, unsuitable for disabled.
BACKGROUND MUSIC: none.
LOCATION: edge of village.
CHILDREN: not under 16.
DOGS: not allowed.
CREDIT CARDS: MasterCard, Visa.
PRICES: [2015] per room B&B single £110–£140, double £125–£155 (rates lower Feb/Mar mid-week). 1-night bookings refused bank holiday weekends.

THE TRADDOCK

♥César award in 2014

There is a 'happy buzz' about the Reynolds family's small hotel, a Grade II listed Georgian manor, says a visitor in 2015. On a wild and wet weekend, the public areas were 'snug, with a crackling fire by the front door, and more well-stuffed armchairs and sofas than any weary traveller could reasonably expect'. The bedrooms vary in size: 'Our room was not one of the most expensive, but was wonderfully rich and rare, with a gilt wicker bedhead, brocade cushions and covers, a lovely Persian rug and sparkly lamps. The tea tray had a proper-sized teapot, a cafetière, biscuits which we hoovered up after an exciting walk, decent mugs and fresh milk in a flask. The small bathroom had a big showerhead, bright lighting, shiny tiles.' The chef, John Pratt, is a follower of the Slow Food Movement; he sources his ingredients locally for dishes like roast rack of Mansergh Hall lamb, fondant potatoes, clapshot purée, redcurrant and rioja reduction. 'Breakfast and dinner left us in need of more walks; good-value wines by the glass.' (Sophie Harrowes)

25% DISCOUNT VOUCHERS

Austwick
LA2 8BY

T: 01524 251224
F: 01524 251796
E: info@thetraddock.co.uk
W: www.thetraddock.co.uk

BEDROOMS: 12. 1 on ground floor.
OPEN: all year.
FACILITIES: 3 lounges, bar, 2 dining rooms, function facilities, free Wi-Fi, 1½-acre grounds (sun deck), unsuitable for disabled.
BACKGROUND MUSIC: in public areas except 1 lounge.
LOCATION: 4 miles NW of Settle, train Settle, bus.
CHILDREN: all ages welcomed.
DOGS: welcomed, in public rooms on lead, not in dining rooms.
CREDIT CARDS: MasterCard, Visa.
PRICES: [2015] per room B&B from £95, D,B&B from £160. À la carte £32.50. 1-night bookings refused weekends in season.

AYLESBURY Buckinghamshire

Map 2:C3

HARTWELL HOUSE

♔ César award in 1997

Recommended 'without reservation' this year, this 'blissfully quiet' stately mansion, home to Louis XVIII during his exile from France, is run by Richard Broyd's Historic House Hotels for the National Trust. Guests are encouraged to make use of the 'sumptuous' public rooms, which have brocaded sofas, marble fireplaces and rococo ceilings; 'there was a real peacefulness about these spaces'. The bedrooms are in the main house, Hartwell Court (a restored riding school and stables) and the Old Rectory, a Georgian house in the grounds. A room here had a bed in a mezzanine space overlooking 'a spacious living room; plush, old-fashioned but elegant furnishings; the bed was enormous'. In the elegant dining room, chef Daniel Richardson's dishes (on a seasonal menu) have 'beautifully fresh ingredients, simple concoctions and light seasonings'. 'We enjoyed crisp quail's eggs with spinach; venison, and poire belle Hélène.' Breakfast has 'the best porridge we have tasted'. 'The spa is very nice indeed, in particular the indoor pool and outdoor hot tub.' (John and Irene Harding, Anna and Bill Brewer, and others)

25% DISCOUNT VOUCHERS

Oxford Road
Aylesbury
HP17 8NR

T: 01296 747444
F: 01296 747450
E: info@hartwell-house.com
W: www.hartwell-house.com

BEDROOMS: 48, 16 in stable block, some on ground floor, 2 suitable for disabled.
OPEN: all year.
FACILITIES: lift, ramps, 4 drawing rooms, bar, 3 dining rooms, conference facilities, free Wi-Fi, civil wedding licence, spa (swimming pool, 8 by 16 metres), 94-acre grounds (tennis).
BACKGROUND MUSIC: none.
LOCATION: 2 miles W of Aylesbury.
CHILDREN: not under 6.
DOGS: allowed in the suites in Hartwell Court, guide dogs in main house, dining areas.
CREDIT CARDS: Amex, MasterCard, Visa.
PRICES: [2015] per room B&B single £175–£290, double £205–£700. Set dinner £32–£52.

BABBACOMBE Devon

Map 1:D5

THE CARY ARMS

'Courage' is required by drivers making the 'precipitous, twisting descent' to Lana de Savary's small hotel in a 'fabulously secluded cove' near Torquay. 'It is worth the journey and an entry in the Guide,' said an inspector, who received a 'genuine welcome' from the chef and duty manager in 2015. All the bedrooms have a sea view; several have a balcony with a table and chairs. 'My room was spacious: neutral colours emphasised the clean lines; red-framed yacht photographs matched the resplendent leather bed headboard; a capsule coffee machine and complimentary sloe gin were pleasing touches; the bathroom was spotless and inviting.' In the lounge there are binoculars for dolphin-watching. Ben Kingdon cooks superior pub-style food, served in the conservatory, in a bar with the feel of a 'fishermen's pub', or, in warm weather, on a terrace. Seafood is a speciality: 'We shared a succulent prawn, crayfish and rocket pancake on Shrove Tuesday. Loin of pork and a vegetarian risotto were generous in size.' At breakfast, home-made granola and 'thick, sweet bacon and buttery scrambled eggs' provided 'an uplifting start to the day'.

Beach Road
Babbacombe
TQ1 3LX

T: 01803 327110
F: 01803 323221
E: enquiries@caryarms.co.uk
W: www.caryarms.co.uk

BEDROOMS: 8. 2 on ground floor, plus 4 self-catering cottages.
OPEN: all year.
FACILITIES: lounge, bar, restaurant, conservatory, free Wi-Fi, civil wedding licence, treatment room, garden, terrace.
BACKGROUND MUSIC: 'relaxed' radio all day in bar.
LOCATION: by beach.
CHILDREN: all ages welcomed.
DOGS: two dog-friendly rooms and four cottages.
CREDIT CARDS: Amex, MasterCard, Visa.
PRICES: [2015] per room B&B £195–£495. À la carte £30. 1-night bookings sometimes refused.

BARNSLEY HOUSE

Once the home of the celebrated gardener
Rosemary Verey, this late 17th-century gabled
stone manor house is run as a luxury hotel by
the owners of nearby Calcot Manor, Tetbury
(see entry). Michele Mella is the manager. Head
gardener Richard Gatenby has maintained the
glory of the gardens, which were planted with
Verey's signature soft tones, parterres, topiary,
laburnum walk and a potager. A path leads to
a spa with a hydrotherapy pool and a 30-seat
cinema. The potager supplies the vegetables
and herbs for chef Graham Grafton's dishes,
perhaps purple sprouting broccoli, quinoa,
chilli broad beans; confit duck, sauté potatoes,
sprout flowers. Meals are taken in the Potager
restaurant, a 'charming long room with tall
windows'; mirrors help bring the colours of the
garden into the room. When the 'designerish'
features of one bedroom did not please
(oversized bath, awkward stairs), the response
to a request for a move was 'impeccable; no
demur'. The Rosemary Verey Suite has a private
courtyard facing the garden with outdoor
seating. A breakfast buffet has 'chunky toast,
leaf tea, good cooked dishes'.

Barnsley
GL7 5EE

T: 01285 740000
F: 01285 740925
E: info@barnsleyhouse.com
W: www.barnsleyhouse.com

BEDROOMS: 18. 7 in stableyard, 4 in
courtyard, 1 in cottage.
OPEN: all year.
FACILITIES: 2 lounges, bar,
restaurant, cinema, meeting room,
free Wi-Fi, civil wedding licence,
terrace, 11-acre garden (spa, outdoor
hydrotherapy pool), unsuitable for
disabled.
BACKGROUND MUSIC: 'easy listening',
'lounge' music in restaurant.
LOCATION: 5 miles NE of
Cirencester.
CHILDREN: not under 14.
DOGS: allowed in stableyard rooms,
not in grounds.
CREDIT CARDS: Amex, MasterCard,
Visa.
PRICES: per room B&B £200–£310.
À la carte £40. 1-night bookings
refused Sat.

SEE ALSO SHORTLIST

LITTLE BARWICK HOUSE

25% DISCOUNT VOUCHERS

♀César award in 2002

'In a lovely Alice in Wonderland setting' close to the Somerset/Dorset border, Tim and Emma Ford's restaurant-with-rooms is liked for the 'guaranteed comfort, relaxation and good food'. The 'rolling programme of renovation' of the 'beautiful' listed Georgian dower house continues. The 'clean and cosy' country-style bedrooms, which overlook the garden, 'have benefited by Emma Ford's tasteful redecoration. The living rooms were comfortable and inviting, and filled with books and guides to local and regional sites.' Another comment this year: 'Emma was delightfully cheery and accommodating, as her husband quietly laboured away in the kitchen concocting his wonderful meals.' Seasonality, creativity and variation are the focus of Tim Ford's 'extraordinary' menu of modern English dishes 'with much local produce', perhaps dived West Bay scallops, butternut squash purée, pancetta; roasted saddle of wild roe deer, braised red cabbage, beetroot purée and rösti potato. The extensive wine list has many selections by the glass. (Tony Lombard, Bryan and Mary Blaxall, and others)

Barwick
BA22 9TD

T: 01935 423902
F: 01935 420908
E: reservations@barwick7.fsnet.
co.uk
W: www.littlebarwickhouse.co.uk

BEDROOMS: 6.
OPEN: all year except 26 Dec–mid-Jan, lunch only 25 Dec, restaurant closed Sun evenings, Mon and Tues lunch.
FACILITIES: ramp, 2 lounges, restaurant, conservatory, free Wi-Fi, 3½-acre garden (terrace, paddock), unsuitable for disabled.
BACKGROUND MUSIC: none.
LOCATION: ¾ mile outside Yeovil in a rural village location.
CHILDREN: not under 5.
DOGS: allowed in bedrooms, only assistance dogs in restaurant.
CREDIT CARDS: MasterCard, Visa.
PRICES: [2015] per person B&B £60, D,B&B £110. Set dinner £42–£48.
1-night bookings sometimes refused.

BASLOW Derbyshire

Map 3:A6

THE CAVENDISH

♕César award in 2002

Standing in parkland with 'glorious' views over the Chatsworth estate, this 'beautifully kept', traditional hotel is popular with guests visiting the stately home. It is owned by the Duke of Devonshire; the manager, Philip Joseph, 'goes out of his way to make sure guests are satisfied'. 'We had a lovely welcome, and offers of help to take our luggage to our room.' Bedrooms occupy the oldest part of the building (originally a coaching inn) and the newer Devonshire wing; several have been 'delightfully' refurbished. 'Our pleasant bedroom had a magnificent four-poster bed and dual-aspect windows; the bathroom, though small, was spotless.' In the modern Gallery restaurant and the 'peaceful' conservatory Garden Room, chef Mike Thompson serves 'most enjoyable' meals, perhaps a 'flavoursome' feta-braised lamb shoulder 'so tender you didn't need a knife'. A dinnertime power cut, caused by thunderstorms, was 'well dealt with', a guest reported. 'We had a buffet of sandwiches, Eton mess and unlimited wine provided free of charge, which, together with the maître d's bonhomie, kept everyone happy.' (John and Padi Howard, and others)

25% DISCOUNT VOUCHERS

Church Lane
Baslow
DE45 1SP

T: 01246 582311
F: 01246 582312
E: info@cavendish-hotel.net
W: www.cavendish-hotel.net

BEDROOMS: 24. 2 on ground floor.
OPEN: all year.
FACILITIES: lounge, bar, 2 restaurants, 2 meeting rooms, free Wi-Fi, ½-acre grounds (putting), river fishing nearby.
BACKGROUND MUSIC: light classical in Garden Room restaurant.
LOCATION: on A619, in Chatsworth grounds, in the village of Baslow.
CHILDREN: all ages welcomed.
DOGS: not allowed.
CREDIT CARDS: Amex, MasterCard, Visa.
PRICES: [2015] per room B&B single £169–£199, double £234–£349. D,B&B £48 added per person. Set menus £39.50–£59.50 (5% 'service levy' added to all prices). 1-night bookings sometimes refused.

BASLOW Derbyshire

Map 3:A6

FISCHER'S AT BASLOW HALL

♔César award in 1998

Bordered by woodland, with mature landscaped gardens, this restaurant-with-rooms in an Edwardian manor house in the Peak District is liked for the 'impeccable service' and 'excellent cooking'. The welcome from the owners, Max and Susan Fischer, and their staff is 'always warm'. Chef Rupert Rowley's Michelin-starred menu offers a modern twist on classic favourites, with a separate, innovative vegetarian menu: radicchio risotto with herb salad; pan-fried hand-dived scallops in ponzu dressing; quail tempura in mirin aspic. A bespoke new kitchen was completed in 2015: it has a tasting bench where up to four people can dine while watching the chefs at work. In the main house, bedrooms have traditional furnishings, original plasterwork, 'good-quality' mattresses and bedlinens. Vernon, one of two rooms redecorated this year, has views of Chatsworth Hunting Tower on clear days; Belvoir ('cosy double') overlooks Max Fischer's working kitchen garden. The 'well-equipped, spacious' Garden House bedrooms have books and magazines. Breakfast has 'good' cafetière coffee, pastries, 'substantial' cooked dishes.

Calver Road
Baslow
DE45 1RR

T: 01246 583259
F: 01246 583818
E: reservations@fischers-baslow
   hall.co.uk
W: www.fischers-baslowhall.co.uk

BEDROOMS: 11. 5 in Garden House.
OPEN: all year except 25/26 and 31 Dec evening.
FACILITIES: lounge/bar, breakfast room, 3 dining rooms, function facilities, free Wi-Fi, civil wedding licence, 4-acre grounds, unsuitable for disabled.
BACKGROUND MUSIC: none.
LOCATION: edge of village.
CHILDREN: no under-8s in restaurant in evening, no under-5s at lunch, all ages welcomed at Sunday lunch.
DOGS: not allowed.
CREDIT CARDS: Amex, MasterCard, Visa.
PRICES: [2015] per room B&B £150–£270, D,B&B £294–£414. Set menus £55–£128. 1-night bookings refused in Garden House June–Sept weekends.

THE PHEASANT

Guests receive a 'friendly welcome' at this 'lovely' country hotel, once a Lakeland staging post and coaching inn. It stands in 'well-kept, peaceful' gardens that extend towards the surrounding woodland. 'It is nice and quiet despite the nearby main road, which cannot be seen,' said a visitor this year. The traditionally styled bedrooms have a china tea service and a Roberts radio; each has views of the gardens or woodland. 'Our good-sized room had a large canopied bed and two comfy chairs; the bathroom had natural light and lots of instant hot water.' There is a choice of places to eat: the bar provides light lunches, real ales and 70 malt whiskies; the bistro serves 'ample and tasty' meals; in the Fell restaurant, Malcolm Ennis, the new head chef, cooks traditional French/English dishes. 'We ate in the bistro both evenings and found the plainer dishes, such as fish and chips, and pie of the day, to be the best.' A residents' lounge with a log fire is 'a bonus' when the pub, open to locals, is busy. (Lynn Wildgoose)

25% DISCOUNT VOUCHERS

Bassenthwaite Lake
CA13 9YE

T: 017687 76234
F: 017687 76002
E: info@the-pheasant.co.uk
W: www.the-pheasant.co.uk

BEDROOMS: 15. 2 on ground floor in lodge.
OPEN: all year except 25 Dec, restaurant closed Sun eve and Mon.
FACILITIES: 2 lounges, bar, bistro, restaurant, private dining room, free Wi-Fi, 40-acre grounds, lake 200 yds (fishing), unsuitable for disabled.
BACKGROUND MUSIC: none.
LOCATION: 5 miles E of Cockermouth, ¼ mile off A66 to Keswick.
CHILDREN: not under 8, £30 to share parents' room.
DOGS: allowed in lodge bedrooms (£10 charge) and public rooms.
CREDIT CARDS: MasterCard, Visa.
PRICES: [2015] per room B&B £120–£190. À la carte £30. 1-night bookings sometimes refused Sat.

BATH Somerset

Map 2:D1

APSLEY HOUSE

Built in 1830 by the Duke of Wellington as a (rumoured) retreat for his mistress, this elegant Georgian B&B is 'a model of its kind'. Owned by Claire and Nicholas Potts, managed by Miro Mikula and Kate Kowalczyk, it is liked for the 'superb' service and 'good housekeeping'. The 'spacious, light' lounge, with an honesty bar, overlooks the gardens. Bedrooms (spread over several floors) vary in size. Mornington (the former kitchen) has step access to the 'elegant' gardens, a four-poster with built-in spot lighting ('good for reading in bed'), antique furnishings, the original bread oven. First-floor Wellington (once the Duke's bedroom) has a hand-finished king-size bed, high ceilings, south-facing sash window with views across Bath. Many of the bathrooms are newly refurbished; some have a slipper bath and separate shower; the Beau's bathroom has an antique roll-top bath with column plunger. The 'excellent' breakfast, taken in an airy room with large bay windows, has a buffet (fresh fruit, cereals, yogurt) and cooked daily specials (perhaps pancakes, pancetta and maple syrup). A 20-minute walk or a short bus ride to the centre.

141 Newbridge Hill
Bath
BA1 3PT

T: 01225 336966
F: 01225 425462
E: info@apsley-house.co.uk
W: www.apsley-house.co.uk

BEDROOMS: 12. 1 on ground floor, plus 1 self-catering apartment.
OPEN: all year except 24–26 Dec.
FACILITIES: drawing room, bar, dining room, free Wi-Fi, ¼-acre garden, unsuitable for disabled.
BACKGROUND MUSIC: Classic FM in dining room.
LOCATION: 1¼ miles W of city centre.
CHILDREN: all ages welcomed (under-2s free).
DOGS: not allowed.
CREDIT CARDS: Amex, MasterCard, Visa.
PRICES: [2015] per room B&B £99–£240. 1-night bookings refused Sat in peak season.

SEE ALSO SHORTLIST

BATH Somerset

Map 2:D1

THE QUEENSBERRY

A conversion of four 18th-century town houses in a handsome street off the Circus, Laurence and Helen Beere's hotel is 'excellent and good value', says a visitor in 2015. The 'positive, friendly' staff are liked, as are the 'high ceilings and Georgian proportions'. Kimberley Blair is now the manager. 'Our first-floor room was in good decorative order; soft classical music was playing when we entered; the good bathroom had a powerful shower.' A long, narrow room 'was quite hot; lots of storage space; quiet at night'. In the split-level Olive Tree restaurant, the 'outstanding' cooking of chef Chris Cleghorn is admired; his six-course tasting menu (with a matching wine for each course) might include a 'fine' crab lasagne, mousse and bisque, basil and ginger; loin and belly of lamb, pea purée, braised lettuce, morel, wild garlic, mint. But background music at breakfast was not appreciated. The situation is 'perfect and quiet'. A car-parking system (for a small charge) 'works well': 'Our car was taken off us on arrival and delivered back within minutes of our asking.' Useful reductions are given if you book direct with the hotel. (Donald Reid, and others)

4–7 Russel Street
Bath
BA1 2QF

T: 01225 447928
F: 01225 446065
E: reservations@thequeensberry.
  co.uk
W: www.thequeensberry.co.uk

BEDROOMS: 29. Some on ground floor.
OPEN: all year, restaurant closed Mon/Tues lunch.
FACILITIES: lift, 2 drawing rooms, bar, restaurant, meeting room, free Wi-Fi, 4 linked courtyard gardens, car-parking service, unsuitable for disabled.
BACKGROUND MUSIC: in restaurant and bar.
LOCATION: near Assembly Rooms.
CHILDREN: all ages welcomed.
DOGS: not allowed.
CREDIT CARDS: MasterCard, Visa.
PRICES: [2015] per room B&B £124–£445. À la carte £47. 1-night bookings sometimes refused.

SEE ALSO SHORTLIST

BATH Somerset

Map 2:D1

ROYAL CRESCENT HOTEL   NEW

In the middle of John Wood's glorious crescent
with 'a magical vista' across the city, this
luxury hotel returns to the Guide under the
ownership of the Topland group, which has
renovated throughout. Jonathan Stapleton is
the manager. 'It can sometimes be challenging
to meet everyone's needs within our family of
six; the Royal Crescent did so,' says a visitor
this year. The drawing room and library
are beautifully proportioned and furnished;
traditional afternoon tea can be taken ('though
it would have been nice to be offered some
complimentary drinks'). In the Dower House
restaurant, chef David Campbell has 'a modern
take on classic flavours' in his seasonal menus,
which might include scallop sashimi, smoked
eel, avocado wasabi, Asian broth; Anjou squab
pigeon, asparagus, veal sweetbread, wild garlic,
cèpe purée. The best bedrooms are large and
quiet; suites are grand and lavishly furnished.
'Our rooms were recently refurbished and were
large, stylish, fresh.' Breakfast is 'delicious,
copious and varied'. There is a 'good gym and
spa' which has a 'relaxation' pool. Children are
welcomed (though under-12s are not allowed
in the spa).

16 Royal Crescent
Bath
BA1 2LS

T: 01225 823333
F: 01225 339401
E: info@royalcrescent.co.uk
W: www.royalcrescent.co.uk

BEDROOMS: 45. Some on ground
floor.
OPEN: all year.
FACILITIES: lift, ramps, Montagu bar,
drawing room, sitting room, library,
Dower House restaurant, function
facilities, free Wi-Fi, civil wedding
licence, 1-acre garden, spa and bath
house (12-metre 'relaxation' pool,
gym, sauna, treatment rooms).
BACKGROUND MUSIC: in public areas.
LOCATION: ½ mile from city centre.
CHILDREN: all ages welcomed.
DOGS: allowed in rooms with a
private courtyard, not in public
rooms.
CREDIT CARDS: Amex, MasterCard,
Visa.
PRICES: [2015] B&B from £265.
À la carte £65. 1-night bookings
sometimes refused.

SEE ALSO SHORTLIST

TASBURGH HOUSE

With wide views over Bath and the surrounding countryside, this hilltop red brick Victorian guest house is owned and run by Susan Keeling, 'a kind hostess' who provides 'a personal touch'. Grant Atkinson is the manager. On fine days, tea can be taken at tables scattered across the landscaped terraces. A meadow park extends down to the Kennet and Avon Canal, where the towpath makes a pleasant day-time walk to the city, 'even when it is wet': there is a cupboard full of wellies for guests to borrow. The 'charming' lounge has a mix of antique and modern furnishings. Each of the bedrooms is named after an English author; they vary in size and style; all have an en suite bathroom. Browning has an original, hand-painted tiled fireplace and king-size bed; Hardy has a window seat overlooking the gardens; Shelley, Kipling and Wells can accommodate three to four people. An extensive continental breakfast is served in the dining room and the 'pretty' conservatory; cooked dishes cost extra. Susan Keeling tells us she plans to offer guests a three-course gourmet supper on Friday evenings.

25% DISCOUNT VOUCHERS

Warminster Road
Bath
BA2 6SH

T: 01225 425096
F: 01225 463842
E: stay@tasburghhouse.co.uk
W: www.tasburghhouse.co.uk

BEDROOMS: 14. 2 on ground floor.
OPEN: all year except 19–30 Dec.
FACILITIES: drawing room, dining room, conservatory, free Wi-Fi, terrace, 7-acre grounds (canal walks, mooring), unsuitable for disabled, free parking space for each room.
BACKGROUND MUSIC: none.
LOCATION: 1½ miles E of city centre.
CHILDREN: not under 6.
DOGS: not allowed.
CREDIT CARDS: Amex, MasterCard, Visa.
PRICES: [2015] per room B&B (continental breakfast) single from £100, double £100–£180. Cooked breakfast £8.50. Set dinner for groups of 8 or more, by prior arrangement only. 1-night bookings sometimes refused Sat.

SEE ALSO SHORTLIST

BEAMINSTER Dorset

Map 1:C6

BRIDGEHOUSE

In Thomas Hardy's Wessex, Mark and Joanna Donovan's hotel 'combines the charm of an old building with plenty of modern comfort'. A former priest's house flanked by the River Brit, the 700-year-old building has inglenook fireplaces, low ceilings, oak beams; lots of seating in the lounge (in the oldest part). 'You are made to feel welcome the moment you arrive,' is a recent comment. Bedrooms are 'good sized, well furnished'. The largest rooms are in the main house: the quietest face a walled garden. Four smaller rooms and a family suite are in a converted coach house at the back. Pre-dinner drinks can be taken in the public rooms or in the lawned garden. Award-winning chef Stephen Pielesz's modern European menu, served in the Georgian panelled dining room, is seasonal with 'imaginative' dishes like rustic Sharpham arancini; trio of South Coast fish, fragrant rice, Thai green mussel broth. Light lunches and breakfasts are taken in a conservatory. Children are warmly welcomed: the enclosed garden is 'ideal for toddlers to run around in'. Baby monitors are available and babysitting can be arranged.

25% DISCOUNT VOUCHERS

3 Prout Bridge
Beaminster
DT8 3AY

T: 01308 862200
F: 01308 863700
E: enquiries@bridge-house.co.uk
W: www.bridge-house.co.uk

BEDROOMS: 13. 4 in coach house, 4 on ground floor.
OPEN: all year.
FACILITIES: hall/reception, lounge, bar, sunroom/conservatory, restaurant, free Wi-Fi, civil wedding licence, ¼-acre walled garden, alfresco dining.
BACKGROUND MUSIC: light jazz/classical in most public areas.
LOCATION: 50 yards from centre.
CHILDREN: all ages welcomed.
DOGS: allowed in coach house, occasionally in bar.
CREDIT CARDS: Amex, MasterCard, Visa.
PRICES: [2015] per room B&B £95–£200, D,B&B £165–£290. 1-night bookings refused weekends and bank holidays.

BEAULIEU Hampshire

Map 2:E2

THE MASTER BUILDER'S HOUSE NEW

In a 'lovely setting' by a river estuary, this 18th-century building has 'a real feel of history'. Part of Christoph Brooke's Hillbrooke group, it enters the Guide thanks to a positive report by inspectors who liked the 'quirkiness, good value and good food'. The 'charming' public areas have a nautical air (pictures of boats and maritime heroes). 'Dinner in the restaurant was very good: a delicious amuse-bouche and three types of fresh, warm bread; venison soup; a lovely main course of sea bass and crab cake in a warm broth. The service was friendly; just a pity about the muzak, especially at breakfast.' The best bedrooms, with a river view, are in the main house; rooms in the Henry Adams wing, added later, are more modern: 'Ours was on the small side, with only one armchair; it was well lit, with a big bed, green walls on three sides, patterned wallpaper behind the bed; two chests of drawers and a large wardrobe. No view, just a grassy slope.' A walk by the water leads to Beaulieu.

Buckler's Hard
Beaulieu
SO42 7XB

T: 01590 616253
F: 01590 616297
E: enquiries@themasterbuilders.
   co.uk
W: www.themasterbuilders.co.uk

BEDROOMS: 27. 17 in Henry Adams wing, 1 suitable for disabled.
OPEN: all year.
FACILITIES: lounge, bar, restaurant, free Wi-Fi, civil wedding licence, ½-acre garden (alfresco dining).
BACKGROUND MUSIC: in bar and restaurant.
LOCATION: 6 miles NE of Lymington.
CHILDREN: all ages welcomed.
DOGS: welcomed in 9 bedrooms, not allowed in restaurant.
CREDIT CARDS: Amex, MasterCard, Visa.
PRICES: [2015] per room B&B £130, D,B&B £190. À la carte £30.

BEAULIEU Hampshire

Map 2:E2

MONTAGU ARMS

In a pretty village within the New Forest national park, this Georgian country house is a 'very special place', says a visitor in 2015. 'It may not have the trappings of some larger establishments, but we enjoy the ambience and the exceptional welcome and service.' The oak-panelled public rooms are 'country house in style and are well furnished'. In the formal Terrace restaurant, 'the attention and service is professional but relaxed'. The chef, Matthew Tomkinson, has a Michelin star for his cooking of intricate dishes like pressed terrine of rabbit and black pudding, celeriac remoulade, liver parfait; wild South Coast sea bass, garden artichoke purée, serrano ham, red wine sauce. Lighter meals are served in the informal Monty's Inn. The bedrooms might not be 'the latest in design', but they are comfortable; many have a view of the 'picturesque' garden, 'which is a lovely place to relax'. Breakfast in the Terrace restaurant has eggs from the hotel's own hens. Guests can use the SenSpa at a sister hotel, Careys Manor, in nearby Brockenhurst. 'The location is perfect for country lovers.' (Mary Coles)

Palace Lane
Beaulieu
SO42 7ZL

T: 01590 612324
F: 01590 612188
E: stay@montaguarmshotel.co.uk
W: www.montaguarmshotel.co.uk

BEDROOMS: 22.
OPEN: all year, Terrace restaurant closed Mon, Tues lunch.
FACILITIES: lounge, conservatory, bar/brasserie, restaurant, free Wi-Fi, civil wedding licence, garden, access to nearby spa, unsuitable for disabled.
BACKGROUND MUSIC: in Monty's Inn.
LOCATION: village centre.
CHILDREN: all ages welcomed (under-3s stay free), no under-11s in restaurant.
DOGS: not allowed.
CREDIT CARDS: Amex, MasterCard, Visa.
PRICES: [2015] per room B&B £109.50–£184.50. À la carte Monty's Inn £28, Terrace restaurant £75. 1-night bookings sometimes refused.

BEPTON West Sussex

Map 2:E3

PARK HOUSE

'Everything is of the highest quality: the food, the table, the delightful staff.' Praise again in 2015 for the O'Brien family's 'very pretty' Victorian country house close to the South Downs. Returning visitors appreciate the 'intimate, homely feel', the 'gorgeous summer gardens with tables and benches set around in different areas'. There is good walking on the downs, but 'plenty to do' in the hotel grounds – the 'luxurious, spotless spa', the indoor/outdoor pools and the putting; 'we didn't feel the need to leave'. The public rooms are furnished in country house style. The bedrooms are in the main house and three cottages in the grounds. Bay Tree cottage was 'well fitted; a beautiful bed and linen; our own private patio with garden furniture and a parasol'. A room in the main house was 'smart and newly done'. Chef Callum Keir sources ingredients as locally as possible. Typical dishes on his modern menu: chilled pea and mint soup with lime crème fraîche; sea bass with caramelised oranges, sweet basil gel. Freshly squeezed fruit juices, fruit and muesli at breakfast. (Mary Woods, DB)

Bepton Road
Bepton, nr Midhurst
GU29 0JB

T: 01730 819000
F: 01730 819099
E: reservations@parkhousehotel.com
W: www.parkhousehotel.com

BEDROOMS: 21. 5 on ground floor, 1 suitable for disabled, 9 in cottages in grounds.
OPEN: all year, except Christmas.
FACILITIES: drawing room, bar, dining room, conservatory, function room, free Wi-Fi, civil wedding licence, 9-acre grounds, spa, indoor and outdoor swimming pools (both heated, 15 metres), tennis, pitch and putt.
BACKGROUND MUSIC: in dining room/conservatory.
LOCATION: 2½ miles SW of Midhurst.
CHILDREN: all ages welcomed.
DOGS: allowed in 2 bedrooms (charge), not in public rooms.
CREDIT CARDS: Amex, MasterCard, Visa.
PRICES: [2015] per room B&B from £160, D,B&B from £225. À la carte £45. 1-night bookings refused weekends.

NEWBEGIN HOUSE **NEW**

Close to the centre of a 'fine' East Riding market town, this 'unusually large' Georgian house with a walled garden is the home of Walter and Nuala Sweeney, who welcome B&B guests with 'courtesy and attention'. It enters the Guide thanks to a positive report from regular correspondents. Three generations of the Sweeney family (and their two dogs) live in the house, which is 'full of life, with family members moving about, though never intrusively'. Walter Sweeney, a solicitor and former MP, 'showed us the house and garden, drawing our attention to the history; he gave useful information on the town and about restaurants'. The three spacious bedrooms, in one part of the building, have 'a very comfortable bed, good lighting enabling easy reading; lots of space for clothes and luggage'. Nuala Sweeney prepares 'an excellent breakfast with a wide choice; a bowl of fruit on our table was a nice touch'. Beverley 'deserves a visit for the acclaimed minster and the equally fine parish church, the Georgian quarter and the Saturday market'. (John and Theresa Stewart)

10 Newbegin
Beverley
HU17 8EG

T: 01482 888880
E: wsweeney@
   wsweeney.karoo.co.uk
W: www.newbeginhousebbbeverley.
   co.uk

BEDROOMS: 3.
OPEN: all year except 'when we are on holiday'.
FACILITIES: sitting room, dining room, free Wi-Fi, walled garden, unsuitable for disabled.
BACKGROUND MUSIC: none.
LOCATION: central.
CHILDREN: all ages welcomed.
DOGS: not allowed.
CREDIT CARDS: none accepted.
PRICES: [2015] per room B&B £80. 1-night bookings sometimes refused.

BURGH ISLAND HOTEL

♥ César award in 2012

'A truly memorable stay,' was enjoyed by visitors this year to this Grade II listed hotel on a tidal island at the end of Bigbury beach. Opened in 1929, the 'quirky' building was a favourite retreat of illustrious guests including Agatha Christie and Noël Coward. Today, it 'remains an amazing experience which everyone should enjoy at least once' (according to a Guide hotelier). It was restored in 2006 as an 'Art Deco tour de force' by owners Deborah Clark and Tony Orchard. Named after famous guests, bedrooms are individually decorated in period style; nearly all have views of the sea. 'Our bathroom was bigger than the bedroom and had a sofa by the window.' Black tie is encouraged at dinner, where chef Tim Hall's 'outstanding' daily-changing menus have much local produce and 'plenty of choice', perhaps poached Beesands lobster tail, chickpea and red pepper salad; John Dory, French gnocchi, samphire, girolles. 'When we stayed, the Great Gatsby band played the night away, which totally completed the Art Deco experience.' (Juliette Albone, Annabel Thomas)

Burgh Island
Bigbury-on-Sea
TQ7 4BG

T: 01548 810514
E: reception@burghisland.com
W: www.burghisland.com

BEDROOMS: 25. 1 suite in Beach House, apartment above Pilchard Inn.
OPEN: all year, except 2 weeks in Jan.
FACILITIES: lift, sun lounge, Palm Court bar, dining room, ballroom, billiard room, table tennis, spa, free Wi-Fi, civil wedding licence, 17-acre grounds on 26-acre island (30-metre natural sea swimming pool, tennis).
BACKGROUND MUSIC: 1920s and 1930s in bar, live Wed, Sat with dinner in ballroom.
LOCATION: 5 miles south of Modbury, private garages on mainland.
CHILDREN: not under 5, no under-12s at dinner, high tea.
DOGS: not allowed.
CREDIT CARDS: MasterCard, Visa.
PRICES: [2015] per room D,B&B single £310, double £400–£640. 1-night bookings refused Sat, some bank holidays.

BIGBURY-ON-SEA Devon

Map 1:D4

THE HENLEY

🏆 César award in 2003

'It gets better and better!' Overlooking the tidal Avon estuary, Martyn Scarterfield and Petra Lampe's small Edwardian holiday cottage is popular with return visitors for the 'relaxing' environment and 'friendly, excellent' service. 'On arrival, we were immediately treated to tea and cake at a cliffside table with magnificent views of the bay.' The potted plants, wood-burning stove, comfy sofas and ever-present black Labrador, Caspar, contribute to the homely feel. 'Our spacious room was well presented, with a large, comfortable double bed and fantastic views of the bay; the bathroom had plenty of hot water, fluffy towels and bathrobes,' say visitors this year. Pre-dinner drinks can be taken in the lounge (full of 'nooks and crannies'). Martyn Scarterfield's 'imaginative, tasty' cooking emphasises locally sourced ingredients: perhaps wild mushroom soup, pan-fried John Dory with prawns and asparagus, or fillet steak with peppercorn sauce. 'Breakfast was all you would expect from a good hotel, and more; we enjoyed the porridge with malt whisky, muscovado sugar and cream.' (Simon Rodway, and others)

Folly Hill
Bigbury-on-Sea
TQ7 4AR

T: 01548 810240
F: 01548 810240
E: thehenleyhotel@btconnect.com
W: www.thehenleyhotel.co.uk

BEDROOMS: 5.
OPEN: Mar–end Oct.
FACILITIES: 2 lounges, bar, conservatory dining room, free Wi-Fi (in some areas), small garden (steps to beach, golf, sailing, fishing), Coastal Path nearby, unsuitable for disabled.
BACKGROUND MUSIC: jazz/classical in the evenings in lounge, dining room.
LOCATION: 5 miles S of Modbury.
CHILDREN: not under 12.
DOGS: not allowed in dining room.
CREDIT CARDS: Amex, MasterCard, Visa.
PRICES: [2015] per room B&B single £90, double £120–£150, D,B&B (2-night min.) single £115, double £175–£198. Set dinner £36. 1-night bookings sometimes refused weekends.

BIGGIN HALL

'An outstanding stay.' James Moffett's 'friendly, efficient' hotel offers 'amazing value', and is an 'excellent base' for exploring the Peak District national park. 'Not posh but straightforward', it is popular with walkers, particularly those with canine companions. Dogs are allowed in most bedrooms; the 'comfortably furnished' public rooms remain pet-free. Guests seeking a break from outdoor pursuits might settle in front of one of the fireplaces, with a book from the 'interesting' library. Individually decorated, country house-style bedrooms are spread across the main house and converted outbuildings. One room had a comfortable bed; tea-making facilities; fresh milk in a silent fridge; a newly fitted bathroom. The oak-beamed dining room serves 'excellent, well-designed' daily-changing English classics: honey-glazed Gressingham duck, peppercorn-crushed new potatoes; flat-cap mushroom baked with blue cheese, toasted brioche. Complimentary aperitifs and carafe of wine accompany the meal; cheeseboard and coffee are offered after. A buffet breakfast has hot and cold dishes. 'Sustaining' packed lunches are available. (John Barnes, and others)

Main Street
Biggin-by-Hartington
SK17 0DH

T: 01298 84451
E: enquiries@bigginhall.co.uk
W: www.bigginhall.co.uk

BEDROOMS: 21. 13 in annexes, some on ground floor.
OPEN: all year.
FACILITIES: sitting room, library, dining room, meeting room, free Wi-Fi (in sitting rooms, some bedrooms), civil wedding licence, 8-acre grounds (croquet), River Dove 1½ miles, unsuitable for disabled.
BACKGROUND MUSIC: none.
LOCATION: 8 miles N of Ashbourne.
CHILDREN: not under 12.
DOGS: allowed in courtyard and bothy bedrooms, not in public rooms.
CREDIT CARDS: MasterCard, Visa.
PRICES: [2015] per room B&B £90–£172, D,B&B £130–£212. Set dinner £25. 1-night bookings sometimes refused.

BLAKENEY Norfolk

Map 2:A5

THE BLAKENEY HOTEL

'I love the location overlooking the estuary, the sound of birds, the quirky architecture of the building.' A returning visitor explains the appeal of the Stannard family's large quayside hotel, which faces the salt marshes of Blakeney Point. Another comment (in 2015): 'I cannot fault the comfort and service. The staff are, without exception, courteous and friendly.' The hotel attracts a 'mature clientele' in the off-season; it is popular with families during the school holidays. There are activities to entertain guests of all ages: walks from the door; a dartboard and board games in the games room; plus a shallow indoor swimming pool. There is a 'laid-back, relaxed' atmosphere in the bars and sitting rooms, which are 'in good condition': the lookout lounge has wonderful views. Bedrooms on the ground floor are suitable for guests with dogs. 'An imaginative, well-presented menu is served in the restaurant. I enjoyed a good-sized portion of gravadlax with dill dressing, and the chocolate roulade with sweet strawberries.' Also appreciated: the covers provided to protect vehicles in the car park from evidence of seagulls flying overhead. Breakfast was 'copiously provided'. (Carol Jackson, Moira Jarrett)

Blakeney
NR25 7NE

T: 01263 740797
F: 01263 740795
E: enquiries@blakeneyhotel.co.uk
W: www.blakeneyhotel.co.uk

BEDROOMS: 64. 16 in Granary annexe opposite, some on ground floor.
OPEN: all year.
FACILITIES: lift, ramps, lounge, sun lounge, bar, restaurant, free Wi-Fi, function facilities, heated indoor swimming pool (12 by 5 metres), steam room, sauna, mini-gym, games room, ¼-acre garden.
BACKGROUND MUSIC: none.
LOCATION: on quay.
CHILDREN: all ages welcomed.
DOGS: allowed in some bedrooms, not in public rooms.
CREDIT CARDS: Amex, MasterCard, Visa.
PRICES: [2015] per person B&B £85–£160, D,B&B (2-night min.) £97–£178. Set dinner £29.50, à la carte £37.50. 1-night bookings sometimes refused Fri/Sat, bank holidays.

BLANCHLAND Co. Durham

Map 4:B3

⚜ THE LORD CREWE ARMS

César award: inn of the year

In an 'unbeatable' setting in the North Pennine moors, this old inn has been thoroughly modernised by the owners of Calcot Manor, Tetbury (see entry). They have retained the character of its 900-year history (priest's hole, medieval hand-painted stained glass). 'Highly recommended: the staff unostentatiously went out of their way to make our stay enjoyable.' The bedrooms are in the main building, in The Angel immediately opposite, and in converted miners' cottages facing the village square. 'Our room in the Angel was generously portioned and beautifully appointed; the colour schemes and textiles reflected the local countryside and traditions (heathers and moors). It was supplied with books and magazines; home-made biscuits and fudge on the tea tray.' The Bishop's Dining Room, on the first floor of the main building, has 'beautiful views of the moors': 'The dinner menu was simple and unfussy: delicate mackerel fillets with exceptional pickled spring vegetables; beautifully cooked pork belly with Norfolk shrimps; the cheeses were in good condition.' (David Birnie, and others)

The Square
Blanchland
DH8 9SP

T: 01434 675469
E: enquiries@
   lordcrewearmsblanchland.co.uk
W: www.lordcrewearmsblanchland.
   co.uk

BEDROOMS: 21. 7 in adjacent cottages. 10 in The Angel across road, some on ground floor. 1 suitable for disabled.
OPEN: all year.
FACILITIES: 3 lounges, restaurant, free Wi-Fi, civil wedding licence, beer garden, unsuitable for disabled.
BACKGROUND MUSIC: none.
LOCATION: in village, 9 miles S of Hexham.
CHILDREN: all ages welcomed.
DOGS: allowed in bedrooms, not in dining room.
CREDIT CARDS: MasterCard, Visa.
PRICES: per room B&B £160–£180. À la carte £30. 1-night bookings sometimes refused.

BLEDINGTON Oxfordshire

Map 3:D6

THE KING'S HEAD INN

A stream runs by Archie and Nicola Orr-Ewing's old stone inn, once a 16th-century cider house, in 'a special setting' on the green of a village on the edge of the Cotswolds. It has 'an unspoilt rustic charm', with nooks and crannies, low beams, vintage settles and old hunting prints; Guide inspectors were greeted by ducks and their ducklings on the gravelled drive. Six country cottage-style bedrooms are in the main building; quieter, more spacious accommodation is in a rear courtyard annexe. 'Our small ground-floor room had a comfortable bed and a tiny, functional bathroom.' 'There is a great atmosphere' in the low-ceilinged bar, which is popular with locals and their dogs. In the separate dining areas, Giles Lee, the chef, has 'some interesting modern touches' on his 'delicious' menus. Typical dishes: rabbit and guineafowl terrine, wild mushrooms; rare-breed sirloin steak, pickled red cabbage, rocket and hazelnut salad. 'We very much enjoyed our meal.' Breakfast is served 'with less of a flourish': a 'brief' menu; a 'basic' buffet. The Orr-Ewings also manage the nearby Swan Inn, Swinbrook (see entry).

The Green
Bledington
OX7 6XQ

T: 01608 658365
F: 01608 658902
E: info@kingsheadinn.net
W: www.thekingsheadinn.net

BEDROOMS: 12. 6 in annexe, some on ground floor.
OPEN: all year except 25/26 Dec.
FACILITIES: bar, restaurant, courtyard, free Wi-Fi, children's play area, unsuitable for disabled.
BACKGROUND MUSIC: none.
LOCATION: on village green.
CHILDREN: all ages welcomed.
DOGS: not allowed in bedrooms, restaurant.
CREDIT CARDS: MasterCard, Visa.
PRICES: [2015] per room B&B £100–£130, D,B&B £160–£190. À la carte £28. 1-night bookings refused Sat.

THE OLD RECTORY

In a 'magical setting', at the end of a winding country country lane, this large slate-built Victorian house and its 'magnificent' grounds formed the backdrop for the 'Cornish romance' between Emma Gifford and writer Thomas Hardy. Today, under the ownership of the Searle family, 'the house has been beautifully restored,' says a visitor this year. 'They create the atmosphere of a country house party and show great kindness to guests.' The bedrooms, named for the Hardy love-story, are 'comfortable and private'. Emma's Room has a king-size bed and a restored 'thunderbox' toilet from the 1870s; Mr Hardy's Room, slightly smaller, has a high ceiling, an antique carved double bed. 'The large garden, alive with birds and butterflies, is a delightful place to wander.' The Searles are green tourism gold award holders: much of the produce for breakfast and an (optional) evening meal comes from the Victorian walled kitchen garden, the Searles's own hens and ducks, rare-breed pigs and Jacob sheep, and hive of bees. The meals are taken communally; bring your own wine at dinner (no corkage charge). (Catherine Storr, and others)

St Juliot
Boscastle
PL35 0BT

T: 01840 250225
F: 01840 250225
E: sally@stjuliot.com
W: www.stjuliot.com

BEDROOMS: 4. 1 in stables (linked to house).
OPEN: all year, except Christmas/New Year.
FACILITIES: sitting room, breakfast room, conservatory, free Wi-Fi, 3-acre garden (croquet lawn, 'lookout'), unsuitable for disabled.
BACKGROUND MUSIC: none.
LOCATION: 1½ miles NE of Boscastle.
CHILDREN: not under 12.
DOGS: only allowed in stables (£10 per stay).
CREDIT CARDS: MasterCard, Visa.
PRICES: per room B&B £75–£110. 2-course dinner (by arrangement; bring your own bottle) £17.50. 1-night bookings refused weekends and busy periods.

THE MILLSTREAM

In the village where King Canute failed to stop the incoming tide, the Wild family's hotel 'appeals strongly to a mature clientele who value the traditional decor and ambience', said Guide inspectors. There are many returning visitors who consider it 'like an old friend'. Clare Sherlock, née Wild, is the manager; the staff are 'mainly young and enthusiastic'; standards of service and housekeeping are 'high'. Two suites are in the 'pretty' garden. 'Ours had a smallish bedroom with French windows opening on to a private garden; a decent-sized sitting room with a comfy sofa.' A first-floor room overlooking the front garden 'had a small balcony, floral fabrics, good reading lights, a fridge; an immaculate bathroom'. There are two dining options: in the main restaurant, which has well-spaced tables, chef Neil Hiskey serves a modern menu of dishes like roasted beetroot, goat's curd, pear and walnuts; stone bass, cèpe gnocchi, red wine emulsion. More informal meals can be taken in Marwick's brasserie, which is open to non-residents. Breakfast has an extensive menu; an express breakfast is served in the lounge until 11.30 am.

Bosham Lane
Bosham, nr Chichester
PO18 8HL

T: 01243 573234
F: 01243 573459
E: info@millstreamhotel.com
W: www.millstreamhotel.com

BEDROOMS: 35. 2 in cottage, 7 on ground floor, 1 suitable for disabled.
OPEN: all year.
FACILITIES: lounge, bar, restaurant (pianist Fri and Sat), brasserie, conference room, free Wi-Fi, civil wedding licence, 1¼-acre garden, Chichester Harbour 300 yards.
BACKGROUND MUSIC: all day in bar, lounge and restaurant.
LOCATION: 4 miles W of Chichester.
CHILDREN: all ages welcomed, £20 B&B to share adult's room.
DOGS: not allowed.
CREDIT CARDS: all major cards.
PRICES: [2015] per room B&B £159–£229, D,B&B £184–£244. À la carte £35.50. 1-night bookings refused Sat.

BOURTON-ON-THE-HILL Gloucestershire Map 3:D6

THE HORSE AND GROOM

♀César award in 2012

Brothers Tom and Will Greenstock have run this Grade II listed Georgian pub-with-rooms in a Cotswold village for ten years. Tom Greenstock, who directs the front-of-house, is quickly 'on first-name terms' with guests. His brother's artisan cooking has long been admired by Guide readers. He finds the ingredients for his 'imaginative, unpretentious' dishes from the inn's vegetable garden and from neighbouring farms (the bottle of milk at breakfast might bear the name of the cow that produced it). His blackboard menu might include home-cured salt cod fritters; Dexter beef, ale and horseradish pie; vanilla and gingernut cheesecake, poached winter rhubarb. There is no guest lounge: the bar is a 'cheerful, informal' place to sit by a fire listening to local gossip, and the garden is well supplied with tables and benches. The well-equipped bedrooms are spacious for a pub; 'nice touches' include home-made biscuits, fresh milk in a flask. Light sleepers might prefer a room overlooking the garden; in road-facing rooms heavy curtains 'provide good soundproofing'. Croissants at breakfast, 'warm, buttery, flaky', are a 'delight'. (J and MB)

Bourton-on-the-Hill
nr Moreton-in-Marsh
GL56 9AQ

T: 01386 700413
F: 01386 700413
E: greenstocks@
  horseandgroom.info
W: www.horseandgroom.info

BEDROOMS: 5.
OPEN: all year except 25/31 Dec, restaurant closed Sun eve except on bank holiday weekends.
FACILITIES: bar/restaurant, free Wi-Fi, 1-acre garden, unsuitable for disabled.
BACKGROUND MUSIC: none.
LOCATION: village centre.
CHILDREN: all ages welcomed.
DOGS: not allowed.
CREDIT CARDS: Diners, MasterCard, Visa.
PRICES: [2015] per room B&B single £80, double £120–£170. À la carte £27. 1-night bookings refused weekends.

BOWNESS-ON-WINDERMERE Cumbria Map 4: inset C2

LINDETH FELL

♥ Cesar award in 2009

'Nothing stands still,' say the Kennedy family, who have decided to run their country house on the fells overlooking Lake Windermere as a 'luxury B&B' rather than a hotel. They have turned the restaurant into a bar and lounge. Dinner is no longer served: afternoon tea, which can be taken from 12.30 pm, has been expanded, and a range of cold platters (fish, meat, cheese and ploughman's) can be taken in the bar, the lounges, on the terrace or in the bedroom. Also new in 2015 is a biomass boiler; Wi-Fi reception has been upgraded in the bedrooms; all rooms have a decanter of sherry, and master rooms have been given a Nespresso coffee machine. Diana Kennedy and her daughters, Sheena and Joanna, are 'charming and friendly as usual', and the house is 'welcoming and comfortable', say returning visitors. The drawing rooms have deep sofas; one has books and magazines for guests who want to read. The bedrooms, which vary in size, are individually styled. Breakfast has a well-stocked buffet and a wide choice of cooked dishes.

Lyth Valley Road
Bowness-on-Windermere
LA23 3JP

T: 015394 43286
F: 015394 47455
E: kennedy@lindethfell.co.uk
W: www.lindethfell.co.uk

BEDROOMS: 14. 1 on ground floor.
OPEN: all year except Jan.
FACILITIES: ramp, hall, 2 lounges, dispense bar, dining room, free Wi-Fi, 7-acre grounds (gardens, croquet, putting, bowls, tarn, fishing permits).
BACKGROUND MUSIC: none.
LOCATION: 1 mile S of Bowness on A5074.
CHILDREN: all ages welcomed, ('on request') in some bedrooms.
DOGS: only assistance dogs allowed.
CREDIT CARDS: MasterCard, Visa.
PRICES: [2015] per person B&B £68–£115, 1-night bookings sometimes refused weekends, bank holidays.

SEE ALSO SHORTLIST

LINTHWAITE HOUSE

'A superb setting in extensive gardens.' High above Lake Windermere, Mike Bevans and Simon Doddrell's smart hotel wins fresh praise from a reader in 2015. Andrew Nicholson is the manager. Period and contemporary features are combined in the 'spacious' public rooms which have potted plants, memorabilia. An enclosed veranda faces the gardens. The atmosphere is 'relaxed but also elegant'; the service 'impeccable, always attentive'. Smart casual dress is suggested for the restaurant where chef Chris O'Callaghan's daily-changing four-course modern menu 'gave good choice'. The presentation is 'excellent' of dishes like goat's cheese and gingerbread truffles, pickled raspberry and beetroot; roasted pheasant breast, creamed leeks, fermented garlic. 'The only minus was the intrusive taped music.' The bedrooms vary in size and outlook: some face the lake, others the garden. 'Our room was well-nigh perfect, with a small sitting area overlooking a pond. The decor was modern and restful, with beds of high quality; a very good bathroom.' The Loft Suite has a separate lounge, a retractable glass roof panel and a telescope. (Clive Blackburn, and others)

Crook Road
Bowness-on-Windermere
LA23 3JA

T: 015394 88600
F: 015394 88601
E: market@linthwaite.com
W: www.linthwaite.com

BEDROOMS: 30. Some on ground floor.
OPEN: all year.
FACILITIES: ramp, two lounges, bar, conservatory, 3 dining rooms, function facilities, free Wi-Fi, civil wedding licence, 14-acre grounds.
BACKGROUND MUSIC: gentle piano music in bar and dining rooms.
LOCATION: 1 mile S of Bowness, Windermere.
CHILDREN: no under-7s in dining rooms after 7 pm.
DOGS: allowed in two external bedrooms, not in public areas.
CREDIT CARDS: Amex, MasterCard, Visa.
PRICES: [2015] per person B&B from £95, D,B&B from £135. À la carte £52. 1-night bookings sometimes refused weekends.

SEE ALSO SHORTLIST

WOOLLEY GRANGE

Wellington boots flank the entrance of Nigel Chapman's characterful, family-friendly Jacobean stone manor house in 'glorious' countryside. 'Like the country home of a wealthy family friend, it is a bit shabby around the edges; charmingly so if you have the right attitude,' Guide inspectors said. Public rooms are filled with curios and antique furniture; young guests have much diversion (play areas, garden games, a fairy trail) in the rambling grounds. 'The den was a hit with our children,' said a visitor in 2015. 'We even managed time on our own in the afternoon.' Bedrooms vary considerably in size and style: a family room had a snug antechamber large enough to accommodate two cots; a 'spacious, charming' room had 'great views on two sides'. Four rooms were refurbished in 2015. There is a good variety of 'tasty' children's meals in the Orangery; in the restaurant, chef Mark Bradbury's seasonal menus might include 'rich, well-cooked' pork belly, red cabbage, fondant potato. Breakfast toast is served at table, with softened butter and 'generous dollops' of jam; a buffet has thick yogurt, dried and stewed fruit, jugs of milk and juice. (Zoe Hinton, and others)

Woolley Green
Bradford-on-Avon
BA15 1TX

T: 01225 864705
E: info@woolleygrangehotel.co.uk
W: www.woolleygrangehotel.co.uk

BEDROOMS: 25. 11 in annexes, 2 on ground floor, 1 suitable for disabled.
OPEN: all year.
FACILITIES: 2 drawing rooms, 2 restaurants, cinema, meeting rooms, free Wi-Fi, crèche, spa, heated indoor and outdoor swimming pools (12 metres), civil wedding licence, 14-acre grounds (kitchen garden, children's play areas, fields).
BACKGROUND MUSIC: 'easy listening' in restaurants.
LOCATION: 1 mile NE of Bradford-on-Avon.
CHILDREN: all ages welcomed.
DOGS: not allowed in restaurants.
CREDIT CARDS: Amex, MasterCard, Visa.
PRICES: [2015] per room B&B £120–£500, D,B&B £190–£570. À la carte £40. 1-night bookings sometimes refused.

BRAITHWAITE Cumbria

Map 4: inset C2

THE COTTAGE IN THE WOOD

'We got the warmest welcome we have ever received from any hotel.' Praise this year for Kath and Liam Berney's restaurant-with-rooms deep in the Whinlatter forest. In the converted 17th-century coaching inn, chef Chris Archer's modern European dinners are served in the conservatory-style dining room, which has 'great views' over the garden (and red squirrels) towards the Skiddaw mountain range. Menus feature much regional, local and foraged produce, perhaps milk-fed veal, potato gnocchi, asparagus, morels. 'I ordered the chocolate dessert three times during our stay.' A visitor this year enjoyed the 'delicious' turbot, but would have liked more variety on the menu. Equipped with home-made shortbread, and tea- and coffee-making facilities, bedrooms vary in size: the Garden Room had 'lots of space and a beautiful bathroom'; a smaller Cottage Room was 'clean and well appointed – perfectly good for a two-night stay'. Breakfast is 'a lovely experience': yogurts, fresh fruit, home-made jam and marmalade; a dish of duck egg and crispy bacon on sourdough bread was 'a great way to start a day on the fells'. (John Patterson, Hilary Blakemore)

25% DISCOUNT VOUCHERS

Magic Hill
Whinlatter Forest
Braithwaite
CA12 5TW

T: 017687 78409
E: relax@thecottageinthewood.co.uk
W: www.thecottageinthewood.co.uk

BEDROOMS: 9. 1 in the garden with separate entrance.
OPEN: all year except Christmas, restaurant closed Mon.
FACILITIES: lounge, restaurant, free Wi-Fi, drying room, secure bicycle storage, terraced garden, 2 acres of woodland, only restaurant suitable for disabled.
BACKGROUND MUSIC: none.
LOCATION: 5 miles NW of Keswick.
CHILDREN: not under 10.
DOGS: not allowed.
CREDIT CARDS: MasterCard, Visa.
PRICES: [2015] per room B&B £88–£210. Set menu £45, tasting menu £65. 1-night bookings refused weekends.

BRAMPTON Cumbria

Map 4:B3

FARLAM HALL

♀César award in 2001

In Hadrian's Wall country, this traditional country house hotel (Relais & Châteaux) has been owned and managed by the Quinion family for 40 years. Guests comment on their 'warm and attentive welcome' and 'consistently high-quality service'. 'The hospitality cannot be faulted.' The Victorian decor reflects the building's 19th-century heritage. 'Our very floral bedroom looked out over beautiful lawns (on which croquet was set) and magnificent mature trees,' said a visitor this year. 'There was a beautiful piece of Victorian furniture which acted as a dressing table; two magnifying mirrors (a lot of hotels have none).' The Hay Loft, a spacious room with floor-to-ceiling windows, is reached by an outdoor staircase ('ideal for guests who want to come and go at odd times'). In the dining room, dinner is served by waitresses 'dressed in striking black gowns'. Barry Quinion cooks modern country house dishes, perhaps terrine of chicken, bacon and wild mushrooms; loin of spring lamb, roasted ratatouille, parsnip purée. 'Breakfast was waitress service, no buffet.' (Barbara Watkinson, and others)

Hallbankgate
Brampton
CA8 2NG

T: 01697 746234
F: 01697 746683
E: farlam@farlamhall.co.uk
W: www.farlamhall.co.uk

BEDROOMS: 12, 1 in stables, 2 on ground floor.
OPEN: all year except 25–30 Dec, 4–21 Jan, restaurant closed midday (light lunches by arrangement) except New Year's Day, Mothering and Easter Sun.
FACILITIES: ramps, 2 lounges, restaurant, free Wi-Fi, civil wedding licence, 10-acre grounds, unsuitable for disabled.
BACKGROUND MUSIC: none.
LOCATION: on A689, 2½ miles SE of Brampton (not in Farlam village).
CHILDREN: not under 5.
DOGS: not allowed in restaurant, or unattended in bedrooms.
CREDIT CARDS: Amex, MasterCard, Visa.
PRICES: [2015] per person D,B&B £160–£185. Set dinner £48–£50. 1-night bookings sometimes refused.

THE WHITE HORSE

♀César award in 2014

In an area of outstanding beauty on the north Norfolk coast, the Nye family's small hotel has 'tranquil views over the salt marshes to little sailing boats beyond'. Visitors this year found it 'charming; attractively decorated with a nautical theme'. It is liked for the 'relaxed ambience', 'friendly staff' and 'good value' (though breakfast disappointed one visitor). The 'freshest' fish (from nearby ports) and shellfish (mussels from the bottom of the garden) are enjoyed in the conservatory restaurant. Chef Fran Hartshorne's modern menu might include local oysters; roast sea trout, saffron Norfolk Peer potatoes, wild garlic Parmesan, Heirloom tomato salsa. 'Service was impeccable.' The bedrooms, decorated in seaside colours, are in the main house and in a garden annexe, which, with its sedum roof, 'folds into the landscape'. These 'spacious and light' rooms, 'like a beach hut', have matting and laminated flooring; good storage and a large bathroom. Each has a small terrace and direct access from the car park; they are popular with walkers (the Coastal Path borders the grounds) and dog-owners. (Jane and Martin Bailey, and others)

Main Road
Brancaster Staithe
PE31 8BY

T: 01485 210262
F: 01485 210930
E: reception@whitehorsebrancaster.co.uk
W: www.whitehorsebrancaster.co.uk

BEDROOMS: 15. 8 on ground floor in annexe, 1 suitable for disabled.
OPEN: all year.
FACILITIES: 2 lounge areas, public bar, conservatory restaurant, dining room, free Wi-Fi, ½-acre garden (covered sunken garden), harbour sailing.
BACKGROUND MUSIC: 'light' in bar all day.
LOCATION: centre of village just E of Brancaster.
CHILDREN: all ages welcomed.
DOGS: allowed in annexe rooms (£10 per night) and bar.
CREDIT CARDS: MasterCard, Visa.
PRICES: [2015] per room B&B £100–£190, D,B&B (Nov–Mar only) £150–£190. À la carte £30.

THE WATERSIDE INN

In a 16th-century village on the banks of the River Thames, chef/patron Alain Roux's restaurant-with-rooms has long held three Michelin stars for the 'excellent', classic French cooking. The dining room has white linens, green silk banquettes and large picture windows overlooking the river; here, the seven-course 'menu exceptionnel', which must be taken by the entire table, is rich but none the less recommended. The flavours are 'beautiful' although one recent guest 'started to flag when the pigeon – after the amuse-bouche, the ceviche, the foie gras and the lobster – was brought out'. A lighter three-course 'menu gastronomique' is served at lunch, Wednesdays to Sundays. 'The service was very attentive.' 'Impeccable' bedrooms are in the main building and in two cottages in the grounds; one, in Ryepeck Cottage, has a private garden that runs down to the river. A standard room was 'small but pretty, with a soft bed and an excellent, strong shower'. A 'delicious' breakfast of freshly squeezed juice, yogurt and buttery pastries is brought to the room. 'A great experience.' (ANR)

Ferry Road
Bray
SL6 2AT

T: 01628 620691
F: 01628 784710
E: reservations@waterside-inn.co.uk
W: www.waterside-inn.co.uk

BEDROOMS: 11. 3 in cottages.
OPEN: 29 Jan–25 Dec, closed Mon/Tues.
FACILITIES: restaurant, private dining room (with drawing room and courtyard garden), free Wi-Fi, civil wedding licence, riverside terrace (launch for drinks/coffee), unsuitable for disabled.
BACKGROUND MUSIC: none.
LOCATION: 3 miles SE of Maidenhead.
CHILDREN: not under 12.
DOGS: not allowed.
CREDIT CARDS: all major cards.
PRICES: [2015] per room B&B £240–£395. À la carte £160, menu exceptionnel £160.

BROOKS GUESTHOUSE

A 1960s office block that became a hostel for
backpackers, Carla and Andrew Brooks's
contemporary hotel is situated beside Bristol's
vibrant St Nicholas food market, and close
to the popular bars and restaurants of the
waterfront. Entry is through wrought iron
gates into a large, paved courtyard where
breakfast and drinks can be taken in summer.
The owners have 'imaginatively' refurbished
the building in a simple, clean style: in the
open-plan public areas, there are leather sofas
on wooden floors; pine tables in the breakfast
area. Inner-city 'glamping' is possible in four
retro aluminium caravans on the roof, which
have built-in storage, a compact bathroom. The
bedrooms in the main house are also small: the
style is contemporary – half-height panelling,
plantation-style shutters. To save space there
are no wardrobes; storage is on hooks and
coat-hangers. The quietest rooms overlook the
courtyard (there can be some noise at weekends
from the surrounding pubs). Breakfast, prepared
in an open kitchen, has fruit and yogurt
pots topped with granola, daily blackboard
specials which might include eggs Benedict or
Florentine; a 'grab and go' option.

25% DISCOUNT VOUCHERS

Exchange Avenue
St Nicholas Market
Bristol
BS1 1UB

T: 0117 930 0066
F: 0117 929 9489
E: info@
    brooksguesthousebristol.com
W: www.brooksguesthousebristol.
    com

BEDROOMS: 27. 4 in Airstream
caravans on roof, 1 on ground floor
suitable for disabled.
OPEN: all year except 24/25 Dec.
FACILITIES: lounge/dining room, free
Wi-Fi, courtyard garden.
BACKGROUND MUSIC: contemporary
in lounge.
LOCATION: central, next to
St Nicholas Market.
CHILDREN: all ages welcomed.
DOGS: not allowed.
CREDIT CARDS: Amex, MasterCard,
Visa.
PRICES: [2015] per room B&B
£67–£149.

BRISTOL

NUMBER THIRTY EIGHT CLIFTON

♔ Cesar award in 2013

'Standards are being well maintained,' says a visitor this year to Adam and Mike Dorrien-Smith's luxury B&B at the top of Clifton Downs. Jarek Eliasz is the 'cheerful' manager. The interiors of the five-storey Georgian merchant's house are 'well done with a limited palette of neutral colours complementing the modern artwork'. The bedrooms are on six floors. 'Our rooms at the back had a superb view over rooftops, and were quiet. The bathrooms were excellent, with a separate, rather deep bath (no grab handles), and the only proper-sized shower cubicle I have encountered in a B&B.' Another visitor would have liked a table and chair to use a laptop in her room. All rooms have tea- and coffee-making facilities. There are sofas, coffee tables, magazines and local information in the ground-floor lounge. Breakfast, which can be taken in the room (no charge) or in a dining room, is 'very good' with 'attentive staff, super-fresh croissants and decaf tea on request'. The setting is liked: 'The zoo (with a baby pygmy hippopotamus) is within walking distance, as are local restaurants.' (David Fowler, and others)

38 Upper Belgrave Road
Clifton, Bristol
BS8 2XN

T: 0117 946 6905
E: info@number38clifton.com
W: www.number38clifton.com

BEDROOMS: 9.
OPEN: all year.
FACILITIES: lounge, breakfast room, free Wi-Fi, terrace, unsuitable for disabled.
BACKGROUND MUSIC: jazz/soul/classical all day.
LOCATION: Clifton, Bristol
CHILDREN: not under 12.
DOGS: guide dogs only.
CREDIT CARDS: all major cards.
PRICES: [2015] per room B&B £110–£225.

BROADWAY Worcestershire

Map 3:D6

THE BROADWAY HOTEL

Once a retreat for the abbots of Pershore, this 16th-century stone house was the first hotel in the small Cotswolds Hotels and Inns chain. 'The staff retained a welcoming approach throughout,' says a visitor this year. Other praise: 'We enjoyed our stay: the public areas are particularly pleasing and well executed.' There is a 'cool, modern' atrium restaurant (Tattersalls Brasserie), and a smaller, 'rather dark' lounge. Brasserie meals are served from noon: there is 'ample variety' on the monthly-changing menu with dishes like Innes goat's cheese curd, heritage beetroots; stone bass fillet, samphire, chorizo and brown shrimps, salsa verde. The traditional bedrooms, named after winners of the Cheltenham Gold Cup, are individually styled. 'Our ground-floor room was not over-large but it faced the pretty garden.' Breakfast (served at table except for jugs of fruit juice) is a 'delight, particularly fresh scrambled eggs with a copious quantity of smoked salmon, and home-made Drambuie marmalade'. EF Benson took Broadway as his model for Riseholme in his Lucia novels; its main street is 'a gem of medieval domestic architecture'. (Anthony Bradbury, Bryan and Mary Blaxall)

The Green
Broadway
WR12 7AA

T: 01386 852401
F: 01386 853879
E: info@broadwayhotel.info
W: www.cotswold-inns-hotels.co.uk/broadway

BEDROOMS: 19. 1 on ground floor.
OPEN: all year.
FACILITIES: bar, sitting room, brasserie, free Wi-Fi, small garden.
BACKGROUND MUSIC: none.
LOCATION: in village centre.
CHILDREN: all ages welcomed.
DOGS: allowed in some bedrooms (£10 charge), not in brasserie, on leads in public rooms.
CREDIT CARDS: Amex, MasterCard, Visa.
PRICES: [2015] per room B&B £170–£210, D,B&B £234–£274. À la carte £38.

BROADWAY Worcestershire

Map 3:D6

DORMY HOUSE **NEW**

Guide inspectors this year 'found a welcoming atmosphere' at the Sorensen family's hotel which stands on a ridge above a pretty Cotswolds village. Tom Aspey is the manager. Built around a 17th-century farmhouse, the much-extended hotel has had a contemporary make-over. There is a 'well-equipped' spa at the rear. Guests enter to 'big vases of fresh flowers, a large, well-stocked fruit bowl by reception, a carafe of orange juice and glasses'. Individually decorated bedrooms are in the main house and annexes in the grounds. 'Our ground-floor room facing a grassy courtyard had an enormous bed, plentiful storage and excellent (if complicated) lighting; the large bathroom had a lovely heated floor.' There is a choice of places to eat: the Garden Room restaurant serves modern dishes, perhaps bill-to-tail terrine, grapefruit, chicory; the 'relaxed, rustic' Potting Shed has sandwiches and sharing platters. A family visiting in 2015 praised the welcome for children: 'The staff beautifully took us all in their stride.' Breakfast, overlooking the lawn and rose beds, is 'memorable': 'delicious' muesli and granola; home-made preserves; toast from chunky bread; 'first-class' cooked dishes.

Willersey Hill
Broadway
WR12 7LF

T: 01386 852711
E: reservations@dormyhouse.co.uk
W: dormyhouse.co.uk

BEDROOMS: 38. 8 in Danish Court, 5 in Lavender Lodge, 2 suitable for disabled.
OPEN: all year.
FACILITIES: 4 lounges, Garden Room and Potting Shed restaurants, free Wi-Fi, civil wedding licence (for pagoda in garden), gardens, spa (16-metre indoor swimming pool, gym, treatment rooms).
BACKGROUND MUSIC: 'laid back' in public areas.
LOCATION: 1½ miles E of Broadway.
CHILDREN: all ages welcomed.
DOGS: welcomed (£25 charge) in 4 bedrooms, lounges, not allowed in restaurants.
CREDIT CARDS: Amex, MasterCard, Visa.
PRICES: [2015] B&B from £230, D,B&B from £320. Set menu (Garden Room) £45, à la carte (Potting Shed) £28. 1-night bookings sometimes refused.

BROADWAY Worcestershire

Map 3:D6

RUSSELL'S

♥César award in 2006

On one of the longest, most picturesque High Streets in England, Andrew Riley's restaurant-with-rooms occupies the former showroom of pioneering furniture designer Sir Gordon Russell. Next door is a museum dedicated to his work. 'Excellent food; great value for money,' says a returning visitor this year. Behind the historic Cotswold stone exterior, interiors are contemporary and chic. In the air-conditioned bedrooms, modern styling blends with original architectural features. 'We enjoyed our huge suite, which had a whirlpool bath.' A room in the loft (facing the high street and hills) has A-frame beams, a king-size bed, a seating area with two armchairs; a natural stone bathroom. There is an honesty bar on the landing. An iron and ironing board are available on request. Breakfast, lunch and dinner are served in the L-shaped dining room (bare floorboards, exposed beams). Neil Clarke cooks a daily-changing menu of modern dishes, perhaps pressed head pig terrine, red wine-glazed salsify; Bibury trout, soused beetroot, saffron potatoes. Another comment: 'Excellent in pretty well all respects.' (Tom and Sarah Mann)

The Green
20 High Street
Broadway
WR12 7DT

T: 01386 853555
F: 01386 853964
E: info@russellsofbroadway.co.uk
W: www.russellsofbroadway.co.uk

BEDROOMS: 7. 3 in adjoining building, 2 on ground floor.
OPEN: all year, restaurant closed Sun night.
FACILITIES: ramp, residents' lounge, bar, restaurant, private dining room, free Wi-Fi, patio (heating, meal service), unsuitable for disabled.
BACKGROUND MUSIC: 'ambient' in restaurant.
LOCATION: village centre.
CHILDREN: all ages welcomed.
DOGS: not allowed.
CREDIT CARDS: Amex, MasterCard, Visa.
PRICES: [2015] per room B&B £120–£300. Set menus £14–£22, à la carte £50. 1-night bookings refused weekends.

THE PIG

'Not grand, exactly; neither is it a shabby country pile; like that last bowl of porridge Goldilocks tried, it is just right.' Warm praise comes from a trusted Guide correspondent this year for this informal hotel in the New Forest. It is a 'great place for children, with lots of space for gambolling, and so many things to hold their interest. Our enormous room had plenty of storage; a huge bathroom and roll-top bath; bunk beds for the children in their own room. We had a plate of home-baked goodies as a gift, with personalised piggy biscuits for the children.' The popular restaurant ('buzzy, atmospheric') emphasises local produce and 'has a decided bias towards meat'. 'Melt-in-the-mouth' pork belly, dressed Lymington crab ('with a fat dollop of luscious fennel mayonnaise') and an 'imaginative, citrusy trifle scented with kaffir' characterise the menu. Breakfast has an 'excellent' buffet (pastries, granola with thick yogurt) and a 'delicious' full English; good coffee, brought to the table. Sister hotels are in Southampton, Pensford and Studland (see entries). (M. Astella Saw)

Beaulieu Road
Brockenhurst
SO42 7QL

T: 01590 622354
E: info@thepighotel.com
W: www.thepighotel.co.uk

BEDROOMS: 29. 10 in stable block (100 yds), some on ground floor.
OPEN: all year.
FACILITIES: 2 lounges, bar, restaurant, free Wi-Fi, civil wedding licence, Potting Shed spa, kitchen garden, 14-acre grounds.
BACKGROUND MUSIC: in restaurant and lounges.
LOCATION: 2 miles E of Brockenhurst.
CHILDREN: all ages welcomed.
DOGS: no.
CREDIT CARDS: Amex, MasterCard, Visa.
PRICES: [2015] room £149–£385. Breakfast £10–£15, à la carte £35. 1-night bookings refused at weekends.

AT THE CHAPEL **NEW**

On the main street of a small, fashionable Somerset town, this former congregational chapel is now a bakery, café, wine shop and restaurant with bedrooms. The Grade II listed 19th-century building has been 'stylishly' converted by the owner, Catherine Butler. Guide inspectors this year were 'warmly greeted' by 'friendly' staff and the smell of freshly baked bread. The main dining room is a 'wonderful open space with lots of light from the original windows'; 'vast' pizzas, and modern dishes (perhaps slow-cooked shoulder of lamb, tzatziki, flatbread) are on the menu. 'Busy in the evening, this is clearly the place to visit in town.' The 'spare, modern' bedrooms are decorated with original art. 'Our large, high-ceilinged room had lovely bed linens and puffy pillows; the stunning marble-tiled bathroom had huge vaulted windows and a freestanding bath.' In the morning, 'delicious' croissants are left outside the door for breakfast in the room. 'Somerset butter and home-made strawberry jam in a fridge; decent tea and ground coffee on the tray.' Cooked breakfasts are available in the dining room, at extra cost.

High Street
Bruton
BA10 0AE

T: 01749 814070
E: mail@atthechapel.co.uk
W: www.atthechapel.co.uk

BEDROOMS: 8.
OPEN: all year.
FACILITIES: club room, restaurant, free Wi-Fi, terrace, unsuitable for disabled.
BACKGROUND MUSIC: none.
LOCATION: 7 miles SE of Shepton Mallet.
CHILDREN: all ages welcomed.
DOGS: not allowed.
CREDIT CARDS: Amex, MasterCard, Visa.
PRICES: [2015] per room B&B (continental) £100–£250. À la carte £35.

BRYHER Isles of Scilly

HELL BAY HOTEL

The 'end-of-the-world' quality appealed to a visitor this year to Robert Dorrien-Smith's small hotel. It faces the jagged rocks of Hell Bay on the smallest of the inhabited Scilly Isles. The only access is by small boat from neighbouring islands; guests are met at the quay. The hotel's large lounge has a lofty ceiling, with 'tree-like' supports echoed in the curved wooden top of the fireplace. There is an open fire in the adjoining bar. Robert Dorrien-Smith's unrivalled collection of Cornish art is displayed here: 'I had forgotten how wonderful it was; worth the visit alone,' said a day-visitor. In the kitchen, chef Richard Kearsley cooks a short menu of modern dishes like halibut gravadlax, sauce gribiche; haunch of West Country venison, turnip gratin, chocolate jus. The bedrooms, decorated in bright seaside colours, are off an open internal courtyard. Most face the sea and have a balcony or a terrace. 'Being able to walk to the best little beach in England with just a towel over my shoulder was a bonus.' (Amanda Gay, and others)

Bryher
TR23 0PR

T: 01720 422947
F: 01720 423004
E: contactus@hellbay.co.uk
W: www.hellbay.co.uk

BEDROOMS: 25 suites. In 5 buildings, some on ground floor, 1 suitable for disabled.
OPEN: 11 Mar–24 Oct.
FACILITIES: lounge, games room, bar, 2 dining rooms, free Wi-Fi, gym, sauna, large grounds (heated swimming pool, 15 by 10 metres, children's playground, par 3 golf course), beach 75 yds.
BACKGROUND MUSIC: none.
LOCATION: W coast of island, boat from Tresco (reached by boat/ helicopter from mainland) or St Mary's.
CHILDREN: all ages welcomed (high tea at 5.30).
DOGS: allowed (£12 a night charge), not allowed in public rooms.
CREDIT CARDS: MasterCard, Visa.
PRICES: [2015] per person B&B £85–£285, D,B&B £120–£320. Set dinner £42.50.

BUCKDEN Cambridgeshire

Map 2:B4

THE GEORGE

Once a 19th-century coaching inn, Anne and Richard Furbank's 'well-modernised' hotel stands on the main street of a village on the Great North Road. It is liked today by locals who come for the popular Sunday lunch. There is a wood-burning fire in the entrance hall; the public areas are 'smart and stylish'. Staff are 'efficient and friendly'. Named after famous Georges (Orwell, Eliot, etc), the bedrooms vary in size: two standard rooms have an en suite shower room; others have a bath. 'Our room wasn't big, but we had a decent, comfortable bed and a reasonable-sized bathroom. On a hot and humid day, the room was cool, and a fan could have been provided if needed. There was some noise from the kitchen just below.' Rooms have no tea/coffee-making facilities, but 'tea was brought promptly at 7 am'. A biscuit barrel on the landing is 'a nice touch'. Chef Benaissa El Akil is the new chef in the brasserie; his 'excellent' modern British dishes have a Mediterranean touch. A typical dish: a 'generous' portion of 'tender duck breast with plenty of vegetables'. (Peter Anderson, and others)

25% DISCOUNT VOUCHERS

High Street
Buckden
PE19 5XA

T: 01480 812300
F: 01480 813920
E: manager@thegeorgebuckden.com
W: www.thegeorgebuckden.com

BEDROOMS: 12. 3 suitable for disabled.
OPEN: all year.
FACILITIES: lift, bar, lounge, restaurant, private dining rooms, free Wi-Fi, civil wedding licence, courtyard.
BACKGROUND MUSIC: varied in public areas.
LOCATION: village centre.
CHILDREN: all ages welcomed.
DOGS: allowed in foyer lounge and courtyard.
CREDIT CARDS: Amex, MasterCard, Visa.
PRICES: [2015] per room B&B £95–£150, D,B&B from £150. À la carte £35.

BUDE Cornwall

Map 1:C3

THE BEACH

In a fine position above Summerleaze beach, Susie and Will Daniel's contemporary hotel has a terrace with 'lovely sea views'. In warm weather, light meals and cocktails (like the signature Summerleaze Sunrise) can be taken here while watching the surfers ride the waves below. There is a chrome-topped bar with orange leather chairs; the restaurant has rustic wooden tables, wicker chairs. Joe Simmons is now the chef; classically trained, he uses local produce for his modern dishes, perhaps slow-cooked belly pork rillette, orange marmalade chutney, brioche; roasted grey mullet, Thai-influenced curry of clams, mussels, prawns, caramelised tomato and samphire. The bedrooms, decorated in New England style, have limed oak furniture, Lloyd Loom chairs. The best rooms have a sea view, a super king-size bed; a walk-in shower and a separate bath in the bathroom. Some (including a ground-floor room) have a private terrace, others a Juliet balcony. The 'seaside atmosphere' is appreciated. Breakfast has a comprehensive buffet and a good selection of cooked dishes. Summerleaze has a seawater swimming pool set in the rocks. (FM)

25% DISCOUNT VOUCHERS

Summerleaze Crescent
Bude
EX23 8HJ

T: 01288 389800
F: 01288 389820
E: enquiries@thebeachatbude.co.uk
W: www.thebeachatbude.co.uk

BEDROOMS: 16. 1 on ground floor.
OPEN: all year except 25/26 Dec.
FACILITIES: lift, 2 bars, restaurant, free Wi-Fi, terrace.
BACKGROUND MUSIC: all day in public areas.
LOCATION: above Summerleaze beach.
CHILDREN: all ages welcomed.
DOGS: not allowed.
CREDIT CARDS: Amex, MasterCard, Visa.
PRICES: [2015] per room B&B £120–£215, D,B&B £170–£265. À la carte £30.

THE LAMB INN

Occupying a row of medieval weavers' cottages on a tree-lined street of limestone houses, this 'lovely' old inn, part of a small group of Cotswold hotels, has log fires in the public areas, and a walled garden where guests may take drinks and alfresco meals in fine weather. Bill Ramsay is the manager. 'Comfortable', 'slightly old-fashioned' bedrooms are individually styled; each has a tea tray with home-made flapjacks. The rooms vary in size: Shepherd has a fireplace and a four-poster bed; Allium, the largest room, has a roll-top bath in a spacious bathroom. Two large lounges have books, magazines and plenty of seating. Local ales, deli boards and pub classics are served in the flagstoned bar; dogs are welcomed here with a bowl of water, a biscuit and a special menu. In the restaurant overlooking the courtyard terrace, modern British dishes and an eight-course tasting menu might include Evesham asparagus, smoked duck egg, cauliflower, pea shoots; fillet of beef, ox cheek tortellini, broccoli, quinoa crisps. Breakfast is 'first class': freshly squeezed juices, home-made jams and Drambuie marmalade; a good selection of hot dishes.

Sheep Street
Burford
OX18 4LR

T: 01993 823155
F: 01993 822228
E: info@lambinn-burford.co.uk
W: www.cotswold-inns-hotels.co.uk/lamb

BEDROOMS: 17.
OPEN: all year.
FACILITIES: 2 lounges, bar, restaurant, free Wi-Fi, courtyard, ½-acre garden, unsuitable for disabled.
BACKGROUND MUSIC: none.
LOCATION: 500 yds from centre.
CHILDREN: all ages welcomed.
DOGS: allowed in some bedrooms, not in restaurant.
CREDIT CARDS: Amex, MasterCard, Visa.
PRICES: [2015] per room B&B £165–£275, D,B&B from £237. Set menu £36–£42, tasting menu £58.

SEE ALSO SHORTLIST

BURNHAM MARKET Norfolk

Map 2:A5

THE HOSTE

Variously a manor house, a coaching inn and the host of a livestock auction market, this 16th-century building is today the centrepiece of a sprawling hotel owned by Brendan and Bee Hopkins. Bedrooms are in the main house, a courtyard wing, Vine House across the green, and Railway House, a ten-minute walk away (where one of the rooms is in a refurbished railway carriage on the old train tracks). Each has a particular character: some main-house rooms have a terrace; Vine House rooms have antiques and gilt mirrors; those in the Railway House, more smartly decorated, have railway memorabilia. 'Our courtyard room was slightly over the top – silver furnishings, silvery wallpaper – but the essentials were right: a large, comfortable bed, quality bedlinen, excellent lighting, a decent bathroom.' Guests have a choice of eating places: in the dining room, James O'Connor, the chef, serves modern dishes (perhaps roast sea bass, crab ravioli, spinach, bisque sauce); informal meals may be taken in the conservatory, the garden room and, in good weather, the wisteria-clad walled garden. Breakfast has 'exceptionally good' local sausages; vegetarian options.

The Green
Burnham Market
PE31 8HD

T: 01328 738777
F: 01328 730103
E: reservations@thehoste.com
W: www.thehoste.com

BEDROOMS: 62. 6 on ground floor, 6 in courtyard wing, 8 in Vine House, 8 in Railway House (1 in railway carriage), 3 three-bedroom cottages.
OPEN: all year.
FACILITIES: bar, lounge, conservatory, garden room, restaurant, private dining lodge, free Wi-Fi, civil wedding licence, spa, terrace garden (at Vine House).
BACKGROUND MUSIC: varied in all public areas except bar.
LOCATION: village centre.
CHILDREN: all ages welcomed.
DOGS: allowed in some bedrooms (£15 per night), public rooms.
CREDIT CARDS: Amex, MasterCard, Visa.
PRICES: [2015] per room B&B £130–£350. À la carte £35. 1-night bookings sometimes refused weekends.

BURRINGTON Devon

Map 1:C4

NORTHCOTE MANOR

'An oasis of calm and tranquillity', this 18th-century manor house stands in extensive grounds in the Taw valley. It is managed by the chef, Richie Herkes, for the owner, Jean-Pierre Mifsud. The staff are 'universally' charming, say fans. The spacious public rooms have polished wooden floors, oriental rugs. On the drawing room and restaurant walls, three striking murals by Barrington Barber, commissioned by a previous owner, tell the story of the site from its early monastic days. The setting in the restaurant is formal, but the seasonal menus are contemporary, with dishes like chicken boudin, wilted baby spinach, white truffle cream; pavé of Cornish cod, green asparagus spears, braised leeks, leek and potato sauce. There is a six-course gourmet menu. The bedrooms are individually decorated and 'have all the necessities' (fresh fruit, mints and home-made shortbread are supplied). The Heron suite has a freestanding bath in the bedroom; a separate bathroom with a walk-in shower. 'Our lovely ground-floor room was great for our dog.' The Lake, Llangammarch Wells (see entry), is under the same ownership. (Annabel Thomas, and others)

Burrington
EX37 9LZ

T: 01769 560501
F: 01769 560770
E: rest@northcotemanor.co.uk
W: www.northcotemanor.co.uk

BEDROOMS: 16. 1 suitable for disabled.
OPEN: all year.
FACILITIES: ramps, 2 lounges, bar, 2 restaurants, free Wi-Fi, civil wedding licence, 25-acre grounds.
BACKGROUND MUSIC: classical in public areas.
LOCATION: 3 miles S of Umberleigh.
CHILDREN: no under-10s in restaurant after 7 pm.
DOGS: welcomed in some bedrooms, not in restaurants.
CREDIT CARDS: Amex, MasterCard, Visa.
PRICES: [2015] B&B per room £170–£280, D,B&B £260–£340. Set dinner £45, gourmet menu £90.

BURTON BRADSTOCK Dorset

Map 1:D6

THE SEASIDE BOARDING HOUSE **NEW**

On a cliff above Chesil Bay, this former B&B has been transformed into a sophisticated restaurant-with-rooms by Mary-Lou Sturridge and her business partner, Anthony Mackintosh, both formerly of the Groucho Club, London. 'Laid-back and friendly', it 'has much to recommend it', say Guide inspectors in 2015. 'Everything is done in good taste, and everyone is obliging.' Jonny Jeffery, the manager, 'brought us extra (free-range) coat-hangers, gave us a drink in the bar, and came to chat during dinner; a chair in the bedroom was quickly changed when we asked'. There is a 'blissful lack of background music' in the long, narrow dining room which faces the sea. 'Dinner had good ingredients, unfussily presented; sea trout on spinach; perfectly prepared turbot (vegetables cost extra); delicious lemon tart. Not cheap, but enjoyable, with well-paced service.' There is a small, quiet library. The decor in the bedrooms is 'elegant, with restrained shades of grey; our room had an unusually high bed, big windows with a view of the sea, shelves of interesting books; a Roberts radio but no TV (you can request one). A beautiful, big bathroom.'

Cliff Road
Burton Bradstock
DT6 4RB

T: 01308 897 205
E: info@theseasideboardinghouse.com
w: theseasideboardinghouse.com

BEDROOMS: 8.
OPEN: all year.
FACILITIES: bar, library, restaurant, free Wi-Fi, unsuitable for disabled.
BACKGROUND MUSIC: none.
LOCATION: 3 miles SE of Bridport.
CHILDREN: all ages welcomed (in 1 family room).
DOGS: welcomed in 2 bedrooms, bar, not allowed in restaurant.
CREDIT CARDS: Amex, MasterCard, Visa.
PRICES: [2015] per room B&B £180–£200. À la carte £35.

CAMBRIDGE Cambridgeshire

Map 2:B4

DUKE HOUSE [NEW]

Close to the main colleges, Liz and Rob Cameron's 'excellent' B&B is in a smartly refurbished Victorian house, once the student home of the Duke of Gloucester. 'We very much enjoyed our stay,' said a guest in 2015, whose positive report earns it an upgrade to a full entry. Tea, coffee and a sweet treat are served in the 'pleasant' sitting room; the library has 'serious books, paperback novels and magazines'. Some of the pretty bedrooms retain original features such as a Victorian fireplace; those on the second floor are reached via 'steep' stairs. 'Our first-floor room had two armchairs and a small dressing table; the roomy bathroom had modern fittings. The duvets were the best we have ever slept under – light and cosy.' A communal fridge on the landing contains fresh milk, and cold drinks 'paid for on the honour system'. Breakfast can be taken in the small courtyard garden on warm days. No evening meals are served, but the Clarendon Arms down the street is 'an excellent "proper" pub with home-cooked food and real ales'. (Michael Gwinnell)

1 Victoria Street
Cambridge
CB1 1JP

T: 01223 314773
E: info@dukehousecambridge.co.uk
W: www.dukehousecambridge.co.uk

BEDROOMS: 5. 1 in adjacent cottage, plus self-catering apartment.
OPEN: all year except 23–29 Dec.
FACILITIES: sitting room, breakfast room, balcony, free Wi-Fi, courtyard, limited parking (by arrangement), unsuitable for disabled.
BACKGROUND MUSIC: none.
LOCATION: central.
CHILDREN: not under 10.
DOGS: not allowed.
CREDIT CARDS: Diners, MasterCard, Visa.
PRICES: [2015] per room B&B from £130. 1-night bookings sometimes refused.

SEE ALSO SHORTLIST

PENDRAGON COUNTRY HOUSE

In North Cornish countryside, this former Victorian rectory is run as a small guest house by Nigel and Sharon Reed; his mother, Sue, is a partner. 'We arrived early to a warm welcome,' said visitors in 2015. 'While we were shown the house, our bags appeared magically in our room.' The Reeds have furnished the house with Victorian antiques and 'well-chosen' pictures; the Red room has books and games, information leaflets on the area; there's an honesty bar in the Green room. Bedrooms vary in size and decor: Bedivere has a solid cherry-wood bed, a shower cabinet and a roll-top bath big enough for two; Lamorak has double-aspect windows and a king-size four-poster bed; Tristram, the largest, can accommodate a family and has a Cornish tin ceiling. Children are welcomed: baby monitors and a listening service are available. Nigel Reed, a 'good cook', serves a set menu (likes and dislikes discussed beforehand) of dishes like Cornish yarg cheese and coppa salad; slow-roasted and pressed belly of pork, crushed new potatoes. Breakfast has home-made muesli, home-baked bread and pastries; kipper and 'the tastiest' rarebit among the cooked options.

Old Vicarage Hill
Davidstow
Camelford
PL32 9XR

T: 01840 261131
E: enquiries@
pendragoncountryhouse.com
W: www.pendragoncountryhouse.
com

BEDROOMS: 7. 1 on ground floor suitable for disabled.
OPEN: all year except 23–28 Dec, restaurant closed Sun.
FACILITIES: sitting room, bar, Orangery breakfast/dining room, private dining room, free Wi-Fi, civil wedding licence, 1¼-acre grounds.
BACKGROUND MUSIC: none.
LOCATION: 3½ miles NE of Camelford.
CHILDREN: all ages welcomed.
DOGS: allowed in 1 bedroom, sitting room (£5 per night).
CREDIT CARDS: all major cards.
PRICES: per room B&B single £60–£65, double £95–£140. D,B&B £22.50 added per person. Set menu £25–£32.

CANNINGTON Somerset

Map 1:B5

BLACKMORE FARM

At the foot of the Quantock hills, 'Blachamore' estate is listed in the Domesday Book. Today the (relatively newer) Grade I listed 15th-century manor house and converted outbuildings welcome B&B guests, and house a farm shop and café. The owners, Ann and Ian Dyer, run the farm alongside greeting visitors. In 2015, they added four extra bedrooms and a 'retreat', a 'cosy' shepherd's hut in the grounds. The newest rooms are on the ground floor in the Wagon House; they have views across fields to the hills. Many original features are retained in the manor house: stone archways, medieval garderobes and cob-and-lime-plaster walls. An ancient front door opens on to the Great Hall, which has an inglenook fireplace, a full suit of armour, and a long oak refectory table (where a generous communal breakfast is served). Ploughman's lunches and quiches are available in the café, and Blackmore Farm ice cream. Children may roam the gardens and watch the cows being milked. Indoors, myriad nooks and crannies invite games of hide-and-seek on wet days. There is good walking from the door.

Blackmore Lane
Cannington
TA5 2NE

T: 01278 653442
E: dyerfarm@aol.com
W: www.blackmorefarm.co.uk

BEDROOMS: 10. 6 on ground floor in annexes, 1 in grounds.
OPEN: all year.
FACILITIES: lounge/TV room, hall/breakfast room, free Wi-Fi, 1-acre garden (stream, coarse fishing).
BACKGROUND MUSIC: none.
LOCATION: 3 miles NW of Bridgwater
CHILDREN: all ages welcomed.
DOGS: not allowed.
CREDIT CARDS: Diners, MasterCard, Visa.
PRICES: [2015] per person B&B £55–£60. 1-night bookings refused bank holiday weekends.

CARLISLE Cumbria

Map 4:B2

WILLOWBECK LODGE

Amid mature weeping willows, and beech and oak trees, this alpine-style guest house is run by 'friendly' owners Liz and John McGrillis. The 'spacious, superbly furnished' bedrooms have a contemporary finish; two dormer rooms have French windows and a Juliet balcony. Willow, the largest room, is decorated in pastel colours; a dressing room, with mirrored wardrobes, leads to a bathroom with a corner bath and separate shower. All rooms have a view of the duck pond; they have under-floor heating and free Wi-Fi, and are equipped with a hospitality tray with chocolates and biscuits. All rooms have en suite facilities. The guest lounge has a wall of books, a big window overlooking the pond and a patio. It 'feels like a private home, not a hotel'. On five days a week from 10 am to 6 pm, light meals can be taken in Fini's Kitchen (the classic dishes with a modern twist are 'inspired by the hearty, wholesome cooking of my late grandmother, Josephine "Fini" McGrillis', says the host). Willowbeck is close to the M6 (no road noise); 'a great place to stop on the way to or from Scotland'.

Lambley Bank
Scotby
Carlisle
CA4 8BX

T: 01228 513607
F: 01228 501053
E: info@willowbeck-lodge.com
W: www.willowbeck-lodge.com

BEDROOMS: 4.
OPEN: all year except 21 Dec–2 Jan, restaurant closed Sun/Mon.
FACILITIES: lounge, lounge/dining room, conference/function facilities, free Wi-Fi, civil wedding licence, 1½-acre garden (stream, pond), unsuitable for disabled.
BACKGROUND MUSIC: 'at owners' discretion'.
LOCATION: 3 miles E of Carlisle.
CHILDREN: not under 12.
DOGS: not allowed.
CREDIT CARDS: MasterCard, Visa.
PRICES: per room B&B £100–£140 (£10 reduction for single occupancy). Set dinner £25.

AYNSOME MANOR

♥César award in 1998

'In a quiet part of the South Lakes away from the tourist crowds', this 'exceptionally good' 17th-century manor house hotel has long been run by its owners, Christopher and Andrea Varley. It is popular with travellers who seek traditional values, and appreciate the 'high standards and wonderful atmosphere'. There are modern and antique touches in the lounges (high-backed chairs, patterned carpets, brass scuttles). Guests can read by the open wood-burning fireplace or, on fine days, on one of many benches in the gardens. A visitor this year 'was delighted to be given a large, well-equipped bedroom with shower room attached, though I had booked a single room'. In the Georgian dining room, chef Gordon Topp's daily-changing menu focuses on fresh, locally sourced ingredients: 'The portions are generous; a huge seafood ragout was hard to fault; enjoyable pork fillet with a side dish of vegetables. An excellent meal.' Breakfast has a 'wide choice – good bread'. 'The service is friendly and prompt; the prices are reasonable,' said a returning visitor. (Dorothy Brining, William Smethurst)

25% DISCOUNT VOUCHERS

Aynsome Lane
Cartmel
nr Grange-over-Sands
LA11 6HH

T: 01539 536653
F: 01539 536016
E: aynsomemanor@btconnect.com
W: www.aynsomemanorhotel.co.uk

BEDROOMS: 12. 2 in cottage (with lounge) across courtyard.
OPEN: all year except 23–28 Dec, 2–29 Jan, lunch served Sun only, Sun dinner for residents only.
FACILITIES: 2 lounges, bar, dining room, free Wi-Fi (ground floor and some first-floor bedrooms only), ½-acre garden, unsuitable for disabled.
BACKGROUND MUSIC: none.
LOCATION: ¾ mile outside village.
CHILDREN: not under 5.
DOGS: allowed (£5.50 a night), not in public rooms.
CREDIT CARDS: Amex, MasterCard.
PRICES: [2015] per room B&B £95–£150, D,B&B £162–£195. Set dinner £29. 1-night bookings occasionally refused weekends.

CHAGFORD Devon

Map 1:C4

PARFORD WELL

Owner Tim Daniel escaped from London to run this 'professional but personal' B&B within Dartmoor national park. Arriving guests are greeted with afternoon tea and home-made cake. On fine days, visitors can sit in the pretty walled garden and look out across the unspoilt countryside of the River Teign valley; there is a supply of books and board games, and a wood-burning stove for wet days, in the elegantly furnished lounge. The 'very comfortable' bedrooms are decorated in a country house/ modern style with wooden furniture and tasteful fabrics; one has a private bathroom across the corridor, the others have facilities en suite. The 'superb' breakfast is made to order by Tim Daniel, using fresh, locally sourced ingredients where possible: fruit salad, full English, coffee and juice. Guests eat communally in the dining room, or in a private side room if they prefer. There are 'wonderful' walks from the doorstep, to the wooded valley or the open moorland, as well as the nearby 20th-century Castle Drogo, completed in 1930. No lunches or dinners; the pub opposite serves locally crafted beer and food. (CA)

Sandy Park
Chagford
TQ13 8JW

T: 01647 433353
E: tim@parfordwell.co.uk
W: www.parfordwell.co.uk

BEDROOMS: 3.
OPEN: all year.
FACILITIES: sitting room, 2 breakfast rooms, free Wi-Fi, ½-acre garden, unsuitable for disabled.
BACKGROUND MUSIC: none.
LOCATION: in hamlet 1 mile N of Chagford.
CHILDREN: not under 8.
DOGS: not allowed.
CREDIT CARDS: none.
PRICES: per room B&B £90–£110. 1-night bookings sometimes refused weekends in season.

CHETTLE Dorset

Map 2:E1

CASTLEMAN

♥César award in 2004

Occupying a former dower house in a historic Dorset village, this 'relaxed', 'good-value' restaurant-with-rooms is loved by visitors who return for the 'gorgeous, unspoilt and atmospheric' setting, and the 'charming, helpful, laid-back' staff. It is run by Barbara Garnsworthy and her brother, Brendan – 'real personalities'. 'They looked after our three generations very well,' said guests who stayed for a family celebration this year. 'We thought the younger members would think it totally uncool, but they have actually returned since, as it reminded them of a country hotel in rural France.' Bedrooms 'need careful selection': most are 'spacious, with a wonderful outlook', though housekeeping might 'need greater attention' in others. The 'delightful' dining room looks out on to fields and lawns, 'with not another building in sight'; here, Barbara Garnsworthy and Richard Morris's 'first-class' menus use fruit and vegetables from the kitchen garden. Breakfast has fresh orange juice, local sausages, home-baked bread and 'wonderful' plum jam. 'Richard cooks the finest scrambled eggs.' (Alec Frank)

25% DISCOUNT VOUCHERS

Chettle
nr Blandford Forum
DT11 8DB

T: 01258 830096
F: 01258 830051
E: enquiry@castlemanhotel.co.uk
W: www.castlemanhotel.co.uk

BEDROOMS: 8 (1 family).
OPEN: Mar–Jan, except 25/26, 31 Dec, restaurant closed midday except Sun.
FACILITIES: 2 drawing rooms, bar, restaurant, free Wi-Fi, 2-acre grounds (stables for visiting horses), riding, fishing, shooting, cycling nearby, only restaurant suitable for disabled.
BACKGROUND MUSIC: none.
LOCATION: village, 1 mile off A354 Salisbury–Blandford, hotel signposted.
CHILDREN: all ages welcomed.
DOGS: not allowed.
CREDIT CARDS: MasterCard, Visa.
PRICES: [2015] per room B&B £100–£115. À la carte £30.

CHILLATON Devon

Map 1:D3

TOR COTTAGE

Hillside woodlands, home to deer, pheasants and shy badgers, rise behind this rustic B&B in a secluded spot at the end of a long, tree-lined track. Maureen Rowlatt is the 'charming' owner. 'She did all she could to make our stay comfortable,' guests said this year. Bedrooms are in the main house and in converted outbuildings (a craftsman's workshop, an ancient cart house, a modest cottage) in the gardens; each has a log fire, a well-equipped kitchenette, a private terrace and garden. Reached by a woodland walk, the most private room, Laughing Waters, is a New England-style bed-sitting room with steps leading down to a stream; it has a barbecue area, and a veranda with a rocking chair. Dinner is not provided (several restaurants and pubs are within easy driving distance), but a generous picnic platter of sandwiches, Cornish pasties, pudding, cheeses and chutney is available, by arrangement, to be consumed in the bedroom. A copious breakfast has an extensive choice of fruits, cereals and yogurt; hot dishes, ordered the day before, include kedgeree and a vegetarian option. (Sue and Colin Raymond)

nr Lifton
Chillaton
PL16 0JE

T: 01822 860248
F: 01822 860126
E: info@torcottage.co.uk
W: www.torcottage.co.uk

BEDROOMS: 5. 4 in garden.
OPEN: mid-Jan–mid-Dec.
FACILITIES: sitting room, large conservatory, breakfast room, free Wi-Fi (in conservatory only), 28-acre grounds (2-acre garden, heated swimming pool (14 by 5 metres, May–Sept), barbecue, stream, bridleway, walks), river (fishing ½ mile), unsuitable for disabled.
BACKGROUND MUSIC: none.
LOCATION: ½ mile S of Chillaton.
CHILDREN: not under 14.
DOGS: not allowed.
CREDIT CARDS: MasterCard, Visa.
PRICES: per person B&B (min. 2 nights) £75–£77.50. 1-night bookings sometimes refused.

CAPTAINS CLUB HOTEL

There is an ocean-going feel to this 'modern, stylish', nautical-inspired hotel. Set on the banks of the River Stour, it has a riverside terrace and floor-to-ceiling windows. 'It is a welcoming and comfortable place to stay,' says a regular Guide correspondent this year. 'The decking by the river seemed to be busy at all times of the day with guests and lots of locals. There were plenty of well-trained staff, looked over by hard-working managers who were not afraid to get stuck in.' The 'unfussy' menu in the restaurant was liked. Chef Andrew Gault buys for freshness, quality and sustainability: steaks are served with hand-cut chips; bream with red pepper and tomato tapenade; aubergine with curried lentils, a cucumber and pomegranate salad. The contemporary bedrooms overlook the water. 'Ours was of a good size, with an interesting view; plenty of space for lounging around in.' Breakfast is 'especially good; an extensive choice of both hot and cold items'. The harbour teems with winged and web-footed birdlife. River trips can be taken on a luxury motor launch. (Lynn Wildgoose)

Wick Ferry
37 Wick Lane
Christchurch
BH23 1HU

T: 01202 475111
F: 01202 490111
E: enquiries@captainsclubhotel.
   com
W: www.captainsclubhotel.com

BEDROOMS: 29. 2 suitable for disabled.
OPEN: all year.
FACILITIES: lifts, lounge, bar, restaurant, function facilities, civil wedding licence, free Wi-Fi, terrace, spa (hydrotherapy pool, sauna, treatments).
BACKGROUND MUSIC: in public areas, live pianist Sat evening.
LOCATION: on Christchurch quay.
CHILDREN: all ages welcomed.
DOGS: allowed in suites, not in public rooms.
CREDIT CARDS: Amex, MasterCard, Visa.
PRICES: [2015] per room B&B £249–£299, D,B&B from £329. Min. 2-night stay at peak periods.

CIRENCESTER Gloucestershire

Map 3:E5

KINGS HEAD HOTEL   **NEW**

Staff, say Guide inspectors in 2015, display an
'obvious desire to satisfy the customer' at Mark
and Alison Booth's sympathetically renovated
medieval coaching inn on the market square.
Alongside original features of the hotel's long
history (beams, restored fireplaces, a Roman
mosaic in the reception area), individually
designed, 'state-of-the-art' bedrooms have a
Mac mini-computer system and a Nespresso
machine. A standard room, reached via 'a long,
twisting landing', had a king-size bed, two
'comfortable' upholstered armchairs, a fridge
with complimentary mineral water and fresh
milk. Another room, with a four-poster bed,
had a 'vast' copper bath in the bathroom. Air
conditioning was 'effective but noisy'. Service is
'friendly and informal' in the popular, open-
plan bar and dining area, in a covered inner
courtyard with a wood-burning stove. Chef
David Watts uses 'outstanding' local ingredients
in his modern dishes: 'We enjoyed parsnip and
apple soup, venison and sirloin steak. Portions
were well judged.' Breakfast has freshly
squeezed juice, 'succulent' local bacon and
'very tasty' Gloucestershire Old Spot sausages.
Parking can be tricky.

24 Market Place
Cirencester
GL7 2NR

T: 01285 700900
E: info@kingshead-hotel.co.uk
W: kingshead-hotel.co.uk

BEDROOMS: 45. 1 suitable for
disabled.
OPEN: all year.
FACILITIES: lifts, ramp, lounge, bar,
restaurant, private dining rooms,
meeting rooms, spa (treatments,
steam room, sauna), free Wi-Fi,
civil wedding licence, rooftop
garden.
BACKGROUND MUSIC: various in
public areas.
LOCATION: town centre.
CHILDREN: all ages welcomed.
DOGS: allowed by prior arrangement
(charge), not in restaurant.
CREDIT CARDS: Amex, MasterCard,
Visa.
PRICES: [2015] per person B&B from
£120, D,B&B from £155. À la carte
£35. 1-night bookings sometimes
refused.

CLEARWELL Gloucestershire

Map 3:D4

TUDOR FARMHOUSE

In a 'remote' position in the Royal Forest of Dean, this 'relaxing' hotel occupies an 'attractively converted' farmhouse surrounded by 'imaginative' gardens and expansive countryside. Guests receive a 'warm and genuine' welcome from Hari and Colin Fell, the owners; service is 'outstanding'. Visitors in 2015 found the hotel 'pleasantly full for late February'. Four bedrooms are in the main house (up a steep spiral staircase); others are in a refurbished barn and cider house in the grounds. All are decorated in a contemporary country style. 'Our room was lovely: comfortable beds, sumptuous linen, an exceptional hot drinks tray; good lighting – you could sit up in bed and read.' In the restaurant, chef Martin Adams uses home-grown and foraged ingredients in his 'very good' modern menus, perhaps a 'tender, flavourful' confit pork belly, burnt apple purée, roasted shallots, beetroot fondant. In the summer, guests may take al fresco meals and afternoon tea in the cottage garden. 'Excellent' breakfasts have freshly squeezed juices, fruit, croissants, 'wonderful' local honey; 'full marks for marmalade almost as good as my mother makes'. (Gwyn Morgan, MC)

25% DISCOUNT VOUCHERS

High Street
Clearwell
GL16 8JS

T: 01594 833046
F: 01594 837093
E: info@tudorfarmhousehotel.co.uk
W: www.tudorfarmhousehotel.co.uk

BEDROOMS: 20. 8 on ground floor, 9 in barn, 7 in cider house.
OPEN: all year.
FACILITIES: lounge, bar, restaurant, free Wi-Fi, 14-acre grounds.
BACKGROUND MUSIC: 'discreet' in restaurant and lounge.
LOCATION: 7 miles SE of Monmouth.
CHILDREN: all ages welcomed.
DOGS: not allowed.
CREDIT CARDS: Amex, MasterCard, Visa.
PRICES: [2015] per room B&B £100–£230. À la carte £35. 2-night stays only in selected rooms weekends May–Sept.

CLEE STANTON Shropshire

Map 3:C5

TIMBERSTONE

'A very welcoming couple', Tracey Baylis and Alex Read, greet guests with tea or coffee at their 'delightful' rural B&B in this 'lovingly extended' stone cottage in the Clee hills. The open-plan lounge/dining room has books, games and a wood-burning stove; glass doors lead to the terrace. Under old oak beams and in the more modern extension, country-style bedrooms are simply furnished; each has a tea tray with hot chocolate, infusions and shortbread biscuits. They vary in size and decor: Clay has French doors opening on to a balcony; Oak and Slate have a sofa bed to accommodate a family; Dhustone has a large double-ended bath in the bathroom. Tracey Baylis's 'delicious' communal dinners, served by arrangement, 'would have done credit to a posh restaurant': her traditional dishes use local, home-grown and organic ingredients where possible, perhaps loin of pork, creamy wholegrain mustard and cider sauce. Breakfast has home-made preserves and bread, eggs from the house's hens, and 'a large choice' of cooked dishes. Tracey Baylis, a reflexologist, can provide treatments in a garden studio. (JM)

25% DISCOUNT VOUCHERS

Lackstone Lane
Clee Stanton
SY8 3EL

T: 01584 823519
E: timberstone1@hotmail.com
W: www.timberstoneludlow.co.uk

BEDROOMS: 4. Plus summer house retreat in summer.
OPEN: all year except 25 Dec and 1 Jan.
FACILITIES: lounge/dining room, conservatory, free Wi-Fi, ½-acre garden, treatment room, unsuitable for disabled.
BACKGROUND MUSIC: none.
LOCATION: 5 miles NE of Ludlow.
CHILDREN: all ages welcomed.
DOGS: allowed by arrangement, not in public rooms.
CREDIT CARDS: MasterCard, Visa.
PRICES: [2015] per room B&B £95. Set menus £20–£24.50.

CLIPSHAM Rutland

Map 2:A3

BEECH HOUSE & OLIVE BRANCH

💐 César award in 2012

'Highly recommended' this year, Sean Hope and Ben Jones's informal pub/restaurant-with-rooms is on a tree-lined street in a village near Stamford. Louise Williams is the manager: 'The staff are very welcoming.' Sean Hope is the chef, serving 'excellent' meals in the restaurant, a series of rooms with stained beams, log fires. His seasonal menu might include wild mushroom and tarragon risotto; plaice with grapes and caper mash. The bedrooms are in Beech House, a restored Georgian building across the road (umbrellas are provided). 'Our room, Biscuit, had a king-size bed, good storage and plenty of space; we enjoyed sitting on the lovely private patio at the end of a long day hiking.' Apple, a smaller room, had 'a French painted chest of drawers, a large bed, good lighting; home-made biscuits, fresh milk in a fridge on the landing'. Breakfast, 'laid in a delightfully restored barn with a feature fireplace with a proper fire', has a 'superb selection of hot and cold dishes, locally made bread and jams, and marmalade made in the pub'. (Tara Varco, and others)

Main Street
Clipsham
LE15 7SH

T: 01780 410355
F: 01780 410000
E: beechhouse@theolivebranchpub.com
W: www.theolivebranchpub.com

BEDROOMS: 6. 2 on ground floor, family room (also suitable for disabled) in annexe.
OPEN: all year, pub closed evening 25 Dec/1 Jan.
FACILITIES: ramps, pub, dining room, breakfast room, free Wi-Fi, small front garden.
BACKGROUND MUSIC: classical/jazz in pub.
LOCATION: in village 7 miles NW of Stamford.
CHILDREN: all ages welcomed.
DOGS: allowed in ground-floor bedrooms and bar.
CREDIT CARDS: MasterCard, Visa.
PRICES: [2015] per room B&B £115–£195. Set dinner £29.50, à la carte £30.50.

COWAN BRIDGE Lancashire

Map 4: inset D2

HIPPING HALL

♀César award in 2008

Once owned by resourceful blacksmiths, this early 18th-century country pile stands in lovely countryside where Lancashire, Yorkshire and Cumbria meet. It is the first of three ventures by Andrew Wildsmith, who abandoned a PhD in chemistry to follow his 'retired' father into the hotel business, applying the trusted formula of 'simple things done well'. 'Once again a very enjoyable weekend' was enjoyed by visitors who returned in 2015, with praise for the 'impressively comfortable' bedrooms, 'furnished in modern country style', the 'smart' stone-tiled bathrooms, and the young staff, 'happy to serve the guests'. Tatham Suite, in the oak-beamed roof space, is a smart blend of modern luxury and rusticity. Dinner from a daily-changing menu is served in a 15th-century galleried Great Hall. Oli Martin, promoted to head chef, displays a 'vibrant cooking style' in dishes like Cartmel valley rabbit, lardo, celery, borlotti beans; Lakeland beef fillet, beef short ribs, pied bleu mushrooms, radish. Broken Beck runs past a 13th-century wash house in the 'well-kept' grounds. A 'generous' breakfast is cooked to order. (David and Kate Wooff)

Cowan Bridge
LA6 2JJ

T: 015242 71187
E: info@hippinghall.com
W: www.hippinghall.com

BEDROOMS: 10. 3 in cottages, 1, on ground floor, suitable for disabled.
OPEN: all year, lunch, weekends only.
FACILITIES: lounge, orangery, restaurant, free Wi-Fi in lounge only, civil wedding licence, 3-acre garden.
BACKGROUND MUSIC: in lounge, restaurant.
LOCATION: 2 miles SE of Kirkby Lonsdale, on A65.
CHILDREN: not under 12.
DOGS: allowed in 2 bedrooms and orangery.
CREDIT CARDS: MasterCard, Visa.
PRICES: [2015] per room B&B £159–£419, D,B&B £80 added per couple. Set dinner £55, tasting menu £65, lunch £29.50, tasting menu £39.50.

CROFT-ON-TEES Co. Durham

Map 4:C4

CLOW BECK HOUSE

♀César award in 2007

Near the confluence of the Clow Beck and the River Tees, Heather and David Armstrong's 'unexpected' farmhouse hotel and restaurant stands in 'beautifully landscaped, immaculately kept' gardens. The 'warmth of feeling' from the Armstrongs made a recent visitor 'feel at home'. The lounge is 'bright and attractive', with sofas, a piano and lots of books. Divided across the main house and a group of converted stone outbuildings, the 'comfortable, well-equipped' bedrooms are individually decorated, 'flamboyant but not "over the top"': the bold drapery of the half-tester in one would suit a jester; in another chandeliers hang from carved wooden ceiling roses. In another room a Japanese-style headboard is overlooked by a portrait of Audrey Hepburn. The gardens are well suited for afternoon tea; walkers might warm up in the knot garden before heading for a riverside trek to Croft, to find the family pew of Ava Lovelace (mathematician and Lord Byron's daughter). David Armstrong's 'good, wholesome' menu includes a separate vegetarian selection. Breakfast has 'excellent' scrambled eggs, 'David's Special Porridge'.

Monk End Farm
Croft-on-Tees
DL2 2SP

T: 01325 721075
F: 01325 720419
E: reservations@clowbeckhouse.
co.uk
W: www.clowbeckhouse.co.uk

BEDROOMS: 13. 12 in garden buildings. 1 suitable for disabled.
OPEN: all year except 24 Dec–10 Jan.
FACILITIES: ramps, lounge, restaurant, free Wi-Fi, small conference facilities, 2-acre grounds in 100-acre farm.
BACKGROUND MUSIC: classical, 'easy listening' in restaurant at mealtimes.
LOCATION: 3 miles SE of Darlington.
CHILDREN: all ages welcomed.
DOGS: not allowed.
CREDIT CARDS: Amex, MasterCard, Visa.
PRICES: per room B&B single £90, double £140. À la carte £37.

CRUDWELL Wiltshire

Map 3:E5

THE RECTORY HOTEL

'Viewed from a lovely gravel path, the first sight of this pretty hotel – and its three quirky piggy statues – captures the epitome of the place: warm, inviting, with a country-cottage feel, yet with an individuality of its own.' Praise this year from Guide inspectors, for Julian Muggridge and Jonathan Barry's 'laid-back', family-friendly hotel set in three acres of greenery. Past the lollies and dog biscuits at reception, bedrooms, in 'a quaint higgledy-piggledy maze of upstairs corridors', have a 'tasteful' mix of antique and modern furniture. 'Our bright, spacious room had very comfortable armchairs, gorgeous bedside tables and lamps, and a Roberts radio.' The grounds are 'a plus': a 'pretty' formal garden with a pond, a large lawn with croquet and cricket sets, a 'splendid' pool with 'plenty of loungers to relax on'. Drinks and 'delicious' canapés are taken in the 'comfortable' lounge; in the dining room, chef Peter Fairclough's 'tempting' dinners might include pork belly 'packed with flavour'. 'My lamb chump in red wine jus was perfectly cooked; a request for mint sauce was met with an individual, freshly made creation within minutes – immensely minty, probably the nicest I've ever tasted.'

25% DISCOUNT VOUCHERS

Crudwell, nr Malmesbury
SN16 9EP

T: 01666 577194
F: 01666 577853
E: info@therectoryhotel.com
W: www.therectoryhotel.com

BEDROOMS: 12.
OPEN: all year, restaurant closed lunchtime.
FACILITIES: lounge, bar, dining room, free Wi-Fi, meeting facilities, civil wedding licence, 3-acre garden, heated outdoor swimming pool (10 by 15 metres), unsuitable for disabled.
BACKGROUND MUSIC: 'light' background music in bar and dining room in evening.
LOCATION: 4 miles N of Malmesbury.
CHILDREN: all ages welcomed.
DOGS: not allowed in dining room.
CREDIT CARDS: Amex, MasterCard, Visa.
PRICES: per room B&B £105–£195. Set dinner £26.50–£32.50. 1-night bookings refused bank holidays.

DARTMOUTH Devon

Map 1:D4

DART MARINA

'Faultless Towers' was the verdict of returning visitors to Richard Seton's hotel on the River Dart. And this before an upgrading with the creation of the new Britannia rooms, one of which a later visitor describes as 'excellent'. All bedrooms overlook the sparkling waters; some have a balcony. The palette is chic and calming, housekeeping is 'immaculate'. The manager, Paul Downing, is attentive: 'He listens to everything suggested to him… and has a wonderful staff in every department.' Yachts bob at anchor or skim past the dining-room windows, where chef Peter Alcroft is 'second to none': his menus might include carpaccio of West Country beef; plaice fillet paupiettes, shallot, parsley-crushed new potatoes, bouillabaisse saffron cream. Vegetarian options are creative, perhaps potato and ricotta gnocchi, broad beans, sage and lemon butter sauce. Breakfast has a buffet of cereals, fresh fruit salad, compotes, croissants; 'generous' cooked dishes. Facial treatments are a speciality in the spa which has a small swimming pool. You can ride the Dartmouth Steam Railway, then down a pint at the quayside Floating Bridge Inn. (Mary Woods, Neville and Betty Kenyon)

Sandquay Road
Dartmouth
TQ6 9PH

T: 01803 832580
F: 01803 835040
E: pauld@dartmarinahotel.com
W: www.dartmarina.com

BEDROOMS: 49. 4 on ground floor, 1 suitable for disabled, plus 3 apartments.
OPEN: all year, restaurant closed lunchtime Mon–Sat.
FACILITIES: lounge/bar, restaurant, free Wi-Fi, river-front terrace, small garden with seating, spa (heated indoor swimming pool, 8 by 4 metres, gym).
BACKGROUND MUSIC: varied in restaurant.
LOCATION: on waterfront.
CHILDREN: all ages welcomed.
DOGS: in some rooms (£10 per stay), not allowed in restaurant.
CREDIT CARDS: MasterCard, Visa.
PRICES: per room B&B £170–£425, D,B&B £230–£485. À la carte £42.50. 1-night bookings usually refused Sat.

SEE ALSO SHORTLIST

DARTMOUTH Devon

Map 1:D4

NONSUCH HOUSE

♔ César award in 2000

'Homely and unique', Kit and Penny Noble's Edwardian guest house stands at the top of a hill overlooking the Dart estuary. 'They are caring and friendly hosts,' says a visitor in 2015. There are 'glorious' south-facing views over the river from the conservatory dining room and the bedrooms. In summer, the terrace is the place to be; in cooler months, there is a log fire in the residents' lounge. 'We have time to discuss anything and to be ready to take a guest anywhere locally if they are unable to drive,' the couple say. Chilled water and fresh milk are provided in the spacious bedrooms, which are individually decorated. Kit Noble sees what is available on the day before preparing his dinner menu on four nights a week (guests are asked in advance about likes and dislikes). His dishes, which have 'the occasional Kiwi twist', might include cauliflower soup, Parmesan and truffle oil; John Dory fillets roasted with lemon and herbs. A 'great' breakfast has home-toasted granola; home-made bread and jams; apple juice from a nearby orchard. (Colin Adams, and others)

Church Hill
Kingswear
Dartmouth
TQ6 0BX

T: 01803 752829
E: enquiries@nonsuch-house.co.uk
W: www.nonsuch-house.co.uk

BEDROOMS: 4.
OPEN: all year except Christmas 2015, 2 weeks Jan, dining room closed midday, evening Tues/Wed/Sat.
FACILITIES: ramps, lounge, dining room/conservatory, free Wi-Fi, ¼-acre garden (sun terrace), rock beach 300 yds (sailing nearby), membership of local gym and spa.
BACKGROUND MUSIC: none.
LOCATION: 5 mins' walk from ferry to Dartmouth.
CHILDREN: not under 12.
DOGS: not allowed.
CREDIT CARDS: MasterCard, Visa.
PRICES: [2015] per room B&B £115–£195. Dinner £39.50. 1-night bookings usually refused weekends.

SEE ALSO SHORTLIST

DEDHAM HALL & FOUNTAIN HOUSE RESTAURANT

The guest lounge at Jim and Wendy Sarton's 15th-century manor house in deepest Constable country is hung with works by artists who have attended residential painting courses here. It is an informal, quirky place, perhaps not to all tastes. Those in favour enjoy the old-fashioned ambience, the 'wonderful quiet, just the sound of bees buzzing in the lavender'. Bedrooms in the house and converted barns are 'large and comfortable', with Persian rugs and yet more pictures; bathrooms are 'huge'. The cooking for the Fountain restaurant is straightforward: 'generous' portions of locally sourced seasonal ingredients in dishes like avocado and smoked salmon mousse; beef fillet, wild mushrooms, red wine; lemon tart, vanilla ice cream. 'None of this itsy-bitsy nouvelle cuisine; vegetables taste like vegetables should.' Breakfast is 'beautifully cooked'. The art courses are held from February to early November. Constable's Flatford Mill, not two miles' walk from Dedham, is a tourist honeypot, but Dedham Vale is all around. Another artist, England's finest painter of horses, Sir Alfred Munnings, lived at Castle House, now a gallery with his studio.

Brook Street
Dedham
CO7 6AD

T: 01206 323027
E: sarton@dedhamhall.demon.
co.uk
W: www.dedhamhall.co.uk

BEDROOMS: 20. 16 in annexe, some on ground floor, suitable for disabled.
OPEN: all year except Christmas/New Year, restaurant closed Sun/Mon Nov–Feb.
FACILITIES: ramps, 2 lounges, 2 bars, dining room, restaurant, studio, free Wi-Fi, 6-acre grounds (pond, gardens).
BACKGROUND MUSIC: none.
LOCATION: end of village High Street.
CHILDREN: all ages welcomed.
DOGS: not allowed.
CREDIT CARDS: MasterCard, Visa.
PRICES: per room B&B single £65, double £110, D,B&B single £95, double £170. À la carte £30.

THE SUN INN

In the Dedham Vale, this 'friendly' restaurant-with-rooms occupies a 15th-century building restored by owner Piers Baker. Visitors this year enjoyed the hotel's location ('ideal for visiting Constable country') and the 'helpful, very pleasant young staff'. 'The cosy beamed and wood-panelled sitting room and bar have open fires, a knowledgeable barman, and a good art gallery.' The bedrooms are 'freshly decorated and sparkling'. One has 'a Victorian-style bedstead, good reading lights; not a lot of space for sitting; an exemplary bathroom'; another had 'low beams and a fireplace, stylish furniture including a wide four-poster bed; a power shower'. Two rooms are accessed by a 'lovely' external Elizabethan staircase. Jack Levine, who is now the chef, serves an Italian-influenced, seasonal menu of dishes like roast tomato and onion soup, basil mascarpone; wild sea bass baked with artichokes, asparagus, chives, crème fraîche. Bicycles can be hired from the hotel for exploring the countryside, perhaps a nearby vineyard ('quite a find'); a picnic can be arranged for an additional cost. 'A really comfortable short break.' (Sara Price, and others)

High Street
Dedham
CO7 6DF

T: 01206 323351
E: office@thesuninndedham.com
W: www.thesuninndedham.com

BEDROOMS: 7.
OPEN: all year except 24–27 Dec.
FACILITIES: lounge, bar, dining room, free Wi-Fi, 1-acre garden (covered terrace, children's play area), unsuitable for disabled.
BACKGROUND MUSIC: jazz/blues/folk in lounge and bar.
LOCATION: central, opposite St Mary's church, 5 miles NE of Colchester.
CHILDREN: all ages welcomed.
DOGS: not allowed.
CREDIT CARDS: Amex, MasterCard, Visa.
PRICES: [2015] per room B&B £135, D,B&B £190. À la carte £25–£30.

DITTISHAM Devon

FINGALS

NEW

There is a 'most relaxing' ambience at Richard and Sheila Johnston's 'characterful' B&B in a secluded valley near Dittisham village. 'Abundant in quiet and calm, it is not "wow" or glitzy – this is its appeal. Richard and Sheila look after you very well, without pretension,' said returning guests this year, securing Fingals a full Guide entry. The 'comfortably and artistically' extended 17th-century manor house has oak beams, log fires, antique carpets and an honesty bar; country-style bedrooms, including a large room suitable for a family, are individually decorated with antiques and original art. Children have much diversion, including board games, a piano and an 'excellent' conservatory swimming pool; bicycles are available to borrow. Communal dinners, using plenty of organic local produce, are served two nights a week, or by arrangement; children can be given 'an ample and appropriate high tea'. Taken on the terrace in good weather, breakfast is 'delicious': freshly squeezed orange juice, freshly baked croissants, local sausages. 'We will return with family again and again.' Four rooms were converted into self-catering in 2015. (Rowena Moore, Ellie Grayson)

25% DISCOUNT VOUCHERS

Old Coombe Manor Farm
Dittisham
TQ6 0JA

T: 01803 722398
F: 01803 722401
E: info@fingals.co.uk
W: www.fingals.co.uk

BEDROOMS: 4. 1 in separate building by stream.
OPEN: Mar–4 Jan, closed Christmas.
FACILITIES: dining room, honesty bar, sitting room, free Wi-Fi, games room, indoor swimming pool (8 by 4 metres), 1¾-acre garden, grass tennis court, unsuitable for disabled.
BACKGROUND MUSIC: classical in bar and dining room.
LOCATION: in hamlet, 1 mile from village.
CHILDREN: all ages welcomed.
DOGS: allowed in bedrooms, not in public rooms or grounds.
CREDIT CARDS: Amex, Diners, Visa.
PRICES: [2015] per room B&B £90–£160, D,B&B £162–£232. À la carte £36. 1-night bookings sometimes refused.

DODDISCOMBSLEIGH Devon

Map 1:C4

THE NOBODY INN

Between the Haldon hills and the Teign valley, Sue Burdge's 'lovely old pub' is reached down a maze of country lanes near Exeter. The modern history of the building can be traced back to 1591, but it became an inn 200 years before that. In 2015, Nick Crosley was appointed manager; Rudi Horvath joined as the chef. In the 'atmospheric, popular' beamed bar, there is an 'enormous' whisky selection ('262 at last count'), 'good' cask ale, an 'excellent' wine list, which can be enjoyed in 'cosy' spots in front of the inglenook fireplace. Allergens are listed on the menu, which can be taken in the 'small, light' restaurant: it might include potted confit rabbit, carrot and orange salad; pumpkin and sage risotto. The bedrooms upstairs are 'incredibly peaceful' (although there might be 'some noise before closing time'); decorated in a modern country style, they have tea/coffee-making facilities. Breakfast has 'particularly good' preserves; it is ordered the night before and served at an agreed time. The village church has some fine medieval stained glass (Cromwell's wreckers failed to find it in the hidden valley).

Doddiscombsleigh
EX6 7PS

T: 01647 252394
F: 01647 252978
E: info@nobodyinn.co.uk
W: www.nobodyinn.co.uk

BEDROOMS: 5. 1 with bathroom across corridor.
OPEN: all year except 1 Jan.
FACILITIES: 2 bars, restaurant, free Wi-Fi (may be patchy), garden, patio, parking, unsuitable for disabled.
BACKGROUND MUSIC: none.
LOCATION: in village 6 miles SW of Exeter.
CHILDREN: not under 5 for overnight stays, not under 14 in 1 bar.
DOGS: not allowed.
CREDIT CARDS: MasterCard, Visa.
PRICES: [2015] per room B&B double £75–£105. À la carte £26.

THE RED LION FREEHOUSE

In a peaceful country village, this 'ancient thatched pub' is 'exceptionally relaxed and friendly', say visitors this year. Another comment: 'We were celebrating a December birthday so decided to stay the night to avoid the drive home in the dark. What a great decision.' Owned by chef/patron Guy Manning and his American wife, Brittany, the Red Lion has a Michelin star for its 'exciting' menu with modern dishes like steamed Atlantic halibut, hand-rolled farfalle, peas, shiitakes, clams, crab bisque. Wooden tables are 'nicely laid' in the restaurant: 'My Wiltshire rib of beef was top class as were the chips and the plaice goujons starter.' The bedrooms are in a restored bungalow across the road. 'Our room was a joy: a delightful riverside terrace and outlook; an elegant decor without being fussy. Simply the best shower on a heated floor; every last detail, both practical and tasteful, had been anticipated.' Some traffic noise was heard in a room near the road but it was 'totally quiet at night'. 'Altogether a great night out.' (JS and F Waters, Richard and Sheila Owen)

East Chisenbury
SN9 6AQ

T: 01980 671124
E: troutbeck@redlionfreehouse.com
W: www.redlionfreehouse.com

BEDROOMS: 5. On ground floor, in adjacent building.
OPEN: all year.
FACILITIES: pub/restaurant, free Wi-Fi, 1-acre garden.
BACKGROUND MUSIC: in pub/restaurant.
LOCATION: in village.
CHILDREN: all ages accepted.
DOGS: allowed in pub, 1 bedroom.
CREDIT CARDS: Diners, MasterCard, Visa.
PRICES: [2015] per room B&B from £150. À la carte £60.

GRAVETYE MANOR

'All was quite perfect' according to visitors to this luxury country house hotel (Relais & Châteaux). Once the home of William Robinson, pioneer of the English natural garden, the Elizabethan manor house has been restored by owners Jeremy and Elizabeth Hosking, inside and out. Head gardener Tom Coward upholds Robinson's legacy in the extensive grounds, mixing native and exotic plants, bulbs and grass in the wild meadows and Victorian glasshouses; the 'glorious gardens are full of exuberant colour'. The gardens spill inwards as bold flower displays in the wood-panelled Arts and Crafts public rooms (sourced, it is said, from the estate), where easy chairs sit before log fires. The newly refurbished bedrooms mix traditional with modern. 'Our splendid corner room had a comfortable king-size bed and a sitting area with magazines and a flask of Gravetye spring water.' Head chef George Blogg's diverse modern British menu reaps the benefits of the kitchen garden, from vegan kohlrabi lasagne, sautéed forest mushroom, garden chard to Cornish brill, saffron quinoa, cauliflower textures. Freshly squeezed juices and an 'excellent' full English at breakfast.

Vowels Lane
East Grinstead
RH19 4LJ

T: 01342 810567
F: 01342 810080
E: info@gravetyemanor.co.uk
W: www.gravetyemanor.co.uk

BEDROOMS: 17.
OPEN: all year.
FACILITIES: 2 lounges, bar, restaurant, 2 private dining rooms, free Wi-Fi, civil wedding licence, 1,000-acre grounds (woodland, ornamental and kitchen gardens, meadow, orchard, lake, croquet lawn), only restaurant suitable for disabled.
BACKGROUND MUSIC: none.
LOCATION: 4 miles SW of East Grinstead.
CHILDREN: not under 7.
DOGS: not allowed.
CREDIT CARDS: Amex, MasterCard, Visa.
PRICES: [2015] per room B&B £260, D,B&B £405. A la carte £70. 1-night bookings sometimes refused at weekends.

EAST HOATHLY East Sussex

Map 2:E4

OLD WHYLY

In the East Sussex countryside, this Grade II listed Georgian manor house has medieval origins and a history spotted with drinkers, card players and deer poachers. Today, run as an upmarket B&B by Sarah Burgoyne, it is 'better than ever', say regular Guide correspondents this year. 'The house is beautiful, the garden glorious.' The 'well-proportioned' drawing room has a large open fire, books, paintings and 'fine' furniture. Decorated in country house style, the bedrooms have views of the grounds. Beds are turned down in the evening, and home-made biscuits and fresh milk left on the tea tray. Guests meet at 7 pm for pre-dinner drinks and canapés; communal dinners are served in the candlelit dining room or, in warm weather, under the vine-covered pergola on the terrace. An 'accomplished' cook, Sarah Burgoyne uses home-grown produce, and eggs laid by her hens and ducks, in her seasonal dishes. With home-made marmalade and jams, and honey from the bees in the orchard, 'Sarah's breakfasts are the best'. 'Delicious' picnic hampers can be provided for guests heading to nearby Glyndebourne. (Tom and Catrin Treadwell)

London Road
East Hoathly
BN8 6EL

T: 01825 840216
E: stay@oldwhyly.co.uk
w: www.oldwhyly.co.uk

BEDROOMS: 4.
OPEN: all year.
FACILITIES: drawing room, dining room, free Wi-Fi, 3-acre garden in 30-acre grounds, heated outdoor swimming pool (10 by 5 metres), tennis, unsuitable for disabled.
BACKGROUND MUSIC: none.
LOCATION: 1 mile N of village.
CHILDREN: all ages welcomed.
DOGS: not allowed indoors.
CREDIT CARDS: none.
PRICES: [2015] per room B&B £98–£145. Set dinner £35, Glyndebourne hamper £38 per person. 1-night bookings sometimes refused weekends in high season.

THE ROYAL OAK

'Every detail has been thought of' at Sarah and Charles Ullmann's 19th-century pub/inn at the foot of the South Downs. Walkers coming off the moors will appreciate the open fire, leather sofas and beer (brewed in nearby Arundel) in the 'popular, stylish' pub. There is waitress service, proper linen napkins and 'subdued' lighting in the adjacent restaurant; terrace and garden seating is available in clement weather. The food is 'first class'. James Dean is now the chef: he cooks 'favourites with a modern twist', turning to local producers for his ingredients. Typical dishes: broad bean, pea and chive risotto; roast rump of South Downs lamb, méli-mélo of spring vegetables, wild garlic-crushed potatoes, red wine jus. The 'comfortable, well-equipped' bedrooms are above the restaurant and in cottages behind. Individually decorated, they have oak beams, fresh flowers, board games, views over farmland and the moors. Breakfast has 'ample' variety: home-made muesli, fresh fruit; full 'Sussex' cooked to a 'high quality'. The inn is a good base for outdoors and sporting folk, a few miles from both the South Downs Way and Chichester Harbour.

25% DISCOUNT VOUCHERS

Pook Lane
East Lavant
PO18 0AX

T: 01243 527434
E: info@royaloakeastlavant.co.uk
W: www.royaloakeastlavant.co.uk

BEDROOMS: 5. Plus 2 self-catering cottages nearby.
OPEN: all year.
FACILITIES: bar/restaurant, free Wi-Fi, terrace (outside meals), small garden, unsuitable for disabled.
BACKGROUND MUSIC: jazz/pop in restaurant.
LOCATION: 2 miles N of Chichester.
CHILDREN: all ages welcomed.
DOGS: not allowed.
CREDIT CARDS: all major cards.
PRICES: [2015] per room B&B £90–£300. À la carte £35. 1-night bookings refused weekends, bank holidays.

EASTBOURNE East Sussex

Map 2:E4

BELLE TOUT LIGHTHOUSE

'The views are fantastic' from this 'lovely and unusual place', a decommissioned lighthouse on the chalk cliffs of Beachy Head. It is owned by David Shaw; Ian Noall is the manager. Individually decorated bedrooms are in the original tower and a more recent extension; each has an en suite shower, tea- and coffee-making facilities, TV with a DVD- and CD-player. Guests are encouraged to discuss their room choice before booking. 'Ian was very helpful, asking if I preferred view or space – I chose view,' a Guide inspector said. A dual-aspect room had views of the present Beachy Head lighthouse through one window, and of grazing sheep on nearby farms through the other. There was 'a lot packed into the space: a soft, comfortable bed, two director's chairs, plenty of storage; the tiny bathroom had everything I needed'. A sitting room on an upper floor has 'comfy chairs and sofas, a wood-burning stove, a guest fridge and lots of local information'. Up 80 steps, the former lantern room is 'a great place for stargazing or ship-spotting'. Breakfast is 'a generous affair': home-made muesli, home-baked muffins, a daily cooked special.

Beachy Head Road
Eastbourne
BN20 0AE

T: 01323 423185
E: info@belletout.co.uk
W: www.belletout.co.uk

BEDROOMS: 6.
OPEN: all year, except 20 Dec–15 Jan.
FACILITIES: lounge, breakfast room, free Wi-Fi (in some rooms and some public areas only), terrace, garden, unsuitable for disabled.
BACKGROUND MUSIC: none.
LOCATION: 3 miles W of Eastbourne.
CHILDREN: not under 15.
DOGS: not allowed.
CREDIT CARDS: MasterCard, Visa.
PRICES: [2015] per room B&B from £145. Min. 2-night stay, 1-night bookings only accepted 7–10 days in advance.

SEE ALSO SHORTLIST

ECKINGTON Worcestershire

Map 3:D5

ECKINGTON MANOR · NEW

On a working farm where pedigree herds of
Aberdeen Angus and Highland cattle, Lleyn
sheep and Old Spot pigs are raised, Judy
Gardner has converted a clutch of old buildings
into a hotel, cookery school and popular
restaurant. Guide inspectors in 2015 enjoyed
the 'tranquil, comfortably rural' setting, their
'beautifully beamed' bedroom, and the 'refined
cuisine at reasonable prices'. Accommodation
is in the former milking parlour and cider mill,
and the 17th-century Lower End House, where
the 'stylish' lounge has an honesty bar. 'Our
room had a striking glass chandelier, two velvet
easy chairs, a super king-size bed, crisp white
bedlinen; a well-designed, pretty bathroom.
No biscuits or home-made cake – strange, for a
cookery place.' Across the 'pleasant' courtyard
('the walk was prettily lit with candlelight and
lanterns'), 'every table was full' in the 'stark,
modern' restaurant, where chefs Sue Ellis and
Mark Stinchcombe's modern dishes might
include 'delicious and perfectly cooked' fillet
of brill, leeks, mussels, cider, fennel. Breakfast
has 'nice' yogurt, 'boring' toast, little jars of
preserves; 'good' cooked ingredients. 'We left on
a happy note.'

25% DISCOUNT VOUCHERS

Hammock Road
Eckington
WR10 3BJ

T: 01386 751600
F: 01386 751362
E: info@eckingtonmanor.co.uk
W: www.eckingtonmanor.co.uk

BEDROOMS: 17. All in courtyard
annexes, 1 suitable for disabled.
OPEN: all year, restaurant closed
Sun, Mon.
FACILITIES: lift, 3 reception rooms,
restaurant, function rooms, free
Wi-Fi, civil wedding licence,
cookery school, 260-acre grounds
(lawns, herb garden, orchard,
working farm).
BACKGROUND MUSIC: none.
LOCATION: 4 miles SW of Pershore.
CHILDREN: not under 8.
DOGS: allowed in some bedrooms,
not in public rooms.
CREDIT CARDS: Amex, MasterCard,
Visa.
PRICES: per room B&B £95–£249,
D,B&B from £145. Set menus
£32–£38.

EDENBRIDGE Kent

Map 2:D4

STARBOROUGH MANOR

At the top of a tree-lined gravel driveway, this 18th-century manor house was in a decrepit state when bought by Jonathan and Lynn Matthias. 'The restoration is very impressive,' say Guide inspectors visiting in 2015. 'Lynn Matthias is a chatty host and welcomed us with tea, scones still warm from her Aga, whipped cream and home-made jam.' The bedrooms and communal guest areas are 'immaculate and well lit: our second-floor room was the largest; it had a comfortable king-size bed, heavy duvet, comprehensive hospitality tray, Wi-Fi. Bathrooms are well equipped, with fluffy towels, bathrobes, quality goodies.' Guests have use of a first-floor sitting room, which has television, a library of books to borrow, games and DVDs. A second sitting room/study is for those wanting to work or to read quietly. No evening meals are served: a kitchen and dining room are available (for an extra charge). Breakfast has a 'generous array of cereals, fruit and yogurt on the table'; cooked dishes to order. The meal is taken communally in the 'spectacular' kitchen, or in the garden in fine weather.

Moor Lane, Marsh Green
Edenbridge
TN8 5QY

T: 01732 862152
E: lynn@starboroughmanor.co.uk
W: www.starboroughmanor.co.uk

BEDROOMS: 4.
OPEN: all year.
FACILITIES: 2 sitting rooms, dining room, free Wi-Fi, 13-acre grounds, unsuitable for disabled.
BACKGROUND MUSIC: none.
LOCATION: 1½ miles W of Edenbridge.
CHILDREN: all ages welcomed.
DOGS: not allowed.
CREDIT CARDS: MasterCard, Visa.
PRICES: [2015] per room B&B single £90–£100, double £140. 1-night bookings sometimes refused weekends in summer.

EMSWORTH Hampshire

Map 2:E3

36 ON THE QUAY

♥César award in 2011

'A great experience', Ramon and Karen Farthing's restaurant-with-rooms is in a 17th-century building on the harbour of a pretty town. Gary Pearce is the chef ('his cooking didn't disappoint,' says a visitor in 2015). In the 'immaculately appointed' dining room, he serves a modern menu, perhaps seared scallops, cauliflower panna cotta, coconut crumble; roast loin of fallow deer, spelt risotto, game bolognese, salt-baked swede. 'The quality and presentation of the dishes was superb; service was friendly, knowledgeable and efficient.' Original features, such as exposed beams from the 15th century, have been retained. Bedrooms, with a spice theme, have views across the harbour or the village; a two-bedroom cottage has its own garden and parking. Cinnamon was 'comfortably warm with a large bed; ultra-modern fittings contrasting with the ancient building; very good lighting'. A 'compact' room was 'beautifully decorated; fixtures and fittings of the highest order'. A continental breakfast has muesli, yogurt, fresh fruit, toast, croissants; 'decent coffee', 'packaged juice alas'. (Ian Malone, Michael and Margaret Cross, Mary Coles)

47 South Street
Emsworth
PO10 7EG

T: 01243 375592
E: info@36onthequay.co.uk
W: www.36onthequay.co.uk

BEDROOMS: 7. 2 in cottages across road (can be let weekly), plus 2-bed cottage.
OPEN: all year except 24–26 Dec, first 2 weeks Jan, restaurant closed Sun/Mon.
FACILITIES: bar area, restaurant, free Wi-Fi, small terrace, limited parking, only restaurant suitable for disabled.
BACKGROUND MUSIC: none.
LOCATION: on harbour.
CHILDREN: all ages welcomed.
DOGS: allowed in 1 cottage, by arrangement.
CREDIT CARDS: Amex, MasterCard, Visa.
PRICES: [2015] per room B&B £100–£200, D,B&B from £200. Set dinner £57.95.

ERMINGTON Devon

Map 1:D4

PLANTATION HOUSE

'Lovely' extra touches (fruit, biscuits, fresh milk, a small decanter of brandy, 'all replenished each day') create a 'very special feel' at this small hotel, a Grade II listed Georgian rectory in south Devon. Owner/chef Richard Hendey's 'friendly informality is delightful', says a visitor in 2015. Contemporary furnishings and artefacts, tropical plants and 'artistically arranged' flowers from the garden are found throughout. A bedroom overlooking the countryside was 'very spacious with a large, comfortable bed and a great modern bathroom'. Richard Hendey is a 'first-class' chef, using ingredients from nearby farms, or foraged: wild garlic, rock samphire, etc. He adapts his classic menu to guests' preferences; the four-course dinner might include slow-cooked Devon duckling, crisp Maris Piper chive potato cake, wild garlic dauphinoise. 'He was happy to serve us a light meal one evening.' Breakfast is 'particularly good', with home-made bread, fresh orange juice, proper leaf tea, eggs from their own hens. Several reporters noted the 'excellent fresh fruit salad with a little Greek yogurt' and the 'Devon' cooked breakfast ('no insipid egg-and-bacon at this hotel'). (GC, Robert and Rosemary Ingram)

Totnes Road
Ivybridge
Ermington
PL21 9NS

T: 01548 831100
E: info@plantationhousehotel.co.uk
W: www.plantationhousehotel.co.uk

BEDROOMS: 8.
OPEN: all year, restaurant closed midday, some Sunday evenings.
FACILITIES: lounge/bar, 2 dining rooms, free Wi-Fi, terrace, garden, unsuitable for disabled.
BACKGROUND MUSIC: classical/easy jazz throughout, if required.
LOCATION: 10 miles E of Plymouth.
CHILDREN: 'well-behaved' children welcomed.
DOGS: not allowed.
CREDIT CARDS: Amex, MasterCard, Visa.
PRICES: [2015] per room B&B single £75, double £95–£230. D,B&B £36 added per person. Set dinner £36. 1-night bookings sometimes refused.

EVESHAM Worcestershire

Map 3:D6

THE EVESHAM HOTEL

♥César award in 1990

A self-confessed 'quirky' establishment, this family-friendly hotel has been run by John and Sue Jenkinson for 40 years. They have appointed David Field as manager, and stepped back 'to concentrate on the bits we really enjoy'. 'The style is homely, a little old-fashioned,' say Guide inspectors in 2015. 'It is lots of fun, characterful and memorable. Our children had a great time.' Young visitors have an indoor swimming pool; a play area with table tennis and table football; a climbing frame and slide in the garden. One of the two family suites has an Alice-in-Wonderland theme with a secret nook under the beams. Children under 12 stay free when sharing a room with their parents. A formal vegetable garden has been added to the salad and herb garden to supply the kitchen. The chef, Paul Napper, serves a short menu of 'delicious' dishes like salmon and caper fishcakes; slow-cooked pork belly, sage mash. Vegetarians have their own menu. 'A good-value family hotel where everyone will have a good time.'

25% DISCOUNT VOUCHERS

Cooper's Lane, off Waterside
Evesham
WR11 1DA

T: 01386 765566
F: 01386 765443
E: reception@eveshamhotel.com
W: www.eveshamhotel.com

BEDROOMS: 37. 9 on ground floor, 2 suitable for disabled.
OPEN: all year.
FACILITIES: 2 lounges, bar, restaurant, private dining room, free Wi-Fi, children's play area, indoor swimming pool (5 by 12 metres), 2½-acre grounds (croquet, putting, swings).
BACKGROUND MUSIC: none.
LOCATION: 5 mins' walk from centre, across river.
CHILDREN: all ages welcomed.
DOGS: allowed in bedrooms (small charge), but only guide dogs allowed in public rooms.
CREDIT CARDS: Amex, MasterCard, Visa.
PRICES: per room B&B single from £85, double from £115, D,B&B single from £105, double from £155. À la carte £28. 1-night bookings sometimes refused.

THE CROWN HOTEL

In large gardens opposite the green of a pretty Exmoor village, this 'interesting' coaching inn has been run by the owners, Sara and Dan Whittaker and her father, Chris Kirkbride, for almost ten years. Visitors this year 'were warmly greeted by Sara; her father carried our bags to our room' . There is 'a friendly atmosphere' in the bar, which is well frequented by locals and visitors ('this is where it is all at,' was an overheard comment). In the smart red-and-black restaurant, chef Raza Muhammad's menu combines modern dishes (eg, ham hock and guineafowl terrine, apple and cider chutney) with grills. A similar menu can be taken in the bar. 'Upgrading remains a work in progress; our favourite room had improved furniture; thick curtains reduced any local traffic noise' (perhaps an early morning tractor). The inn is pet friendly (even your horse can be accommodated in stabling). 'The village is an excellent place for exploring a lovely area; returning in the evening to the Crown is the icing on the cake.' (Jack Hanmer, Kay and Peter Rogers)

Exford
Exmoor National Park
TA24 7PP

T: 01643 831554
E: info@crownhotelexmoor.co.uk
W: www.crownhotelexmoor.co.uk

BEDROOMS: 16.
OPEN: all year.
FACILITIES: lounge, residents' bar, public bar, restaurant, meeting room, free Wi-Fi, 3-acre grounds (trout stream, water garden, terrace garden), stabling, unsuitable for disabled.
BACKGROUND MUSIC: 'mixed' in bar and restaurant in evening.
LOCATION: on village green.
CHILDREN: all ages welcomed.
DOGS: welcomed, but not allowed in restaurant.
CREDIT CARDS: MasterCard, Visa.
PRICES: [2015] per room B&B single £69, double £125–£145. À la carte £30.

FAVERSHAM Kent

Map 2:D5

READ'S

♔César award in 2005

Near the old market town of Faversham, this 'impressive yet homely' Georgian manor house is run with 'friendly professionalism' as a restaurant-with-rooms by Rona and David Pitchford. The accommodation is 'anything but a second thought' to the food, say visitors. The interiors are 'simultaneously classy and cosy'. The bedrooms, 'comfortable and not fussy', are individually decorated. Cedar has window seats overlooking a magnificent cedar tree, 'thick curtains, rich fabrics; extremely restful bed; Laurel has a 'super' four-poster bed. There is a 'well-stocked' pantry between the bedrooms. No distracting background music in the candlelit restaurant, where Michelin-starred chef David Pitchford's seasonal menu is served 'by an obviously happy staff'. Herbs and vegetables come from the hotel's own kitchen garden. The tasting menu is 'good value and special'. Typical dishes: Ellie's dairy goat's curd, pickled beetroot terrine; halibut, crushed new potatoes, confit lemon, champagne and chive velouté. Breakfast is 'simple and enjoyable', with home-made jams, 'delicious' home-pressed apple juice and an 'excellent' hot selection. (DS, and others)

Macknade Manor
Canterbury Road
Faversham
ME13 8XE

T: 01795 535344
F: 01795 591200
E: enquiries@reads.com
W: www.reads.com

BEDROOMS: 6.
OPEN: all year except 25–27 Dec, 1st week Jan, restaurant closed Sun/Mon.
FACILITIES: ramp, sitting room/bar, restaurant, private dining room, free Wi-Fi, civil wedding licence, 4-acre garden (terrace, outdoor dining), only restaurant suitable for disabled.
BACKGROUND MUSIC: none.
LOCATION: ½ mile SE of Faversham.
CHILDREN: all ages welcomed.
DOGS: not allowed in public rooms.
CREDIT CARDS: Amex, MasterCard, Visa.
PRICES: [2015] per room B&B single £125–£185, double £165–£195, D,B&B £135–£240 per person. Set dinner £60.

THE CARPENTERS ARMS **NEW**

'Outstanding: the bedrooms are stunning and well thought out; the cooking highlighted the freshest of ingredients.' Guide inspectors in 2015 were impressed by this pub-with-rooms in a Domesday village near Thirsk. It is owned by the small Provenance Inns group, which has added bedrooms in a building arranged around a kitchen garden; each has a private patio. 'Light streamed into our room, which was decorated in caramel and cream; it had a two-seater sofa and two armchairs by a gas flame fire; a built-in honesty bar and a tea tray with fresh milk and biscuits; one of the two built-in wardrobes had drying facilities, a boon for walkers, fishers and shooters; the information pack was comprehensive.' One room is equipped for disabled visitors; two smaller rooms are in the main building. 'Good bistro' dishes are served in the two dining areas: 'We enjoyed chilli and lime chicken; a seafood pasta with mussels, clams, prawns, fish; rhubarb crumble.' Breakfast has a buffet table with freshly squeezed juices, cereals, yogurts and fresh fruits; 'excellent' poached eggs and smoked haddock. 'The pleasant staff were available when needed.'

Felixkirk
YO7 2DP

T: 01845 537369
E: enquiries@
    thecarpentersarmsfelixkirk.com
W: www.
    thecarpentersarmsfelixkirk.com

BEDROOMS: 10. 8 in garden annexe, 1 suitable for disabled.
OPEN: all year.
FACILITIES: bar/sitting area, 2 dining rooms, free Wi-Fi, garden.
BACKGROUND MUSIC: 'easy listening' in public areas.
LOCATION: in village 3 miles NE of Thirsk.
CHILDREN: all ages welcomed.
DOGS: welcomed in certain bedrooms, bar and some dining areas.
CREDIT CARDS: Amex, MasterCard, Visa.
PRICES: [2015] per room B&B £120–£185. À la carte £28.

MOONFLEET MANOR

In 'romantic' Dorset countryside overlooking Chesil Beach, this 'pretty' Georgian house is part of the child-friendly Luxury Family Hotels group. Parents needn't feel guilty as their children disappear to the twice-daily crèche, say inspectors. 'It doesn't feel like a dumping ground; they made papier mâché jewellery trees, and had a ball in the lovely playroom which was full of toys and dressing-up clothes.' There is also much to keep children busy in the garden (a climbing frame and a sandpit); there are nightly family films in the cinema room. Morning coffee and afternoon tea are served in two large lounges, which have 'big sofas, piles of newspapers'; a family snug has games and books. Families can ask for extra beds in the parents' bedroom, or have an interconnecting room for the children. The smallest children can take high tea at 5 pm; families can eat together until 7.30, when 'exhausted' parents can dine alone (listening devices are available). Breakfast ('awesome', said a five-year-old visitor) has a big buffet with freshly squeezed juice, 'delicious' jams and cereals; 'very good' cooked options.

Fleet Road
Fleet
DT3 4ED

T: 01305 786948
F: 01305 774395
E: info@moonfleetmanorhotel.co.uk
W: www.moonfleetmanorhotel.co.uk

BEDROOMS: 36. 6 in annexes, 3 on ground floor.
OPEN: all year.
FACILITIES: 2 lounges, family snug, restaurant, indoor playroom, crèche, cinema room, free Wi-Fi, civil wedding licence, indoor swimming pools, terrace, 15-acre garden (play areas).
BACKGROUND MUSIC: contemporary in restaurant.
LOCATION: 7 miles W of Weymouth.
CHILDREN: all ages welcomed.
DOGS: allowed in bedrooms (£10 charge per day), not in public rooms.
CREDIT CARDS: Amex, MasterCard, Visa.
PRICES: [2015] per room B&B £120–£475, D,B&B £190–£545. À la carte £40. 1-night bookings sometimes refused.

FLETCHING East Sussex

Map 2:E4

THE GRIFFIN INN

Owned by the Pullan family, this 16th-century Grade II listed coaching inn, with beams, horse brasses and 'country-style bedrooms', is in a pretty village overlooking the Ouse valley. 'We cannot praise the staff too highly,' said Guide inspectors, 'from the courteous, friendly welcome to the perfectly timed service in the restaurant.' The 'busy, relaxed', beamed pub attracts diners and locals in for a drink in front of open fires and framed images of country living; a permanent barbecue area in the garden is popular in the summer. In the well-lit, L-shaped dining room, chef Matt Starkey serves modern European dishes, perhaps slow-cooked pork belly, mustard mash, quince jus; chargrilled courgette linguini, lemon and mint. 'Focaccia and olive oil for dipping, served before the meal, was delicious.' The bedrooms, spread across three annexes, are 'nicely decorated in a shabby-chic style; ours had an original cast-iron fireplace, good storage; small shower with good pressure, double-sided make-up mirror in the bathroom. A nice touch was an iPhone docking station.' Breakfast has 'locally sourced' jams and honey; 'really delicious sausages'.

High Street
Fletching
TN22 3SS

T: 01825 722890
F: 01825 722810
E: info@thegriffininn.co.uk
W: www.thegriffininn.co.uk

BEDROOMS: 13. 4 in coach house. 5 in Griffin House next door, 4 on ground floor.
OPEN: all year except 25 Dec.
FACILITIES: ramps, 2 lounge bars (1 with TV), restaurant, free Wi-Fi, terrace, 2-acre garden.
BACKGROUND MUSIC: none.
LOCATION: 3 miles NW of Uckfield.
CHILDREN: all ages welcomed.
DOGS: welcomed.
CREDIT CARDS: Amex, MasterCard, Visa.
PRICES: [2015] per room B&B £70–£150. À la carte £30.

FOWEY Cornwall

Map 1:D3

FOWEY HALL

♧ Cesar award in 2015

'It can't be bettered.' Overlooking the Fowey estuary, this Victorian mansion, part of Nigel Chapman's Luxury Family Hotels group, is 'outstanding', a Guide inspector said. 'It sets a benchmark on how to cater for children and adults. It is well managed and standards are high.' Family-focused facilities include a crèche, an outdoor play area and a games room; young beachgoers may borrow wellingtons, fishing nets, buckets and spades. The 'swish but comfy' drawing room has a log fire; there is no bar, but 'everything – including a marvellous choice of sherries – is delivered with courtesy and promptness'. Bedrooms are in the main house, a garden wing and a coach house a short open-air walk away. 'Our large room was a proper retreat: it had a divinely comfortable bed, easy chairs and plenty of hanging space; the bathroom had lots of huge towels and a freestanding roll-top bath.' At dinner, chef James Parkinson's modern dishes are 'glorious'; in the morning, 'the breakfast buffet table groans with poached fruits, yogurts, cereals, juices and breads'.

Hanson Drive
Fowey
PL23 1ET

T: 01726 833866
E: info@foweyhallhotel.co.uk
W: www.foweyhallhotel.co.uk

BEDROOMS: 36. 8 in coach house, some on ground floor, 2 suitable for disabled.
OPEN: all year.
FACILITIES: 2 lounges, library/snug, 2 restaurants, free Wi-Fi, crèche, games rooms, civil wedding licence, spa, 12-metre indoor swimming pool, 7-acre grounds (trampoline, zip wire).
BACKGROUND MUSIC: 'easy listening' in restaurants.
LOCATION: ½ mile from town centre.
CHILDREN: all ages welcomed.
DOGS: allowed in main house bedrooms (£15), not in restaurant.
CREDIT CARDS: all major cards.
PRICES: [2015] per room B&B £180–£700, D,B&B £250–£770. À la carte £42. 1-night bookings refused at weekends.

THE OLD QUAY HOUSE **NEW**

On the waterfront of a pretty town, this tall and narrow Victorian seamen's mission has been turned into a hotel by Jane and Roy Carson. 'It is amazing how they squeezed it into such a tiny plot, but they did, spectacularly so,' say Guide inspectors, restoring The Old Quay House to a full entry. 'The contemporary bedrooms are clean and fresh, and they serve very good food. The staff are young, likeable and willing.' Visitors arriving by car are encouraged to drop off baggage before parking up the hill (cost included), a ten-minute walk away. 'Our corner room, reached by two flights of steps, had a side view of the estuary; the woven rattan frame of a large standing mirror matched the headboard and seating; plenty of hanging space in the wardrobe; good attention to detail in the extras. In the restaurant, Ryan Kellow has returned as chef: 'We enjoyed steamed mussels with an unusual and tasty coconut and Thai chilli sauce; succulent wood pigeon breasts and a rabbit ballottine came with lightly and sweetly pickled red cabbage.'

28 Fore Street
Fowey
PL23 1AQ

T: 01726 833302
F: 01726 833668
E: info@theoldquayhouse.com
W: www.theoldquayhouse.com

BEDROOMS: 11.
OPEN: all year, lunch Apr–Oct only.
FACILITIES: open-plan lounge, bar, restaurant with seating area, free Wi-Fi, civil wedding licence, waterside terrace, unsuitable for disabled.
BACKGROUND MUSIC: 'relaxed' at mealtimes.
LOCATION: central, on waterfront.
CHILDREN: not under 12.
DOGS: not allowed.
CREDIT CARDS: Amex, MasterCard, Visa.
PRICES: [2015] per room B&B £190, D,B&B £265. Set dinner £37.50.

ESLINGTON VILLA

In a handsome Victorian building standing
in landscaped gardens, Nick and Melanie
Tulip run their small hotel with 'attentive',
'unfailingly pleasant and helpful' staff. Colin
Edgar is the manager. The hotel is well located
for travellers to Newcastle; despite its proximity
to the A1, 'the gardens mean the place feels
quite rural', say visitors this year. Public areas
have mainly traditional artwork, photographs
and antiques; the terrace is 'ideal for alfresco
drinks'. 'Comfortable' bedrooms are in the main
house and an annexe with its own entrance;
individually decorated, they range in style
from the traditional (four-poster bed, antique
furniture) to the modern (bold wallpaper, bright
colours). Guests who had a room window
open on a warm night this year said that 'trains
were heard regularly'. Pre-dinner drinks are
taken in the lounge and bar. In the restaurant,
chef Jamie Walsh cooks 'good' modern dishes:
'The locally sourced sirloin of beef deserves a
special mention.' Breakfast in the conservatory
or dining room has freshly baked croissants,
organic nutty granola, a variety of fruit juices;
cooked dishes include grilled Craster kippers
and a poached egg.

25% DISCOUNT VOUCHERS

8 Station Road
Low Fell
Gateshead
NE9 6DR

T: 01914 876017
F: 01914 200667
E: home@eslingtonvilla.co.uk
W: www.eslingtonvilla.co.uk

BEDROOMS: 18. 3, on ground floor,
in annexe.
OPEN: all year except 25/26 Dec,
1 Jan.
FACILITIES: ramp, lounge/bar,
conservatory, restaurant, private
dining room, conference/function
facilities, free Wi-Fi, 2-acre garden
(patio).
BACKGROUND MUSIC: jazz/pop in
public rooms.
LOCATION: 2 miles S of town centre,
off A1.
CHILDREN: all ages welcomed.
DOGS: not allowed.
CREDIT CARDS: Amex, MasterCard,
Visa.
PRICES: [2015] per room B&B single
£79.50–£109.50, double £110.50–
£160. Set dinner £24.50–£28.50.

STOCK HILL HOUSE

'It is a world of its own: you leave the reality of outside life behind.' A guest in 2015 was impressed by the 'lovely' ambience at Nita and Peter Hauser's traditional hotel/restaurant. It stands in landscaped grounds with huge trees, terraced lawns, statues and flowerbeds. 'Nita made us feel so welcome,' is another comment. Up a beech-lined drive, the late Victorian mansion is decorated throughout in period style. 'Very comfortable' public rooms have paintings, curios and fine fabrics; a log fire burns in the lounge. Bedrooms, in the main building and the former coach house, are furnished with antiques; most have views of the gardens. In the restaurant, Peter Hauser cooks 'exceptional' daily-changing, Austrian-influenced dishes using local game and meat, and herbs and vegetables from the kitchen garden. Afternoon tea, with home-baked cake, may be taken in the lounges or the bedroom. Breakfast has home-made yogurts, marmalade and preserves, and honey from the Hausers' bees. Close to the borders of Dorset, Somerset and Wiltshire, the hotel is well located for Sherborne Castle, Kingston Lacy and Stourhead. (Geoffery Smith, Mary and Rodney Milne-Day, APP Frankl)

25% DISCOUNT VOUCHERS

Stock Hill
Gillingham
SP8 5NR

T: 01747 823626
F: 01747 825628
E: reception@stockhillhouse.co.uk
W: www.stockhillhouse.co.uk

BEDROOMS: 9. 2, on ground floor, in coach house.
OPEN: all year.
FACILITIES: 2 lounges, restaurant, breakfast room, private dining room, free Wi-Fi (mainly in Reception area), 10-acre grounds (tennis, croquet, small lake), unsuitable for disabled.
BACKGROUND MUSIC: none.
LOCATION: 1 mile W of Gillingham.
CHILDREN: all ages welcomed.
DOGS: not allowed.
CREDIT CARDS: MasterCard, Visa.
PRICES: per person D,B&B £120–£160. Set dinner £40.

GRASMERE Cumbria

THE GRASMERE HOTEL

'It would be hard to beat such excellence in a small hotel,' said trusted correspondents in 2015 visiting Rob van der Palen and Anton Renac's renovated Victorian hotel. Although in the village, it has its own car park. 'The rooms are all quiet despite the traffic outside.' Bordered by the River Rothay, the garden is a 'haven of peace'. Wordsworth, a ground-floor room, was 'small but well equipped with French doors on to the garden; a huge walk-in closet, comfortable twin beds and excellent heating'. De Quincey is 'spacious with king-size bed, comfortable armchairs, pleasant colours and fabrics, well-thought-out lighting with a dimmer switch'. The lounge has good seating, 'strategically placed' low tables and a log fire. 'Thoughtful' touches include packed lunches; trays by the front door for walkers' muddy boots, 'which were cleaned and returned'. Anton Renac's European menu might include Portobello mushroom sautéed with garlic and basil; sea bass with crab salad; Grasmere gingerbread and meringue ice cream tart. 'The trio of lamb was wonderful.' Breakfast has fresh fruit salad, 'well-cooked' vegetarian and meaty hot dishes. (Janet and Dennis Allom)

Broadgate
Grasmere
LA22 9TA

T: 015394 35277
E: info@grasmerehotel.co.uk
W: www.grasmerehotel.co.uk

BEDROOMS: 11.
OPEN: all year except 3–28 Jan.
FACILITIES: lounge, restaurant, free Wi-Fi, 1-acre garden, unsuitable for disabled.
BACKGROUND MUSIC: classical at breakfast, 'easy listening' rest of day.
LOCATION: in village.
CHILDREN: not under 10.
DOGS: by arrangement, allowed in some bedrooms (£10 per stay), not in public rooms.
CREDIT CARDS: MasterCard, Visa.
PRICES: [2015] per person B&B £57–£70, D,B&B £78–£91. Set dinner £21 residents, £30 non-residents. 1-night bookings refused Sat in 2015, all week from 2016.

GRASMERE Cumbria

Map 4: inset C2

OAK BANK

'Friendly hospitality and fine food.' More praise this year for Glynis and Simon Wood's small hotel, a rough-hewn vernacular building, a short walk from William Wordsworth's grave. The 'imaginative' cooking of chef Darren Comish again earns plaudits ('the content and quality matches any top London restaurant'). His menu of modern variations of classic dishes might include wild sea trout, spiced quinoa, lemongrass velouté; Goosnargh duck, red wine figs, butternut squash sorbet. It is served 'efficiently and without fuss'. The bedrooms are being refurbished: four rooms on the second floor have been reconfigured into three larger rooms this year. 'We were delighted by the lovely welcome and the home-made shortbreads and decanter of sherry waiting in our room.' A log fire in the lounge 'gives the place a homely feel: great to relax in'. Local beers can be taken in the lounge or on shaded wooden benches in the closed mature garden. 'Breakfast was top quality': cereals, a daily fruit smoothie, cooked dishes and pots of tea/coffee. Good bus connections from the door. (Gwyn Morgan, John and Theresa Stewart)

Broadgate
Grasmere
LA22 9TA

T: 015394 35217
F: 015394 35685
E: info@lakedistricthotel.co.uk
W: www.lakedistricthotel.co.uk

BEDROOMS: 13. 1 on ground floor.
OPEN: all year except 20–26 Dec, 2–21 Jan, 1–5 May, 7–18 Aug.
FACILITIES: lounge, bar, dining room, conservatory dining room, free Wi-Fi, garden, unsuitable for disabled.
BACKGROUND MUSIC: classical at breakfast, 'easy listening'/light jazz at dinner in bar lounge and dining rooms, none in front lounge.
LOCATION: in village.
CHILDREN: not under 10.
DOGS: allowed in 2 bedrooms, front lounge.
CREDIT CARDS: Diners, MasterCard, Visa.
PRICES: per person B&B £60–£92, D,B&B £110–£117. Set dinner £40–£58. 1-night bookings usually refused weekends.

GREAT MILTON Oxfordshire

Map 2:C3

LE MANOIR AUX QUAT'SAISONS

♔ César award in 1985

In extensive grounds with sculptures, ponds, an orchard and a Japanese tea garden, Raymond Blanc's luxury hotel is a good choice for a 'special occasion'. Philip Newman-Hall is the long-serving manager. The candlelit conservatory restaurant has held two Michelin stars since 1985; the 'excellent' five- and seven-course modern French menus cooked by Raymond Blanc and Gary Jones showcase the heritage fruit, organic vegetables and micro herbs grown in the two-acre kitchen garden. Typical dishes: terrine of garden beetroot, horseradish sorbet; fillet of Cornish brill, oyster, cucumber, wasabi. 'It was the best meal I have ever had.' Elegant accommodation is in the honey-stone 15th-century manor house and the garden courtyard; individually decorated bedrooms have 'nice touches' such as fresh fruit, sugared almonds and a decanter of Madeira wine. Spacious suites, down a path from the main house, have a private terrace and garden. Children are welcomed with a toy box, garden games and their own menu; the on-site cookery school has cooking courses for young guests. Garden tours can be booked.

Church Road
Great Milton
OX44 7PD

T: 01844 278881
F: 01844 278847
E: manoir.mqs@belmond.com
W: www.belmond.com/lemanoir

BEDROOMS: 32. 22 in garden buildings, some on ground floor, 1 suitable for disabled.
OPEN: all year.
FACILITIES: ramps, 2 lounges, champagne bar, restaurant, private dining room, free Wi-Fi, cookery school, civil wedding licence, 27-acre grounds.
BACKGROUND MUSIC: none.
LOCATION: 8 miles SE of Oxford.
CHILDREN: all ages welcomed.
DOGS: allowed in some bedrooms, not in public rooms, kennels provided.
CREDIT CARDS: all major cards.
PRICES: [2015] per room B&B £595–£805. Set dinner £138–£159.

GULWORTHY Devon

Map 1:D4

THE HORN OF PLENTY

NEW

'Imagine what your ideal country house should be like, and you have the Horn of Plenty.' On a 'beautiful' hillside overlooking a wooded valley, guests receive a 'genuine and warm welcome' at Julie Leivers and Damien Pease's smartly refurbished hotel. 'It is very comfortable, with good food; the service is first class,' says a guest this year, whose enthusiastic report earns the hotel a full entry in the Guide. The 19th-century house was built for a local mine captain (the area has a rich copper-mining past); today, 'well-furnished, well-decorated' accommodation is divided between the main house and a converted coach house a minute's walk away (umbrellas are provided). 'Our large room in the garden annexe had a spectacular view over the Tamar valley from the balcony; the bathroom had plenty of storage space. A minor quibble: the flaky Wi-Fi.' Chef Scott Paton's 'pretty', 'well-executed' modern dishes are served in the restaurant overlooking the countryside. 'My crab, prawn and mango salad starter was excellent; scallops were equally good. I would have liked more vegetables.' 'We will return.' (Robert Sanger, Peter Anderson)

Gulworthy
PL19 8JD

T: 01822 832528
F: 01822 834390
E: enquiries@thehornofplenty.
co.uk
W: www.thehornofplenty.co.uk

BEDROOMS: 16. 12 in Coach House (20 yds), 7 on ground floor, 1 suitable for disabled.
OPEN: all year.
FACILITIES: bar, library, drawing room, restaurant, free Wi-Fi, civil wedding licence, 5-acre grounds.
BACKGROUND MUSIC: 'soft, atmospheric, contemporary' at meal times in drawing room, restaurant.
LOCATION: 3 miles SW of Tavistock.
CHILDREN: all ages welcomed.
DOGS: allowed by prior arrangement in designated coach house rooms, not in public rooms.
CREDIT CARDS: MasterCard, Visa.
PRICES: [2015] per room B&B £110–£245, D,B&B £180–£315. Set dinner £49.50, tasting menu £65.

HALNAKER West Sussex

Map 2:E3

THE OLD STORE

'Standards remain the highest' at Patrick and Heather Birchenough's B&B on the edge of the South Downs. Once home of the village bakery and shop, the Grade II listed 17th-century brick-and-flint house now has seven 'immaculate', recently redecorated bedrooms each with an en suite shower room. Arriving guests are greeted with tea and a slice of the hostess's home-made cake – 'such a delight after a long journey'. Room 5 is a king-size double, with space for a cot; Room 6 has twin beds, beamed ceiling, views over the fields to Chichester Cathedral. Breakfast is taken in the old shop floor, still lined with the original delicatessen shelves. There are home-made preserves, oven-fresh bread and 'delicious' hot dishes cooked to order: pancakes with bacon, smoked salmon and scrambled egg, a full English. Guests are welcome to take their morning cuppa into the semi-circular garden peppered with benches and framed with herbaceous borders and with a kitchen garden at the bottom end. There are restaurants in nearby Chichester for evening meals; the Anglesey Arms is within walking distance ('take a torch for the journey back!').

Stane Street
Halnaker
PO18 0QL

T: 01243 531977
F: 01243 531977
E: theoldstore4@aol.com
W: www.theoldstoreguesthouse.co.uk

BEDROOMS: 7. 1 on ground floor.
OPEN: Mar–Dec.
FACILITIES: lounge, breakfast room, free Wi-Fi, ¼-acre garden with seating, unsuitable for disabled.
BACKGROUND MUSIC: none.
LOCATION: 4 miles NE of Chichester.
CHILDREN: all ages welcomed.
DOGS: not allowed.
CREDIT CARDS: MasterCard, Visa.
PRICES: [2015] per person B&B £35–£50 (higher for Goodwood 'Festival of Speed' and 'Revival' meetings). 1-night bookings refused weekends in high season.

HAMBLETON HALL

♀César award in 1985

In fine gardens overlooking Rutland Water, this country house hotel has long been run by owners Tim and Stefa Hart. 'We received a warm welcome,' say returning visitors in 2015, who were accompanied to their second-floor room ('with a stunning view over the lake') by a receptionist and a porter. 'It was elegantly arranged with armchairs and cream furniture on a lush carpet of the same hue; the built-in wardrobe with mirrored panelled doors was a clever touch; the bathroom was exemplary and well equipped. We indulged in excellent tea and biscuits in the main lounge.' Pre-dinner drinks come with 'interesting amuse-bouche'. The chef, Aaron Patterson, has a Michelin star for his modern cooking: 'They were happy to serve me two dishes from the starter menu; crab meat in a biscuit tuile with a small scoop of brown crab ice cream; then queen scallops on a sweet and sour sauce. Each came decorated with mixed curly salads at the side. Service was prompt, carried in by courteous foreign students.' (Francine and Ian Walsh)

Hambleton Hall
Oakham
Hambleton
LE15 8TH

T: 01572 756991
F: 01572 724721
E: hotel@hambletonhall.com
W: www.hambletonhall.com

BEDROOMS: 17. 2-bedroomed suite in pavilion.
OPEN: all year.
FACILITIES: lift, ramps, hall, drawing room, bar, restaurant, 2 private dining rooms, free Wi-Fi, civil wedding licence, 17-acre grounds (swimming pool, tennis).
BACKGROUND MUSIC: none.
LOCATION: 3 miles SE of Oakham, Rutland.
CHILDREN: only children 'of a grown-up age' in restaurant in evening.
DOGS: not allowed in public rooms, nor unattended in bedrooms (£10 per night per dog).
CREDIT CARDS: all major cards.
PRICES: [2015] per room B&B single £195–£220, double £265–£540. Set dinner £68–£80. 1-night bookings sometimes refused weekends.

HAROME North Yorkshire

Map 4:D4

THE STAR INN   NEW

'A very comfortable refuge.' Andrew Pern's characterful inn regains its place in the Guide this year thanks to a positive report from a trusted correspondent in 2015. The medieval inn is in a 'quiet, attractive' village in the North York Moors. Its Michelin-starred restaurant occupies the main building; in the Cross House Lodge opposite, individually styled bedrooms have various quirks, such as a rope-slung bed or a piano. 'My large room had a central snooker table, and quality antique-reproduction furnishings; a single bed frame doubled as a second sofa. There was a good supply of magazines and books; a tea tray had chocolate bars and shortbread biscuits. A useful guide included details of walks and expeditions.' In the restaurant, Andrew Pern and Steve Smith's modern Yorkshire cooking might include 'good' black pudding bread; 'nicely rare' sirloin steak. Presided over by two 'splendid' candelabras, breakfast in the Wheelhouse is 'an experience not to be missed': slices of salmon, cheese and ham; pots of jam, lemon curd and marmalade; a slab of honeycomb; 'beautifully smoked' bacon and 'scrambled eggs that melted in the mouth'. (Robert Gower)

High Street
Harome
YO62 5JE

T: 01439 770397
E: reservations@
   thestarinnatharome.co.uk
W: www.thestaratharome.co.uk

BEDROOMS: 9. All in Cross House Lodge opposite, 3 on ground floor.
OPEN: all year, restaurant closed Sun dinner, Mon lunch.
FACILITIES: lounge, restaurant, The Wheelhouse private dining room, civil wedding licence, terrace, 2-acre garden, unsuitable for disabled.
BACKGROUND MUSIC: 'gentle jazz' in lounge.
LOCATION: village centre.
CHILDREN: all ages welcomed (children's menu).
DOGS: by arrangement in certain bedrooms, not in public rooms.
CREDIT CARDS: MasterCard, Visa.
PRICES: [2015] per room B&B £150–£260. Set menus £20–£25, à la carte £50.

HARWICH Essex

Map 2:C5

THE PIER AT HARWICH

Sea-lovers and marine history buffs will be drawn to Paul Milsom's Victorian quayside hotel/restaurant overlooking the Stour and Orwell estuaries and Old Harwich's historic Ha'Penny Pier; the Mayflower Museum is close by. The blue-and-white palazzo exterior is striking, the maritime heritage of its location reflected in its public spaces, which have antique figureheads, vintage ferry company posters and nautical clocks. The theme stops short of the individually decorated bedrooms: one room was 'sophisticated', 'richly coloured' and adorned with 'quirky pastoral paintings'. Sea-facing rooms, at the front, have 'panoramic views of the water, and the many ferries and fishing boats that come and go'. The lively Ha'Penny bistro ('quick and simple food') and the Harbourside restaurant ('more elaborate dishes and full service') both specialise in the fruits of the sea. Chef John Goff's frequently changing menu might include locally caught lobster thermidor gratinated with mustard, brandy and cheese sauce; pan-fried fillet of bream, courgette, gnocchi, pancetta, lemon beurre blanc. Breakfast has a buffet of cereals, pastries and juices; a 'full regional' with Suffolk sausages and kippers.

The Quay
Harwich
CO12 3HH

T: 01255 241212
F: 01255 551922
E: pier@milsomhotels.com
W: www.milsomhotels.com

BEDROOMS: 14. 7 in annexe, 1 on ground floor.
OPEN: all year, restaurant closed Mon/Tues.
FACILITIES: ramps, bar, lounge (in annexe), restaurant, bistro, free Wi-Fi, civil wedding licence, small front terrace.
BACKGROUND MUSIC: 'easy listening' in bar and bistro.
LOCATION: on quay.
CHILDREN: all ages welcomed.
DOGS: allowed in bar and bedrooms.
CREDIT CARDS: all major cards.
PRICES: [2015] per room B&B £120–£230. À la carte £45.

BLACK ROCK HOUSE

On a quiet residential street on a hill above the town, this 'handsome' Victorian villa is run as a B&B by the owner/manager Yuliya Vereshchuk. 'She is a terrific host who works really hard to keep everything immaculate,' says a visitor in 2015. 'It was nice to have an open fire lit in the lounge on the two evenings we spent in the house. It had an interesting selection of books about Hastings and Sussex; useful information on restaurants in the town.' The large hall has an elegant staircase, a bowl of apples on the table, a selection of DVDs and more books. 'Everything has been thought of' in the bedrooms: a carafe of filtered water; home-made biscuits and a cafetière; fresh milk in a fridge. The turret room has a 'restrained modern look' and a 'huge' bathroom. Breakfast has a buffet of granola, muesli, fruit compote, 'a wide variety of fresh fruit'. 'Yuliya was quick to call help from a neighbour to jump start our car. She replaced a fridge in the room expeditiously when it stopped working.' (Michael Gwinnell)

25% DISCOUNT VOUCHERS

10 Stanley Road
Hastings
TN34 1UE

T: 01424 438448
E: enquiries@black-rock-hastings.
co.uk
W: www.hastingsaccommodation.
com

BEDROOMS: 5.
OPEN: all year except Christmas/New Year, a few weeks in winter.
FACILITIES: lounge, breakfast room, free Wi-Fi, terrace, unsuitable for disabled.
BACKGROUND MUSIC: lounge and breakfast room.
LOCATION: central.
CHILDREN: not under 10, family room available.
DOGS: not allowed.
CREDIT CARDS: Amex, MasterCard, Visa.
PRICES: [2015] per room B&B single £85–£90, double £120–£155, family room £150. 1-night bookings refused bank holidays, weekends.

SEE ALSO SHORTLIST

HASTINGS East Sussex

SWAN HOUSE

By the 'charming' 14th-century St Clement's church in Hastings Old Town, this timber-framed Tudor cottage (built in 1490) is run as a contemporary B&B by the owner, Brendan McDonagh. He has given the house a 'restful, pleasing' interior, and furnished it with an 'eclectic' mix of antiques, paintings and bric-a-brac. The large lounge has a beamed ceiling, white walls, a huge stone fireplace; two long linen-covered settees. The Garden Room, on the ground floor, has an ornate French bed, a carved mahogany chandelier; double oak doors lead directly to the patio garden. Upstairs, the Renaissance Suite is ideal for a family; it has two large bedrooms and a shared en suite shower room. The Artisan Room is decorated with muted colours and vibrant furnishings; it has a stained-glass window; in the bathroom are intricate shell panelling, tongue and groove painted walls and nautical rope wall lights. Breakfast has Greek yogurt with prunes and honey, fruit smoothies, organic muesli; cooked dishes might include smoked haddock with poached egg; kippers with parsley butter; creamed mushrooms on toast. Permits are provided for nearby car parks.

25% DISCOUNT VOUCHERS

1 Hill Street
Hastings
TN34 3HU

T: 01424 430014
E: res@swanhousehastings.co.uk
W: www.swanhousehastings.co.uk

BEDROOMS: 4. 1 on ground floor.
OPEN: all year except 24–26 Dec.
FACILITIES: lounge/breakfast room, courtyard garden, free Wi-Fi, unsuitable for disabled.
BACKGROUND MUSIC: none.
LOCATION: in old town, near seafront.
CHILDREN: not under 5.
DOGS: not allowed.
CREDIT CARDS: Amex, MasterCard, Visa.
PRICES: per room B&B £120–£150.

SEE ALSO SHORTLIST

HATCH BEAUCHAMP Somerset

Map 1:C6

FROG STREET FARMHOUSE

'We had an idyllic stay in picture-book English countryside.' Praise this year for Louise and David Farrance's B&B surrounded by gardens and farmland. 'Perfect hosts', the Farrances are 'helpful, friendly, so accommodating'. 'We arrived in the late afternoon, and David insisted on making us a pot of tea, served with a slice of beautiful home-made cake.' Covered with wisteria in season, the listed longhouse dates back to the 15th century; its traditional character (beamed ceilings, flagstone floors) has been maintained. Country-style bedrooms have a 'lovely, comfortable' bed and a tea tray with fresh milk. They vary in size and decor: Willow has exposed brick walls and antique furniture; the Snug has its own entrance and, in cool months, a log fire. In the evening, Louise Farrance cooks 'tasty' dinners for six or more guests, by arrangement. Breakfast is 'simple and delicious', with home-made jams and marmalade, local sausages, and eggs from the farm's free-range hens. The fields surrounding the farmhouse have thoroughbred horses; during jump season, the Farrances can organise a full day's racing, on request. (Linda Addis, and others)

Hatch Beauchamp
TA3 6AF

T: 01823 481883
E: frogstreet@hotmail.com
W: www.frogstreet.co.uk

BEDROOMS: 4. 1 with private entrance.
OPEN: all year except Dec/Jan.
FACILITIES: 1 lounge, dining room, free Wi-Fi, 150-acre grounds (gardens, farmland), unsuitable for disabled.
BACKGROUND MUSIC: optional in dining room.
LOCATION: 5 miles SE of Taunton.
CHILDREN: all ages welcomed.
DOGS: not allowed.
CREDIT CARDS: all major cards (charges may apply).
PRICES: [2015] per person B&B £45, D,B&B from £67.50 (2 courses).

SEE ALSO SHORTLIST

THE GEORGE HOTEL

'As reliable as ever', this 15th-century former coaching inn, in a Peak District village, is owned by Eric Marsh, 'a brilliant host who has created a happy ship'. James Fair is now the manager. 'The individual members of staff appear to feel that anything they do to improve a visitor's stay is their responsibility. The presentation and ambience of the hotel have improved. Our bedroom had new ceiling lights (good for reading in bed); the small bathroom had been thoughtfully renewed. When we reported that a lamp wasn't working, it was fixed while we were out.' A 'big, comfortable room' at the back was 'very quiet'; rooms at the front have double-glazed windows. In the 'cosy' restaurant, the 'brilliant' cooking of long-serving chef Helen Prince 'is even better'. Trusted correspondents in 2015 enjoyed 'generous portions of sea trout and shrimp rillette, light and full of flavour; sweet and moist rack of lamb'. Breakfast has 'wonderful' American pancakes; chef's own marmalade, 'as good as ever'. 'Always a pleasure to return.' The village is a good base for outdoor pursuits. (Peter Anderson, Kay and Peter Rogers, Padi Howard)

25% DISCOUNT VOUCHERS

Main Road
Hathersage
S32 1BB

T: 01433 650436
F: 01433 650099
E: info@george-hotel.net
W: www.george-hotel.net

BEDROOMS: 24.
OPEN: all year.
FACILITIES: lounge/bar, restaurant, 2 function rooms, free Wi-Fi, civil wedding licence, courtyard, only restaurant suitable for disabled.
BACKGROUND MUSIC: light jazz in restaurant.
LOCATION: in village centre.
CHILDREN: all ages welcomed.
DOGS: not allowed.
CREDIT CARDS: Amex, MasterCard, Visa.
PRICES: [2015] per room B&B £95–£180. Set dinner £36.95 (5% 'service levy' added to all prices). 1-night bookings sometimes refused.

CASTLE HOUSE

Close to the cathedral, this 'excellent' small hotel is owned by local farmer David Watkins. It occupies a Grade II listed Regency villa and a Georgian town house down the street. The ancient castle moat runs through the garden of the main house. 'The staff were all very friendly and efficient,' wrote regular Guide correspondents, who 'had a thoroughly enjoyable stay'. Bedrooms in the main building are traditionally furnished; many have views over the garden and moat. 'Our spacious suite, recently refurbished, was spotless; it had a large and comfortable sitting area.' Another comment: 'Our junior suite was very well appointed: good-quality furniture, excellent lighting, a marble bathroom and a walk-in wardrobe.' A minute's walk away, rooms in Number 25, the town house, are more modern, with under-floor heating in the bathroom, and a box of local produce. The public rooms are in the main house. In the Castle restaurant, chef Claire Nicholls cooks 'outstanding' modern dishes, perhaps rack of lamb, rosemary and spinach spaetzle, butternut squash. Lighter meals are available in the bar. Breakfast has 'good' cooked dishes. (R and JB, LW)

25% DISCOUNT VOUCHERS

Castle Street
Hereford
HR1 2NW

T: 01432 356321
E: info@castlehse.co.uk
W: www.castlehse.co.uk

BEDROOMS: 24. 8 in town house (a short walk away), some on ground floor, 1 suitable for disabled.
OPEN: all year.
FACILITIES: lift, lounge, bar/bistro, restaurant, free Wi-Fi, civil wedding licence, terrace, garden.
BACKGROUND MUSIC: light jazz in public areas.
LOCATION: central.
CHILDREN: all ages welcomed.
DOGS: not allowed.
CREDIT CARDS: Amex, MasterCard, Visa.
PRICES: [2015] per room B&B £110–£230, D,B&B £150–£275. À la carte £40, tasting menu £50. 1-night bookings sometimes refused.

HEXHAM Northumberland

BATTLESTEADS

'We were once again impressed with the quality of accommodation, food and facilities,' say guests returning to this eco-friendly hotel and restaurant on the edge of the Northumberland national park this year. Owners Dee and Richard Slade, with 'invariably friendly, helpful and efficient' staff, run the extended 18th-century farmhouse along green lines: the heating and hot-water system is carbon neutral; the walled garden was developed to encourage wildlife; an observatory opened in 2015. Bedrooms are in the main house and a new timber lodge in the grounds. 'Our large, comfortable double bedroom was like a junior suite. It was practically designed, with well-thought-out bedside lighting; the bathroom was scented with a vase of sweet peas from the garden.' In the restaurant, chef Edward Shilton's 'excellent' modern British dishes use much locally sourced meat and home-grown produce. The hotel is well placed for visitors exploring Hadrian's Wall or taking moor walks ('the drying room is a boon for walkers'); 'it's also well worth taking Richard's offered tour of the gloriously varied and colourful garden'. (Stephen and Pauline Glover)

Wark-on-Tyne
nr Hexham
NE48 3LS

T: 01434 230209
F: 01434 230039
E: info@battlesteads.com
W: www.battlesteads.com

BEDROOMS: 22. 4 on ground floor, 5 in lodge, 2 suitable for disabled.
OPEN: all year except 25 Dec.
FACILITIES: bar, dining room, function facilities, free Wi-Fi, civil wedding licence, 2-acre grounds (walled garden, kitchen garden, dark sky observatory).
BACKGROUND MUSIC: jazz in public areas.
LOCATION: edge of village, 12 miles N of Hexham.
CHILDREN: all ages welcomed.
DOGS: allowed in public rooms, by arrangement in bedrooms (£10).
CREDIT CARDS: Amex, MasterCard, Visa.
PRICES: [2015] per room B&B from £115, D,B&B from £160. À la carte £27.50.

SEE ALSO SHORTLIST

BYFORDS

A 'posh B&B' in a converted ironmonger's premises in this Georgian market town's oldest house sounds improbable, but guests find 'beautifully furnished' character rooms with bare brick walls and oak floors. Byfords succeeds in being all things to all (hungry) comers. Iain and Clair Wilson employ a young staff who 'impress with their enthusiasm'. At breakfast there are 'jugs of freshly squeezed juices', porridge, 'big jars of home-made preserves', fruit salads, croissants, fresh espresso. An 'extensive choice of cooked dishes with good ingredients' includes fish from Cley ('Cly') Smokehouse; Norfolk kippers with slow-roast tomato, lemon, parsley butter; haddock and prawn kedgeree, poached free-range egg – even 'breakfast pizza'. The bedrooms have fresh flowers, home-made biscuits, tea, coffee, chilled milk, all manner of 'modern gizmos'. Marbled bathrooms have under-floor heating. With an all-day café-restaurant and a store-deli 'like a busy takeaway', selling breads, pies, sandwiches, cakes, coffees and speciality foods, it's not fine dining, 'just simpler food' – a miscellany of sandwiches, pasties, soups, sharing plates, salads, pizza, tagine. Vegetarians have plenty of choice.

1–3 Shirehall Plain
Holt
NR25 6BG

T: 01263 711400
E: queries@byfords.org.uk
W: www.byfords.org.uk

BEDROOMS: 16. 1 suitable for disabled.
OPEN: all year.
FACILITIES: ramps, 5 internal eating areas, free Wi-Fi, deli.
BACKGROUND MUSIC: in eating areas.
LOCATION: central, private secure parking.
CHILDREN: all ages welcomed.
DOGS: not allowed.
CREDIT CARDS: Amex, MasterCard, Visa.
PRICES: [2015] per room B&B £175–£255. À la carte £27.

UNDERLEIGH HOUSE

At their converted Victorian cottage and barn in the Peak District national park, Vivienne and Philip Taylor are 'very helpful' hosts, says a visitor this year. 'They provided much local information, recommended local pubs and restaurants, even made reservations for us.' The Taylors are committed to following good environmental practices: they have installed a photovoltaic solar system, and encourage biodiversity in the garden. Breakfast is tailored to allow guests to experience 'some of the Peak District's finest produce'. Served at a long communal table, it includes bacon and sausages from the village butcher, and 'is quite a ceremony'. 'You are given an explanation of the jams, mueslis, etc.' Bedrooms upstairs have views over the hills. 'Twitchers' should ask for ground-floor Townhead: glazed doors on two sides lead to the garden, and have close views of the woodpeckers and tits that visit the hanging feeders. All rooms have a large bed, an en suite bathroom, tea/coffee-making facilities, a mini-fridge. There is good walking and mountain biking from the doorstep. Packed lunches and refreshments, and a place to dry waterproofs on return, are provided. (JM)

Lose Hill Lane
off Edale Road
Hope
S33 6AF

T: 01433 621372
F: 01433 621324
E: info@underleighhouse.co.uk
W: www.underleighhouse.co.uk

BEDROOMS: 4.
OPEN: all year except Christmas/
New Year, Jan.
FACILITIES: lounge, breakfast
room, free Wi-Fi, ¼-acre garden,
unsuitable for disabled.
BACKGROUND MUSIC: none.
LOCATION: 1 mile N of Hope.
CHILDREN: not under 12.
DOGS: not allowed.
CREDIT CARDS: MasterCard, Visa
(both 1.75% surcharge).
PRICES: per room B&B £95–£125.
1-night bookings refused Fri/Sat,
bank holidays.

SEE ALSO SHORTLIST

HOUGH-ON-THE-HILL Lincolnshire

MAP 2:A3

THE BROWNLOW ARMS

A 'winning combination of gastropub, local inn and restaurant-with-rooms', Paul and Lorraine Willoughby's 17th-century inn is in a 'pretty stone village' in East Lincolnshire. The restaurant, popular with villagers and visitors alike, has a 'grand, informal air'. 'Lorraine and her staff, all local, serve with care; ripples of laughter ran through the three adjoining rooms,' said a visitor this year. Chef Ruaraidh Bealby's 'imaginative' menus have 'a great deal of choice' of modern dishes, perhaps baked goat's cheese, truffled honey; 'perfectly pink' venison, dauphinoise potatoes. 'Attention to detail' has been shown in the bedrooms which are in the main building and a barn conversion. A pub room had 'a carefully chosen', 'restful' decor, good linen, comfortable beds and 'pleasing furniture and prints'. Earlier visitors found their room a 'perfect place in which to hunker down on a wet weekend'. In the bathroom are 'lovely, thick' towelling robes, slippers; 'a hot, powerful shower'. No residents' lounge but 'there is a bar with an open fire and a range of armchairs and sofas, with plenty of space to hide'. (David Berry, A and BB)

High Road
Hough-on-the-Hill
NG32 2AZ

T: 01400 250234
E: armsinn@yahoo.co.uk
W: www.thebrownlowarms.com

BEDROOMS: 7. 3 on ground floor in barn conversion.
OPEN: all year except 25/26 Dec, 1 Jan, restaurant closed midday Mon–Sat, Sun evening, Mon evening.
FACILITIES: bar, 3 restaurants, free Wi-Fi, unsuitable for disabled.
BACKGROUND MUSIC: 'easy listening' in public areas.
LOCATION: in village, 7 miles N of Grantham.
CHILDREN: not under 8.
DOGS: not allowed.
CREDIT CARDS: MasterCard, Visa.
PRICES: [2015] per room B&B single £70, double £110. À la carte £40.

HUNTINGDON Cambridgeshire

Map 2:B4

THE OLD BRIDGE

'Wine buffs will have a blast' at John Hoskins's ivy-clad 18th-century town house hotel on the banks of the River Ouse; more than 30 wines can be ordered by the glass on the extensive wine list. The 'friendly' owner, who runs a wine shop on the premises, has an 'exceptional knowledge of wine' and 'keeps a watchful eye on the dynamic young staff', say visitors in 2015. As popular with locals as visitors, the 'casual, cosy' lounge and bar areas have log fires, historic features. 'Our bedroom (plush without a whiff of pretension) had a tasteful mix of traditional and bold contemporary furnishings; a large closet; wonderfully spacious bathroom with luxurious towels, products.' Many of the rooms overlook the river or garden. Those facing the road are triple glazed. In the 'atmospheric' Terrace restaurant, chef Jack Woolner cooks 'simple but well-executed British dishes', perhaps cauliflower and Cheddar soup with chives; boned and rolled ham hock, honey and mustard, crisp potato. Breakfast is 'equally impressive': home-made compotes, fresh fruit, and a 'good selection of cooked dishes'. (Bill and Anna Brewer)

1 High Street
Huntingdon
PE29 3TQ

T: 01480 424300
F: 01480 411017
E: oldbridge@huntsbridge.co.uk
W: www.huntsbridge.com

BEDROOMS: 24. 2 on ground floor.
OPEN: all year.
FACILITIES: ramps, lounge, bar, restaurant, private dining room, wine shop, business centre, civil wedding licence, free Wi-Fi, 1-acre grounds (terrace, garden), river (fishing, jetty, boat trips), unsuitable for disabled.
BACKGROUND MUSIC: none.
LOCATION: 500 yds from town centre, parking, station 10 mins' walk.
CHILDREN: all ages welcomed.
DOGS: allowed in bedrooms, lounge and bar, not in restaurant.
CREDIT CARDS: MasterCard, Visa.
PRICES: [2015] per room B&B £89–£230, D,B&B £180–£260. Set menus £19–£24 (not Sat eve), à la carte £35.

IREBY Cumbria

Map 4: inset B2

OVERWATER HALL

♀César award in 2015

Deer and red squirrel may be seen on the approach to this 'comfortable, friendly hotel' in the northern Lake District. The Grade II listed Georgian mansion is run in an informal style by the owners Stephen Bore and Angela and Adrian Hyde. Dogs are 'genuinely' welcome at no extra charge (the Guide award was for dog-friendly hotel): they have the run of the 18 acres of grounds including a woodland broad walk, and are allowed in bedrooms and one of the two lounges (though 'not on chairs, please'). Human visitors also enjoy the service: 'Angela and her team couldn't have been more helpful.' Afternoon tea is served with home-made biscuits: 'The shortbread is superb.' The 'really comfortable' bedrooms are 'well provisioned' (flowers, fresh milk), and have a 'lovely' bathroom. A ground-floor room opens on to the garden; unusual turret rooms, with their curved walls and huge windows, have great character. Adrian Hyde's locally sourced menu is 'as good as ever'; perhaps roast pork belly, parsnip and apple rösti; butternut squash risotto with piperade. Breakfast has Aspatrian eggs, Wigton bacon, Frizington kippers. (M and AS)

Ireby
CA7 1HH

T: 017687 76566
F: 017687 76921
E: welcome@overwaterhall.co.uk
W: www.overwaterhall.co.uk

BEDROOMS: 11. 1 on ground floor.
OPEN: all year, except 2 weeks early Jan.
FACILITIES: drawing room, lounge, bar area, restaurant, free Wi-Fi, civil wedding licence, 18-acre grounds, Overwater tarn 1 mile.
BACKGROUND MUSIC: light instrumental in restaurant in evening.
LOCATION: 2 miles NE of Bassenthwaite Lake.
CHILDREN: all ages welcomed, not under 5 in restaurant (high tea at 5.30 pm).
DOGS: welcomed, not allowed in 1 lounge, restaurant.
CREDIT CARDS: MasterCard, Visa.
PRICES: [2015] per person B&B £80–£125. Set dinner £48. 1-night bookings refused Sat.

BANK HOUSE

NEW

25% DISCOUNT VOUCHERS

'A busy, well-situated town hotel', Anthony and Jeannette Goodrich's Grade II* listed Georgian town house on the quayside 'lived up to expectations', say Guide inspectors in 2015. 'It is well used by locals throughout the day'; staff are 'welcoming and helpful'. 'The whole place has been imaginatively decorated, and there are lots of little public rooms to sit or eat in.' Individually styled bedrooms have a mix of antique and modern furniture; many have river views. 'Our comfortable first-floor room was one of the largest we have ever stayed in. It had a superking-size bed, a three-seater sofa, an easy chair, a large coffee table, a marble-and-cast iron fireplace; the bathroom, with a freestanding claw-footed bath, was memorable. We watched the last of a glorious sunset through the huge windows.' Chef Stuart Deuchars's 'beautifully cooked' modern brasserie dishes are taken in the 'sympathetically updated' dining rooms or, in balmy weather, in the courtyard or riverside terrace. Breakfast has 'good' coffee; sausages, bread and jam are all home made. The Goodriches also own the Rose & Crown, Snettisham (see Shortlist entry).

King's Staithe Square
King's Lynn
PE30 1RD

T: 01553 660492
E: info@thebankhouse.co.uk
W: www.thebankhouse.co.uk

BEDROOMS: 11.
OPEN: all year.
FACILITIES: bar, 3 dining rooms, private dining room, free Wi-Fi, riverside terrace, only dining rooms suitable for disabled.
BACKGROUND MUSIC: 'low-key, mellow jazz' in bar and dining rooms ('but can be turned down or off').
LOCATION: on the quayside, in old town.
CHILDREN: all ages welcomed.
DOGS: allowed in bar, not in bedrooms.
CREDIT CARDS: Amex, MasterCard, Visa.
PRICES: [2015] per room B&B £110–£150, D,B&B £150–£190. À la carte £27.

CONGHAM HALL `NEW`

'A lovely country hotel', this ivy-clad Georgian house stands in pretty gardens amid parkland near the Queen's estate at Sandringham. It gains a full entry in the Guide after returning to the ownership of the experienced hotelier Nicholas Dickinson; Julie Woodhouse is the manager. The 'charming' house has a spacious lounge and library; 'a nice understated decor'; there are 'lots of sitting areas'. Spacious bedrooms in the main house are 'pretty, with flowery curtains and nice watercolours'; a 'good, unfussy bathroom'; they face the walled garden and cricket pitch in the front of the house, or lawns and parkland at the rear. The style is more contemporary in the garden rooms, each of which has a private patio. In the restaurant, chef Nick Claxton-Webb uses apples from the orchard, and many home-grown vegetables and herbs, in his imaginative modern menus, which have dishes like slow-cooked saddle and smoked tenderloin of Norfolk lamb, sautéed potatoes, carrot purée, wilted spinach. Treatments can be taken in a spa, which has a swimming pool, sauna and steam room. Children are welcomed.

Lynn Road
Grimston
King's Lynn
PE32 1AH

T: 01485 600250
F: 01485 601191
E: info@conghamhallhotel.co.uk
W: www.conghamhallhotel.co.uk

BEDROOMS: 26. 11 garden rooms, 1 suitable for disabled.
OPEN: all year.
FACILITIES: sitting room, bar, library, restaurant; free Wi-Fi, civil wedding licence, conference facilities, terrace, spa, 12-metre swimming pool, 30-acre grounds, herb garden.
BACKGROUND MUSIC: 'mellow' in bar and restaurant.
LOCATION: 6 miles E of King's Lynn.
CHILDREN: all ages welcomed.
DOGS: welcomed in some bedrooms, library.
CREDIT CARDS: Amex, MasterCard, Visa.
PRICES: [2015] per room D,B&B £199–£349. À la carte £45. 1-night bookings sometimes refused.

SUN INN

Near the churchyard in this historic market town on the banks of the River Lune, this white-painted 17th-century inn is owned and run by Lucy and Mark Fuller, with 'warm, friendly' staff. There are log fires, leather chesterfields and real ales in the beamed bar; bedrooms are decorated in contemporary style with handcrafted furniture. Thoughtful touches include Cumbrian biscuits, fresh milk and earplugs; a dog bowl, towel and treats in dog-friendly bedrooms. 'My second-floor room had exposed beams, fine furniture; the modern bathroom was well equipped and sparkling clean.' In the restaurant, Carter at the Sun Inn, chef Sam Carter cooks modern British dishes, perhaps ox cheek, horseradish, shallots. 'The local roast lamb was so good I had it both evenings; puddings were light and scrumptious; the service was faultless.' Breakfast is 'superb': freshly squeezed orange juice, home-made granola, fresh and poached fruit, croissants; sausages from the local butcher. A stroll through the churchyard leads to riverside and woodland walks; raincoats, wellingtons and walking boots are available to borrow. Residents are given free permits for the town's car parks. (TL)

6 Market Street
Kirkby Lonsdale
LA6 2AU

T: 015242 71965
E: email@sun-inn.info
W: www.sun-inn.info

BEDROOMS: 11.
OPEN: all year, bar and restaurant closed Mon lunch.
FACILITIES: bar, restaurant, free Wi-Fi, unsuitable for disabled.
BACKGROUND MUSIC: classical (mornings) and jazz (rest of day) in bar.
LOCATION: town centre.
CHILDREN: all ages welcomed.
DOGS: allowed in 8 bedrooms, bar.
CREDIT CARDS: MasterCard, Visa.
PRICES: [2015] per room B&B £108–£182, D,B&B £164–£246. À la carte £40. 1-night bookings refused Sat.

♕ AUGILL CASTLE

César award: family hotel of the year

'There is something here for everyone,' says a visitor this year to Wendy and Simon Bennett's turreted Gothic castle in the Eden valley. A multi-generational party (aged from three to 67) had 'an absolute blast, not a moment of boredom'. Another comment: 'On the outside it looked like a storybook castle with lavish gardens; on the inside, it had nicely renovated bathrooms, comfortable bedrooms and common areas.' Couples will enjoy Haygarth (with a two-person bathtub) or the Gatehouse (a private garden, king-size four-poster bed). Children will appreciate the tree houses and Augill's Little Cooks classes. Meals are eaten communally at a large oak table in front of 'an invitingly warm log fire'. This year, a locally sourced 'Four Counties' à la carte menu has been introduced, with dishes like potted Morecambe shrimp; Lancashire fish pie, a creamy mash topping. The Yorkshire Dales and the northern lakes are close by, but there is no need to leave the castle: 'You can spend an afternoon playing knights and princesses or just sit in the cinema watching a film with popcorn.' (Tony Swindells, and others)

25% DISCOUNT VOUCHERS

Kirkby Stephen
CA17 4DE

T: 01768 341937
E: office@stayinacastle.com
W: www.stayinacastle.com/

BEDROOMS: 15. 2 on ground floor, 4 in Stable House, 2 in Orangery.
OPEN: all year, dinner by arrangement, lunch for groups by arrangement.
FACILITIES: hall, cinema, drawing room, library (honesty bar), music (sitting) room, conservatory, dining room, free Wi-Fi, civil wedding licence, 15-acre grounds (landscaped garden, tennis).
BACKGROUND MUSIC: none.
LOCATION: 3 miles NE of Kirkby Stephen.
CHILDREN: all ages welcomed.
DOGS: not allowed.
CREDIT CARDS: Amex, MasterCard, Visa.
PRICES: [2015] per room B&B £180–£240, D,B&B £240–£300. À la carte dinner £27. 1-night bookings sometimes refused.

LANGAR Nottinghamshire

Map 2:A3

LANGAR HALL

♥ César award in 2000

'Quite a character', Imogen Skirving began to take in guests when she inherited her family's 19th-century stuccoed and apricot-washed Georgian mansion more than 30 years ago. She continues to run it in hands-on style as if 'entertaining friends in the country'. With a close association with the Nottingham-born designer Paul Smith, it is the place to stay at in the area, notably for cricket commentators, barristers and other professionals. Bedrooms are themed (Bohemia was once an artist's studio), or named after previous guests (Cartland, although no longer pink, is a 'romantic' room). Edwards, overlooking the gardens, has its original four-poster bed and 1830s porcelain bathtub. A short walk across the croquet lawn, Agnews is a 'quiet, private' chalet in the garden: it has sloping ceilings, its own veranda, large shower, but no bath. Housekeeping is 'superb'. The drawing room has a mix of antiques and artefacts from Imogen Skirving's travels (particularly to India). In the restaurant, chefs Gary Booth and Ross Jeffrey serve seasonal dishes, perhaps Belvoir hare, parsley root and pear; caramelised chicory tarte Tatin.

25% DISCOUNT VOUCHERS

Church Lane
Langar
NG13 9HG

T: 01949 860559
F: 01949 861045
E: info@langarhall.co.uk
W: www.langarhall.com

BEDROOMS: 12. 1 on ground floor, 1 in garden chalet.
OPEN: all year.
FACILITIES: ramps, sitting room, study, library, bar, garden room, restaurant, free Wi-Fi, civil wedding licence, 30-acre grounds (gardens, children's play area), unsuitable for disabled.
BACKGROUND MUSIC: none.
LOCATION: 12 miles SE of Nottingham.
CHILDREN: all ages welcomed by arrangement.
DOGS: small dogs on a lead allowed by arrangement, not unaccompanied.
CREDIT CARDS: MasterCard, Visa.
PRICES: [2015] per room B&B single £95–£140, double £110–£199, D,B&B (Sun and Mon) £30 added per person. Set dinner (not on Sat) £30, à la carte £40.

LANGHO Lancashire

Map 4:D3

NORTHCOTE

NEW

In an 'outstanding' location in the Ribble valley, considerable investment has been put into refurbishing this 19th-century manor house (Relais & Châteaux). It stands in 'well-established' gardens. Run by chef/patron Nigel Haworth and his business partner, Craig Bancroft, it continues to be 'an old favourite of local residents'. Newspapers are 'thoughtfully provided' for reading by the wood fire in the 'comfortable' public areas ('the too-loud background music was unfortunate'). 'A convivial atmosphere was encouraged by one of the owners doing his rounds,' say Guide inspectors in 2015, restoring Northcote to a full entry. 'Well-equipped' bedrooms are in the main house and the new garden lodge. 'Our spacious room had a comfortable bed, reading material, a desk, chairs and a table; the large bathroom had plenty of surfaces for "stuff".' In the chandelier-lit restaurant, Nigel Haworth and Lisa Allen hold a Michelin star for their modern menus. 'The food was of a high standard, including a particularly good smoked eel and shrimp Caesar. Some of the wine pairings suggested for each course were expensive; on request, cheaper, very good substitutes were provided.'

Northcote Road
Langho
BB6 8BE

T: 01254 240555
F: 01254 246568
E: reception@northcote.com
W: www.northcote.com

BEDROOMS: 26. 8 on ground floor, 2 suitable for disabled.
OPEN: all year.
FACILITIES: lift, ramp, lounges, cocktail bar, restaurant, private dining/meeting room, free Wi-Fi, civil wedding licence, 3-acre garden.
BACKGROUND MUSIC: varied in restaurant and bar.
LOCATION: 5½ miles N of Blackburn, on A59.
CHILDREN: all ages welcomed.
DOGS: not allowed.
CREDIT CARDS: Amex, MasterCard, Visa.
PRICES: [2015] per room B&B from £305, D,B&B from £365. Set dinner £65, tasting menu £85.

LASTINGHAM North Yorkshire

Map 4:C4

LASTINGHAM GRANGE

♛ César award in 1991

'A model of what a country hotel should be.' In a historic village on the edge of the North York Moors, Bertie Wood, his mother, Jane, and brother, Tom, run their 'lovely' traditional hotel in this creeper-covered 17th-century farmhouse. The Woods are the 'most welcoming', 'hands-on' hosts; their staff are 'beyond praise'. Overlooking the terrace and the 'delightful' rose garden, the lounge has an open fire, armchairs and lots of books; bedrooms are 'old-fashioned but spotlessly clean and comfortable'. In the dining room, chefs Paul Cattaneo and Sandra Thurlow serve 'first-class', traditional English dishes, perhaps roast rack of Kirkbymoorside lamb, Yorkshire sauce. 'It is remarkable that they manage a completely different menu every evening, but when we particularly enjoyed some halibut, they were happy to provide it again the following night.' Tea and 'delicious' warm scones with butter, cream and jam are served every afternoon; they may be taken on the terrace in good weather. 'Superb walking on the moors from the door; a truly charming hotel, unusual in this day and age.' (John and Cherry Hopkins, and others)

25% DISCOUNT VOUCHERS

High Street
Lastingham
YO62 6TH

T: 01751 417345
F: 01751 417358
E: reservations@lastinghamgrange.com
W: www.lastinghamgrange.com

BEDROOMS: 12. Plus cottage in village.
OPEN: Mar–end Nov.
FACILITIES: ramps, hall, lounge, dining room, laundry facilities, free Wi-Fi in public areas, 12-acre grounds (terrace, garden, adventure playground, croquet, boules), unsuitable for disabled.
BACKGROUND MUSIC: none.
LOCATION: 5 miles NE of Kirkbymoorside.
CHILDREN: all ages welcomed (adventure playground, special meals).
DOGS: not allowed in public rooms or unattended in bedrooms.
CREDIT CARDS: Amex, MasterCard, Visa.
PRICES: [2015] per room B&B from £145, D,B&B from £165. Set dinner £39.95, à la carte £30.

LAVENHAM Suffolk

Map 2:C5

THE GREAT HOUSE

César award in 2009

At the heart of a 'beautiful' medieval town, chef/proprietor Régis Crépy has run this restaurant-with-rooms with his wife, Martine, for 30 years. The 14th-century house (with Georgian additions) on the market square is a 'comfortable, welcoming' place. 'The staff are always wanting to help, and quick to learn guests' names', says a reader in 2015, returning for his fourth visit. The public rooms have contemporary flourishes; up uneven stairs, the individually decorated bedrooms have 'ancient beams', 'modern knick-knacks' and 'an aura of great comfort'. 'We had their Grand Room, with two double king-size beds, matching chaises longues, and a double-fronted view of the market place. The bathroom, down a quaint stairway, was of a good size, with bathrobes and slippers.' In the elegant restaurant, long-serving chef Enrique Bilbault cooks 'magnificent' French dishes. 'A splendid soup of Jerusalem artichokes with quail's eggs; scallops in a tangy broth; a tender beef fillet.' A 'substantial' breakfast has French bread, 'good' conserves, stewed fruits, a 'well-cooked' full English. (David Grant, A and MK)

Market Place
Lavenham
CO10 9QZ

T: 01787 247431
F: 01787 248007
E: info@greathouse.co.uk
W: www.greathouse.co.uk

BEDROOMS: 5.
OPEN: Feb–Dec, restaurant closed Sun night, Mon, Tues midday.
FACILITIES: lounge/bar, restaurant, free Wi-Fi, patio dining area, ½-acre garden, unsuitable for disabled.
BACKGROUND MUSIC: 'easy listening' in restaurant.
LOCATION: town centre, by Market Cross, near Guildhall, free public car park.
CHILDREN: all ages welcomed.
DOGS: not allowed.
CREDIT CARDS: Amex, MasterCard, Visa.
PRICES: [2015] per room B&B £129–£249, D,B&B £199–£304. Set dinner £35, à la carte £47 (Sat only). 1-night bookings sometimes refused Sat.

SEE ALSO SHORTLIST

LEAMINGTON SPA Warwickshire

Map 3:C6

EIGHT CLARENDON CRESCENT

Guests appreciate the peaceful aspect of Christine and David Lawson's B&B, a Grade II listed Regency house overlooking its own private dell, in the north end of the spa town. 'The only sounds you hear are the chimes of the grandfather clock,' a regular correspondent said. Another comment: 'At night, I was surprised by how few sounds entered my open window. I'd never have thought I was close to the centre of town.' The 'immaculately presented' house is furnished with 'many fine antiques'. The 'spacious' drawing room has fresh flowers and a grand piano 'which we would be delighted to hear you play', the hosts say. Upstairs, the bedrooms are individually decorated in neutral colours; each has a TV and tea/coffee-making facilities; one has a private bathroom across the corridor. An 'excellent' communal breakfast, prepared by Christine Lawson, is served around an antique table. It has home-made bread and preserves, fresh fruit, 'perfectly cooked' bacon and eggs. Special diets are catered for. Evening meals are not provided, but the Lawsons can recommend restaurants within walking distance. More reports, please.

8 Clarendon Crescent
Leamington Spa
CV32 5NR

T: 01926 429840
F: 01926 424641
E: lawson@lawson71.fsnet.co.uk
W: www.eightclarendoncrescent.
   co.uk

BEDROOMS: 4. 1 with private bathroom.
OPEN: all year except Christmas–New Year, Easter, occasional holidays.
FACILITIES: drawing room, dining room, free Wi-Fi, ¾-acre garden (private dell), unsuitable for disabled.
BACKGROUND MUSIC: none.
LOCATION: close to centre.
CHILDREN: all ages welcomed.
DOGS: not allowed.
CREDIT CARDS: none.
PRICES: [2015] per room B&B single £50, double £85.

LEDBURY Herefordshire

Map 3:D5

THE FEATHERS

For almost 500 years, this black-and-white-timbered Tudor pile has been run as an inn on the High Street of a medieval town. The 'lovely old building' is today owned by David Elliston. The history and original character (beamed rooms, 'quirky' staircase, leaded windows) have been carefully maintained. Visitors in 2015 found their room 'very good', the food and the attitude of the staff 'excellent', but encountered inconsistency when booking. Bedrooms have coffee/tea facilities, bathrobes, free Wi-Fi. Coaching rooms have original Tudor beams; 'very comfortable, clean' rooms in the converted Victorian ballroom are light, with a high ceiling and modern furnishings. 'Busy' Fuggles brasserie has thickly hung hops on the ceiling; in the more intimate Quills restaurant, chef Suzie Isaac's modern dishes might include hot-and-sour chargrilled baby aubergine, herbed rice; Cotswold venison loin, root vegetables, curly kale. In warm weather, light meals and drinks might be taken in the walled garden. A 'good choice' of fruit; cereals; 'very tasty' full English is 'cheerfully served' at breakfast; 'good coffee'. Hotel guests enjoy free access to the inn's spa which has a swimming pool.

25% DISCOUNT VOUCHERS

High Street
Ledbury
HR8 1DS

T: 01531 635266
F: 01531 638955
E: enquiries@feathers-ledbury.co.uk
W: www.feathers-ledbury.co.uk

BEDROOMS: 22. 1 suite in cottage, also self-catering apartments.
OPEN: all year.
FACILITIES: lounge, bar, brasserie, restaurant, free Wi-Fi, function/conference/wedding facilities, spa (swimming pool, 11 by 6 metres, whirlpool, gym), civil wedding licence, courtyard garden (fountain, alfresco eating), unsuitable for disabled.
BACKGROUND MUSIC: none.
LOCATION: town centre, parking.
CHILDREN: all ages welcomed.
DOGS: welcomed in bedrooms and public areas, only guide dogs in restaurant and brasserie.
CREDIT CARDS: all major cards.
PRICES: [2015] per room B&B £150–£240, D,B&B £165–£250. Set menu (Sun–Thurs) £18.95–£22, à la carte £30. 1-night bookings occasionally refused weekends.

LEWDOWN Devon

Map 1:C3

LEWTRENCHARD MANOR   NEW

Back in the hands of the Murray family, this 'beautiful old manor house in lovely surroundings' returns to a full entry after a report by Guide inspectors who 'could not find fault'. A 'Victorian/Elizabethan fantasy', it was the ancestral home of the Reverend Sabine Baring-Gould, who wrote 'Onward, Christian Soldiers'. The public rooms and the grand staircase have oak panelling and family portraits. Some of the bedrooms are in the main house; some others are in a courtyard a short walk away. 'Our front room had a gilded leather frieze above the panelling; lots of light from low leaded windows facing three ways on to the gardens; an alcove with a chaise longue and a stunning carved period wardrobe.' Rooms are serviced during dinner. The restaurant, which overlooks the courtyard, has chandeliers, silverware on white cloths. The chef, Matthew Peryer, cooks 'excellent' modern dishes. 'We enjoyed a cauliflower cream pre-starter; succulent roasted quail legs; tender chicken breast with a dauphinoise potato cake on a fabulous sauce. The staff are all brisk, efficient, amiable and welcoming; the ambience is truly luxurious.'

Lewdown
EX20 4PN

T: 01566 783222
F: 01566 783332
E: info@lewtrenchard.co.uk
W: www.lewtrenchard.co.uk

BEDROOMS: 14.
OPEN: all year.
FACILITIES: lounge, bar, library, restaurant, function facilities, free Wi-Fi, civil wedding licence, 12-acre garden.
BACKGROUND MUSIC: none.
LOCATION: 10 miles N of Tavistock.
CHILDREN: not under 8 at dinner.
DOGS: allowed in bedrooms, and lounge areas on a lead 'if no one objects'.
CREDIT CARDS: Amex, MasterCard, Visa.
PRICES: [2015] per room B&B from £155, D,B&B from £245. Set dinner £49.50. 1-night bookings sometimes refused.

LICHFIELD Staffordshire

Map 2:A2

NETHERSTOWE HOUSE

'Solid red brick' Netherstowe, originally a
19th-century mill house and former woollen
manufactory, has been turned into a small
hotel by the Heathcote family; Ben Heathcote
is manager. The city setting is not bucolic, but
a 'dense, tree-lined drive' screens the building
from a modern housing estate. The 'diligent'
staff are welcoming. The bedrooms are divided
between the main house and 'spacious, well-
equipped' apartments in the courtyard, which
have a kitchen. A house room, with a four-
poster bed, was liked for its 'original fixtures
and fittings (exposed floorboards, panelling
and a fireplace); a well-appointed bathroom
big enough to party in'. A winter visitor was
less happy with her 'cold, characterless' room.
There is a choice of eating places: the cellar
Steakhouse Brasserie or the dining room, where
chef Stephen Garland uses local, sustainable
ingredients. A 'Fantastic Friday' dinner proved
'a wonderful creation', including cocktails, an
amuse-bouche, a 'most delicate' consommé with
'melting yet crisp oxtail; poached chicken breast,
seared foie gras, shiitake mushrooms, chicken
skin crisp'. Verdict: 'All in all a most enjoyable
stay.' (Trudi Burton, and others)

Netherstowe Lane
Off the Mill Pond
Lichfield
WS13 6AY

T: 01543 254270
F: 01543 419998
E: info@netherstowehouse.com
W: www.netherstowehouse.com

BEDROOMS: 9. Plus 8 serviced
apartments in annexe.
OPEN: all year, restaurant closed Sun
dinner.
FACILITIES: 2 lounges, bar, 2 dining
rooms, free Wi-Fi, gymnasium,
2-acre grounds.
BACKGROUND MUSIC: instrumental
compilations in public rooms all
day.
LOCATION: 2 miles NE of city centre.
CHILDREN: all ages welcomed.
DOGS: not allowed.
CREDIT CARDS: Amex, MasterCard,
Visa.
PRICES: [2015] per room B&B
£105–£195, D,B&B £185–£215.
À la carte £45.

LIFTON Devon

Map 1:C3

THE ARUNDELL ARMS

♔ César award in 2006

Country pursuits and the pleasures of a sporting life attract visitors to this 'very nice' hotel in a village near the Devon–Cornwall border. 'An excellent combination of relatively simple accommodation and outstanding cooking', it has been run by members of the Fox-Edwards family – 'lovely people' – for more than 50 years. It has an award-winning fishing school and 20 miles of rights on the River Tamar and its tributaries; fly-fishing is a 'major feature'. Non-fishing guests are also 'made very welcome'. The 'unfussy' bedrooms are decorated in country house style, with prints and antiques. A 'quiet, comfortable' room had a 'large bathroom with lots of storage space'. Three bedrooms in Church Cottage, opposite the main house, have been refurbished this year. Popular with locals, the 'convivial' bar has a log fire in the winter months, and ales from a local brewery half an hour's drive away. In the more formal dining room, Steve Pidgeon, the long-serving chef, serves 'great' British dishes, perhaps pork tenderloin, wood mushroom mousseline, savoy cabbage, smoked bacon. 'A good cooked breakfast set us up for the day.' (PA, and others)

25% DISCOUNT VOUCHERS

Fore Street
Lifton
PL16 0AA

T: 01566 784666
F: 01566 784494
E: reservations@arundellarms.com
W: www.arundellarms.com

BEDROOMS: 26. 4 on ground floor, 3 in Church Cottage opposite.
OPEN: all year.
FACILITIES: ramp, lounge, cocktail bar, village pub, restaurant, brasserie, conference/meeting rooms, games room, free Wi-Fi, skittle alley, civil wedding licence, garden (lake), 20 miles fishing rights on River Tamar and tributaries, fishing school, secure bicycle storage.
BACKGROUND MUSIC: none.
LOCATION: 3 miles E of Launceston, 1 mile from A30.
CHILDREN: all ages welcomed.
DOGS: welcomed, not allowed in restaurant.
CREDIT CARDS: Amex, MasterCard, Visa.
PRICES: per person B&B from £90, D,B&B from £130. Set dinner £35, à la carte £30.

LODSWORTH West Sussex

Map 2:E3

THE HALFWAY BRIDGE

Flanked by the rolling countryside and ancient woodland of the South Downs, Sam and Janet Bakose's refurbished 17th-century coaching inn is popular with walkers. Locals and families are likewise drawn by the 'welcoming' atmosphere in the bar, where visitors can take local ales on barstools hand made out of old whisky barrels. The 'stylish' bedrooms are in the converted Cowdray Barns behind the main building, and have views of the lawns or the woods. There are umbrellas and a boot tray in the lobby for wet days. One room had 'good-quality mahogany furniture, a black leather armchair and a large, comfortable bed'; exposed beams, brickwork; full-length windows with wooden shutters; a refrigerator with fresh milk ('hurray!'); fresh coffee. 'Housekeeping throughout was of a high standard.' Guide inspectors experienced 'first-class service from enthusiastic young staff' in the 'small, intimate' dining areas. 'Upmarket pub food' is served: Sussex savoury pork sausages, mash potato, caramelised onion gravy; a 'delicious' clementine sponge pudding. Breakfast has a 'wide range of delicious cooked dishes', including vegetarian options, to set you up for trekking the Downs.

Lodsworth
GU28 9BP

T: 01798 861281
E: enquiries@halfwaybridge.co.uk
W: www.halfwaybridge.co.uk

BEDROOMS: 7. In converted barns.
OPEN: all year.
FACILITIES: bar, restaurant, free Wi-Fi, terrace, unsuitable for disabled.
BACKGROUND MUSIC: light jazz in bar and restaurant.
LOCATION: 3 miles W of Petworth.
CHILDREN: all ages welcomed.
DOGS: allowed in bar, not in bedrooms.
CREDIT CARDS: Amex, MasterCard, Visa.
PRICES: per room B&B £140–£230. À la carte £34. 1-night bookings refused weekends.

LONGHORSLEY Northumberland

Map 4:B3

THISTLEYHAUGH FARM

♔César award in 2011

Guests are 'guaranteed a warm welcome' at this 'beautiful' Georgian farmhouse on the banks of the River Coquet. It is owned and run by Enid Nelless, 'who makes it so special, with her friendliness and easy conversation'. The Nelless family have farmed locally for three generations; the house, on the family's 720-acre organic livestock farm, is 'a peaceful spot – except for the sheepdogs rounding up the squealing pigs, which was great fun to watch'. There are 'lovely furniture and ornaments' in the public rooms; the spacious bedrooms are decorated with art and antiques. 'Our room was very large and well equipped, with lots of storage, exquisite bedlinen; fresh milk in the fridge, and home-made biscuits. The splendid roll-top bath had a powerful shower over it.' Guests meet for a glass of sherry in the garden room before dinner; evening meals, cooked by Enid Nelless and her daughter-in-law, Zoë, are taken communally. A typical dish: 'delicious' roast organic lamb from the farm, with seasonal vegetables. Breakfast is 'very good and set us up for a day's walking'. (MH, and others)

25% DISCOUNT VOUCHERS

Longhorsley
NE65 8RG

T: 01665 570629
F: 01665 570629
E: thistleyhaugh@hotmail.com
W: www.thistleyhaugh.co.uk

BEDROOMS: 5.
OPEN: all year except Christmas/New Year, Jan, dining room closed Sat eve.
FACILITIES: 2 lounges, garden room, dining room, free Wi-Fi, 720-acre farm, ¼-acre garden (summer house), fishing, shooting, golf, riding nearby, unsuitable for disabled.
BACKGROUND MUSIC: none.
LOCATION: 10 miles N of Morpeth, W of A697.
CHILDREN: all ages welcomed.
DOGS: not allowed (kennels nearby).
CREDIT CARDS: MasterCard, Visa.
PRICES: per person B&B £50, D,B&B £75.

LOOE Cornwall

Map 1:D3

THE BEACH HOUSE

With 'panoramic views' over Whitsand Bay and Looe Island, this 'very friendly' seaside B&B is run by 'warm' hosts, Rosie and David Reeve. 'Rosie looked after us superbly,' said a recent visitor. Arriving guests are offered tea and home-made cake. The 'immaculately clean' bedrooms have 'beachy' accents: cushioned bamboo chairs, bright fabrics, complemented by original seascape paintings. Three of the five 'comfortable, well-appointed' rooms are sea facing; Fistral has a private balcony. Two bedrooms at the back of the house have access to the light garden room, overlooking the bay. All have an en suite bathroom; a fridge and tea/coffee-making facilities, with fresh milk, 'regularly replenished'. Breakfast ('fantastic') is ordered the evening before and served at an agreed time in the bright dining room. There is a 'well-varied' buffet (fresh fruit salad, home-made muffins, etc). Freshly cooked hot dishes include a full English; pancakes; scrambled eggs with smoked salmon. On the doorstep is a small, sandy beach with rock pools to explore; the Reeves can recommend local restaurants. Private parking is an asset. Good walking from the door. (CM)

Marine Drive
Hannafore
Looe
PL13 2DH

T: 01503 262598
F: 01503 262298
E: enquiries@thebeachhouselooe.
  co.uk
W: www.thebeachhouselooe.co.uk

BEDROOMS: 5.
OPEN: all year except 23–25 Dec.
FACILITIES: garden room, breakfast room, free Wi-Fi, terrace, ½-acre garden, beach opposite, unsuitable for disabled.
BACKGROUND MUSIC: classical radio in dining room.
LOCATION: ½ mile from centre.
CHILDREN: children over 16 welcomed.
DOGS: not allowed.
CREDIT CARDS: MasterCard, Visa.
PRICES: per room B&B £80–£130. 1-night bookings refused weekends, high season.

SEE ALSO SHORTLIST

LORTON Cumbria

NEW HOUSE FARM

In the Lorton Vale, away from Lake District tourists, Hazel Thompson's unpretentious guest house is surrounded by the glorious landscape of the fells. She has restored and furnished the Grade II listed 17th-century farmhouse 'beautifully', retaining period features (oak-beamed ceilings, flagged floors and open fires). The 'excellent, clean' bedrooms are individually decorated. Low Fell, in the oldest part of the main house, has a queen-size bed with solid oak headboard; a Victorian bathroom with a large slipper bath. Whiteside has a king-sized brass bed; a double airbath. The Old Dairy, in the converted barn, has an exposed stone wall; a hand-carved four-poster bed; separate wardrobe area. Each room has coffee/tea-making facilities, freshly baked biscuits; views of open fields 'surrounded by fells'. The outside rooms do not have a Wi-Fi signal. In the dining room, Hazel Thompson's traditional English menu might include local poached salmon with pesto sauce; steak and kidney with herb dumplings. Lunches and teas are served in a converted byre with seating arranged in the old stalls. Breakfast has fruit, porridge; cooked dishes 'straight from the Aga'. (DP)

Lorton
CA13 9UU

T: 07841 159818
E: hazel@newhouse-farm.co.uk
W: www.newhouse-farm.com

BEDROOMS: 5. 1 in stable, 1 in Old Dairy.
OPEN: all year except Christmas/New Year.
FACILITIES: 3 lounges, dining room, free Wi-Fi in main house, civil wedding licence, 17-acre grounds (garden, hot tub, streams, woods, field, lake and river, safe bathing 2 miles), unsuitable for disabled.
BACKGROUND MUSIC: none.
LOCATION: 2 miles S of Lorton.
CHILDREN: not under 6.
DOGS: 'clean and dry' dogs allowed in bedrooms (£20 charge per night), not in public rooms.
CREDIT CARDS: MasterCard, Visa.
PRICES: per person B&B £50–£90, D,B&B £82–£122. Set dinner £34–£38.

LOUTH Lincolnshire

THE OLD RECTORY AT STEWTON

At the end of a quiet lane opposite a Norman church, this early Victorian former rectory 'stands out' among the accommodation in the Lincolnshire Wolds. Alan and Linda Palmer are 'relaxed and charming' hosts. The large gardens with lawns and mature trees of this 'delightfully quirky' house are frequented by finches, herons, squirrels and badgers. Walkers and cyclists will enjoy the chalk hills of the Wolds; children and pets will want to explore the 'nooks and crannies' of both public and guest rooms. Visitors have use of the large sitting room with plush rugs, leather sofas, books, magazines; and the bright and cosy conservatory with wicker armchairs, fresh flowers and views of the gardens. The bedrooms are 'beautifully presented, clean'; comfortable beds; art and artefacts that reflect the owners' travels. One bathroom has checkerboard tiles and a slipper bath; another a staircase and wooden floors. Small families can be accommodated in the four-person suite, which has a separate lounge and a sofa bed. Young guests are received in an 'easy manner'. Breakfast is 'taken seriously'; ingredients sourced from the area.

Stewton
Louth
LN11 8SF

T: 01507 328063
E: alanjpalmer100@aol.com
W: www.louthbedandbreakfast.co.uk

BEDROOMS: 4. 1 with private bathroom.
OPEN: all year except Christmas/New Year.
FACILITIES: sitting room, breakfast room, free Wi-Fi in some parts of house, 3-acre garden, unsuitable for disabled.
BACKGROUND MUSIC: none.
LOCATION: in hamlet 2½ miles SE of Louth.
CHILDREN: all ages welcomed.
DOGS: allowed in bedrooms only (£5 charge per visit).
CREDIT CARDS: MasterCard, Visa.
PRICES: [2015] per room B&B £65–£80.

LOWER BOCKHAMPTON Dorset

Map 1:D6

YALBURY COTTAGE

♥ César award in 2015

Near the River Frome, this 'lovely little hotel' is within walking distance of Thomas Hardy's birthplace. Personally run by owners Ariane and Jamie Jones, it is a converted cluster of 350-year-old thatched cottages. New praise came in 2015. Jamie Jones is the 'friendly face' front-of-house. 'The staff go the extra mile to ensure you are happy,' is one comment. 'Perfect service from start to finish.' The host is also the chef, serving 'generous' portions of 'beautifully cooked' dishes in a dining room which has oak beams and inglenook fireplaces. 'I had scallops followed by tender venison; the following night, I chose dressed crab followed by an excellent pork en croute.' A vegetarian dish was thought 'excellent'. The wine list is 'well priced'. Bedrooms are decorated in simple, rustic style. 'Ours was fine, with a big bed and a rural outlook.' 'Ours was better than adequate.' Breakfast 'had delicious home-made chunky marmalade, freshly squeezed orange juice, a good cooked plate'. 'The whole experience is excellent value.' (Peter Anderson, Carol Jackson)

Lower Bockhampton
DT2 8PZ

T: 01305 262382
E: enquiries@yalburycottage.com
W: www.yalburycottage.com

BEDROOMS: 8. 6 on ground floor.
OPEN: all year except 22 Dec–19 Jan.
FACILITIES: lounge, restaurant, free Wi-Fi (in some parts of hotel), unsuitable for disabled.
BACKGROUND MUSIC: 'easy listening' in lounge at dinner.
LOCATION: 2 miles E of Dorchester.
CHILDREN: all ages welcomed, but not under 12 in restaurant after 8 pm.
DOGS: welcomed, not allowed in restaurant.
CREDIT CARDS: MasterCard, Visa.
PRICES: [2015] per room B&B single £75–£85, double £99–£120, D,B&B single £99–£115, double £160–£180. Set dinner £32.50–£37.50.

LUDLOW Shropshire

Map 3:C4

MR UNDERHILL'S

♀César award in 2000

Named after a cat (no longer around), Chris and Judy Bradley's 'unpretentious' restaurant-with-rooms, in this lovely old market town, stands on the banks of the River Teme. 'Dinner was both excellent and excellent value,' an impressed guest said. Pre-dinner drinks may be taken in the 'very pleasant' riverside garden in good weather. In the candlelit restaurant, self-taught chef Chris Bradley holds a Michelin star for his 'inventive' eight-course, no-choice (until dessert) seasonal menus. 'We loved our experience: a delicious almond velouté, outstanding duck liver custard, wonderfully tender venison accompanied by braised venison cannelloni. Dessert was a rhubarb tart with olive-scented ice cream.' Accommodation is in 'tastefully decorated' modern suites with a sitting area and views over the garden and river. In an oak-framed annexe off the courtyard, the 'spacious, comfortable' Shed has armchairs by the French windows overlooking the weir. Breakfast has freshly squeezed orange juice and 'irresistible' dishes; 'proper, old-fashioned' marmalade; 'a wonderfully light black pudding and fried bread'. (P and AC, and others)

Dinham Weir
Ludlow
SY8 1EH

T: 01584 874431
W: www.mr-underhills.co.uk

BEDROOMS: 4. 1 in annexe.
OPEN: all year except Christmas/New Year, 2 weeks June and Oct, restaurant closed Mon/Tues.
FACILITIES: small lounge, restaurant, function facilities, ½-acre courtyard, riverside garden (fishing, swimming), unsuitable for disabled.
BACKGROUND MUSIC: none.
LOCATION: below castle, on River Teme, station ½ mile, parking.
CHILDREN: not 2–8.
DOGS: not allowed.
CREDIT CARDS: MasterCard, Visa.
PRICES: per room B&B £245–£360. Set menu £69.50. 1-night bookings sometimes refused Sat.

SEE ALSO SHORTLIST

LUDLOW Shropshire

Map 3:C4

OLD DOWNTON LODGE   NEW

In rolling Shropshire countryside, a cluster of old stone and brick farm buildings (some medieval, some Georgian) has been remodelled into a restaurant-with-rooms by Willem and Pippa Vlok. 'It is a stunning place with wonderful food,' said Guide inspectors in 2015. The bedrooms and restaurant are in buildings around a courtyard with 'delightful', formal parterre gardens; there are seating areas, 'lots of plants and flowers'. A large lounge bar is in a converted barn with a wood-burner, oak beams, limewashed white rafters. In the dining room, which dates to Norman times, chef Karl Martin serves daily-changing five- and seven-course tasting menus. 'The dishes were delicate with wonderful flavours; perhaps not for a trencherman but great for a special occasion.' Service is 'good, attentive; the owner was around in the evening and morning'. The bedrooms have been fashioned from various buildings. 'Ours had a soaring roof, exposed stone walls, a huge bed. The understated style was rustic and calm, with pleasing fabrics. There were quality fittings, interesting lamps.' Breakfast is 'local and wholesome'. Popular with shooting parties; good walking from the door.

Downton on the Rock
Ludlow
SY8 2HU

T: 01568 771826
E: bookings@olddowntonlodge.
   com
W: www.olddowntonlodge.com

BEDROOMS: 10. In buildings around courtyard.
OPEN: all year, except Christmas, restaurant closed Sun, Mon.
FACILITIES: sitting room, museum room, free Wi-Fi in public areas only, civil wedding licence, ½-acre courtyard, unsuitable for disabled.
BACKGROUND MUSIC: soft classical in sitting room and dining room.
LOCATION: 6 miles W of Ludlow.
CHILDREN: not under 12.
DOGS: allowed in some bedrooms by prior arrangement.
CREDIT CARDS: MasterCard, Visa.
PRICES: [2015] per room B&B £125, D,B&B £195. Set dinner £40–£50.

SEE ALSO SHORTLIST

LURGASHALL West Sussex

THE BARN AT ROUNDHURST

NEW

Surrounded by 'beautiful' countryside, Moya and Richard Connell's 'delightful, friendly' B&B is on the family's 'neat and tidy' organic farm within the South Downs national park. 'We spotted an alpaca happily grazing among the sheep,' Guide inspectors said this year. The star of the site is a 'very impressive' renovated 17th-century threshing barn, 'an enormous, soaring space' with a lounge and an eating area (a four-course dinner is served here three nights a week). Up a 'beautiful winding staircase', visitors have access to an honesty bar, library, board games and DVDs. Around a 'secluded' flagstone courtyard, bedrooms are in converted stables; 'lush vegetation ensures that each has privacy'. 'Our rustic beamed room had a huge bed, plaid blankets, and space to sit. The lovely, spacious, modern bathroom had a powerful shower.' Breakfast is 'perfect': interesting fruit salads, a buffet with fresh juices, freshly baked bread, and jars of muesli and granola; cooked dishes using organic bacon, sausages and eggs from the farm. There are 'stunning walks with exquisite views' from the door; picnics can be provided.

Lower Roundhurst Farm
Jobson's Lane
Lurgashall
GU27 3BY

T: 01428 642535
E: bookings@thebarnatroundhurst.com
W: http://thebarnatroundhurst.com/

BEDROOMS: 6.
OPEN: all year.
FACILITIES: open-plan lounge/dining area, library/bar, free Wi-Fi, small garden on 250-acre farm.
BACKGROUND MUSIC: mixed in lounge.
LOCATION: 2 miles S of Haslemere, Surrey.
CHILDREN: all ages welcomed.
DOGS: not allowed.
CREDIT CARDS: all major cards.
PRICES: [2015] per room B&B £120–£200. Set menu £40.

BRITANNIA HOUSE

Two minutes from the water in this 'lively' seaside town, 'enthusiastic, amiable' host Tobias Feilke has created 'a warm and homely environment' in his B&B. It occupies two houses opposite each other: one a historic 19th-century building, the other more modern. There are 'quirky' decorations and 'good attention to detail' throughout; the house is 'spotless'. Guests enter the main building into a hallway decorated with 'an eclectic collection' of hats and a suit of armour. On the first floor, a 'bright and cheerful' sitting room, with large sofas and plenty of books and magazines, has wide views of the harbour and marina. In good weather, a small but 'lush' evergreen courtyard garden is a nice place to sit. The bedrooms are individually styled; a two-storey apartment has a living room and its own balcony. 'Our ground-floor room was lavishly decorated in neo-classical style, with brocade curtains and classical prints. The comfortable bed had good-quality linens, a plump duvet, lovely pillows.' A 'hearty' breakfast, with 'delicious' locally sourced bacon, is served at a 'convivial' communal table in the country-style kitchen.

Station Street
Lymington
SO41 3BA

T: 01590 672091
E: enquiries@britannia-house.com
W: www.britannia-house.com

BEDROOMS: 5. 2 on ground floor.
OPEN: all year except Christmas.
FACILITIES: lounge, kitchen/breakfast room, free Wi-Fi, courtyard garden, unsuitable for disabled.
BACKGROUND MUSIC: none.
LOCATION: 2 mins' walk from High Street/quayside, parking.
CHILDREN: not under 8.
DOGS: not allowed.
CREDIT CARDS: MasterCard, Visa.
PRICES: [2015] per room B&B from £75. 1-night bookings refused weekends.

LIME WOOD

In a 'dream location', 'smack bang in the middle of the New Forest', this 'relaxed', family-friendly country house hotel occupies a 'stunning' Regency manor house in extensive grounds adjoining forest and parkland. It is part of the small Lime Wood group owned by Jim Ratcliffe; Kenneth Speirs manages, with 'extremely friendly and professional' staff. 'We liked the lack of airs and graces,' said one guest. 'From the public spaces to the bedrooms, every little detail has been thought of.' Public rooms are filled with artwork, ceramics, and a mix of antique and modern furniture; the 'cosy, intimate' library full of 'fabulous' books is 'like a wealthy relative's den'. 'Gorgeous' bedrooms are spread out between the main house and several 'beautifully designed' buildings in the grounds; many have a private garden or balcony overlooking the forest. In the informal Hartnett Holder & Co. restaurant, chefs Angela Hartnett and Luke Holder cook seasonal menus with a strong Italian influence, perhaps braised veal shank, roast cipolline onions, bone marrow, Parmesan-crusted fennel. Breakfast in the Scullery is 'delightful'. (AL, BW, and others)

Beaulieu Road
Lyndhurst
SO43 7FZ

T: 02380 287177
F: 02380 287199
E: info@limewood.co.uk
W: www.limewoodhotel.co.uk

BEDROOMS: 32. 5 on ground floor, 2 suitable for disabled, 16 in pavilions and cottages in the grounds.
OPEN: all year.
FACILITIES: lifts, ramps, 2 bars, 3 lounges, 2 restaurants, private dining rooms, civil wedding licence, free Wi-Fi, spa (16-metre swimming pool), 14-acre gardens (outdoor hot pool).
BACKGROUND MUSIC: in some communal areas.
LOCATION: in New Forest, 12 miles SW of Southampton.
CHILDREN: all ages welcomed.
DOGS: allowed in outside bedrooms, not in the main house.
CREDIT CARDS: Amex, MasterCard, Visa.
PRICES: [2015] room from £315. Breakfast £13.50–£18.50, à la carte £50. 1-night bookings refused most weekends, bank holidays.

MARAZION Cornwall

Map 1:E1

MOUNT HAVEN HOTEL & RESTAURANT

'Welcoming and relaxed', Mike and Orange Trevillion's 'beautifully quiet' hotel has 'wonderful' views of St Michael's Mount. 'We really enjoyed our stay,' say visitors in 2015. 'There was no demand for pre-authorisation of a card on check-in; nice to be trusted for a change.' Reached by 'lots of steep stairs' (help is offered with luggage), most of the bedrooms have sea views; a room facing away from the water has a private patio garden with seating. 'Our comfortable, well-serviced deluxe room had loungers on the large terrace; an espresso machine, ground coffee for the cafetière, a variety of teas, decent biscuits, fresh milk in the fridge.' A lounge/bar opens on to a decked terrace for alfresco drinks and meals. In the restaurant, chef Nathan Williams's 'very good' modern dishes might include assiette of Cornish swine (sausage roll, crispy belly, maple-roasted loin), sage and onion croquette potato. Breakfast is praised: 'no self-service toasters'; 'particularly nice muesli, a decent compote'; 'an excellent full English, with well-sourced sausages and bacon – and the omelettes were even better'. (Kevin Seymour, Alice Sennett)

Turnpike Road
Marazion
TR17 0DQ

T: 01736 710249
E: reception@mounthaven.co.uk
W: www.mounthaven.co.uk

BEDROOMS: 18. Some on ground floor.
OPEN: all year except 20 Dec–10 Feb.
FACILITIES: lounge/bar, restaurant, free Wi-Fi in public areas, healing room (holistic treatments), sun terrace, ½-acre grounds (rock/sand beaches 100 yds), unsuitable for disabled.
BACKGROUND MUSIC: varied all day in bar and restaurant.
LOCATION: 4 miles E of Penzance, car park.
CHILDREN: all ages welcomed.
DOGS: allowed in garden bedrooms and bar.
CREDIT CARDS: MasterCard, Visa.
PRICES: per room B&B £120–£250, D,B&B £170–£300. À la carte £25.

SEE ALSO SHORTLIST

MARGATE Kent

Map 2:D5

SANDS HOTEL

On the seafront, yards from the Turner Contemporary, Nick Conington's 'smartly renovated' Victorian hotel has a 'grandstand outlook over one of the best beaches in the South-East'. Tina Kennedy is the manager. Staff are 'friendly and efficient', a guest said this year. All but two of the 'tastefully decorated' bedrooms overlook the sea or the lively Old Town; most sea-view rooms have their own balcony; guests can enjoy 'huge bay views' from the roof terrace. 'Our stylish town-view room had attractive artwork, very comfortable twin beds with high-quality linens; good lighting for reading. Some nocturnal noise from the high street, but our earplugs provided a good night's sleep.' The glass-fronted Bay restaurant, 'clearly the focal point of the hotel', serves modern European dishes; in good weather, alfresco meals may be taken on the 'spacious' balcony overlooking Margate Sands. 'Very good' breakfasts have fresh fruit, yogurts and French pastries; hot dishes are cooked to order. In the summer, Melt, the gelato bar downstairs, has milkshakes, sundaes and ice cream sodas. (Michael Gwinnell)

16 Marine Drive
Margate
CT9 1DH

T: 01843 228228
E: info@sandshotelmargate.co.uk
W: www.sandshotelmargate.co.uk

BEDROOMS: 20. 1 suitable for disabled.
OPEN: all year.
FACILITIES: lift, bar, restaurant, free Wi-Fi, civil wedding licence, roof terrace, ice cream parlour.
BACKGROUND MUSIC: varied, in public areas.
LOCATION: town centre.
CHILDREN: all ages welcomed (family rooms, children's menus).
DOGS: not allowed.
CREDIT CARDS: MasterCard, Visa.
PRICES: [2015] per room B&B £120–£200, D,B&B £180–£260. À la carte £30–£40.

SEE ALSO SHORTLIST

THE OLD RECTORY HOTEL

♀ César award in 2014

'An attractive house in a beautiful garden; excellent dinner and breakfast.' Praise comes in 2015 from a trusted correspondent for Huw Rees and Sam Prosser's small hotel in an 'idyllic backwater', a hamlet close to the Exmoor coast. Another comment: 'The most attractive aspect was the attention paid by the hosts; running this hotel is their passion.' Public areas are 'tasteful with well-chosen textiles', 'uncluttered and aesthetically furnished'. There are 'plenty of magazines in the conservatory, reference books in the lounge'. The dining room, where guests are served at a single sitting, is 'elegantly dressed with immaculate white cloths'. Huw Rees is the chef; his short menu might include smoked duck and asparagus salad, sesame dressing; fillet of Lundy turbot, Noilly Prat sauce. Vegetables are served separately. The bedrooms are in the main house and an adjacent coach house. They are furnished in traditional style: lighting is 'good' as is storage space. Breakfast has local apple juice, perhaps mushroom eggs Florentine. 'The host mended a suitcase and drew a helpful map for my journey home.' (Helge Rubinstein, and others)

Berry's Ground Lane
Martinhoe
EX31 4QT

T: 01598 763368
E: reception@oldrectoryhotel.co.uk
W: www.oldrectoryhotel.co.uk

BEDROOMS: 11. 2 on ground floor, 3 in coach house.
OPEN: Mar–Nov.
FACILITIES: 2 lounges, orangery, dining room, free Wi-Fi, 3-acre grounds.
BACKGROUND MUSIC: 'very quiet jazz' in dining room 'so it doesn't feel like a hushed morgue'.
LOCATION: 4 miles W of Lynton.
CHILDREN: not under 14.
DOGS: not allowed.
CREDIT CARDS: Amex, MasterCard, Visa.
PRICES: [2015] per room B&B £180–£225, D,B&B £220–£270.

SEE ALSO SHORTLIST

MASHAM North Yorkshire

Map 4:D4

SWINTON PARK

🏆 César award in 2011

The 19th-century addition of a tower, turrets and battlements to the ancestral seat of the Earl of Swinton created this mock-Gothic castle which is run in relaxed style by Mark and Felicity Cunliffe-Lister. They have furnished it with antiques and family portraits to recreate an 'authentic stately-home experience'. It might be 'elegant, even luxurious', say visitors but it is 'never stuffy'. Families are made 'to feel particularly welcome' (the Guide César award was for family hotel of the year): children will find a play room full of toys; kites and bikes in a boot room; countless other activities in the parkland. The smallest children are not forgotten: there are baby bathtime products and wipes; babysitting can be arranged. There are spa treatments for teenagers. The bedrooms and suites are on the first and second floors (a lift is available); many are large; they 'had everything we could ever need', is a recent comment. In the restaurant, Samuel's, chef Simon Crannage uses produce from the walled kitchen garden for his seasonal dishes, perhaps poached halibut, cauliflower, broccoli, chervil and verjus sauce.

25% DISCOUNT VOUCHERS

Masham
HG4 4JH

T: 01765 680900
F: 01765 680901
E: reservations@swintonpark.com
W: www.swintonpark.com

BEDROOMS: 31. 4 suitable for disabled.
OPEN: all year, restaurant closed midday Mon–Fri.
FACILITIES: lift, ramps, 3 lounges, library, bar, restaurant, free Wi-Fi, banqueting hall, spa, games rooms, civil wedding licence, 200-acre grounds (many activities).
BACKGROUND MUSIC: classical in evening in bar and dining room.
LOCATION: 1 mile SW of Masham, Yorkshire.
CHILDREN: all ages welcomed.
DOGS: allowed, not in public rooms, unattended in bedrooms.
CREDIT CARDS: Diners, MasterCard, Visa.
PRICES: [2015] per room B&B £195–£469, D,B&B £275–£535. Set dinner £55.

MAWGAN PORTH Cornwall

Map 1:D2

BEDRUTHAN HOTEL AND SPA

✤César award in 2012

'Everything was relaxing and comfortable,' says a visitor this year to this 'fantastic' family-friendly hotel on the north Cornish coast. Owned and managed by sisters Emma Stratton, Deborah Wakefield and Rebecca Whittington, it has 'magnificent views, superb food and lovely service; even the dog was greeted with a little parcel of biscuit bones'. Another comment (in 2015): 'They really do seem to have thought of everything.' Decorated in a Cornish-meets-Scandinavian style, public rooms are 'airy, spacious, with some great local art'; a new gallery has replaced the adult games room this year. 'Spotless' bedrooms are full of colour; many have sea views. In the bar, 'the Cornwall-inspired cocktails were amazing', as was the food served in the Herring restaurant. (Light meals are available in the Wild Café.) 'The children's activities are a godsend': swimming pools, playgrounds; kites and binoculars are available to borrow. Adult visitors might seek the adult-only spa or cinema club. 'Breakfasts are fantastic.' The Scarlet (see next entry) is a child-free sister hotel. (Sharon Stell, Diana Goodey)

Mawgan Porth
TR8 4BU

T: 01637 860860
F: 01637 860714
E: stay@bedruthan.com
W: www.bedruthan.com

BEDROOMS: 101. 1 suitable for disabled.
OPEN: all year except Christmas, Jan, open New Year.
FACILITIES: lift, 2 lounges, 2 bars, Herring restaurant, Wild Café, free Wi-Fi, poolside snack bar, ballroom, 4 children's clubs, spa (indoor swimming pool), civil wedding licence, 5-acre grounds (heated swimming pools, tennis, playing field).
BACKGROUND MUSIC: 'laid-back' in bar and Wild Café.
LOCATION: 4 miles NE of Newquay.
CHILDREN: all ages welcomed.
DOGS: welcomed, not in restaurants.
CREDIT CARDS: MasterCard, Visa.
PRICES: [2015] per room B&B single from £79, double from £139, D,B&B single from £95, double from £172. À la carte £30. 1-night bookings sometimes refused.

MAWGAN PORTH Cornwall

Map 1:D2

THE SCARLET

On a Cornish cliff-top, this 'fabulous' eco-friendly hotel is 'a perfect sanctuary', say visitors this year. Owned by sisters Emma Stratton, Deborah Wakefield and Rebecca Whittington, it has thrift-planted roofs, beach-view hot tubs dotting the cliff-face and a reed-filtered outdoor swimming pool. Throughout is a 'fresh, uncluttered, modern design', with artwork by local artists. Each of the 'well-decorated, spacious' bedrooms has an outside space; 'brilliant ambient lighting; no coffee/tea-making facilities but the staff will bring whatever you need'. Many of the sea-facing rooms have 'stunning uninterrupted views'. Chef Tom Hunter's menu is 'a highlight', with dishes like turbot, truffled celeriac, roasted baby gems, sauce vierge. The Anywhere Anytime menu provides lighter dishes. 'We had an excellent late lunch on our balcony (no room-service charge).' The healthy smorgasbord can be packed into a picnic for a coastal trek ('if you can bear leaving the hotel'). The Ayurvedic spa has a 'soothing, otherworldly' atmosphere. Breakfast (à la carte, 'very good') is served with a carafe of fruit juice. Its sister is Bedruthan Hotel and Spa (see previous entry). (Marcia Ballard, and others)

Tredragon Road
Mawgan Porth
TR8 4DQ

T: 01637 861800
F: 01637 861801
E: stay@scarlethotel.co.uk
W: www.scarlethotel.co.uk

BEDROOMS: 37. 2 suitable for disabled.
OPEN: all year except Jan.
FACILITIES: lift, lobby, bar, lounge, library, restaurant, free Wi-Fi, civil wedding licence, spa (indoor swimming pool, 4 by 13 metres, steam room, hammam, treatment room), natural outdoor swimming pool (40 sq metres), seaweed baths.
BACKGROUND MUSIC: all day in bar and restaurant.
LOCATION: 4 miles NE of Newquay.
CHILDREN: normally not under 16.
DOGS: welcomed in selected bedrooms, public areas except restaurant, bar and library.
CREDIT CARDS: MasterCard, Visa.
PRICES: [2015] per room B&B £210–£480, D,B&B £275–£545. Set dinner £43.50. 1-night bookings refused Fri/Sat.

BUDOCK VEAN

On a quiet bend in the Helford river, the Barlow family's traditional hotel is 'a super family-run place'. 'We very much enjoyed our stay: the staff, the ambience, the gardens and the facilities were excellent,' says a visitor this year. The hotel stands in extensive grounds with gardens, terraced ponds, waterfalls and its own nine-hole golf course. Inside, regular guests like the 'old-fashioned' atmosphere, 'reminiscent of the 1940s', in which visitors are encouraged to dress up for dinner. 'Well-appointed' bedrooms have bathrobes and slippers, a tea tray; the best rooms overlook the gardens and golf course. 'Signature' bedrooms have recently been refurbished. Lunch may be taken in the conservatory, cocktail bar and lounges; in the formal restaurant, chef Darren Kelly cooks 'very good' daily-changing four-course dinners. Typical dishes: pan-seared Falmouth Bay scallops, pancetta, chive butter; roast fillet of local pork, grain mustard mash, Bramley apple purée. There is much to see and do: the hotel's river boat cruises up and down the many creeks; bicycle hire can be arranged; local walking maps are available to borrow. (Alice Sennett, and others)

Helford Passage
Mawnan Smith
TR11 5LG

T: 01326 252100
F: 01326 250892
E: relax@budockvean.co.uk
W: www.budockvean.co.uk

BEDROOMS: 57. 4 self-catering cottages.
OPEN: all year except 3–22 Jan.
FACILITIES: lift, ramps, 3 lounges, conservatory, 2 bars, restaurant, snooker room, free Wi-Fi, civil wedding licence, 65-acre grounds (covered heated swimming pool, 15 by 8 metres), spa, 9-hole golf course, tennis.
BACKGROUND MUSIC: live piano or guitar music in evening in restaurant and cocktail bar.
LOCATION: 6 miles SW of Falmouth.
CHILDREN: no under-7s in dining room after 7 pm.
DOGS: allowed in some bedrooms, not in public rooms.
CREDIT CARDS: all major cards.
PRICES: [2015] per person B&B £73–£141, D,B&B £88–£156. Set dinner £41.

THE TALBOT INN

♀César award in 2015

'Friendly and informal', this former coaching inn has been renovated in 'simple, modern style' by the owners Charlie Luxton, Dan Brod and Matt Greenlees (the manager). The building is entered through an inner courtyard with tables and chairs; on one side is a 'lovely' sitting room with sofas, magazines. On the other is the bar where guests check in. It is linked by narrow corridors to a series of dining areas. One of the bedrooms is on the ground floor; the others are reached up a steep staircase (help is given with luggage). A room at the front had a window seat, a high ceiling and a walk-in wardrobe; there was sisal flooring, 'excellent reading lights on the side tables'. The chef, Pravin Nayar, serves a seasonal menu in the 'intimate' dining areas, mixing pub classics with dishes like Brixham sea bass, radishes, heritage tomatoes, poached egg, brown butter, horseradish. At weekends, food is grilled over a charcoal and wood fire in the coach house and served at long shared tables. The Beckford Arms, Tisbury (see entry), is under the same ownership.

Selwood Street
Mells
BA11 3PN

T: 01373 812254
E: info@talbotinn.com
W: www.talbotinn.com

BEDROOMS: 8. 1 on ground floor.
OPEN: all year except 25 Dec.
FACILITIES: bar, restaurant, snug, map room, sitting room, dining room, grill, free Wi-Fi, courtyard, garden.
BACKGROUND MUSIC: in public areas.
LOCATION: in village.
CHILDREN: all ages welcomed.
DOGS: welcomed, in 1 bedroom, dining areas.
CREDIT CARDS: MasterCard, Visa.
PRICES: [2015] per room B&B £95–£150. À la carte £29.

MILTON ABBOT Devon

Map 1:D3

♣ HOTEL ENDSLEIGH

César award: country house hotel of the year

Tall, ancient trees tower over this 'beautiful' estate of gardens and woodlands, streams and waterfalls, follies and grottos. On the banks of the River Tamar, the 19th-century hunting and fishing lodge is today an 'unpretentious and comfortable' family-friendly luxury hotel owned by Olga Polizzi. She has restored the building 'with charm and taste', said Guide inspectors, who found it 'a glorious place, run with a generous spirit'. Adam Cornish is the manager; the 'friendly but never over-attentive staff quickly know you by name'. There are many public spaces to relax in: a library 'full of real books', several outside loggias, and finely decorated sitting rooms (including one with hand-painted wallpaper). The grounds are scattered with loungers, croquet, table tennis – 'so much to do you never need leave the estate'. The bedrooms are 'charmingly done'; most have views of the gardens. Chef Robert Wright's modern menus are served in the panelled dining room; they might include fillet of brill, butter beans, wild garlic. Afternoon tea is a 'lavish' affair; breakfast has an 'excellent' buffet, 'lovely, chunky' brown toast, leaf tea. 'Almost magical.'

25% DISCOUNT VOUCHERS

Milton Abbot
PL19 0PQ

T: 01822 870000
F: 01822 870578
E: mail@hotelendsleigh.com
W: www.hotelendsleigh.com

BEDROOMS: 17. 1 on ground floor, also 1 in lodge (1 mile from main house).
OPEN: all year.
FACILITIES: drawing room, library, card room, bar, 2 dining rooms, free Wi-Fi, civil wedding licence, terraces, 108-acre estate (fishing, ghillie available).
BACKGROUND MUSIC: none.
LOCATION: 7 miles NW of Tavistock, train/plane Plymouth or Exeter.
CHILDREN: all ages welcomed (children's menu, baby-listening, games).
DOGS: welcomed, not in restaurant, or 'near afternoon tea table'.
CREDIT CARDS: Amex, MasterCard, Visa.
PRICES: [2015] per room B&B from £190, D,B&B from £250. Set dinner £44. 1-night bookings refused weekends.

MORETON-IN-MARSH Gloucestershire

Map 3:D6

THE REDESDALE ARMS

Returning visitors were 'delighted' this year by this old coaching inn, on the main street of a medieval market town. Robert Smith is the 'hands-on' owner/manager, who greets his guests with a 'warm welcome'; the staff provide 'terrific' service. Dating back to 1650, the mellow Cotswold stone building has an oak-beamed interior; there are old passages in the bars and restaurant, and an open fire in the residents' lounge. James Hitchman is the new chef, cooking 'excellent' modern British dishes in the restaurant, perhaps pan-fried Brixham sea bass fillet, wild mushroom risotto, truffle oil. Bedrooms in the main house are decorated ('appropriately') in traditional country style; those in the converted stable block, a short walk across the courtyard, are more modern. 'Ours was very comfortable, with close attention to detail throughout, especially the lighting.' The rooms vary in size: some courtyard rooms have a private garden, lounge or balcony; junior suites with a sofa bed can accommodate a family. Breakfast has hot and cold buffets 'to suit every taste'; hot toast is brought to the table. 'An ideal situation for exploring the Cotswolds.'(John Frood, Dr Malcolm Godfrey)

High Street
Moreton-in-Marsh
GL56 0AW

T: 01608 650308
F: 01608 654055
E: info@redesdalearms.com
W: www.redesdalearms.com

BEDROOMS: 32. 25 in annexe across courtyard, 1 suitable for disabled.
OPEN: all year.
FACILITIES: 3 lounge bars, 2 restaurants, heated open dining area, free Wi-Fi.
BACKGROUND MUSIC: in all public areas.
LOCATION: town centre.
CHILDREN: all ages welcomed.
DOGS: not allowed.
CREDIT CARDS: MasterCard, Visa.
PRICES: [2015] per room B&B from £100, D,B&B from £140. À la carte £35. 1-night bookings refused Sat Apr–Oct.

SEE ALSO SHORTLIST

ST MARY'S INN   **NEW**

In countryside near Morpeth, the administration building of a disused Victorian hospital has been remodelled into a 'pub and B&B' by Peter Candler, who also runs nearby Jesmond Dene House, Newcastle upon Tyne (see entry). 'The clever renovation has created a new type of place to stay and eat,' say Guide inspectors who 'came in anticipation and were not disappointed'. A modern glass porch and bar 'belie a traditional pub interior; mismatched chairs and tables in booths and separate rooms, some with a wood-burning stove'. A double-height bedroom 'was well thought out and designed, with excellent lighting. The huge bed had a striking wrought iron frame; plenty of shelf space in the large, tiled bathroom.' In the evening, the dining areas were busy. Chef Michael Penaluna serves a 'mix of classic pub grub and local specialities with a modern twist. We enjoyed a good old-fashioned prawn cocktail, generously served; a huge plateful of fish and chips with mushy peas and tartar sauce; roast onion tart with Mordon Blue cheese and salad. The prices were reasonable for the quality; service was swift and knowledgeable.'

St Mary's Lane
St Mary's Park
Morpeth
NE61 6BL

T: 01670 293293
E: hello@stmarysinn.co.uk
W: www.stmarysinn.co.uk

BEDROOMS: 11. 1 suitable for disabled.
OPEN: all year.
FACILITIES: bar, dining room, private dining room, free Wi-Fi.
BACKGROUND MUSIC: 'easy listening' in bar.
LOCATION: 2¾ miles W of Stannington.
CHILDREN: all ages welcomed.
DOGS: welcomed, 1 dog-friendly room, bar.
CREDIT CARDS: all major cards.
PRICES: [2015] per person B&B £80. Set dinner £25.

MORSTON Norfolk

Map 2:A5

MORSTON HALL

♔César award in 2010

'We are forever grateful that we found this great hotel in the Guide,' say trusted correspondents returning to Tracy and Galton Blackiston's restaurant-with-rooms. In 1992, Galton Blackiston was persuaded by Delia Smith to open a hotel in his native Norfolk; by 1999 he had a Michelin star. The former 17th-century farmhouse stands in 'fabulous' gardens in a coastal Norfolk village. The bedrooms are in the main house and a pavilion in the grounds. A house room had 'a comfortable bed, a tea-maker and a Nespresso machine'. Pavilion rooms have underfloor heating, an outdoor terrace; a large bath and a walk-in shower. At 7.30 pm, guests assemble for drinks and canapés before a daily-changing, seven-course dinner in the dining room or conservatory. There is no choice (dietary requirements catered for). 'Portions are always small enough that we could enjoy it all without feeling full.' Typical dishes: quail Scotch egg; cock-a-leekie; showcase of rabbit; long-shore cod, girolles; confit loin of lamb. Breakfast is 'simply delicious'. Packed lunches are available for those wishing to explore the luminous landscape of salt marsh and dunes.

Morston
NR25 7AA

T: 01263 741041
F: 01263 740419
E: reception@morstonhall.com
W: www.morstonhall.com

BEDROOMS: 13. 6 in garden pavilion on ground floor.
OPEN: all year except Christmas, Jan, restaurant closed midday except Sun.
FACILITIES: hall, lounge, orangery, conservatory, restaurant, free Wi-Fi, 2-acre garden (pond, croquet).
BACKGROUND MUSIC: none.
LOCATION: 2 miles W of Blakeney.
CHILDREN: all ages welcomed.
DOGS: Welcomed in bedrooms (£5 per night), not in rooms where food is served.
CREDIT CARDS: Amex, MasterCard, Visa.
PRICES: [2015] per person D,B&B £155–£200. Set dinner £66, Sunday lunch £37. 1-night bookings sometimes refused Sat.

MOUSEHOLE Cornwall

Map 1: E1

THE OLD COASTGUARD

Brothers Charles and Edmund Inkin have brought to this Victorian hotel the winning 'keep it simple' philosophy that has won them praise at Felin Fach and Zennor (see entries). Visitors this year received a 'very warm welcome'; they enjoyed the 'excellent' and 'friendly' service, and the relaxed ethos throughout. Renovation continues: four bathrooms have been upgraded this year. Rooms vary in size; several have a balcony. All have 'excellent linen', cafetière coffee, leaf tea, a retro radio, fresh flowers, good books. St Clements was 'comfortable, and had great views of both sea and harbour', but kitchen smells, although 'more appetising than overpowering', were a drawback. There are sofas and striped armchairs in a sun lounge with a glass wall that runs the length of the ground floor. Matt Smith has returned as chef: his bistro-style food is served at wooden tables in the bar and dining area: fish stew, mussels, fennel, aïoli; beef rump, butter-pressed potato, charred onion, greens. At breakfast there is Cornish apple juice, home-made soda bread to toast, smoked salmon with scrambled eggs. (Michael Eldridge, SA Mathieson)

The Parade
Mousehole
TR19 6PR

T: 01736 731222
E: bookings@oldcoastguardhotel.co.uk
W: www.oldcoastguardhotel.co.uk

BEDROOMS: 14.
OPEN: all year except 24/25 Dec, 4 days in Jan.
FACILITIES: bar, sun terrace, dining room, free Wi-Fi, enclosed garden with path to beach.
BACKGROUND MUSIC: Radio 4 at breakfast, selected music during meals.
LOCATION: edge of village, 3 miles S of Newlyn.
CHILDREN: all ages welcomed, under-5s stay free.
DOGS: welcomed (treats, towels, dog bowls), not allowed in dining room.
CREDIT CARDS: MasterCard, Visa.
PRICES: [2015] per room B&B £130–£220, D,B&B £180–£270. À la carte £43. 1-night bookings sometimes refused Sat.

MULLION COVE Cornwall

Map 1:E2

MULLION COVE HOTEL

Romantic Robert Baden Powell, the Boy Scouts movement founder, brought his bride for a week's honeymoon in 1912 to this hotel on the cliff-top overlooking a small fishing harbour. Be prepared for an 'uncompromising white block' exterior, built by the Great Western Railway and opened in 1898, and within, 'thoughtful, smiling' staff and 'comfortable furniture throughout'. There has been much renovation by the owners, the Grose family. Many of the bedrooms have a sea view. A round tower room has 'fabulous views from three-aspect bay windows'. Chef Fiona Were cooks a daily-changing menu of 'stunning' dishes and 'isn't afraid to combine textures and tastes'. The menu might include salt and pepper squid with citrus miso, coriander, fennel, Ugli salad; roasted sea trout, saffron potatoes, rainbow chard, mussel chowder. Food is available all day in the bar. Unusual breakfast options include scrambled tofu; grilled hogs pudding (pork with spices). A late cancellation of a suite due to illness was handled with grace: 'The hotel won in me now a devoted and loyal guest who will go there at the earliest opportunity.'

25% DISCOUNT VOUCHERS

Cliff Road
Mullion Cove
TR12 7EP

T: 01326 240328
F: 01326 240998
E: enquiries@mullion-cove.co.uk
W: www.mullion-cove.co.uk

BEDROOMS: 30. Some on ground floor.
OPEN: all year.
FACILITIES: lift, 3 lounges, bar, restaurant, free Wi-Fi, 3-acre garden, heated outdoor swimming pool (11 by 5.5 metres), unsuitable for disabled.
BACKGROUND MUSIC: none.
LOCATION: on edge of village.
CHILDREN: all ages welcomed.
DOGS: allowed in some bedrooms, 1 lounge.
CREDIT CARDS: Amex, MasterCard, Visa.
PRICES: [2015] per room B&B £95–£335, D,B&B £151–£391. Set dinner £35, à la carte £28.

EES WYKE COUNTRY HOUSE

'It is nearly as perfect a little place as I have ever lived in,' wrote Beatrix Potter, who arrived at the village of Near Sawrey in 1896 with pony and phaeton. She spent three summers at this elegant Georgian house. Today, run as a guest house by Richard and Margaret Lee, it remains 'a lovely house in a beautiful setting with all the tranquillity one could wish for'. The Lees, 'charming hosts who do all they can to make their guests welcome', keep the house 'immaculate', say visitors. 'Our bedroom was superbly decorated with a modern, well-designed bathroom and fresh bedlinen and soft, fluffy towels.' This year, five rooms have been refurbished. In the evening, Richard Lee cooks a five-course daily-changing menu based on local, seasonal produce, served in a dining room with lovely views. Duck confit, perhaps; noisettes of lamb, wine jus; pear poached in wine and cassis with Cointreau crème Chantilly. Breakfast is 'a treat that can't be missed', with fresh-baked bread and croissants, freshly squeezed juices, local sausages, Loch Fyne kipper or finnan haddock. (Philip and Viv Waltham)

Near Sawrey
LA22 0JZ

T: 015394 36393
E: mail@eeswyke.co.uk
W: www.eeswyke.co.uk

BEDROOMS: 8. 1 on ground floor.
OPEN: all year, except Christmas.
FACILITIES: 2 lounges, restaurant, free Wi-Fi, veranda, 1-acre garden, unsuitable for disabled.
BACKGROUND MUSIC: none.
LOCATION: edge of village 2½ miles SE of Hawkshead on B5285.
CHILDREN: not under 12.
DOGS: not allowed.
CREDIT CARDS: MasterCard, Visa.
PRICES: per room B&B £90–£155, D,B&B £177–£242. Set dinner £43.50. 1-night bookings sometimes refused.

NETHER WESTCOTE Oxfordshire

Map 3:D6

THE FEATHERED NEST

❦César award in 2013

It is five years since Tony and Amanda Timmer transformed this 300-year-old malthouse in a Cotswold village into a smart pub and restaurant. They are committed to sustainability and to supporting their rural community: half the staff are local, and regular village get-togethers are held. There are flagstone floors and a log fire in the bar, where cask ales are stocked. 'Light floods' into the dining room which has French doors opening on to a terrace and the garden. There is a pylon-free view of the Evenlode valley. The chef, Kuba Winkowski, looks to the kitchen garden and local farms for ingredients for his sophisticated modern menus. Typical dishes: spring white truffle tagliatelle with parmesan; grilled Ibérico feather loin, chunky chips, chorizo, garlic mushroom. Everything is 'peaceful' at night in the bedrooms which have a contemporary decor. They are well equipped: a Nespresso coffee machine, fresh flowers, fruit, chocolates; books and current magazines; free-range hangers in the wardrobe; extra directional reading lamp. Breakfast has chunky toast, leaf tea and home-made compotes and preserves; 'tasty' cooked dishes.

Chipping Norton
Nether Westcote
OX7 6SD

T: 01993 833030
F: 01993 833031
E: info@thefeatherednestinn.co.uk
W: www.thefeatherednestinn.co.uk

BEDROOMS: 4.
OPEN: all year except 25 Dec, restaurant closed Mon except bank holidays.
FACILITIES: bar, dining room, garden room, free Wi-Fi, civil wedding licence, unsuitable for disabled.
BACKGROUND MUSIC: jazz in bar and restaurant.
LOCATION: in village 5 miles S of Stow-on-the-Wold.
CHILDREN: not under 12 (if in own room).
DOGS: allowed in bar, not in bedrooms.
CREDIT CARDS: Amex, MasterCard, Visa.
PRICES: [2015] per room B&B single £150–£200, double £180–£230. À la carte £50. 1-night bookings refused weekends.

HOTEL TERRAVINA

♀César award in 2009

'Welcoming hosts' Gérard and Nina Basset brought a wealth of experience with them when they transformed this red brick Victorian villa on the edge of the New Forest into a stylish, modern hotel. Co-founder of the Hotel du Vin chain and a Master of Wine, he has been voted the World's Best Sommelier; she was a hotel inspector at the age of 21; they met working at Chewton Glen, New Milton (see next entry). This year, they have promoted Charlotte Barrington to general manager. In the 'attractively furnished', air-conditioned bedrooms there are capsule coffee machines, chilled milk, Egyptian cotton sheets; seven rooms have a patio or roof terrace. Bathrooms have a deluge shower. In the open kitchen of the Californian-inspired restaurant, chef Gavin Barnes cooks dishes like roast and braised New Forest venison, garlic kale, pommes Anna, chestnuts. The wine is, of course, central to the experience. A recent comment: 'Our stay was enhanced by the delicate flavours of the food, complemented by the wine from an extensive selection.' There is a private dining room for wine events and wine dinners.

174 Woodlands Road
Netley Marsh
SO40 7GL

T: 02380 293784
F: 02380 293627
E: info@hotelterravina.co.uk
W: www.hotelterravina.co.uk

BEDROOMS: 11. 3 on ground floor, 1 suitable for disabled.
OPEN: all year.
FACILITIES: ramp, lounge, bar, restaurant, private dining room, free Wi-Fi, civil wedding licence, 1½-acre grounds (heated outdoor swimming pool).
BACKGROUND MUSIC: none.
LOCATION: in village, NW of Southampton, 2 miles W of Totton.
CHILDREN: all ages welcomed.
DOGS: not allowed.
CREDIT CARDS: Amex, MasterCard, Visa.
PRICES: [2015] per room B&B £165–£265. À la carte £45, tasting menus £65. 2-night bookings preferred at weekends

NEW MILTON Hampshire

Map 2:E2

CHEWTON GLEN

'Faultless' service is reported by a visitor this year to this luxury country house hotel (Relais & Châteaux) on the edge of the New Forest. It is privately owned; Andrew Stembridge is managing director. Families are warmly welcomed: children have a welcome activity pack, mini-robes and slippers, access to a cupboard full of games; there's a kids' club and allocated times for swimming in the pool. All ages will want to climb the gangplank to the tree-house suites in the woods, which have a wood-burning stove and a whirlpool tub on the wrap-around terrace. Bedrooms in the main house have a mix of antiques and modern furnishings. In the dining room, chef Luke Matthews serves an 'eclectic' menu of dishes like roast pumpkin and sage risotto; line-caught Cornish sea bass, cauliflower, grapes and Parmesan velouté. For breakfast, guests in the tree-house suites are given a hamper; they can walk to the main house for a cooked dish. An extensive range of treatments is offered in the award-winning spa. Christchurch's shingle beach is a short walk away. (Chris Kilroy, and others)

Christchurch Road
New Milton
BH25 6QS

T: 01425 275341
F: 01425 272310
E: reservations@chewtonglen.com
W: www.chewtonglen.com

BEDROOMS: 70. 14 on ground floor, 12 tree-house suites in grounds, 1 suitable for disabled.
OPEN: all year.
FACILITIES: 3 lounges, bar, restaurant, function rooms, free Wi-Fi, civil wedding licence, spa, indoor 17-metre swimming pool, 130-acre grounds, outdoor 15-metre heated swimming pool, tennis centre, par-3 golf course.
BACKGROUND MUSIC: 'subtle' in public areas.
LOCATION: on S edge of New Forest.
CHILDREN: all ages welcomed.
DOGS: allowed in tree-house suites only, not in public rooms.
CREDIT CARDS: Amex, MasterCard, Visa.
PRICES: [to Mar 2016] per room £325–£1,595. Breakfast £26, à la carte £70. 1-night bookings refused weekends.

NEW ROMNEY Kent

Map 2:E5

ROMNEY BAY HOUSE

♀César award in 2012

'More like a home than a hotel', Clinton and
Lisa Lovell's 1920s house has a 'stunning
position' between a golf course and the sea on
the Kent coast. It was designed by Sir Clough
Williams-Ellis, creator of Portmeirion in
north Wales (see entry), for American actress
Hedda Hopper. 'Everything was perfect,' says a
visitor this year, who enjoyed a 'superb' dinner.
'Welcoming hosts', the Lovells have a 'sure sense
of detail'. The drawing room has pastel colours,
shelves with china cups, stripped pine and floral
sofas, a log fire and an honesty bar. In the 'light,
bright' upstairs lounge, you can spot France on a
clear day with the help of the telescope provided.
The 'thoughtful touches' in the bedrooms
(bathrobes, mineral water, binoculars and
sewing kit) are appreciated. On four evenings
a week, the host cooks a four-course dinner (no
choice but ingredients are discussed in advance).
Served in a conservatory dining room, it might
include 'delicious' smoked fish, 'perfectly
cooked' duck breast. Breakfast, 'freshly prepared
and delightfully served', has 'excellent home-
made compotes, wonderful bacon'. (Michael
Blanchard, and others)

25% DISCOUNT VOUCHERS

Coast Road
Littlestone
New Romney
TN28 8QY

T: 01797 364747
E: romneybayhouse@aol.co.uk
W: www.romneybayhousehotel.
co.uk

BEDROOMS: 10.
OPEN: all year except 2 weeks
Christmas, open New Year, dining
room closed midday, Sun/Mon/
Thurs evenings.
FACILITIES: 2 lounges, bar,
conservatory, dining room, free
Wi-Fi, small function facilities,
1-acre garden, unsuitable for
disabled.
BACKGROUND MUSIC: none.
LOCATION: 1½ miles from New
Romney.
CHILDREN: not under 14.
DOGS: not allowed.
CREDIT CARDS: Amex, MasterCard,
Visa.
PRICES: [2015] per room B&B
£95–£160. Set dinner £45. 1-night
advance bookings refused weekends.

NEWBIGGIN-ON-LUNE Cumbria

Map 4:C3

BROWNBER HALL

Owners Hilary and Andrew Woodward run their peaceful B&B in this 19th-century country house. Standing in extensive mature gardens, it has views across open farmland to the Howgill Fells and the North Pennines beyond. The Woodwards offer a warm welcome, said a visitor arriving 'on a wet and stormy winter evening'. 'Hilary greeted us, offered assistance with our luggage and showed us to a spacious double room facing open fields. A wood-burning stove in the lounge and efficient central heating kept us warm.' Bedrooms, on the first floor, vary in size; some may accommodate a family. Many have views of the countryside and hills. Dinner is not provided, but there is an honesty bar and 'a wide selection' of local recommendations in the lounge; previous guests found The Black Swan, Ravenstonedale (see entry), 'a good choice for an evening meal'. Breakfast has 'ample choice': 'unpackaged butter and marmalade, good toast'; local ingredients in the hot dishes. Walkers are welcomed: the B&B is on the Coast to Coast and Dales High Way long-distance walking routes; free walking guides and maps are available. (NP, and others)

Brownber Hall
Newbiggin-on-Lune
CA17 4NX

T: 015396 23208
F: 0872 1155373
E: enquiries@brownberhall.co.uk
W: www.brownberhall.co.uk

BEDROOMS: 10. 2 partial en suite, with a separate bathroom.
OPEN: Apr–Sept.
FACILITIES: lounge (honesty bar), dining room, free Wi-Fi, terrace, garden, unsuitable for disabled.
BACKGROUND MUSIC: soft folk/ classical in public areas.
LOCATION: 5 miles SW of Kirkby Stephen.
CHILDREN: not under 12.
DOGS: welcomed (numbers are limited).
CREDIT CARDS: MasterCard, Visa.
PRICES: [2015] per room B&B single £35–£55, double £70–£90. 1-night bookings refused bank holiday weekends.

NEWCASTLE UPON TYNE Tyne and Wear Map 4:B4

JESMOND DENE HOUSE

♔César award in 2013

'A country house almost in the city', Peter Candler's Arts and Crafts mansion is at the head of a wooded valley close to the centre. A visitor in 2015 found it 'unexpectedly delightful and surprisingly peaceful, given its proximity to the city'. Historic features are blended with contemporary flourishes in the Grade II listed building: wood-panelling and stained-glass windows stand alongside contemporary artwork, some on loan from local universities. The bedrooms are decorated in subtle shades, with bursts of colour. They are well equipped and generously supplied (fruit and mineral water, bathrobes and slippers, magazines). 'My room was beautifully appointed and spacious; the bathroom was huge.' Staff are 'very helpful', readily providing maps for local walks. Chef Michael Penaluna serves 'imaginative' dishes, perhaps roast hake, clam and mussel broth, curly kale.' 'Breakfast is extraordinarily varied, encompassing everything from full English to a continental cheese and meat selection, pastries and a whole honeycomb. I wouldn't think of staying anywhere else.' (Sara Hollowell, and others)

Jesmond Dene Road
Newcastle upon Tyne
NE2 2EY

T: 0191 212 3000
F: 0191 212 3001
E: info@jesmonddenehouse.co.uk
W: www.jesmonddenehouse.co.uk

BEDROOMS: 40. 8 in adjacent annexe, 2 suitable for disabled.
OPEN: all year.
FACILITIES: lift, 2 lounges, cocktail bar, restaurant, conference/function facilities, free Wi-Fi, civil wedding licence, 2-acre garden.
BACKGROUND MUSIC: 'easy listening' in public areas at mealtimes.
LOCATION: 2 miles from city centre.
CHILDREN: all ages welcomed.
DOGS: not allowed.
CREDIT CARDS: Amex, MasterCard, Visa.
PRICES: [2015] per room B&B from £140, D,B&B from £200. À la carte £45, tasting menu £75.

NEWLANDS Cumbria

Map 4: inset C2

SWINSIDE LODGE

At the foot of Cat Bells, Mike and Kath Bilton's small country hotel, a 'friendly' Georgian house, is minutes from Derwentwater. Pheasants, ducks and red squirrels wander on the lawns. Inside, the two sitting rooms are filled with fresh flowers, books and local maps. Bedrooms vary in size and decoration (some are small); all have views of Lake District peaks, and 'nice touches' including 'local guides, a sewing kit, tea/coffee tray with home-made biscuits, mineral water'. Beds are turned down in the evening. Long-serving chef Clive Imber's 'tasty, generous and colourful' four-course, daily-changing menus are served at 7.30 pm in the candlelit dining room. Typical dishes might include Flookburgh crab salad, apple, horseradish; roast Cumbrian lamb, stuffed courgettes, parsnips, apricots. The 'excellent' breakfasts have local ham with poached eggs. 'Welcoming' hosts with 'the personal touch', the Biltons are happy to provide advice on the best walks in the area; packed lunches, with sandwiches and home-made energy bars, are available to order. (Gareth and Ros Gunning, and others)

25% DISCOUNT VOUCHERS

Grange Road
Newlands, nr Keswick
CA12 5UE

T: 017687 72948
F: 017687 73312
E: info@swinsidelodge-hotel.co.uk
W: www.swinsidelodge-hotel.co.uk

BEDROOMS: 7.
OPEN: all year except Dec, Jan.
FACILITIES: 2 lounges, dining room, free Wi-Fi, 1-acre garden, unsuitable for disabled.
BACKGROUND MUSIC: radio/CDs in reception.
LOCATION: 2 miles SW of Keswick.
CHILDREN: not under 12.
DOGS: allowed in some bedrooms (£10), not in public rooms.
CREDIT CARDS: MasterCard, Visa.
PRICES: [2015] per person D,B&B £96–£139. Set menu £45.

THE PACKHORSE INN **NEW**

Beside a medieval packhorse bridge in a village near Newmarket, this flint-and-brick inn has been 'revitalised' by Philip Turner's small Chestnut Inns group. It is run by the chef, Chris Lee, and his wife, Hayley. 'The public areas are smart and the bedrooms have an appealing look,' said a Guide inspector in 2015. 'Check-in was friendly and efficient; no paperwork required.' Four 'characterful' bedrooms are in the main house: 'Our room was decorated in warm colours, with lime wood French-style furniture, a good king-size bed, brass bedside lamps, a mirror in a huge frame. The bathroom had a double-ended bath and a separate shower; fresh milk and home-made biscuits were provided with the tea tray.' Four more compact rooms, equipped for disabled visitors, are in a renovated coach house. A double-aspect fireplace stands between the bar and the restaurant. 'The food was exciting, different; all the dishes had surprising elements; the bread was home made; a dark chocolate crème brûlée with orange jelly was an intense taste experience.' A staff member was helpful providing information for local walks.

Bridge Street
Moulton
Newmarket
CB8 8SP

T: 01638 751818
E: info@thepackhorseinn.com
W: www.thepackhorseinn.com

BEDROOMS: 8. 4 on ground floor in coach house suitable for disabled.
OPEN: all year.
FACILITIES: bar/restaurant, function room, free Wi-Fi, courtyard.
BACKGROUND MUSIC: 'low' in public rooms.
LOCATION: opposite village green.
CHILDREN: all ages welcomed.
DOGS: welcomed in courtyard rooms (£10 a night).
CREDIT CARDS: MasterCard, Visa.
PRICES: (2015) per room B&B £85–£175, D,B&B from £160. À la carte £34.

THE ROCK INN NEW

In a hamlet below Haytor Rocks, just inside Dartmoor national park, this 18th-century country inn has been owned (and 'cherished') by the Graves family for more than 30 years. It earns an upgrade to a full entry after a visit in 2015 by a Guide inspector: 'The family clearly know what people want, and give it to them; the staff also know what they are doing. Everything worked in our cosy small room, which was painted a pretty pale yellow; during dinner the curtains were drawn and the room was tidied. Nice pictures everywhere; exposed beams painted black; good views across the valley.' There are books, board games and jigsaw puzzles ('for rainy days') in the 'lovely' public rooms. Dinner, served in four areas, is popular locally. 'Delicious scallops with black pudding, cauliflower purée; roast hake with spring vegetable risotto; a side dish of perfectly cooked vegetables. Lots of wines by the glass.' There is no buffet at breakfast apart from help-yourself jugs of juice. 'Orders were taken quickly: great poached eggs, a wonderful kipper.' Walkers are 'well catered for with maps and guidebooks'.

Haytor Vale
Newton Abbot
TQ13 9XP

T: 01364 661305
F: 01364 661242
E: info@rock-inn.co.uk
W: www.rock-inn.co.uk

BEDROOMS: 9.
OPEN: all year except 25/26 Dec.
FACILITIES: bar, 4 dining rooms, free Wi-Fi, ¼-acre garden, unsuitable for disabled.
BACKGROUND MUSIC: none.
LOCATION: 3 miles W of Bovey Tracey.
CHILDREN: all ages welcomed.
DOGS: welcomed in some bedrooms, bar, 1 dining room.
CREDIT CARDS: Diners, MasterCard, Visa.
PRICES: [2015] per room B&B £95–£160, D,B&B £155–£220. Set dinner £19.95–£24.95, à la carte £30. 1-night bookings sometimes refused.

NEWTON AYCLIFFE Co. Durham

Map 4:C4

THE COUNTY

'Experienced hoteliers', Colette Farrell and Stuart Dale are the 'hands-on' owners of this restaurant-with-rooms, a former pub opposite the green of a village just off the A1(M). 'It is a wonderful place, well kept and bustling,' said a returning visitor. The bedrooms are in the adjacent building which has a small lounge for residents ('useful if the pub is busy and you don't want to sit in your room') and a patio. Rooms have 'good lighting', 'plentiful storage with lots of hangers', tea- and coffee-making facilities. A large double room has two leather armchairs; a walk-through dressing area; a good-sized bathroom; 'lovely views across the green'. Local ales are served in the bar, which is popular with villagers. Stuart Dale, the chef, produces 'exceptional' meals, which are served by a 'well-trained and friendly team' in the open-plan restaurant. His menu might include Yorkshire smoked chicken Caesar salad; Hartlepool smoked haddock, poached hen's egg, grain mustard mash, Chardonnay cream sauce. A 'proper, freshly cooked' breakfast has 'excellent' bacon, 'decent granary bloomer bread'. 'A really comfortable place to stay; a delight to visit.' (LW)

13 The Green
Aycliffe Village
DL5 6LX

T: 01325 312273
E: info@thecountyaycliffevillage.
com
W: www.thecountyaycliffevillage.
com

BEDROOMS: 7 in annexe.
OPEN: all year except 25/26 Dec.
FACILITIES: bar, restaurant, free
Wi-Fi, unsuitable for disabled.
BACKGROUND MUSIC: 'easy listening'
in public areas.
LOCATION: 1 mile from junction 59
on A1(M).
CHILDREN: all ages welcomed.
DOGS: not allowed.
CREDIT CARDS: Amex, MasterCard,
Visa.
PRICES: [2015] per room B&B single
£49, double £70–£120. À la carte £25.

NORTH WALSHAM Norfolk

Map 2:A6

BEECHWOOD HOTEL

Near the north Norfolk coast, Lindsay Spalding and Don Birch's small hotel, a creeper-clad Georgian house, is 'more than just good', says a visitor this year. Another comment: 'A perfect welcome: we were helped with our bags as soon as we got out of our car; we were given complimentary tea and scones which we took in the evening sunshine in the leafy garden.' The bedrooms are in the main house and a newer wing: 'Ours was clean, beautifully furnished and well maintained: a freestanding bath and a powerful shower in the large bathroom.' In the restaurant, chef Steven Norgate's cooking is given 'top marks': he follows a fair-trade philosophy for his ten-mile dinner (produce comes from as close to the hotel as possible). 'I enjoyed a delicious pre-starter of pea and broccoli velouté; crab, asparagus and poached egg; a duo of monkfish and hake, samphire and sautée potatoes; we had coffee with chocolates and brandy snaps in the bar.' The wine list is 'well priced'. Breakfast has kippers from Cley smokehouse; sausages from a Swafield butcher. (Jack Hanmer, Carol Jackson)

25% DISCOUNT VOUCHERS

20 Cromer Road
North Walsham
NR28 0HD

T: 01692 403231
F: 01692 407284
E: info@beechwood-hotel.co.uk
W: www.beechwood-hotel.co.uk

BEDROOMS: 17. Some on ground floor, 1 suitable for disabled.
OPEN: all year, except Christmas, restaurant closed midday Mon–Sat.
FACILITIES: 2 lounges, bar, restaurant, free Wi-Fi, 1-acre garden (croquet).
BACKGROUND MUSIC: none.
LOCATION: near town centre.
CHILDREN: not under 10.
DOGS: welcomed (3 'dog' bedrooms).
CREDIT CARDS: MasterCard, Visa.
PRICES: [2015] per room B&B single £90, double £100–£175. Set dinner £40. 1-night bookings sometimes refused Sat.

THE WHEATSHEAF

The 'youthful buzz' generated by a 'cool staff who seem to enjoy themselves' is liked at this modern conversion of a former coaching inn in a Cotswold market town. Owned by restaurateurs Sam and Georgie Pearman, it is managed by Tom Hughes. There are flagstone floors in the bar, which is favoured by locals; polished wooden floors in the two dining areas which have well-spaced mismatched tables and chairs. A series of portraits on canvas (of Wills board members, bought at auction) decorate the walls. The chef, Ethan Rodgers, cooks simple rustic dishes like devilled kidneys; saffron-baked cod with clams. Bedrooms come in three sizes: good, very good, and excellent. A 'very good' room had a freestanding bath and washbasin in the room ('a clever way of keeping the original proportions'); a dramatic canvas of a gunslinger on the wall. 'Nice complimentary snacks' are provided as is a 'have you forgotten?' pack with a toothbrush and paste, other bathroom extras. Breakfast has freshly squeezed orange juice, local apple juice; 'decent' cereals; 'proper' toast, home-made preserves. Cooked dishes cost extra. (DS, and others)

West End
Northleach
GL54 3EZ

T: 01451 860244
E: reservations@
  cotswoldswheatsheaf.com
W: www.cotswoldswheatsheaf.com

BEDROOMS: 14. 3 on ground floor, 2 in annexe.
OPEN: all year.
FACILITIES: sitting room, 2 bars, dining room, 2 private dining rooms, free Wi-Fi, garden.
BACKGROUND MUSIC: varied in public areas all day.
LOCATION: town centre.
CHILDREN: all ages welcomed.
DOGS: welcomed, 3 dog-friendly bedrooms, on lead in restaurant.
CREDIT CARDS: Amex, MasterCard, Visa.
PRICES: [2015] per room B&B (continental) £120–£180. À la carte £33.

NORWICH Norfolk

THE OLD RECTORY

Visitors this year to this small hotel and restaurant 'were invited upon arrival to a poolside glass of Pimm's on the sunny patio'. Chris and Sally Entwistle's ivy-covered Grade II listed Georgian house is in a leafy conservation area close to the centre of Norwich. They are 'hands-on' owners, providing local information, lending maps and bus timetables; their staff are 'efficient and friendly'. The traditionally furnished bedrooms are in the main building and an adjoining Victorian coach house; period features (exposed beams, fireplaces) have been retained. 'Our top-floor bedroom was spacious and restfully decorated; it had dual-aspect views over the gardens with their magnificent trees. Both bedroom and bathroom were well equipped and comfortable. Downstairs we could sit with drinks and read the menu on the big, squashy sofas in the drawing room.' Chef James Perry's 'imaginative, colourful' dishes might include potted Cromer crab, pickled cucumber; locally sourced 'melt-in-the-mouth' roasted meats. 'The panna cotta was the star for me.' Breakfast has home-made fruit compotes, Norfolk eggs, hot dishes to order. (Mary Hewson)

25% DISCOUNT VOUCHERS

103 Yarmouth Road
Thorpe St Andrew
Norwich
NR7 0HF

T: 01603 700772
F: 01603 300772
E: enquiries@oldrectorynorwich.com
W: www.oldrectorynorwich.com

BEDROOMS: 8. 3 in coach house.
OPEN: all year except Christmas/New Year, restaurant closed Sun and Mon except bank holiday weekends when open Sun.
FACILITIES: drawing room, dining room, conservatory, free Wi-Fi, 1-acre garden, unheated swimming pool, unsuitable for disabled.
BACKGROUND MUSIC: classical/jazz at dinner in drawing/dining rooms.
LOCATION: 2 miles E of Norwich.
CHILDREN: all ages welcomed.
DOGS: only assistance dogs allowed.
CREDIT CARDS: Amex, MasterCard, Visa.
PRICES: [2015] per room B&B £99–£175, D,B&B (min. 2 nights) £125–£230. Set dinner £30–£35. 1-night bookings refused weekends (spring, summer).

SEE ALSO SHORTLIST

NORWICH Norfolk

Map 2:B5

38 ST GILES

Jan and William Cheeseman run their upmarket B&B in this 'handsome' Georgian town house, on a street of independent shops 'in the ancient heart of the town'. The Grade II listed building has been 'stylishly' renovated: there are polished floorboards, modern fittings, and contemporary works by local artists. The 'spotless' bedrooms are individually decorated: one has handmade rugs and a chaise longue; a spacious family suite has a sofa bed; an 'enormous' top-floor bedroom with silk curtains overlooks rooftops and gardens. Each room has 'divine' home-made cake and fresh milk; 'luxurious' linens. Breakfast, served on handmade crockery, is 'a cut above': 'light and fluffy' buttermilk pancakes are served with Norfolk bacon; poached eggs are 'just right'; 'delicious' bread, preserves and granola are home made. 'We sat for hours over breakfast, and there was no attempt to move us on – just the occasional, sincere offer of more coffee.' Private parking, reached via a 'slightly convoluted drive through narrow lanes', is nearby. The B&B is within walking distance of many of the city's attractions and eating places; Norwich Cathedral is close by.

38 St Giles Street
Norwich
NR2 1LL

T: 01603 662944
E: 38stgiles@gmail.com
W: www.38stgiles.co.uk

BEDROOMS: 7. 1 on ground floor.
OPEN: all year except Christmas.
FACILITIES: breakfast room, free Wi-Fi, private parking.
BACKGROUND MUSIC: Radio 3 at breakfast.
LOCATION: central.
CHILDREN: all ages welcomed.
DOGS: not allowed.
CREDIT CARDS: MasterCard, Visa.
PRICES: [2015] per room B&B from £130.

SEE ALSO SHORTLIST

NOTTINGHAM Nottinghamshire

Map 2:A3

HART'S HOTEL

♀César award in 2007

There are 'lovely views over the city from a height' from this modern, purpose-built hotel on the former ramparts of Nottingham's medieval castle. Owned by Tim Hart (who also has Hambleton Hall, Hambleton, see entry), it is a few minutes' walk from the centre. Hart's is liked for its 'great position' and the quiet, enclosed courtyard garden where afternoon tea or drinks before dinner can be taken. Bedrooms are 'very modern, small but well equipped'. Garden rooms have French doors leading out to a terrace with seating. A system of louvred shutters in the bedrooms 'works very well' as air conditioning in warm weather. Returning visitors write of the 'excellent, caring staff'. There is a small gym, and in-room spa treatments can be booked. Chef Dan Burridge's menus of modern British dishes change daily in the busy Hart's restaurant close by, perhaps Cornish plaice, new potatoes, spinach, saffron hollandaise. The wine list, compiled by Tim Hart, includes a range from small producers. Breakfast (charged extra) can be taken in the bedroom or from a buffet in the bar.

25% DISCOUNT VOUCHERS

Standard Hill
Park Row
Nottingham
NG1 6GN

T: 0115 988 1900
F: 0115 947 7600
E: reception@hartshotel.co.uk
W: www.hartsnottingham.co.uk

BEDROOMS: 32. 2 suitable for disabled.
OPEN: all year, restaurant closed 1 Jan.
FACILITIES: lift, ramps, reception/lobby, bar, restaurant (30 yds), free Wi-Fi, conference/banqueting facilities, small exercise room, civil wedding licence, small garden, private car park with CCTV.
BACKGROUND MUSIC: light jazz in bar.
LOCATION: city centre.
CHILDREN: all ages welcomed.
DOGS: not allowed in public rooms, or unattended in bedrooms.
CREDIT CARDS: Amex, MasterCard, Visa.
PRICES: [2015] room £129–£269. Breakfast £9–£14 per person, set dinner £24, à la carte £33.

THE GRANGE AT OBORNE

Once the main farmhouse of Oborne, this 200-year-old house, built of stone from the Purbeck hills, stands in formal gardens (floodlit at night). It is now a 'pleasant, comfortable' family-run hotel, well placed for visiting Sherborne and the surrounding area. The owners, Karenza and Ken Mathews, their daughter, Jennifer, and her husband, Jonathan (who manage on a day-to-day basis), are 'much in evidence', say visitors. The staff are 'extremely helpful'; the facilities for, and the hospitality shown to, disabled visitors have been admired by readers. The bedrooms are individually decorated in traditional and modern style; some have an original fireplace, some a balcony with views of the Dorset hills, or a French window on to the garden. All rooms have an en suite shower or bathroom, coffee/tea-making facilities. Chef Simon Clewlow serves 'well-prepared, nicely presented' seasonal dishes in the candlelit dining room, perhaps goat's cheese panna cotta; West Bay hake, Dorset watercress pesto. A comprehensive breakfast selection has a buffet with cold meats and cheese, croissants; cooked options include smoked salmon and scrambled eggs, kippers. (PG)

Oborne
DT9 4LA

T: 01935 813463
F: 01935 817464
E: reception@thegrange.co.uk
W: www.thegrangeatoborne.co.uk

BEDROOMS: 18. 1 suitable for disabled.
OPEN: all year, except 28–31 Dec.
FACILITIES: lounge, bar, restaurant, 2 function rooms, free Wi-Fi, civil wedding licence, ¾-acre garden.
BACKGROUND MUSIC: 'easy listening' at mealtimes, in public rooms.
LOCATION: 2 miles NE of Sherborne by A30.
CHILDREN: all ages welcomed.
DOGS: only guide dogs allowed.
CREDIT CARDS: Amex, MasterCard, Visa.
PRICES: [2015] per room B&B single £88–£139, double £99–£169, D,B&B single £113–£164, double £149–£219. Set dinner £28–£35. 1-night bookings sometimes refused Sat in summer.

OLD HUNSTANTON Norfolk

THE NEPTUNE

NEW

A short stroll from the sea, Kevin Mangeolles and his wife, Jacki, run their restaurant-with-rooms in this 18th-century coaching inn. 'The owners are much in evidence: Kevin at reception and as chef; Jacki in the smart dining room,' says a guest this year, whose report earns the inn an upgrade to a full entry. Kevin Mangeolles has a Michelin star for his modern European cooking; his menus feature local meat and produce, and locally landed fish and Brancaster lobsters. A typical dish: fillet of brill, oyster mayonnaise, Pink Fir Apple potatoes, wild broccoli. 'Excellent and very light, dinner was served with a welcome absence of "flunkery" – we weren't asked all the time if "everything was OK"'. The compact bedrooms, 'nicely done up in New England style', have an en suite shower room. 'Our room had a Nespresso coffee machine, a variety of teabags, delicious home-made biscuits and fresh milk; the wardrobes were in a separate sitting room. The bathroom, though minute, was well appointed, with good soaps and towels.' Breakfast is 'excellent': 'divine' yogurt and fruit compote, pastries, 'good' coffee.

85 Old Hunstanton Road
Old Hunstanton
PE36 6HZ

T: 01485 532122
E: reservations@theneptune.co.uk
W: www.theneptune.co.uk

BEDROOMS: 5.
OPEN: all year, except 26 Dec, 3 weeks Jan, 10 days Nov, Mon.
FACILITIES: residents' lounge, bar, restaurant, free Wi-Fi, unsuitable for disabled.
BACKGROUND MUSIC: jazz in bar in evening.
LOCATION: village centre, on A149.
CHILDREN: not under 8.
DOGS: not allowed.
CREDIT CARDS: Amex, MasterCard, Visa.
PRICES: [2015] per room B&B £145, D,B&B £245. A la carte £56, tasting menu £70.

OLDSTEAD North Yorkshire

Map 4:D4

THE BLACK SWAN AT OLDSTEAD

César award in 2014

'The welcome is warm and attentive' at the Banks family's restaurant-with-rooms, in the North York Moors national park. Tom and Ann Banks are the hands-on owners; their eldest son, James, is the manager; his brother, Tommy, the chef, has a Michelin star for his 'fantastic' modern cooking. There have been considerable additions this year: a refurbished Georgian house across the yard has five new bedrooms; an extensive kitchen garden now provides most of the produce used in the restaurant. In the 'rustic but sophisticated' dining room, 'the food merits its Michelin star'. 'We enjoyed the smoked venison tartare, and coley with mussels, samphire and a quail's egg.' The bedrooms are decorated with 'well-chosen' antiques: 'there was beautiful china, even in the bathrooms'. Breakfast has 'lovely' home-made preserves, 'copious' smoked salmon and scrambled eggs, 'excellent' coffee. 'We had to leave early for a morning meeting and asked if they could push breakfast forward. Our order was taken in the evening, and both chef and waitress came in especially early for us.' (F and IW)

Oldstead
YO61 4BL

T: 01347 868387
E: enquiries@blackswanoldstead.
   co.uk
W: www.blackswanoldstead.co.uk

BEDROOMS: 9. 4, on ground floor, in annexe, 5 in Ashberry House, 50 yds away.
OPEN: all year except 2 weeks Jan.
FACILITIES: bar, restaurant, private dining room, free Wi-Fi, small garden, 2½-acre kitchen garden and orchard.
BACKGROUND MUSIC: in bar and restaurant.
LOCATION: in village 7 miles E of Thirsk.
CHILDREN: all ages welcomed in bar, not under 18 to stay.
DOGS: not allowed.
CREDIT CARDS: MasterCard, Visa.
PRICES: [2015] per room D,B&B £250–£410. Set meals £32–£55, tasting menu £80.

ORFORD Suffolk

Map 2:C6

THE CROWN AND CASTLE

♔ Cesar award in 2013

'Peaceful and comfortable, a good place to unwind.' This small hotel/restaurant stands near the castle quayside in a Suffolk village. Ruth and David Watson are its owners with Tim Sunderland the partner/manager. The staff 'work hard to good effect, striking the right balance between formality and informality', says a visitor in 2015. 'Tasteful' bedrooms with 'very comfy' beds are divided between the main building and the garden. They have 'good lighting and plenty of storage space'. 'Our wonderful room had a glorious view across the water.' In the 'cosy, modern' restaurant, chef Charlene Gavazzi serves an Italian-influenced menu. 'We enjoyed fresh dressed crab; chicken liver pâté with pickled courgettes; Cornish gurnard in sea food broth with tortellini. All delicious.' A separate vegetarian menu was welcomed. There is a special table in the restaurant area where dogs may sit with their owners. Breakfast 'cooked from scratch, so really hot and fresh' is a highlight. 'Good, fresh orange juice, real bread; excellent sausage, black pudding, bacon and egg.' (Lynn Wildgoose, Andrew Kleissner)

Orford
nr Woodbridge
IP12 2LJ

T: 01394 450205
E: info@crownandcastle.co.uk
W: www.crownandcastle.co.uk

BEDROOMS: 21. 10 (all on ground floor) in garden, 3 (on ground floor) in terrace.
OPEN: all year.
FACILITIES: lounge/bar, restaurant, private dining room, gallery, free Wi-Fi, 1-acre garden.
BACKGROUND MUSIC: none.
LOCATION: market square.
CHILDREN: not under 8 in hotel and Trinity restaurant (any age at lunch).
DOGS: allowed in 5 garden rooms, in restaurant (at 'doggie table'), limited number in bar.
CREDIT CARDS: MasterCard, Visa.
PRICES: per room B&B £115–£240, D,B&B £185–£310. À la carte £35. 1-night bookings refused Fri/Sat.

PEN-Y-DYFFRYN

♀ César award in 2003

'An old rectory in an Arcadian setting in a beautiful valley', Miles and Audrey Hunter's small country hotel is close to the border with Wales. 'A pleasant place with character', the silver-stone former Georgian rectory stands in 'enchanting' gardens. Most of the 'immaculate' bedrooms have the view: 'Our room had a lovely double-aspect outlook over the garden and valley; it had too much furniture as did the whole hotel.' Four rooms in a converted coach house have a private stone-walled patio with outdoor seating. 'Ours, in elegant contemporary style, was well equipped; the bathroom was state of the art.' Tea and cake can be taken on the hotel's terrace or, on cold days, in front of a log fire in the public rooms. 'Little vases of sweet peas on the table were a nice touch' in the restaurant, where 'tables are tightly packed'. Chef David Morris cooks 'lovely food' on a daily-changing four-course menu which might include medallion of rare breed pork loin, Shropshire Blue cheese sauce, quince jelly. (David Birnie, Francine and Ian Walsh, Tara Varco)

25% DISCOUNT VOUCHERS

Rhydycroesau
Oswestry
SY10 7JD

T: 01691 653700
E: stay@peny.co.uk
W: www.peny.co.uk

BEDROOMS: 12. 4, each with patio, in coach house, 1 on ground floor.
OPEN: all year except Christmas.
FACILITIES: 2 lounges, bar, restaurant, free Wi-Fi, 5-acre grounds (summer house, dog-walking area), unsuitable for disabled.
BACKGROUND MUSIC: 'quiet' light classical or pop in 1 lounge, restaurant in evening.
LOCATION: 3 miles W of Oswestry.
CHILDREN: not under 3.
DOGS: allowed in some bedrooms, not in public rooms after 6 pm.
CREDIT CARDS: MasterCard, Visa.
PRICES: [2015] per person B&B £66–£97, D,B&B £95–£130. Set dinner £40. 1-night bookings occasionally refused Sat.

OLD BANK

♀Cesar award in 2011

On the High Street opposite All Souls College, Jeremy Mogford's contemporary hotel is a conversion of three stone buildings (one a former bank). Quod, the bar and brasserie in the former banking hall, is popular with town and gown. It has a seasonal menu of dishes like Caesar salad; salmon fishcakes, spinach, sorrel sauce. The staff are 'accommodating and friendly; any small imperfections (there were a lot of new staff) were swiftly rectified,' says a visitor in 2015. 'Our room was spectacular, with a south-facing balcony and an enormous bay window.' Tea and coffee are available in the small library downstairs, if the Bodleian Library opposite feels too far away. A collection of young British art (Sandra Blow, Gary Hume) is displayed in the corridors and bedrooms. Breakfast has 'an extensive choice of cooked food; I recommend the smoked salmon and scrambled eggs'. 'The city-centre car park is a bonus, although access is pretty tight.' Old Parsonage (see next entry) is under the same ownership. Old Bank will be closed in January 2016 for refurbishment. (Matt and Kelly Rose-Clarke, and others)

92–94 High Street
Oxford
OX1 4BJ

T: 01865 799599
E: reception@oldbank-hotel.co.uk
W: www.oldbank-hotel.co.uk

BEDROOMS: 42. 1 suitable for disabled.
OPEN: all year, except Jan (for refurbishment).
FACILITIES: lift, residents' library/bar, bar/grill, dining terrace, 2 meeting/private dining rooms, free Wi-Fi, small garden.
BACKGROUND MUSIC: none.
LOCATION: central, car park.
CHILDREN: all ages welcomed.
DOGS: not allowed.
CREDIT CARDS: Amex, MasterCard, Visa.
PRICES: [2015] per room B&B from £206, D,B&B from £267. À la carte £35. 1-night bookings often refused Sat.

SEE ALSO SHORTLIST

OXFORD Oxfordshire

Map 2:C2

OLD PARSONAGE

Behind high walls next to St Giles church, Jeremy Mogford's luxury hotel in a 17th-century building is liked for its 'intimate, club-like atmosphere'. An old stone gate opens on to a sunny walled terrace where drinks and meals can be taken on warm days. The lobby has an ancient fireplace; to the side is a 'dark' club room. In contrast, on the first floor is a recently added 'lovely, light' library ('well stocked with interesting books'). The colours in the public areas are predominately grey, plum, deep red and purple. The bedrooms, in a similar palate, are decorated with charcoal prints of Oxford. Bloomsbury portraits from Jeremy Mogford's extensive art collection enliven the walls of the restaurant. Michael Wright is now the chef. He serves a 'seasonal menu of classics' such as rabbit, leek and sage pie, carrots, creamed potatoes. Breakfast has 'tasty ingredients' in the cooked selection; 'proper bread' for the toast, home-made preserves, and freshly squeezed juice. Spa treatments are available in the bedroom; the hotel offers a complimentary daily walking tour (recommended) and free bicycle use.

1 Banbury Road
Oxford
OX2 6NN

T: 01865 310210
F: 01865 311262
E: reservations@
   oldparsonage-hotel.co.uk
W: www.oldparsonage-hotel.co.uk

BEDROOMS: 35. 10 on ground floor, 2 suitable for disabled.
OPEN: all year.
FACILITIES: lounge, library, bar/restaurant, free Wi-Fi, civil wedding licence, terrace, 2 small gardens.
BACKGROUND MUSIC: no.
LOCATION: NE end of St Giles, small car park.
CHILDREN: all ages welcomed.
DOGS: allowed in designated bedrooms, reception area.
CREDIT CARDS: Amex, MasterCard, Visa.
PRICES: [2015] per room B&B from £235, D,B&B from £315. Set dinner £42.50, à la carte £35–£40 (12½% discretionary service charge added).

SEE ALSO SHORTLIST

PADSTOW Cornwall

THE SEAFOOD RESTAURANT **NEW**

'Exemplary food served by focused and attentive staff in stunning surroundings; the hotel reception and bedroom were of a complementary standard.' Inspectors in 2015 were impressed by Rick and Jill Stein's celebrated restaurant-with-rooms, which returns to the Guide after a period without reports. 'The dining room is spectacular': in the centre is a large bar with zinc top and high stools, behind which cooks are preparing cold dishes. The chef, Stephane Delourme, serves an extensive menu with Asian influences: 'We enjoyed delicious crisp smoked mackerel, Thai green mango and green papaya salad; pan-fried monkfish with garlic and fennel, with red-hot bird's-eye chillies; a light-as-a-feather soufflé beignet. The well-trained staff were smartly dressed.' A wheelchair-accessible lift can be taken to the bedrooms above: 'Our room had a side view over rooftops to Rock across the estuary; a large bed, a comfy sofa and a table; the bathroom was exceptional with a freestanding bath.' Breakfast, also in the restaurant, has a 'fine' buffet, four kinds of fish among the cooked choices. The Steins have four other places to stay in the town.

Riverside
Padstow
PL28 8BY

T: 01841 532700
E: reservations@rickstein.com
W: www.rickstein.com

BEDROOMS: 16.
OPEN: all year except Christmas.
FACILITIES: lounge, reading room, restaurant, free Wi-Fi.
BACKGROUND MUSIC: in restaurant.
LOCATION: village centre.
CHILDREN: all ages welcomed, not under 3 in restaurant.
DOGS: welcomed in some bedrooms.
CREDIT CARDS: Diners, MasterCard, Visa.
PRICES: [2015] per room B&B from £113, D,B&B from £139. À la carte £52.

PENSFORD Somerset

Map 2:D1

THE PIG NEAR BATH

'Fresh and appealing', this 'glorious' honey-stone Georgian mansion 'with bags of style' 'fits the new sense of "cool"', Guide inspectors said. A 'grander' sister to The Pig, Brockenhurst (see entry), it is part of Robin Hutson and David Elton's small Home Grown Hotels group. Open fires burn in 'beautiful' fireplaces in the public rooms; there are magazines, potted herbs, 'slouchy' leather armchairs and settees. Handsomely decorated bedrooms are in the main building, coach house and cottages in the grounds (umbrellas provided). 'Our spacious room had bare floorboards, a topless four-poster bed, a Roberts radio; excellent and generously sized bathroom goodies in the large bathroom.' In the conservatory restaurant ('like eating in a greenhouse'), chef Kamil Oseka uses much home-grown produce in his modern meals; the menu lists ingredients 'literally picked this morning' in the short journey garden to plate. A typical dish: Barnsley pork chop, with nettle salsa verde, tomato salad and goat's cheese curd. Breakfast has a 'comprehensive' buffet of fresh fruit, pastries, 'lovely' brown eggs, 'yogurt in funny little milk churns'; 'distinctively smoked salmon'; 'a very fine kipper'.

Hunstrete House
Pensford
BS39 4NS

T: 01761 490490
E: reservations@thepighotel.com
W: www.thepighotel.com

BEDROOMS: 29. 5 in gardens, some on ground floor, 1 suitable for disabled.
OPEN: all year.
FACILITIES: lounge, bar, library, restaurant, private dining room, billiard room, free Wi-Fi, civil wedding licence, treatment rooms, kitchen garden, wild flower meadow, deer park.
BACKGROUND MUSIC: all day in public areas.
LOCATION: 7 miles SW of Bath.
CHILDREN: all ages welcomed.
DOGS: not allowed.
CREDIT CARDS: Amex, MasterCard, Visa.
PRICES: [2015] room £149–£275. Breakfast £10–£15, à la carte £35. 1-night bookings refused weekends, Christmas/New Year.

PETERSFIELD Hampshire

JSW

Chef/patron Jake (Saul) Watkins is an 'accommodating' host at his restaurant-with-rooms, a former coaching inn in a market town within the South Downs national park. His philosophy is simplicity on the plate and in the decor of the building. The bedrooms, reached off a wide landing, are 'fresh and light'. Three overlook the street, the fourth faces a rear courtyard. They have 'a comfortable bed with a duvet, a desk, a wardrobe, a large flat-screen TV, free Wi-Fi; a modern bathroom'. The 'welcoming' restaurant has subdued lighting, pristine linen and settings. Jake Watkins has a Michelin star for his flavoursome cooking. His menu might include scallops, celeriac purée, mushrooms and nasturtium; duck, hay-baked parsnip, salted orange purée and sea beet. The 700-strong wine list is evenly split between Old- and New-World wines; 14 selections are available by the glass. In the morning, a continental breakfast tray is brought to the bedroom: it might have orange juice, muesli, toast, home-made marmalade and lemon curd. The croissants and pastries come from Rungis market in Paris. 'A good place for a gastronomic experience.'

20 Dragon Street
Petersfield
GU31 4JJ

T: 01730 262030
E: jsw.restaurant@btconnect.com
W: www.jswrestaurant.com

BEDROOMS: 4.
OPEN: all year except 24 Dec–10 Jan, Sun night, Mon/Tues.
FACILITIES: restaurant, free Wi-Fi, courtyard, unsuitable for disabled.
BACKGROUND MUSIC: none.
LOCATION: town centre.
CHILDREN: 'quiet babies', not under 7.
DOGS: not allowed.
CREDIT CARDS: Amex, MasterCard, Visa.
PRICES: [2015] per room D,B&B £195–£310. À la carte £49.50.

PETWORTH West Sussex

THE OLD RAILWAY STATION

On a disused railway line bordered by woodland, this B&B with a difference occupies a renovated Victorian station building and four restored Pullman carriages. Hosts Gudmund Olafsson and Catherine Stormont give a 'warm welcome' to guests, who check in at the original ticket office window. Most of the bedrooms are in the British-built carriages, each divided into two rooms with a separate entrance. Long and narrow, with Edwardian fittings and furnishings, they are 'comfortable and well furnished. Our bathroom was surprisingly spacious, with a proper bath.' Two larger rooms in the main building, reached by a spiral staircase, were refurbished this year, as was the waiting room. The nearby road can be busy, but visitors report 'virtually no traffic at night; all we heard was owls'. There are leather-buttoned sofas and chairs, a wood-burning fireplace, 'intriguing railwayana' in the waiting room, where tea and coffee are served. Breakfast ('splendid, unhurried') is taken here or in the carriages or the waiting room. 'Perfect scrambled eggs, excellent sausages, freshly ground coffee'. Evening meals can be found at a nearby pub (walking distance).

Station Road
Petworth
GU28 0JF

T: 01798 342346
F: 01798 343033
E: info@old-station.co.uk
W: www.old-station.co.uk

BEDROOMS: 10. 8 in Pullman carriages. 1 suitable for disabled.
OPEN: all year except 23–26 Dec.
FACILITIES: lounge/bar/breakfast room, free Wi-Fi, platform/terrace, 2-acre garden.
BACKGROUND MUSIC: soft 1930s/1940s in waiting room at breakfast time.
LOCATION: 1½ miles south of Petworth.
CHILDREN: not under 10.
DOGS: not allowed.
CREDIT CARDS: Amex, MasterCard, Visa.
PRICES: [2015] per room B&B £90–£240.

THE WHITE SWAN   **NEW**

In a market town known as 'the gateway to the moors', this 'well-established' 16th-century coaching inn is upgraded to a full entry after good reports by regular correspondents. Owned by the Buchanan family for 30 years, it is managed by Catherine Feather. Praise in 2015: 'The staff were consistently smiling and caring.' 'Excellent service, good food, value for money. A good centre for coast and country.' In the main building, bedrooms are traditionally styled; more modern rooms are in the Hideaway, the converted stables across the open courtyard. The Bothy, an adjacent barn, houses the beamed lounge, with sofas, a wood-burning stove, newspapers and magazines; toys, board games and colouring pens for children are at the ready. The porch entrance in the Hideaway is a good place to stow dog-walking kit overnight. Children have their own menus and an early dinner hour; digital baby monitors are available, so parents can eat in the restaurant worry-free. Chef Darren Clemmit serves 'honest food in Yorkshire portions', perhaps roast moorland grouse with game crisps, watercress. Breakfast has cereals, fresh fruit and cooked options. (John Baynham, Margery Miller)

Market Place
Pickering
YO18 7AA

T: 01751 472288
F: 01751 475554
E: welcome@white-swan.co.uk
W: www.white-swan.co.uk

BEDROOMS: 21. 9 in annexe.
OPEN: all year.
FACILITIES: ramps to ground-floor facilities, lounge, bar, club room, restaurant, private dining room, conference/meeting facilities, free Wi-Fi, small terrace (alfresco meals), 1½-acre grounds.
BACKGROUND MUSIC: none.
LOCATION: central.
CHILDREN: all ages welcomed.
DOGS: welcomed, not allowed in restaurant (owners can dine with dogs in snug).
CREDIT CARDS: Amex, MasterCard, Visa.
PRICES: [2015] per room B&B from £129, D,B&B from £156. À la carte £25. 1-night bookings sometimes refused.

PICKHILL North Yorkshire

THE NAG'S HEAD

In a pretty Domesday village close to the A1, this old coaching inn is run in personal style by Janet and Edward Boynton, who are 'hard-working and hands-on' hosts. The inn is much liked by readers for the 'excellent service without pretension' and for the 'invention, quality of cooking and delivery' of the meals (a report this year). Food is served in the restaurant, which has a library theme ('a huge bookcase crammed with books, large mirrors'), the lounge bar or the tap room (which stocks well-kept Yorkshire ales). 'The cooking is excellent,' said Guide inspectors in 2015 who enjoyed 'large portions of dishes with local ingredients,' a tartlet of asparagus, sundried tomatoes and blue cheese; smoked haddock on curried risotto. A typical comment: 'We have never eaten the same dish twice and everything was delicious.' Bedrooms, including a suite in an adjacent building, are 'plain but comfortable', with 'plenty of hot water, and lovely fluffy towels and robes'. 'A peaceful sleep is guaranteed.' Breakfast has a small buffet; good ingredients in the cooked dishes. 'The prices are very reasonable.' (Robert Gower, and others)

25% DISCOUNT VOUCHERS

Pickhill
YO7 4JG

T: 01845 567391
F: 01845 567212
E: enquiries@nagsheadpickhill.co.uk
W: www.nagsheadpickhill.co.uk

BEDROOMS: 12. 6 in annexe, 3 on ground floor.
OPEN: all year except 24/25 Dec.
FACILITIES: ramps, lounge, bar, restaurant, free Wi-Fi, meeting facilities, lawn (croquet).
BACKGROUND MUSIC: varied in lounge, bar and restaurant.
LOCATION: 5 miles NW of Thirsk.
CHILDREN: all ages welcomed.
DOGS: allowed in 2 bedrooms (not unattended).
CREDIT CARDS: Amex, MasterCard, Visa.
PRICES: [2015] per person B&B £40–£48.50. À la carte £25.

PORLOCK Somerset

Map 1:B5

THE OAKS

On the edge of a village where Exmoor national park meets the sea, Tim and Anne Riley's small, traditional hotel attracts many return visitors. 'We can do no better than confirm that they are excellent hosts,' says a regular this year. An earlier comment: 'They are so kind and they think of everything.' The imposing Edwardian house, in gardens with lawns and oak trees, overlooks the village and the sea. Tim Riley carries luggage to the bedroom and welcomes guests with tea and home-made cakes. All the spacious bedrooms have a view; they are supplied daily with fresh milk and fruit. In the evening, guests gather in the lounge for pre-dinner drinks served by the host. Tables in the dining room are arranged around the windows where, in summer, diners can watch a coastal sunset. Anne Riley has 'a passion and enthusiasm for traditional English cooking'; her 'excellent' daily-changing menu might include cream of pear and watercress soup; Dover sole, sautéed leeks, tartar sauce. Everything is home made, from her breakfast marmalade, to his bread and after-dinner chocolates. (Michael and Jenifer Price)

Porlock
TA24 8ES

T: 01643 862265
F: 01643 863131
E: info@oakshotel.co.uk
W: www.oakshotel.co.uk

BEDROOMS: 7.
OPEN: Apr–Nov, open Christmas.
FACILITIES: 2 lounges, bar, restaurant, free Wi-Fi, 2-acre garden, pebble beach 1 mile, unsuitable for disabled.
BACKGROUND MUSIC: none.
LOCATION: edge of village.
CHILDREN: not under 8.
DOGS: not allowed.
CREDIT CARDS: MasterCard, Visa.
PRICES: per room D,B&B £230–£250. Set dinner £37.50.

DRIFTWOOD HOTEL

♥César award in 2010

Standing in 'beautifully landscaped' gardens overlooking Gerrans Bay, Paul and Fiona Robinson's upscale seaside hotel has a 'relaxed' atmosphere and 'friendly and courteous' staff. 'The presence of the owners is key to setting a welcoming tone devoid of pretension,' say visitors in 2015. 'We stayed in the only available room, in the eaves on the top floor; it was snug but had a comfortable bed, a spotless large bathroom and a bird's eye view from a window seat of the garden and the sea.' A tall visitor found this room constricting. It can be used as a family suite: 'A separate children's room had been made up for us with two cots and a selection of children's books.' Pre-dinner drinks can be taken on the terrace on balmy evenings; in the restaurant, chef Chris Eden holds a Michelin star for his 'very special' modern European menus. 'It was great to see a lightness of touch in the cooking: a simple John Dory with intense flavours; a spiced pineapple and lemon dessert was so good I had two helpings.' (Mr and Mrs Sachak-Patwa)

Rosevine
nr Portscatho
TR2 5EW

T: 01872 580644
F: 01872 580801
E: info@driftwoodhotel.co.uk
W: www.driftwoodhotel.co.uk

BEDROOMS: 14. 4 in courtyard, also 2 in cabin (2 mins' walk).
OPEN: 5 Feb–6 Dec.
FACILITIES: 2 lounges, bar, restaurant, children's games room, free Wi-Fi, 7-acre grounds (terraced gardens, private beach, safe bathing), unsuitable for disabled.
BACKGROUND MUSIC: jazz or classical in restaurant.
LOCATION: N side of Portscatho.
CHILDREN: all ages welcomed, early supper for children, no very young children in restaurant in evenings.
DOGS: not allowed.
CREDIT CARDS: Amex, MasterCard, Visa.
PRICES: (2015) per room B&B £170–£280, D,B&B £235–£295. Set dinner £55. 1-night bookings refused weekends.

PURTON Wiltshire

Map 3:E5

THE PEAR TREE AT PURTON

♛César award in 2015

'The room, the service and the food were all excellent,' says a visitor returning in 2015 to this small hotel on the outskirts of a Saxon village. It is run by a mother and daughter, Anne and Alix Young, assisted by Alix's husband Tim. The 'charming' building, a 16th-century former vicarage, has been sympathetically extended. Adam Conduit has been promoted to head chef in the conservatory restaurant. He cooks modern British dishes like crab tian, chilli and avocado; corn-fed chicken breast, wild mushroom, Bath soft cheese, port and redcurrant sauce. 'The carpeted floor and lack of background music create a peaceful feel,' said a Guide inspector. The bedrooms are 'spacious and comfortable', with good amenities ('it was well equipped and not at all designerish'). In good weather, tea and drinks can be taken in the garden with its 'lovely' herbaceous borders. 'Not only do the Youngs run an excellent hotel, they also produce their own honey, and their own wine from vines on the large wild meadow at the rear.' Families are welcomed; so are dogs. (Gwyn Morgan, and others)

Church End
Purton
SN5 4ED

T: 01793 772100
F: 01793 772369
E: anne@peartreepurton.co.uk
W: www.peartreepurton.co.uk

BEDROOMS: 17. Some on ground floor.
OPEN: all year except 25 Dec evening and 26 Dec.
FACILITIES: ramps, lounge/bar, library, restaurant, free Wi-Fi, function/conference facilities, civil wedding licence, 7½-acre grounds (vineyard, croquet, pond, jogging route).
BACKGROUND MUSIC: none.
LOCATION: 5 miles NW of Swindon.
CHILDREN: all ages welcomed.
DOGS: welcomed, not unattended in bedrooms and not allowed in restaurant.
CREDIT CARDS: Amex, MasterCard, Visa.
PRICES: [2015] per room B&B £109–£149, D,B&B £160–£210. À la carte £35.

THE YORKE ARMS

♀Cesar award in 2000

In an 'unbeatable Dales location', by the green in a village surrounded by woodland, Bill and Frances Atkins's 'friendly' restaurant-with-rooms occupies an 18th-century shooting lodge. The 'rustic' entrance gives no hint to the 'divine' meals that are served within. Frances Atkins cooks 'the best Michelin one-star menu we have tasted for a long time', said trusted reporters in 2015. 'The imaginative combinations of ingredients throughout our ample three-course menu offered exquisite, interesting flavours. The marinated smoked duck and hazelnut starter was faultless; the slow-cooked loin of hare fabulous. Puddings were outstanding.' Bedrooms are in the main house and newer two-storey suites in the courtyard; the two-bedroom Ghyll Cottage is 'comfortable and attractive'. 'Our bedroom had a stone mullioned window overlooking the green, robust but simple modern furniture, a comfy bed. The new bathroom had copious goodies.' Breakfast has a 'generous basket of excellent breads and croissants, home-made jam, strong coffee'; cooked dishes include an 'excellent' smoked haddock. (Francine and Ian Walsh)

Ramsgill-in-Nidderdale
nr Harrogate
HG3 5RL

T: 01423 755243
F: 01423 755330
E: enquiries@yorke-arms.co.uk
W: www.yorke-arms.co.uk

BEDROOMS: 16. 4 in courtyard, 2 in Ghyll Cottage.
OPEN: all year except 24/25 Dec, Sun dinner for residents only, closed Mon.
FACILITIES: ramp, lounge, bar, 2 dining rooms, free Wi-Fi in drawing room and some bedrooms, function facilities, 2-acre grounds, unsuitable for disabled.
BACKGROUND MUSIC: classical in dining rooms.
LOCATION: centre of village.
CHILDREN: not under 12.
DOGS: allowed by arrangement in 1 bedroom, bar area.
CREDIT CARDS: Amex, MasterCard, Visa.
PRICES: [2015] per room D,B&B £345–£430. Tasting menu £85, à la carte £65.

THE BLACK SWAN

♥César award in 2013

'Definitely off the beaten track', Alan and Louise Dinnes's 'thoroughly dependable' country-pub-with-rooms sits amid upland pastures at the foot of the Howgill fells. Visitors this year praised 'the friendliness and helpfulness of the staff'. The 'well-populated' pub is 'inviting', as is the streamside garden. The Dinneses have continued with refurbishment: they have created an additional dog-friendly room (also equipped for disabled visitors), upgraded several bathrooms, renovated bar areas, and improved the garden facilities. Bedrooms vary in size and decor: one has an iron bedframe, a log-burning stove; others are decorated in soft colours. Ground-floor rooms are 'large, comfortable' and have 'a particularly inviting bed'. All rooms have tea/coffee-making facilities, Wi-Fi, a bathroom with hand-made soaps (for sale in the pub-owned village shop). Bryan Parsons is the new chef this year, serving meals in the bar or dining room. Breakfast has a daily special, 'excellent' fresh orange juice. 'The cooked breakfast is irresistible, really sets you up for a day of exploring.' (Trevor Lockwood, John and Teresa Stewart)

25% DISCOUNT VOUCHERS

Ravenstonedale
CA17 4NG

T: 015396 23204
F: 015396 23204
E: enquiries@blackswanhotel.com
W: www.blackswanhotel.com

BEDROOMS: 16. 5 in annexe, 2 on ground floor suitable for disabled.
OPEN: all year.
FACILITIES: bar, lounge, 2 dining rooms, free Wi-Fi, beer garden in wooded grounds, tennis and golf in village.
BACKGROUND MUSIC: 'easy listening' in public areas, all day.
LOCATION: in village 5 miles SW of Kirkby Stephen.
CHILDREN: all ages welcomed.
DOGS: allowed in 4 ground-floor bedrooms, not in restaurant.
CREDIT CARDS: Amex, MasterCard, Visa.
PRICES: [2015] per room B&B £75–£145. À la carte £25.

REETH North Yorkshire

THE BURGOYNE

In 'delightful James Herriot motoring country', this Georgian Grade II listed country house hotel is owned by Mo and Julia Usman. She is a 'pleasant hostess; the staff were delightful', says a visitor in 2015. The bedrooms have 'lovely' views of the surrounding countryside. The lounges have fresh flowers, original features ('fancy' cornices, carved stone ceilings, fine joinery). 'Our large, ground-floor room was warm and comfortable, with good lighting; a large, clean, well-equipped bathroom; French doors on to a patio. The coffee table stacked with books, a selection of teas/coffee, etc.' Guests assemble at 7 pm for drinks and meal orders ('although stragglers can hold up dinner for everyone, as no one eats until all are ready'). In the dining room, chef Paul Salonga 'has some excellent dishes in his repertoire, especially aubergine and mushroom fritters; duck breast served on apple mash; service was pleasant if inexperienced'. Breakfast was 'outstanding: a vast array of fruit, yogurt; cooked choice was wide (eggs all ways, fish in many guises), including a fry-up to please the most active walkers'. There is good walking from the front door.

On the Green
Reeth
DL11 6SN

T: 01748 884292
F: 01748 884292
E: enquiries@theburgoyne.co.uk
W: www.theburgoyne.co.uk

BEDROOMS: 10. 1 on ground floor suitable for disabled.
OPEN: all year.
FACILITIES: ramp, 2 lounges, dining room, free Wi-Fi, ½-acre garden.
BACKGROUND MUSIC: 'easy listening' on low during meals.
LOCATION: village green.
CHILDREN: all ages welcomed.
DOGS: welcomed, not allowed in dining room.
CREDIT CARDS: MasterCard, Visa.
PRICES: [2015] per room B&B £110–£220, D,B&B £200–£310. Set dinner £45.

RICHMOND North Yorkshire

Map 4:C3

❦ THE COACH HOUSE AT [NEW] MIDDLETON LODGE

César award: newcomer of the year

'Another exciting newcomer in the north.' Trusted Guide correspondents were impressed in 2015 by James Allison's restaurant-with-rooms, a 'sensitive' conversion of the Georgian buildings on a large estate close to Scotch Corner. The bedrooms are in the honey-stoned mansion and in converted stables around a neatly planted courtyard. The 'original features and the character' of the old buildings have been preserved. The tack room and garden rooms are on the ground floor; each has a private outdoor sitting area. Three hayloft rooms are up a worn stone staircase. 'Our room was amazing; it had original beams and wooden shutters combined with modern underfloor heating. A three-seat sofa at the end of a huge bed faced a wood-burning stove with a basket of logs.' In the double-height restaurant, chef Gareth Rayner produces a 'fine and interesting menu'. His 'excellent' dishes 'bring different flavours together well; we enjoyed blowtorched mackerel, broccoli, pickled shallots; sea bream, Israeli couscous, wild garlic and crab beignet'. (Pat and Jeremy Temple)

Kneeton Lane
Middleton Tyas
Richmond
DL10 6NJ

T: 01325 377 977
F: 01325 377 065
E: info@middletonlodge.co.uk
W: www.middletonlodge.co.uk

BEDROOMS: 14. 5 in coach house, 3 in hayloft, 1 in tack room, 1 suitable for disabled.
OPEN: all year except Christmas, closed Mon/Tues.
FACILITIES: bar, restaurant, free Wi-Fi, civil wedding licence, garden, kitchen garden in 200-acre grounds.
BACKGROUND MUSIC: 'relaxed' in public areas.
LOCATION: 1 mile N of village, E of Scotch Corner.
CHILDREN: all ages welcomed.
DOGS: not allowed.
CREDIT CARDS: Amex, MasterCard, Visa.
PRICES: [2015] per room B&B £155–£220. À la carte £30.

SEE ALSO SHORTLIST

MILLGATE HOUSE

♥ Cesar award in 2011

'A beautiful house with lovely things', Austin Lynch and Tim Culkin's early Georgian home stands just off the square of this market town on the edge of the Dales. Its sheltered garden ('full of interest') was chosen by Alan Titchmarsh as one of Britain's best gardens in 2015. Heavily planted, it has terraces which lead down to the fast-flowing River Swale. The owners, who are 'eager to share their knowledge of the area', have packed the 'magnificent' drawing room with an eclectic collection of antiques, fine silver and china, souvenirs, books and original paintings. These treasures spill over into the bedrooms, two of which face the gardens. The third bedroom has its own bathroom across the hall. An 'excellent' breakfast, served with silver cutlery at mahogany tables in a well-proportioned dining room, has an extensive buffet of fresh fruit, cereals and croissants. Cooked choices include kippers, locally sourced bacon and sausages, and eggs cooked to order. Dinner is served only to groups of 16 or more. The owners, who have two whippets, welcome visiting dogs.

Richmond
DL10 4JN

T: 01748 823571
E: oztim@millgatehouse.demon.
  co.uk
W: www.millgatehouse.com

BEDROOMS: 3. Also self-catering facilities for 12.
OPEN: all year.
FACILITIES: hall, drawing room, dining room, free Wi-Fi, ⅓-acre garden, unsuitable for disabled.
BACKGROUND MUSIC: none.
LOCATION: town centre.
CHILDREN: all ages welcomed, 'depending on the children'.
DOGS: not in public rooms, or unattended in bedrooms.
CREDIT CARDS: none.
PRICES: per room B&B £110–£145.

SEE ALSO SHORTLIST

BINGHAM

'With beautiful views of the Thames', this smart hotel/restaurant is formed from two Grade II listed houses built in 1740, with lawns running down to the river. Owned by Ruth and Samantha Trinder, it is managed by Erick Kervaon. Lady Ann Bingham, who rented the property in the 19th century, added a river-facing room to link the buildings. It now houses the 'magnificent' bar/lounge which has a double-height ceiling, mirrored walls, a glass chandelier, silver-leaf; drinks, afternoon tea and light meals can be taken here. There are striking floral displays in the public areas. In the plush dining room (heavy silk curtains, a gold fabric mural), Andrew Cole is now the chef. His short market menu of modern British dishes (available from Monday to Thursday, and at 6.30 pm on Friday) might include celery soup, slow-cooked duck egg, rye crumbs; guineafowl, spring green salsa, sweetcorn. A more extensive carte is served on Friday evening and Saturday. Meals can be taken alfresco on a terrace in warmer weather. The best bedrooms have a view of the river; they are decorated in Art Deco style.

61–63 Petersham Road
Richmond-upon-Thames
TW10 6UT

T: 020 8940 0902
E: info@thebingham.co.uk
W: www.thebingham.co.uk

BEDROOMS: 15.
OPEN: all year, restaurant closed Sun evening.
FACILITIES: bar, restaurant, function room, free Wi-Fi, civil wedding licence, terrace, garden, unsuitable for disabled.
BACKGROUND MUSIC: mixed in lounge bar and restaurant.
LOCATION: ½ mile S of centre.
CHILDREN: all ages welcomed.
DOGS: not allowed.
CREDIT CARDS: all major cards.
PRICES: [2015] per room B&B from £165. Set dinner £25–£30, à la carte £40 (plus 12½% discretionary service charge).

ST ENODOC

In a fashionable resort on the Camel estuary, this child-friendly hotel has a light, Mediterranean decor with bright colours and original artwork. There are stone floors, open spaces in the public areas. Many of the 'well-designed' bedrooms have views of the estuary; they have a 'peaceful, coordinated' decor, 'good storage', 'lovely' daily replenished biscuits on the tea tray. Bathrooms are 'well equipped', with 'well-designed' lighting. There has been a change in the eating arrangements this year. The Michelin-starred Restaurant Nathan Outlaw has moved to Port Isaac. Daytime and evening meals are taken in Outlaw's where Tom Brown is head chef. His seasonal menus might include dishes like Boxeater beef tartare, seaweed mayonnaise; mushroom miso, spring vegetables. An evening meal is served for children at 5 pm. For rainy days, children have a games room (ping pong, table football, board games). Breakfast is 'very good': 'delicious porridge, succulent kippers, excellent coffee'; daily specials. Walkers will enjoy the circular trail from Rock to St Miniver, passing both St Enodoc Church (the burial place of Sir John Betjemen) and Sharp's Brewery for refreshment.

Rock
PL27 6LA

T: 01208 863394
F: 01208 863970
E: info@enodoc-hotel.co.uk
W: www.enodoc-hotel.co.uk

BEDROOMS: 20.
OPEN: all year except 20 Dec–end Jan.
FACILITIES: lounge, library, billiard room, 2 restaurants, free Wi-Fi, spa, heated outdoor swimming pool (May–Sept, 9 by 4.5 metres), terrace, garden, only restaurants suitable for disabled.
BACKGROUND MUSIC: none.
LOCATION: outskirts of village.
CHILDREN: all ages welcomed, not under 10 in restaurant in evening.
DOGS: not allowed.
CREDIT CARDS: Amex, MasterCard, Visa.
PRICES: [2015] per room B&B £170–£495, D,B&B (not high season) from £215. Set dinner £35–£45.

THE ROSE AND CROWN

'An escape from the real world,' says a visitor in 2015 to this 18th-century coaching inn beside a Saxon church. Now owned by the Robinson family of Headlam Hall, Darlington (see Shortlist entry), it is managed by Sarah Gregory. 'It is most appealing, inside and out,' said other visitors, who received a friendly welcome. 'Our bag was carried to our room in the main house, which overlooked the village green and the old stocks. The furnishings were traditional; everything was gleaming and polished; the only drawback captive hangers.' Each of the five rooms in a single-storey courtyard building has an outdoor seating area. Next door, the converted 17th-century Monk's Cottage has a residents' lounge with an honesty bar. An open fire burns in the bar which has oak settles, antique chairs. Chef Dave Hunter's seasonal menu can be taken here or in the oak-panelled dining room. He uses local produce for his modern dishes, perhaps roast pigeon breast, leg croquette, boulangère potato, thyme-infused sauce. A 'good breakfast' has a 'notable selection of teas'. 'Our favourite hotel; warm and comfy; we managed a walk in the glorious countryside despite the bad weather.' (Shirley Gray, and others)

25% DISCOUNT VOUCHERS

Romaldkirk
DL12 9EB

T: 01833 650213
E: hotel@rose-and-crown.co.uk
W: www.rose-and-crown.co.uk

BEDROOMS: 14. 2 in Monk's Cottage, 5 in rear courtyard, some on ground floor.
OPEN: all year except 23–27 Dec.
FACILITIES: residents' lounge, lounge bar, Crown Room (bar meals), restaurant, free Wi-Fi, boot room, fishing (grouse shooting, birdwatching) nearby.
BACKGROUND MUSIC: 'easy listening' in restaurant.
LOCATION: village centre.
CHILDREN: all ages welcomed.
DOGS: welcomed.
CREDIT CARDS: Amex, MasterCard, Visa.
PRICES: [2015] per person B&B £57.50–£67.50, D,B&B £89. À la carte £32.

ROSS-ON-WYE Herefordshire

Map 3:D5

WILTON COURT

Enveloped by the 'peaceful atmosphere' of the River Wye, Helen and Roger Wynn's riverbank restaurant-with-rooms is liked for the 'good food' and 'friendly, efficient service'. In their absence, 'everything was spot on,' say visitors in 2015. Once an Elizabethan magistrates' court, the building is steeped in history. The Riverview restaurant is now located in the old courtroom; bedrooms on the first floor were once the magistrates' chambers. In the oldest part of the building, rooms have original exposed beams and restored stone fireplaces. There are large beds. Bedrooms facing the Wye have views of swans, kingfishers, even otters; those overlooking the gardens take in mature willows and the landscaped lawns. Each is individually decorated with bright fabrics and bold wallpaper. Public spaces have ancient beams, leaded windows and curios picked up on the Wynns' travels. In the bright and spacious restaurant, chef Rachael Williams's market menu might include goat's cheese and red onion tartlet; duo of sea bass and red mullet, roast peppers, pak choi, brown shrimp butter. Breakfast has organic porridge and kippers ('as tasty as they get'). (Richard Morgan-Price, and others)

Wilton Lane
Ross-on-Wye
HR9 6AQ

T: 01989 562569
F: 01989 768460
E: info@wiltoncourthotel.com
W: www.wiltoncourthotel.com

BEDROOMS: 10.
OPEN: all year except first 2 weeks Jan.
FACILITIES: sitting room, bar, restaurant, private dining room, free Wi-Fi, civil wedding licence, 1-acre grounds, only restaurant suitable for disabled.
BACKGROUND MUSIC: none.
LOCATION: ½ mile from centre.
CHILDREN: all ages welcomed.
DOGS: welcomed, but not in restaurant.
CREDIT CARDS: Amex, MasterCard, Visa.
PRICES: [2015] per room B&B £135–£185, D,B&B £185–£235. Set dinner £29.50–£32.50, à la carte £37.50. 1-night bookings refused weekends Apr–Oct.

ROSTHWAITE Cumbria

Map 4: inset C2

❦ HAZEL BANK **[NEW]**

César award: walking hotel of the year

In a beautiful Lake District valley, this 'charming' stone house, built in 1840, returns to the Guide under the ownership of the MacRae family. 'It is a welcoming, relaxed place,' say inspectors in 2015. 'The whole family runs the hotel: Gary is the enthusiastic host, helped by his eldest son; his wife, Donna, is the cook; Rachael, the granny, is also involved.' The house, which stands in large grounds that run down to a river, has been 'transformed from a gloomy place into one that is bright and welcoming'. It is popular with walkers: six walks of varying length and difficulty start at the door; packed lunches can be provided; a drying room is available. 'Our bedroom had white paintwork, light patterned wallpaper; walnut bedside tables, powerful reading lights. It was well equipped; a good selection on the hospitality tray; a sherry decanter; chocolates.' Dinner, in a 'pleasant, light' dining room, is 'excellent'. The short four-course menu might include risotto of wild pea and river trout; roast duo of Cumbrian chicken, pommes boulangère. Breakfast has a wide choice; 'very good scrambled eggs'.

Borrowdale
Rosthwaite
CA12 5XB

T: 017687 77248
F: 017687 77373
E: info@hazelbankhotel.co.uk
w: www.hazelbankhotel.co.uk

BEDROOMS: 7. 1 on ground floor.
OPEN: all year except 6 Dec–28 Jan.
FACILITIES: lounge, dining room, drying room, free Wi-Fi, 4-acre grounds (croquet, woodland walks).
BACKGROUND MUSIC: none.
LOCATION: 6 miles S of Keswick.
CHILDREN: not under 15.
DOGS: not allowed.
CREDIT CARDS: MasterCard, Visa.
PRICES: per person B&B £70–£78, D,B&B £92–£104. Set dinner £29. Min. 2-night stay.

THE PEACOCK AT ROWSLEY NEW

On the edge of a Peak District village, this creeper-covered Grade II listed 17th-century building, once the dower house to nearby Haddon Hall, is upgraded to a full entry thanks to a positive report by a regular Guide correspondent. Owned by Lord Edward Manners, it is run to 'high standards', says a visitor in 2015. 'The staff are friendly and efficient.' Original features (mullioned windows, leaded lights, open stone fireplaces) complement modern soft furnishings in the 'cosy' bar. The bedrooms are individually furnished with antiques, Manners family portraits and fine fabrics. Some overlook the gardens designed by Arne Maynard, that run down to the River Derwent. Rooms facing the busy road have double-glazed windows. Meals can be taken in the restaurant or the bar. Chef Dan Smith's British modern menu is 'consistently good; the "real steal" is the lighter lunch menu: normal-size starter and dessert, and a half-size main, but these are Derbyshire portions and half-size is still very adequate'. There is 'good fishing on both the Derwent and Wye, a huge bonus'. The only irritant: 'Cooked breakfast costs extra.' Dogs are welcomed. (Peter Anderson)

Bakewell Road
Rowsley
DE4 2EB

T: 01629 733518
F: 01629 732671
E: reception@thepeacockatrowsley.com
w: www.thepeacockatrowsley.co.uk

BEDROOMS: 15.
OPEN: all year except 24–26 Dec, 2 weeks Jan.
FACILITIES: lounge, bar, restaurant, free Wi-Fi, civil wedding licence, ½-acre garden on river, unsuitable for disabled.
BACKGROUND MUSIC: none.
LOCATION: edge of village.
CHILDREN: not under 10 at weekends.
DOGS: not allowed in public rooms.
CREDIT CARDS: Amex, MasterCard, Visa.
PRICES: [2015] per room B&B single £110–£125, double £180–£240, D,B&B single £145–£160, double £250–£310. A la carte £55. 1-night bookings sometimes refused.

RUSHLAKE GREEN East Sussex

STONE HOUSE

Henry VII was on the throne when the original timber-frame, tile-hung house was built by the Roberts Dunn family, whose descendants still live here. The later Tudor, gabled building with massive oak staircase and a Georgian wing, is run in a very personal way as a 'delightful' small hotel. It is traditionally furnished throughout, with antiques, paintings, family photographs, floral fabrics, chintzes, Staffordshire dogs. A log fire burns in the 'gorgeous' library. The 'comfortable' rooms are individually styled; two have a four-poster bed. The veteran owner, Peter Dunn, greets guests with old-fashioned courtesy and charm. His portrait hangs on the panelled walls of a dining room with brick floor, and silver candlesticks on the tables. Jane Dunn cooks 'superb' dinners using vegetables and herbs from the walled kitchen garden, game from the estate, fish from the South Coast. Typical dishes: nettle soup with wild garlic; saddle of wild rabbit, thyme and three-mustard sauce. Staff are 'delightful', grounds and garden – with two lakes and woodland – are 'beautifully kept'. A picnic hamper on wheels can be provided for taking to nearby Glyndebourne. (Alex McTavish)

Rushlake Green
TN21 9QJ

T: 01435 830553
F: 01435 830726
E: stonehousehotel@aol.co.uk
W: www.stonehousesussex.co.uk

BEDROOMS: 7.
OPEN: all year except 23 Dec–4 Jan, 29 Jan–12 Feb.
FACILITIES: drawing room, library, dining room, billiard room, free Wi-Fi, 1,000-acre estate (6½-acre garden, farm, woodland, croquet, shooting, pheasant/clay-pigeon shooting, 2 lakes, rowing, fishing), unsuitable for disabled.
BACKGROUND MUSIC: none.
LOCATION: 4 miles SE of Heathfield, by village green.
CHILDREN: not under 9.
DOGS: allowed in bedrooms, not in public rooms.
CREDIT CARDS: MasterCard, Visa.
PRICES: [2015] per room double/twin £195–£290. À la carte £34. 1-night bookings refused weekends 16 May–1 Sept.

RYE East Sussex

Map 2:E5

JEAKE'S HOUSE

♕ César award in 1992

Once the 'deeply cherished home' of American
writer Conrad Aiken, this 17th-century wool
store and adjoining Elders House is run as a
B&B by Jenny Hadfield. 'Very nice owner and
staff, splendid breakfast,' said a visitor this
year. The house stands on a cobbled street in
this former Cinque Port town rich in literary
associations. Bags are carried to the bedrooms
which are reached along a warren of corridors
(some are up steep staircases). Some rooms are
named after the literary figures associated with
the town. Elizabeth Fry was 'bathed in sunlight
and felt light and airy', but its four-poster was
thought to be small. There are warm colours
and traditional furnishings throughout. Some
rooms have low beams, others uneven floors. An
open fire might burn in the parlour. An honesty
bar is 'useful before departing for dinner' at
one of Rye's many restaurants. Tables are set
with crisp white cloths in a galleried hall for
breakfast which has a buffet of cereals and fruit;
perhaps oak-smoked haddock, devilled kidneys;
home-made jams. 'Discreet' background music
is played. (Peter Morris, and others)

Mermaid Street
Rye
TN31 7ET

T: 01797 222828
E: stay@jeakeshouse.com
W: www.jeakeshouse.com

BEDROOMS: 11.
OPEN: all year.
FACILITIES: parlour, bar/library,
breakfast room, free Wi-Fi,
unsuitable for disabled.
BACKGROUND MUSIC: classical in
breakfast room.
LOCATION: town centre.
CHILDREN: not under 8.
DOGS: allowed, on leads 'and always
supervised' (£5 a night), not in
breakfast room.
CREDIT CARDS: MasterCard, Visa.
PRICES: [2015] per person B&B
£58–£70.

SEE ALSO SHORTLIST

ST AGNES Cornwall

Map 1:D2

ROSE IN VALE

In summer, swags of roses adorn the Doric porch of James and Sara Evans's 'elegant' if much extended Georgian country house in a secluded valley, in the village of Mithian. 'Tireless' Sara Evans looks after everything front-of-house, the staff are 'utterly charming', say returning visitors this year. There has been a change in the kitchen. Joint head chefs James and Tom Bennett ('not related', strangely) make inventive use of seasonal, local produce in such dishes as duo of Cornish duck (breast and confit spring roll), fondant potato, dates, julienne of vegetables; roast monkfish, lemon, charred chorizo, samphire, saffron potato. 'Loud pianola music' was not liked. The bedrooms are individually styled. The Rose suite, with views over the wooded valley, has a four-poster bed; in the bathroom a double spa bath and a separate shower. Some ground-floor rooms have a wet room suitable for disabled guests. The solar-heated swimming pool is a big plus. 'The staff were good at briefing us on the rip tides in the bay where we were competing in a bellyboarding championship.'

Mithian
St Agnes
TR5 0QD

T: 01872 552202
E: reception@roseinvalehotel.co.uk
W: www.roseinvalehotel.co.uk

BEDROOMS: 22. 7 on ground floor, 2 suitable for disabled, 3 in garden annexes.
OPEN: all year except 1 week end Nov, Jan.
FACILITIES: lift, sitting room, snug, lounge, drawing room, restaurant, free Wi-Fi, civil wedding licence, 9-acre grounds, outdoor swimming pool (15 by 33 metres).
BACKGROUND MUSIC: piano music in restaurant and bar in evening.
LOCATION: 2 miles E of St Agnes.
CHILDREN: not under 12.
DOGS: allowed in some bedrooms, elsewhere on leads, not in restaurant.
CREDIT CARDS: MasterCard, Visa.
PRICES: [2015] per room B&B £120–£380. À la carte £37.50.

ST IVES Cornwall

Map 1:D1

BOSKERRIS HOTEL

A 'compelling view' of Carbis Bay can be enjoyed from the public rooms and outdoor decked terrace of Jonathan and Marianne Bassett's small hotel. They have given the public areas an 'immaculate' modern look, with white-painted walls; floor-to-ceiling windows flood the rooms with light. It opens on to a large 'delightful decked terrace', 'ideal' in good weather for afternoon tea, early-evening drinks or a light meal. Many of the bedrooms have a sea view; the Celebration room has a sunken bath looking over the bay. 'Our room was immaculate in shades of white and cream; a spotless modern bathroom with a huge shower.' An informal Mediterranean supper is available on five nights a week (eg, carpaccio of beef, horseradish celeriac; lamb tagine). There is good information on the restaurants in St Ives, which can be reached by train: the station is a short walk down the hill ('more testing on the way back'). An 'excellent' breakfast has an 'above-average' buffet with freshly squeezed orange juice, fruit, home-made muesli; 'delicious' local ingredients for the cooked dishes. The Coastal Path passes nearby.

Boskerris Road
Carbis Bay
St Ives
TR26 2NQ

T: 01736 795295
E: reservations@boskerrishotel.co.uk
W: www.boskerrishotel.co.uk

BEDROOMS: 15. 1 on ground floor.
OPEN: Mar–Nov, restaurant closed Sun/Mon.
FACILITIES: lounge, bar, restaurant, private dining/meeting room, free Wi-Fi, decked terrace, 1½-acre garden.
BACKGROUND MUSIC: jazz/Latin.
LOCATION: 1½ miles from centre (5 mins by local train), car park.
CHILDREN: not under 8.
DOGS: not allowed.
CREDIT CARDS: Amex, MasterCard, Visa.
PRICES: [2015] per room B&B £150–£275. À la carte £30. 1-night bookings sometimes refused.

SEE ALSO SHORTLIST

HASTINGS HOUSE

Steps from the sea, Seng and Elisabeth Loy's 'immaculate' B&B is a four-storey Victorian house given a 'modern, stylish' interior. The greeting is warm (a welcoming drink might be offered). All of the bedrooms have large windows; some have a sea view. They are individually decorated with bold colours and striking designs. Room 5 ('lovely') has black and brown leather furnishings; a view of the pier. Room 1 has an open-plan layout with a power shower in a closet tucked around the corner. Room 7 can accommodate two adults and a child. Room 6, in deep orange colours, has a large freestanding bath in the bathroom. The attention to detail and extra touches like flowers in the room, a hospitality tray with tea and coffee, are liked. The lounge has a marble-topped bar, leather chairs, a wooden floor; the dining room overlooks the garden with views out to sea. Breakfast has fresh fruit, croissants, pains au chocolat; among the cooked options are brioche French toast, pancakes, perhaps smoked salmon and scrambled eggs or a full English. Events and functions are catered for.

25% DISCOUNT VOUCHERS

9 Warrior Square
St Leonards-on-Sea
TN37 6BA

T: 01424 422709
F: 01424 420592
E: info@hastingshouse.co.uk
W: www.hastingshouse.co.uk

BEDROOMS: 8.
OPEN: all year.
FACILITIES: bar/lounge, dining room, free Wi-Fi, small terrace, unsuitable for disabled.
BACKGROUND MUSIC: none.
LOCATION: seafront, 1 mile from town centre.
CHILDREN: all ages welcomed.
DOGS: not allowed.
CREDIT CARDS: MasterCard, Visa.
PRICES: [2015] per room B&B single £80–£110, double £95–£145. 1-night bookings refused weekends and bank holidays.

ST LEONARDS-ON-SEA East Sussex

⚜ ZANZIBAR INTERNATIONAL HOTEL

César award: eccentric hotel of the year

'With an exotic name, themed bedrooms, showers that say "welcome" and "goodbye", there is a splendidly quirky feel about this small seafront hotel.' Guide inspectors this year enjoyed the informal charm of Max O'Rourke's 'relaxed' hotel: 'First names are used from the start; we were given drinks in the garden while our suitcases were carted up three flights of stairs.' Big windows and plentiful mirrors 'fill the building with light during the day'. The themed bedrooms, which vary in size, reflect the owner's passion for travel. 'We chose Antarctica because of the sea view. It had white walls and floor, pale green upholstery, a chandelier like icicles; a high ceiling contributed to a spacious feel; a chaise longue and sofa by the window, a small fridge with drinks and goodies. Loud muzak played in the public areas.' 'Delicious, utterly unpretentious' meals are served in the 'pleasant' restaurant, Pier Nine: 'Very fresh plaice and sea bass; the £10 lunch is excellent value. We liked the note that accompanied our morning newspaper, giving the weather forecast and suggesting an outing of the day.'

9 Eversfield Place
St Leonards-on-Sea
TN37 6BY

T: 01424 460109
E: info@zanzibarhotel.co.uk
W: www.zanzibarhotel.co.uk

BEDROOMS: 8. 1 on ground floor.
OPEN: all year.
FACILITIES: bar area, restaurant, free Wi-Fi, garden, beach across road, unsuitable for disabled.
BACKGROUND MUSIC: 'easy listening' in bar, restaurant.
LOCATION: seafront, 650 yds W of Hastings pier, free parking.
CHILDREN: not under 5.
DOGS: not allowed.
CREDIT CARDS: Amex, MasterCard, Visa.
PRICES: [2015] per room B&B from £115, D,B&B from £184. À la carte £35.

ST MARY'S Isles of Scilly

Map 1: inset C1

STAR CASTLE

♕César award in 2009

There are 'stunningly beautiful views across the islands' from the Francis family's hotel, in a star-shaped, 16th-century castle on Garrison Hill. James Francis is the manager; long-serving staff are 'friendly and helpful'. Bedrooms are in the castle and single-storey buildings in the grounds (a short open-air walk away); garden suites have a veranda. 'My single Guard House room on the ramparts had tiny windows looking out on to the harbour. On the windowsill, a pewter tankard with fresh dahlias was a nice touch.' Guests have a choice of places to eat: the summertime Conservatory specialises in seafood; the 'atmospheric and historic' Castle restaurant has a 'wonderful' candlelit ambience and 'excellent' food (perhaps 'very good' seared venison). At breakfast, 'delicious' bacon and tomatoes are 'cooked to perfection'. The hotel is a ten-minute walk up a hill from the harbour; for guests arriving by ferry, luggage is brought from the boat to the room. Robert Francis, James's father, has established a vineyard on the island. The first bottles were reserved for hotel guests to enjoy with lobster caught 'by Robert himself'.

The Garrison
St Mary's
TR21 0JA

T: 01720 422317
F: 01720 422343
E: info@star-castle.co.uk
W: www.star-castle.co.uk

BEDROOMS: 38. 27 in 2 garden wings.
OPEN: all year, B&B only Nov–Jan except Christmas/New Year.
FACILITIES: lounge, bar, 2 restaurants, free Wi-Fi, civil wedding licence, 3-acre grounds (covered swimming pool, 12 by 3 metres, tennis), beach nearby, unsuitable for disabled.
BACKGROUND MUSIC: none.
LOCATION: ¼ mile from town centre, boat (2¾ hours)/helicopter.
CHILDREN: welcomed, not under 5 in restaurants.
DOGS: welcomed in garden rooms, not in restaurants.
CREDIT CARDS: Amex, MasterCard, Visa.
PRICES: [2015] per person B&B (Nov–Jan) from £75, D,B&B £85–£201. À la carte £34.50.

IDLE ROCKS

On the harbour, with nothing between it and the sea, David and Karen Richards's luxury hotel has been a seaside destination for 100 years. Award-winning hotelier Anthony Chapman has joined as general manager this year. Guide inspectors were impressed by the renovation of the building: 'It has a well-presented nautical style with vibrant colours, big paintings, huge planters full of orchids.' The terrace is 'perfect' for enjoying a glass of wine in good weather. 'Our bedroom (exquisitely furnished with a delightful raspberry pink scheme) had a large, very comfortable bed, well-designed curtains, Juliet window with views of the water; a huge shower, good-quality smellies. Of especial note was the tiny motion-sensor-operated night light in the bathroom and the evening turn-down service – so nice to come back to after dinner!' The dining room 'is cleverly laid out in three tiers so everyone gets the sea view'. A new chef was being appointed as the Guide went to press. Breakfast has 'really good marmalade'. Children are welcomed: they have a playroom with toys and puzzles; high tea is served at the chef's table.

Harbourside
St Mawes
TR2 5AN

T: 01326 270270
E: info@idlerocks.com
W: www.idlerocks.com

BEDROOMS: 19. 1 room suitable for disabled.
OPEN: all year, except 3–4 weeks Jan.
FACILITIES: lounge, bar, kids' room, boot room, free Wi-Fi, terrace.
BACKGROUND MUSIC: 'mixed' in public areas.
LOCATION: by the harbour.
CHILDREN: all ages welcomed.
DOGS: allowed in 2 bedrooms, not in public rooms.
CREDIT CARDS: all major cards.
PRICES: [2015] per room B&B £195–£350. Set menu £27. À la carte £55. 1-night bookings sometimes refused.

TRESANTON

♥César award in 2009

Originally a yachting club, Olga Polizzi's 'superb' luxury hotel has views over Falmouth Bay towards St Anthony's lighthouse. Standing on a steep hill ('the climb is worth it for plant lovers'), the hotel has 'bags of charm': fresh flowers, original paintings, 'quirky mosaic floors' in some rooms. Bedrooms ('relaxed, but not overdone') are spread across a cluster of buildings; some are reached via stairs through 'well-planted' gardens. Each is individually decorated in a subtle seafaring theme (nautical stripes, antiques), and has Cornish objets d'art. One room has a wood-burning stove and a crow's nest terrace; another a balcony with deckchairs. In the tongue-and-grooved restaurant, chef Paul Wadham's Mediterranean menu is influenced by the day's catch, with 'fresh ingredients, simply done'; his menu might include breaded Fal prawns, wild bass and crab cakes. The cinema, playroom, children's garden and kids' club during school holidays will keep youngsters busy. Older explorers will enjoy a cruise on the private yacht. There is a sister hotel: Hotel Endsleigh, Milton Abbot (see entry). (CR, and others)

27 Lower Castle Road
St Mawes
TR2 5DR

T: 01326 270055
F: 01326 270053
E: info@tresanton.com
W: www.tresanton.com

BEDROOMS: 30. In 5 houses.
OPEN: all year.
FACILITIES: 2 lounges, bar, restaurant, cinema, playroom, conference facilities, free Wi-Fi, civil wedding licence, terrace, ¼-acre garden, by sea (48-foot yacht, rigid inflatable boat), unsuitable for disabled.
BACKGROUND MUSIC: none.
LOCATION: on seafront, valet parking (car park up hill).
CHILDREN: all ages welcomed, no under-6s in restaurant in evening.
DOGS: allowed in some bedrooms, and in dogs' bar, not in sitting rooms or restaurant.
CREDIT CARDS: Amex, MasterCard, Visa.
PRICES: [2015] per room B&B £200–£580, D,B&B from £280. Set lunch £23–£27, à la carte £45. 1-night bookings refused weekends in high season.

SALCOMBE Devon

Map 1:E4

SALCOMBE HARBOUR HOTEL
NEW

In a prime position on the water's edge of a 'wonderful' Devon estuary, this Victorian hotel has been redeveloped to 'a very high standard' by Harbour Hotels. The modern design has 'many lovely touches and an impressive sea theme', says a regular correspondent, recommending an upgrade to a full entry. 'The level of service exceeded expectations; the staff were professional and willing to please.' The bedrooms, decorated in pale blues and maritime stripes, are on four floors (the views are best on the higher levels; some rooms face inland). 'Our room, which had a balcony facing the beaches across the estuary, was difficult to fault; we liked the decanters of gin and sherry and the proper coffee machine.' In the restaurant, which has sitting areas for pre-dinner drinks, chef Alex Aitken makes full use of locally landed fish and shellfish in his contemporary menus ('the fish soup was delicious'). An 'excellent' spa has an indoor swimming pool, treatment rooms, a sauna and a cool room. Valet service is appreciated in a town of narrow streets and limited parking. (Ian Dewey, BW)

Cliff Road
Salcombe
TQ8 8JH

T: 01548 844444
E: salcombe@harbourhotels.co.uk
W: www.salcombe-harbour-hotel.co.uk

BEDROOMS: 50. 2 suitable for disabled.
OPEN: all year.
FACILITIES: bar/lounge, Jetty restaurant, civil wedding licence, spa (indoor swimming pool, 15 by 5 metres, fitness suite, treatment rooms), free Wi-Fi.
BACKGROUND MUSIC: in public areas.
LOCATION: town centre.
CHILDREN: all ages welcomed.
DOGS: welcomed in some bedrooms, not in public rooms.
CREDIT CARDS: all major cards.
PRICES: (2015) per room B&B £155–£545, D,B&B £210–£580. 1-night bookings sometimes refused.

SEE ALSO SHORTLIST

SEAHAM Co. Durham

Map 4:B4

SEAHAM HALL NEW

'Informal and relaxed, but nevertheless wonderfully pleasant and civilised', this 'stylish' contemporary hotel sits in 'beautifully landscaped' grounds minutes from the beach. 'We were very impressed,' say trusted correspondents this year, whose report earns Seaham Hall a full entry in the Guide. The extended 18th-century manor house was acquired in 2012 by private owners, who have carried out considerable renovation. Ross Grieve is the manager; staff are 'friendly, helpful and attentive'. ('One niggle: the inescapable background music.') Guests have a choice of eating places: Byrons Bar & Grill has an emphasis on seafood; pan-Asian Ozone is 'informal but stylish'; light meals are taken in the lounges or on terraces overlooking the garden and the sea. 'We showed an interest in the wine list at dinner, and were invited for a tour of the wine cellar the next day.' Some of the modern bedrooms have a private garden. 'Our spacious suite had a king-size bed with a wonderfully soft duvet and pillows: utter luxury.' The spa has 'all the facilities imaginable', including a heated pool 'lovely for relaxing in'. (Stephen and Pauline Glover)

Lord Byron's Walk
Seaham
SR7 7AG

T: 0191 5161400
F: 0191 5161410
E: hotel@seaham-hall.com
W: www.seaham-hall.com

BEDROOMS: 20. 1 suitable for disabled.
OPEN: all year.
FACILITIES: lift, 2 lounges, bar, 2 restaurants, private dining room, conference facilities, free Wi-Fi, civil wedding licence, spa (treatment rooms, outdoor hot tubs, sun terrace, fitness suite, 20-metre heated swimming pool), 37-acre grounds (terraces, putting green).
BACKGROUND MUSIC: contemporary in public areas, spa.
LOCATION: 5 miles S of Sunderland.
CHILDREN: all ages welcomed.
DOGS: not allowed.
CREDIT CARDS: all major cards.
PRICES: [2015] per room B&B from £265, D,B&B from £325. À la carte £45.

SEAHOUSES Northumberland

Map 4:A4

ST CUTHBERT'S HOUSE

In this colourful harbour village on the 'beautiful' Northumberland coast, this former Presbyterian church has been 'lovingly' restored into a B&B by musicians Jill and Jeff Sutheran, 'great hosts'. The 'very comfortable' bedrooms, decorated in classic colours, have solid wood furniture. 'My spacious room could not be faulted for the sense of style; it had a good shower room.' Two rooms are on the ground floor (one equipped for visitors with mobility problems). The Sutherans employed local craftsmen to convert the church to dramatic effect: the former pulpit overlooks the double-height chapel which houses the lounge ('good seating, local information') and the breakfast area. There's an honesty bar stocked with local ales. Breakfast has bread from the nearby bakery, award-winning sausages, home-made preserves (including marmalade with chilli) and honey from the Sutherans' own bees. Local fish is a feature of the cooked choices (Seahouses is the birthplace of the original kipper): perhaps 'delicious' kipper pâté ('the best ever'), kipper fillets, smoked haddock kedgeree. There is much to see in the area: Bamburgh Castle and the Farne Islands are nearby. (Gwyn Morgan, SP)

192 Main Street
Seahouses
NE68 7UB

T: 01665 720456
E: stay@stcuthbertshouse.com
W: www.stcuthbertshouse.com

BEDROOMS: 6, 2 on ground floor, 1 suitable for disabled.
OPEN: all year, except Christmas/New Year, occasionally in 'quieter periods'.
FACILITIES: lounge/breakfast room, free Wi-Fi, small garden.
BACKGROUND MUSIC: none.
LOCATION: 1 mile from harbour.
CHILDREN: not under 12.
DOGS: not allowed.
CREDIT CARDS: MasterCard, Visa.
PRICES: per room B&B £120. 1-night bookings sometimes refused.

SHAFTESBURY Dorset

Map 2:D1

LA FLEUR DE LYS

In a 'friendly little town with plenty of individual shops', this restaurant-with-rooms is run by the 'charming, hands-on' owners, David and Mary Griffin-Shepherd and Marc Preston. 'Outstanding food, immaculate rooms, professional yet very helpful owners,' said one visitor. There is a 'welcoming' lounge/bar; pre-dinner drinks (and afternoon tea) can also be taken, in fine weather, in a pretty courtyard garden. Mary Griffin-Shepherd is in charge of front-of-house; her husband and Marc Preston are the chefs, serving a seasonal menu of 'well-executed and presented' dishes like home-smoked quail; sole fillets, asparagus, lemon-infused butter. Guests can choose between two and three courses; some dishes carry a supplement. The 'immaculate' bedrooms, each named after a grape variety, have a small refrigerator, tea-making facilities with fresh milk and home-made biscuits. Sauvignon was 'small, but clean and comfortable'. Superior rooms have a sofa and a laptop computer. Bedroom windows at the front are double glazed. An 'excellent' breakfast has freshly squeezed orange juice, porridge, butter and marmalade in pots. (CS, and others)

Bleke Street
Shaftesbury
SP7 8AW

T: 01747 853717
E: info@lafleurdelys.co.uk
w: www.lafleurdelys.co.uk

BEDROOMS: 8. 1 on ground floor.
OPEN: all year, restaurant closed Sun night, midday Mon and Tues, 3 weeks in Jan.
FACILITIES: lounge, bar, dining room, conference room, free Wi-Fi, small courtyard.
BACKGROUND MUSIC: none.
LOCATION: N edge of town centre.
CHILDREN: all ages welcomed.
DOGS: not allowed.
CREDIT CARDS: Amex, MasterCard, Visa.
PRICES: [2015] per room B&B single £90–£100, double £105–£165. Set meals £28–£35. 1-night bookings sometimes refused.

HOTEL RIVIERA

NEW

'It's the little things that count' at the Wharton family's traditional hotel on the esplanade overlooking Lyme Bay. A regular correspondent's positive report in 2015 earns it an upgrade to a full entry. 'Things like the bed being turned down, the room tidied and the curtains drawn as one is at dinner; like the barman remembering which wines you like; like the breakfast toast arriving at the precise time you want it, so that it's hot when you apply the butter.' The 'smart, comfortable' hotel occupies a fine Regency terrace two minutes from the town centre; many bedrooms have sea views. 'My small, first-floor room was spotlessly clean and well equipped; there was a very good shower over the bath.' There is 'a timeless feel' in the 'spacious' dining room, where chef Martin Osedo's 'flawlessly served, beautifully presented' daily-changing menus might include whole lemon sole, new potatoes, asparagus, truffle butter. Served at table, breakfast is 'extensive and absolutely delicious'. 'It's quite a treat to have, even at breakfast, the starched linen napkin unfolded and placed across one's lap.' (Trevor Lockwood)

The Esplanade
Sidmouth
EX10 8AY

T: 01395 515201
F: 01395 577775
E: enquiries@hotelriviera.co.uk
W: www.hotelriviera.co.uk

BEDROOMS: 26.
OPEN: all year, except Jan–mid-Feb 2016.
FACILITIES: lift, ramp, lounge, bar, restaurant, function facilities, free Wi-Fi, terrace, opposite pebble/sand beach (safe bathing).
BACKGROUND MUSIC: 'soft' in bar and restaurant, occasional live piano music in bar.
LOCATION: central, on the esplanade.
CHILDREN: all ages welcomed.
DOGS: small dogs allowed in some bedrooms, not public rooms.
CREDIT CARDS: all major cards.
PRICES: [2015] per person B&B £109–£211, D,B&B £99–£232. Set dinner £38–£42, à la carte £44.

SEE ALSO SHORTLIST

SOAR MILL COVE Devon

Map 1:E4

SOAR MILL COVE HOTEL

In extensive grounds above a sandy cove in an area of outstanding natural beauty, this 'welcoming' hotel has a 'pleasant, settled feel'. The owner/manager Keith Makepeace has recently renovated the public areas and bedrooms. 'It is much improved in looks since the last time we were there,' said a visitor this year. 'The restaurant is lighter, and the lounge has attractive seating. Both have large windows facing the view over sloping lawns, green meadows with sheep and cattle, and out to the sea.' There is no background music. The chef, Ian MacDonald, serves a five-course menu (individual courses can be taken) of locally sourced produce with dishes like yellow-fin tuna, oriental spices; duo of cumin-spiced lamb, caramelised root vegetables, shallot purée, port and redcurrant sauce. Each of the bedrooms has a private patio with sun loungers. Family suites have a separate bedroom for children, and plenty of storybooks. Young visitors will find much to do if they can be dragged away from the beach: there is entertainment in the summer (movie nights, baking, etc); a games room has pool and table tennis. (CE)

25% DISCOUNT VOUCHERS

Soar Mill Cove
TQ7 3DS

T: 01548 561566
F: 01548 561223
E: Keith@soarmillcove.co.uk
W: www.soarmillcove.co.uk

BEDROOMS: 22. All on ground floor.
OPEN: all year, except Jan, closed New Year.
FACILITIES: lounge, 2 bars, restaurant (pianist), coffee shop, free Wi-Fi, indoor swimming pool (15 by 10 metres), treatment room (hairdressing, reflexology, aromatherapy, etc), civil wedding licence, 10-acre grounds (tennis, children's play area), sandy beach.
BACKGROUND MUSIC: none.
LOCATION: 3 miles SW of Salcombe.
CHILDREN: all ages welcomed (children's tea, baby-listening service, free cots, baby meals, games room, children's entertainment in summer).
DOGS: well-behaved dogs allowed in bedrooms, coffee shop only.
CREDIT CARDS: Amex, MasterCard, Visa.
PRICES: [2015] per room B&B from £169, D,B&B from £229.

THE LYNCH COUNTRY HOUSE

On the edge of a medieval market, this 'beautiful' country house has 'understated Georgian elegance'. On the top of a ridge leading down to the River Cary (Lynch means 'terrace on the face of a down'), it stands in gardens 'worth making a journey to enjoy'; they have a large lawned area, topiary, a rill, many specimen trees and flowers; a lake with ornamental fish and resident black swans. Owned by retired jazz musician Roy Copeland, the house is managed as a B&B by Lynne Vincent. The 'intimate' interior has been restored and furnished with antiques and jazz memorabilia. Light floods the centre of the building thanks to a 'sun bonnet' lantern on the apex of the roof. The best bedrooms, on the first floor of the main building, have a high ceiling, sash windows facing the garden. Smaller rooms are at the top of the house; four ground-floor rooms are in a coach house in the garden. Breakfast, in a bright orangery, has freshly squeezed orange juice, French yogurts. The White Hart, Market Place (see Shortlist), is recommended for dinner. (ML, and others)

4 Behind Berry
Somerton
TA11 7PD

T: 01458 272316
F: 01458 272590
E: enquiries@
thelynchcountryhouse.co.uk
W: www.thelynchcountryhouse.co.uk

BEDROOMS: 9. 4, in coach house, on ground floor.
OPEN: all year (limited opening, no breakfast at Christmas/New Year).
FACILITIES: breakfast room, small sitting area, free Wi-Fi, 2½-acre grounds (lake), unsuitable for disabled.
BACKGROUND MUSIC: none.
LOCATION: N edge of town.
CHILDREN: all ages welcomed.
DOGS: allowed in 1 coach house room (not unattended), not in public rooms.
CREDIT CARDS: Amex, MasterCard, Visa.
PRICES: [2015] per room B&B single £70–£95, double £80–£115.

THE PIG IN THE WALL

Set into the medieval city walls, this 'smart, shabby chic' B&B hotel occupies a 'charming' 19th-century building in the 'interesting' old town. It is part of the small Home Grown Hotels group of Pig hotels, owned by Robin Hutson and David Elton. 'We were particularly struck by the ethos of the place. Even the staff – efficient young people – seem immensely delighted by it,' Guide inspectors said. Guests enter through the deli bar 'where people enjoy good-looking nibbles and drinks by an open fire'. In the bedrooms, decorated by Judy Hutson, 'everything is modern and well thought out'. 'Our room had a beamed ceiling and an original decorative iron fireplace. The comfortable super-king-size bed had crisp white linens: we slept well.' 'Piggy bits' (perhaps a Hampshire charcuterie platter) are served in the deli bar; for dinner, a free shuttle service takes guests to sister hotel The Pig, Brockenhurst (see entry), which is 'magical at night'. Breakfast is a help-yourself buffet with 'a nice selection of most things one would require of a continental breakfast'; 'good' coffee is brought by the cup.

8 Western Esplanade
Southampton
SO14 2AZ

T: 02380 636900
E: reservations@
 thepiginthewall.com
W: www.thepighotel.com

BEDROOMS: 12. 2 on ground floor.
OPEN: all year.
FACILITIES: open-plan lounge, bar, deli counter, free Wi-Fi, unsuitable for disabled.
BACKGROUND MUSIC: in public areas.
LOCATION: central.
CHILDREN: all ages welcomed.
DOGS: not allowed.
CREDIT CARDS: Amex, MasterCard, Visa.
PRICES: [2015] room £130–£190. Breakfast £10.

SEE ALSO SHORTLIST

SOUTHWOLD Suffolk

Map 2:B6

THE SWAN

Adnams Brewery and the 350-year-old Swan are as prominent a feature of Southwold as the Victorian lighthouse of which the hotel annexe rooms have a view. In early 2015 the Swan was closed for a 'refresh' that has brought a cleaner, more modern look. The contemporary, dog-friendly, family-oriented Lighthouse rooms, with 'coastal theme' decor and outside seating, surround the garden and had no need of updating. A guest who slept in Mr Crisp's Room – named after William Crisp, elected the town's first mayor in 1836 – found something like the Great Bed of Ware but better upholstered, 'enough to sleep six, and on a well-sprung mattress too'. Fluffy towels, walk-in shower and oval bath in the bathroom. Guests can eat in the bar or restaurant, from a short menu. Chef Rory Whelan gives a modern twist to local ingredients – Bunwell venison loin, dauphine potatoes, Jerusalem artichoke, savoy, wild mushrooms, fig, port reduction; Binham Blue, mushrooms and spinach millefeuille, cauliflower, chicory, apple. At breakfast there is Greek yogurt, cured East Anglian ham, Broadside bacon, locally smoked kippers. Holistic treatments can be taken in Priya Spa. (DB)

Market Place
Southwold
IP18 6EG

T: 01502 722186
F: 01502 724800
E: reception@adnams.co.uk
W: www.adnams.co.uk

BEDROOMS: 42. 17 in garden annexe on ground floor, 1 suitable for disabled.
OPEN: all year.
FACILITIES: lift, drawing room, bar, restaurant, private dining room, free Wi-Fi (in main building only), civil wedding licence, garden, treatment room.
BACKGROUND MUSIC: none.
LOCATION: town centre.
CHILDREN: all ages welcomed, free B&B for under-12s.
DOGS: allowed in Lighthouse rooms (£10 charge), reception.
CREDIT CARDS: MasterCard, Visa.
PRICES: [2015] per room B&B single £115–£125, double £185–£255. Set dinner £35.

THE GEORGE

In 'the finest stone town in England', according to Sir Walter Scott, this 'quintessential English inn' by the River Welland is as popular a meeting point now as it was when stagecoaches changed horses here. Returning guests this year were pleased that Lawrence Hoskins's 'comfortable, well-organised' hotel had not changed: 'Extremely good, with lots of helpful, long-serving staff.' Hours may be spent in the enclosed Monastery Garden (misnamed: there was never a monastery), or 'over afternoon tea in the courtyard – especially nice on a sunny Saturday afternoon when a pianist plays. The sound pleasantly drifted up to our room.' Bedrooms vary in size: 'Our bright, spacious room had a fireplace and two comfortable antique-style chairs by the window; perfectly placed bedside lights; a large bathroom.' The Oak Room serves a classic British menu ('decent value for money'): beef sirloin carved at the table; a sweets trolley appears at dessert. 'An excellent half-lobster starter.' Breakfast in the Garden Room was 'very good: a nice buffet (excellent scrambled eggs, lovely local yogurt), choice of cooked dishes'. (Lynn Wildgoose, and others)

71 St Martins
Stamford
PE9 2LB

T: 01780 750750
F: 01780 750701
E: reservations@
   georgehotelofstamford.com
W: www.georgehotelofstamford.com

BEDROOMS: 47.
OPEN: all year.
FACILITIES: ramps, 2 lounges, 2 bars, 2 restaurants, 4 private dining rooms, business centre, free Wi-Fi, civil wedding licence, 2-acre grounds (courtyard, gardens), only public areas suitable for disabled.
BACKGROUND MUSIC: none.
LOCATION: ½ mile from centre.
CHILDREN: all ages welcomed.
DOGS: allowed, not unattended in bedrooms, only guide dogs in restaurants.
CREDIT CARDS: all major cards.
PRICES: [2015] per room B&B single £100–£135, double £170–£260. À la carte £50.

SEE ALSO SHORTLIST

STANTON WICK Somerset

THE CARPENTER'S ARMS

'One of the pleasures of the Guide is that it introduces us to delightful places which we would not otherwise have found. This most appealing pub, well away from main roads and towns, is one such place.' Praise from a regular correspondent this year for this stone-built inn in the Chew valley. Part of a small West Country chain, it is managed by Simon Pledge; Chris Dando is the chef. Converted from a row of miners' cottages, it is 'a maze of rooms with nooks and crannies and low beams: they have a restful, elegant decor'. The contemporary bedrooms have 'good furniture, fittings and lighting; a modern, well-stocked bathroom'. 'Our room was small but adequate for a short stay; we liked the flask of fresh milk on the hospitality tray.' Chris Dando's 'superb' menus might include dishes like confit of duck, sauté potato, spinach, red wine and thyme sauce. 'I wish that I had been warned about the size of the delicious speciality breads; whole loaves too enticing to leave.' A 'tasty' breakfast is served at table. (Mary Hewson, Kay and Peter Rogers)

Stanton Wick
BS39 4BX

T: 01761 490202
F: 01761 490763
E: carpenters@buccaneer.co.uk
W: www.the-carpenters-arms.co.uk

BEDROOMS: 12.
OPEN: all year except evenings 25/26 Dec, 1 Jan.
FACILITIES: bar, 2 restaurants, function room, free Wi-Fi, patio, secure parking, only public areas suitable for disabled.
BACKGROUND MUSIC: none.
LOCATION: 8 miles S of Bristol, 8 miles W of Bath.
CHILDREN: all ages welcomed.
DOGS: allowed in bar and outside areas only.
CREDIT CARDS: Amex, MasterCard, Visa.
PRICES: [2015] per room B&B single £75, double £110, D,B&B single £92.50, double £145. À la carte £27.

STRATFORD-UPON-AVON Warwickshire   Map 3:D6

THE ARDEN

'Fall out of bed and into the RSC.' This red brick hotel, across a 'traffic-restricted' road from the Royal Shakespeare Theatre in Elizabethan Stratford, is 'ideally located'. A joint venture between Sir Peter Rigby's Eden Hotel Collection and the RSC, it is managed by Josefine Blomqvist. It is 'professionally run and very comfortable', say visitors. The bright, contemporary interiors have been 'tastefully' done; one lounge features portraits of noted actors in their Shakespearean roles. The 'comfortable' bedrooms are chic and 'well furnished', with a 'good, modern' en suite bathroom. Rooms at the back overlook the Elizabethan knot garden, where, it is rumoured, Shakespeare crafted his works, although the building itself is Georgian. The restaurant caters for theatre-going schedules, with early and late dinners on offer. Meals can be taken in the brasserie restaurant or outdoor terrace; late suppers are available in the 'comfortable' lounge. Chef Abhijeet Dasalkar's modern menu might include pancetta-wrapped pork fillet, mustard mash, spring cabbage, red wine jus. The breakfast has a 'good traditional English, served by efficient and courteous staff'. (AK)

44 Waterside
Stratford-upon-Avon
CV37 6BA

T: 01789 298682
F: 01789 206989
E: enquiries@
   theardenhotelstratford.com
W: www.theardenhotelstratford.com

BEDROOMS: 45. 1 on ground floor suitable for disabled.
OPEN: all year.
FACILITIES: lounge, restaurant, bar, free Wi-Fi, civil wedding licence, terrace, small knot garden.
BACKGROUND MUSIC: mixed in public areas.
LOCATION: town centre.
CHILDREN: all ages welcomed.
DOGS: not allowed.
CREDIT CARDS: Amex, MasterCard, Visa.
PRICES: [2015] per room B&B £150–£405, D,B&B £200–455. Set meals £25, à la carte from £33.50. 1-night bookings sometimes refused Sat.

SEE ALSO SHORTLIST

CHERRY TREES

In 'an ideal position' for theatre-goers, this modern B&B is a short walk across the Avon footbridge to the town. The owners, Tony Godel and Royd Laidlow, are 'brilliant' hosts. 'They welcomed us with a beautiful home-made apple cake to go with our tea, and gave me a copy of the recipe.' Tony Godel, a former stage manager, is 'great to talk to about productions' at the Royal Shakespeare Company's theatres. The 'spacious, well-equipped, spotlessly clean' bedrooms have a king-size bed, sitting area, 'proper' fresh milk in the mini-fridge; the bathrooms are 'comfortably large, with a wonderful power shower and heated towels'. Two suites (Garden, Terrace) have access to the landscaped contemporary gardens and 'beautiful' pond. 'Tiffany' (Art Nouveau theme) has a newly renovated bathroom. Breakfast, served in the conservatory, 'is the best ever: the full English breakfast is perfectly cooked, tasty sausage, thick slices of bacon; not in the least bit greasy; lovely home-made bread'; porridge with Drambuie-soaked raisins; freshly ground coffee and juice. Private parking means you can 'forget the car and enjoy the town'. (Enid Proud, Colin Adams)

Swan's Nest Lane
Stratford-upon-Avon
CV37 7LS

T: 01789 292989
E: cherrytreesstratforduponavon@gmail.com
W: www.cherrytrees-stratford.co.uk

BEDROOMS: 3. All on ground floor.
OPEN: 13 Feb–23 Nov.
FACILITIES: breakfast room, free Wi-Fi, garden.
BACKGROUND MUSIC: none.
LOCATION: central, near river.
CHILDREN: not under 12.
DOGS: not allowed.
CREDIT CARDS: MasterCard, Visa.
PRICES: per room B&B £110–£135. 1-night bookings sometimes refused.

SEE ALSO SHORTLIST

STUCKTON Hampshire

Map 2:E2

THE THREE LIONS

Jayne and Mike Womersely count ex-Python John Cleese – along with Prince Andrew, Madonna and Status Quo – among former guests at their 'English auberge' in a converted New Forest farmhouse. This is a child-friendly, dog-friendly, informal operation. Guests are encouraged 'to come and go as they please'. Mike Womersely quit a job as head chef at a smart country house hotel and relinquished a Michelin star to take over The Three Lions, and to concentrate on a 'more rustic country cooking', using ingredients grown, raised and foraged locally. Waiter service, in a brasserie reminiscent of an outmoded pub, is 'friendly and smart', lunch or dinner 'a leisurely affair'. The menu might include wild mushroom salad, garlic croutons; loin of local pork, stuffing and crackling. Four of the bedrooms are in a wooden single-storey chalet-style building in the garden; others (preferred by a reader this year) are in the main house. A superior room was recently adapted to accommodate a family. Breakfast croissants and jams are home made. Bookings must be made by telephone.

25% DISCOUNT VOUCHERS

Stuckton
SP6 2HF

T: 01425 652489
F: 01425 656144
E: the3lions@btinternet.com
W: www.thethreelionsrestaurant.co.uk

BEDROOMS: 7. 4 in courtyard block on ground floor.
OPEN: all year except last 2 weeks Feb, restaurant closed Sun night/Mon.
FACILITIES: ramps, conservatory, meeting/sitting room, public bar, restaurant, free Wi-Fi (in bar, conservatory, adjoining three rooms), 2-acre garden (sauna, whirlpool).
BACKGROUND MUSIC: none.
LOCATION: 2 miles E of Fordingbridge.
CHILDREN: all ages welcomed.
DOGS: allowed in bedrooms, conservatory (£10 charge for up to two dogs).
CREDIT CARDS: MasterCard, Visa.
PRICES: [2015] per room B&B single £79, double £125. Set dinner Tues–Thurs £29.50. À la carte £42.

STUDLAND Dorset

Map 2:E2

🦌 THE PIG ON THE BEACH NEW

César award: romantic hotel of the year

Above the 'magnificent' beach at Studland Bay, Robin Hutson's newest addition to his litter of Pigs occupies an 'imaginative' conversion of a 'rambling', turreted Gothic building. 'A relaxed version of a country house, it is noticeably enjoyed by guests of all ages,' said Guide inspectors this year. Staff are 'ever cheerful, informal but well trained'; guests are greeted and immediately shown to their room – 'so much nicer than hanging around a reception desk'. 'Delightfully quirky' public rooms have 'squashy seating', sea paintings and stuffed wildlife; bedrooms are in the main house, and dovecotes and shepherds' huts in the grounds. 'Our room overlooking a field of grazing sheep had mismatched country furniture, a Roberts radio; the enormous, comfy bed had good bedside lighting.' In the 'wonderful' conservatory dining room, 'the cooking is appetising: pink loin of lamb, an unusual but tasty shoulder of lamb potato cake'. Breakfast brings 'a treasure trove' of a buffet: jugs of freshly squeezed juice; fresh-baked pastries. The original Pig is in Brockenhurst; sister hotels are in Southampton and Pensford (see entries).

Manor House
Manor Road
Studland
BH19 3AU

T: 01929 450288
E: info@thepighotel.com
W: www.thepighotel.com

BEDROOMS: 23. Some on the ground floor, 2 Dovecot hideaways, Harry's Hut in grounds.
OPEN: all year.
FACILITIES: bar, lounge, snug, restaurant, private dining room, free Wi-Fi, 2 treatment cabins, garden.
BACKGROUND MUSIC: all day in public areas.
LOCATION: above Studland Beach.
CHILDREN: all ages welcomed.
DOGS: not allowed.
CREDIT CARDS: MasterCard, Visa.
PRICES: [2015] per room £145–£300. Breakfast £10–£15, à la carte £35. 1-night bookings sometimes refused.

STURMINSTER NEWTON Dorset

Map 2:E1

PLUMBER MANOR

♕César award in 1987

The Prideaux-Brunes's Jacobean manor would have been known to Thomas Hardy in his years at Sturminster, where he wrote The Return of the Native. It has been a family-run hotel since 1972, and the recent return of a guest after 30 years' absence was 'much akin to seeing again an old friend who hadn't really changed at all despite the intervening years, except to age along with the rest of us'. Richard Prideaux-Brune, front-of-house, 'was charmingly the same as before, and if brother Brian's fantastic cookery is anything to judge by, he hasn't changed either'. Richard's wife, Alison, is 'everywhere'. Bedrooms are big, traditionally furnished, with florals and sprigs, comfortable, but some may be 'in need of refreshing'. In the gallery there is a portrait given by Charles II to a forebear, possibly one of his mistresses. The daily-changing menu includes such dishes as roast pork loin, apricots, rosemary jus; spinach and Cambozola roulade, spicy tomato coulis. A stream runs through the gardens. 'A true escape, a complete and utter bolt-hole; we were cosseted.' (Caroline and Richard Faircliff)

Sturminster Newton
DT10 2AF

T: 01258 472507
F: 01258 473370
E: book@plumbermanor.com
W: www.plumbermanor.com

BEDROOMS: 16. 10 on ground floor in courtyard.
OPEN: all year except Feb.
FACILITIES: lounge, bar, 3 dining rooms, gallery, free Wi-Fi, 2-acre grounds (garden, tennis, croquet, stream).
BACKGROUND MUSIC: none.
LOCATION: 2 miles SW of Sturminster Newton.
CHILDREN: all ages welcomed, by prior arrangement.
DOGS: allowed in 4 bedrooms, not in public rooms.
CREDIT CARDS: MasterCard, Visa.
PRICES: [2015] per room B&B single £120–£145, double £160–£240. Set dinner £30–£38. À la carte £42.

STRATTONS

♀César award in 2003

Les Scott, the co-owner, with his wife, Vanessa, of this 'eclectic', family-friendly hotel, leads guests down the garden path – and beyond. (A keen runner, he happily takes like-minded visitors to his favourite tracks and trails, perhaps spotting deer along the way.) The hotel occupies a restored Queen Anne villa off the town square. It is run on sustainable lines by the Scotts' daughter, Hannah, and her husband, Dominic Hughes, with a team of 'friendly, helpful' staff. 'Imaginatively designed' bedrooms are spread out in the main house and converted buildings (cottages, a stable, a printing workshop) in the grounds; each is filled with 'varied and unusual ornaments and decorations', perhaps a carved four-poster bed (Red Room), a Michelangelo-style fresco (Boudoir) or a mermaid mosaic (Portico). In the restaurant, chef Julia Hetherton's modern British cooking uses vegetables and herbs from the kitchen garden. A typical dish: slow-cooked rare-breed pork belly, boulangère potatoes, cauliflower cheese. Children are welcomed: there are baby-listening facilities, a children's menu; games, books and toys in the lounges. (J and MB)

4 Ash Close
Swaffham
PE37 7NH

т: 01760 723845
е: enquiries@strattonshotel.com
w: www.strattonshotel.com

BEDROOMS: 14. 6 in annexes, 1 on ground floor.
OPEN: all year except 1 week at Christmas.
FACILITIES: drawing room, reading room, restaurant, free Wi-Fi, terrace, café/deli, 1½-acre garden.
BACKGROUND MUSIC: 'chill-out'/jazz in lounges, restaurant, café/deli.
LOCATION: central, parking.
CHILDREN: all ages welcomed.
DOGS: allowed in some bedrooms (£6.50 per day), lounges. Not in restaurant.
CREDIT CARDS: Amex, MasterCard, Visa.
PRICES: [2015] per room B&B £155–£185, D,B&B £209–£239. À la carte £30. 1-night bookings refused weekends and bank holidays.

THE SWAN INN `NEW`

By a bridge over the pretty River Windrush, this 'lovely old inn' has a 'picture-perfect English setting'. Leased from the Devonshire estate (the late dowager duchess – Debo Mitford – was brought up in the village), it is managed by Daniel Manlup for Nicola and Archie Orr-Ewing (see The King's Head Inn, Bledington). It returns to a full entry after a positive report by a reader and an enthusiastic endorsement by an inspector. The inn has been styled in homage to the Mitford sisters; large black-and-white pictures of the family are displayed throughout. In the bar and restaurant, chef Matthew Laughton serves 'very good' gastropub dishes, perhaps a 'proper Caesar salad with all the expected ingredients, rare these days'; service was 'good despite the obvious popularity with locals'. The bedrooms, 'done in restrained modern style', are in converted stables at the back and a recently renovated riverside cottage across the road. 'Our lovely cottage room, decorated in grey and cream, overlooked the river; it had lots of storage; a freestanding tub in the large bathroom.' You can walk along the river to Burford. (Suzanne Lyons, and others)

25% DISCOUNT VOUCHERS

Swinbrook
OX18 4DY

T: 01993 823339
E: info@theswanswinbrook.co.uk
W: www.theswanswinbrook.co.uk

BEDROOMS: 11. 7 on ground floor, 5 in riverside cottage.
OPEN: all year except Christmas/New Year.
FACILITIES: bar, restaurant, free Wi-Fi, garden, orchard, unsuitable for disabled.
BACKGROUND MUSIC: in bar and restaurant.
LOCATION: 2 miles E of Burford.
CHILDREN: all ages welcomed.
DOGS: not allowed.
CREDIT CARDS: MasterCard, Visa.
PRICES: [2015] per room B&B £125–£195, D,B&B from £165. À la carte £35.

TALLAND-BY-LOOE Cornwall

Map 1:D3

TALLAND BAY HOTEL

Close to the Coastal Path and uncrowded Cornish beaches, Vanessa Rees's 18th-century manor house overlooks subtropical gardens. Pets are warmly welcomed ('they need a break, too'). The hotel is 'very well run', and furnished with a sense of fun. 'Everywhere you looked there was something of interest,' said a visitor this year, who praised the 'friendly, efficient but unobtrusive staff'. Another comment (in 2015): 'It is full of quirky and interesting artistic pieces that give it a relaxing and fun ambience.' The 'magical' situation is enhanced by fantastical garden statuary. No two bedrooms are the same: you might have a sleigh bed or a modern four-poster, jazzy tiled fireplace, freestanding bath, stars, stripes, larky pictures and ornaments. Dinner and Sunday lunch are served in the dining room; lunch otherwise is in the recently added conservatory ('where your four-legged friend is very welcome'). The extensive menu ranges from simple English (soup, beer-battered catch of the day, steaks) to more exotic dishes (Thai fishcakes, lamb kleftiko). 'An excellent meal in the restaurant' was marred only by loud pop music. At breakfast the full English might include hog's pudding. (Vivienne Lewitt, Stuart Clee)

Porthallow
Talland-by-Looe
PL13 2JB

T: 01503 272667
F: 01503 272940
E: info@tallandbayhotel.co.uk
W: www.tallandbayhotel.co.uk

BEDROOMS: 22. 3 in cottages, 6 on ground floor.
OPEN: all year.
FACILITIES: lounge, bar, restaurant, conservatory, free Wi-Fi, civil wedding licence, patio, 2-acre garden.
BACKGROUND MUSIC: in bar and restaurant.
LOCATION: 2½ miles SW of Looe.
CHILDREN: all ages welcomed.
DOGS: welcomed, not allowed in restaurant.
CREDIT CARDS: MasterCard, Visa.
PRICES: [2015] per room B&B £100–£260, D,B&B from £176. À la carte £35.

TAPLOW Berkshire

Map 2:D3

CLIVEDEN HOUSE

'A very special place where affluent hotel-goers can experience luxurious country house living as it used to be.' Visitors were impressed in 2015 by the restoration of this illustrious stately home on the River Thames. Under the same private ownership as Chewton Glen, New Milton (see entry), it is managed by the 'remarkable' Sue Williams. 'The huge panelled salon is impressive with its dark panelling, coats of armour, tapestries. The bar, which faces the glorious garden, is light.' In the 'beautiful' restaurant, hung with chandeliers, chef André Garrett serves 'exquisite' meals: 'We enjoyed small portions of grilled turbot in a delicate sauce; everything was very pretty; service was attentive without ever being obsequious.' The recently refurbished bedrooms are 'stunning'; 'opulent' Lady Astor overlooks the garden; Lord Astor is 'more austere'; each room is different. A family group staying in Spring Cottage, in the 'beautiful' grounds (owned by the National Trust), was impressed with the 'exceptional' service. 'The cottage was furnished to the highest standard and lacked for nothing. We had a good time in the spa. Expensive, but worth every penny.' (Annabel Thomas, CE)

Bourne End Road
Taplow
SL6 0JF

T: 01628 668561
F: 01628 661837
E: reservations@clivedenhouse.co.uk
W: www.clivedenhouse.co.uk

BEDROOMS: 44. Some on ground floor, plus Spring Cottage in grounds.
OPEN: all year.
FACILITIES: lift, Great Hall, library, boudoir, restaurant, private dining rooms, snooker room, free Wi-Fi, civil wedding licence, spa, indoor and (heated) outdoor 15-metre swimming pools, terrace, tennis, 376-acre National Trust gardens.
BACKGROUND MUSIC: none.
LOCATION: 10 miles NW of Windsor.
CHILDREN: all ages welcomed.
DOGS: welcomed, not allowed in restaurant.
CREDIT CARDS: Amex, MasterCard, Visa.
PRICES: [2015] per room B&B £445–£1,535, D,B&B from £635. À la carte £70. 1-night bookings occasionally refused.

LAUNCESTON FARM

In the rolling chalklands of the Tarrant valley, this stylish B&B occupies a 'well-renovated' Grade II listed Georgian farmhouse on the Worrall family's organic farm. The 'lovely old house' stands in 'attractive' walled gardens. Arriving guests are greeted with tea and home-made cake. In the sitting room is an open fireplace and honesty bar; there is also a small library. The individually styled bedrooms, up a spiral staircase, overlook the garden and the adjacent orchard where the farm's hens roam about. 'Our spacious room had a very comfortable bed, good bedside lighting, wooden wardrobe hangers, home-made biscuits; shutters at the windows; a roll-top bath and good shower.' There is a heated doghouse for canine visitors (free of charge). Cordon bleu-trained Sarah Worrall serves a 'rustic' breakfast using farm-fresh ingredients; preserves and marmalade are home made. Monday and Friday evening meals can be arranged, and guests can eat at the local pub, five minutes' walk away. Those interested in where their food comes from might opt for Jimi Worrall's tour of the farm. There are circular walks from the gate. (MC)

Tarrant Launceston
DT11 8BY

T: 01258 830528
E: info@launcestonfarm.co.uk
W: www.launcestonfarm.co.uk

BEDROOMS: 6.
OPEN: all year.
FACILITIES: 2 lounges, library, dining room, breakfast room, free Wi-Fi, terrace, 1-acre walled garden, outdoor 11-metre heated pool, unsuitable for disabled.
BACKGROUND MUSIC: classical during breakfast.
LOCATION: 5 miles NE of Blandford Forum.
CHILDREN: not under 12.
DOGS: allowed in a purpose-built Dog House, not in house.
CREDIT CARDS: MasterCard, Visa.
PRICES: per room B&B single £65 (Sun–Thurs), double £100–£125. Set dinner (Mon and Fri only) £30. 1-night bookings refused May/Sept, and bank holidays.

TAUNTON Somerset

Map 1:C5

THE CASTLE AT TAUNTON

♀César award in 1987

There has been 'regime change' at this 'excellent town hotel' as Kit Chapman has stepped down as chairman to allow 'younger generation stepping into the driving seat'. His son, Nicholas, has been appointed chairman, becoming the third generation of the family to run the medieval castle that has been extended and rebuilt over centuries. In late spring, its crenellated facade is festooned with wisteria. Marc Mac Closkey is the manager. 'The best thing about it was our bedroom and the food,' says a recent visitor. On Wednesday to Saturday nights, head chef Liam Finnegan cooks dinner for the 'charming' Castle Bow restaurant, with dishes like Brixham scallops, Jerusalem artichokes, hazelnut vinaigrette; Devon blue cheese tartlet, root vegetables, spinach, pickled red onion. Meals in the 'vibrant', 'excitingly modern', 'out of keeping' BRAZZ brasserie are simpler: fish and chips, fishcakes, burgers. The bedrooms, designed by Nicholas's mother, Louise, have extras like bathrobes, bottled water. Breakfast has home-made bread, jams and muesli, eggs Benedict, Florentine, Royale – or simply boiled, with soldiers.

Castle Green
Taunton
TA1 1NF

T: 01823 272671
F: 01823 336066
E: reception@the-castle-hotel.com
W: www.the-castle-hotel.com

BEDROOMS: 44.
OPEN: all year, Castle Bow restaurant closed Sun/Mon/Tues.
FACILITIES: lift, ramps, lounge/bar, BRAZZ, Castle Bow restaurant (Wed–Sat evenings), private dining/meeting rooms, free Wi-Fi, civil wedding licence, ½-acre garden, unsuitable for disabled.
BACKGROUND MUSIC: 'easy listening' in lounge, restaurant and brasserie.
LOCATION: central.
CHILDREN: all ages welcomed.
DOGS: allowed in bedrooms (£15 a night), not allowed in public rooms.
CREDIT CARDS: Amex, MasterCard, Visa.
PRICES: [2015] per room B&B from £160, DB&B from £199. À la carte (Castle Bow) £35, (BRAZZ) £25. 1-night bookings sometimes refused.

TEFFONT EVIAS Wiltshire

Map 2:D1

HOWARD'S HOUSE

César award in 2010

'The whole feeling is of comfort and homeliness' at this mellow stone dower house standing in 'lovely' gardens, say visitors in 2015. The small hotel is owned by a partnership that includes the chef, Nick Wentworth. His mother-in-law, Noële Thompson, and Simon Greenwood are the managers, offering 'a warm welcome'. There is a 'blazing fire' in the lounge in cool weather; guests sit here for afternoon tea and toast, or pre-dinner drinks and canapés. 'The food is a great attraction' in the restaurant, where Nick Wentworth uses seasonal produce in his modern menus. Typical dishes: home-smoked goose breast salad, sweet pickled vegetables, onion marmalade; roasted local partridge, game chips, bread sauce 'the best I remember outside home cooking'. Upstairs, bedrooms vary in size and aspect. 'Our spacious, comfortable room had a couple of armchairs and a view over the garden; the lighting could have been a little brighter. The well-equipped bathroom was cleaned immaculately each day.' Breakfast is 'outstanding': freshly squeezed fruit juices, fruit compotes, yogurts; 'a full range' of cooked dishes. (Ann and Philip Carlisle, SP)

25% DISCOUNT VOUCHERS

Teffont Evias
SP3 5RJ

T: 01722 716392
E: enq@howardshouse.co.uk
W: www.howardshousehotel.co.uk

BEDROOMS: 9.
OPEN: all year except 23–27 Dec.
FACILITIES: lounge, snug, restaurant, free Wi-Fi, 2-acre grounds (garden terrace, croquet), river, fishing nearby, only restaurant suitable for disabled.
BACKGROUND MUSIC: light jazz during meals.
LOCATION: 10 miles W of Salisbury.
CHILDREN: all ages welcomed.
DOGS: allowed (£15 surcharge) in bedrooms, not in public rooms.
CREDIT CARDS: Amex, MasterCard, Visa.
PRICES: [2015] per room B&B single £120, double £190–£210. Set menu from £25, à la carte £45.

TEMPLE SOWERBY Cumbria

TEMPLE SOWERBY HOUSE

Run with 'enthusiasm and professionalism' by its owners, Paul and Julie Evans, this Grade II listed red brick mansion is in a village in the Eden valley. Standing in two acres of 'atmospheric' walled gardens, it is a 17th-century farmhouse with a Georgian wing added. The classically styled public rooms are 'immaculate'. The bedrooms vary in size and style: superior rooms at the front have high ceilings and a view over the village green; each has a modern bathroom, some with an aqua-spa bath, others with a walk-in shower. Two ground-floor rooms in a converted coach house in the grounds are good for dog-owners. In the conservatory-style restaurant, which faces the garden, the 'exquisite' cooking of the chef, Ashley Whittaker, is much praised. He blends British and classical French techniques in his modern menu which might include cured mackerel and salmon, sour cream, pickles; loin and leg of wild rabbit, nettle and potato terrine, butternut ketchup and rabbit sauce. Breakfast is served entirely at table. Wine weekends and painting courses are among the short breaks available. (PA)

Temple Sowerby
CA10 1RZ

T: 017683 61578
F: 017683 61958
E: stay@templesowerby.com
W: www.templesowerby.com

BEDROOMS: 12. 2 on ground floor, 4 in coach house (20 yds).
OPEN: all year except Christmas.
FACILITIES: 2 lounges, bar, restaurant, conference/function facilities, free Wi-Fi, civil wedding licence, 2-acre garden (croquet).
BACKGROUND MUSIC: none.
LOCATION: village centre.
CHILDREN: not under 12.
DOGS: by arrangement in 2 bedrooms, not allowed in public rooms or gardens.
CREDIT CARDS: MasterCard, Visa.
PRICES: [2015] per room B&B from £99, D,B&B (min. 2 nights) from £190. Set dinner £33–£43.

CALCOT MANOR

♦César award in 2001

Adults and children 'coexist happily' at this luxury hotel in a converted 14th-century farmhouse in 'admirable' gardens in the Cotswold countryside. It is part of the small Calcot Hotels group; Paul Sadler is the manager. Bedrooms are spread between the main house and a collection of medieval stone barns and stables around a courtyard; individually decorated in soothing colours, each has books, magazines, fresh fruit and biscuits. There are real ales and a log fire in the Gumstool Inn; informal meals here are 'popular with people of all ages'. Chef Michael Benjamin's modern dishes, perhaps herb-crusted rack of local lamb, jabron potatoes, crispy sweetbreads, are served in the Conservatory restaurant. Breakfast is 'top class': freshly squeezed juices, plenty of cooked options, a daily smoothie special. Children have much to occupy their days: nature trails, play areas, indoor and outdoor swimming pools; horse riding can be arranged. Three miles of cycle paths lead around the manor; bicycles, packed lunches are available. Barnsley House, Barnsley (see entry), is under the same ownership.

Tetbury
GL8 8YJ

T: 01666 890391
F: 01666 891244
E: frontdesk@calcotmanor.co.uk
W: www.calcotmanor.co.uk

BEDROOMS: 35. 10 (family) in cottage, 13 around courtyard, on ground floor.
OPEN: all year.
FACILITIES: ramps, lounge, 2 bars, 2 restaurants, cinema, crèche, free Wi-Fi, civil wedding licence, 250-acre grounds (tennis, heated outdoor 8-metre swimming pool, children's play area, spa with 16-metre swimming pool).
BACKGROUND MUSIC: in restaurants.
LOCATION: 3 miles W of Tetbury.
CHILDREN: all ages welcomed.
DOGS: allowed in courtyard bedrooms, not in public rooms.
CREDIT CARDS: Amex, MasterCard, Visa.
PRICES: [2015] per room B&B from £250, D,B&B from £330. À la carte £40. 1-night bookings refused weekends.

SEE ALSO SHORTLIST

TIMBLE North Yorkshire

Map 4:D3

THE TIMBLE INN   **NEW**

In a quiet village in the Washburn valley, this grade II listed 18th-century coaching inn 'received a thumbs-up from us all as a base to explore the area and to feed the body and spirit'. Run as a restaurant-with-rooms by Paul Radcliffe, with 'cheery, professional and helpful' staff, it gains a full entry thanks to a positive report from a regular correspondent this year. The candlelit restaurant has flagstoned floors and exposed brick walls, a wood-burning stove in winter. Chef Mandy Pulford's 'outstanding' modern British dishes might include trio of Nidderdale lamb (loin, shoulder, cheek), sweet potato purée, spinach. 'There are just four stools at the bar for a drink before dinner, but staff will bring drinks over to the residents' lounge in the adjoining building.' 'Comfortable, well-appointed' bedrooms vary in size and decor; visitors should discuss their room choice before booking. 'The width of the beds varies, and some en suites have only a shower.' 'Breakfast was the best I have had for many years – it's such a change to have everything freshly prepared, and served.' (John Bennett)

Timble
LS21 2NN

T: 01943 880530
E: info@thetimbleinn.co.uk
W: www.thetimbleinn.co.uk

BEDROOMS: 9. 1 on ground floor, 2 in cottages, 4 with own private entrance.
OPEN: all year, restaurant closed Sun eve, Mon/Tues.
FACILITIES: bar, restaurant, residents' lounge, free Wi-Fi, garden, unsuitable for disabled.
BACKGROUND MUSIC: none.
LOCATION: 9 miles W of Harrogate.
CHILDREN: all ages welcomed, not in restaurant after 7 pm.
DOGS: not allowed.
CREDIT CARDS: MasterCard, Visa.
PRICES: [2015] per room B&B from £110, D,B&B from £150. À la carte £37. 1-night bookings sometimes refused.

THE BECKFORD ARMS

Between a Gothic arch and the quiet country lanes, 'there is a slight sensation of entering another world' at this Georgian coaching inn. Dan Brod and Charlie Luxton's ivy-covered hotel is 'traditional in some ways' (log fires, cosy bar, wooden floors, a resident dog), said Guide inspectors. 'But it has an airy, modern feel, with large windows, a spacious, pretty sitting room, and a bright conservatory dining room, opening on to a charming terrace.' Bedrooms in the main building are 'comfortable and elegantly decorated, if a bit small'. Two rooms in a 'luxurious' converted farm building (five minutes down the lane) are 'a mixture of country chic and metropolitan loft style'; there are country views from the large bed or the roll-top bath; a 'gorgeous' wood-burning stove; a fridge 'packed with goodies'. The bathroom has a 'state-of-the-art' shower. Chef Nigel Everett's seasonal menu is 'seriously good'; it might include Beckford pig salad (hock, smoked cheeks, crisped ear). Or settle for a pork pie with home-made chutney at the bar. Breakfast has home-made jams, eggs Benedict, waffles and maple syrup.

Fonthill Gifford
Tisbury
SP3 6PX

T: 01747 870385
E: info@beckfordarms.com
W: www.beckfordarms.com

BEDROOMS: 10. 2 in lodge nearby.
OPEN: all year except 25 Dec.
FACILITIES: sitting room, bar, restaurant, private dining room, free Wi-Fi, function facilities, 1-acre garden.
BACKGROUND MUSIC: light background jazz in public areas.
LOCATION: in village, 1 mile N of Tisbury.
CHILDREN: all ages welcomed.
DOGS: allowed in 1 bedroom, public areas.
CREDIT CARDS: MasterCard, Visa.
PRICES: [2015] per room B&B £95–£120, D,B&B £150–£175. À la carte £30–£35. 1-night bookings sometimes refused.

SEE ALSO SHORTLIST

TITCHWELL Norfolk

TITCHWELL MANOR

On the north Norfolk coast, Ian and Margaret Snaith's contemporary hotel occupies a former Victorian farmhouse with views across open marshes to the North Sea. Individually designed bedrooms are in the main house and converted outbuildings in the grounds. Some, around a pretty garden square with lavender and herbs, have French doors leading to outside seating overlooking farmland. The best Manor Rooms, with bold, contemporary prints and vintage furnishings, have sea views. The Potting Shed, which stands apart, has its own veranda, a log-burner and a large roll-top bath. Afternoon tea and informal brasserie meals (perhaps fish pie, Parmesan croquettes) are taken in the Eating Rooms. In the Conservatory restaurant, chef Eric Snaith, the owners' son, serves 'excellent' modern European dishes, perhaps Jerusalem artichoke, quail's egg, Wiltshire truffle; Norfolk lamb, parsley root, hazelnut. 'The breakfasts are some of the best we have had': a buffet has 'a plentiful array' of cereals, yogurt and fruit; cooked dishes have sausages, bacon and black pudding from rare-breed pigs. The RSPB Titchwell Nature Reserve is nearby; walkers and birdwatchers are welcomed. (CR, and others)

nr Brancaster
Titchwell
PE31 8BB

T: 01485 210221
E: info@titchwellmanor.com
w: www.titchwellmanor.com

BEDROOMS: 27. 12 in herb garden, 4 in converted farm building, 1 in Potting Shed, 2 suitable for disabled.
OPEN: all year.
FACILITIES: lounge, bar, 2 restaurants, free Wi-Fi, civil wedding licence, ¼-acre walled garden.
BACKGROUND MUSIC: in public rooms.
LOCATION: on coast road, 5 miles E of Hunstanton.
CHILDREN: all ages welcomed (sand pit, games, DVDs).
DOGS: not allowed in main restaurant.
CREDIT CARDS: Amex, MasterCard, Visa.
PRICES: per room B&B from £95, D,B&B (min. 2 nights) from £155. Set menus £55–£65, à la carte £35.

SEE ALSO SHORTLIST

THE STAGG INN

♀ Cesar award in 2013

'A most relaxed place', this unpretentious white-painted inn is owned by Steve (the chef) and Nicola Reynolds. 'Everyone from the owner to the waitress serving breakfast was extremely friendly,' said a visitor this year. Meals can be taken in the bar (popular with locals) and the dining room. 'At dinner, Nicola Reynolds was very much in charge, greeting guests and taking orders. Our meal was delicious; the highlights were scallops with the tastiest pickled cauliflower; sea bass, leeks and samphire; a wonderful trio of crèmes brûlées (vanilla, coffee and lavender). Service was relaxed; there was no sense of rush.' The best bedrooms are in a part-Georgian, part-Victorian former vicarage, in 'beautifully kept' gardens, 300 yards from the inn. They have antique furniture, wrought iron beds, original features (fireplaces and high ceilings). Transport is offered to guests preferring not to walk on the country road. Bedside lighting is 'as good as it gets' in dog-friendly rooms in the main building. There are home-produced sausages at breakfast; 'perfect poached eggs'; Marmite and home-made jams. (Glen Balmer, and others)

25% DISCOUNT VOUCHERS

Titley
nr Kington
HR5 3RL

T: 01544 230221
F: 01544 231390
E: reservations@thestagg.co.uk
W: www.thestagg.co.uk

BEDROOMS: 7. 3 at Old Vicarage (300 yds).
OPEN: all year except Mon/Tues, 25/26 Dec, 1 Jan, 1 week in Jan/Feb, first 2 weeks in Nov.
FACILITIES: (Old Vicarage) sitting room, free Wi-Fi, 1½-acre garden, (Stagg Inn) bar, restaurant areas, free Wi-Fi, small garden, unsuitable for disabled, 'ample parking'.
BACKGROUND MUSIC: none.
LOCATION: on B4355 between Kington and Presteigne (3 miles from each).
CHILDREN: all ages welcomed.
DOGS: only allowed in pub, some pub bedrooms.
CREDIT CARDS: Amex, MasterCard, Visa.
PRICES: [2015] per room B&B £100–£150. À la carte £35. 1-night bookings sometimes refused.

TUDDENHAM MILL

'Very stylish,' say visitors this year, who enjoyed their stay at this 18th-century mill (Grade II listed), which has been given a modern make-over with bedrooms added in two wood-clad buildings. It is owned by Agellus Hotels (a small East Anglian group). The old building has been 'nicely restored': the mill race, grinding stones, original beams and stonework have been highlighted. Three of the bedrooms are in the original building; other rooms are in the wood-clad additions. 'Our huge room had many high-quality extras; an ultra-modern bathroom.' Other visitors liked their 'light, modern' room, which had painted floorboards, original art, minimal furniture; French windows opened on to a deck with seating. In the restaurant on the first floor of the main building, the cooking of the chef, Lee Bye, is acclaimed. He uses regional produce for his menus which might include crispy hen's egg parsley soup, kohlrabi, Parmesan; hake fillet, peas à la française, cockles, gem lettuce, cider noisette. 'Good food, and an excellent breakfast, cooked to order.' A vegetarian was 'well looked after'. (Evan Jon Hughes)

High Street
Tuddenham
IP28 6SQ

T: 01638 713552
E: info@tuddenhammill.co.uk
W: www.tuddenhammill.co.uk

BEDROOMS: 15. 12 in 2 separate buildings, 8 on ground floor, 1 suitable for disabled.
OPEN: all year.
FACILITIES: bar, restaurant, 2 function rooms, free Wi-Fi, 12-acre grounds.
BACKGROUND MUSIC: 'modern' in bar and restaurant.
LOCATION: in village, 8 miles NE of Newmarket.
CHILDREN: all ages welcomed.
DOGS: welcomed in some bedrooms (£15 a night).
CREDIT CARDS: MasterCard, Visa.
PRICES: [2015] per room B&B £185–£345. À la carte £38, early dining (Sun–Fri 6.30–7.30 pm) £19.50, tasting menu £49.50. 1-night bookings refused weekends.

TWO BRIDGES Devon

Map 1:D4

PRINCE HALL

In a 'wonderful position' on Dartmoor, Fi and Chris Daly's 'welcoming', dog-friendly hotel is liked for the 'peace and seclusion' that surround it, say visitors this year. The staff are 'delightful'; there is a 'relaxed' atmosphere and a 'laid-back attitude' throughout. 'It is an excellent place for visiting dogs – and their owners.' The high-ceilinged lounge and bar have a 'comfortable', 'lived-in' feel and 'glorious' moor views. Upstairs, country-style bedrooms overlooking moorland or neighbouring farm buildings are well equipped, with a refreshment tray and 'delicious' water from the hotel's own well. Guests who enjoyed their 'spacious' moor-view room this year regretted an uncomfortable mattress and a temperamental shower. A daily-changing dinner menu is served in the 'light and airy' restaurant looking towards the River Dart. 'Good', 'well-presented' modern dishes might include loin of West Country venison, celeriac fondant, confit shallots, chorizo crumb. 'Vegetarians are well catered for.' Served at table, breakfast has home-baked bread, 'tasty' home-made preserves, leaf tea. 'The wildlife guide they gave us was extremely good, and enhanced our whole experience.'

Two Bridges
PL20 6SA

T: 01822 890403
E: info@princehall.co.uk
W: www.princehall.co.uk

BEDROOMS: 8. Plus Shepherd's Hut in grounds.
OPEN: all year.
FACILITIES: 2 lounges, dining room, free Wi-Fi in bar/lounge, civil wedding licence, terrace, 5-acre grounds, only ground floor suitable for disabled.
BACKGROUND MUSIC: 'easy listening' in restaurant and lounges.
LOCATION: 1 mile E of Two Bridges.
CHILDREN: not under 10.
DOGS: welcomed (treats, facilities for food storage and dog washing, pet-friendly garden and grounds), not in restaurant.
CREDIT CARDS: MasterCard, Visa.
PRICES: [2015] per person B&B £80–£90, D,B&B £95–£110. Set dinner £39.50–£47.50. 1-night bookings sometimes refused.

ULLSWATER Cumbria

Map 4: inset C2

HOWTOWN HOTEL

🦚 César award in 1991

'A place to get away from it all.' Guide inspectors in 2015 loved this stone-built Lake District hotel, which the Baldry family has run for more than a century. 'It unashamedly sticks to its old-fashioned values; all the better for it. It is so retro, it's almost trendy: the decor, the cooking style; the Lalique glass bowls on a window sill in the dining room, china sets in one of the three guest lounges.' Bookings are made by telephone and confirmed in writing. In the simple bedrooms 'everything is spotless, well decorated, not dowdy'. Modern equipment is absent: no Wi-Fi; no music; no mobile signal; no toiletries other than a bar of soap. A gong announces meals in the 'beautifully laid' dining room. 'We had perfectly poached salmon and an excellent steak, with a good supply of vegetables served with silver spoons; the bread-and-butter pudding was light and delicious. Loose tea in a fine china pot is brought to your room before breakfast which has preserves in individual bowls, butter balls, proper toast.' Packed lunches are available; superb walking from the door.

Ullswater
CA10 2ND

T: 01768 486514
W: www.howtown-hotel.com

BEDROOMS: 15. 4 in annexe, 4 self-catering cottages for weekly rent.
OPEN: Mar–1 Nov.
FACILITIES: 3 lounges, TV room, 2 bars, dining room, no Wi-Fi, 2-acre grounds, 200 yds from lake (private foreshore, fishing), walking, sailing, climbing, riding, golf nearby, unsuitable for disabled.
BACKGROUND MUSIC: none.
LOCATION: 4 miles S of Pooley Bridge, bus from Penrith station 9 miles.
CHILDREN: all ages welcomed (no special facilities).
DOGS: allowed in some bedrooms (£4 per night charge), not in public rooms.
CREDIT CARDS: none.
PRICES: [2015] per person D,B&B £94. Set dinner £27. 1-night bookings sometimes refused.

THE BAY HORSE

♥Cesar award in 2009

'Utter peace' reigns at this 18th-century former staging post which is 'beautifully situated' on Morecambe Bay. Robert Lyons and Lesley Wheeler's inn is 'a place from a bygone age of service and style', says a visitor this year. Their 'touch is evident throughout': 'Lesley's supervision keeps everything moving nicely.' In the bar/restaurant, Robert Lyons serves traditional British dishes: 'His cooking is always excellent; no attempt at fine dining, but very satisfying.' 'We had a large portion of venison medallions; steak and kidney pie was provided willingly although it was not on the menu.' The bedrooms are small and simple, 'but it is a pub and the rates reflect that'. 'You can lie in bed and look out across the sands and watch the birds as the tide comes in and out.' In warmer weather, 'it is lovely and relaxing to sit on the balcony with a refreshment before or after dinner'. On colder weekends, 'the open fire in the bar made it difficult to venture outside'. Breakfast is 'biblical': it has freshly squeezed orange juice, hot dishes cooked to order, home-made jams. (Lynn Wildgoose, WK Wood)

Canal Foot
Ulverston
LA12 9EL

T: 01229 583972
F: 01229 580502
E: reservations@thebayhorsehotel.co.uk
W: www.thebayhorsehotel.co.uk

BEDROOMS: 9.
OPEN: all year, restaurant closed Mon midday (light bar meals available).
FACILITIES: bar lounge, restaurant, free Wi-Fi, picnic area, unsuitable for disabled.
BACKGROUND MUSIC: mixed 'easy listening', all day in public areas.
LOCATION: 8 miles NE of Barrow-in-Furness.
CHILDREN: not under 10.
DOGS: allowed in bedrooms and bar, not in restaurant.
CREDIT CARDS: all major cards.
PRICES: [2015] per room B&B £95–£120, D,B&B (min. 2 nights Fri–Sat or Sat–Sun) £155–£180. À la carte £37. 1-night bookings refused bank holidays.

UPPER SLAUGHTER Gloucestershire

Map 3:D6

LORDS OF THE MANOR

♀César award in 2015

The 'quality and ambience' of this country house hotel is 'self-evident as you walk past the neatly cropped box hedges from the car park' to the honey-stoned building. Under private ownership, it is managed by Paul Thompson. Trusted Guide correspondents on a return visit in 2015 found it 'was even better than before'. In the hall, 'the smiling receptionist had the paperwork ready; the porter had already taken our bags'. The bedrooms are reached by corridors overlooking internal courtyards. 'Our large room on the first floor had a splendid view from the window seats over the gardens. We took afternoon tea in traditional grand old English style in the lounge.' In the dining room, 'well-spaced tables are elegantly set with white linen and sparkling glass; we enjoyed Richard Picard-Edwards's Michelin-starred cooking, in particular Cornish crab with potato, cucumber and caviar; beef two ways (slow cooked and steak)'. Breakfast has a 'comprehensive cold buffet of cereals, fruits, cheese, meat, croissants and pastries; scrambled egg with, if anything, an over-generous quantity of smoked salmon; and good coffee'. (Francine and Ian Walsh)

Upper Slaughter
GL54 2JD

T: 01451 820243
F: 01451 820696
E: reservations@lordsofthemanor.com
W: www.lordsofthemanor.com

BEDROOMS: 26. 1 on ground floor.
OPEN: all year.
FACILITIES: 2 lounges, bar, restaurant, free Wi-Fi in bar and drawing room, civil wedding licence, terrace, 8-acre grounds, unsuitable for disabled.
BACKGROUND MUSIC: none.
LOCATION: in village, 3 miles SW of Stow-on-the-Wold.
CHILDREN: all ages welcomed, no under-7s in restaurant in evening (high tea served).
DOGS: 'on request', not allowed in restaurant.
CREDIT CARDS: Amex, MasterCard, Visa.
PRICES: [2015] per room B&B £249–£490, D,B&B from £384. Set menus £72.50. 1-night bookings sometimes refused.

UPPINGHAM Rutland

Map 2:B3

LAKE ISLE HOTEL & RESTAURANT

Named after the WB Yeats poem ('for its sentiments of peace, relaxation and tranquillity'), this Grade II listed 17th-century hotel/restaurant in the oldest part of the town is 'very well run indeed'. The service provided by Richard and Janine Burton is 'uniformly pleasant and efficient without being effusive'. The 'beautiful presentation' of the rooms bears witness to an 'experienced hand', say Guide readers. The bedrooms, standard and those with a whirlpool bath, are divided between the main house and two small cottages in the courtyard. Recent visitors found their room 'immaculately clean, unfussy', with a king-size bed, comfortable sitting area, good lighting and storage. In the restaurant, chef Stuart Mead's 'good, imaginative' British menu changes daily and seasonally, with dishes like duck liver parfait, white-wine-and-thyme-preserved apricots; Glamorgan sausages, sticky sage-braised shallots and apples. 'It was all very good.' Breakfast has 'a notably good choice with a few original touches', including salmon and haddock fishcakes and compote of prunes and apricots in Earl Grey and cinnamon syrup.

16 High Street East
Uppingham
LE15 9PZ

T: 01572 822951
F: 01572 824400
E: info@lakeisle.co.uk
W: www.lakeisle.co.uk

BEDROOMS: 12. 2 in cottages.
OPEN: all year, restaurant closed Sun night, Mon lunch.
FACILITIES: lounge, bar, restaurant, free Wi-Fi, unsuitable for disabled.
BACKGROUND MUSIC: in restaurant.
LOCATION: town centre.
CHILDREN: all ages welcomed.
DOGS: allowed in bedrooms (£10–£20 charge), not in public areas.
CREDIT CARDS: MasterCard, Visa.
PRICES: [2015] per room B&B single £59.50–£69.50, double £85–£110, D,B&B single £89.50–£99.50, double £145–£165. À la carte £35.

VENTNOR Isle of Wight

Map 2:E2

HILLSIDE

With 'superb views across the sea', this small hotel has a 'modern, fresh' decor and an extensive collection of bold contemporary art. 'Exceptional standards of service' are provided by the owner, Gert Bach, and his staff, say visitors. Backing on to National Trust land at the foot of St Boniface Down, the Grade II listed thatched villa has been given a bright Scandinavian feel, reflecting the owner's Danish heritage. Most of the bedrooms face the sea: each has a bespoke Vi-Spring bed; neutral colours; vintage Welsh blankets; Danish lighting; underfloor heating in the bathroom. 'Our room was pleasant, comfortable.' In the restaurant, chef Gerald Frutier uses home-grown ingredients for his menus (meals must be ordered in advance). After dinner, coffee is served in the 'gorgeous conservatory'; 'the staff offered soft Welsh wool shawls in the cooling evening'. Meals can be taken on a terrace in warm weather. A short walk away in Ventnor, the Hillside Bistro, under the same ownership, has 'similar standards'. Breakfast 'reflects the quality of dinner': it has home-made yogurt and preserves; cooked dishes have home-made sausages.

25% DISCOUNT VOUCHERS

151 Mitchell Avenue
Ventnor
PO38 1DR

T: 01983 852271
E: mail@hillsideventnor.co.uk
W: www.hillsideventnor.co.uk

BEDROOMS: 12. Plus 2 self-catering apartments.
OPEN: all year, restaurant closed Sun.
FACILITIES: bar, lounge, restaurant, conservatory, free Wi-Fi, civil wedding licence, terrace, 5-acre garden, unsuitable for disabled.
BACKGROUND MUSIC: none.
LOCATION: top of town, at foot of St Boniface Down.
CHILDREN: not under 12.
DOGS: not allowed.
CREDIT CARDS: MasterCard, Visa.
PRICES: [2015] per room B&B single £68–£133, double £146–£186, D,B&B £99 per person. Min. 2-night bookings preferred.

SEE ALSO SHORTLIST

THE NARE

♀ César award in 2003

'A year spent without a visit to The Nare is a year wasted,' say devotees returning in 2015 to Toby Ashworth's luxury seaside hotel on the 'breathtaking' Roseland Peninsula. 'The staff exude friendliness; guests' individual preferences are remembered for next time.' The hotel is 'resonant of a bygone era': 'proper' shoe cleaning, evening turn-down, hot-water bottle in winter, silver service. The public rooms are 'charming and traditional with a modern twist', with fresh flowers, wing chairs, low tables, original Cornish artwork. 'Our spacious seaview room was full of home comforts, lovely antiques, a patio overlooking the gardens.' Guests are expected to dress for the occasion in the dining room, where chef Richard James serves a 'delicious' table d'hôte menu. À la carte and family meals are taken in the Quarterdeck restaurant. Children are welcomed: they receive a gift on arrival and have a library of books. A comprehensive breakfast (buffet and cooked options) is taken in the dining room or in guests' rooms. The hotel's yacht, Alice Rose, is available for a day on the Fal and Helford rivers. (Peter Govier, and others)

Carne Beach
Veryan-in-Roseland
TR2 5PF

T: 01872 501111
F: 01872 501856
E: tgha@narehotel.co.uk
W: www.narehotel.co.uk

BEDROOMS: 37. Some on ground floor, 1 in adjacent cottage, 5 suitable for disabled.
OPEN: all year.
FACILITIES: lift, ramps, lounge, drawing room, sun lounge, gallery, study, bar, billiards, light lunch/supper room, 2 restaurants, conservatory, free Wi-Fi, indoor 10-metre swimming pool, gym, 2-acre grounds, heated 15-metre swimming pool, tennis.
BACKGROUND MUSIC: none.
LOCATION: S of Veryan, on coast.
CHILDREN: all ages welcomed.
DOGS: allowed in bedrooms, not in public areas (except for assistance dogs).
CREDIT CARDS: Amex, MasterCard, Visa.
PRICES: [2015] per room B&B £284–£815. Set dinner £50, à la carte £50.

THE FIVE ARROWS

Built on the site of a coaching inn to house the architects and craftsmen who built Waddesdon Manor, this half-timbered building is a small hotel with 'good vibes'. It is run by the Rothschild family trust for the National Trust; Alex McEwen is the manager. 'The staff were friendly, the room was comfortable, the food good,' says a regular Guide correspondent this year. Five bedrooms recently added in a converted coach house are spacious: 'Ours had a super king-size bed, a comfy leather armchair and a Windsor-style smaller chair; it was decorated in modern classic colours. It overlooked the main road; the faint hum of traffic did not bother us.' Rooms in the main house are more traditional in style. There is no residents' lounge, but in warm weather guests can sit in the courtyard garden. In the dining room, chef Karl Penny serves modern dishes: 'We especially enjoyed crab and cod fishcakes; cherry tomato tartlet; a pudding of almond cake and pistachio ice cream.' Breakfast has a 'good' cold buffet; a wide choice of hot dishes. (GC)

High Street
Waddesdon
HP18 0JE

T: 01296 651727
F: 01296 658596
E: five.arrows@nationaltrust.org.uk
W: www.thefivearrows.co.uk

BEDROOMS: 16. 5 in Old Coach House, 3, in courtyard, on ground floor.
OPEN: all year.
FACILITIES: bar, restaurant, free Wi-Fi, civil wedding licence, 1-acre garden, unsuitable for disabled.
BACKGROUND MUSIC: none.
LOCATION: in village.
CHILDREN: all ages welcomed.
DOGS: not allowed.
CREDIT CARDS: Amex, MasterCard, Visa.
PRICES: [2015] per room B&B from £105, D,B&B from £160. À la carte £30.

WAREHAM Dorset

Map 2:E1

THE PRIORY

♦César award in 1996

'It just keeps getting better.' This 'well-run' country hotel on the banks of the River Frome is owned by Anne Turner and her brother-in-law, Stuart Turner. 'The atmosphere is exceptionally friendly,' say returning visitors in 2015. The 'glorious' riverside gardens of the former priory are an 'eruption' of bloom from early spring to autumn, attracting butterflies and birds: 'especially lovely' for afternoon tea or a pre-prandial stroll. On colder days, there is a log fire in the beamed lounge ('a winter delight'), with its pew benches and antique furniture. Bedrooms, in the main house and converted boathouse, have board games, books, fresh fruit. 'Our room in the Boathouse had its own thermostat control; a comfortable four-poster without fussy drapes; good seating, a separate dressing area; a splendid bathroom with a walk-in shower, huge whirlpool bath.' In the Abbot's Cellar restaurant, chef Stephan Guinebault serves French-influenced dishes. 'The steak I had was perfectly cooked, very tender.' 'Breakfasts in the garden rooms are very good indeed: eggs just right, delicious porridge.' (Elizabeth and Richard Pratt, Bill Bennett)

25% DISCOUNT VOUCHERS

Church Green
Wareham
BH20 4ND

T: 01929 551666
F: 01929 554519
E: reservations@theprioryhotel.co.uk
W: www.theprioryhotel.co.uk

BEDROOMS: 18. Some on ground floor (in courtyard), 4 suites in Boathouse.
OPEN: all year.
FACILITIES: ramps, lounge, drawing room, bar, 2 dining rooms, free Wi-Fi, 4-acre gardens (croquet, river frontage, moorings, fishing), unsuitable for disabled.
BACKGROUND MUSIC: none.
LOCATION: town centre.
CHILDREN: not under 14.
DOGS: not allowed.
CREDIT CARDS: MasterCard, Visa.
PRICES: [2015] per room B&B £220–£380, D,B&B £265–£425. Set dinner £47.50. 1-night bookings sometimes refused.

WATERMILLOCK Cumbria

RAMPSBECK   NEW

'A classic country house', John Brooksbank's whitewashed hotel stands in extensive gardens with 'spectacular' views over Lake Ullswater. It returns to a full entry after positive reports in 2015: 'We received a warm welcome; all the staff are very friendly'; 'A superb break in a lovely location; we had a stylish and well-equipped bedroom and bathroom.' Alison Mathewson is the manager. The drawing room has an ornate ceiling and a marble fireplace. Afternoon tea and light meals can be taken on a terrace in warm months. Most of the bedrooms face the lake or garden. 'Our elegant room had a sumptuous bed, and lovely views through an enormous window.' Another comment: 'The real highlight was the food: well cooked and served beautifully.' Chef Ben Wilkinson prepares modern British fare, perhaps cured Arctic char, caviar, horseradish ice cream, spiced beetroot jelly; Cumbrian beef sirloin, a fritter of beef cheek, smoked marrow. 'The mushroom cappuccino was gorgeous; the chef was superb with vegetarians.' Breakfast has 'a great choice of well-cooked local ingredients'. 'I cannot wait to go back.' (Pat Woodward, Mary Coles, Trudi Burton)

Watermillock
CA11 0LP

T: 01768 486442
F: 01768 486688
E: enquiries@rampsbeck.co.uk
W: www.rampsbeck.co.uk

BEDROOMS: 19.
OPEN: all year.
FACILITIES: 3 lounges, bar, restaurant, free Wi-Fi, civil wedding licence, 18-acre grounds (croquet), lake frontage (fishing, sailing, windsurfing, etc).
BACKGROUND MUSIC: 'easy listening' in bar and restaurant..
LOCATION: 5½ miles SW of Penrith.
CHILDREN: not under 10 in restaurant at night.
DOGS: allowed in 4 bedrooms (£15 per stay), allowed in hall only.
CREDIT CARDS: Diners, MasterCard, Visa.
PRICES: [2015] per person B&B from £85, D,B&B from £135. Set meals £50.95–£68.95.

STOBERRY HOUSE

'Finer views are hard to find,' says a visitor to this elegant B&B. It stands in a 'beautifully laid-out' garden with sculptures, wildlife ponds, a gazebo and plenty of outdoor seating. The owners, Frances and Tim Meeres Young, are 'fantastic hosts'. The sitting rooms in the converted 18th-century coach house have prints, fresh flowers, books and board games; there are 'things to view at every turn'. In the main building and a studio a short stroll away, 'well-appointed' accommodation is 'of the highest standard'. Rooms are equipped with dressing gowns, slippers, a drinks tray, fresh fruit and flowers; guests staying in the main house have access to a pantry for light snacks. 'The biggest treat is breakfast', where 'much is home cooked by Frances using fresh local produce, often from her own potager'. The 'fabulous' continental selection has an 'extensive' choice of yogurts, cheeses, hams, freshly baked breads, pastries and scones, and home-made jams; a porridge menu (at extra charge) includes an option with a 'generous tot of whisky'. 'On a fine day, several hours could be spent exploring the grounds.' (RG)

Stoberry Park
Wells
BA5 3LD

T: 01749 672906
F: 01749 674175
E: stay@stoberry-park.co.uk
W: www.stoberry-park.co.uk

BEDROOMS: 5. 1 in studio cottage.
OPEN: all year except 15 Dec–31 Jan.
FACILITIES: 3 sitting rooms, breakfast room, free Wi-Fi, 6½-acre grounds, unsuitable for disabled.
BACKGROUND MUSIC: none.
LOCATION: outskirts of Wells.
CHILDREN: all ages welcomed (in designated rooms).
DOGS: not allowed.
CREDIT CARDS: MasterCard, Visa.
PRICES: [2015] per room B&B (continental) £65–£145. Cooked breakfast £5.50.

THE CAT INN

♀César award in 2014

Opposite a 'lovely' old church in a village on the Sussex Weald, Andrew Russell's 16th-century inn has many fans. 'The welcome was warm, and the owner and staff were helpful and considerate,' say visitors this year. 'Mr Russell carried our bag to the room and settled us in. There was a friendly atmosphere in the bar, which was well patronised by locals.' Alex Jacquemin has been promoted to head chef: 'The standard of food has reached a new level,' says a returning guest. His menus mix modern dishes with classics, perhaps salt-baked beetroot salad, candied hazelnuts, honey, goat's curd; steak, mushroom and ale pie, Sussex vegetables. 'We enjoyed our meals and the service was good.' Bedrooms ('very comfortable') are well equipped: they have a king-size bed, a Nespresso machine; 'fresh milk in a flask'; 'good' lighting and 'a proper mirror'. Breakfast has good cooked dishes; 'butter not in a foil wrap, but freshly presented'. On the western edge of the Ashdown Forest, there is good walking; nearby gardens include Wakehurst Place and Nymans. (Jean and David Jukes, Chris Savory)

North Lane
West Hoathly
RH19 4PP

T: 01342 810369
E: thecatinn@googlemail.com
W: www.catinn.co.uk

BEDROOMS: 4.
OPEN: all year, restaurant closed 25 Dec and Sun evening.
FACILITIES: bar, 3 dining areas, free Wi-Fi, small terrace, unsuitable for disabled.
BACKGROUND MUSIC: none.
LOCATION: in village.
CHILDREN: not under 7.
DOGS: not allowed in dining room.
CREDIT CARDS: MasterCard, Visa.
PRICES: [2015] per room B&B from £120. À la carte £28.

WHASHTON North Yorkshire

THE HACK & SPADE

Down a single-track lane, this 'unpretentious' stone-built restaurant-with-rooms has been the hub of this Yorkshire village since 1806. Owners Jane and Andy Ratcliffe still host the local domino club every Thursday. 'Jane Ratcliffe is a pleasant host who looked after us well,' says a visitor in 2015. A 'bright, airy' hallway from the small bar leads to the 'wonderful' bedrooms which overlook the village green. Simply furnished, one room has 'the largest bed we'd ever seen'; a 'comfortable' tub chair by the window; 'ample' storage; a 'smart, well-lit' bathroom, with 'plenty of space' for toiletries, a freestanding bath, separate walk-in rain shower. Jane Ratcliffe's blackboard menu is served in the candlelit restaurant, separated by a log-burning fire from the adjacent sitting area; a double-edged spade and an 'eye-catching' display of fishing rods are on the walls (reflections of once and current village occupations). She serves 'generous' portions of dishes like Hebridean peat-smoked salmon; chicken breast, Yorkshire blue cheese, pine nuts. The sky's the limit at breakfast: 'No menu here, just the question: "What would you like?"' (Richard Bright, Peter Bell)

Whashton
DL11 7JL

T: 01748 823721
E: reservations@hackandspade.com
W: www.hackandspade.com

BEDROOMS: 5.
OPEN: all year except Christmas/ New Year, last 2 weeks Jan.
FACILITIES: lounge, restaurant, free Wi-Fi, only restaurant suitable for disabled.
BACKGROUND MUSIC: classical in lounge and dining room.
LOCATION: 4 miles NW of Richmond.
CHILDREN: not under 7.
DOGS: not allowed.
CREDIT CARDS: MasterCard, Visa.
PRICES: [2015] per room B&B £120–£130. À la carte £25.

WHITEWELL Lancashire

Map 4:D3

THE INN AT WHITEWELL

'Eccentric, homely and run with considerable style', third-generation hotelier Charles Bowman's cheerful hotel stands above the Forest of Bowland, in 'some of the most beautiful countryside I have ever seen', says a visitor this year. Binoculars are provided for the casual twitcher; fishing rods for the idle fisherman; an extensive range of wines and cask ales for the occasional carouser. 'All I could hear at night, from a splendid four-poster, was the sound of the River Hodder tumbling along beyond the gardens.' Bedrooms are individually styled and have antiques, rich fabrics, Georgian prints, modern amenities; some have a log fire or a restored Victorian/Edwardian cabinet bath. One bedroom was 'huge and long', with a 'good-sized' bed; free-range hangers in an old-fashioned wardrobe; a bay window overlooking the river. 'The view from the dining room is simply fabulous.' Chef Jamie Cadman's modern menu uses local ingredients in dishes like roasted Burholme Lonk lamb roast, crushed new potatoes, lemon and mint jelly. Breakfast has freshly squeezed orange juice, 'nicely cooked bacon, mushrooms, flavoursome sausages'. (Michael Craddock)

Whitewell
BB7 3AT

T: 01200 448222
F: 01200 448298
E: reception@innatwhitewell.com
W: www.innatwhitewell.com

BEDROOMS: 23. 4 (2 on ground floor) in coach house, 150 yds.
OPEN: all year.
FACILITIES: 3 bars, restaurant, boardroom, private dining room, free Wi-Fi, civil wedding licence, 5-acre garden, 7 miles fishing (ghillie available), unsuitable for disabled.
BACKGROUND MUSIC: none.
LOCATION: 6 miles NW of Clitheroe.
CHILDREN: all ages welcomed.
DOGS: welcomed, not allowed in dining room.
CREDIT CARDS: MasterCard, Visa.
PRICES: [2015] per room B&B £128–£253. À la carte £40.

CROSSWAYS HOTEL

A visit to Clive James and David Stott's restaurant-with-rooms has become 'an annual ritual' for a long-time Guide reader who reports this year: 'Happily, it's as good as ever.' Within easy access of Glyndebourne, this popular retreat is thought 'very good value', even during the opera season. Lying at the foot of the South Downs national park, the white Georgian house stands in two acres of 'delightful' Sussex countryside; its garden contains a 'stylish' gazebo and a duck pond. The bright and airy bedrooms are individually styled, with modern and traditional touches; some showers 'might be ready for renovation'. Guests enjoyed the 'badinage' over dinner in the restaurant: 'David recites the menu, which evolves slowly from year to year and seems even tastier than previous (good) experiences.' The cooking, which now has 'a slightly lighter feel', uses locally sourced meats, seasonal game, and vegetables from the garden. 'I enjoyed thinly sliced calf's liver; hake in Parmesan crust; good puddings.' Breakfast highlights include home-made marmalade, and eggs from 'just down the road'. (Richard Parish, and others)

25% DISCOUNT VOUCHERS

Lewes Road
Wilmington
BN26 5SG

T: 01323 482455
F: 01323 487811
E: stay@crosswayshotel.co.uk
W: www.crosswayshotel.co.uk

BEDROOMS: 7. Also self-catering cottage.
OPEN: all year except 23 Dec–23 Jan, restaurant closed Sun/Mon.
FACILITIES: breakfast room, restaurant, free Wi-Fi, 2-acre grounds (duck pond), unsuitable for disabled.
BACKGROUND MUSIC: none.
LOCATION: 2 miles W of Polegate on A27.
CHILDREN: not under 12.
DOGS: not allowed.
CREDIT CARDS: Amex, MasterCard, Visa.
PRICES: [2015] per room B&B £145–£170, D,B&B £220–£240. Set dinner £41.

THE LION INN

'Clearly the place to be in Winchcombe,' says a visitor in 2015 to Annie Fox-Hamilton's 'fine modern inn', which is 'decorated with wit and imagination'. A beamed suite in a converted outbuilding, reached by a wooden staircase, 'had a small balcony, sitting area and separate bedroom, with muted grey walls and sisal flooring, a large, beautifully crafted vase of flowers and a mix-match of auction house finds. The decent-sized bathroom had a big walk-in drench shower. A wonderful giant chest served as a coffee table, but no TV (Scrabble and cards instead) and no radio.' There might be some noise in rooms above the bar and in the courtyard (diners eating alfresco, etc.) 'but the sounds cease after closing'. The cooking of chef Alex Dumitrache is 'first class': 'We enjoyed crab frittata on chickpeas; the freshest hake with Brussel sprout tops and samphire.' Nearby is a heritage railway and Sudeley Castle, home of Henry VIII's Katherine Parr, the wife who survived him. (DB)

37 North Street
Winchcombe
GL54 5PS

T: 01242 603300
E: reception@thelionwinchcombe.co.uk
W: www.thelionwinchcombe.co.uk

BEDROOMS: 7. 2 accessed by external staircase.
OPEN: all year.
FACILITIES: club room, bar, restaurant, free Wi-Fi, courtyard garden, only public areas suitable for disabled.
BACKGROUND MUSIC: in bar and restaurant.
LOCATION: town centre.
CHILDREN: all ages welcomed.
DOGS: allowed in bedrooms (£15), not in restaurant.
CREDIT CARDS: MasterCard, Visa.
PRICES: [2015] per room B&B from £110. À la carte £30. 1-night bookings sometimes refused.

GILPIN HOTEL AND
LAKE HOUSE

♥César award in 2000

'A happy atmosphere: friendly staff, flowers in every room.' Fresh praise in 2015 from returning visitors for this 'superb' country house hotel (Relais & Châteaux). It stands in lovely grounds with a terrace, pond, waterfall and croquet lawn. 'Everything was as good as or better than we remembered.' Two generations of the Cunliffe family run the hotel: Barney and Zoë Cunliffe are in day-to-day charge, working with his parents, John and Christine. In April 2015, the family appointed a new chef, Hrishikesh Desai, who secured the post in a TV audition (Alex Polizzi's Chefs on Trial). He oversees the cooking of modern dishes like sticky chicken wings and duck heart, artichoke, crispy rice; roast fillet of brill, hand-rolled macaroni, brown shrimps, lettuce salad. The Edwardian house has Arts and Crafts features blended with modern touches. The bedrooms, individually decorated, vary in size. 'Our junior suite had a terrace overlooking the garden where we could sit and read the newspapers; it was well equipped, with a tea-maker and fresh milk in the fridge.' (James and Lesley Rudd, WS)

25% DISCOUNT VOUCHERS

Crook Road
Windermere
LA23 3NE

T: 015394 88818
E: hotel@thegilpin.co.uk
W: www.thegilpin.co.uk

BEDROOMS: 26. 6 in orchard wing, 6 in Lake House (½ mile from main house).
OPEN: all year.
FACILITIES: ramps, bar, 2 lounges, 3 dining rooms, free Wi-Fi, 22-acre grounds (ponds, croquet), free access to nearby country club, golf course opposite, unsuitable for disabled.
BACKGROUND MUSIC: none.
LOCATION: on B5284, 2 miles SE of Windermere.
CHILDREN: not under 7.
DOGS: not allowed.
CREDIT CARDS: all major cards.
PRICES: [2015] per room B&B £215–£535, D,B&B £295–£615. Set dinner £58–£85. 1-night bookings sometimes refused.

SEE ALSO SHORTLIST

WINDERMERE Cumbria

Map 4: inset C2

HOLBECK GHYLL

'An enjoyable experience', Stephen and Lisa Leahy's ivy-covered Arts and Crafts house has a 'friendly, relaxed' atmosphere. 'It doesn't feel formal or stuffy in the slightest,' say guests who enjoyed 'a peaceful stay' this year. 'The public rooms couldn't be cosier: there are roaring fires, comfortable furniture arranged around lamps, and staff on hand to bring you drinks.' 'Very pleasant' bedrooms are in the main house, a lodge, and cottages in the grounds. 'Our attractive Lodge room had a stunning view over Lake Windermere. There was a large bed with lovely, plump pillows, two armchairs by the windows; up a winding staircase, a mezzanine level had a sofa and TV. A hot-water bottle was put in the bed at turn-down – a most welcome touch.' In the elegant dining room, chef David McLaughlin's modern menu divides opinions: one visitor found a scallop dish 'fresh and tasty, but not particularly inventive'; a guest in 2015 thought the food 'very good'. Breakfast, with a 'nice buffet' of fruit, cereals and croissants, is served in a 'stunning' oak-panelled room. (Bill and Anna Brewer, and others)

Holbeck Lane
Windermere
LA23 1LU

T: 015394 32375
F: 015394 34743
E: stay@holbeckghyll.com
W: www.holbeckghyll.com

BEDROOMS: 29. 1 suitable for disabled, 13, including 3 suites, outside the main house, plus 2-bedroom and 4-bedroom cottages.
OPEN: all year except first 2 weeks Jan.
FACILITIES: ramp, 2 lounges, bar, restaurant, private dining rooms, conference facilities, free Wi-Fi, civil wedding licence, small spa, 17-acre grounds (tennis, putting).
BACKGROUND MUSIC: piano in lounge and restaurant in evening.
LOCATION: 4 miles N of Windermere.
CHILDREN: all ages welcomed, not under 8 in restaurant.
DOGS: allowed in lodge rooms.
CREDIT CARDS: Amex, MasterCard, Visa (charge for credit card use).
PRICES: per room B&B from £170, D,B&B from £295. Set dinner £70. 1-night bookings sometimes refused Sat.

SEE ALSO SHORTLIST

THE WOLD COTTAGE

In landscaped grounds within a 300-acre farm, this red brick Georgian country house has a 'wonderful rural location'. The 'welcoming' hosts, Katrina and Derek Gray, greet visitors with tea and cakes on arrival; the home from home atmosphere is enjoyed by visitors. The cottage is run on a B&B basis, with evening meals by arrangement. The bedrooms, four in the main house and two in a barn extension, are named after people associated with the house: 'each is uniquely and beautifully furnished'. Two have a four-poster bed. Rooms are well equipped with tea- and coffee-making facilities, biscuits, chocolate or cake, plus local mineral water. A 'light and airy barn room was well appointed; plenty of hot water and toiletries'. Evening meals, cooked by Katrina Gray and served by her husband, are taken in the candlelit dining room. She places importance on the provenance of the produce; fruit and vegetables are grown in the garden, and local organic flour is used for making fresh bread every morning. The 'excellent' breakfast has locally smoked fish, cereals, fresh fruit, yogurt; full English. (DP)

25% DISCOUNT VOUCHERS

Wold Newton
YO25 3HL

T: 01262 470696
F: 01262 470696
E: katrina@woldcottage.com
W: www.woldcottage.com

BEDROOMS: 6. 2 in converted barn, 1 on ground floor, 2 self-catering cottages.
OPEN: all year.
FACILITIES: lounge, dining room, free Wi-Fi in public areas, 3-acre grounds (croquet) in 300-acre farmland.
BACKGROUND MUSIC: none.
LOCATION: just outside village.
CHILDREN: all ages welcomed.
DOGS: not allowed.
CREDIT CARDS: MasterCard, Visa.
PRICES: per person B&B £55–£90, D,B&B £83–£118. 1-night bookings sometimes refused.

THE SARACEN'S HEAD

Hidden in a 'lovely roadside setting in the middle of Norfolk countryside', Tim and Janie Elwes's ivy-covered Tuscan-style Georgian inn, with its unusual curved dormer windows and arches, is liked for its 'honest-to-goodness food and accommodation'. The Elweses are 'welcoming, relaxed, friendly' hosts: 'Our bags were willingly carried up to our quiet, "roomy" bedroom.' The modern rooms have 'plenty of storage'; coffee/tea-making facilities; flat-screen television; plug-in Internet access ('the speed might be slower than you're used to'). The 'spacious', newly renovated bathrooms have dark wooden floors, 'modern' washbasin, heated towel rail. The family room has enough space for a travel cot. Chef Mark Sayers serves a 'local, fresh, seasonal' menu in the two dining rooms ('one is more homey, with red brick walls and a wood-burner') or the 'cosy' bar. One visitor this year found the side dishes 'inconsistent, but the main courses were generous and very good. We enjoyed the broad-bean-and-chickpea cakes, and some very good duck.' There are 'lots of guides, maps and books' in the small sitting room upstairs, for planning North Norfolk exploration. (PA, and others)

Wall Road
Wolterton
NR11 7LZ

T: 01263 768909
F: 01263 768993
E: info@saracenshead-norfolk.co.uk
W: www.saracenshead-norfolk.co.uk

BEDROOMS: 6.
OPEN: all year except Christmas, 2 weeks late Feb/early Mar, restaurant closed Sun evening, Mon, Tues lunchtime except summer.
FACILITIES: lounge, bar, restaurant, free Wi-Fi, courtyard, 1-acre garden, unsuitable for disabled.
BACKGROUND MUSIC: in bar and dining rooms.
LOCATION: 5 miles from Aylsham.
CHILDREN: all ages welcomed.
DOGS: welcomed, not allowed in restaurant.
CREDIT CARDS: MasterCard, Visa.
PRICES: [2015] per room B&B single £70, double £100, D,B&B £165. À la carte £30.

WOOLACOMBE Devon

Map 1:B4

WATERSMEET

There is an 'easy, relaxed' atmosphere at this 'excellent' traditional hotel, once an Edwardian gentleman's retreat, above Woolacombe Bay. It is owned by Amanda James; 'first-class' staff are 'most helpful'. In a 'glorious setting' above a quiet, sandy beach, the hotel has 'impressive' Atlantic views across the bay to Lundy Island. All but three bedrooms look out to sea; some have a wooden balcony or a garden terrace. A third-floor suite under a sloping attic ceiling has panoramic views of the beach. In the restaurant overlooking the bay, chef John Prince cooks classic British dishes, perhaps roast sirloin of Exmoor beef, cauliflower cheese purée, steak and tongue pudding, truffle mash. An informal bistro serves simpler meals (mussels and chips; confit duck leg); afternoon tea, with freshly baked scones and local clotted cream, is served in the 'well-kept' lounge or, in good weather, on the terrace or lawn. New this year, a snug treatment room is available for massages and reflexology treatments. The South West Coast Path is nearby; the hotel has much information on local walks. (R and PJ, SH)

Mortehoe
Woolacombe
EX34 7EB

T: 01271 870333
F: 01271 870890
E: info@watersmeethotel.co.uk
W: www.watersmeethotel.co.uk

BEDROOMS: 25. 3 on ground floor, 1 suitable for disabled.
OPEN: all year except Jan.
FACILITIES: lift, lounge, bar, restaurant, bistro, function room, free Wi-Fi, civil wedding licence, terrace, treatment room, ½-acre gardens, heated indoor and outdoor swimming pools, sandy beach below.
BACKGROUND MUSIC: mixed in lounge all day.
LOCATION: by the sea, 4 miles SW of Ilfracombe.
CHILDREN: all ages welcomed, no under-8s in restaurant in evening.
DOGS: not allowed.
CREDIT CARDS: MasterCard, Visa (3% surcharge on credit cards).
PRICES: [2015] per room B&B £160–£250, D,B&B £220–£310. Set dinner £42.

WOOTTON COURTENAY Somerset

DUNKERY BEACON COUNTRY HOUSE

NEW

'Ideal for walkers', Jane and John Bradley's Edwardian hunting lodge on Exmoor earns an upgrade from the Shortlist after a positive report from readers who had 'another hugely enjoyable stay'. The elegant veranda and the lounge have dramatic views across the moor and towards the summit of Dunkery Beacon. Night skies, unpolluted by artificial light, can be viewed through a Newtonian reflector telescope. The country-style bedrooms also have the views: several have a four-poster bed, another a sleigh bed; they are supplied with fresh milk and spring water. 'We appreciated the attention to detail; it was noted that we asked for Earl Grey tea; a supply appeared on our bedroom tray the next day.' Mobile phone reception is limited (a landline is available). On four nights a week, dinner is served in the Coleridge restaurant. 'Jane's experience in the wine trade is demonstrated in an impressive wine list; this is complemented by John's expertise in the kitchen.' The short menu might include potted prawns and crab; garlic roast rump of Somerset lamb, soft polenta, sautéed kale, minted pea salsa. (Andrew and Hannah Butterworth)

25% DISCOUNT VOUCHERS

Wootton Courtenay
TA24 8RH

T: 01643 841241
E: info@dunkerybeacon
accommodation.co.uk
W: www.dunkerybeacon
countryhouse.co.uk

BEDROOMS: 8. 1 on ground floor.
OPEN: mid-Feb–2 Jan. Restaurant closed Sun/Mon/Tues.
FACILITIES: lounge, restaurant, breakfast room, free Wi-Fi in public areas, some bedrooms, ¾-acre garden, unsuitable for disabled.
BACKGROUND MUSIC: varied in restaurant.
LOCATION: 4 miles SW of Dunster.
CHILDREN: not under 10.
DOGS: allowed in 2 bedrooms (£5 per night), not in public rooms.
CREDIT CARDS: MasterCard, Visa.
PRICES: [2015] per room £80–£130, D,B&B £127–£177. Set dinner £23.50–£26.95. 1-night bookings refused Fri/Sat.

YARM North Yorkshire

JUDGES

In 'lovely manicured parkland', this 'immaculate Victorian country house hotel' is owned by the Downs family; Tim Howard is the manager. 'The service throughout, from unstarchy staff, was exemplary,' says a trusted Guide reporter. 'The proportions of the main staircase would grace a stately home twice the size; the decorations and furnishings were a little tired, perhaps. Our sumptuous bedroom was spacious, the bed was of Olympic proportions. Some nice touches: complimentary sherry, chocolates, fruit, home-made biscuits, fresh milk in the minibar. The bathroom was large and well lit.' Guests have access to the on-site gym and beauty clinic. In the dining room, chef John Schwarz specialises in modern British cuisine. 'The cooking was excellent, the menu interesting. Unusual canapés (deep-fried cheese, sago crisps, hummus); pigeon breast with rocket salad; venison with red cabbage, boudin noir.' Breakfast in the conservatory, overlooking blossoming trees and squirrels on the lawns, was 'good': 'plenty of cooked options and freshly squeezed juice, served by an affable waitress'. The Wi-Fi, upgraded this year, 'worked well in the bedroom'. (Francine Walsh, and others)

25% DISCOUNT VOUCHERS

Kirklevington Hall
Kirklevington
Yarm
TS15 9LW

T: 01642 789000
F: 01642 782878
E: thoward@judgeshotel.co.uk
W: www.judgeshotel.co.uk

BEDROOMS: 21. Some on ground floor.
OPEN: all year.
FACILITIES: ramps, lounge, bar, restaurant, private dining room, free Wi-Fi, function facilities, business centre, civil wedding licence, 36-acre grounds (paths, running routes), access to local spa and sports club.
BACKGROUND MUSIC: none.
LOCATION: 1½ miles S of centre.
CHILDREN: all ages welcomed.
DOGS: not allowed.
CREDIT CARDS: all major cards.
PRICES: [2015] per room B&B £145–£230, D,B&B £220–£315. Set dinner £39.50, à la carte £58.

MIDDLETHORPE HALL & SPA

Built in 1713 for the diarist Lady Mary Wortley Montagu, this 'rare example of a perfect William and Mary mansion is undeniably splendid and interesting', says a Guide inspector in 2015. Now owned by the National Trust, it is run as a hotel by Historic House Hotels; Lionel Chatard is the manager. 'Service is attentive and welcoming'; staff were 'neither supercilious nor obsequious'. Public rooms are 'spacious and elegant', with 'fire-lit halls' and 'a magnificently carved staircase; an ample quota of antiques, rugs, gilt mirrors and oil paintings'. The bedrooms are divided between the main house (these are 'grand and large') and a restored coach house (umbrellas are provided for wet days). 'Our coach house room was cosy with wallpapers and bathroom tiles from yesteryear – soft stripes and florals.' In the panelled dining rooms, which overlook the gardens, chef Nicholas Evans serves a modern British menu of 'elaborate' dishes, perhaps fillets of lemon sole, lobster macaroni, roast salsify, red wine jus. Dinner service was 'polished, correct'. Breakfast 'passed the porridge test with flying colours; delicious poached haddock'.

Bishopthorpe Road
York
YO23 2GB

T: 01904 641241
F: 01904 620176
E: info@middlethorpe.com
W: www.middlethorpe.com

BEDROOMS: 29. 17 in courtyard, 2 in garden, 1 suitable for disabled.
OPEN: all year.
FACILITIES: drawing room, sitting rooms, library, bar, restaurant, free Wi-Fi, civil wedding licence, 20-acre grounds, spa (indoor swimming pool, 10 by 5 metres).
BACKGROUND MUSIC: none.
LOCATION: 1½ miles S of centre.
CHILDREN: not under 6.
DOGS: welcomed in garden suites, not in public rooms.
CREDIT CARDS: Amex, MasterCard, Visa.
PRICES: [2015] per room B&B single £139–£179, double £199–£499, D,B&B from £129 per person. Set dinner £43–£69, à la carte £60. 1-night bookings refused weekends in summer.

SEE ALSO SHORTLIST

ZENNOR Cornwall

Map 1:D1

THE GURNARD'S HEAD

♀ César award in 2009

'This very individual inn oozes character and generosity.' Next to a Coastal Path in 'wildest' west Cornwall, Charles and Edmund Inkin's 'laid-back, well-run' yellow-painted inn welcomes children and pets alike. There are open fires, wooden floors and a library of paperbacks. Bedrooms are 'far from luxurious, but cosy, warm and lacking nothing; little touches such as Welsh blankets and fresh flowers give the place a lived-in atmosphere'. Rooms have views of the sea on one side, 'romantic views of the hills and cows walking up the road in the morning' on the other. The dining room has 'a lovely atmosphere, efficient service, gulpable wines'; new head chef Jack Clayton's menu is seasonal and locally sourced. Breakfast brings 'honest fare': pressed Cornish apple juice; home-made soda bread and jams; full English with hog's pudding. The bar is known to be quite boisterous on weekends. There is a rolling calendar of workshops: sketching, foraging, yoga. The Inkin brothers also run The Old Coastguard, Mousehole, and The Felin Fach Griffin, Felin Fach, in Wales (see entries). (JR, and others)

25% DISCOUNT VOUCHERS

Treen
Zennor
TR26 3DE

T: 01736 796928
E: edmund@eatdrinksleep.ltd.uk
W: www.gurnardshead.co.uk

BEDROOMS: 7.
OPEN: all year except 24/25 Dec.
FACILITIES: bar area, small connecting room with sofas, dining room, 3-acre garden, unsuitable for disabled.
BACKGROUND MUSIC: Radio 4 at breakfast, selected music at other times, in bar and restaurant.
LOCATION: 7 miles SW of St Ives, on B3306.
CHILDREN: all ages welcomed.
DOGS: welcomed, not allowed in dining room.
CREDIT CARDS: MasterCard, Visa.
PRICES: [2015] per room B&B from £110, D,B&B from £160. À la carte £29. 1-night bookings sometimes refused.

SCOTLAND

Shieldaig village, on Loch Shieldaig

SUMMER ISLES

NEW

Originally a fishing inn, Terry Mackay's 'remote but accessible' hotel has 'stunning views' across to the Summer Isles. It returns to a full entry thanks to a positive report from a regular correspondent. The public rooms are 'well furnished'. In the candlelit restaurant, the new chef, Victoria Edwards, serves a three-course set meal of dishes like roast rump of lamb, slow-cooked mutton croquette, rosemary jus; a six-course tasting menu is available. Meals can also be taken in the bar where seafood is a speciality: 'Our starter of dressed crab was generous and delicious; the main course of 16 fresh langoustines served with a separate Marie Rose sauce was wonderful.' The bedrooms are in the main house and in cottages and log cabins in the grounds. 'Our nice cottage room had a seating area looking out to Tanera Mòr; a decent bed; the large bathroom was slightly dated. Umbrellas were provided for the short walk to the main building.' There are fresh flowers on the table at breakfast: 'I had a lovely peat-smoked chestnut brown Finnan haddock with spinach and a poached egg.' (David Birnie)

Achiltibuie
by Ullapool
IV26 2YG

T: 01854 622282
F: 01854 622251
E: welcome@summerisleshotel.com
W: www.summerisleshotel.com

BEDROOMS: 13. 10 in annexe and cottages, 1 suitable for disabled.
OPEN: Apr–Oct, Christmas house party.
FACILITIES: cocktail bar and lounge, pub, restaurant, free Wi-Fi, wedding facilities, 1-acre garden.
BACKGROUND MUSIC: classical/traditional in bars and restaurant.
LOCATION: NW of Ullapool.
CHILDREN: not under 8 in restaurant.
DOGS: allowed in outside bedrooms (£20 per stay), not allowed in public rooms.
CREDIT CARDS: MasterCard, Visa.
PRICES: [2015] B&B per room single £130–£200, double £170–£340. Set dinner £39–£59, à la carte £39.

LOCH MELFORT HOTEL

A room with a view is assured at Calum and Rachel Ross's country hotel in 17-acre grounds: all bedrooms in the main house and the cedar-framed annexe look out over the Sound of Jura to the islands of Islay, Jura and Scarba, while the Asknish Bay restaurant has picture windows for an inside-outside feel. Chef Michael Knowles's menus feature langoustines, Islay scallops, Isle of Seil oysters, crabs and lobsters fresh from local waters. Typical dishes: yellow pepper and ricotta mousse; hake, squid ink risotto, smoked haddock sauce. Simpler dining is available in the Chartroom II Bistro, with children's favourites like burgers, pizza, haddock and chips, and soups and light main courses on an all-day menu. The walkway to the Cedar Wing is partly open to the elements, but the climate is temperate, warmed by the North Atlantic Drift, and these large rooms have a balcony, or a terrace with patio doors opening on to the grounds. Rooms in the main house are 'cosy'. The hotel's three highland cattle roam at will; ducks bob on a pond. Visit at azalea time: Arduaine Garden is next door.

Arduaine
by Oban
PA34 4XG

T: 01852 200233
F: 01852 200214
E: reception@lochmelfort.co.uk
W: www.lochmelfort.co.uk

BEDROOMS: 25. 20 in Cedar Wing annexe, 10 on ground floor, 1 suitable for disabled.
OPEN: Feb–Dec, closed Mon–Wed Feb/Mar, Nov/Dec, open Christmas/New Year.
FACILITIES: sitting room, library, bar/bistro, restaurant, wedding facilities, free Wi-Fi, 17-acre grounds (including National Trust for Scotland's Arduaine Garden).
BACKGROUND MUSIC: modern Scottish in restaurant and bistro.
LOCATION: 19 miles S of Oban.
CHILDREN: all ages welcomed, under-2s free.
DOGS: allowed in 6 bedrooms (£9 per night), not in public rooms.
CREDIT CARDS: MasterCard, Visa.
PRICES: [2015] per person B&B £75–£136, D,B&B £108–£156, £30 single supplement. Set menu £39.50, à la carte £41.

BALCARY BAY HOTEL

In a 'beautiful setting' on the Solway coast (once the haunt of smugglers), Graeme Lamb's 'well-maintained' hotel is liked for the 'tranquillity' and traditional comforts. It appeals to the mature guest who values the 'old-fashioned' touches such as sheets and blankets rather than a duvet, tea-making facilities of fresh milk and a china teapot, and an extra dish of vegetables at dinner. A complimentary box of chocolates and fresh fruit in the bedroom were also appreciated. The dress code in the restaurant is 'smart casual' (no jeans). Chef Craig McWilliam's cooking is praised: 'We enjoyed some excellent meals on an up-to-date menu; very good ballottine of rabbit, wonderful duck terrine.' Galloway beef and Stewartry lamb are speciality. Another comment: 'The four-course meal provides satiety for hearty eaters, yet allowing those like ourselves, with a smaller appetite, to enjoy the canapés and the petits fours.' The hotel's upgrading programme 'continues under the expert hands of [manager] Elaine Ness', says a visitor this year. Three ground-floor rooms have a patio and sea view; some rooms overlook the mature, landscaped grounds. (Anne Thackray, MT)

Shore Road
Auchencairn
Castle Douglas
DG7 1QZ

T: 01556 640217
F: 01556 640272
E: reservations@balcary-bay-hotel.co.uk
W: www.balcary-bay-hotel.co.uk

BEDROOMS: 20. 3 on ground floor.
OPEN: 29 Jan–1 Dec.
FACILITIES: 2 lounges, bar, conservatory, restaurant, free Wi-Fi (lounge only), 3½-acre grounds, unsuitable for disabled.
BACKGROUND MUSIC: none.
LOCATION: on shore, 2 miles SW of village.
CHILDREN: all ages welcomed.
DOGS: allowed in bedrooms, not in public rooms.
CREDIT CARDS: MasterCard, Visa.
PRICES: per person B&B £77–£93, D,B&B £91–£119. À la carte £42. 1-night bookings usually refused weekends.

SEE ALSO SHORTLIST

25%
DISCOUNT VOUCHER

THE GOOD HOTEL GUIDE 2016
Use this voucher to claim a 25% discount off the normal price for bed and breakfast at hotels with a `25% DISCOUNT VOUCHERS` sign. **You must request a voucher discount at the time of booking and present this voucher on arrival. Further details and conditions overleaf.**
Valid to 5th October 2016.

25%
DISCOUNT VOUCHER

THE GOOD HOTEL GUIDE 2016
Use this voucher to claim a 25% discount off the normal price for bed and breakfast at hotels with a `25% DISCOUNT VOUCHERS` sign. **You must request a voucher discount at the time of booking and present this voucher on arrival. Further details and conditions overleaf.**
Valid to 5th October 2016.

25%
DISCOUNT VOUCHER

THE GOOD HOTEL GUIDE 2016
Use this voucher to claim a 25% discount off the normal price for bed and breakfast at hotels with a `25% DISCOUNT VOUCHERS` sign. **You must request a voucher discount at the time of booking and present this voucher on arrival. Further details and conditions overleaf.**
Valid to 5th October 2016.

25%
DISCOUNT VOUCHER

THE GOOD HOTEL GUIDE 2016
Use this voucher to claim a 25% discount off the normal price for bed and breakfast at hotels with a `25% DISCOUNT VOUCHERS` sign. **You must request a voucher discount at the time of booking and present this voucher on arrival. Further details and conditions overleaf.**
Valid to 5th October 2016.

25%
DISCOUNT VOUCHER

THE GOOD HOTEL GUIDE 2016
Use this voucher to claim a 25% discount off the normal price for bed and breakfast at hotels with a `25% DISCOUNT VOUCHERS` sign. **You must request a voucher discount at the time of booking and present this voucher on arrival. Further details and conditions overleaf.**
Valid to 5th October 2016.

25%
DISCOUNT VOUCHER

THE GOOD HOTEL GUIDE 2016
Use this voucher to claim a 25% discount off the normal price for bed and breakfast at hotels with a `25% DISCOUNT VOUCHERS` sign. **You must request a voucher discount at the time of booking and present this voucher on arrival. Further details and conditions overleaf.**
Valid to 5th October 2016.

CONDITIONS

1. Hotels with a **25% DISCOUNT VOUCHERS** sign have agreed to give readers a discount of 25% off their normal bed-and-breakfast rate.
2. One voucher is good for the first night's stay only, at the discounted rate for yourself alone or for you and a partner sharing a double room.
3. Hotels may decline to accept a voucher reservation if they expect to be fully booked at the full room price.

CONDITIONS

1. Hotels with a **25% DISCOUNT VOUCHERS** sign have agreed to give readers a discount of 25% off their normal bed-and-breakfast rate.
2. One voucher is good for the first night's stay only, at the discounted rate for yourself alone or for you and a partner sharing a double room.
3. Hotels may decline to accept a voucher reservation if they expect to be fully booked at the full room price.

CONDITIONS

1. Hotels with a **25% DISCOUNT VOUCHERS** sign have agreed to give readers a discount of 25% off their normal bed-and-breakfast rate.
2. One voucher is good for the first night's stay only, at the discounted rate for yourself alone or for you and a partner sharing a double room.
3. Hotels may decline to accept a voucher reservation if they expect to be fully booked at the full room price.

CONDITIONS

1. Hotels with a **25% DISCOUNT VOUCHERS** sign have agreed to give readers a discount of 25% off their normal bed-and-breakfast rate.
2. One voucher is good for the first night's stay only, at the discounted rate for yourself alone or for you and a partner sharing a double room.
3. Hotels may decline to accept a voucher reservation if they expect to be fully booked at the full room price.

CONDITIONS

1. Hotels with a **25% DISCOUNT VOUCHERS** sign have agreed to give readers a discount of 25% off their normal bed-and-breakfast rate.
2. One voucher is good for the first night's stay only, at the discounted rate for yourself alone or for you and a partner sharing a double room.
3. Hotels may decline to accept a voucher reservation if they expect to be fully booked at the full room price.

BOATH HOUSE

♀César award in 2013

In 'delightful' grounds with award-winning gardens, this pale stone Georgian mansion is run as a luxury hotel by the owners Wendy and Don Matheson; their son, Sam, is the manager. The family have restored an endangered building, designed by renowned Aberdeen architect Archibald Simpson for Sir James Dunbar. 'Our large room looked out on to the wonderful kitchen gardens. It was beautiful in every way; the furniture was good, and there was an excellent tea tray. At one window, there was a table with two comfortable upholstered chairs. The bathroom was large, with a roll-top bath and an over-bath shower.' There may be noise from the main road at the front. In the dining room, which has views through French windows to a lake, chef Charlie Lockley is a follower of the Slow Food Movement. He uses local produce for the 'exceptional' dishes on a no-choice menu: 'We were given salmon, duck and rhubarb, all beautifully cooked.' Breakfast 'was like an elegant, well-presented dinner: apple juice, fruit smoothies; bacon, black pudding, duck eggs; toast and delicious marmalade'. (Barbara Watkinson)

Boath House
Auldearn
IV12 5TE

T: 01667 454896
F: 01667 455469
E: info@boath-house.com
W: www.boath-house.com

BEDROOMS: 8, 1, in cottage (50 yds), suitable for disabled.
OPEN: all year.
FACILITIES: 2 lounges, whisky bar/library, orangery, restaurant, health/beauty spa, free Wi-Fi, wedding facilities, 22-acre grounds (woods, gardens, meadow, streams, trout lake).
BACKGROUND MUSIC: none.
LOCATION: 2 miles E of Nairn.
CHILDREN: all ages welcomed, not under 8 in dining room at dinner.
DOGS: allowed in some bedrooms, not in public rooms.
CREDIT CARDS: MasterCard, Visa.
PRICES: (2015) per room B&B single £190–£260, double £260–£365, D,B&B £345–£450. Set dinner £45–£70.

COSSES COUNTRY HOUSE

In 'a little hidden valley' near the village, this low-built, whitewashed house, with a single-storey byre conversion, is run as a guest house by 'charming' owners Susan and Robin Crosthwaite. Visitors are greeted with tea and home-made fruitcake. In the evening, the hostess, author of *A Country Cook's Garden in South West Scotland*, cooks a daily-changing dinner menu based on local produce and home-grown fruit and vegetables. Guests sit down together to such 'delicious' dishes as crab cakes, Cosses salad leaves, sweet chilli balsamic dressing, olive bread; Highland roe deer, brandy and spring onion sauce. The smallest bedroom is in the main house; guests cross the courtyard to the other rooms. The Ailsa Suite was 'spotless', prettily furnished, 'hung with Susan's own watercolours'. Its bathroom had a bath and a walk-in shower (the Iona Suite and the Garden Room have a bath). For rainy days there is a games room with table tennis and a half-size snooker table, as well as use of the utility room to dry clothes. Breakfast has home-baked bread and 'any cooked breakfast you could think of'.

Ballantrae
KA26 0LR

T: 01465 831363
F: 01465 831598
E: enquiries@cossescountryhouse.com
W: www.cossescountryhouse.com

BEDROOMS: 3. All on ground floor, 2 across courtyard.
OPEN: all year except Christmas/New Year and 'occasional' closures.
FACILITIES: drawing room, dining room, games room (table tennis, darts), free Wi-Fi, 12-acre grounds.
BACKGROUND MUSIC: none.
LOCATION: 2 miles E of Ballantrae.
CHILDREN: not under 12.
DOGS: allowed by arrangement in 1 suite, not in public rooms.
CREDIT CARDS: MasterCard, Visa.
PRICES: [2015] per person B&B £55–£65, D,B&B £90–£100. À la carte £35.

GLENAPP CASTLE

In extensive grounds overlooking Ailsa Craig, this 19th-century sandstone castle (once the seat of the Earl of Inchcape) has been restored by the McMillan family. The work was overseen by Fay (née McMillan) Cowan and her husband, Graham, who run it as a luxury hotel (Relais & Châteaux). Visitors comment on the 'exemplary' service: 'The staff are friendly, no standing on ceremony.' The castle has been furnished with fine paintings, Middle Eastern rugs, antiques. The library has floor-to-ceiling bookshelves. Guests have exclusive access to the gardens, which have a huge Victorian glasshouse, rare plants and shrubs, a walled garden and woodland walks. In the formal dining room, chef Tyron Ellul looks to local producers to supply modern British dishes like braised Jacob's ladder of beef, beer-pickled onions, bone marrow and sage; pavé of spring lamb, potato and haggis terrine, crisp shoulder, mint jus. The spacious bedrooms have an open fire; there are wide beds, books, 'everything for your comfort'. Two palatial master rooms have ornate cornice work. Children are welcomed; a ground-floor suite has two connecting bedrooms, each with its own bathroom.

25% DISCOUNT VOUCHERS

Glenapp Castle
Ballantrae
KA26 0NZ

T: 01465 831212
F: 01465 831000
E: info@glenappcastle.com
W: www.glenappcastle.com

BEDROOMS: 17. 7 on ground floor.
OPEN: 27 Mar–3 Jan, except 22–28 Dec.
FACILITIES: ramp, lift, drawing room, library, 2 dining rooms, wedding facilities, free Wi-Fi, 36-acre gardens (tennis, croquet), fishing, golf nearby, access to spa.
BACKGROUND MUSIC: none.
LOCATION: 2 miles S of Ballantrae.
CHILDREN: all ages welcomed, junior dinner or 'well-behaved' children can join parents in dining room.
DOGS: allowed in 2 bedrooms (not unaccompanied), not in public rooms (no charge).
CREDIT CARDS: Amex, MasterCard, Visa.
PRICES: [2015] per room B&B £435, D,B&B £470 (min. 2-night stay). Set dinner £65. 1-night bookings refused at bank holidays, New Year.

NO. 45

Set back from the road on the outskirts of the
Deeside burgh closest to the royal residence at
Balmoral, this Victorian house is run as a B&B
by the owners Gordon Waddell and Penella
Price. In 2015 they stopped serving evening
meals 'to concentrate on developing a home
from home atmosphere'. The character of the
house has been retained: a royal stag's head from
the Glenlivet estate stands above the original
pitch pine staircase. Guests are encouraged
to make use of the lounge and drawing room
where a log fire might burn. The bar has
also been closed but a drinks licence has been
retained. A ground-floor bedroom has a wet
room and French windows to the garden.
An upstairs room has a king-size four-poster.
Each room is individually styled, with views
of garden or hillside. 'Tasty' breakfast dishes,
served in a 'large, airy' conservatory, include 'a
good selection' of hot and cold dishes: porridge
with cream and Drambuie; smoked salmon on
a potato scone. Ballater's former station, built to
serve Balmoral, houses the visitor centre in what
was once Queen Victoria's waiting room.

45 Braemar Road
Ballater
AB35 5RQ

T: 01339755420
F: 0871 989 5933
E: mail@no45.co.uk
W: www.no45.co.uk

BEDROOMS: 8. 1 on ground floor.
OPEN: May–Oct.
FACILITIES: ramp, library, drawing
room, lounge, conservatory, free
Wi-Fi, 1-acre garden.
BACKGROUND MUSIC: none.
LOCATION: village outskirts.
CHILDREN: all ages welcomed.
DOGS: not allowed.
CREDIT CARDS: Amex, MasterCard,
Visa.
PRICES: [2015] per room B&B £100–
£120. 1-night bookings sometimes
refused Sat in season.

KINLOCH HOUSE

'A wonderfully relaxed place to stay,' says a visitor this year to the Allen family's creeper-clad Victorian country house hotel (Relais & Châteaux) in the Perthshire hills. The staff might appear inconspicuous, 'but if you want something, just ask at reception and it happens straight away'. The public rooms have log fires, antiques, paintings, mantel clocks, rugs, rich damasks and ornaments. The landing is hung with oil-painting portraits. The 'lovely' bedrooms are large and 'beautifully furnished'; the beds are made with sheets and blankets. Most have a view of a landscape dotted with grazing Highland cattle and soft-fruit farms. 'I like the idea of being asked to order dinner before 6 pm; it avoids the indecision when under pressure at the table.' The dining room is dressed with crystal, silver and white linen. The chef, Steve McCallum, serves a short modern menu of dishes like hot quail salad with artichokes; sea bream with white wine and chive sauce, spinach, mussels. 'Not the cheapest hotel but it feels good value when everything is so well organised behind the scenes.' (William Wood, and others)

Dunkeld Road
Blairgowrie
PH10 6SG

T: 01250 884237
F: 01250 884333
E: reception@kinlochhouse.com
W: www.kinlochhouse.com

BEDROOMS: 15. 4 on ground floor.
OPEN: all year except 13–29 Dec.
FACILITIES: ramp, bar, lounge, drawing room, conservatory, dining room, private dining room, free Wi-Fi, wedding facilities, 25-acre grounds.
BACKGROUND MUSIC: none.
LOCATION: 3 miles W of Blairgowrie, on A923.
CHILDREN: no under-6s in dining room at night.
DOGS: not allowed.
CREDIT CARDS: MasterCard, Visa.
PRICES: [2015] per room B&B £185–£325, D,B&B £291–£431. Set dinner £53. 1-night bookings refused at busy periods.

TIGH AN DOCHAIS

Built ten years ago to designs by RIBA-award-winning architects Dualchas to exploit natural light and the constantly changing views of the bay, islands and mountains, Neil Hope and Lesley Unwin's B&B is run 'to the highest standards'. A galvanised steel bridged walkway leads to the upper storey entrance, where the lounge has floor-to-ceiling windows, sofas, bare oak floorboards, underfloor heating, a wood-burning stove and a bookcase crammed with 'thoughtfully chosen' books. There are more 'fantastic views' from the 'comfortable, spacious, well-maintained' bedrooms below, which have sliding doors leading on to a larch deck, and are equipped with binoculars. The 'delightful hosts' offer tea and shortbread on arrival, and provide 'helpful information on the area'. Breakfast, served at a communal table in the lounge, might include smoked haddock or kippers, hand-made sausages from the nearby Orbost organic farm, black pudding from Stornoway, home-made bread, muffins and yogurt. There is no restaurant, but Neil Hope will cook a 'delicious' evening meal by arrangement: the menu might include Orbost venison or pork; catch of the day with local vegetables; blackberry sponge.

13 Harrapool
Isle of Skye
Broadford
IV49 9AQ

T: 01471 820022
E: hopeskye@btinternet.com
W: www.skyebedbreakfast.co.uk

BEDROOMS: 3. All on ground floor.
OPEN: Apr–Nov.
FACILITIES: lounge, dining area, free Wi-Fi, ½-acre garden, unsuitable for disabled.
BACKGROUND MUSIC: Celtic occasionally at breakfast.
LOCATION: 1 mile E of Broadford.
CHILDREN: all ages welcomed.
DOGS: not allowed.
CREDIT CARDS: MasterCard, Visa.
PRICES: [2015] per room B&B £95. Set dinner £25.

🏅 KILMICHAEL COUNTRY HOUSE

César award: Scottish hotel of the year

'A very special small hotel which feels like a well-cared-for home. Excellent service is given in a personal way.' A Guide inspector was greeted in the wooded drive by peacocks (there are 22 of them, 'but no bother to visitors'); then by name at the door by Geoffrey Botterill, who owns Kilmichael with Antony Butterworth (who cooks). 'He made us very welcome and gave us tea and melt-in-the-mouth shortbread. He was interesting and informative about the Isle of Arran.' The ground-floor Rose Room was 'spacious, with rose-patterned curtains and bedspread, fresh-cut flowers; good lighting'. Drinks and canapés are taken in one of the two drawing rooms, which 'have ornaments, pictures and books from all over the world'. A set menu is served in the 'light' dining room (it is shown ahead of time and changes can be made). 'The meals are first class with interesting dishes; a warm salad of figs and chicken livers with leaves and flowers from the potager; guineafowl marinated in rum and lime juice.' Breakfast has 'delicious compotes', new-laid eggs from the hen coop, home-made jams.

Glen Cloy
Brodick, Isle of Arran
KA27 8BY

T: 01770 302219
E: enquiries@kilmichael.com
W: www.kilmichael.com

BEDROOMS: 7. 3 in converted stables (20 yds), some on ground floor, 4 self-catering cottages.
OPEN: Apr–Oct, restaurant closed Sun–Tues.
FACILITIES: 2 drawing rooms, dining room, free Wi-Fi (in drawing rooms), 3-acre grounds (burn), unsuitable for disabled.
BACKGROUND MUSIC: none.
LOCATION: 1 mile SW of village.
CHILDREN: not under 12.
DOGS: not allowed in public rooms, on lead in grounds.
CREDIT CARDS: Diners, MasterCard, Visa.
PRICES: [2015] per room B&B single £78–£98, double £130–£205. Set dinner £45. 1-night bookings sometimes refused Sat.

SEE ALSO SHORTLIST

POPPIES HOTEL AND RESTAURANT

Facing west towards the River Teith and distant hills in a 'beautiful and accessible' area, this modernised Victorian mansion is run as a small hotel and restaurant by the owners, John and Susan Martin. They show 'great attention to detail, and generally do all the jobs', said Guide inspectors. 'They were concerned and warm without being intrusive.' Pre-dinner drinks are taken in the Oak Bar (made from locally sourced wood), which has an extensive selection of malt whiskies. Steven Eastcroft has joined as chef this year; in the 'nicely decorated' dining room, he serves modern dishes like lobster and prawn terrine, asparagus salad, avocado oil; herb-crusted rack of lamb, roasted courgette, potato cake, minted Cabernet jus. 'Discreet' background music is played. The bedrooms are individually decorated: 'Our spotless room was spacious and warm; we enjoyed the view from two armchairs in front of the big bay window; there was a tray for making tea; water was piping hot in the modern and stylish bathroom.' There are two family rooms (children are welcomed and have their own menu). Breakfast is 'excellent'. 'Good value.'

25% DISCOUNT VOUCHERS

Leny Road
Callander
FK17 8AL

T: 01877 330329
F: 01877 332679
E: info@poppieshotel.com
W: www.poppieshotel.com

BEDROOMS: 9. 1 on ground floor.
OPEN: 25 Jan–24 Dec.
FACILITIES: reception, bar, restaurant, free Wi-Fi, small front garden, unsuitable for disabled.
BACKGROUND MUSIC: in bar and restaurant.
LOCATION: ¼ mile W of town.
CHILDREN: all ages welcomed.
DOGS: allowed in 2 bedrooms, not in public rooms.
CREDIT CARDS: Amex, MasterCard, Visa.
PRICES: per room B&B £80–£115, D,B&B £20 added per person. Early evening menu £13.95–£17.95, à la carte £30.

DUNVALANREE IN CARRADALE

'What a great place. It has those extra touches that make a special experience; we felt really welcome.' This year's praise for Alan and Alyson Milstead's restaurant-with-rooms in an Edwardian house on the Mull of Kintyre, overlooking the golf course and sandy Port Righ Bay. Home-made shortbread in the room proved 'positively addictive' to one visitor. 'Bathrobes, binoculars and a guest folder to help you plan days show real thought for guests.' The bedrooms are individually furnished and decorated. Two at the back share a bathroom and are ideal for a family. 'The highlight was the food; quality ingredients blended by a talented cook; it was not simple stuff done well, it was clever, interesting food, excellently cooked.' At 7 pm guests gather for drinks while Alan Milstead plays 'ebullient' host; his wife cooks a daily-changing menu, using local fish, shellfish and farm produce. The meal is a leisurely affair, served in a dining room overlooking the cliff-top garden and sea. At breakfast eggs are from the Milsteads' own hens. 'A great spot, handy for ferries to the islands.' (Jim Naismith)

Port Righ
Carradale
PA28 6SE

T: 01583 431226
E: book@dunvalanree.com
W: www.dunvalanree.com

BEDROOMS: 5. 1 on ground floor suitable for disabled.
OPEN: all year except Christmas.
FACILITIES: lounge, dining room, free Wi-Fi, 1/3-acre garden.
BACKGROUND MUSIC: in dining room Radio 2 in morning, jazz in evening.
LOCATION: on edge of village 15 miles N of Campbeltown.
CHILDREN: all ages welcomed, £22 B&B for small children.
DOGS: allowed in bedrooms only.
CREDIT CARDS: MasterCard, Visa.
PRICES: (2015) per person B&B £50–£70, D,B&B £74–£95. À la carte £29.

CHIRNSIDE HALL

Readers arriving for their yearly stay at Tessa
and Christian Korsten's late Georgian, Tudor-
gabled mansion, were welcomed by the hostess
'like old friends'. She was, writes a first-time
guest, 'much in evidence from dawn till dusk',
as 'receptionist, dining room host and general
factotum' – and always 'cheerful'. 'We had a
large second-floor room with a splendid sofa
and an excellent light tiled bathroom.' The
returnees' room had a four-poster, sofa, and
views of the Cheviots. 'The soft furnishings have
been renewed in tasteful grey/blue Welsh wool.'
In one of the two 'large' lounges, sofa covers had
similarly been renewed, 'in plains and plaids in
complementing colours'. There are open fires in
public rooms; antlers bristle on walls. 'Meals are
straightforward, nothing Cordon Bleu, but of
good quality.' Chef Tim Holmes sources local,
seasonal ingredients. Praise for carpaccio of
tuna, coriander, lime and lemon salad; slow-
roast pork belly, apple meatballs, mash, mustard
velouté, samphire. At breakfast there were
kippers with parsley butter, smoked haddock
with chive cream sauce, fruit compote with
crème fraîche and nuts. 'We will return.' (GC,
Anthony Bradbury)

Chirnside
TD11 3LD

T: 01890 818219
F: 01890 818231
E: reception@chirnsidehallhotel.
com
W: www.chirnsidehallhotel.com

BEDROOMS: 10.
OPEN: all year except Mar.
FACILITIES: 2 lounges, dining
room, private dining room, free
Wi-Fi, billiard room, fitness room,
library/conference rooms, wedding
facilities, 5-acre grounds, unsuitable
for disabled.
BACKGROUND MUSIC: 'easy listening'
in corridor.
LOCATION: ½ mile E of Chirnside,
NE of Duns.
CHILDREN: all ages welcomed.
DOGS: allowed, not unattended in
bedrooms, nor in public rooms.
CREDIT CARDS: Amex, MasterCard,
Visa.
PRICES: [2015] per person B&B single
£100, double £90, D,B&B single
£130, double £115.

THE COLONSAY

Built in 1750 as an inn for the islanders, this whitewashed hotel in a rugged landscape overlooking the harbour has not only a kitchen garden but its own oyster farm. Owners Jane and Alex Howard opened their doors to guests in 2007 after a stylish renovation – painted floorboards, open fires, sea colours of green, grey and blue. Hugo Arnold, food writer and hotel and restaurant consultant, leads occasional foraging groups. Ivan Lisovyy is the manager. There is plenty of comfortable seating in the public rooms; the bar is 'buzzy' with locals. The 'simply furnished' bedrooms are 'warm' but airy. The 'relaxed, unpretentious' feel continues in the restaurant, which has views of the harbour, and a wood-burning stove. The seasonal menu is based on local produce – 'lovely' soups, shellfish, lamb, beef, pork with organic salads and vegetables, hand-cut chips, newly baked bread, Scottish cheeses. White linen tablecloths, and Egyptian sheets on the beds are touches of luxury. Hot breakfasts are 'well cooked and tasty'. Golden eagles, grey seal and otters are among the wildlife. Colonsay House gardens are renowned for their rhododendrons.

Isle of Colonsay
PA61 7YP

T: 01951 200316
F: 01951 200353
E: hotel@colonsayestate.co.uk
W: www.colonsayholidays.co.uk

BEDROOMS: 9.
OPEN: Mar–Nov, Christmas, New Year, check-in days Fri, Sat, Sun, Wed, Thurs.
FACILITIES: conservatory lounge, log room, bar, restaurant, free Wi-Fi on ground floor, accommodation unsuitable for disabled.
BACKGROUND MUSIC: none.
LOCATION: 400 yds W of harbour.
CHILDREN: all ages welcomed, children under 12 free if sharing with parents.
DOGS: allowed in 2 bedrooms, public rooms except restaurant.
CREDIT CARDS: MasterCard, Visa.
PRICES: per room B&B £75–£150, D,B&B £30 added per person. À la carte £25–£30.

COUL HOUSE

Reached by a long, graded drive, this Georgian house has 'beautiful views to the south'. It is run as a small hotel by the 'proud owners', Stuart and Susannah Macpherson. The atmosphere is 'relaxed and friendly', say visitors this year. The Macphersons have restored the integrity of a house which was split in two in the 1960s and run as competing guest houses. They continue to refurbish, and to reinstate original features. A painting over the fireplace in the octagonal dining room depicts a visit by Queen Victoria in 1888. In the dining room, the cooking of chef Garry Kenley is admired: 'Delicately balanced brown crab and tomato soup; halibut on smoked prawns, savoy cabbage, bacon; an artful hot banana crêpe and excellent Scottish cheeses. A brilliant effort by the kitchen.' Bedrooms are generously furnished and have views of gardens and woodlands or mountains. A ground-floor room is 'pretty in blues and turquoise'. There are home-smoked or cured meats and home-baked bread at breakfast. In the grounds there is a Douglas fir planted in 1827 by the great plant-hunter David Douglas himself. (David Birnie, Hilary Murray)

Contin
by Strathpeffer
Ross-shire
IV14 9ES

T: 01997 421487
F: 01997 421945
E: stay@coulhouse.com
W: www.coulhousehotel.com

BEDROOMS: 21. 4 on ground floor.
OPEN: all year except Christmas.
FACILITIES: ramp, bar, lounge and front hall, restaurant, free Wi-Fi, conference/wedding facilities, 8-acre garden (children's play area, 9-hole pitch and putt).
BACKGROUND MUSIC: 'mixed' in bar, classical in restaurant.
LOCATION: 17 miles NW of Inverness.
CHILDREN: all ages welcomed, discounts up to age 15.
DOGS: welcomed (£5 per day).
CREDIT CARDS: Amex, MasterCard, Visa.
PRICES: per room B&B £95–£325. À la carte £37.50.

CRINAN HOTEL

In a 'superb position for scenery gazing', this hotel has long been the hub of a fishing village at the north end of the Crinan Canal. It is run with 'friendly informality' by Nick and Frances Ryan, who have been at the helm for nigh on half a century. Fans commend the charm and the ambience. Some guests might find the decor dated. But everyone enjoys the 'marvellous views' from the simply furnished bedrooms; some have a balcony. The local fishing fleet is based yards from the hotel, and lands lobster, prawns and white fish which supply the kitchens. There is a choice of places to eat: in the Westward restaurant, chef Gregor Bara serves a short set menu of dishes like risotto of West Coast crab, cream cheese and chives; grilled lemon sole, crushed potatoes, beurre blanc. A more extensive menu can be taken in the popular Seafood Bar. In season a no-choice menu is served in Lock 16, a rooftop restaurant. Frances Ryan (the painter Frances Macdonald) displays her own work and holds exhibitions of contemporary artists. Boat trips can be arranged.

25% DISCOUNT VOUCHERS

Crinan
PA31 8SR

T: 01546 830261
F: 01546 830292
E: reception.crinan@btconnect.com
W: www.crinanhotel.com

BEDROOMS: 20.
OPEN: all year except Christmas.
FACILITIES: lift, ramps, 2 lounges, gallery bar, Seafood Bar, 2 restaurants, coffee shop, free Wi-Fi in public areas, treatment room (health and beauty), wedding facilities, patio, ¼-acre garden.
BACKGROUND MUSIC: none.
LOCATION: village centre, waterfront.
CHILDREN: all ages welcomed.
DOGS: dogs welcomed (bring dog's own bedding, £10 surcharge to cover additional cleaning).
CREDIT CARDS: Diners, MasterCard, Visa.
PRICES: [2015] per room B&B £200–£260, D,B&B £260–£320. Set dinner Westward restaurant £35, Lock 16 (June to Sept) £65, Seafood Bar à la carte £30.

THE THREE CHIMNEYS AND
THE HOUSE OVER-BY

♀César award in 2001

An offer of tea and scones with jam and cream on arrival was 'enjoyed enormously' by guests who'd made a long drive to reach Eddie and Shirley Spear's Michelin-starred restaurant-with-rooms on Loch Dunvegan. They sat down later in the evening to the 'beautifully executed' eight-course Isle of Skye tasting menu. A new chef, Paul Hughes, joined in 2015, as did a new manager, Scott Davies. The Spears tell us they 'remain firmly at the helm of their business' as they celebrate their 30th year at the Three Chimneys. The menus will continue to be based on the 'authentic provenance' of local ingredients (especially Skye seafood). The unfussy bedroom suites in the building next door have loch views. 'Our room had a patio door with steps leading down to the garden. Everything we could have wished for in a hotel room was catered for; the bathroom was spacious and well lit.' There is a breakfast buffet, with hot food to order. A telescope is provided to watch seabirds – perhaps even porpoises. (John Holland, David Birnie)

Colbost
Dunvegan
IV55 8ZT

T: 01470 511258
F: 01470 511358
E: eatandstay@threechimneys.co.uk
W: www.threechimneys.co.uk

BEDROOMS: 6. All on ground floor in separate building, 1 suitable for disabled.
OPEN: all year except 1 Dec–14 Jan, restaurant closed for lunch Nov–Feb and Sun Oct–May.
FACILITIES: ramps, 3 public rooms, free Wi-Fi, garden on loch.
BACKGROUND MUSIC: 'gentle Scottish' at breakfast and in evenings.
LOCATION: 4 miles W of Dunvegan.
CHILDREN: no under-5s at lunch, no under-8s at dinner, tea at 5 pm.
DOGS: not allowed.
CREDIT CARDS: Amex, MasterCard, Visa.
PRICES: per room B&B £345. Set dinner £65–£90.

BEALACH HOUSE

♥César award in 2009

The journey might be challenging (the final mile-and-a-half is on a rough forestry track), but the welcome is 'warm' at Jim and Hilary McFadyen's small guest house. The former shepherd's croft, which has been extended with mini-baronial flourishes, stands in a remote glen with 'fabulous' views. The bedrooms are well equipped: each has tea- and coffee-making facilities with fresh chilled milk. Bathrooms have a power shower; one has a bath. In the lounge are a wood-burning stove, books, board games, and a jigsaw always in progress. Dinner is a sociable affair (visitors say they 'enjoy meeting other guests') at a communal table. As far as possible, everything on Hilary McFadyen's menus is home made or home grown; from bread and marmalade to petits fours, and fruit and vegetables from the garden. Typical dishes: chicken pork and apricot terrine; sea bass, roast cherry tomatoes, basil pesto dressing. Breakfast 'can be as light or hearty as you require': the daily special might be smoked haddock kedgeree. In the grounds you can catch sight of golden eagles, trespassing red and roe deer, even pine martens.

Salachan Glen
Duror
PA38 4BW

T: 01631 740298
E: enquiries@bealachhouse.co.uk
W: www.bealachhouse.co.uk

BEDROOMS: 3.
OPEN: mid-Mar–end Oct, dining room closed Mon evening.
FACILITIES: lounge, conservatory, dining room, free Wi-Fi, 8-acre grounds, unsuitable for disabled.
BACKGROUND MUSIC: none.
LOCATION: 2 miles S of Duror, off A828.
CHILDREN: not under 14.
DOGS: not allowed.
CREDIT CARDS: MasterCard, Visa.
PRICES: per room B&B £90–£110. Set dinner £25–£30. 1-night bookings sometimes refused.

ARDMOR HOUSE

For 15 years, Robin Jack has been welcoming guests to his B&B, a bay-fronted Victorian house with a small, flower-filled front garden. He has 'a little help', he says, from his partner, Barry, and 'our lovely dog, Vera, who will always give you an excited welcome'. He promises to provide insider information: readers vouch that he is 'a great help, responding readily to requests, and giving us a proper briefing on arrival'. His guide to the cafés, restaurants, shops and activities is 'the best we have come across in hotels'. The bedrooms are large, contemporary and 'immaculate'. There are king-size beds; power showers and Scottish toiletries in the bathroom. In the dining room at breakfast there are newspapers, fresh flowers, and a view across to Pilrig Park, former grounds of 17th-century Pilrig House (now apartments, once home to Robert Louis Stevenson's forebears). There is a buffet of cereals, fresh fruit, juices, home-made oatcakes, and bread for toasting; cooked dishes include porridge; local sausages and bacon; smoked bacon, potato waffle and maple syrup. Buses from 'just outside' service the city centre.

74 Pilrig Street
Edinburgh
EH6 5AS

T: 0131 5544944
F: 0131 5544944
E: info@ardmorhouse.com
W: www.ardmorhouse.com

BEDROOMS: 5. 1 on ground floor.
OPEN: all year.
FACILITIES: breakfast room, free Wi-Fi, small front garden.
BACKGROUND MUSIC: classical in breakfast room.
LOCATION: Leith, 1 mile NE of city centre.
CHILDREN: all ages welcomed.
DOGS: allowed by arrangement.
CREDIT CARDS: Diners, MasterCard, Visa.
PRICES: per room B&B £95–£170. 1-night bookings may be refused at weekends in peak season.

SEE ALSO SHORTLIST

THE BONHAM

'A civilised retreat from the noise of Edinburgh at Festival time,' say returning visitors this year, of their stay at this smart hotel. It occupies three late Victorian houses on a leafy crescent. David Barkley is the manager for the small Town House group. The chic bedrooms are individually styled: 'Our third-floor room, with a splendid view over the Firth of Forth, was lovely and comfortable. There was an abundance of drawers, though not enough hanging space (you need coats in Edinburgh even in August).' In the public areas, original carved wood panelling and classical detailing mix happily with a permanent contemporary art collection. The Consulting Room bar recalls the building's stint as a medical clinic. In the bay-windowed dining room, chef Maciej Szymik creates such inventive, modern dishes as truffle potato and egg-yolk ravioli, pickled mushrooms, mushroom velouté; braised beef cheeks, mashed potato, curly kale, bordelaise sauce. Background music plays ('why does a hotel as good as this inflict music on guests?'). 'We like The Bonham a lot and will continue to stay there.' (Elspeth and John Gibbon, and others)

35 Drumsheugh Gardens
Edinburgh
EH3 7RN

T: 0131 226 6050
F: 0131 226 6080
E: reception@thebonham.com
W: www.thebonham.com

BEDROOMS: 49. 1 suitable for disabled.
OPEN: all year, restaurant closed Mon/Tues.
FACILITIES: reception lounge, bar, restaurant, free Wi-Fi, wedding facilities.
BACKGROUND MUSIC: jazz and classical in public areas.
LOCATION: West End, free parking.
CHILDREN: all ages welcomed.
DOGS: welcomed in bedrooms (£30 charge), not allowed in public rooms.
CREDIT CARDS: Amex, MasterCard, Visa.
PRICES: [2015] per room B&B from £129. Set dinner £18–£22, à la carte £37. 1-night bookings sometimes refused.

SEE ALSO SHORTLIST

MILLERS64

Two sisters with the hospitable impulse present their Victorian town house as a smart but welcoming B&B. With just three guest bedrooms, and bags of enthusiasm, Louise and Shona Clelland have plenty of time for their visitors. 'Louise has the perfect attitude as a host,' report returning admirers. 'She is always available and aware, but never makes you feel that you're under her watch.' Contemporary styling sits well with original features. Park Suite was 'immaculately kept; luxurious in a modern and simple way; it was extremely spacious, as was our bathroom'. Although just off busy Leith Walk – past the French Gothic St Paul's Church with its dramatic spire and important stained glass by Daniel Cottier – the situation is quiet. Complimentary home-made shortbread and fudge were provided with tea and coffee facilities. Breakfast, served at a communal table, has home-made pastries, muffins, oatcakes, jams and compotes; the full Scottish comes with potato scones (black pudding and/or haggis extra), and there is a vegetarian alternative. You can catch a bus outside, or walk to the city centre in 20 minutes – 15 if you go at a smart pace. (Anna and Bill Brewer)

64 Pilrig Street
Edinburgh
EH6 5AS

T: 0131 4543666
F: 0131 4543666
E: reservations@millers64.com
W: www.millers64.com

BEDROOMS: 3.
OPEN: all year.
FACILITIES: dining room, patio, free Wi-Fi, unsuitable for disabled.
BACKGROUND MUSIC: none.
LOCATION: Leith.
CHILDREN: not under 12.
DOGS: not allowed.
CREDIT CARDS: none.
PRICES: [2015] per room B&B £85–£150. 1-night bookings refused weekends, min. 3-night stay Christmas/New Year, during Festival.

SEE ALSO SHORTLIST

ISLE OF ERISKA HOTEL, SPA AND ISLAND

♘César award in 2007

When Robin and Sheena Buchanan-Smith bought Eriska, at the mouth of Loch Creran, in 1973, they planned to take paying guests in summer to support a non-profit retreat in winter. Their son Beppo had a different vision, and today oversees a luxury Relais & Châteaux hotel with Michelin-starred restaurant in the family's Victorian Scottish Baronial mansion. A rickety chain bridge leads from the mainland to this leisure island. Bedrooms are 'super', large and 'well furnished' in contemporary style. Bathrooms are big and 'elegant', staff are 'friendly' and 'very professional'. Dinner is served in a panelled dining room. Ross Stovold cooks a daily-changing menu of West Coast produce. Sample: halibut, smoked mussels, seaweed-braised potatoes, pickled oarweed; Scotch beef sirloin, barbecued kohlrabi, watercress, onion gravy. The Stables Spa therapists are Espa trained and there is now a Rasul Mud room. Indoor sports include badminton and tennis, outdoors there is golf, clay-pigeon shooting, croquet, windsurfing, sailing – perhaps badger- or seal-watching.

Benderloch
Eriska
PA37 1SD

T: 01631 720371
F: 01631 720531
E: office@eriska-hotel.co.uk
W: www.eriska-hotel.co.uk

BEDROOMS: 25. 5 spa suites, 2 garden cottages, 2 Hilltop Reserves, some on ground floor.
OPEN: all year except Jan.
FACILITIES: ramp, drawing room, reception room, main hall, library, free Wi-Fi, leisure centre, heated swimming pool (17 by 6 metres), gym, sauna, treatments, wedding facilities, tennis, 350-acre private island, 6-hole par 22 golf course.
BACKGROUND MUSIC: none.
LOCATION: 12 miles N of Oban.
CHILDREN: all ages welcomed, but no under-5s in leisure centre, and special evening meal arrangements.
DOGS: welcomed, not allowed in public rooms or in spa suites.
CREDIT CARDS: Amex, MasterCard, Visa.
PRICES: [2015] per room B&B £350, D,B&B £450. Set dinner £55. 2-night min. stay. .

THE GRANGE

Everything is 'immaculately presented' at John and Joan Campbell's Victorian Gothic house with a turret and pointed gable, which stands in secluded landscaped gardens sloping down to Loch Linnhe. There are loch views from the dining room and the three bedrooms, which are supplied with 'just about everything', from glassware and candles, lamps, cushions and ornaments, to fresh fruit, a decanter of sherry, binoculars and even playing cards. The Turret Room has a Louis XV bed, a chandelier, armchairs. Rob Roy has a king-size bed, and a bathroom with both a bath and a walk-in shower. In a garden room there is an elegant sitting area approached through an arch between bed and bathroom. Furniture is of 'the highest quality'. Joan Campbell welcomes guests with offers of tea and home-made shortbread, and talks them through how things are run. Breakfast, served until 9 am, has fresh fruit; porridge with whisky and honey; smoked haddock with cream sauce; pancakes with bacon and maple syrup; the owners say they are happy 'to accommodate all tastes'. The town centre is within walking distance.

Grange Road
Fort William
PH33 6JF

T: 01397 705516
E: joan@thegrange-scotland.co.uk
W: www.grangefortwilliam.com

BEDROOMS: 3.
OPEN: Mar–Nov.
FACILITIES: lounge, breakfast room, 1-acre garden, unsuitable for disabled.
BACKGROUND MUSIC: none.
LOCATION: edge of town.
CHILDREN: not under 16.
DOGS: not allowed.
CREDIT CARDS: MasterCard, Visa (only to hold room).
PRICES: [2015] per person B&B £65–£70.

SEE ALSO SHORTLIST

GRASSHOPPERS

'Highly recommended: it is just like a very upmarket hostel,' said a youthful visitor this year to Brooke Noble's unusual hotel. It occupies the 'penthouse' sixth floor of the former head office of the Caledonian Railway Company, beside Central Station. The entrance lobby today serves as offices for Virgin and ScotRail ('not hotel-like at all') and gives no hint of what awaits when you step out of the lift. Cool colours, Scandinavian styling, oak floors, are all contained within the lofty rooms of an early-Edwardian (1905) block. Some windows look over the station's glass roof. 'We loved the views and the little touches, especially cakes on your arrival.' The bedrooms vary in size; they are well designed, and bathrooms have a power shower. The kitchen is at the hub, and tea and coffee are always available. Suppers are home cooked, served at wooden tables: soup, smoked haddock, apple pie, the ingredients locally sourced. At breakfast there is porridge, eggs and bacon cooked to order by 'friendly, willing staff'; cold meats, cheese, fruit, and specials 'to reflect important national and European days'.

6th floor, Caledonian Chambers
87 Union Street
Glasgow
G1 3TA

T: 0141 222 2666
F: 0141 248 3641
E: info@grasshoppersglasgow.com
W: www.grasshoppersglasgow.com

BEDROOMS: 29.
OPEN: all year except 3 days Christmas, no evening meals Fri–Sun.
FACILITIES: breakfast/supper room, free Wi-Fi, unsuitable for disabled.
BACKGROUND MUSIC: none.
LOCATION: by Central Station.
CHILDREN: all ages welcomed.
DOGS: welcomed.
CREDIT CARDS: Mastercard.
PRICES: [2015] per room B&B £95, DB&B £115. À la carte £17.

SEE ALSO SHORTLIST

GLENFINNAN HOUSE HOTEL

Liked for the 'warmth and comfort', the MacFarlane family's Victorian mansion has a 'lovely' situation, with lawns stretching down to Loch Shiel, Ben Nevis in the distance. Manja and Duncan Gibson are the long-serving managers. Originally an 18th-century inn, the building was remodelled and extended by Alexander MacDonald XII of Glenaladale, whose profligate predecessor commissioned the monument to the 1745 Jacobite Rebellion on the opposite shore. Public rooms have fresh flowers, 'roaring log fires', and paintings exploring Jacobite history. Dinner can be taken in the bar or the restaurant. Chef Duncan Gibson is classically trained in the French style: his menu might include fillet of turbot, spinach, cocotte potatoes, salmon caviar sauce. A home-from-home atmosphere is cultivated: there are no keys to the bedrooms, no television or telephone. The 'vast' Jacobite Suite has loch views, a four-poster, a spa bath and walk-in shower. Extra touches include 'upmarket' biscuits and shortbread on the tea tray, and locally made toiletries. 'At breakfast there could be smoked venison, kippers or smoked salmon; croissants, home-made jam and cafetière coffee.' (A and EW)

25% DISCOUNT VOUCHERS

Glenfinnan
PH37 4LT

T: 01397 722235
F: 01397 722249
E: availability@glenfinnanhouse.com
W: www.glenfinnanhouse.com

BEDROOMS: 14.
OPEN: 18 Mar–31 Oct.
FACILITIES: ramps, drawing room, bar/lounge, playroom, restaurant, wedding facilities, free Wi-Fi, 1-acre grounds, playground, unsuitable for disabled.
BACKGROUND MUSIC: Scottish in bar and restaurant.
LOCATION: 15 miles NW of Fort William.
CHILDREN: all ages welcomed.
DOGS: not in restaurant (or on soft furnishings).
CREDIT CARDS: Amex, MasterCard, Visa.
PRICES: [2015] per room B&B single £70–£80, double £140–£240. À la carte £30.

GLENFINNAN Highland

THE PRINCE'S HOUSE

'I cannot believe you will get a friendlier welcome or more attentive service than you do here,' writes a visitor this year to Kieron and Ina Kelly's small hotel at the head of Loch Shiel. An inn stood here on the August day when Bonnie Prince Charlie raised the standard at Glenfinnan to proclaim the start of the doomed Jacobite Rebellion of 1745. The wood-panelled restaurant and two of the bedrooms occupy the building's 17th-century core; the 'Stuart Room' is appropriately furnished with a Jacobean four-poster. Reservations are essential in the restaurant where Kieron Kelly's set four-course menu is tailored to the number of diners. It might include turbot, leek, oyster and beetroot; roast rack and slow-cooked shoulder of lamb, Madeira jus. More casual dining is available in the spacious bar, which has a vaulted ceiling. The home-baked bread and home-made ice cream are 'outstanding'. Breakfast has freshly squeezed orange juice; 'excellent' porridge. In the immediate vicinity can be found some of the 'most remote and beautiful' scenery in the Western Highlands. (AJ Gillingwater)

25% DISCOUNT VOUCHERS

by Fort William
Glenfinnan
PH37 4LT

T: 01397 722246
E: princeshouse@glenfinnan.co.uk
W: www.glenfinnan.co.uk

BEDROOMS: 9.
OPEN: mid-Mar–end Oct, 1 week from 27 Dec, restaurant open Easter–end Sept.
FACILITIES: lounge/bar, bar, dining room, free Wi-Fi, small front lawn, only bar suitable for disabled.
BACKGROUND MUSIC: classical in restaurant, 'easy listening' in bar.
LOCATION: 15 miles NW of Fort William.
CHILDREN: all ages welcomed.
DOGS: allowed in bar only.
CREDIT CARDS: Amex, MasterCard, Visa.
PRICES: per room B&B £110–£175. Set menu (in restaurant) £45, à la carte (in bar) £28.

CULDEARN HOUSE

'A four-square Scottish dwelling house', William and Sonia Marshall's Victorian granite villa is set back from the road next to woodland, a stroll from the centre of the Speyside town. The owners take 'tremendous pride' in their hotel, and 'should be congratulated for the warmth, welcome and quality', says a visitor. Open fires burn in original marble fireplaces. The style is traditional, with the atmosphere of a lived-in home – sofas, books, clocks, ornaments. Each of the 'excellent' bedrooms is individually furnished; the bathrooms are 'pristine'. In the evening, guests are given amuse-bouche with drinks in the lounge. Sonia Marshall is the cook, serving a daily-changing menu of seasonal dishes, perhaps warm leek and Stilton tart, pear dressing; saddle of Morayshire lamb, port and plum jus. Breakfast has 'generous servings of coffee', a small buffet; 'good' cooked options include an 'excellent' kipper. For a post-dinner drink, William Marshall can offer an extensive selection of single malts and single cask whiskies (there are 50 distilleries within 25 miles of Culdearn House). Whisky breaks are a speciality. (DB)

Woodlands Terrace
Grantown-on-Spey
PH26 3JU

T: 01479 872106
F: 01479 873641
E: enquiries@culdearn.com
W: www.culdearn.com

BEDROOMS: 6. 1 on ground floor.
OPEN: all year.
FACILITIES: lounge, dining room, free Wi-Fi, ¾-acre garden, unsuitable for disabled.
BACKGROUND MUSIC: none.
LOCATION: edge of town.
CHILDREN: not under 10.
DOGS: not allowed.
CREDIT CARDS: Diners, MasterCard, Visa.
PRICES: per person B&B £75–£85, D,B&B £100–£125. À la carte £45.

SEE ALSO SHORTLIST

GORDON'S

For 30 years Gordon and Maria Watson have run their restaurant-with-rooms in a converted terrace house built in the early 1800s. He is the chef, working alongside their son, Garry, who, having completed his training further afield, is 'increasingly taking over the mantle'. Maria Watson supervises the 'friendly' service front-of-house. 'Memorable' meals are taken in the recently refurbished restaurant (exposed stone wall, sage and grape wallpapers, good lighting, central chandeliers by a Spanish designer). The short set menu of modern dishes might include roast scallops, crispy chicken wings, Jerusalem artichoke, hazelnut; loin of Highland roe deer, mushroom ravioli, purple cabbage, venison and juniper jus. Home-baked bread is 'warm, light and moreish'. The bedrooms, created by a local designer, have bold bedspreads and wallpaper, modern furnishings. The largest, Thistle, has a decorative cornice ceiling, a tropical chic colour scheme; in the bathroom, a roll-top bath and separate shower. Close by is Lunan Bay, one of Scotland's most beautiful beaches, overlooked by the jagged ruins of the 12th-century Red Castle, built for William the Lion to repel Viking invaders. (RG)

Main Street
Inverkeilor
DD11 5RN

T: 01241 830364
E: gordonsrest@aol.com
W: www.gordonsrestaurant.co.uk

BEDROOMS: 5. 1 on ground floor in courtyard annexe.
OPEN: all year except 3 weeks Jan, restaurant open to residents only on Mon.
FACILITIES: lounge, restaurant, free Wi-Fi in reception, small garden.
BACKGROUND MUSIC: none.
LOCATION: in village.
CHILDREN: not under 12.
DOGS: not allowed.
CREDIT CARDS: MasterCard, Visa.
PRICES: per room B&B £110–£150. Set dinner £55.

ARGYLL HOTEL

NEW

'What an amazing little hotel,' says a 2015 visitor to this 19th-century former crofter's house with 1970s extension, restoring the Argyll to a main entry after a period without reports. Another visitor, for whom Iona has been 'a very special place' since childhood, booked knowing that the rooms would be compact: 'This is, after all, a remote small island, not some luxury resort with all mod cons. That for us is the charm.' A seafront room had 'a heavenly view' across to the Isle of Mull. Owners Wendy and Rob MacManaway are 'charming', the staff 'friendly and efficient'. At dinner, chef Richard Shwe uses local produce, with fruit and vegetables from the hotel's organic garden, to produce such 'delicious and interesting' dishes as carrot and cabbage spring roll, sweet and sour rhubarb, mustard seed caviar; loin of hogget, blue cheese croquettes, trotter sauce, purple sprouting broccoli. A buffet breakfast is included in the price; cooked items such as Iona hogget sausage, organic eggs, mushrooms and tattie scones charged extra. 'Being here makes even a committed atheist feel holy!' (Richard Macey, Robert Sanger)

Isle of Iona
PA76 6SJ

T: 01681 700334
F: 01681 700510
E: reception@argyllhoteliona.co.uk
W: www.argyllhoteliona.co.uk

BEDROOMS: 17. 7 in annexe.
OPEN: Mar–Oct.
FACILITIES: 3 lounges, conservatory, dining room, free Wi-Fi in dining room and west lounge, wedding facilities, beachfront garden, unsuitable for disabled.
BACKGROUND MUSIC: jazz, 'easy listening' in dining room.
LOCATION: village centre.
CHILDREN: all ages welcomed.
DOGS: welcomed, not allowed in dining room and 1 guest lounge.
CREDIT CARDS: MasterCard, Visa.
PRICES: B&B per room £62–£185, D,B&B from £85 per person. À la carte £35. 1-night bookings sometimes refused.

KILBERRY INN

♔César award in 2010

'There are unconfirmed reports that the Queen dined here during her 80th birthday cruise,' according to the website of this small restaurant-with-rooms. The owners' lips are sealed, but if Her Majesty did visit, she would have found rustic charm amid bewitching scenery. Since 2005, owners Clare Johnson and David Wilson have been building a reputation for the warmth of their welcome, while her cooking has earned a Michelin Bib Gourmand. He shakes or stirs a 'cocktail of the day' as guests peruse menus based on West Coast ingredients. 'Our eighth yearly visit,' say fans returning in 2015. 'We particularly enjoyed lamb tagine with bulgar wheat and aubergine yogurt, whole langoustine, and chocolate brownie with poached pear and chocolate sauce.' Local fish and shellfish are star turns. A fried breakfast has Stornoway black pudding and tattie scone. Granola, marmalade and jams are home made. There are five unfussy double rooms with en suite shower at the back, around a courtyard garden; 'Arran' has a sitting room. Order a packed lunch for a day at a deserted beach. (GC)

Kilberry, by Tarbert
PA29 6YD

T: 01880 770223
E: relax@kilberryinn.com
w: www.kilberryinn.com

BEDROOMS: 5, all on ground floor.
OPEN: Tues–Sun 13 Mar–mid-Dec.
FACILITIES: bar/dining room, smaller dining room, Wi-Fi (some areas), unsuitable for disabled.
BACKGROUND MUSIC: 'gentle' during lunch and dinner.
LOCATION: 16 miles NW of Tarbert, on B8024.
CHILDREN: no under-12s.
DOGS: allowed 'by arrangement' in 1 bedroom, not in public rooms.
CREDIT CARDS: MasterCard, Visa.
PRICES: [2015] per room D,B&B £215. A la carte £35. 1-night bookings sometimes refused.

ARDANAISEIG

'Beautifully situated' on the shores of Loch Awe, this rambling manor house is 'full of character', say Guide inspectors in 2015. 'A pleasingly old-fashioned air of country-house grandeur – with some eccentricity – pervades the public rooms. The owner, antique dealer Bennie Gray, has filled the house with suitably grand – and some quirky – pieces. The light-filled drawing room has large (modern) sofas, antique tables, fireplace, mirrors and art; two oversized, rather outré golden throne-like chairs.' A 'slightly cheeky' ambience is reflected in the 'unstuffy attitude of the friendly staff'. The public rooms, and many of the bedrooms, have a loch view. 'Our very comfortable room had a huge four-poster bed, sofa, chairs and tables by the window so you could sit and gaze at the view; a well-appointed bathroom; fresh flowers were a nice touch. Dinner was excellent: scallops with a subtly flavoured cumin sauce; tender sirloin of beef with mash, cèpes and crispy shards of bacon.' Breakfast has a wide selection of cooked dishes. 'It was nice to stroll down to the loch accompanied by deer.'

Kilchrenan
PA35 1HE

T: 01866 833333
F: 01866 833222
E: hello@ardanaiseig.com
W: www.ardanaiseig.com

BEDROOMS: 19. Some on ground floor, 1 in boatshed, 1 self-catering cottage.
OPEN: all year except Christmas.
FACILITIES: drawing room, library/bar, restaurant, free Wi-Fi, wedding facilities, 240-acre grounds on loch, unsuitable for disabled.
BACKGROUND MUSIC: none.
LOCATION: 4 miles E of Kilchrenan.
CHILDREN: all ages welcomed.
DOGS: allowed in bedrooms (£20 charge), not in public rooms.
CREDIT CARDS: all major cards.
PRICES: [2015] per room B&B £218–£363, D,B&B from £299. À la carte £40, tasting menu £60.

KILLIECRANKIE HOTEL

♔César award in 2011

'Outstanding: our favourite Scottish hotel.'
Henrietta Fergusson's whitewashed 19th-
century dower house in wooded grounds at
the entrance to the Pass of Killiecrankie has
long been popular with Guide readers. It
is a 'wonderfully relaxing place'; Henrietta
Fergusson, an 'open-hearted' host, personally
greets guests, and oversees the 'very efficient and
friendly' staff. The bedrooms vary in size and
style: each has 'comfortable' bed, neutral walls,
heavy curtains, fresh flowers and Egyptian
cotton sheets. Meals can be taken in the dining
room or the conservatory bar (which has a
lengthy list of whiskies). Chef Mark Easton
cooks a daily-changing menu using local
ingredients (some from the kitchen garden).
Wild mushroom ragout, say, with Rannoch-
smoked chicken breast, tagliatelle, chive cream
sauce; shallot and petit pois tortellini, Parmesan,
leek cream sauce. The waiters in their Scotch
Potch mixed-plaid trousers raise the occasional
eyebrow and smile. The house stands in fine
gardens with trim lawns, a rose garden and a
view of Fonvuik hill across the River Garry.
(A and EW, and others)

25% DISCOUNT VOUCHERS

Killiecrankie
PH16 5LG

T: 01796 473220
F: 01796 472451
E: enquiries@killiecrankiehotel.
co.uk
W: www.killiecrankiehotel.co.uk

BEDROOMS: 10. 2 on ground floor.
OPEN: 18 Mar–2 Jan.
FACILITIES: ramp, sitting room, bar
with conservatory, dining room,
breakfast conservatory, free Wi-Fi,
5-acre grounds, unsuitable for
disabled.
BACKGROUND MUSIC: none.
LOCATION: hamlet 3 miles W of
Pitlochry.
CHILDREN: all ages welcomed.
DOGS: welcomed, not in eating areas,
some bedrooms.
CREDIT CARDS: none.
PRICES: [2015] per person D,B&B
£120–£150. Set dinner £42. 1-night
bookings sometimes refused
weekends.

THE CROSS AT KINGUSSIE

The welcome is 'warm' from Derek and Celia Kitchingman at their restaurant-with-rooms in a former tweed mill in a 'very quiet' area of Kingussie. The loudest noise might be the sound of the River Gynack rushing past the terrace. David Skiggs was appointed chef in 2014. In the beamed restaurant, he serves a three-course set meal (included in the special rate for residents) and a six-course tasting menu. 'We enjoyed our meals (excepting sous vide meat, which is not to our taste),' say visitors in 2015. 'The food is of high quality.' There are books and games for a rainy day in two lounges. The bedrooms, recently renovated, have contemporary furniture, soft colours inspired by the surrounding hills. The largest rooms overlook the river; one has a balcony. Breakfast, which can be provided for guests arriving on the sleeper at 7.30 am, has a comprehensive buffet of cereals, fruit salad, berries, freshly baked croissants and home-made preserves; bacon and sausages come from Mr Gow, the local butcher; fish options include kipper and smoked salmon. (GC, and others)

Tweed Mill Brae
Ardbroilach Road
Kingussie
PH21 1LB

T: 01540 661166
E: relax@thecross.co.uk
W: www.thecross.co.uk

BEDROOMS: 8.
OPEN: closed Christmas and Jan, except Hogmanay.
FACILITIES: 2 lounges, restaurant, free Wi-Fi, 4-acre grounds, only restaurant suitable for disabled.
BACKGROUND MUSIC: none.
LOCATION: 440 yds from village centre.
CHILDREN: all ages welcomed.
DOGS: allowed by arrangement, not in public rooms.
CREDIT CARDS: Amex, MasterCard, Visa.
PRICES: [2015] per room B&B £110–£180, D,B&B £200–£280. Set dinner £55, tasting menu £60.

KIRKBEAN Dumfries and Galloway

CAVENS

Built for tobacco merchant Richard Oswald, a British commissioner who helped to negotiate the Treaty of Paris, this mid-18th-century manor house stands in large grounds offering plenty of peace for 21st-century visitors. A recent guest commented on a 'restful' atmosphere (rendering low background music 'unnecessary'). The Fordyce family run their home as a comfortable country hotel. The public areas are unapologetically old-fashioned, with 'lovely traditional furniture' – oil paintings, antiques, a grand piano. Most of the bedrooms are large, and have a sofa, books, 'lovely china' on the hospitality tray. Bathrooms are modern, 'well equipped' and 'pristine'. Angus Fordyce is the cook, serving a fixed-price market menu and a short à la carte. Typical dishes: pan-fried whole lemon sole; panna cotta. Tables are set with starched white linen and silverware; the meal is 'well served' by the 'smiling' staff. The choice at breakfast is wide, with 'well-presented' cooked dishes. You can play croquet, take tea on the terrace or, on rainy days, by the fire. (MH)

25% DISCOUNT VOUCHERS

Kirkbean
by Dumfries
DG2 8AA

T: 01387 880234
F: 01387 880467
E: enquiries@cavens.com
W: www.cavens.com

BEDROOMS: 6. 1 on ground floor.
OPEN: Mar–Nov, exclusive use by groups at Christmas/New Year.
FACILITIES: 2 sitting rooms, dining room, meeting facilities, free Wi-Fi, 20-acre grounds, unsuitable for disabled.
BACKGROUND MUSIC: light classical all day in one sitting room, dining room.
LOCATION: 13 miles S of Dumfries.
CHILDREN: all ages welcomed.
DOGS: allowed by arrangement, not in public rooms or unattended in bedrooms.
CREDIT CARDS: MasterCard, Visa.
PRICES: per room B&B £100–£200. D,B&B £150–£250. Set dinner £25, à la carte £35. 1-night bookings refused Easter, bank holidays.

GLENHOLME COUNTRY HOUSE

Retired diplomat Laurence Bristow-Smith and his artist wife, Jennifer, welcome guests to their 'interesting and very comfortable' home, a Victorian mansion set back from the road. A visitor this year was impressed: 'They are welcoming and helpful without being intrusive, and are fine cooks (and waiters).' The bedrooms are named after prominent Victorian political figures. Curzon, which has 'every comfort', overlooks the garden to 'a lovely view of the hills beyond'. It has a colonial four-poster bed, vintage fabrics and 'empire reds' reflecting Curzon's standing as Viceroy of India. In the library is a 'fascinating collection of well-thumbed books'. The three-course dinner is served in a 'beautifully furnished' room hung with landscapes commissioned from the artist Alan Rankle. 'Guests are invited to say what they do not or cannot eat and we build a menu based on that,' say the hosts. It might include salmon and ginger wonton, soya and balsamic sauce; rack of Galloway lamb, red wine sauce. 'We liked being able to bring our own wine.' A 'generous' bespoke breakfast is cooked to order. (David Waddington)

Tongland Road
Kirkcudbright
DG6 4UU

T: 01557 339422
E: info@glenholmecountryhouse.com
W: www.glenholmecountryhouse.com

BEDROOMS: 4.
OPEN: all year except Christmas, New Year.
FACILITIES: library, lounge, dining room, hall, free Wi-Fi, 2-acre garden, unsuitable for disabled.
BACKGROUND MUSIC: none.
LOCATION: 1 mile N of town.
CHILDREN: not under 12.
DOGS: not allowed.
CREDIT CARDS: MasterCard, Visa.
PRICES: [2015] per room B&B single £90–£100, double £100–£125. Set dinner £35. 1-night bookings sometimes refused in high season.

KYLESKU HOTEL

♥César award in 2014

'This was the most modest, least expensive hotel of our trip, and the most enjoyable.' Praise comes again this year for Tanja Lister and Sonia Virechauveix's 17th-century inn in a 'wonderful, peaceful' position by the old ferry slipway on a sea loch. There have been significant changes in 2015: the 'absolutely charming' owners have not rested on their laurels. There is a new garden deck; four new bedrooms have been added, two with a balcony. 'They blend well with the superb setting,' says a visitor in 2015. A guest who regretted that she could not get a sea-view bedroom (they are quickly booked up) liked her large room, which was 'well decorated with a very stylish, statement headboard'. And at dinner, 'we had a corner table with the most lovely view to the mountains, and were bathed in sunshine'. Sonia Virechauveix is the chef: she cooks with the freshest local ingredients. 'We had half a lobster each, followed by langoustine and scallops; date pudding, salted caramel sauce and ice cream. It was all wonderful.' Guests can eat in the restaurant, in the popular bar or alfresco. Boat trips can be taken from the harbour. (Barbara Watkinson, Colin Adams)

Kylesku
IV27 4HW

T: 01971 502231
E: info@kyleskuhotel.co.uk
W: www.kyleskuhotel.co.uk

BEDROOMS: 11. 4 in annexe.
OPEN: mid-Feb–New Year.
FACILITIES: lounge, bar, restaurant, free Wi-Fi in bar and lounge, small garden (tables for outside eating), unsuitable for disabled.
BACKGROUND MUSIC: modern popular in bar.
LOCATION: 10 miles S of Scourie, 30 miles north of Ullapool.
CHILDREN: all ages welcomed.
DOGS: allowed, £10 a night to max £40.
CREDIT CARDS: MasterCard, Visa.
PRICES: [2015] per room B&B £100–£140. À la carte £25.

LANGASS LODGE

Above Loch Langass, this 'handsome' white-painted sporting lodge, with a modern extension, is run as a small hotel by owners Niall and Amanda Leveson Gower. Guide inspectors, on a 'happy' stay in 2015, liked the 'stylish' decor and the 'friendly, efficient' service. The lodge has a 'cosy bar with a traditional feel; a conservatory-like sitting room-cum-extension to the bar, with sofas and tables where you can eat; and a bright, airy dining room'. Derek Maclean is now the chef, serving a menu that has daily variations: 'The smoked fish was delicious – one night thinly sliced scallops, hot- and cold-smoked salmon and pâté; next night gravadlax; fillet steak medallions were perfectly cooked; a very good cheeseboard; tasty chocolate fondant.' A covered walkway links the lodge with hillside bedrooms: 'Ours was warm and spacious with comfy twin beds, armchairs, wooden floors, rugs; French windows opened on to a little terrace with a lovely outlook of garden – and children's play area.' Amanda Leveson Gower 'suggested walks and provided maps'; North Uist is a paradise for wildlife, especially birds.

Locheport
Isle of North Uist
HS6 5HA

T: 01876 580285
F: 01876 580385
E: langasslodge@btconnect.com
W: www.langasslodge.co.uk

BEDROOMS: 11. 1 suitable for disabled.
OPEN: all year except Christmas.
FACILITIES: lounge, bar, restaurant, free Wi-Fi, wedding facilities, 11-acre garden in 200-acre grounds.
BACKGROUND MUSIC: in evening in bar, sometimes restaurant.
LOCATION: 7½ miles SW of Lochmaddy.
CHILDREN: all ages welcomed.
DOGS: welcomed, £5 charge.
CREDIT CARDS: MasterCard, Visa.
PRICES: [2015] per room B&B single £75–£100, double £95–£149. À la carte £36.

THE ALBANNACH

It is 25 years since Lesley Crosfield and Colin Craig opened their restaurant-with-rooms in a walled garden above this small fishing port. Picture windows in the dining room look over a deep sea loch to the dome of Suilven. The chef/proprietors have a Michelin star for their five-course set menu which changes daily, reflecting what is in season, which might mean roe deer with candy beetroot and truffled squash, scallops and monkfish, foraged chanterelles, croft rhubarb parfait. Canapés and petits fours top and tail the meal. Fish is landed at the harbour, jams and honey are from local crofters, many vegetables, fruit and herbs from the garden. A visitor this year found the meal 'excellent'. The Loft suite is a 'lovely room' with a sitting area facing the view. 'We had an enormous and very elegant bathroom with double sinks. Quite the best of our trip.' The large Penthouse suite has a bath 'big enough for two'. The Caberfeidh pub in the village, under the same ownership, has tapas-style tasting plates as well as local seafood. (Barbara Watkinson)

Baddidarroch
Sutherland
Lochinver
IV27 4LP

T: 01571 844407
E: info@thealbannach.co.uk
W: www.thealbannach.co.uk

BEDROOMS: 5. 1 in byre.
OPEN: 12 Mar–3 Jan, closed Mon.
FACILITIES: ramp, snug, conservatory, dining room, free Wi-Fi, ½-acre garden, unsuitable for disabled.
BACKGROUND MUSIC: none.
LOCATION: ½ mile from village.
CHILDREN: not under 12.
DOGS: not allowed.
CREDIT CARDS: MasterCard, Visa.
PRICES: [2015] per room D,B&B £280–£385. Set dinner £70. 1-night bookings generally refused Sat.

SEE ALSO SHORTLIST

THE DOWER HOUSE

♀César award in 2008

Wisteria swags this tucked-away, single-storey Georgian stone cottage-orné. It stands in flower-filled gardens with a fishpond, bordered by the rivers Beauly and Conon. William Ewart Gladstone used to come here for a spot of shooting. Since 1989 Mena and Robyn Aitchison have run it as a much-loved guest house, although, with log fires, antiques, rugs, book-lined walls and winged fireside chairs, it retains the feeling of a family home. Guests are welcomed by the hostess front-of-house; her husband cooks. 'We were thoroughly spoiled,' says a visitor who enjoyed two 'splendid' nights in 2015. Another comment: 'Both the Aitchisons are indeed charming. Inevitably one sees a lot more of Mena, but Robyn did emerge from the kitchen from time to time, and was equally delightful.' The three bedrooms and one suite have individual character. At dinner the three-course, no-choice set menu is based on fresh, local, seasonal ingredients. The cooking is modern British, 'and quality was very high'. 'An excellent meal included a memorable asparagus, pea and mint risotto.' 'A treasure chest.' (Colin Adams, and others)

Highfield
Muir of Ord
IV6 7XN

T: 01463 870090
F: 01463 870090
E: info@thedowerhouse.co.uk
W: www.thedowerhouse.co.uk

BEDROOMS: 4. All on ground floor.
OPEN: Apr–Oct.
FACILITIES: lounge, dining room, TV room, free Wi-Fi, wedding facilities, 4-acre grounds, unsuitable for disabled.
BACKGROUND MUSIC: none.
LOCATION: 14 miles NW of Inverness. 1 mile N of Muir of Ord.
CHILDREN: no under-5s at dinner (high tea at 5).
DOGS: allowed in bedrooms, not in public rooms.
CREDIT CARDS: MasterCard, Visa.
PRICES: [2015] per room B&B £140, D,B&B £216.

BARLEY BREE

Husband-and-wife team Alison and Fabrice Bouteloup have done 'a wonderful job' converting an early 19th-century coaching inn, in this conservation village (pronounced 'Mew-thil'), to an award-winning restaurant-with-rooms. In the bistro-style dining room there are bare floorboards (re-laid in 2015 'to improve the experience for heel-wearing customers'), exposed beams and brickwork, around a central wood-burning stove. Fabrice Bouteloup brings French flair to the cooking of local, seasonal ingredients. On the daily-changing menu you might find saffron risotto with wild garlic scallops; ox cheek slow cooked on the custom-built French stove. The menu can be 'tweaked' to accommodate vegetarians and guests with food allergies. The waiting staff are young, 'friendly and efficient'. Alison Bouteloup has selected a wine list that has good by-the-glass and carafe choices. Coffee can be taken in the guest lounge. The contemporary bedrooms are 'impeccable', individually styled. The 'huge' corner room was not plagued by traffic noise, even on a Saturday night. The cooked Scottish breakfast is 'delicious', with options of porridge, croissants and home-baked crusty bread.

6 Willoughby Street
Muthill
PH5 2AB

T: 01764 681451
F: 01764 910055
E: info@barleybree.com
W: www.barleybree.com

BEDROOMS: 6.
OPEN: all year except Christmas, closed on occasional periods shown on website, restaurant closed Mon and Tues.
FACILITIES: lounge, restaurant, free Wi-Fi in lounge, small terrace, unsuitable for disabled.
BACKGROUND MUSIC: jazz in lounge in evening.
LOCATION: village centre.
CHILDREN: all ages welcomed.
DOGS: not allowed.
CREDIT CARDS: MasterCard, Visa.
PRICES: [2015] per room B&B £110–£150. À la carte £42.

THE MANOR HOUSE

Built as a dower house for the Duke of Argyll's Oban estate, this listed Georgian stone mansion on the south shore of the bay is run as a small hotel/restaurant by owners Leslie and Margaret Crane. Gregor MacKinnon is the 'laid-back and efficient' manager. The 'pristine' public areas are decorated in Scottish country house style (rich colours, tartan), and have 'interesting books and pictures'. There are fine views from Nelson's Bar. Bedrooms are 'prettily decorated'; each has sheets and blankets on the bed, a tea tray, fresh fruit and chocolates, free Wi-Fi. Some rooms are small ('cosy'); five have a view of the harbour; one is on the ground floor. In the dining room ('obviously the place to eat in Oban'), the tables are 'nicely set' with crisp white table linen, fresh flowers and candles; 'quiet' background music is played. Chef Shaun Squire's 'excellent' daily-changing menu of modern dishes might include haggis, neeps and tatties, Stornoway black pudding; duo of pork, dauphinoise potatoes, baked apples. Breakfast has a mixed buffet and table service 'with plenty of choice'. (CB)

Gallanach Road
Oban
PA34 4LS

T: 01631 562087
F: 01631 563053
E: info@manorhouseoban.com
W: www.manorhouseoban.com

BEDROOMS: 11. 1 on ground floor.
OPEN: all year except 25/26 Dec.
FACILITIES: 2 lounges, bar, restaurant, free Wi-Fi, wedding facilities, 1½-acre grounds, unsuitable for disabled.
BACKGROUND MUSIC: traditional in bar and dining room.
LOCATION: ½ mile from centre.
CHILDREN: not under 12.
DOGS: by arrangement, not allowed in public rooms.
CREDIT CARDS: all major cards.
PRICES: [2015] per room B&B £110–£235, D,B&B £195–£310. Set dinner £37.50–£42.50.

SEE ALSO SHORTLIST

CRAIGATIN HOUSE AND COURTYARD

When Martin and Andrea Anderson came from London in June 2007 to this stone-built Victorian house in a wooded location, it was as paying guests. They planned to use it as a base from which to scout for a suitable property to run as their own B&B. Then they chatted with the owner – and by October Craigatin House was theirs. One room at a time, they set about making the place over, introducing contemporary interiors, with bold use of colours, Zoffany wallpapers and Farrow & Ball paint finishes. Seven of the rooms are in the house; seven in converted stables. A cheap modern conservatory has been replaced by a double-height, light-filled cedarwood extension to accommodate dining area and lounge, heated by a wood-burning stove. Hand-made biscuits, bottled water and tea and coffee facilities are provided. The breakfast choice includes apple pancakes with bacon or caramelised banana; smoked-haddock omelette; porridge with a dash of whisky, cream and soft brown sugar. The Andersons are messianic about their adopted Highland town, happy to recommend local restaurants, places to see and things to do.

25% DISCOUNT VOUCHERS

165 Atholl Road
Pitlochry
PH16 5QL

T: 01796 472478
E: enquiries@craigatinhouse.co.uk
W: www.craigatinhouse.co.uk

BEDROOMS: 14. 7 in courtyard, 2 on ground floor, 1 suitable for disabled.
OPEN: Feb–Dec, Hogmanay but not Christmas.
FACILITIES: lounge, 2 dining rooms, free Wi-Fi, 2-acre garden.
BACKGROUND MUSIC: light jazz and soul in dining room in morning.
LOCATION: central.
CHILDREN: not under 13.
DOGS: not allowed.
CREDIT CARDS: MasterCard, Visa.
PRICES: [2015] per room B&B £95–£122 (single prices by arrangement). 1-night bookings refused Sat.

SEE ALSO SHORTLIST

PITLOCHRY Perth and Kinross

DALSHIAN HOUSE

The sign board at the foot of the private drive
to this 18th-century house promises 'genuine
Scottish hospitality'; recent visitors concur.
'A lovely stay', 'warm, friendly', 'home
baking', 'extremely comfortable' are typical
comments. Martin and Heather Walls welcome
visitors unobtrusively. In the lounge there are
magazines, a wood-burning stove, sofas, tartan
carpet. The bedrooms – including a family
room under the eaves, with a king-size double
bed and two singles – are individually styled,
mixing traditional furniture with modern decor
and artworks. An 'exceptional' breakfast has
fruit compotes, porridge with an (optional)
slug of whisky, the full Scottish (which comes
with roasted vine tomatoes, mushrooms and
a potato scone), perhaps eggs Benedict with
smoked salmon or French toast with maple
syrup and bacon. The situation is secluded, amid
woodland, with a well-kept garden in which to
sit and take tea and to watch for red squirrels.
Pitlochry has a fair choice of restaurants and
food pubs, and the internationally renowned
Festival Theatre. The walk into town is a
pleasure – but the return by night might call for
a taxi or a good torch.

25% DISCOUNT VOUCHERS

Old Perth Road
Pitlochry
PH16 5TD

T: 01796 472173
E: dalshian@btconnect.com
W: www.dalshian.co.uk

BEDROOMS: 7.
OPEN: all year except Christmas.
FACILITIES: lounge, dining room, free
Wi-Fi, 1-acre garden, unsuitable for
disabled.
BACKGROUND MUSIC: none.
LOCATION: 1 mile S of centre.
CHILDREN: all ages welcomed.
DOGS: allowed by arrangement, not
in public rooms.
CREDIT CARDS: MasterCard, Visa.
PRICES: [2015] per person B&B
£35–£45.

SEE ALSO SHORTLIST

THE GREEN PARK

♥César award in 2015

In a prime position on the banks of Loch Faskally, close to Pitlochry golf course, this traditional hotel is run by two generations of the McMenemie family. The original house was built for sisters Grace and Jane Cowan, celebrated hostesses. The McMenemies have extended the building 'without allowing modernity to prejudice the elegance', while maintaining the tradition of hospitality. Visitors comment on 'the incredibly personal service offered to guests, and the awesome attention to detail'. In the main lounge, an amalgamation of the two principal Victorian rooms, a vast buffet of tea and coffee, biscuits and home-made cakes is available free from late morning until 5 pm. In the large dining room, where window tables are at a premium, chef Chris Tamblin serves a daily-changing menu of 'superb' Franco-Scottish dishes like salmon, sole and pistachio terrine; fillet of pork, thyme mousse, chorizo and bean cassoulet. Guests can choose from a library of 3,000 books, take advantage of a jigsaw puzzle area or watch red squirrels from the sun lounge. Breakfast has the 'greatest range of choices we have ever seen'. (AW)

25% DISCOUNT VOUCHERS

Clunie Bridge Road
Pitlochry
PH16 5JY

T: 01796 473248
F: 01796 473520
E: bookings@thegreenpark.co.uk
W: www.thegreenpark.co.uk

BEDROOMS: 51. 13 on ground floor, 1 suitable for disabled.
OPEN: all year except 17–27 Dec.
FACILITIES: 2 lifts, 3 lounges, library, bar, restaurant, free Wi-Fi, 3-acre garden.
BACKGROUND MUSIC: none.
LOCATION: northern edge of town.
CHILDREN: all ages welcomed.
DOGS: allowed, not in public rooms.
CREDIT CARDS: MasterCard, Visa.
PRICES: [2015] per person B&B £78–£89, D,B&B £90–£114. Set menus £23–£27.

SEE ALSO SHORTLIST

KNOCKENDARROCH HOUSE HOTEL

NEW

Experienced hoteliers Struan and Louise Lothian have created 'a feeling of friendliness' at this small hotel. A Victorian stone mansion with baronial entrance tower on a quiet street, it has 'beautiful views across the Tummel valley'. The Lothians have refurbished throughout since buying the property in late 2014. Guide inspectors in 2015 were impressed: 'A lovely place to stay, good value given the quality of the food, service and comfort.' Each of the two lounge areas has a log fire; they have been given a clean country house look. Original Scottish contemporary art is hung throughout. The bedrooms are decorated in 'fresh and tasteful' colours. 'Our room at the side had a good-sized bed; two armchairs, a dressing table and a wardrobe with plenty of drawers and hanging space.' Drinks before dinner come with 'delicious hot canapés'. The chef, Graeme Stewart, serves 'original and tasty' dishes. 'We enjoyed Hebridean scallops; lamb and guineafowl nicely cooked and presented.' A 'wonderful' breakfast is served by Louise Lothian. The Pitlochry theatre, which was born in a marquee in the grounds, is across the river.

25% DISCOUNT VOUCHERS

Higher Oakfield
Pitlochry
PH16 5HT

T: 01796 473473
E: bookings@knockendarroch.co.uk
W: www.knockendarroch.co.uk

BEDROOMS: 12.
OPEN: 6 Feb–20 Dec.
FACILITIES: lounge, restaurant, 1½ acres woodland garden, free Wi-Fi, unsuitable for disabled.
BACKGROUND MUSIC: eclectic 'easy listening' at dinner.
LOCATION: central.
CHILDREN: not under 10.
DOGS: not allowed.
CREDIT CARDS: Amex, MasterCard, Visa.
PRICES: [2015] per room B&B £125–£195, D,B&B £150–£245. Set dinner £42. 1-night bookings sometimes refused.

SEE ALSO SHORTLIST

POOL HOUSE `NEW`

On the shores of Loch Ewe, this 'quirky' guest house has 'all the attributes of a small boutique hotel of outstanding quality'. It returns to the Guide thanks to a positive report from a regular correspondent this year. 'It is entirely run by the charming Harrison family: Peter Harrison, the patriarch, is much in evidence, serving meals in the dining room. Two daughters share the work of meeting and greeting, and ensuring the house is kept in tip-top condition. A son-in-law, John Moir, is an outstanding and largely self-taught chef.' The 300-year-old house is filled with antiques, paintings and curios, deep sofas, a Victorian piano; there are four suites, each with a sitting room and views across the bay. 'Our four-poster bedroom was a little dark, but the sunny, spacious sitting room overlooked the loch, and we watched otters from our window. Despite the impractical Edwardian bathing machine, the bathroom looked wonderful.' In the nautical-themed dining room, John Moir's four-course modern Scottish menus, including perhaps butter roast saddle of venison, haggis mash, Drambuie and peppercorn sauce, are 'unsurpassed'. (John Holland)

by Inverewe Garden
Poolewe
IV22 2LD

T: 01445 781272
E: stay@pool-house.co.uk
W: www.pool-house.co.uk

BEDROOMS: 4. Plus 2 self-catering cottages.
OPEN: Mar–Nov, dining room closed Mon eve (except bank holidays).
FACILITIES: reception room, drawing room/library, dining room, private dining room, billiard/whisky room, free Wi-Fi in public areas, ¼-acre garden, unsuitable for disabled.
BACKGROUND MUSIC: none.
LOCATION: 6 miles NE of Gairloch.
CHILDREN: not under 12.
DOGS: allowed in some bedrooms (£10 charge), billiard/whisky room.
CREDIT CARDS: Amex, MasterCard, Visa.
PRICES: [2015] per room B&B £275–£375. Set menu £45–£49. 1-night bookings refused weekends.

THE AIRDS HOTEL

An 18th-century ferry inn on the shores of Loch Linnhe is run as a luxury hotel (Relais & Châteaux) by Shaun and Jenny McKivragan, who, in 2002, bought not just the hotel but a formidable gastronomic reputation. Today's chef, Jordan Annabi, wins plaudits for his cooking of fresh, fished and foraged ingredients. In the dining room, 'everything is beautifully arranged', say visitors this year. 'Watchful staff stand behind chairs to place napkins on laps, remove plates promptly. Dinner was very good, including an extra starter, a velouté; we enjoyed some fine venison, and quail.' The public rooms are traditionally styled, with log fires, ample sofas and antiques. The 'beautifully furnished' bedrooms, many with loch views, vary in size and price. A decanter of Whisky Mac, and soft bathrobes are extra touches. No buffet at breakfast but an 'impressive' menu, including 'porridge and a wee dram, a nice granola with berries; scrambled eggs were less good'. 'We hired bikes and took the ferry to Lismore Island; it's not as flat as it might appear.' (Jill and Mike Bennett)

Port Appin
PA38 4DF

T: 01631 730236
F: 01631 730535
E: airds@airds-hotel.com
W: www.airds-hotel.com

BEDROOMS: 11. 2 on ground floor, also self-catering cottage.
OPEN: all year except Mon, Tues in Nov–Jan.
FACILITIES: 2 lounges, conservatory, snug bar, restaurant, wedding facilities, free Wi-Fi, 1-acre garden (croquet, putting), unsuitable for disabled.
BACKGROUND MUSIC: none.
LOCATION: 25 miles N of Oban.
CHILDREN: all ages welcomed, but no under-8s in dining room after 7.30 (high tea at 6.30).
DOGS: welcomed (£10 a day), not in public rooms.
CREDIT CARDS: MasterCard, Visa.
PRICES: [2015] per room B&B £250–£510. Set dinner £55.

SEE ALSO SHORTLIST

KNOCKINAAM LODGE

'Perfect: a tranquil setting, cosy log fire, big
bed and superb food.' A visitor who first came
on business to Sian and David Ibbotson's stone
hunting lodge returned for his honeymoon this
year. 'It will be our go-to anniversary break.'
The lodge's secluded setting, sheltered by a
horseshoe of wooded hills, is why it was chosen
for Winston Churchill's meeting with General
Eisenhower to plan the D-Day landings in
1944. Guests can steep in the same 100-year-old
enamelled bath as the war-time leader, in the
Churchill suite, which has a sitting area with
an original fireplace. The Hannay room on the
second floor has a separate lounge; a window
seat in the bathroom has views to Northern
Ireland. The chef, Tony Pierce, holds a Michelin
star for his modern menus with dishes like
leek, potato and truffle soup; roast breast of
Goosnargh duck, sweet and sour red cabbage.
'They were happy to provide a non-menu
dessert when asked.' Children can take high
tea or join their parents for an early dinner.
Breakfast has much choice. (Ian Shaw)

25% DISCOUNT VOUCHERS

Knockinaam Lodge
Portpatrick
DG9 9AD

T: 01776 810471
F: 01776 810435
E: reservations@knockinaamlodge.com
W: www.knockinaamlodge.com

BEDROOMS: 10.
OPEN: all year.
FACILITIES: 2 lounges, bar,
restaurant, free Wi-Fi, wedding
facilities, 30-acre grounds, only
restaurant suitable for disabled.
BACKGROUND MUSIC: 'easy listening'/
classical in restaurant in evening.
LOCATION: 3 miles S of Portpatrick.
CHILDREN: no under-12s in dining
room after 7 pm (high tea at 6).
DOGS: allowed in some bedrooms,
not in public rooms.
CREDIT CARDS: Amex, MasterCard,
Visa.
PRICES: [2015] per person D,B&B
single £175–£325, double £145–£220.
Set dinner £67.50. 1-night bookings
sometimes refused.

VIEWFIELD HOUSE

♥César award in 1993

A relatively modest Georgian house appears today as a Victorian extravaganza thanks to the present owner's great-grandfather. On his return from planting indigo in India, Harry Macdonald called in Alexander Ross, architect of Inverness Cathedral, to extend in all directions. Although not on cathedral proportions, several of the rooms are huge. The mansion has passed down to Hugh Macdonald, who creates the feeling of a house party (if you want a drink, ask for it; there isn't a bar). 'Fabulous, one of the nicest places we stayed on our visit to Scotland,' said a visitor from America this year, who appreciated the use of washing machine and drier. Walls bristle with antlers. Ancestral portraits look down. Log fires blaze. Public rooms are adorned with mementoes of the Raj. Portree is the capital of Skye, but the house stands quietly in wooded grounds with views of Portree Bay. 'You can walk into town.' Evening meals, by prior arrangement, are 'fantastic'. Breakfasts are hearty, with a good choice of cooked eggs, bacon, fish, as well as a cold buffet. (Beth Parks)

25% DISCOUNT VOUCHERS

Viewfield Road
Portree
Isle of Skye
IV51 9EU

T: 01478 612217
F: 01478 613517
E: info@viewfieldhouse.com
W: www.viewfieldhouse.com

BEDROOMS: 11. 1, on ground floor, suitable for disabled.
OPEN: 8 Apr–mid-Oct.
FACILITIES: ramp, drawing room, morning/TV room, dining room, free Wi-Fi, 20-acre grounds (croquet, swings).
BACKGROUND MUSIC: none.
LOCATION: S side of Portree.
CHILDREN: all ages welcomed.
DOGS: allowed in bedrooms, not allowed in public rooms.
CREDIT CARDS: MasterCard, Visa.
PRICES: [2015] per person B&B £75–£90. Set dinner £25.

MOOR OF RANNOCH HOTEL

♕ César award in 2015

In a village on the West Highland railway line, Scott Meikle and Stephanie Graham's 'beautifully remote hotel' stands at the end of the road on the edge of a moorland wilderness. The absence of 'modern-day essentials' – there is no Wi-Fi, no mobile phone signal, no television or radio – ensures a 'convivial time' with guests 'talking to each other' in a 'relaxed atmosphere'. 'Our bedroom was simple and stylish with stunning views from both windows,' says a visitor this year. The view is equally good from the dining room where Stephanie Graham serves an 'excellent' daily-changing menu of Aga-cooked dishes, perhaps trout, pea purée, potato salad; black-pudding-stuffed pork fillet, pear relish. On a pre-breakfast amble you might 'see the London train emerge from the mist over the moor'. Visitors who arrive on the overnight sleeper are welcome to take breakfast which has porridge with Drambuie and cream, and a full Scottish with home-made tattie scones. The owners are 'informative and entertaining', providing local knowledge on 'walks, Munros and train times'. (Katharine Dolby, Dermot Stewart)

Rannoch Station
PH17 2QA

T: 01882 633238
E: info@moorofrannoch.co.uk
W: www.moorofrannoch.co.uk

BEDROOMS: 5.
OPEN: 11 Feb–end Oct.
FACILITIES: lounge, bar, dining room, no Wi-Fi, unsuitable for disabled.
BACKGROUND MUSIC: none.
LOCATION: end of road, 36 miles W of Pitlochry.
CHILDREN: all ages welcomed.
DOGS: welcomed.
CREDIT CARDS: all major cards.
PRICES: [2015] per room B&B single £85, double £115. Set meals £24–£30.

THE BRIDGE INN
AT RATHO

NEW

By a bridge over the Union Canal in a village
near Edinburgh, Graham and Rachel Bucknall's
'lively' restaurant and pub-with-rooms has 'an
informal air', say Guide inspectors in 2015.
'Efficiently run by cheerful young women; a
casual place with character.' The 'smart' ground
floor has a busy bar on one side; on the other, a
bar-cum-parlour (each room has an open fire),
leading to a 'light-filled' dining room; there
are also tables outside on a terrace. Chef Ben
Watson's imaginative dishes include meat from
the owners' rare breed pigs and sheep at nearby
Ratho Hall. 'The food was delicious: Cullen
skink, scallops and black pudding with carrot
and ginger purée; roast loin of venison with port
gravy and scrumptious croquettes filled with
pulled venison shoulder.' The bedrooms are on
the first floor. 'Ours was small but not cramped,
with a large bed; only one bedside table and
lamp. It overlooked the road (some traffic, but
we weren't bothered by it) to the canal basin.'
Breakfast was 'very good; enormous, with two
of everything'.

27 Baird Road
Ratho
EH28 8RA

T: 0131 333 1320
F: 0131 333 3480
E: info@bridgeinn.com
W: www.bridgeinn.com

BEDROOMS: 4.
OPEN: all year, accommodation
closed 24/25 Dec.
FACILITIES: 2 bars, restaurant, free
Wi-Fi, terrace (beer garden, boat
shed), only bar and restaurant
suitable for disabled.
BACKGROUND MUSIC: 'relaxed' all day.
LOCATION: in village, 7 miles W of
Edinburgh.
CHILDREN: all ages welcomed.
DOGS: allowed in bar only.
CREDIT CARDS: Amex, MasterCard,
Visa.
PRICES: [2015] per room £70–£120.
À la carte £27. 1-night bookings
sometimes refused.

FOVERAN

In a starkly beautiful landscape overlooking
Scapa Flow, this award-winning restaurant-
with-rooms is a Doull family affair. Chef/
director Paul Doull runs the kitchen; his wife,
Helen, manages the front-of-house, while his
brother, Hamish, and sister-in-law, Shirley, take
care of the facilities and administration. The
homely decor of the single-storey restaurant
and lounge reflects the family's 'enthusiasm
and pride in all things Orcadian'. A tapestry
on display is by Leila Thomson, a cousin. The
kitchen and restaurant were renovated in early
2015. Paul Doull's menus showcase Orcadian
produce in dishes like North Ronaldsay mutton
patties; monkfish with smoked garlic, chorizo
and tomato sauce. Shellfish is a speciality: a
whole lobster can be ordered (with 24 hours'
notice). The service is 'friendly and helpful' in
the restaurant, which is popular with locals. The
lounge, which enjoys 'wonderful' sea views, has
good seating and an open fire. The bedrooms
are spruce and comfortable. Breakfast has
home-baked bread and bannocks, home-made
preserves; the cooked dishes have free-range
eggs and black pudding. No lunch: check-in is
from 4.30 pm unless by arrangement. (JB)

St Ola
Kirkwall
KW15 1SF

T: 01856 872389
F: 01856 876430
E: info@thefoveran.com
W: www.thefoveran.com

BEDROOMS: 8. All on ground floor.
OPEN: mid-May–mid-Sept, by
arrangement at other times,
restaurant closed Sun evening end
Sept–late May.
FACILITIES: lounge, restaurant,
12-acre grounds (private rock
beach), unsuitable for disabled.
BACKGROUND MUSIC: Scottish, in
evening, in restaurant.
LOCATION: 3 miles SW of Kirkwall.
CHILDREN: all ages welcomed.
DOGS: not allowed.
CREDIT CARDS: MasterCard, Visa.
PRICES: [2015] per person B&B
£55–£78, D,B&B £80–£103.
À la carte £35.

SCARISTA HOUSE

Q César award in 2012

'We couldn't have celebrated a 50th birthday in a more beautiful place; the setting and peacefulness are remarkable.' Tim and Patricia Martin's whitewashed Georgian manse stands above white shell sands on the remote west coast of Harris. 'It is a very special place thanks to the wonderfully laid-back but professional service; it has character, simplicity but most of all fantastic food,' says a regular Guide correspondent. There are rugs on wooden floors, comfortable sofas, open fires; a wealth of books and good art in both the downstairs library (where guests might be joined by the resident dogs and cat) and in the pet-free first-floor drawing room. Three bedrooms are in the main house; the others are in a converted outbuilding, where a 'light-filled' room had a 'wonderful view of the bay'. A set meal is served at dinner which is taken in two adjoining areas. Locally sourced ingredients are the backbone of the menu which might include Inverawe smoked venison, garden salad, Lewis quail's egg; Harris Minch langoustines, garlic and herb butter, Dijon mayonnaise, garden vegetables. The Martins welcome visiting children and pets. (NM)

Scarista
Isle of Harris
HS3 3HX

T: 01859 550238
E: bookings@scaristahouse.com
W: www.scaristahouse.com

BEDROOMS: 6. 3 in annexe.
OPEN: Mar–18 Dec, closed 17–31 Oct.
FACILITIES: 2 sitting rooms,
2 dining rooms, free Wi-Fi in most bedrooms and all public areas, wedding facilities, 1-acre garden, unsuitable for disabled.
BACKGROUND MUSIC: none.
LOCATION: 15 miles SW of Tarbert.
CHILDREN: all ages welcomed, early supper provided for young children.
DOGS: by arrangement in bedrooms, library.
CREDIT CARDS: Amex, MasterCard, Visa.
PRICES: [2015] per room B&B £215–£240. Set meals £43.50–£51.

TORAVAIG HOUSE

'Gloriously' positioned, with views of the Sound of Sleat and ruined Knock Castle, this whitewashed hotel is owned by Ken Gunn and Anne Gracie. A master mariner, he offers guests trips aboard his yacht, Solus a Chuain (Light of the Ocean), to the islands of Rhum and Eigg. A visitor this year received a friendly welcome at reception. 'Our room, Colonsay, was of a generous size; nicely decorated'; it had a bay window with a sea view; the bathroom, with a good shower, was 'slightly cramped'. Public areas are smart, comfortable and contemporary. There is a marble fireplace with open fire in the 'lovely' drawing room. A new head chef, Scott Galloway, serves a short daily-changing menu of modern dishes like scallops, wild garlic linguine, confit lemon, roast chicken sauce; Black Isle beef fillet, carrot, banana shallot tart Tatin, horseradish, red wine. The background music at dinner and breakfast was found 'annoying'. Freshly cooked dishes in the morning include Mallaig kippers, Skye smoked salmon, French toast with berries. Duisdale House nearby (see Shortlist) is under the same ownership.

Knock Bay
Sleat
Isle of Skye
IV44 8RE

T: 01471 820200
F: 01471 833404
E: info@skyehotel.co.uk
W: www.skyehotel.co.uk

BEDROOMS: 9.
OPEN: all year.
FACILITIES: lounge, dining room, free Wi-Fi, wedding facilities, 2-acre grounds, unsuitable for disabled.
BACKGROUND MUSIC: ambient all day in public areas.
LOCATION: 7 miles S of Broadford.
CHILDREN: all ages welcomed.
DOGS: not allowed.
CREDIT CARDS: MasterCard, Visa.
PRICES: per person B&B £85–£139, D,B&B £124–£184. Set dinner £48, à la carte £35.

SEE ALSO SHORTLIST

CREAGAN HOUSE

'A delightful place to stay', Gordon and Cherry Gunn's restaurant-with-rooms is housed in an 'intriguing' building, an extended 17th-century farmhouse where the 1970s dining room is styled as if it were a medieval great hall. 'She greeted us in a pleasant way and gave us some welcome tea and shortbread biscuits,' say visitors this year. 'We were invited down for drinks and spicy nuts before dinner in the dramatic dining room. It looks as though it could be medieval: a huge fireplace (with a gas fire) and Scottish lions rampant; lovely old wooden tables; the crockery with the signature lions rampant is from a local potter.' Gordon Gunn's cooking is much praised: 'We loved the Scottish flavours and recommend a "smokie in a pokie" [smoked haddock and fresh salmon, cooked in amontillado sherry and served with a pastis butter sauce], also the famous and rare Gigha halibut.' The bedrooms have antiques, fine fabrics. 'Our room was small but perfectly adequate, with tea tray and a nice bathroom overlooking the garden, hens and car park.' To the rear is wooded Glen Ample; in front, the A84. (Jill and Mike Bennett)

25% DISCOUNT VOUCHERS

Strathyre
FK18 8ND

T: 01877 384638
F: 01877 384319
E: eatandstay@creaganhouse.co.uk
W: www.creaganhouse.co.uk

BEDROOMS: 5. 1 on ground floor.
OPEN: 18 Mar–late Oct; closed Wed/Thurs.
FACILITIES: lounge, restaurant, private dining room, free Wi-Fi, 1-acre grounds.
BACKGROUND MUSIC: none.
LOCATION: just N of village.
CHILDREN: all ages welcomed.
DOGS: not allowed in public rooms.
CREDIT CARDS: MasterCard, Visa.
PRICES: per person B&B £67.50–£90, D,B&B £105–£127.50. Set dinner £37.50.

KILCAMB LODGE

An 18th-century stone house with Victorian east and west wings, Kilcamb Lodge stands amid meadow and woodland grazed by red deer. Its lawns run down to Loch Sunart. Variously home to an admiral, a church minister and a teacher, and once barracks for the troops of Bonnie Prince Charlie, it is today run as a small hotel by Sally and David Ruthven-Fox; Paul Arcari is the manager. The atmosphere is 'relaxed and friendly', with 'homely' lounges and 'log fires everywhere'. The spacious bedrooms, each of which has a loch view, have been refurbished in 2015; upgraded bathrooms have a power shower. Lunch and dinner are served in the candlelit dining room and the more informal brasserie. A new arrangement with Tiree-based fishing boat Kirsty Ann supplies fish for the daily specials on chef Gary Phillips's menus. They might include dishes like Kilcamb seafood platter; West Coast sea bass, tomato and olive tart. At breakfast there are home-made croissants, granola, porridge, berry compote, kippers with parsley and lemon butter, Inverawe smoked salmon, as well as the full Scottish.

Strontian
PH36 4HY

T: 01967 402257
F: 01967 402041
E: enquiries@kilcamblodge.co.uk
W: www.kilcamblodge.co.uk

BEDROOMS: 11.
OPEN: all year, except Jan.
FACILITIES: drawing room, lounge bar, dining room, brasserie, free Wi-Fi, wedding facilities, 11-acre grounds, unsuitable for disabled.
BACKGROUND MUSIC: jazz/classical/guitar in dining room (lunch time), brasserie (evening).
LOCATION: edge of village.
CHILDREN: not under 5.
DOGS: allowed in 4 bedrooms, not in public rooms.
CREDIT CARDS: MasterCard, Visa.
PRICES: [2015] per room B&B £120–£180, D,B&B £240–£415. À la carte £35.

TRIGONY HOUSE

Originally a 19th-century shooting and fishing lodge for Closeburn Castle, Adam and Jan Moore's 'relaxed' country house stands in ideal walking country, in the gentle, rolling countryside of the Nithsdale valley. It is close to, but screened from, the main road, by wooded grounds. The hotel is so pet-friendly that 'well-behaved' dogs receive a welcome pack. Japanese oak panelling in the hallway, an Art Deco staircase and half-landing window date from a 1930s makeover. 'Spotless' bedrooms are individually designed. The Garden Suite has a conservatory sitting room, and a bathroom with power shower, 'fragrant Scottish toiletries, large towels'. Jan Moore is the 'chatty and helpful' front-of-house. Her husband specialises in what he describes as '19th-century rustic cuisine', with the emphasis on local, organic produce, including fruit and vegetables from the walled kitchen garden. A 'delicious' dinner might include warm crispy duck salad, roasted red onion, orange dressing; cassoulet of local pork, flageolet beans, Gressingham duck. 'Can't wait to go back!' 'We will be there again,' are typical readers' comments. The Duke of Buccleuch's Drumlanrig Castle is three miles away.

25% DISCOUNT VOUCHERS

Closeburn
Thornhill
DG3 5EZ

T: 01848 331211
F: 01848 331303
E: info@trigonyhotel.co.uk
W: www.countryhousehotelscotland.com

BEDROOMS: 9. 1 on ground floor.
OPEN: all year except 24–26 and 31 Dec.
FACILITIES: lounge, bar, dining room, free Wi-Fi, wedding facilities, 4-acre grounds, unsuitable for disabled.
BACKGROUND MUSIC: jazz in bar in evening.
LOCATION: 1 mile S of Thornhill.
CHILDREN: all ages welcomed.
DOGS: 'well behaved' dogs welcomed.
CREDIT CARDS: Amex, MasterCard, Visa.
PRICES: per room B&B £110–£155, D,B&B £185–£225. À la carte £35. 1-night bookings sometimes refused Sat.

FORSS HOUSE

The River Forss wraps itself around this 'lovely old' Georgian house in wooded grounds popular with anglers, and rushes over falls on its way to the sea a mile away. A crenellated trophy room built by Major CRE Radclyffe, author of Big Game Shooting in Alaska (1904), is now the entrance hall (no moose or bears). The eccentric Major is still present in spirit and photographs, but the life and soul for nearly 30 years has been the manageress. 'The delightful Anne Mackenzie ensures everything runs smoothly with a liberal layer of humour,' says a visitor this year. From the 'slightly old-fashioned' ground floor, wide stairs with an iron balustrade ascend to the bedrooms. Cairnmore is 'a large room with huge en suite' and lots of fresh fruit. Another room had 'a very modern bathroom with roll-top bath by the window and a walk-in shower'. At dinner there are 'interesting menus of simply cooked local produce'. Breakfast in the conservatory has 'perfect finnan haddock and poached egg; very good croissants'. There are 300 whiskies in the bar. (David Birnie, Barbara Watkinson)

25% DISCOUNT VOUCHERS

Forss
by Thurso
KW14 7XY

T: 01847 861201
F: 01847 861301
E: anne@forsshousehotel.co.uk
W: www.forsshousehotel.co.uk

BEDROOMS: 14. 3 in main house on ground floor, 4 in River House, 2 in Fishing Lodge.
OPEN: all year except 24 Dec–4 Jan.
FACILITIES: trophy room/reception, dining room, conservatory, bar and Radclyffe Room, free Wi-Fi, wedding facilities, 20-acre grounds.
BACKGROUND MUSIC: in public areas.
LOCATION: 5 miles W of Thurso.
CHILDREN: all ages welcomed, under-5s free.
DOGS: not allowed in main building.
CREDIT CARDS: all major cards.
PRICES: [2015] per room B&B single £99–£135, double £135–£185, D,B&B single £137–£170, double £205–£260. À la carte £35.

TIRORAN HOUSE

The welcome is warm at Laurence and Katie Mackay's former Victorian hunting lodge. Set in 'lovely' wooded grounds (with a 'wonderful' garden) running down to Loch Scridain, it has views across to the Ross of Mull. Guests are received in house-party fashion. Introductions will be made (perhaps over complimentary tea and home-made cakes on arrival) and conversation will flow over pre-dinner drinks and canapés in one of the 'charming' sitting rooms. Dinner is served at 8 pm by 'delightful' staff. Two or three 'imaginative' choices at each course (vegetarians and others with special dietary requirements can be catered for, with notice). Chef Craig Ferguson uses local ingredients in his 'modern Scottish' dishes: fillet of salmon with wild leeks and Loch Spelve mussel broth; saddle of Forres lamb, brioche herb crust, sweetbreads, garlic purée, wild leek, fondant potato. The amply and traditionally furnished bedrooms vary in size and style. The large East Room has views over the loch; double doors open on to a spacious bathroom. 'Well-trained' dogs are welcomed in five rooms, each of which has a private entrance.

25% DISCOUNT VOUCHERS

Tiroran
Isle of Mull
PA69 6ES

T: 01681 705232
E: info@tiroran.com
W: www.tiroran.com

BEDROOMS: 11. 2 on ground floor, 4 in annexes.
OPEN: all year, New Year, except Dec, Jan.
FACILITIES: 2 sitting rooms, dining room, conservatory, free Wi-Fi, 17½-acre gardens in 56-acre grounds, beach with mooring, wedding facilities, unsuitable for disabled.
BACKGROUND MUSIC: none.
LOCATION: N side of Loch Scridain.
CHILDREN: all ages welcomed.
DOGS: allowed in 5 bedrooms, not in public rooms.
CREDIT CARDS: MasterCard, Visa.
PRICES: [2015] per room B&B £175–£220, D,B&B £271–£316. À la carte £48 (£36 for Sun night supper). 1-night bookings sometimes refused.

HIGHLAND COTTAGE

There was merely 'a tolerable inn' here when
Dr Johnson and James Boswell stayed in 1773.
Today's visitors are more glowing in their
praise for this purpose-built hotel, on a hill
overlooking the 'unbelievably pretty' harbour
of Mull's principal town. 'Excellent', 'friendly',
'comfortable', 'cosy', readers write. Owners
David and Jo Currie are career hoteliers, always
present, 'chatty and helpful'. The modest-sized
rooms are individually furnished; bathrooms
have a bath and temperature-controlled
shower. Ulva, and Staffa (with four-poster bed),
overlook the bay, Calve Island and the Sound
of Mull. Jo Currie cooks a 'stunning' three-
course dinner (a choice of two dishes at each
course) based on local, seasonal ingredients,
which might include smoked venison carpaccio,
peppered pear; halibut, boulangère potatoes,
leek, smoked-mussel cream sauce; lemon posset,
home-made shortbread. Vegetarian options
are 'no problem, given notice'. Aperitifs are
served in the conservatory. Public rooms have
an 'old-fashioned, slightly cluttered feel', though
'nothing is shabby'. The summer Mendelssohn
on Mull Festival celebrates the composer's visit
in 1829, which inspired his Hebrides Overture.

25% DISCOUNT VOUCHERS

Breadalbane Street
Tobermory
Isle of Mull
PA75 6PD

T: 01688 302030
E: davidandjo@highlandcottage.
   co.uk
W: www.highlandcottage.co.uk

BEDROOMS: 6. 1 on ground floor.
OPEN: Apr–mid-Oct.
FACILITIES: 2 lounges, restaurant,
free Wi-Fi, garden.
BACKGROUND MUSIC: none.
LOCATION: on hill above the town.
CHILDREN: not under 10.
DOGS: not allowed in public rooms.
CREDIT CARDS: MasterCard, Visa.
PRICES: [2015] per room B&B £135–
£165. Set dinner £39.50. 1-night
bookings refused weekends.

SEE ALSO SHORTLIST

THE CEILIDH PLACE

'Highly recommended' by a guest this year, Jean Urquhart's 'unique' hotel/bar/bookshop is close to the harbour of this fishing village. It began life in 1970 when Jean Urquhart's actor husband, the late Robert Urquhart, opened a café in a boatshed where musicians could sing for their supper. From there it grew into adjacent cottages, creating a warren of public rooms. The 'enormous' beamed lounge has a log fire, an honesty bar and a pantry for tea or coffee. Simple, country-style bedrooms are supplied with thoughtfully chosen books, a radio but no TV, and no hospitality tray because 'we don't like UHT milk and instant coffee'. In the buzzy dining room, chef Scott Morrison serves 'eclectic Scottish' fare 'with spice', using mainly local, organic produce. Comments have been mixed: 'Friendly service from European staff,' says a reader who enjoyed an 'excellent dinner'. A returning visitor in 2015 was less impressed and thought the staff 'needed more training'. The menu might have local fish and shellfish – smoked haddock chowder, mussels in cream sauce, spiced crab, for instance; perhaps braised ox cheek, beef and ale casserole.

25% DISCOUNT VOUCHERS

12–14 West Argyle Street
Ullapool
IV26 2TY

T: 01854 612103
F: 01854 613773
E: stay@theceilidhplace.com
W: www.theceilidhplace.com

BEDROOMS: 13. 10 with facilities en suite, plus 11 in Bunkhouse across road.
OPEN: all year except 7–21 Jan.
FACILITIES: bar, parlour, café/bistro, restaurant, bookshop, conference/function/wedding facilities, free Wi-Fi, 2-acre garden, only public areas suitable for disabled.
BACKGROUND MUSIC: 'eclectic' in public areas.
LOCATION: village centre, large car park.
CHILDREN: all ages welcomed.
DOGS: welcomed, not in breakfast room.
CREDIT CARDS: MasterCard, Visa.
PRICES: per person B&B £62–£84 (rooms in Bunkhouse from £23). À la carte £27.

SEE ALSO SHORTLIST

BURRASTOW HOUSE

In remote 'Waas', overlooking Vaila Sound, and protected from the sea by a crenellated wall, this 18th-century former merchant laird's house has been a hotel since 1980. It was much altered and extended in the early 1900s, and in 1995 acquired a new wing. Flemish owner Pierre Dupont creates the ambience of a private home, with peat fires, a 'cosy' lounge and library. There is no bar; guests jot down the drinks to which they help themselves. In the main house the Laird's Room, with tester bed, and Vaila (a four-poster double and a twin) overlook the waters where otters fish. Rooms in the extension are more modern. Over a breakfast of porridge, fresh croissants, perhaps locally smoked kippers, Mr Dupont asks who would like dinner – a three-course set menu of uncomplicated fare based on seasonal, local ingredients – lamb from the hills, halibut, turbot, crab and lobster. 'Don't be abrupted or shocked,' he says, 'by the asking of your desires as breakfast the next morning; Pierre simply wants to please you to start off your day agreeable' – which is the spirit of the place.

Walls
Shetland
ZE2 9PD

T: 01595 809307
E: info@burrastowhouse.co.uk
W: www.burrastowhouse.co.uk

BEDROOMS: 7. 3 in extension, 2 on ground floor.
OPEN: Apr–Oct.
FACILITIES: sitting room, library, dining room, free Wi-Fi in library, wedding facilities, unsuitable for disabled.
BACKGROUND MUSIC: none.
LOCATION: 2 miles from Walls, 27 miles NW of Lerwick.
CHILDREN: all ages welcomed, half price.
DOGS: not allowed.
CREDIT CARDS: MasterCard, Visa.
PRICES: [2015] per person B&B £60, D,B&B £95.

WALES

Conwy castle and river

HARBOURMASTER HOTEL

♥César award in 2005

'There is a real sense of Welshness,' says a visitor in 2015 at Glyn and Menna Heulyn's small hotel. Composed of three characterful converted buildings, it stands on the quayside of this pretty Regency town. Another guest commented on the 'very friendly' staff, and the 'lively, relaxed' feel in the public areas: 'The bar had a real buzz about it, and it was good to hear Welsh being spoken by so many.' Brightly decorated bedrooms are in the original building, a converted grain store next door, and a historic cottage. 'Every room is a delight,' say regular guests. 'We enjoyed the panoramic views from our spacious room, Aeron Queen, and watched a beautiful, golden sunset over the harbour on our first evening.' A small single room in the main house was 'clean, comfortable and well equipped, with a lovely view over the sea'. Chef Ludo Dieumegard's 'excellent' modern Welsh dishes are served in the bar and restaurant. 'We had a superb bar meal, with a delicious crab, chilli and garlic linguine.' A 'tasty' breakfast has 'all the extras you could wish for'. (Euan Balmer, Mike Craddock)

Pen Cei
Aberaeron
SA46 0BT

T: 01545 570755
F: 01545 570762
E: info@harbour-master.com
W: www.harbour-master.com

BEDROOMS: 13. 2 in cottage, 1 suitable for disabled.
OPEN: all year except 24 evening–26 Dec.
FACILITIES: lift, ramps, bar, restaurant, free Wi-Fi, pebble beach (safe bathing nearby).
BACKGROUND MUSIC: 'light' in bar all day.
LOCATION: central, on harbour.
CHILDREN: under-5s in cottage only.
DOGS: not allowed.
CREDIT CARDS: Amex, MasterCard, Visa.
PRICES: [2015] per room B&B £110–£250, D,B&B £160–£300. Set dinner £25–£30, à la carte £30. 1-night bookings refused weekends.

ABERDYFI Gwynedd

Map 3:C3

TREFEDDIAN HOTEL

'A real joy: we have been visiting for 40 years, and the standard has not changed.' Praise this year, from one of many repeat visitors, for the Cave family's 'lovely' hotel on a bluff with 'glorious' views across Cardigan Bay. Another comment, in 2015: 'It is refreshing to go somewhere that maintains tradition.' Out of season, the hotel is popular with older guests who enjoy the sociable public areas (including an adults-only lounge and a library with a card table) and the traditional values (like the dress code for dinner – 'gentlemen are required to wear a jacket or tie'). In the school holidays, it is busy with young families: 'The [newly renovated] swimming pool, snooker and children's room appeal to the grandchildren.' 'Well-equipped' bedrooms have views of the sea, or toward the hills of the Snowdonia national park. In the formal dining room, the chef, Tracy Sheen, cooks 'good' daily-changing English/French menus that 'always have one conservative and one more exciting main course'; a children's menu is served at 5.15 pm. 'An ideal place to really relax.' (Dorothy Brining)

Tywyn Road
Aberdyfi
LL35 0SB

T: 01654 767213
F: 01654 767777
E: info@trefwales.com
W: www.trefwales.com

BEDROOMS: 59.
OPEN: early Jan–early Dec.
FACILITIES: lift, 3 lounges, bar lounge, restaurant, games room (snooker, table tennis, air hockey), free Wi-Fi, fitness centre, indoor swimming pool (6 by 12 metres), beauty salon, 15-acre grounds (lawns, sun terrace, tennis, putting green).
BACKGROUND MUSIC: none.
LOCATION: ½ mile N of village.
CHILDREN: all ages welcomed.
DOGS: allowed in 1 lounge, some bedrooms.
CREDIT CARDS: MasterCard, Visa.
PRICES: [2015] per person D,B&B £70–£138. Set dinner £29.50. 1-night bookings sometimes refused.

THE ANGEL HOTEL

'A social hub' of this historic market town on the edge of the Brecon Beacons national park, this former coaching inn is 'very much a town hotel – and all the better for it', a Guide inspector said. The inn was bought and refurbished by the local Griffiths family; William Griffiths is now at the helm. Decorated with contemporary artworks (mother Pauline Griffiths runs an adjacent art shop and gallery), the public areas are 'well done'. The Foxhunter Bar, often busy with locals, has leather sofas, wooden tables, vintage settles; award-winning afternoon teas are taken in a 'pretty' lounge. In the Oak Room restaurant, chef Wesley Hammond's modern British menus might include braised lamb shoulder, leek and wild garlic purée, confit potatoes. Accommodation is spread between the main house, converted stables and two cottages nearby: standard rooms are 'comfortable if old-fashioned'; renovated rooms have a modern decor (four rooms have been upgraded this year). Rooms overlooking the front may have some street noise. The Griffiths family also co-owns, with Shaun Hill, the Michelin-starred Walnut Tree restaurant, a ten-minute drive away.

15 Cross Street
Abergavenny
NP7 5EN

T: 01873 857121
F: 01873 858059
E: info@angelabergavenny.com
W: www.angelabergavenny.com

BEDROOMS: 34. 2 in adjacent mews, plus 2 two-bedroom cottages.
OPEN: all year except 24–27 Dec.
FACILITIES: ramps, lift, lounge, 2 bars, tea room, restaurant, private function rooms, free Wi-Fi, civil wedding licence, courtyard.
BACKGROUND MUSIC: soft instrumental in restaurant and tea room.
LOCATION: town centre.
CHILDREN: all ages welcomed.
DOGS: allowed in bedrooms (£25 charge), bar, not in restaurant or tea room.
CREDIT CARDS: Amex, MasterCard, Visa.
PRICES: [2015] per room B&B from £111, D,B&B from £161. Set dinner £25, à la carte £30. 1-night bookings sometimes refused.

ABERSOCH Gwynedd

PORTH TOCYN HOTEL

♥César award in 1984

Steps from the Welsh Coast Footpath, with 'stupendous' views over Cardigan Bay, this 'lovely, wacky' hotel has been run by three generations of the Fletcher-Brewer family since 1948. Occupying three old miners' cottages, it has an unstuffy feel; children are made very welcome. Families may take advantage of baby-listening services, a guest fridge and microwave, a games room and a snug with books and television; a children's high tea is served at 5.30 pm. Furnished with country antiques, the bedrooms (most with sea views) have watercolours, prints and books; some are suitable for a family, others for guests travelling alone. 'Our spacious room had views over the sea to Snowdonia.' In the well-regarded restaurant overlooking the bay, chefs Louise Fletcher-Brewer and Ian Frost cook 'excellent' daily-changing modern menus. Typical dishes: pan-seared scallops, minted garden pea purée; grilled locally caught sea bass, vegetable and barley broth. An alternative light supper menu (bangers and mash, smoked salmon and dressed salad, etc) is available for those 'who do not want fine dining night after night'. (GC, and others)

Bwlch Tocyn
Abersoch
LL53 7BU

T: 01758 713303
F: 01758 713538
E: bookings@porthtocynhotel.co.uk
W: www.porthtocynhotel.co.uk

BEDROOMS: 17. 3 on ground floor.
OPEN: week before Easter–early Nov.
FACILITIES: ramp, sitting rooms, children's rooms, cocktail bar, dining room, free Wi-Fi, 20-acre grounds (swimming pool, 10 by 6 metres, heated May–end Sept, tennis), telephone to discuss disabled access.
BACKGROUND MUSIC: none.
LOCATION: 2 miles outside village.
CHILDREN: all ages welcomed (high tea for under-5s; no babies or young children at dinner).
DOGS: by arrangement, not allowed in public rooms.
CREDIT CARDS: MasterCard, Visa.
PRICES: [2015] per room B&B single £78.50–£93.50, double £107–£187. Set dinner £39–£46. 1-night bookings occasionally refused.

ABERYSTWYTH Ceredigion

GWESTY CYMRU

'An excellent hotel with a warm welcome', Huw and Beth Roberts's stylish restaurant-with-rooms is on the Victorian promenade of this lively resort town. The name translates as 'Welsh hotel', and the Grade II listed terrace house has been refurbished with a sense of national identity at heart: much of the custom-designed oak furniture is handmade in Wales; slate accents recall the country's once-flourishing industry. Inspired by the bold colours of the surrounding landscape (the red sky at night, the sand dunes at Ynyslas), modern bedrooms have abstract oil paintings; each also has bathrobes and a tea tray. An attic room with exposed beams and an original stone wall connects with an adjacent single to accommodate a family. In the restaurant, William Ainsworth, the new chef, serves modern Welsh dishes, perhaps pan-fried red mullet, Welshman's caviar polenta; lamb rump, sautéed kale, leeks. Alfresco meals may be taken on the terrace in warm weather. 'Breakfast is freshly cooked and excellent.' Well placed for Royal Pier, the castle and the cliff railway; many walks along the Wales Coastal Path, up Constitution Hill. (David Kershaw)

19 Marine Terrace
Aberystwyth
SY23 2AZ

T: 01970 612252
F: 01970 623348
E: info@gwestycymru.co.uk
W: www.gwestycymru.co.uk

BEDROOMS: 8. 2 on ground floor.
OPEN: all year except 23 Dec–3 Jan, restaurant closed for lunch Tues.
FACILITIES: bar, restaurant, terrace, free Wi-Fi, secure parking (book in advance), unsuitable for disabled.
BACKGROUND MUSIC: 'easy listening' in reception and restaurant.
LOCATION: central, on seafront.
CHILDREN: all ages welcomed at lunch, no under-5s to stay or in restaurant in evenings.
DOGS: not allowed.
CREDIT CARDS: MasterCard, Visa.
PRICES: [2015] per room B&B single £70–£80, double £90–£165, D,B&B (Nov–Mar, Sun–Thurs, excluding half-term) single £85–£125, double £150–£165. À la carte £30.

BRYNIAU GOLAU

♕ César award in 2014

'Delightful hosts who make their guests feel like friends', Katrina Le Saux and Peter Cottee run their small guest house in a 'beautiful' Victorian mansion on a secluded hillside overlooking Lake Bala. It is an elegant, homely place: the sitting room has a log fire and an honesty bar; the terrace, ideal for pre-dinner drinks at sunset, has views towards the Arenig mountain; the gardens have 'lots of little corners for relaxation'. Bedrooms are named after the adjacent mountain ranges: Berwyn and Arenig have an antique four-poster bed; Aran has a large bath overlooking the lake. All are well equipped with electric blankets, and tea- and coffee-making facilities. Two nights a week, Peter Cottee, 'an excellent cook', will prepare a three-course dinner by arrangement: his 'unpretentious' dishes might include prawn and avocado cocktail; pan-fried sole fillet, aubergine compote, gratin potatoes. A communal breakfast is served in a room with a grand piano: granola, breads and preserves are home made; honey comes from the hosts' own bees. Many walks directly from the town; the owners provide drying facilities and cycle storage. (LF, and others)

25% DISCOUNT VOUCHERS

Bryniau Golau
Llangower
Bala
LL23 7BT

T: 01678 521782
E: katrinalesaux@hotmail.co.uk
W: www.bryniau-golau.co.uk

BEDROOMS: 3.
OPEN: Mar–Dec (not Christmas).
FACILITIES: sitting room, dining room, free Wi-Fi, ½-acre garden (terrace), unsuitable for disabled.
BACKGROUND MUSIC: none.
LOCATION: 2 miles SE of Bala.
CHILDREN: babes in arms, and over 12.
DOGS: not allowed.
CREDIT CARDS: MasterCard, Visa.
PRICES: [2015] per room B&B £110–£120, D,B&B £137.50–£147.50. Set dinner £27.50. 1-night bookings refused weekends and peak times.

LLWYNDU FARMHOUSE

'A super little hotel', Paula and Peter Thompson's 'tranquil' 16th-century farmhouse stands at the base of the Rhinog Mountains, overlooking Cardigan Bay. 'We received a splendid welcome from Paula and Peter, who gave discreet and laid-back service,' say visitors in 2015. 'The most enchanting experience was the views across the bay where one day we saw a sunset to compare with anywhere; it was magical.' Simply furnished bedrooms retain the quirky aspects of the house: 'Our room in the old part had a bathroom tucked among oak beams, and stone walls.' In a converted granary, four rooms which have direct access to the garden have a high ceiling and exposed timbers – these are 'great for a family'. The Thompsons adhere to the Slow Food Movement; in the candlelit dining room, 'the evening meals were a highlight'. Peter Thompson's 'skilful, locally sourced, home-cooked food' might include Welsh Black beef rib-eye steak, red onion and crab apple marmalade. A supper for children can be arranged. Breakfast is cooked to order, using sausages and smoked bacon from the local butcher. Good beach walks. (Pamela and Christopher Morrison)

Llanaber
Barmouth
LL42 1RR

T: 01341 280144
F: 01341 281236
E: intouch@llwyndu-farmhouse.
co.uk
W: www.llwyndu-farmhouse.co.uk

BEDROOMS: 7. 4 in granary, 1 on ground floor.
OPEN: all year except 25/26 Dec, restaurant closed Sun evening.
FACILITIES: lounge, restaurant, free Wi-Fi, 4-acre garden, unsuitable for disabled.
BACKGROUND MUSIC: eclectic occasionally in restaurant 'but not usually at breakfast'.
LOCATION: 2 miles N of Barmouth.
CHILDREN: all ages welcomed.
DOGS: not allowed.
CREDIT CARDS: MasterCard, Visa.
PRICES: [2015] per person B&B £55–£65, D,B&B £85–£95. À la carte £29.95. 1-night bookings refused peak weekends.

BEAUMARIS Isle of Anglesey

Map 3:A3

YE OLDE BULLS HEAD

'Highly recommended.' There are ancient timbers, antique furniture, historic artefacts and real ales in David Robertson and Keith Rothwell's inn, which has been welcoming travellers to the ferry port since the 15th century. Modern-day guests are welcomed by the 'young, helpful and friendly' staff. Accommodation is in the main house, a converted hayloft and an updated 16th-century building 100 yards away. A 'superb, spacious and comfortable' room in the main building had a king-size bed and a 'lavish' bathroom; a tea tray with fresh milk and home-made shortbread biscuits. 'There is much in the way of creaking and plumbing noises through the night.' In The Townhouse, brightly decorated, air-conditioned rooms are 'modern and well equipped'; a suite with a sofa bed can accommodate a family. 'We like having a choice of restaurants,' said previous guests: informal meals are taken at the 'bright and cheerful' brasserie; in the Loft restaurant, chef Hefin Roberts cooks 'excellent' modern British dishes, perhaps fillet of locally reared beef, braised ox cheek, roast garlic mashed potato, celeriac purée. (Tara M. Varco, and others)

Castle Street
Beaumaris, Isle of Anglesey
LL58 8AP

T: 01248 810329
F: 01248 811294
E: info@bullsheadinn.co.uk
W: www.bullsheadinn.co.uk

BEDROOMS: 26. 2 on ground floor, 1 in courtyard, 13 in The Townhouse adjacent, 1 suitable for disabled.
OPEN: all year, except 25/26 Dec, Loft restaurant closed lunch, Sun/Mon nights.
FACILITIES: lift (in The Townhouse), lounge, bar, brasserie, restaurant, free Wi-Fi, sea 200 yds, only brasserie, bar and The Townhouse suitable for disabled.
BACKGROUND MUSIC: 'chill-out' in brasserie.
LOCATION: central.
CHILDREN: all ages welcomed, no under-7s in restaurant.
DOGS: allowed in some bedrooms, bar.
CREDIT CARDS: Amex, MasterCard, Visa.
PRICES: [2015] per room B&B single from £82.50, double from £105. Set dinner (restaurant) £47.50, à la carte (brasserie) £28.

TY MAWR

🔍 César award in 2011

'Hospitable' hosts Annabel and Stephen Thomas run their small country hotel in this 16th-century farmhouse on the edge of the Brechfa forest. It has a 'peaceful', rustic atmosphere: the public areas have exposed stone walls, fireplaces, and artwork and pottery by local Carmarthenshire artists. The 'manicured' garden, where guests take al fresco afternoon tea in good weather, runs down to the River Marlais. Simply decorated bedrooms have tea- and coffee-making facilities and dressing gowns; two ground-floor rooms are popular with guests who travel with their dog. 'Our immaculate room was like a suite; it had a large bed, a good sitting area, a well-appointed bathroom and all the amenities you might expect.' Pre-dinner drinks and canapés are served in the lounge or on the patio; in the restaurant, residents and locals enjoy the 'informal ambience' over Stephen Thomas's cooking. 'Dinner was divine: we had perfectly prepared lobster and a gorgeous fillet of beef with oxtail.' At breakfast, a buffet holds fresh fruit salad, cereals and local yogurts; hot dishes include home-cured bacon and laver bread oatcakes. (GN, RM-P, and others)

25% DISCOUNT VOUCHERS

Ty Mawr Country Hotel
Brechfa
SA32 7RA

T: 01267 202332
E: info@wales-country-hotel.co.uk
W: www.wales-country-hotel.co.uk

BEDROOMS: 6. 2 on ground floor.
OPEN: all year.
FACILITIES: sitting room, bar, breakfast room, restaurant, free Wi-Fi, 1-acre grounds, unsuitable for disabled.
BACKGROUND MUSIC: classical in restaurant.
LOCATION: village centre.
CHILDREN: not under 12.
DOGS: by arrangement (no charge), not allowed in breakfast room, restaurant.
CREDIT CARDS: Amex, MasterCard, Visa.
PRICES: [2015] per room B&B double £115–£130, D,B&B £160–£175. Set dinner £25–£30 per person, à la carte £30.

CRICKHOWELL Powys

Map 3:D4

GLANGRWYNEY COURT

'Everything is top notch' at this Grade II listed Palladian house. It has been restored and 'beautifully furnished' by the owners, Christina and Warwick Jackson, who run it as an upmarket B&B. An impressive cantilevered staircase leads to the bedrooms in the main house, which vary in size and aspect and are priced accordingly. Furnished with antiques, interesting artwork and pretty porcelain, they are well equipped, with tea- and coffee-making facilities, a TV and DVD-player, bathrobes. One room has its own bathroom across the landing. A huge, curved window over the stairs overlooks the gardens to the Black Mountains. There is a ground-floor room in the garden courtyard. The public rooms are decorated in keeping with the age of the house. Guests are encouraged to relax with a book, perhaps in front of a log-burning stove; there is a well-stocked honesty bar (and crystal glasses) in the library, where floor-to-ceiling windows face the house's extensive parkland and Blorenge mountain. At breakfast, the jams and marmalade are home made; bacon, sausages, eggs and apple juice come from nearby farms.

Glangrwyney
Crickhowell
NP8 1ES

T: 01873 811288
F: 01873 810317
E: info@glancourt.co.uk
W: www.glancourt.co.uk

BEDROOMS: 9. 1, on ground floor, in courtyard, 4 cottages in grounds.
OPEN: all year except 25/26 Dec.
FACILITIES: sitting room, library/honesty bar, dining room, free Wi-Fi, civil wedding licence, 4-acre garden (croquet, boules, tennis) in 33-acre parkland, unsuitable for disabled.
BACKGROUND MUSIC: on request.
LOCATION: 2 miles SE of Crickhowell, off A40.
CHILDREN: all ages welcomed.
DOGS: allowed in courtyard room only, not in main house.
CREDIT CARDS: MasterCard, Visa.
PRICES: [2015] per room B&B £115–£145. 1-night bookings sometimes refused weekends.

GLIFFAES

♀César award in 2009

'There is nowhere else more calming' than the 'magnificent' grounds of Susie and James Suter's sporting hotel by the River Usk, a long-time visitor says. The 19th-century Italianate building stands in 'beautiful' gardens that 'add to the magic of its setting on the bluff' over the river. It is popular with fisherfolk who enjoy a private stretch of the trout- and salmon-laden waters. Overlooking the garden or the river, 'immaculate' bedrooms are individually decorated, with charming touches: a superior room has a wisteria-covered balcony; a smaller standard room has its original Delft-tiled fireplace and plenty of books. Four garden-view rooms are in a cottage across the lawn from the main house. In the restaurant, Karl Cheetham's 'excellent' dinners use local produce, perhaps British rose veal tagliata, gnocchi, asparagus, pancetta. Special diets are catered for: 'Every member of staff was aware of our needs and the chef ensured that all the menu options were accessible to us.' At breakfast, a buffet table has freshly squeezed juice, home-made muesli and freshly baked pastries; cooked items include Welsh bacon and sausages. (DW)

25% DISCOUNT VOUCHERS

Gliffaes Road
Crickhowell
NP8 1RH

T: 01874 730371
F: 01874 730463
E: calls@gliffaes.com
W: www.gliffaeshotel.com

BEDROOMS: 23. 4 in annexe, 1 on ground floor suitable for disabled.
OPEN: all year except 28 Dec–25 Jan.
FACILITIES: ramp, 2 sitting rooms, conservatory, bar, dining room, free Wi-Fi, civil wedding licence, 33-acre garden (tennis, croquet, fishing).
BACKGROUND MUSIC: jazz/classical in bar in evening.
LOCATION: 3 miles W of Crickhowell.
CHILDREN: all ages welcomed.
DOGS: not allowed indoors (kennels available).
CREDIT CARDS: Amex, MasterCard, Visa.
PRICES: [2015] per room B&B £118–£275, D,B&B from £190. À la carte £42. 1-night bookings refused high season weekends.

THE OLD VICARAGE

Guests are greeted with afternoon tea and cake at this small guest house, in a red brick Victorian vicarage in the hills of the Welsh Marches. Helen and Tim Withers are the 'charming, helpful' owners, who run it along green lines: local and organic food and drink producers are prioritised; electric vehicle charging is available; bicycles can be hired; a discount is given to guests arriving by public transport. Named after rivers, 'pleasant, comfortable' bedrooms 'lack nothing': each is well equipped with bathrobes, organic toiletries, bottles of mineral water, locally handmade woollen blankets. Pre-dinner drinks are taken in the lounge. In the dining room, Tim Withers serves an Aga-cooked dinner six nights a week, using vegetables and herbs from the kitchen garden. 'It is simple, no-nonsense cooking which does not bow to fashion,' says one visitor (a fellow Guide hotelier). Typical dishes on the short menu: Hafod Cheddar cheese soufflé; pot-roast Welsh lamb, orange and laver bread sauce, dauphinoise potatoes. Breakfast has local bacon, traditionally cured kippers, and eggs from the house's free-range hens. (KM, and others)

25% DISCOUNT VOUCHERS

Dolfor
SY16 4BN

T: 01686 629051
F: 01686 207629
E: tim@theoldvicaragedolfor.co.uk
W: www.theoldvicaragedolfor.co.uk

BEDROOMS: 4.
OPEN: all year except Christmas/ New Year, dining room closed Sun.
FACILITIES: drawing room, dining room, free Wi-Fi, 2-acre garden, unsuitable for disabled.
BACKGROUND MUSIC: none.
LOCATION: 3 miles S of Newtown.
CHILDREN: all ages welcomed.
DOGS: not allowed.
CREDIT CARDS: Amex, MasterCard, Visa.
PRICES: [2015] per person B&B £37.50–£60, D,B&B £67.50–£90. Set dinner £25–£30. 1-night bookings sometimes refused.

Y GOEDEN EIRIN

ǪCésar award in 2008

Named in homage to a book of Welsh stories,
The Plum Tree (as it translates) is a converted
cowshed in pastureland facing the three peaks
of Yr Eifl in Snowdonia. We were sorry to learn
of the death of the joint owner, John Rowlands,
in February 2015. His widow, Eluned, tells us
she has decided to continue to accept guests
on a B&B basis. Welsh is the first language of
a house devoted to Welsh culture and arts.
Eluned Rowlands is a serious art collector:
many original works are displayed. Two of the
bedrooms, Cwt Môr and Cwt Mynydd (sea and
mountain rooms), are in renovated outbuildings;
each has underfloor heating, shelves stacked
with books in English and Welsh; they are
equipped with a carafe of sherry, fresh fruit and
Welsh cakes. A spacious room in the main house
has a small dressing room; a bathroom with a
bath and a separate shower. Eluned Rowlands
bakes her own bread for breakfast, which has
freshly squeezed orange juice, local produce for
the cooked dishes, Fairtrade tea and coffee (a
green philosophy is followed throughout).

Dolydd
LL54 7EF

T: 01286 830942
E: eluned.rowlands@tiscali.co.uk
W: www.ygoedeneirin.co.uk

BEDROOMS: 3. 2 in annexe.
OPEN: all year except Christmas/
New Year.
FACILITIES: dining room, lounge by
arrangement, free Wi-Fi, 20-acre
pastureland, unsuitable for disabled.
BACKGROUND MUSIC: none.
LOCATION: 3 miles S of Caernarfon.
CHILDREN: not under 12.
DOGS: not allowed.
CREDIT CARDS: none, cash or cheque
payment requested on arrival.
PRICES: per room B&B single £65,
double £90–£100.1-night bookings
sometimes refused weekends.

EGLWYSFACH Powys

Map 3:C3

YNYSHIR HALL

In a 'beautiful setting in lovely countryside', this 'pretty' manor house was once Queen Victoria's country retreat. Today, it is a luxury hotel/restaurant (Relais & Châteaux), owned by Joan and Rob Reen, and John and Jenny Talbot, and run with 'very welcoming' staff. Rob Reen is an artist; his striking oil paintings are hung throughout the hotel. Decorated in bold colours, the 'comfortable' bedrooms have an 'opulent' feel. Many have views of the gardens and the mountains beyond; two garden suites have a patio or balcony, and a separate living room with a fireplace and log burner. Guests help themselves from a bottle of sherry in the room; tea and coffee are brought on request (at a charge). Chef Gareth Ward received a Michelin star in 2015 for his 'superlative' modern British cooking – 'some of the best we've ever had,' said visitors this year. In the formal restaurant, which has picture windows with views of the Cambrian Mountains, his tasting menus are 'full of wonderful bursts of flavour', perhaps mackerel, black sesame, fermented cabbage. 'We very much enjoyed ourselves.' (Frances Thomas)

Eglwysfach
SY20 8TA

T: 01654 781209
F: 01654 781366
E: info@ynyshirhall.co.uk
W: www.ynyshirhall.co.uk

BEDROOMS: 10. 2 garden suites, 1 in studio annexe, 3 on ground floor, 1 suitable for disabled.
OPEN: all year.
FACILITIES: ramp, drawing room, bar lounge, breakfast room, restaurant, free Wi-Fi, civil wedding licence, 14-acre gardens in 1,000-acre bird reserve.
BACKGROUND MUSIC: in bar and restaurant.
LOCATION: 6 miles SW of Machynlleth.
CHILDREN: not under 9 in evening in restaurant.
DOGS: allowed in some bedrooms by arrangement, not in public rooms.
CREDIT CARDS: Amex, MasterCard, Visa.
PRICES: [2015] per room B&B £215–£950, D,B&B £315–£1,050. Set dinner £55–£100. 1-night bookings refused on busy weekends.

AEL Y BRYN

Guests are 'welcomed as friends' at this rural B&B, in a 'magnificent' setting near the Pembrokeshire coast. 'The owners, Robert Smith and Arwel Hughes, are what makes this such a special place,' wrote one visitor. Said another: 'They are congenial, adaptable, generous, hospitable.' This former prisoner-of-war camp has been restored 'with flair and imagination', according to Guide inspectors. There are 'interesting' objects (good paintings, an 'amazing' collection of antique glass) in the public rooms. 'Large windows bring in the wonderful surrounding countryside.' Bedrooms vary in size and aspect; all are 'superbly equipped' with books, guides, biscuits, chocolates. In the evening, a communal dinner is served, by arrangement, under 'striking' chandeliers in the baronial-style dining room (guests bring their own wine). 'The food is wonderful: fresh, innovative, served with a genuine authenticity. Arwel produces two delicious desserts at the end of the meal.' Breakfast is laid out in 'spectacular' fashion: home-made jams, croissants in a basket, a 'magnificent' fruit salad, 'good' coffee; 'lots of choice' of cooked dishes. (Rosemary Albone)

Ael y Bryn
Eglwyswrw
SA41 3UL

T: 01239 891411
E: stay@aelybrynpembrokeshire.co.uk
W: www.aelybrynpembrokeshire.co.uk

BEDROOMS: 4. All on ground floor.
OPEN: all year except Christmas/New Year.
FACILITIES: library, music room, dining room, conservatory (telescope), free Wi-Fi, courtyard, 2½-acre garden (wildlife pond, stream, bowls court).
BACKGROUND MUSIC: 'easy listening'/classical in dining room and music room.
LOCATION: ½ mile N of village.
CHILDREN: not under 14.
DOGS: not allowed.
CREDIT CARDS: Amex, MasterCard, Visa.
PRICES: [2015] per room B&B £100–£130. Set dinner £24–£28.

THE FELIN FACH GRIFFIN

♥ César award in 2013

Entering through the front door of this roadside inn, visitors find themselves in an open sitting area with leather sofas, books, magazines and a log fire. The inn, which has been owned and run in a relaxed manner for 15 years by brothers Charles and Edmund Inkin, is 'ridiculously welcoming'; families and dogs are greeted with equal warmth. Handsome bedrooms have fresh flowers, home-made biscuits, Welsh blankets, books and a Roberts radio; there is no TV ('as we think it conspires against a relaxing, enjoyable stay', the owners say). Head gardener Joe Hand provides vegetables and fruit from the organic kitchen garden for chef Max Wilson's short seasonal menus; typical dishes might include Helford crab, pickled apple, coriander; roast Bwlch venison, honey-glazed parsnip, red cabbage. Breakfast in the library has local apple juice and home-made soda bread. The inn sits between the Brecon Beacons and the Black Mountains; long-serving manager Julie Bell has a collection of walks to share. The brothers run The Gurnard's Head, Zennor, and The Old Coastguard, Mousehole, in similar style (see entries).

25% DISCOUNT VOUCHERS

Felin Fach
LD3 0UB

T: 01874 620111
E: enquiries@felinfachgriffin.co.uk
W: www.felinfachgriffin.co.uk

BEDROOMS: 7.
OPEN: all year except 24/25 Dec, 4 days in Jan.
FACILITIES: bar area, dining room, breakfast room, private dining room, no Wi-Fi, limited mobile phone signals, 3-acre garden (stream, kitchen garden), only bar/dining room suitable for disabled.
BACKGROUND MUSIC: Radio 4 at breakfast, 'carefully considered music at other times'.
LOCATION: 4 miles NE of Brecon, in village on A470.
CHILDREN: all ages welcomed (games, books, children's menu).
DOGS: allowed in bedrooms, at some tables in bar.
CREDIT CARDS: MasterCard, Visa.
PRICES: [2015] per room B&B £125–£165, D,B&B £177.50–£217.50. Set menus £28.50, à la carte £35. 1-night bookings occasionally refused.

THE MANOR TOWN HOUSE

'Friendly owners' Helen and Chris Sheldon
run their 'delightful' B&B in this Grade II
listed Georgian house (painted cornflower blue)
near the town square of this lively old fishing
town. The lounges have deep sofas, books,
magazines and fresh flowers; in good weather,
cream teas with home-baked cakes are taken on
the terrace overlooking Lower Town harbour
and Fishguard Bay. Many of the individually
decorated bedrooms have an original fireplace
and antique furniture; some have views of the
sea. All have tea- and coffee-making facilities,
a TV and DVD-player; dressing gowns are
provided. Children are welcomed: three
bedrooms are large enough to accommodate
a family (travel cots and fold-out beds are
available on request). Breakfast, which may
be taken in the room, has waffles, fresh fruit,
Greek yogurt; bacon and sausages from the
local butcher. Special diets are catered for, by
arrangement. In the evening, the hosts are ready
with recommendations of eating places nearby.
There are coastal and hill walks to be had
(packed lunches available); the Pembrokeshire
Coastal Path can be joined in the wooded valley
below the garden.

11 Main Street
Fishguard
SA65 9HG

T: 01348 873260
E: enquiries@manortownhouse.
com
W: www.manortownhouse.com

BEDROOMS: 6.
OPEN: all year except 24–27 Dec.
FACILITIES: 2 lounges, breakfast
room, free Wi-Fi, small walled
garden, unsuitable for disabled.
BACKGROUND MUSIC: classical at
breakfast.
LOCATION: town centre.
CHILDREN: all ages welcomed.
DOGS: not allowed.
CREDIT CARDS: MasterCard, Visa.
PRICES: [2015] per room B&B £90–
£110. 1-night bookings sometimes
refused peak weekends.

GLYNARTHEN Ceredigion

Map 3:D2

PENBONTBREN

♛César award in 2012

There is a 'very happy atmosphere' at this luxury B&B, a conversion of a 19th-century livestock farm surrounded by 'beautiful' countryside. 'Great hosts' Richard Morgan-Price and Huw Thomas are the 'extremely friendly' owners. Free-range hens roam the grounds. 'Richard and Hugh have obviously spent a lot of time and effort in the gardens.' Accommodation, complete with home-made Welsh cakes, is in 'spacious' suites in converted farm buildings (a former stable, a granary, an old mill and a threshing barn); a new, smaller, gable-roofed garden room with a terrace and a covered pergola has been added this year. 'Our room was spotless and so well equipped. I cannot think of anything they had not supplied that we might have needed.' Breakfast, served on 'crisp white linen' in another converted barn, is 'a delight': a buffet has freshly squeezed juice, organic yogurt, cereals and fresh fruit; cooked options include local Rhydlewis smoked salmon and a traditional Welsh breakfast with laver bread. The hosts are ready with recommendations for dinner nearby; a farm shop close by sells mainly Welsh produce for a simple supper. (AT)

25% DISCOUNT VOUCHERS

Glynarthen
Llandysul
SA44 6PE

T: 01239 810248
F: 01239 811129
E: contact@penbontbren.com
W: www.penbontbren.com

BEDROOMS: 6. 5 in annexe, 1 in garden, 3 on ground floor, 1 suitable for disabled.
OPEN: all year except 3 days at Christmas.
FACILITIES: breakfast room, free Wi-Fi, 32-acre grounds.
BACKGROUND MUSIC: none.
LOCATION: 5 miles N of Newcastle Emlyn.
CHILDREN: all ages welcomed.
DOGS: allowed in bedrooms, not in breakfast room.
CREDIT CARDS: MasterCard, Visa.
PRICES: per room B&B £120. 1-night bookings sometimes refused weekends.

CASTLE COTTAGE

On a steep road behind Harlech Castle, Glyn and Jacqueline Roberts have run their contemporary restaurant-with-rooms since 1989. It has 'an amazing setting with wonderful views'. Decorated in an understated style with 'high-quality fittings', bedrooms are in the main building and an adjoining annexe (a stone-built former 16th-century coaching inn); some have views of the sea and the Rhinog Mountains. They are well equipped with tea- and coffee-making facilities, slippers, a desk fan, an iPod docking station, bottles of water and a bowl of fresh fruit; individual heating is guest controlled. Glyn Roberts is the chef in the restaurant, where his 'delicious' modern Welsh dishes use much locally caught seafood and locally reared meat, perhaps Rhydlewis smoked salmon, chilled melon, mango; roasted sucking pig, sage potatoes, Calvados jus. Canapés are taken in the bar before dinner. An early dinner can be prepared for young children, by arrangement. Tables are laid with home-made jam and marmalade at breakfast; a buffet has freshly squeezed juices, home-made muesli, local yogurt with Welsh honey; a good choice of hot dishes is cooked to order. (IM)

Y Llech
Harlech
LL46 2YL

T: 01766 780479
E: glyn@castlecottageharlech.co.uk
W: www.castlecottageharlech.co.uk

BEDROOMS: 7. 4 in annexe, 2 on ground floor.
OPEN: all year except Christmas and 3 weeks Nov, restaurant closed Sun–Wed in winter months.
FACILITIES: bar, lounge, restaurant, free Wi-Fi, unsuitable for disabled.
BACKGROUND MUSIC: radio at breakfast, 'discreet' CDs at dinner in bar/restaurant.
LOCATION: town centre.
CHILDREN: all ages welcomed.
DOGS: not allowed.
CREDIT CARDS: MasterCard, Visa.
PRICES: [2015] per room B&B £130–£175. Set menus £35–£45.

MILEBROOK HOUSE

♦ César award in 2015

'Pleasant' owners Beryl and Rodney Marsden
run their 'delightful' small hotel in this
18th-century stone dower house in 'lovely'
countryside. Three generations of the family
are involved in its running: daughter Joanne
manages front-of-house with 'friendly, caring'
staff; granddaughter, Katie, is the chef. 'The
family were clearly in evidence and we were
courteously received by them.' Regular guests
like the 'settled and reassuring feel'; others
find it 'old-fashioned': 'It is a nice place to
stay, if a bit eccentric,' said one visitor this
year. 'Clean', 'comfortable' bedrooms are
simply and traditionally furnished. 'Our large,
ground-floor room was very quiet, with lovely
views over the Teme valley; the good-sized
bathroom had plenty of storage space.' Katie
Marsden's 'homely' dishes may be taken in the
bar, the restaurant or, in the summer, on the
terrace; typical dishes: 'excellent' pigeon breast
salad; 'tender' Welsh Black rib-eye steak. 'We
entertained friends to dinner and all of us
were more than satisfied.' The house stands in
extensive grounds that lead to the River Teme.
(John Bell, Kay and Peter Rogers)

25% DISCOUNT VOUCHERS

Knighton
LD7 1LT

T: 01547 528632
E: hotel@milebrookhouse.co.uk
W: www.milebrookhouse.co.uk

BEDROOMS: 10. 2 on ground floor.
OPEN: all year, restaurant closed
Mon lunch, Sun night and Mon
Nov–Feb.
FACILITIES: lounge, bar, 2 dining
rooms, free Wi-Fi, 3½-acre grounds
on river (terraces, pond, croquet,
fishing).
BACKGROUND MUSIC: in bar and
restaurant in evening.
LOCATION: on A4113, 2 miles E of
Knighton.
CHILDREN: not under 8.
DOGS: not allowed.
CREDIT CARDS: MasterCard, Visa.
PRICES: [2015] per room B&B £144,
D,B&B £199. À la carte £32.

THE FALCONDALE

Up a drive bordered by bluebells in season, Chris and Lisa Hutton's 'striking' Italianate hotel is 'run with good traditional taste and without pretension'. Guests praise the 'very pleasant' staff and 'excellent' service: 'Lisa makes everyone feel so welcome.' The public areas are 'roomy and well decorated': the lounge has a baby grand piano, 'deep seats and stacks of glossy magazines'; 'there are interesting pictures everywhere'. Bedrooms vary in size and outlook; each 'has its own character, with individually chosen ornaments, wallpaper, curtain and bedspread'. Many overlook the 'handsome and well-maintained' gardens; the best have a Juliet balcony with views down the Teifi valley. In the 'elegant' dining room ('pristine napery, sparkling glasses'), chef Dafydd Davies's cooking, including a seven-course tasting menu, is praised. 'Each course was delicious, and just the right size so that you had room for the next one.' Breakfast has a 'comprehensive' buffet, with pastries, 'exquisite' yogurt; cooked ingredients are locally sourced. Dogs are welcomed: 'The blankets, bowls and treats for our dogs were a wonderful gesture.' (Maureen Stander, and others)

Falcondale Drive
Lampeter
SA48 7RX

T: 01570 422910
E: info@thefalcondale.co.uk
W: www.thefalcondale.co.uk

BEDROOMS: 18.
OPEN: all year.
FACILITIES: lift, bar, lounge, conservatory, restaurant, free Wi-Fi, civil wedding licence, terrace, 14-acre grounds (lawns, woodland), unsuitable for disabled.
BACKGROUND MUSIC: classical in public and eating areas.
LOCATION: 1 mile N of Lampeter.
CHILDREN: all ages welcomed.
DOGS: welcomed (£10 a night).
CREDIT CARDS: MasterCard, Visa.
PRICES: [2015] per room B&B £100–£190, D,B&B £170–£260. Set dinner/à la carte £40, tasting menu £67.50.

LLANARTHNE Carmarthenshire

Map 3:D2

LLWYN HELYG

'Hands-on' owners Caron and Fiona Jones
'convey a real pleasure' in welcoming guests
to their 'superb' B&B in 'peaceful' countryside
near the National Botanic Garden of Wales. 'We
had a memorable stay,' Guide inspectors said.
The lavishly finished, newly built stone house
('really more of a mansion in size') has 'lots of
stylishly furnished sitting areas around large
hallways and in intimate rooms'. The spacious,
raftered Listening Room has 'squashy sofas' and
'the best sound system we have heard outside
the Albert Hall'. An 'impressive' oak staircase
leads to the bedrooms. 'Our room had a fine
bed with four barley twist posts, plump pillows
and a black Italianate bedcover; large Etruscan
table lamps; black granite occasional tables. The
luxurious bathroom had "his and hers" basins,
a whirlpool bath and a separate walk-in shower
– all very elegant.' No evening meals are served,
but the hosts are happy to recommend nearby
restaurants. 'Caron booked us in at the excellent
Y Polyn five minutes away, and ferried us to
and fro.' A 'fresh, good-quality' breakfast is
'elegantly presented' on fine china.

Llanarthne
SA32 8HJ

T: 01558 668778
E: enquiries@
   llwynhelygcountryhouse.co.uk
W: www.llwynhelygcountryhouse.
   co.uk

BEDROOMS: 3.
OPEN: all year, except Christmas/
New Year.
FACILITIES: 5 lounges, listening
room, breakfast room, free Wi-Fi,
3-acre garden, unsuitable for
disabled.
BACKGROUND MUSIC: none.
LOCATION: 8 miles E of Carmarthen,
8 miles W of Llandeilo.
CHILDREN: not under 16.
DOGS: not allowed.
CREDIT CARDS: MasterCard, Visa.
PRICES: [2015] per room B&B
£125–£150.

TYDDYN LLAN

♥ César award in 2006

Bryan and Susan Webb have run their 'truly lovely' restaurant-with-rooms for 14 years, in this former shooting lodge. It stands in well-maintained lawns and gardens with views of the Berwyn Mountains. It remains 'up to its usual, very high standard', says a returning guest this year. 'Susan Webb is excellent running the front-of-house – her vibrant personality lifts the whole place'; staff are 'efficient and cheerful'. In the restaurant, Bryan Webb has a Michelin star for his 'imaginative' cooking. 'The food is as good as ever. And quality is not at the expense of quantity: even the canapés are substantial.' Typical dishes: Wye valley asparagus, fresh morels, crisp duck egg; local pork (fillet, cheek, belly, black pudding), breaded trotter, shallot and thyme purée. Everything about the house, 'the style, the comfort, the housekeeping, shows meticulous attention to detail'. Country-style bedrooms have dressing gowns, slippers, tea- and coffee-making facilities; a garden suite has patio doors opening on to a secluded garden area. The Webbs are pleased to advise on walks from the door – 'the perfect prelude to dinner'. (Peter Anderson, and others)

25% DISCOUNT VOUCHERS

Llandrillo
LL21 0ST

T: 01490 440264
F: 01490 440414
E: info@tyddynllan.co.uk
W: www.tyddynllan.co.uk

BEDROOMS: 13. 3 with separate entrance, 1, on ground floor, suitable for disabled.
OPEN: all year except 3 weeks Jan, restaurant closed Mon and Tues, Jan–Mar.
FACILITIES: ramp, 2 lounges, bar, 2 dining rooms, free Wi-Fi, civil wedding licence, 3-acre garden.
BACKGROUND MUSIC: none.
LOCATION: 5 miles SW of Corwen.
CHILDREN: all ages welcomed.
DOGS: allowed in some bedrooms (£10 per night), not in public rooms.
CREDIT CARDS: all major cards.
PRICES: per room B&B £180–£320, D,B&B £280–£420. Set dinner £40–£57, tasting menus £70–£85.

BODYSGALLEN HALL AND SPA

♀ César award in 1988

A 'beautiful house in pretty gardens', this Grade I listed 17th-century mansion has a 'stunning outlook' over Snowdonia. It is managed by Matthew Johnson for Historic House Hotels, who run it for the National Trust. 'The staff are extremely friendly,' says a visitor in 2015. 'We never had to wait to be served; room service was almost instantaneous.' There is a 'warren' of public rooms which have oak panelling, portraits; 'pretty fresh flowers'. Each of the sitting rooms has an open fire. In the dining room ('simple, again an open fire'), 'the food was superb'. John Williams has returned as head chef. The separate bistro is closed but is due to reopen in 2016. 'Our smallish bedroom had a chintzy decor; excellent shower pressure in the spacious bathroom, which was up a few steps.' A 'lovely, large room with a four-poster bed' had 'a glorious view over the grounds'. Cottage suites cater for families (children must be over six). 'Spa facilities are excellent: an unusually large swimming pool, and a full range of treatments': pre-booking may be required. (Tanya Howes, Stephen and Pauline Glover)

The Royal Welsh Way
Llandudno
LL30 1RS

T: 01492 584466
F: 01492 582519
E: info@bodysgallen.com
W: www.bodysgallen.com

BEDROOMS: 31. 16 in cottages, 1 suitable for disabled.
OPEN: all year, restaurant closed Mon lunch.
FACILITIES: hall, drawing room, library, bar, dining room, free Wi-Fi, civil wedding licence, 220-acre park (gardens, tennis, croquet), spa (16-metre swimming pool).
BACKGROUND MUSIC: none.
LOCATION: 2 miles S of Llandudno.
CHILDREN: no children under 6 in hotel, under 8 in spa (set swimming times).
DOGS: allowed by arrangement in some cottages, not in bedrooms.
CREDIT CARDS: Amex, MasterCard, Visa.
PRICES: per room B&B single £159–£195, double £179–£265. Dinner £49. 1-night bookings sometimes refused.

SEE ALSO SHORTLIST

LLANDUDNO Conwy

Map 3:A3

OSBORNE HOUSE

Little sister of the Empire Hotel, and sharing its view of promenade, palm trees and beach, this handsome, bay-fronted stone house is managed by Elyse Waddy for the Maddocks family. They have made it over in a style to reflect its 1850s origins. Nothing is stinted in the lavish decor: marble fireplaces, fluted pillars, candelabras, gilded mirrors, porcelain, paintings, antiques and drapes. The accommodation is in six 'atmospheric' suites, which 'take a lot of beating'. 'Ours was beautifully furnished,' said one visitor. Each suite has rugs on wooden floors, 'table lamps everywhere'; a sitting room with a 'lovely, squishy sofa' in front of a large, square coffee table. On the upper floors there are views of the bay and cliff. A continental breakfast can be taken in the suite (or guests can walk the 200 yards to the Empire if they want cooked dishes – or to use the spa). In the café, chef Michael Waddy cooks such bistro-style dishes as fishcakes, mussels, steaks and lamb shank, available all day. The 'good-value' lunch was recommended this year. (BW, and others)

17 North Parade
Llandudno
LL30 2LP

T: 01492 860330
F: 01492 860791
E: sales@osbornehouse.com
W: www.osbornehouse.co.uk

BEDROOMS: 6.
OPEN: all year, except 10 days Christmas, open New Year.
FACILITIES: sitting room, bar, café/bistro, free Wi-Fi, unsuitable for disabled.
BACKGROUND MUSIC: none.
LOCATION: on promenade.
CHILDREN: not under 14.
DOGS: not allowed.
CREDIT CARDS: all major cards.
PRICES: per room B&B £125–£175, D,B&B from £195. Set menu £22.95. 1-night bookings sometimes refused.

SEE ALSO SHORTLIST

THE LAKE

'A pleasant place with comfortable public rooms and very obliging staff.' Praise in 2015 for Jean-Pierre Mifsud's traditional country house hotel which stands in extensive grounds by a lake on the River Irfon. The owner, 'very much in residence' (another comment this year), often mingles with guests in the evening in the three large lounges. Luke Marriott is the manager. In the 'lovely' dining room, the cooking of the chef, Darren Tattersall, is 'very good'. His four-course menu of modern dishes might include sweetcorn bavarois, organic salsa, crisp sourdough; halibut, clam and shrimp chowder. The spacious bedrooms in the main house have traditional furnishings. More contemporary rooms are in a lodge between the house and the Kingfisher spa. 'Our well-appointed room in the annexe was a decent size; the bathroom was also large. It was quiet and dark at night. A plus was that they provided blankets rather than a duvet.' Various treatments are available in the spa. Children are welcomed: they have restricted access to the spa and the restaurant at night. Breakfast is 'good'. (Antony Griew, and others)

25% DISCOUNT VOUCHERS

Llangammarch Wells
LD4 4BS

T: 01591 620202
F: 01591 620457
E: info@lakecountryhouse.co.uk
W: www.lakecountryhouse.co.uk

BEDROOMS: 30. 12 suites in adjacent lodge, 7 on ground floor, 1 suitable for disabled.
OPEN: all year.
FACILITIES: ramps, 3 lounges, orangery, restaurant, free Wi-Fi, spa (15-metre swimming pool), civil wedding licence, 50-acre grounds (tennis).
BACKGROUND MUSIC: none.
LOCATION: 8 miles SW of Builth Wells.
CHILDREN: all ages welcomed.
DOGS: allowed (£10 charge).
CREDIT CARDS: Amex, MasterCard, Visa.
PRICES: per room B&B £145–£260, D,B&B (min. 2 nights) from £205. Set dinner £45.

LLANWRTYD WELLS Powys

CARLTON RIVERSIDE

♀César award in 1998

'Highly recommended' in 2015, this restaurant-with rooms stands by an old stone bridge over the River Irfon. It is run by 'warm, welcoming' hosts Mary Ann and Alan Gilchrist in one of the oldest buildings in this small spa town. The lounge has squishy sofas, board games and books; in the small restaurant overlooking the river, Mary Ann Gilchrist and Luke Roberts's cooking is much admired. The chefs use local produce (Welsh meats, fish and shellfish from Pwllheli) in their modern menus; typical dishes might include pea mousse, Carmarthen ham, pea and shallot salad; Welsh ale-braised feather blade of beef, punchnep, buttered cabbage. Alan Gilchrist, a wine enthusiast, has assembled an extensive wine list with more than 20 half bottles. On the lower ground floor, the Riverside bar (open from Thursday to Sunday evenings) has sofas and home-made pizzas. Simply furnished bedrooms are equipped with a clock radio, TV and a tea tray; they vary considerably in size and aspect. Road noise 'might be a problem'. The 'spacious' Oriental room has a seating area with a coffee table; compact Irfon has a view of the river. (AD and J Lloyd)

25% DISCOUNT VOUCHERS

Irfon Crescent
Llanwrtyd Wells
LD5 4SP

T: 01591 610248
E: carltonriverside@hotmail.co.uk
W: www.carltonriverside.com

BEDROOMS: 4.
OPEN: all year except 22–31 Dec, restaurant closed Sun/Mon.
FACILITIES: lounge, 2 bars, restaurant, free Wi-Fi, unsuitable for disabled.
BACKGROUND MUSIC: classical piano in lounge in evening.
LOCATION: town centre.
CHILDREN: all ages welcomed.
DOGS: not allowed in public rooms except public bar which opens weekends only.
CREDIT CARDS: MasterCard, Visa.
PRICES: [2015] per room B&B £70–£100, D,B&B £125–£150. À la carte £35. 1-night bookings sometimes refused.

SEE ALSO SHORTLIST

LLANGOED HALL

'Spot on as usual.' Praise from a returning guest to this 'splendid' country house hotel on the banks of the River Wye. Former owner Sir Bernard Ashley's collection of mainly 20th-century art is displayed throughout the Jacobean mansion; there are 'many lovely public rooms'. 'Service is impeccable, not the least obsequious,' said Guide inspectors in 2015. 'Everyone addressed us by name.' Individually decorated with antiques and original art, bedrooms have views of the Wye valley; also fresh fruit, a decanter of sherry, bathrobes and slippers. 'We had a large bedroom with views in two directions; excellently furnished, it had a four-poster bed with proper blankets.' 'The food is clearly a feature' in the formal dining room, where chef Nick Brodie showcases local ingredients in his modern menus. 'We had the nine-course tasting menu and copious amounts of wine – all jolly pleasant.' Another comment: 'It was elegantly presented and served, but pricey.' 'Never any piped music, so peace prevails.' Served at the table, breakfast has home-made granola and 'delicious' scrambled duck eggs. (Richard Morgan-Price, Zara Elliott, and others)

Llangoed Hall
Llyswen
LD3 0YP

T: 01874 754525
F: 01874 754545
E: enquiries@llangoedhall.com
W: www.llangoedhall.co.uk

BEDROOMS: 23.
OPEN: all year.
FACILITIES: morning room, drawing room, bar/lounge, restaurant, billiard room, function rooms, free Wi-Fi, civil wedding licence, 17-acre gardens and parklands, unsuitable for disabled.
BACKGROUND MUSIC: none.
LOCATION: 1 mile N of Llyswen.
CHILDREN: all ages welcomed, over-5s only in restaurant.
DOGS: allowed in grounds, not in restaurant or bedrooms (heated kennels).
CREDIT CARDS: MasterCard, Visa.
PRICES: [2015] per room B&B £175–£400, D,B&B from £275. À la carte £70.

PEN-Y-GWRYD HOTEL

🏅César award in 1995

In the lee of Snowdonia, this 'eccentric and old-fashioned' hotel found fame as the training base for the Everest expedition in 1953. Little has changed in the intervening years: it is owned by the same family, and is run today by brothers Nick and Rupert Pullee. It remains in spirit a simple 'hostel-type' place for mountaineers and walkers. There are no locks on the bedroom doors; only five rooms have an en suite bathroom: these are popular with those who find that 'the attractions of trekking down a corridor to a bathroom have faded somewhat' (a comment from a guest this year who first stayed in 1975). 'P-y-G' is not for those who crave instant communication: there is no television or radio in the simple bedrooms; Wi-Fi is available only in the games room. There is now a choice between three or five courses at dinner, served at separate tables promptly at 7.30 pm (don't miss the gong). 'Food fit for explorers, tasty and plentiful' is promised. Local draught beer is available in the bar, which remains a shrine to the Everest expedition.

Nant Gwynant
LL55 4NT

T: 01286 870211
E: escape@pyg.co.uk
W: www.pyg.co.uk

BEDROOMS: 16. 1 on ground floor, garden suite in annexe.
OPEN: mid-Mar–mid-Nov, New Year, occasional winter.
FACILITIES: lounge, bar, games room, dining room, Wi-Fi in games room, chapel, 1-acre grounds (natural unheated 60-metre swimming pool, sauna), unsuitable for disabled.
BACKGROUND MUSIC: none.
LOCATION: between Beddgelert and Capel Curig.
CHILDREN: all ages welcomed.
DOGS: allowed (£2 charge), not in some public rooms.
CREDIT CARDS: Amex, MasterCard, Visa.
PRICES: [2015] per person B&B £43–£55. Set dinner £25–£30. 1-night bookings often refused weekends.

NARBERTH Pembrokeshire

Map 3:D2

♕ THE GROVE

César award: Welsh hotel of the year

Approached by a tree-lined drive, with 'spectacular' views of the Preseli hills, this 'very striking', early 18th-century mansion in landscaped gardens has been restored by Neil Kedward and Zoë Agar, who run it as a small hotel. 'The friendly staff have created a relaxing atmosphere,' say Guide inspectors in 2015. A reader praised the 'warm, genuine service in an outstanding setting'. Another comment: 'It never disappoints.' The owners have 'a happy knack of marrying the used, cherished and previously loved furniture with the new'; Arts and Crafts features stand alongside contemporary paintings. 'We had a warm welcome; our large room had dark green patterned wallpaper, heavy purple drapes; the furniture was mainly Victorian; two easy chairs by the bay window; ample storage; lighting was inadequate.' Peter Whaley has been promoted to head chef: he cooks dishes with produce from the kitchen garden, perhaps lemon sole, garden peas, crispy tartar sauce, lemon oil. At breakfast there are Manx kippers, freshly squeezed orange juice, 'excellent' Danish pastries. (David Birnie, Mary Coles, and others)

Molleston
Narberth
SA67 8BX

T: 01834 860915
F: 01834 861000
E: neil@thegrove-narberth.co.uk
W: www.thegrove-narberth.co.uk

BEDROOMS: 20. 2 in coach house (1 on ground floor), 4 in longhouse, plus 4 self-catering cottages.
OPEN: all year.
FACILITIES: 3 lounges, study/library, cocktail bar, 3 restaurant rooms, free Wi-Fi, civil wedding licence, 26-acre grounds.
BACKGROUND MUSIC: 'easy listening' from breakfast till evening, then jazz, in public areas.
LOCATION: 1½ miles S of Narberth.
CHILDREN: all ages welcomed.
DOGS: welcomed in some rooms, public areas.
CREDIT CARDS: Amex, MasterCard, Visa.
PRICES: [2015] per room B&B £190–£340, D,B&B £298–£448. Tasting menu £78, à la carte £54. 1-night bookings sometimes refused.

SEE ALSO SHORTLIST

CNAPAN

Family photographs line the staircase of this homely restaurant-with-rooms, in a listed Georgian town house in the centre of a small coastal town. It has been owned and run by Judith and Michael Cooper for more than 30 years. 'Lovely, caring people', they welcome their guests with tea and Welsh cakes. The pink-painted house has a 'lived-in and loved' interior: the cosy lounge has a wood-burning stove, maps, magazines and games; the sheltered back garden is ideal for afternoon tea and pre-dinner drinks in clement weather. Individually styled, simple, bright bedrooms have a selection of books and plenty of local information. Each room has a shower; a shared bathroom is available to guests who would prefer a 'relaxing soak'. In the restaurant, residents and locals come for Judith Cooper's 'high-quality' modern dishes, which use many locally grown and produced ingredients. Typical dishes: chicken liver parfait, pear Sauterne chutney, toasted brioche; confit of duck, grilled black pudding, mulled plum. Breakfasts, with kippers and local bacon, are cooked to order. Five minutes to the coastal path.

East Street
nr Fishguard
Newport
SA42 0SY

T: 01239 820575
F: 01239 820878
E: enquiry@cnapan.co.uk
W: www.cnapan.co.uk

BEDROOMS: 5. Plus self-catering cottage.
OPEN: 20 Mar–20 Dec, restaurant closed Tues.
FACILITIES: lounge, bar, restaurant, free Wi-Fi, small garden, only restaurant suitable for disabled.
BACKGROUND MUSIC: jazz/'easy listening' in evenings in dining room.
LOCATION: town centre.
CHILDREN: all ages welcomed (family room).
DOGS: not allowed.
CREDIT CARDS: MasterCard, Visa.
PRICES: [2015] per person B&B £47.50, D,B&B £72.50. À la carte £30. 1-night bookings sometimes refused during peak season and some Saturdays.

SEE ALSO SHORTLIST

LLYS MEDDYG

In a pretty town between the mountains and the sea, this Georgian coaching inn is run as a contemporary restaurant-with-rooms by Ed and Lou Sykes. Pembrokeshire natives, they are keen to showcase the fat of their land: Ed Sykes runs countryside- and seaside-foraging courses, as well as hands-on introductions to butchery, smoking and curing (on-site smokehouse). In the smart dining room and the flagstoned Cellar Bar, modern menus might include home-smoked salmon, cucumber ketchup, apple, wasabi; braised shoulder of lamb, cauliflower, caper cockle jus. Welsh tipples on the drinks list: Penderyn whisky, real ale from Penlon, local beer from the Gwaun Valley brewery, 15 minutes' drive away. In summer, meals may also be taken in the informal Kitchen Garden dining room, which opens on to the 'lovely' enclosed garden. Children are welcomed: meals can be tailored for younger tastes; there are beanbags and garden games to play. Decorated with local art, the bedrooms have a tea tray and a minibar with fresh milk; three have a sofa bed to accommodate a family. 'Breakfast was great fuel for our day's walking.'

East Street
Newport
SA42 0SY

T: 01239 820008
E: info@llysmeddyg.com
W: www.llysmeddyg.com

BEDROOMS: 8. 1 on ground floor, 3 in annexe, plus a cottage.
OPEN: all year except 2 weeks Jan, restaurant closed midday, Mon eve.
FACILITIES: bar, restaurant, sitting room, free Wi-Fi, civil wedding licence, garden, unsuitable for disabled.
BACKGROUND MUSIC: 'more lively and loud' in bar, 'quiet' in restaurant in evening.
LOCATION: central.
CHILDREN: all ages welcomed.
DOGS: allowed in 3 annexe bedrooms, cellar bar.
CREDIT CARDS: Amex, MasterCard, Visa.
PRICES: [2015] per room B&B £100–£160, D,B&B £160–£220. Set dinner £20–£25, tasting menu £50, à la carte £35. 1-night bookings sometimes refused weekends.

SEE ALSO SHORTLIST

PORTMEIRION Gwynedd

Map 3:B3

HOTEL PORTMEIRION

♀César award in 1990

In a 'unique' setting on the coast of Snowdonia national park, this eccentric resort village, developed between 1925 and 1976 by the architect Sir Clough Williams-Ellis, 'offers complete tranquillity'. 'Perched high on the cliff face, the early 20th-century Italianate buildings, with their brightly coloured exteriors, bring a world of fantasy to life,' said visitors this year. Overnight accommodation is in the 'luxuriously appointed' main hotel, the Victorian mansion Castell Deudraeth and a variety of village properties. 'The decor is quirky and generally tasteful: there is always something to look at. Our large room had a commanding view. There was a semi-four-poster bed, an antique desk and dressing table, complimentary sherry and biscuits.' Guide inspectors expressed uncertainty about a lack of 'characterful hospitality', however: a business-like greeting, overly brisk interactions with managers. In the evening, guests choose between Castell Deudraeth's informal brasserie and the Art Deco dining room at the hotel, which serves modern dishes. Breakfast is 'good': laver bread and leek sausage with 'delicious' black pudding; 'pleasingly virile' coffee.

Minffordd
Penrhyndeudraeth
Portmeirion
LL48 6ER

T: 01766 770000
F: 01766 770300
E: reception@portmeirion-village.com
W: www.portmeirion-village.com

BEDROOMS: 57. 14 in hotel, some on ground floor, 1 suitable for disabled; 11 in Castell Deudraeth, 32 in village.
OPEN: all year.
FACILITIES: hall, lift, 3 lounges, bar, restaurant, brasserie in Castell, beauty salon, free Wi-Fi, civil wedding licence, 170-acre grounds, heated swimming pool (8 by 15 metres, May–Sept).
BACKGROUND MUSIC: none.
LOCATION: 2 miles SE of Porthmadog.
CHILDREN: all ages welcomed.
DOGS: not allowed.
CREDIT CARDS: Amex, MasterCard, Visa.
PRICES: [2015] per room B&B £119–£209, D,B&B £169–£259. Set meals £38, à la carte £50. 1-night bookings sometimes refused.

PWLLHELI Gwynedd

Map 3:B2

THE OLD RECTORY

'Helpful and attentive hosts' Gary and Lindsay Ashcroft run their B&B in this 'handsome' Georgian rectory standing in large, well-tended gardens. 'We were given the warmest of welcomes; tea was offered in the sitting room as soon as we were ready,' said a Guide inspector on an earlier visit. 'The Ashcrofts clearly love this place and love what they are doing; everything – from the furniture to the pictures to the pretty cups on the bedroom tea tray – has been chosen with care.' Furnished with antiques and paintings, the large sitting room has books, guides, magazines, a log fire in cooler months; upstairs, traditionally decorated bedrooms, all with garden views, have special touches such as sherry and chocolates. A communal breakfast is taken around one large table: guests help themselves to juices, cereals and yogurts; cooked dishes use local eggs and meats, including bacon cured by 'a butcher down the road'. Vegetarian options are available. Evening meals are not provided, but the hosts have many recommendations of eating places close by. Sandy beaches and cliff walks nearby; packed lunches and picnics can be arranged. (Lesley Winship)

Boduan
Pwllheli
LL53 6DT

T: 01758 721519
E: theashcrofts@theoldrectory.net
W: www.theoldrectory.net

BEDROOMS: 4. Also a self-catering cottage and lodge.
OPEN: all year except Christmas.
FACILITIES: drawing room, dining room, free Wi-Fi (best signal in public rooms), 3½-acre grounds, walking, riding, sailing, unsuitable for disabled.
BACKGROUND MUSIC: none.
LOCATION: 4 miles NW of Pwllheli.
CHILDREN: all ages welcomed.
DOGS: only assistance dogs allowed in house (kennel and run available).
CREDIT CARDS: MasterCard, Visa.
PRICES: [2015] per room B&B from £95. 1-night bookings sometimes refused high season and bank holidays.

PWLLHELI Gwynedd

Map 3:B2

PLAS BODEGROES

Ⓠ César award in 1992

'Our second visit, we thoroughly enjoyed it once again.' Praise this year from repeat guests at Chris and Gunna Chown's restaurant-with-rooms, in a Georgian manor house standing in wooded grounds on the remote Lleyn peninsula. Twenty-eight years after the Chowns opened their enterprise, 'the cooking is still of a very high standard'. Chefs Chris Chown and Hugh Bracegirdle serve 'delicious' canapés with pre-dinner drinks. In the duck-egg-blue dining room, their modern menu might include an 'exceptional' soup with truffle cappuccino; Lleyn pork tenderloin, leek and mustard crumble, smoky bacon sauce. The bedrooms have a Scandinavian influence and views over the garden. 'Our spacious attic room had a large, comfortable bed, and chairs to relax in; the huge bathroom had a circular bath.' 'Good' breakfasts have freshly squeezed juices and 'well-cooked' dishes. 'The staff are all helpful and can't do enough for you.' 'A lovely area to explore.' The veranda is covered in wisteria and roses in season; the 'delightful' garden has an avenue of beeches leading, through a yew-tree gate, to a stream. (Sara Price, Mary Coles)

Nefyn Road
Efailnewydd
Pwllheli
LL53 5TH

T: 01758 612363
F: 01758 701247
E: gunna@bodegroes.co.uk
W: www.bodegroes.co.uk

BEDROOMS: 10. 2 in courtyard cottage.
OPEN: Mar–Nov, closed Sun and Mon except bank holidays.
FACILITIES: lounge, bar, breakfast room, restaurant, free Wi-Fi, 5-acre grounds, unsuitable for disabled.
BACKGROUND MUSIC: none.
LOCATION: 1 mile W of Pwllheli.
CHILDREN: all ages welcomed, but no under-5s in restaurant.
DOGS: not allowed in public rooms, 1 bedroom.
CREDIT CARDS: MasterCard, Visa.
PRICES: per person B&B £65–£95, D,B&B £113.50–£143.50. Set dinner £48.50. 1-night bookings sometimes refused.

FAIRYHILL

In 'wonderful' grounds with woodland, an orchard and an ornamental lake, this small country hotel, in an 18th-century Georgian mansion, has 'a lot of positives', a guest said in 2015. Another comment: 'The perfect place to relax.' It is owned by Andrew Hetherington and Paul Davies; 'the staff are extremely good, all local and all friendly'. Public rooms have log fires and newspapers; in warm weather, 'the patio is a perfect place for a pre-dinner drink'. Most of the modern bedrooms have views over the garden; one has its own fireplace; all have fresh fruit, organic teas and home-made Welsh cakes. 'My big, comfortable room had an excellent bathroom with plenty of storage space.' In the 'relaxed' restaurant, David Whitecross, the chef, provides modern dishes. 'The cooking was fine, if elaborate. I had very good monkfish with salad niçoise; an excellent lemon curd pavé.' Breakfast has 'proper bread' with a toaster. 'The extensive grounds are full of wildlife. We had a happy couple of hours looking for goldcrests, woodpeckers, grey wagtails and wrens.' (Peter Anderson, Diane Goodey)

Reynoldston, Gower
nr Swansea
SA3 1BS

T: 01792 390139
F: 01792 391358
E: postbox@fairyhill.net
W: www.fairyhill.net

BEDROOMS: 8.
OPEN: all year except 24–26 Dec and 4–28 Jan, restaurant closed Mon and Tues, Nov–end Mar.
FACILITIES: lounge, bar, 3 dining rooms, meeting room, free Wi-Fi, civil wedding licence, spa treatment room, 24-acre grounds, unsuitable for disabled.
BACKGROUND MUSIC: 'easy listening' in public areas at mealtimes.
LOCATION: 11 miles W of Swansea.
CHILDREN: not under 8.
DOGS: 'well-behaved' dogs allowed in bedrooms not unattended, none in public rooms.
CREDIT CARDS: MasterCard, Visa.
PRICES: [2015] per room B&B £200–£300, D,B&B (min. 2 nights) £250–£390. Set dinner £35–£45. 1-night bookings refused Sat.

ST DAVID'S Pembrokeshire

CRUG-GLAS

'A good place to stay when visiting St David's.' This Georgian farmhouse is run as a restaurant-with-rooms by the 'hard-working' owners, Perkin and Janet Evans, who have a long association with the farm. Her family had run it for generations. They moved out when she was 13, but when she married the son of the family who had bought the farm, she returned to the land. In the 'lovely' sitting room is a Welsh dresser; guests help themselves from an honesty bar. Dinner is served in the former family dining room. Janet Evans uses ingredients from the nearby fields and waters for her dishes, which might include smoked salmon and prawn cocktail; Gressingham duck, port and plum sauce. The bedrooms are in the main building and in a converted milk parlour and a coach house: 'Our charming suite was spacious; a pleasant mix of modern rugs and cushions on a tiled floor; a modern bathroom with a fancy whirlpool bath.' Breakfast has a generously supplied buffet table ('a superb selection of fruit') and a wide choice of cooked dishes.

25% DISCOUNT VOUCHERS

nr Abereiddy, St David's
Haverfordwest
St David's
SA62 6XX

T: 01348 831302
E: janet@crug-glas.co.uk
W: www.crug-glas.co.uk

BEDROOMS: 7. 2 in outbuildings, 1 on ground floor.
OPEN: all year except 25/26 Dec.
FACILITIES: drawing room, dining room, free Wi-Fi, civil wedding licence, 1-acre garden on 600-acre farm, unsuitable for disabled.
BACKGROUND MUSIC: none.
LOCATION: 3½ miles NE of St David's.
CHILDREN: not under 12.
DOGS: not allowed.
CREDIT CARDS: MasterCard, Visa.
PRICES: [2015] per room B&B £150–£190. À la carte £35.

THE OLD RECTORY
ON THE LAKE

'Wonderful: our visit is an annual highlight.'
Beneath Cadair Idris, personable owners John
Caine and Ricky Francis run their B&B in this
tranquil stone-built house on the shore of Lake
Tal-y-llyn. There are lake views from every
window of the old house; visitors keep an eye
out for the family of otters that calls the lake
home. For human guests, two smartly decorated
upstairs bedrooms have a large freestanding
Victorian-style bathtub; a smaller ground-floor
room has an en suite shower room. All have tea-
and coffee-making facilities and bottles of Welsh
mineral water. The adjacent Rectory Retreat, a
self-contained ground-floor studio apartment
with a kitchen and wet room, is equipped for
visitors with mobility issues; it can be booked on
a B&B basis. Pre-dinner drinks are taken in the
lounge or on the terrace; in the Orangery dining
room, Ricky Francis cooks 'very good' evening
meals six nights a week, using plenty of local
produce. Typical dishes: salad of locally smoked
trout; Welsh pork loin with stuffing. There is
good walking from the front door; the hosts can
provide packed lunches. (DL, Shirley King)

Tal-y-Llyn
LL36 9AJ

T: 01654 782225
E: enquiries@rectoryonthelake.
co.uk
W: www.rectoryonthelake.co.uk

BEDROOMS: 3. 1 on ground floor,
plus Rectory Retreat, a self-catering
apartment on ground floor suitable
for disabled (also available for B&B).
OPEN: all year except Jan, dining
room closed Wed.
FACILITIES: lounge, Orangery dining
room, free Wi-Fi, 1½-acre grounds,
outdoor hot tub.
BACKGROUND MUSIC: none.
LOCATION: on lake 9½ miles E of
Tywyn.
CHILDREN: not under 18.
DOGS: allowed in Rectory Retreat
only.
CREDIT CARDS: MasterCard, Visa.
PRICES: [2015] per person B&B £45–
£60. Set dinner £30. Only 2-night
bookings accepted at weekends.

DOLFFANOG FAWR

'It was superb: dedicated hosts, excellent accommodation, the best lamb we have eaten anywhere for years.' A well-travelled visitor was impressed this year by Lorraine Hinkins and Alex Yorke's 'exceptional' guest house, in a converted 18th-century farmhouse in the Tal-y-llyn valley. 'Friendly and professional' hosts, the owners 'pay attention to detail in every way'. The large lounge has squashy leather seating, a log fire and plenty of books, guides and maps; in good weather, guests sit in the gardens with the nuthatches, woodpeckers and siskins. Bedrooms have a large bed, Melin Tregwynt blankets and local artwork; three have views to Tal-y-llyn lake or the Dyfi hills. Five nights a week, Lorraine Hinkins cooks seasonally inspired dinners, taken communally ('should this not be to your taste, a separate table is available'). 'We had a simple yet seriously good meal. One of the other guests had dietary restrictions and the menu had been devised to take that into consideration, but we would never have known if we hadn't been told afterwards.' Breakfast is 'extremely generous': home-made preserves, home-made bread, dry-cured bacon, eggs cooked any way. (GN, and others)

Tal-y-llyn
Tywyn
LL36 9AJ

T: 01654 761247
E: info@dolffanogfawr.co.uk
W: www.dolffanogfawr.co.uk

BEDROOMS: 4.
OPEN: Mar–end Oct, dining room closed Sun/Mon eve except bank holidays.
FACILITIES: lounge, dining room, free Wi-Fi (in most rooms, though temperamental), ¾-acre garden, unsuitable for disabled.
BACKGROUND MUSIC: none.
LOCATION: by lake 10 miles E of Tywyn.
CHILDREN: not under 7.
DOGS: allowed in bedrooms (£5 per night) and lounge (if other guests don't mind).
CREDIT CARDS: MasterCard, Visa.
PRICES: [2015] per person B&B £50. Set menu £25. 1-night bookings sometimes refused.

THE WHITEBROOK   NEW

'Rethought, refreshed and redecorated, the
Whitebrook has been reborn in the hands of
chef/patron Chris Harrod and his team – and
he fully lives up to the heritage.' Regular Guide
correspondents recommended a main entry for
this restaurant-with-rooms, in a 17th-century
drovers' inn in the wooded Wye valley – 'an
ideal position for Chris to pursue his love of
foraging'. He has a Michelin star for his 'very
special' modern cooking: 'He uses local produce
right down to the flowers in the garden. It
makes it all taste so fresh and different.' Another
comment: 'All was simply described but
elaborately prepared and delicious. The parsnip
croquette with salsify, beer onion and charlock
on the vegetarian menu tasted amazing.'
Bedrooms overlook the valley or the garden; 'all
the rooms have been improved'. Four bedrooms
have been refurbished this year. 'Our good-sized
first-floor room had a very comfortable, big
bed, two chairs; a well-decorated bathroom.'
A smaller room was less liked. Breakfast has
'interesting' cooked dishes, perhaps scrambled
eggs 'elegantly served in a "bird's nest" of
smoked salmon'. (Tony and Ginny Ayers,
Humphrey Norrington, and others)

Whitebrook
NP25 4TX

T: 01600 860254
E: info@thewhitebrook.co.uk
W: www.thewhitebrook.co.uk

BEDROOMS: 8.
OPEN: all year except 26 Dec, first
2 weeks Jan, restaurant closed Mon.
FACILITIES: ramp, lounge/bar,
restaurant, business facilities, free
Wi-Fi in room, terrace, 3-acre
garden, River Wye 2 miles (fishing),
only restaurant suitable for disabled.
BACKGROUND MUSIC: 'chill-out music'
in restaurant.
LOCATION: 6 miles S of Monmouth.
CHILDREN: not under 12.
DOGS: only guide dogs allowed.
CREDIT CARDS: Amex, MasterCard,
Visa.
PRICES: [2015] per room D,B&B
£250–£292. Tasting menu £67,
à la carte £54.

CHANNEL ISLANDS

St Peter Port lighthouse, Guernsey

THE WHITE HOUSE

Ω César award in 1987

'A lovely stay: the island and the hotel are strongly recommended.' Praise in 2015 for the only hotel on this small, car-free island. Tranquillity prevails: no background music is played in the public rooms; there is no clock, no television, no telephone in the bedrooms. Radios are banned on the island's beaches. Guests are greeted at the pretty harbour, and their luggage is transported by tractor to the hotel. Siôn Dobson Jones is the manager. Many of the bedrooms have a sea view: they are spread between the main building and cottages in the grounds (one has a private garden). They vary considerably in size, and have a modern bathroom. Many rooms can be adapted for a family; children are warmly welcomed and can take high tea at 5.15 pm. Dinner in the conservatory restaurant is 'of a high standard'. The chef, Karl Ginniver, serves British dishes using local ingredients, perhaps pan-roasted rack and pulled shank of lamb, spinach, chantenay carrots. Less formal dining is available in the Ship Inn brasserie. 'Walking is the thing: on the beaches, the lanes, the cliff paths.' (Susan Cunningham-Hill)

Herm, via Guernsey
GY1 3HR

T: 01481 750075
F: 01481 710066
E: hotel@herm.com
W: www.herm.com

BEDROOMS: 40. 18 in cottages, some on ground floor.
OPEN: Apr–Sept.
FACILITIES: 3 lounges, 2 bars, 2 restaurants, conference room, wedding facilities, free Wi-Fi, 1-acre garden (tennis, croquet, 7-metre solar-heated swimming pool), beach 200 yds, Herm unsuitable for disabled.
BACKGROUND MUSIC: none.
LOCATION: by harbour, air/sea to Guernsey, then ferry from Guernsey (20 mins).
CHILDREN: all ages welcomed.
DOGS: allowed in 2 bedrooms (£20 per dog per night), not allowed in public rooms except brasserie.
CREDIT CARDS: MasterCard, Visa.
PRICES: [2015] per person B&B from £69, D,B&B £102–£155. Set dinner £32. 1-night bookings sometimes refused.

THE ATLANTIC HOTEL

Standing on the headland above the five-mile beach at St Ouen's Bay, this luxury hotel has 'lovely' views over the Atlantic ocean and Les Mielles, a conservation area of outstanding natural beauty. It has been owned and managed by the Burke family since it was built in 1970 by Henry Burke. With his son, Patrick, now at the helm, service is 'exemplary', a guest said this year. Decorated in 'understated' colours, bedrooms, all with a marble bathroom, are 'exquisitely made up'; they have fresh fruit, tea- and coffee-making facilities, and a daily newspaper. Full-length, sliding windows overlook the water or the adjoining golf course. 'Although some rooms lack a proper balcony, the views over the landscaped gardens towards the extensive beach are spectacular.' In the elegant Ocean restaurant, chef Mark Jordan has a Michelin star for his modern British cooking: he prioritises local ingredients in dishes such as ravioli of Jersey chancre crab, potato and mussel broth; Jersey red mullet, seared foie gras, lentils, lobster velouté. 'We were very impressed.' (Kevin Seymour, JR)

Le Mont de la Pulente
St Brelade
JE3 8HE

T: 01534 744101
F: 01534 744102
E: info@theatlantichotel.com
W: www.theatlantichotel.com

BEDROOMS: 50. Some on ground floor.
OPEN: 6 Feb–3 Jan.
FACILITIES: lift, lounge, library, cocktail bar, restaurant, private dining room, fitness centre (swimming pool, sauna, mini-gym), free Wi-Fi, wedding facilities, 6-acre garden (tennis, indoor and outdoor heated swimming pools, 10 by 5 metres), unsuitable for disabled.
BACKGROUND MUSIC: in restaurant.
LOCATION: 5 miles W of St Helier.
CHILDREN: all ages welcomed (family rooms, 'nursery menu').
DOGS: not allowed.
CREDIT CARDS: all major cards.
PRICES: [2015] per room B&B from £150, D,B&B from £250. Set dinner £55, tasting menu £80, à la carte £65.

LA FRÉGATE · **NEW**

High on a cliff above the pretty harbour, this 18th-century manor house is 'well worth the walk up from the middle of town'. Managed by Simon Dufty for private owners, the hotel earns an upgrade to a full entry this year, thanks to a report from a regular correspondent. 'Well-equipped' modern bedrooms have tea- and coffee-making facilities, a DVD-player, iPod docking station and radio; many have a balcony or terrace to take in the panoramic sea views. 'From the balcony in our room, we looked over the harbour to the neighbouring islands: magical.' In the light and airy restaurant with huge picture windows and 'fantastic' views over town and sea, chef Neil Maginnis's modern British cooking 'deserves all the accolades it has had'. His 'simple, straightforward' dishes feature much local fish and shellfish, perhaps Guernsey scallops, cauliflower purée, spiced chorizo; sea bass, crabmeat risotto, green peas, bacon. In good weather, lunches and pre-dinner drinks may be taken on the terrace. A path through the terraced garden leads to the shops and restaurants in town. (JR)

Beauregard Lane
Les Cotils
St Peter Port
GY1 1UT

T: 01481 724624
F: 01481 720443
E: enquiries@lafregatehotel.com
W: www.lafregatehotel.com

BEDROOMS: 22.
OPEN: all year.
FACILITIES: lounge/bar, restaurant, private dining/function rooms, free Wi-Fi, patio (alfresco dining), ½-acre terraced garden, unsuitable for disabled.
BACKGROUND MUSIC: in bar at meal times.
LOCATION: 5 mins'walk from centre.
CHILDREN: all ages welcomed.
DOGS: not allowed.
CREDIT CARDS: Amex, MasterCard, Visa.
PRICES: [2015] per room B&B £99.50–£420. Set dinner £36, à la carte £45.

SEE ALSO SHORTLIST

LONGUEVILLE MANOR

There is 'a personal touch' at this extended 14th-century manor house, 'the most spectacular and sumptuous on the Channel Islands', says a visitor this year. Standing in extensive grounds with woodland walks, an ornamental lake and a Victorian kitchen garden, the luxury hotel (Relais & Châteaux) has been run by three generations of the Lewis family; today, Malcolm Lewis, his wife, Patricia, and her brother-in-law, Pedro Bento, are at the helm. There are six categories of rooms and suites: some have their own patio with direct access to the gardens; others are spacious enough to accommodate an extra bed for a child. They are all traditionally decorated, and have magazines, board games, fresh flowers and a bowl of fruit. Chef Andrew Baird's 'impressive' French menus are based on local and home-grown produce; they are served in the formal Oak Room (white linens, dark panelling) and the 'lighter', more relaxed Garden Room. Typical dishes: bonbon of chancre crab, toasted pine nuts, guacamole; local pork, crisp pancetta, cauliflower beignet. In summer, alfresco meals may be taken on the swimming pool terrace. (JR)

Longueville Road
St Saviour
JE2 7WF

T: 01534 725501
F: 01534 731613
E: info@longuevillemanor.com
W: www.longuevillemanor.com

BEDROOMS: 30. 8 on ground floor, 2 in cottage.
OPEN: all year.
FACILITIES: lift, ramp, 2 lounges, cocktail bar, 2 dining rooms, free Wi-Fi, function/conference/wedding facilities, spa (treatments, mini gym, spa pool, terrace), 15-acre grounds (croquet, tennis, outdoor heated swimming pool, woodland), sea 1 mile, unsuitable for disabled.
BACKGROUND MUSIC: in bar and restaurant.
LOCATION: 1½ miles E of St Helier.
CHILDREN: all ages welcomed.
DOGS: not allowed in public rooms.
CREDIT CARDS: all major cards.
PRICES: [2015] per room B&B from £195, D,B&B from £275. Set dinner £40–£110, à la carte £60.

LA SABLONNERIE

'It is still wonderful.' Praise this year from a fan on his 'umpteenth' visit to 'this little paradise', on a tranquil, car-free island an hour's ferry ride from Guernsey. Surrounded by secluded cottage gardens with a croquet lawn, the whitewashed 16th-century farmhouse is run as a small hotel by 'welcoming' host Elizabeth Perrée, with 'charming, polite and elegantly presented' staff. 'It was superb – like stepping back into the past, with no television and no Wi-Fi.' Guests are greeted at the harbour on arrival, and taken to the hotel in a pony and trap. In the main house and nearby cottages, simply furnished bedrooms are decorated in a rustic style. Pre-dinner drinks are taken in front of the log fire in the lounge; in the dining room, chef Colin Day's cooking is 'superb' – 'a renewed pleasure every day'. The French-influenced menus use butter, cream, meat, fruit and vegetables from the hotel's own farm and gardens; freshly caught fish and Sark lobster are specialities. In the summer, meals and cream teas may be taken among the lupins, hollyhocks and lavender in the garden. (John Barnes)

Little Sark
Sark, via Guernsey
GY10 1SD

T: 01481 832061
F: 01481 832408
E: reservations@sablonneriesark.com
W: www.sablonneriesark.com

BEDROOMS: 22. Also accommodation in nearby cottages.
OPEN: Easter–Oct.
FACILITIES: 3 lounges, 2 bars, restaurant, Wi-Fi not available, wedding facilities, 1-acre garden (tea garden/bar, croquet), Sark unsuitable for disabled.
BACKGROUND MUSIC: classical/piano in bar.
LOCATION: S part of island, boat from Guernsey (guests will be met at the harbour on arrival).
CHILDREN: all ages welcomed.
DOGS: allowed at hotel's discretion, but not in public rooms.
CREDIT CARDS: MasterCard, Visa.
PRICES: [2015] per person B&B £40–£107.50, D,B&B £69.50–£137. Set menu £29.50, à la carte £49.50 (excluding 10% service charge).

IRELAND

Doorway in Dingle, Co. Kerry

LORUM OLD RECTORY

♥César award in 2014

'The thing that you notice about staying in Lorum Old Rectory is that it is a home,' says a visitor in 2015 to Bobbie Smith's guest house at the foot of Mount Leinster. 'Yes, it is a beautiful stone house, but what makes it is the hospitality and easy friendliness of host Bobbie Smith, and her attention to detail.' A grandfather clock 'ticks quietly' in the hallway. The house is 'grandly decorated throughout; lots of dark wood; the dining room shows off a beautiful silver collection, without seeming cluttered. Its dark red/maroon walls and ceiling were enlivened by a fire and candles at dinner.' Guests take pre-dinner drinks by an open fire in the lounge. Bobbie Smith serves a five-course meal which is taken communally at a mahogany table. 'We dined on goat's cheese bruschetta; celeriac soup; a refreshing sorbet; chicken with mustard, orange and balsamic vinegar sauce; a lemon posset. Delicious. We stayed in a lovely, spacious room with a very comfortable bed. There were books and magazines, along with tea/coffee-making facilities and a bottle of water.' (Sheila Robinson)

25% DISCOUNT VOUCHERS

Kilgreaney
Bagenalstown

T: 00 353 59 977 5282
F: 00 353 59 977 5455
E: bobbie@lorum.com
W: www.lorum.com

BEDROOMS: 4.
OPEN: Feb–Nov.
FACILITIES: drawing room, study, dining room, free Wi-Fi, wedding facilities, 1-acre garden (croquet), 17-acre grounds, unsuitable for disabled.
BACKGROUND MUSIC: none.
LOCATION: 4 miles S of Bagenalstown on R705 to Borris.
CHILDREN: all ages welcomed by arrangement.
DOGS: allowed by arrangement.
CREDIT CARDS: MasterCard, Visa.
PRICES: per person B&B €75–€85. Set dinner €50.

THE MUSTARD SEED AT ECHO LODGE

'A hotel with a bit of magic about it,' says a visitor this year to Daniel Mullane's restaurant-with-rooms in a pretty village. The owner is 'warm and full of character'; his staff are 'charming, confident; they provide a family feel'. 'Time stands still' in the house which has a 'well-proportioned hall; eclectic period furnishing'. In summer, doors open on to a 'flower-bedecked' garden and green lawns. An 'airy and light' atrium has been refurbished. The 'well-tended' orchards and vegetable gardens supply the kitchen with 'a huge variety' of fruit, vegetables and herbs. The 'quality and innovation' of Angel Pirev's cooking impressed. Examples: wild turbot, wild garlic emulsion, seared Kerry scallop, tapioca liver fritter, lime gel; venison loin, fillet carpaccio, black pudding, honey parsnips, purée, jus. A 'very comfy' duplex room was provided with 'all manner of books' and glossy magazines. Some bedrooms have a panoramic view. Bathrooms have a power shower; some have a bath. A 'lovely' breakfast has stewed rhubarb from the garden, eggs from the hotel's hens, home-made soda bread. (Adam Greaves, Dr Helena Shaw)

Ballingarry

T: 00 353 69 68508
F: 00 353 69 68511
E: mustard@indigo.ie
W: www.mustardseed.ie

BEDROOMS: 16. 1, on ground floor, suitable for disabled.
OPEN: all year except 24–26 Dec.
FACILITIES: 3 public rooms, library, entrance hall, sun room, free Wi-Fi (in public areas, some bedrooms), wedding facilities, 12-acre grounds.
BACKGROUND MUSIC: piano on occasion in restaurant.
LOCATION: in village, 18 miles SW of Limerick.
CHILDREN: all ages welcomed.
DOGS: allowed in 1 bedroom, not in public rooms.
CREDIT CARDS: Amex, MasterCard, Visa.
PRICES: [2015] per person B&B from €90, D,B&B from €129. Set menus €46–€60.

STELLA MARIS   **NEW**

On Mayo's rugged north-west coast, this white-painted building dominates Bunatrahir Bay as befits a former coastguard headquarters. It was turned into a hotel by the owners, Frances Kelly, a Mayo-born, US-trained chef, and her American husband, Terence McSweeney. Along the front of the building is a hundred-foot conservatory with uninterrupted sea views. 'We enjoyed watching dolphins frolicking in the bay,' says a visitor who was 'warmly greeted by the owners and given a welcome cup of tea and biscuits'. Ten of the bedrooms have views of the Atlantic Ocean. They are simply furnished 'but comfortable'. Each is named after a famous golf course (Terence McSweeney is a keen golfer); fellow guests might include a party of golfers. The 'lovely' bar has fireplaces, old prints and golf memorabilia. In the restaurant, Frances Kelly serves a daily-changing menu of modern dishes, perhaps oak-smoked Irish salmon, capucine capers; beer-marinated tenderloin and crispy belly of Irish pork, sweet potato purée, oriental-spiced jus. Breakfast, served at table, has freshly squeezed fruit juice; a choice of potato cakes, free-range eggs, and traditional bacon and sausages. (EC)

Ballycastle

T: 00 353 96 43322
F: 00 353 96 43965
E: info@stellamarisireland.com
W: www.stellamarisireland.com

BEDROOMS: 12. 1, on ground floor, suitable for disabled.
OPEN: May–end Sept.
FACILITIES: ramps, lounge, bar, restaurant, conservatory, free Wi-Fi ('most dependable in public areas'), wedding facilities, 3-acre grounds (golf), sea/freshwater fishing, sandy beach nearby.
BACKGROUND MUSIC: none.
LOCATION: 2 miles W of Ballycastle.
CHILDREN: all ages welcomed.
DOGS: not allowed.
CREDIT CARDS: MasterCard, Visa.
PRICES: [2015] per person B&B €90, D,B&B €125. À la carte €45.

BALLYLICKEY Co. Cork

SEAVIEW HOUSE

'Kindly, helpful' Kathleen O'Sullivan remains very much in charge after three decades of running her hotel in the white, bay-windowed Victorian house that she was brought up in, on the edge of this village on the River Ouvane. Returning guests often comment on how everything is much as they remembered it. The 'time-warp' quality is not for everyone, but traditional furniture, antiques, roaring fires, paintings, mantel clocks, winged armchairs and fresh flowers set a 'welcoming' tone. Bedrooms are large, some huge, though sea views may be 'distant' or obscured by trees. Housekeeping is 'meticulous'. The bar is popular with locals. Dinner, served in the dining room or conservatory, is 'decent and home cooked', honest rather than modish, with plenty of choice. Melon boat is served with fresh fruit and orange coulis; Bantry Bay crab salad comes with Marie Rose sauce; West Cork roast lamb with mint sauce. No fads, no gimmicks, all 'fair value'. Chips are 'exceptional', fish a sound choice. The wine list is 'extensive'. There is a 'good' breakfast buffet; cooked items might include lamb's liver and kidneys.

Ballylickey, Bantry Bay
West Cork
Ballylickey

T: 00 353 27 50073
F: 00 353 27 51555
E: info@seaviewhousehotel.com
W: www.seaviewhousehotel.com

BEDROOMS: 25. 2, on ground floor, suitable for disabled.
OPEN: 15 Mar–15 Nov.
FACILITIES: bar, library, 2 lounges, restaurant/conservatory, free Wi-Fi in public rooms, some bedrooms, wedding facilities, 4-acre grounds, riding, golf nearby.
BACKGROUND MUSIC: none.
LOCATION: 3 miles N of Bantry on N71.
CHILDREN: all ages welcomed, special menus and babysitting available.
DOGS: not allowed in public rooms.
CREDIT CARDS: Amex, MasterCard, Visa.
PRICES: [2015] per person B&B €75–€95, D,B&B €95–€105. Set dinner €35–€45.

TEMPLE HOUSE

A leafy half-mile drive leads to this Georgian mansion, remodelled in 1864, in a thousand acres of gardens, pastures and woodland. 'Stay for two or three nights,' urge Roderick and Helena Perceval, who offer 'space and tranquillity, not just a room' at their ancestral home. The estate has belonged to the Perceval family since 1665. There are muddy wellies in the vestibule. Family portraits look down upon the grand staircase leading to the 'large bedrooms with high ceiling and big windows', individually styled, each with a view of the park. The Twins room has twin canopied beds, a dressing table, boudoir chair and 'huge' wardrobe – 'absolutely no TV'. Original features, custom-built furniture and antiques abound, but bathrooms are modern. Guests gather in the mirrored morning room, with French windows overlooking the croquet lawn, for drinks before dinner at a long mahogany table laid with crystal glass and silverware. Ingredients are mainly organic. 'Generous portions' of lamb and 'decent' Irish cheeses are typically offered. At breakfast there is home-made muesli, fruit compote, home-made bread, new-laid eggs, and the full Irish.

Ballinacarrow
Ballymote

T: 00 353 71 918 3329
E: stay@templehouse.ie
W: www.templehouse.ie

BEDROOMS: 6.
OPEN: 1 Apr–15 Nov.
FACILITIES: drawing room, snooker room, dining room, free Wi-Fi, wedding facilities, 1½-acre garden, 1,000-acre estate, unsuitable for disabled.
BACKGROUND MUSIC: none.
LOCATION: 12 miles S of Sligo.
CHILDREN: all ages welcomed.
DOGS: not allowed in house.
CREDIT CARDS: Diners, MasterCard, Visa.
PRICES: [2015] per person B&B €75–€95. Set dinner €47.

CAIRN BAY LODGE

In their 16th year of running their 'very original' B&B in an Edwardian villa looking east over Ballyholme Bay, Chris and Jenny Mullen win consistent praise for the warmth of their welcome and for 'anticipating their guests' every need'. Bedrooms are 'characterful' and 'well appointed', with views of sea or garden, hospitality tray, TV and DVD-player, blackout drapes or curtains, robes, slippers, organic toiletries. Two are for single occupancy; there are two family suites. Public rooms are oak panelled. The guest lounge has a quaint Dutch fireplace, deep leather armchairs and a good choice of books and magazines. Home-made cakes and fresh milk are set out in the afternoon for tea. An 'excellent' breakfast in the dining room has freshly squeezed juices, smoothies, organic porridge with cream, seeds and honey, and such 'tasty' cooked dishes as Copeland Island crab with scrambled egg and chilli jam, smoked salmon omelette with lemon crème fraîche. Light therapy, facials, body massage and organic seaweed treatments are available. The Starfish café, serving breakfast, brunch and coffee, opened in June 2015.

278 Seacliff Road
Ballyholme
Bangor
BT20 5HS

T: 028 9146 7636
F: 028 9145 7728
E: info@cairnbaylodge.com
W: www.cairnbaylodge.com

BEDROOMS: 8.
OPEN: all year.
FACILITIES: lounge, 2 breakfast rooms, free Wi-Fi, beauty salon, ¼-acre garden, unsuitable for disabled.
BACKGROUND MUSIC: in Starfish café 8 am–4 pm.
LOCATION: ¼ mile E of centre.
CHILDREN: all ages welcomed.
DOGS: not allowed.
CREDIT CARDS: Amex, MasterCard, Visa.
PRICES: [2015] per room B&B, single £50–£80, double/twin £75–£90. 1-night bookings sometimes refused.

CARRIG COUNTRY HOUSE AND RESTAURANT

Landscaped and wooded gardens filled with rare shrubs surround this Victorian manor house and former hunting and fishing lodge on the shores of Caragh Lake. Frank and Mary Slattery bought and extended it in 1996, furnishing it throughout with antiques. Front-of-house and living his dream, Frank extends a 'warm welcome' (first names, no formality). The best of the 'old-fashioned and appealing' bedrooms have lake and mountain views. The Presidential Suite has a rosewood canopied bed picked up in Kerala, a sitting room, a spa bath and two dressing rooms. Head chef Patricia Teahan cooks modern Irish dishes with an international twist – mussels, kumara (sweet potato in korma sauce); chargrilled rack of Kerry lamb, thyme and honey baby carrots; lamb shank pie, fig and port purée. The 'excellent' dinner is served in the restaurant (candles, more lake views), by 'caring', 'charming' and 'unpretentious' local women in black skirt and white blouse. Turf fires burn in the 'pleasant' drawing room and smaller lounges. Killorglin is on the scenic Ring of Kerry tourist circuit.

25% DISCOUNT VOUCHERS

Caragh Lake
Killorglin

T: 00 353 66 976 9100
E: info@carrighouse.com
W: www.carrighouse.com

BEDROOMS: 16. Some on ground floor.
OPEN: 4 Mar–6 Nov.
FACILITIES: 2 lounges, snug, library, TV room, dining room, free Wi-Fi, wedding facilities, 4-acre garden on lake.
BACKGROUND MUSIC: 'subtle and varied' in public areas all day, in restaurant during dinner.
LOCATION: 22 miles W of Killarney.
CHILDREN: not under 8 (except infants under 12 months).
DOGS: not allowed in house (kennel available).
CREDIT CARDS: MasterCard, Visa.
PRICES: [2015] per person B&B €75–€175, D,B&B from €99. Set dinner €49.50.

GHAN HOUSE `NEW`

Within castellated walls, this 'pretty' Georgian house in 'attractive' gardens has been run by the Carroll family, with 'extremely friendly, hospitable and efficient' staff, for more than 20 years. It earns an upgrade to a main entry thanks to a positive report this year. 'It is obviously a family concern': the 'beautifully decorated' house is filled with family antiques and photographs; mother Joyce attends to the herb garden; 'the night we dined in, Paul Carroll, the owner, was everywhere'. The 'pleasant' lounge and 'small, well-stocked' bar have log fires, games, books and magazines. In the main house and a garden annexe, the traditionally decorated bedrooms have views of Carlingford Lough or the mountains beyond. 'Our well-furnished corner room had a large and comfortable (possibly antique) bed, a sofa/day bed and a spacious, state-of-the-art bathroom with an enormous power shower and a deep bath.' In the 'elegant' dining rooms, chef Stephane le Sourne cooks Irish dishes with a French influence, perhaps 'tender and bloody roast beef, as ordered'; 'an enjoyable pudding'. Popular with private parties, which the staff handle 'effortlessly'. (Sarah McKie)

Carlingford

T: 00 353 42 937 3682
E: info@ghanhouse.com
W: www.ghanhouse.com

BEDROOMS: 12. 8 in garden annexe.
OPEN: all year except 24–26 Dec, 31 Dec, 1 Jan.
FACILITIES: bar, lounge, restaurant (3 dining areas), free Wi-Fi, conference facilities, wedding facilities, cookery school, large garden, secure bicycle storage, unsuitable for disabled.
BACKGROUND MUSIC: jazz/classical in bar and restaurant.
LOCATION: in town.
CHILDREN: all ages welcomed.
DOGS: allowed in kennels.
CREDIT CARDS: all major cards.
PRICES: [2015] per person B&B from €65, D,B&B from €90. Set menus €33–€45, à la carte €35.

ENNISCOE HOUSE

In woodland at the foot of Mount Nephin, this classic Georgian mansion (said to be the last great house of North Mayo) is the family home of Susan Kellett and her son, DJ. 'This is not a guest house or a hotel,' they say. Guests are 'warmly welcomed' and encouraged to relax in a building 'full of treasures'. A massive front door opens on to a high-ceilinged hall with family portraits and fishing trophies. A huge elliptical staircase leads to the bedrooms; the three largest, at the front of the house, have a canopy or a four-poster bed, views over Lough Conn. The bedrooms at the back of the house look over the walled gardens. Pre-dinner drinks are taken in one of two vast sitting rooms, which have sofas in front of a fire, and also quieter corners for private conversations. Dinner is served by DJ in a room with wild flowers on well-spaced wooden tables. His mother cooks a short menu in 'good country style'. The estate has a heritage centre and a walled garden with a tea room.

25% DISCOUNT VOUCHERS

Castlehill

T: 00 353 96 31112
F: 00 353 96 31773
E: mail@enniscoe.com
W: www.enniscoe.com

BEDROOMS: 6. Plus self-catering units behind house.
OPEN: Apr–Oct, New Year.
FACILITIES: 2 sitting rooms, dining room, free Wi-Fi (in public rooms, some bedrooms), wedding facilities, 160-acre estate (garden, tea room, farm, heritage centre, conference centre, forge, fishing), unsuitable for disabled.
BACKGROUND MUSIC: none.
LOCATION: 2 miles S of Crossmolina.
CHILDREN: all ages welcomed.
DOGS: welcomed, not allowed in public rooms.
CREDIT CARDS: MasterCard, Visa.
PRICES: [2015] per person B&B €80–€120, D,B&B €130–€170. Set menus €45–€50.

BALLYVOLANE HOUSE

♔César award in 2009

In farming and fishing country in north Cork, this Italianate Georgian mansion is the family home of Justin and Jenny Green. International hoteliers, they returned to his home to welcome guests in an 'atmosphere of informality and friendliness'. There are no keys to the bedrooms, which have an old-fashioned wireless rather than television; books and magazines; a Nespresso coffee machine; home-made cordial and biscuits. The beds are large; some bathrooms have a freestanding antique bath. The house is furnished with traditional pieces and family memorabilia. Visiting families can enjoy 'glamping' in the gardens in summer, sleeping in bell tents kitted out with a raised timber bed. Fishing is an important feature: the family has beats on six miles of the salmon-rich River Blackwater; there are three trout lakes in the grounds. A ghillie might well join guests at dinner, generally a communal affair where conversation flows. Teena Mahon cooks country house dishes. Breakfast is served to house and glamping guests until midday. Children are welcomed, and may be taken on a tractor tour of the grounds by the host.

Castlelyons

T: 00 353 25 36349
F: 00 353 25 36781
E: info@ballyvolanehouse.ie
W: www.ballyvolanehouse.ie

BEDROOMS: 6.
OPEN: all year except Christmas/ New Year, closed Sun/Mon except bank holiday weekends.
FACILITIES: hall, drawing room, honesty bar, dining room, free Wi-Fi, wedding facilities, 80-acre grounds (15-acre garden, croquet, 3 trout lakes), unsuitable for disabled.
BACKGROUND MUSIC: none.
LOCATION: 22 miles NE of Cork.
CHILDREN: all ages welcomed.
DOGS: allowed.
CREDIT CARDS: MasterCard, Visa.
PRICES: per room B&B main house €198–€240. Glamping per tent €150–€166. Set dinner €60.

CLIFDEN Co. Galway

THE QUAY HOUSE

♛ César award in 2003

'Warm' hosts Paddy and Julia Foyle welcome B&B guests to their late-Georgian former harbourmaster's house turned monastery, with modern extension, overlooking a small inlet. The public rooms and bedrooms are individually furnished. There are baroque clocks, portraits and seascapes, exotic hunting trophies, antiques and artefacts; everywhere a sense of fun. Peat fires burn in the large sitting rooms, where you can take tea, have a drink, leaf through magazines and coffee-table books. There's a Napoleon-themed bedroom, an African room. All beds have an orthopaedic mattress. The Mirror Room admires itself in a vast gilded looking glass. Spacious bathrooms have a bath and a shower. Each of the seven studio rooms has a kitchenette and a balcony with harbour views. In the conservatory breakfast room, exuberantly adorned with more of the Foyles' eclectic auction finds, 'splendid' dishes might include oysters with smoked salmon, fresh fish, devilled kidneys, with home-made bread and cakes, freshly squeezed orange juice and Irish cheeses.

25% DISCOUNT VOUCHERS

Beach Road
Clifden

T: 00 353 95 21369
F: 00 353 95 21608
E: thequay@iol.ie
W: www.thequayhouse.com

BEDROOMS: 15. 3 on ground floor, 1 suitable for disabled, 7 studios (6 with kitchenette) in annexe.
OPEN: Apr–Oct.
FACILITIES: 2 sitting rooms, breakfast conservatory, free Wi-Fi, small garden, fishing, sailing, golf, riding nearby.
BACKGROUND MUSIC: none.
LOCATION: harbour, 8 mins' walk from centre.
CHILDREN: all ages welcomed.
DOGS: not allowed.
CREDIT CARDS: MasterCard, Visa.
PRICES: per room B&B €135–€150.

SEA MIST HOUSE

Close to the centre of the coastal town, yet in a quiet position, this late Georgian stone house has been run as a B&B since 1999 by the Griffin family. 'The owners must be enthusiastic art collectors,' speculated a visitor who found the walls covered with pictures. The 'beautifully maintained' bedrooms are decorated in restful colours, with patterned cushions and curtains. Bathrooms are well supplied. There is a sofa on the landing, and a bookcase should you wish to read; a television in the communal lounge. The property passed down to Sheila Griffin from her auctioneer grandfather, who bought it in 1920. From the umbrella stand in the hall to the Welsh dresser in the breakfast room – where pretty windows look out on to a flower-filled garden – the ethos is homely. There is no wine licence, but the owner is happy to supply glasses, corkscrew and a fridge for those who wish to bring their own, to enjoy a drink in the lounge. At breakfast, the eggs are from the family's own hens, the bread is home made, the herbs come from the garden.

Seaview
Clifden

T: 00 353 95 21441
E: sheila@seamisthouse.com
W: www.seamisthouse.com

BEDROOMS: 4.
OPEN: Mar–Nov.
FACILITIES: 2 sitting rooms, conservatory dining room, free Wi-Fi (only in garden), ¾-acre garden, unsuitable for disabled.
BACKGROUND MUSIC: none.
LOCATION: just down from the town centre.
CHILDREN: not under 4.
DOGS: not allowed.
CREDIT CARDS: Amex, MasterCard, Visa.
PRICES: per person B&B €40–€60.

HILTON PARK

'Pure tranquillity. You have to work to get here, but you are fully rewarded for every mile travelled.' In a sprawling estate with heritage woodland, gardens and lakes, stands this 'grand and glorious' Italianate mansion. It has been the family seat since it was built in 1704. Today, it is run by Fred and Joanna Madden of the ninth generation. Their home is filled with books, antiques, art, family memorabilia, 'lots of lived-in sofas and chairs, all comfy'. Guests are encouraged to play the 19th-century grand piano in one of the 'beguiling' drawing rooms. Large windows let in the light. Most of the spacious bedrooms, each individually decorated with antiques, overlook the surrounding parkland. A large walled garden, tended to by Fred Madden's mother, Lucy, provides much of the vegetables and fruits used in the kitchen. 'Lucy and Fred, who share the cooking duties, produce tasty, fresh meals', perhaps wild garlic soup; pan-fried John Dory, almond and caper butter. In the vaulted former servants' hall, breakfast has freshly baked bread, home-made green tomato and cardamom jam.

Clones

T: 00 353 47 56007
E: mail@hiltonpark.ie
W: www.hiltonpark.ie

BEDROOMS: 6.
OPEN: Apr–Oct, groups only Nov–Mar.
FACILITIES: drawing room, sitting room, TV room, breakfast room, dining room, games room, free Wi-Fi (in some rooms, public areas), 400-acre grounds (3 lakes, golf course, croquet), unsuitable for disabled.
BACKGROUND MUSIC: none.
LOCATION: 4 miles S of Clones.
CHILDREN: all ages welcomed.
DOGS: not allowed.
CREDIT CARDS: MasterCard, Visa.
PRICES: [2015] per person B&B €90–€110, D,B&B €145–€165. À la carte €55.

DUNLAVIN Co. Wicklow

RATHSALLAGH HOUSE

Farmer Joe O'Flynn bought Rathsallagh at New Year 1979, intending to work the land. 'Lovely people who make you feel welcome', he and his wife, Kay, started to take paying guests. A restaurant followed, and in 1995 a golf club. The building had been converted from Queen Anne stables when the original manor house burnt down in the violent wake of the 1798 rebellion. The family run it in 'low-key' style. The 'fabulous' bedrooms are traditionally furnished. Most bathrooms have bath, walk-in shower, underfloor heating. Abhishek Tiwari cooks modern Irish fare with Mediterranean and Asian influences, using ingredients produced locally, vegetables and herbs from the garden. Rump of Wicklow lamb, for instance, with polenta cake, Mediterranean vegetables, chimchimchurri, rosemary jus; pan-fried cod, confit fennel, sautéed baby potato, pesto cream, fried squid. 'The best breakfast in the county' includes locally made sausages, home-smoked fish and meat, eggs from the free-range hens. There is a beauty spa and a helipad. Rathsallagh House is close to Wicklow national park; it is in prime horse-racing territory, near the Irish National Stud and the Curragh race course.

25% DISCOUNT VOUCHERS

Dunlavin

T: 00 353 45 403112
F: 00 353 45 403343
E: info@rathsallagh.com
W: www.rathsallagh.com

BEDROOMS: 29. 20 in courtyard, 3 in gate lodge.
OPEN: all year except Mon and Tues.
FACILITIES: 2 drawing rooms, bar, dining room, snooker room, free Wi-Fi, wedding facilities, 500-acre grounds (golf course, tennis), 4-acre walled garden.
BACKGROUND MUSIC: none.
LOCATION: 2 miles SW of village.
CHILDREN: not under 6.
DOGS: allowed (in heated kennels).
CREDIT CARDS: all major cards.
PRICES: [2015] per room B&B from €159, D,B&B from €240. À la carte €45.

BALLINKEELE HOUSE

Built at the dawn of the Victorian era, this 'magnificent' Italianate mansion is run as a 'historic family home' by Val Maher and his wife, Laura, fifth-generation owners. Beyond a Corinthian portico, an entrance hall with columns of Wexford granite leads to a hall with a cantilevered staircase adorned with a striking bronze statue. Throughout the house there are original fireplaces, original furniture, paintings and ornaments. Guests sit down together at a mahogany table set with silver candelabras in the rich red dining room. Self-taught cooks, the Mahers offer a daily no-choice menu of 'honest, tasty' dishes (special dietary requirements accommodated), using seasonal, local produce, fruit from the orchard, vegetables and herbs from the walled kitchen garden. Perhaps a soup, game from the estate or Irish salmon, a white chocolate mousse with berries. All bedrooms have traditional furnishings and views of parkland and gardens. Superior rooms have bath and shower. At breakfast there are pancakes, a traditional Irish, freshly squeezed orange juice. In the grounds there is a lake, ponds, a folly built as a ruined castle keep and, in season, glorious rhododendrons.

Ballymurn
Enniscorthy

T: 00 353 53 913 8105
E: info@ballinkeele.ie
W: www.ballinkeele.ie

BEDROOMS: 6. 1 in wing.
OPEN: Feb–Dec, weekends only in December, closed Christmas, open New Year.
FACILITIES: 2 drawing rooms, dining room, free Wi-Fi, 8-acre gardens in 350-acre estate, lakes, ponds, unsuitable for disabled.
BACKGROUND MUSIC: none.
LOCATION: 6 miles SE of Enniscorthy, 10 miles NW of Wexford Town. 6 miles east of Curracloe Beach. 45 minutes from the ferry at Rosslare. 1.5 hours from Dublin.
CHILDREN: all ages welcomed.
DOGS: not allowed.
CREDIT CARDS: MasterCard, Visa.
PRICES: [2015] per person B&B €75–€115, D,B&B €110–€150.

SALVILLE HOUSE

♥César award in 2013

'We loved it all,' says a regular Guide correspondent on a first visit to Gordon and Jane Parker's ever-popular Victorian country house in large grounds on a hilltop. 'It is like staying in a private home; there are no locks on the doors and everything is very informal.' Three of the bedrooms (Pink, Yellow, Blue) are in the main house, and have splendid views over the River Slaney valley and the Blackstairs Mountains. Two other rooms are in a self-contained apartment. Gordon Parker's cooking is a highlight: 'The food was out of this world. There is no choice, and some of the ingredients which were married together seemed unlikely but all of them worked. Asparagus in breadcrumbs was served on a pea purée pancake and topped with a poached egg. It was delicious.' Early suppers are served for guests attending the Wexford opera festival, when a house-party atmosphere can be expected. 'We didn't really need breakfast but it was worth having – freshly squeezed orange juice, home-made plum compote which was still warm, and perfectly poached eggs.' (Sara Price)

Enniscorthy

T: 00 353 53 923 5252
E: info@salvillehouse.com
W: www.salvillehouse.com

BEDROOMS: 5. 2 in apartment at rear.
OPEN: all year except Christmas.
FACILITIES: drawing room, dining room, free Wi-Fi, 5-acre grounds ('rough' tennis, badminton, croquet), golf nearby, beach, bird sanctuary 10 miles, unsuitable for disabled.
BACKGROUND MUSIC: none.
LOCATION: 2 miles S of town.
CHILDREN: all ages welcomed.
DOGS: allowed by arrangement, not in public rooms.
CREDIT CARDS: none.
PRICES: [2015] per person B&B €55. Set dinner €40.

MARLFIELD HOUSE

Imposing gates open on to a wooded drive through the extensive grounds of the Bowe family's Regency mansion (once the Irish residence of the earls of Courtown). Sisters Margaret and Laura Bowe preside in their 'much-loved' building, which they run as a luxurious country house hotel (Relais & Châteaux). It is furnished in grand style with period pieces and mirrors, open fires, paintings, huge floral displays. The bedrooms have equally sumptuous furnishings: antiques, dramatic wallpaper and curtains, a marble bathroom. A large ground-floor room has French windows opening on to the lovely grounds. The formal dining room has a domed conservatory. The kitchen gardens supply much of the seasonal produce for the menus of chef Ruadhan Furlong: in spring perhaps pink rhubarb, rosemary, thyme and wild garlic; meat and fish are sourced from Wexford farms and Kilmore Quay. New in 2015 is The Duck (a terrace, restaurant, bar and shop), which offers more informal meals from Wednesday to Sunday (11.30 am to 9.30 pm). Surplus garden produce is used for a range of jams, chutneys, marmalade and dressings which can be purchased.

25% DISCOUNT VOUCHERS

Courtown Road
Gorey

T: 00 353 53 942 1124
F: 00 353 53 942 1572
E: info@marlfieldhouse.ie
W: www.marlfieldhouse.com

BEDROOMS: 19. 8 on ground floor.
OPEN: Feb–Dec except Christmas, restaurant closed Mon/Tues in Mar/Apr, Oct–Dec.
FACILITIES: reception hall, drawing room, library/bar, restaurant with conservatory, The Duck restaurant/bar/shop, free Wi-Fi in most areas, wedding facilities, 36-acre grounds (gardens, tennis, croquet, wildfowl reserve, lake).
BACKGROUND MUSIC: none.
LOCATION: 1 mile E of Gorey.
CHILDREN: no under-8s at dinner, high tea provided, babysitting available.
DOGS: not allowed in public rooms.
CREDIT CARDS: all major cards.
PRICES: [2015] per person B&B €105–€335, D,B&B €150–€399. Set dinner €64. 1-night bookings sometimes refused Sat.

RAYANNE HOUSE

There is an Art Deco motif in the public rooms of Conor and Bernadette McClelland's 'very individualistic' guest house. A Victorian former merchant's mansion, it stands in large gardens near Belfast. Furniture and ornaments, including a 'fabulous collection of Clarice Cliff', were inherited from Conor's parents, along with their B&B, which the McClellands have taken to a new level, adding an extension. The bedrooms, reached by 'wide landings and sweeping stairs', are smart and contemporary, bathrooms are 'superb'. With the golf course just minutes' walk away, and discounted green fees for Rayanne's guests, the Rory McIlroy room has a golf-themed bathroom in honour of Holywood's famous son. Some rooms face Belfast Lough, from which the Titanic set sail. Chef Conor McClelland serves a seasonal menu for residents, by arrangement, with dishes like herb-encrusted County Down lamb tenderloin, mint, Beaujolais reduction. The 'Titanic Menu' recreates a nine-course feast served to first-class passengers aboard the liner. At breakfast, there are 'out of this world' County Down kippers, boiled organic eggs with Parmesan breadsticks, sausages made to the host's own recipe.

60 Demesne Road
Holywood
BT18 9EX

T: 028 9042 5859
F: 028 9042 5859
E: info@rayannehouse.com
W: www.rayannehouse.com

BEDROOMS: 10. 1, on ground floor, suitable for disabled.
OPEN: all year, 'limited service' Christmas/New Year.
FACILITIES: 2 lounges, dining room, free Wi-Fi, conference facilities, 1-acre grounds.
BACKGROUND MUSIC: light jazz in dining room.
LOCATION: ½ mile from Holywood town centre, 6 miles to Belfast centre.
CHILDREN: all ages welcomed.
DOGS: not allowed.
CREDIT CARDS: Amex, MasterCard, Visa.
PRICES: [2015] per room B&B single £80–£90, double £120–£140. Set menus £35–£69, à la carte £35.

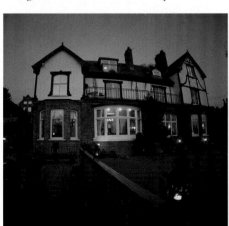

LETTERFRACK Co. Galway

Map 6:C4

ROSLEAGUE MANOR

🏆César award in 2010

On the shores of Ballinakill Bay, this pink-washed
Regency manor house is owned by Mark Foyle.
'I like everything about it,' says its greatest fan
this year, 'the house itself, the setting, the staff,
and the relaxed way in which Mark Foyle runs
it.' The bedrooms are large and individually
furnished, many with lough views. 'I was again in
Room 6. The bathroom has been refitted, with
a slipper bath, a separate shower cubicle, and
a spectacular mirror bordered with seashells.'
There are paintings, antiques, peat fires. The
'magical' conservatory bar opens on to a
courtyard. The gardens are planted with rare
shrubs. Emmanuel Neu cooks 'unfussy' dishes
in 'French country house' style, specialising in
seafood and Leenane Mountain lamb. Praise this
year for turbot, forest mushrooms, lentils; hake
with red and yellow pepper julienne. Service,
in a 'glorious' dining room lit by chandeliers,
although always 'charming', is 'now sharper and
better managed'. Breakfast has 'some unusual
touches' such as garden rhubarb, devilled
kidneys and freshly baked scones. 'Mark
genuinely loves Rosleague, and his stewardship
reflects the depth of his affection.' (Ann Walden)

Letterfrack

T: 00 353 95 41101
F: 00 353 95 41168
E: info@rosleague.com
W: www.rosleague.com

BEDROOMS: 21. 2 on ground floor.
OPEN: Mid-Mar–mid-Nov.
FACILITIES: 2 drawing rooms,
conservatory/bar, dining room, free
Wi-Fi, wedding facilities, 25-acre
grounds (tennis), unsuitable for
disabled.
BACKGROUND MUSIC: none.
LOCATION: 7 miles NE of Clifden.
CHILDREN: all ages welcomed.
DOGS: 'well-behaved dogs' allowed.
CREDIT CARDS: MasterCard, Visa.
PRICES: [2015] per person B&B
€70–€105, D,B&B €95–€135. Set
dinner €34–€48. 1-night bookings
sometimes refused.

NO. 1 PERY SQUARE

The owner, Patricia Roberts, has made changes this year to her popular hotel, an extended Grade I listed townhouse, wrapped around a corner in one of Limerick's finest Georgian terraces. A 'facelift' has seen the guest reception moved, and the refurbishment of the first-floor restaurant, now named Sash. Frederic Duarte has been brought in as chef to oversee the creation of seasonal menus reflecting the period in which the house was built, with modern twists. They use herbs and leaves from the kitchen garden. Typical dishes: mussels with ham hock, artisan cider sauce; chicken, pork and herb stuffing, colcannon, thyme jus. The building retains such fine original features as plaster mouldings and marble fireplaces. Morning coffee, afternoon tea and 'light bites' are served in the Park Room lounge bar. Four bedrooms in the main house are in elegant period style. The modern Club Rooms, overlooking the hotel garden or the Georgian streetscape, are named after Irish poets. Breakfast has freshly squeezed orange juice; the usual cooked offerings, an artisan cheese and charcuterie plate. We would welcome reports on the changes.

Georgian Quarter
1 Pery Square
Limerick

T: 00 353 61 402402
F: 00 353 61 313060
E: info@oneperysquare.com
W: www.oneperysquare.com

BEDROOMS: 20. 2 suitable for disabled.
OPEN: all year except 24 Dec evening, 25/26 Dec, restaurant closed Mon.
FACILITIES: lounge, drawing room, bar, restaurant, private dining room, free Wi-Fi, wedding facilities, terrace, basement spa.
BACKGROUND MUSIC: various in public areas.
LOCATION: central.
CHILDREN: all ages welcomed.
DOGS: not allowed.
CREDIT CARDS: all major cards.
PRICES: [2015] per person B&B from €82.50, D,B&B from €99. Set menus €25–€29, à la carte €45.

SHEEDY'S

For three generations, the Sheedy family has run this small hotel/restaurant on the edge of a town in the Burren best known for its annual matchmaking festival. Today it is run by John Sheedy and his wife, Martina. 'The combination of her management and his cooking is formidable,' says a visitor this year. 'We liked the warmth of her welcome, and the tea and home-made biscuits she offered when we checked in.' There is a 'feeling of well-being over a pre-dinner drink' in the light-filled conservatory at the front of the building. The host 'works his magic on quality local ingredients' in 'perhaps over-generous' dishes like crab claws in garlic and parsley cream; roast rack of lamb, slow-cooked lamb belly, spinach. The bedrooms have a traditional decor: 'Our room was spacious; the bathroom had twin basins, a separate shower, abundant hot water and excellent towels.' There is home-made brown and banana breads and preserves at a buffet-free breakfast. The cooked options include 'something a little different', perhaps goat's cheese, cucumber and tomato. 'You won't find a better Irish fried breakfast.' (Andrew Wardrop)

Sheedys Hotel
Lisdoonvarna

T: 00 353 65 707 4026
F: 00 353 65 707 4555
E: info@sheedys.com
W: www.sheedys.com

BEDROOMS: 11. Some on ground floor, 1 suitable for disabled.
OPEN: Apr–Sept, closed 1 day a week in April.
FACILITIES: ramp, sitting room/library, sun lounge, bar, restaurant, free Wi-Fi, ½-acre garden (rose garden).
BACKGROUND MUSIC: classical at breakfast, light jazz at dinner.
LOCATION: in town 20 miles SW of Galway.
CHILDREN: all ages welcomed.
DOGS: not allowed.
CREDIT CARDS: MasterCard, Visa.
PRICES: [2015] per room B&B €110–€180. À la carte €47. 1-night bookings sometimes refused Sept.

VIEWMOUNT HOUSE `NEW`

On the outskirts of town, beside the golf course, Beryl and James Kearney's beautifully restored Georgian house was once property of the Barons Longford. Today it is run as an 'extremely comfortable, well-appointed' hotel. It earns an upgrade to a main entry after a period without feedback, thanks to a positive report from regular correspondents. 'Beryl Kearney is an excellent, friendly and incredibly hard-working host.' There are period furnishings and features throughout, with a vaulted sitting room and breakfast room, flagstone and timber floors, open fires. The candlelit VM restaurant in the old stables was 'packed with locals – clearly a place to go for a celebration'. Chef Gary O'Hanlon brings a modern twist to classic dishes. 'The early bird menu was good value with large portions. Delicious amuse-bouche, creamy vegetable soup, pork-cheek and salad starter; wonderfully presented salmon and chicken main courses; always a separate dish of veggies, including the best mashed potato ever.' Individually styled bedrooms face the landscaped gardens. At breakfast there are 'the freshest eggs, cooked by Beryl's husband'. (Mary and Rodney Milne-Day)

Dublin Road
Longford

T: 00 353 43 334 1919
E: viewmt@iol.ie
W: www.viewmounthouse.com

BEDROOMS: 12. 7 in modern extension, some on ground floor.
OPEN: all year except 25 Oct–4 Nov, restaurant closed Mon/Tues, 25/26 Dec.
FACILITIES: reception room, library, sitting room, breakfast room, restaurant, free Wi-Fi, wedding facilities, 4-acre grounds.
BACKGROUND MUSIC: none.
LOCATION: 1 mile E of town centre.
CHILDREN: all ages welcomed.
DOGS: not allowed.
CREDIT CARDS: Amex, MasterCard, Visa.
PRICES: [2015] per person €70–€85, D,B&B from €130. Set dinner €60 (early bird €35).

MAGHERALIN Co. Armagh

NEWFORGE HOUSE

🏵César award in 2015

There is a youthful vibrancy about John and Louise Mathers's 'beautiful' guest house in a converted Georgian home that has passed through six generations since 1840. John Mathers spent an 'idyllic' childhood here, with 50 acres as his playground. In 2003, he and his wife began a programme of renovation. Original features have been preserved; there are heirloom antiques throughout – pictures, tapestries, clocks and ornaments. The bedrooms recall the six Mathers wives to have lived here. 'Beaumont' (Louise's maiden name) is styled with tweeds and suede; the bathroom has a marble floor, roll-top bath and walk-in shower. Hanna has a king-size four-poster, and a fireplace in the bathroom. John Mathers cooks a daily-changing seasonal menu, which might include 'fantastic' organic beef dry-aged in Europe's first salt chamber; roast monkfish, mussels, leek cider broth; home-grown produce from the vegetable garden tended by John's father. At breakfast there's apple juice, eggs from the hens in the orchard, oak-smoked kippers, pancakes, the 'traditional Ulster' with black and white pudding, soda and potato breads. 'A gem.' 'Excellent in every way.'

58 Newforge Road
Magheralin
BT67 0QL

T: 028 9261 1255
E: enquiries@newforgehouse.com
W: www.newforgehouse.com

BEDROOMS: 6.
OPEN: Feb–Dec.
FACILITIES: drawing room, dining room, free Wi-Fi, wedding facilities, 2-acre gardens (vegetable garden, orchard) in 50 acres of pastureland, unsuitable for disabled.
BACKGROUND MUSIC: none.
LOCATION: edge of village, 5 miles E of Craigavon.
CHILDREN: not under 10 (except for under-1s).
DOGS: not allowed.
CREDIT CARDS: MasterCard, Visa.
PRICES: [2015] per person B&B £60–£90. Set menu £40.

ROUNDWOOD HOUSE

At their handsome family home, a Palladian villa at the foot of the Slieve Bloom Mountains, Paddy and Hannah Flynn welcome guests in relaxed house-party style. 'Lovely people', they might be joined by a welcoming committee of pets to greet visitors, who are offered tea and home-made biscuits by a log fire in the drawing room, which has 'an intimate feel, with sofas and chairs grouped together'. 'Think of dining as going to a dinner party with friends you haven't met yet,' says Paddy Flynn, who cooks dishes with local and seasonal ingredients on a five-course menu. It is generally taken communally (you can opt to eat privately in the study). A simpler three-course supper is usually available; or an option to take a bowl of soup with an artisan cheese platter. A separate tea can be prepared for children. The bedrooms in the main house are spacious; smaller rooms in the Yellow House (an older building) face a walled garden. Breakfast has a generous sideboard with breads, yogurt, muesli and fruit compote (all home-made); 'superb mushrooms on toast with blue cheese'.

Mountrath

T: 00 353 57 873 2120
F: n/a
E: info@roundwoodhouse.com
W: www.roundwoodhouse.com

BEDROOMS: 10. 4 in garden building.
OPEN: all year except Christmas.
FACILITIES: drawing room, study/library, dining room, playroom, table tennis room, free Wi-Fi, wedding facilities, 18-acre grounds (garden, woodland), golf, walking, river fishing nearby, unsuitable for disabled.
BACKGROUND MUSIC: none.
LOCATION: 3 miles N of village.
CHILDREN: all ages welcomed.
DOGS: not allowed.
CREDIT CARDS: all major cards.
PRICES: [2015] per person B&B €75. Supper €35 (Sun/Mon), set dinner (Tues–Sat) €55.

MORNINGTON HOUSE

In parkland and gardens, in a landscape of lakes and gentle hills, this early 18th-century country house has been home to the O'Hara family since 1858. It was remodelled in 1896, and is run today in house-party spirit by Warwick and Anne O'Hara. On chilly days a fire burns in the drawing room where guests take afternoon tea and home-made cakes on arrival, and gather for aperitifs. Much of the furniture is original and antique; there are fresh flowers, paintings, family photographs. A corner bedroom was typically 'very comfortable, good quality, spotless', with 'cotton bedlinen and fluffy duvet (lovely!)'. The 'modern' bathroom had L'Occitane products and a walk-in shower. A four-course evening meal is taken communally at 8 pm, by prior arrangement, at the large oak table in the dining room, set with silver candelabras. Anne O'Hara cooks modern, seasonal Irish dishes (rack of lamb, say, or braised beef) using produce from the walled garden (sea kale, four varieties of bean, wild sorrel). At breakfast there are home-made jams and nut bread, freshly squeezed orange juice, hot food cooked to order by Warwick O'Hara.

Multyfarnham

T: 00 353 44 937 2191
F: 00 353 44 937 2338
E: stay@mornington.ie
W: www.mornington.ie

BEDROOMS: 4.
OPEN: Apr–Oct, dinner Mon–Sat with 24 hours' notice.
FACILITIES: drawing room, dining room, free Wi-Fi, ¾-acre garden, 50-acre grounds (croquet, bicycle hire), unsuitable for disabled.
BACKGROUND MUSIC: none.
LOCATION: 9 miles NW of Mullingar.
CHILDREN: all ages welcomed.
DOGS: not allowed in house.
CREDIT CARDS: all major cards.
PRICES: [2015] per person B&B €75, D,B&B €120. Set dinner €45.

CURRAREVAGH HOUSE

♔ César award in 1992

'Don't expect TV or sumptuous bedrooms with a walk-in shower' at this Victorian manor in wooded parkland bordering Lough Corrib. 'Just a real break from whatever it was that was bugging you before you arrived.' The house has been run as a hotel by the Hodgson family since 1890. Manager Henry Hodgson is 'a warm and attentive host', his wife, Lucy, 'as master chef makes each meal a delight'. Henry's mother, June, meets and greets. 'A throwback to earlier more gracious days', Currarevagh is 'old-fashioned', with sheets and blankets on the beds in the spacious bedrooms, while an 'Edwardian' breakfast includes freshly squeezed orange juice, home-baked soda bread, local sausages, honey-roast ham, and cheeses. A gong summons diners for a no-choice, four-course menu of 'Irish country house' dishes with a modern spin. Pan-fried mackerel with pistachio crust, beetroot, shallot and apple salad; roast rump of beef, romesco, Maris Peer chips, roast root vegetables. 'Afternoon tea is a delight', the atmosphere in the drawing room is 'convivial'. With so many trees, lough views are at a premium. (Mark Delargy, Richard Parish, Esler Crawford)

25% DISCOUNT VOUCHERS

Oughterard

T: 00 353 91 552312
F: 00 353 91 552731
E: mail@currarevagh.com
W: www.currarevagh.com

BEDROOMS: 12.
OPEN: 17 Mar–31 Oct.
FACILITIES: sitting room/hall, drawing room, library/bar with TV, dining room, free Wi-Fi, 180-acre grounds (lake, fishing, ghillies available, boating, swimming, tennis, croquet), golf, riding nearby, unsuitable for disabled.
BACKGROUND MUSIC: none.
LOCATION: 4 miles NW of Oughterard.
CHILDREN: all ages welcomed.
DOGS: not in public rooms.
CREDIT CARDS: Amex, MasterCard, Visa.
PRICES: per person B&B €70–€90, D,B&B €105–€130. Set dinner €48.

RATHMULLAN HOUSE

A Georgian country house, extended and remodelled in the 1870s, this hotel on the sandy shores of Lough Swilly has been run by the same family since Bob Wheeler and his wife, Robin, took it on in 1962. With the house came Seamus, the donkey, who would carry guests' bags from the pier, and plough the walled garden. Today Mark and Mary Wheeler are in charge. Public rooms retain original features such as marble fireplaces, and have ample seating, open fires, books and paintings. In a 1990s wing, 'spacious and comfortable' bedrooms at ground level have French doors and a patio. Bedrooms in the main building are furnished with carefully chosen antiques. Meals are served in the Cook and Gardener restaurant, which has a 'tented' ceiling, views of the lough. Chef Micheál Harley sources local ingredients, with fresh produce from the walled kitchen garden, perhaps cod, landed at Greencastle, leek velouté, spinach, braised Puy lentils; 30-day-aged Irish beef, potato gratin, roast salsify, red wine jus. Along with cooked dishes, the 'extensive' breakfast buffet has 'interesting home-baked breads' and home-made jams.

Rathmullan

T: 00 353 74 915 8188
F: 00 353 74 915 8200
E: info@rathmullanhouse.com
W: www.rathmullanhouse.com

BEDROOMS: 34. Some on ground floor, 2 suitable for disabled.
OPEN: Feb–Dec, 27 Dec–3 Jan.
FACILITIES: ramps, 4 sitting rooms, library, TV room, cellar bar/bistro, restaurant, free Wi-Fi, 15-metre indoor swimming pool, 7-acre grounds (tennis, croquet).
BACKGROUND MUSIC: none.
LOCATION: ½ mile N of village.
CHILDREN: all ages welcomed.
DOGS: welcomed, allowed in 1 bedroom, but not in public rooms.
CREDIT CARDS: Amex, MasterCard, Visa.
PRICES: [2015] per person B&B €80–€125. À la carte €45. 1-night bookings sometimes refused.

COOPERSHILL

♫César award in 1987

'It was a privilege to be welcomed into the easy grandeur and graciousness of a small stately home in more than 200 years of continuous occupation.' Guide readers enjoyed 'immensely' a visit in 2015 to Simon O'Hara's Georgian mansion which has been owned by seven generations of his family. There are details that 'no hotel furnisher could simulate': busts in niches in the hallway, paintings and original furniture. The stairway is a stags' Valhalla. Simon O'Hara's partner, chef Christina McCauley, trained at Ballymaloe House, Shanagarry (see entry), and prepares a four-course dinner. 'We were the only guests on our first night, so dined in some state, with log fires in both lounge and dining room, and O'Hara ancestors looking down from their portraits. Other nights brought in further guests and conversation was natural and flowed easily. We ate all too well. Simon and Christina are rightly proud of all their home-made, home-grown and locally sourced food.' There are no locks on the doors of the spacious bedrooms; each has a modern en suite bathroom. 'Simon was helpful in advising on excursions.' (Charles Goldie)

25% DISCOUNT VOUCHERS

Riverstown

T: 00 353 71 916 5108
E: ohara@coopershill.com
W: www.coopershill.com

BEDROOMS: 8.
OPEN: Apr–Oct, off-season house parties by arrangement.
FACILITIES: hall, drawing room, dining room, snooker room, free Wi-Fi, wedding facilities, 500-acre estate (garden, tennis, croquet, woods, farmland, river with trout fishing), unsuitable for disabled.
BACKGROUND MUSIC: none.
LOCATION: 11 miles SE of Sligo.
CHILDREN: no children under 12.
DOGS: by arrangement, not unattended in bedrooms, not in public rooms.
CREDIT CARDS: MasterCard, Visa.
PRICES: [2015] per person B&B €99–€122. Set dinner €54.

GROVE HOUSE

'Charming' Swedish owner Katarina Runske welcomes guests to her Victorian house overlooking the harbour, very much as to her family home. Should you want piano lessons, she can teach you – on the baby grand in the dining room. 'We received a friendly welcome with tea and chocolate cake,' says a visitor this year. In the conservatory restaurant, which 'has the ambience of a café with its patterned tablecloths', Katarina Runske's son, Nico, cooks a three-course set dinner with a distinct French accent – moules marinière, rack of lamb Provençal, sole meunière – using seasonal local produce and vegetables from the garden. 'Delicious' and 'good value'. The bedrooms are spacious, with pine floor, books, paintings by local artists. A 'good, well-presented breakfast, no buffet, served by a friendly waitress'. Grove House is proud of its literary associations: GB Shaw, Jack Butler Yeats (brother of the more famous WB) and Edith Somerville are among past guests. The arty ethos continues with occasional music recitals and writers' retreats. The house is 'conveniently located on the edge of the village, with easy parking'. (Elser Crawford)

Colla Road
Schull

T: 00 353 28 28067
F: 00 353 28 28069
E: info@grovehouseschull.com
W: www.grovehouseschull.com

BEDROOMS: 5.
OPEN: Mar–Oct, restaurant closed Sun.
FACILITIES: TV room, sitting room, dining room, free Wi-Fi, wedding facilities, terrace, 2-acre garden, unsuitable for disabled.
BACKGROUND MUSIC: classical and 'casual' in dining room.
LOCATION: outskirts of village.
CHILDREN: all ages welcomed.
DOGS: welcomed, on lead in house.
CREDIT CARDS: MasterCard, Visa.
PRICES: [2015] per room B&B single €40–€65, double €70–€90. Set dinner €30.

BALLYMALOE HOUSE

♀César award in 1984

Since she launched her restaurant more than 50 years ago, Myrtle Allen's Ballymaloe has become a legend and a brand. The venture grew out of the farm that she ran with her late husband, Ivan, espousing the values of 'seasonal, local, organic, home grown'. The house is late Georgian, grafted on to remains of a Norman castle. The farm and garden still supply the table. Myrtle remains a part of it, although her daughters-in-law, Hazel and Darina, respectively, manage the hotel and run the famous cookery school. A 'timeless', 'hospitable' atmosphere. Guests eat in one of the 'cheerful' dining rooms, choosing from five-course menus cooked by chef Gillian Hegarty. Friday night starts with an hors d'oeuvre buffet with fresh shellfish, garden salads, home-made pâtés; on Sunday night, a buffet dinner 'prepared by the Allen family' has 'prime cuts' of local beef, lamb and pork. Bedrooms tend to the pretty and feminine, with fresh flowers, and handmade Ballymaloe soap in the bathroom – several upgraded this year, with a walk-in shower. 'The best place in the world to be,' said a reader.

25% DISCOUNT VOUCHERS

Shanagarry

T: 00 353 21 465 2531
F: 00 353 21 465 2021
E: res@ballymaloe.ie
W: www.ballymaloe.ie

BEDROOMS: 29. 9 in adjacent building, 4 on ground floor, 5 self-catering cottages suitable for disabled.
OPEN: all year except 24–26 Dec, 6 Jan–1 Feb.
FACILITIES: drawing room, 2 small sitting rooms, conservatory, 7 dining rooms, free Wi-Fi, wedding and conference facilities, 6-acre gardens, 400-acre grounds (tennis, swimming pool, 10 by 4 metres), cookery school nearby.
BACKGROUND MUSIC: none.
LOCATION: 20 miles E of Cork.
CHILDREN: all ages welcomed.
DOGS: allowed in 3 rooms with porch, not in public rooms.
CREDIT CARDS: Amex, MasterCard, Visa.
PRICES: [to April 2016] per person B&B €100–€145. Set lunch €40–€45, dinner €50–€70.

INCH HOUSE

NEW

Rescued from near dereliction, this imposing three-storey Georgian mansion on a working farm is run as a 'country house and restaurant' by the 'charming' Egan family. It returns to the Guide after a period without reports, on the recommendation of a trusted correspondent. The venture is a 'labour of love' for the family: father, John Egan, and son Joseph run the farm. John's wife, Nora, runs the house with daughter Mairin Byrne (manager). 'Mairin was not put out when we arrived a day early. She took us straight to our room and served us tea and home-made cake. To work this off we took advantage of a walk fashioned through the grounds by the family's engineer son.' The house has a 'magnificent' divided staircase; rugs on wooden floors; a 'comfortable clutter' of furniture. In the large dining room (popular with locals), chef John Barry's four-course dinner is 'a hearty affair, with helpings to suit a trencherman'. Breakfast has 'lots of fruit, porridge with honey and cream, excellent home-baked bread'. (Esler Crawford)

Bouladuff
Nenagh Road
Thurles

T: 00 353 504 51348
E: info@inchhouse.ie
W: www.inchhouse.ie

BEDROOMS: 5.
OPEN: all year except Christmas/New Year, dining room closed Sun and Mon night.
FACILITIES: drawing room, restaurant, free Wi-Fi in public areas, wedding facilities, 4-acre garden in 250-acre farm, unsuitable for disabled.
BACKGROUND MUSIC: Irish in evening in dining room.
LOCATION: 4 miles NW of Thurles on R498 to Nenagh.
CHILDREN: all ages welcomed.
DOGS: not allowed.
CREDIT CARDS: MasterCard, Visa.
PRICES: [2015] per room €90, D,B&B €140.

SHORTLIST

The Shortlist complements our main section by including potential but untested new entries and appropriate places in areas where we have limited choice. It also has some hotels that have been full entries in the Guide, but have not attracted feedback from our readers.

Three Choirs Vineyards, Newent

Map 2:D4

THE ALMA, 499 Old York Road, SW18 1TF. Tel 020 8870 2537, www. almawandsworth.com. In a former metalworks down a cobbled alley, this remarkably peaceful modern inn has a popular local bar, and comfortable bedrooms in a courtyard annexe. It is run on green lines: solar panels provide energy for hot water and electricity; lights and electrical appliances are programmed to work only when guests are indoors. The Victorian pub (Young & Co's Brewery) has cask ales and beers from local breweries; chef Imants Erbreiders serves gastropub classics in the light, modern dining room at the back of the busy bar. Spacious bedrooms, decorated with bold wallpaper and bespoke furniture, are equipped with a safe, iPod docking station, iron and ironing board; a garden suite has a private terrace with outdoor seating. Breakfast is served until 11 am on weekends. Bar, restaurant (Sunday roasts), function room. Free Wi-Fi. Background music. Civil wedding licence. Use of Virgin spa and gym nearby. Children welcomed (cots). 23 bedrooms (2 on ground floor suitable for disabled). Per room B&B from £139. Dinner £30. (Opposite Wandsworth Town railway station; 15 mins to Waterloo)

THE AMPERSAND, 10 Harrington Road, SW7 3ER. Tel 020 7589 5895, www. ampersandhotel.com. Inspired by the Royal Albert Hall and museums nearby, the rooms and suites in this renovated Victorian building have been given refreshing modern design themes relating to botany, geometry, ornithology, astronomy and music. The hotel has a welcoming ambience, with 'laid-back' staff; Roberto Pajares is the manager. The high-ceilinged bedrooms (some small; 16 allow smoking) have an oversized bedhead, and velvet fabrics; there are free soft drinks in the minibar. Modern Mediterranean dishes are served in the white-tiled basement restaurant, Apero; light meals and afternoon tea are taken in the drawing rooms. Bar, drawing rooms, restaurant, business centre; private dining room. Games room (table tennis), gym; running guides and information on activities in Hyde Park (horse riding, inline skating) available. Free Wi-Fi. Contemporary background music. Lifts. Children (cots) and dogs welcomed. Public parking nearby (reservation required). 111 bedrooms and suites (some suitable for disabled). Room only from £174. À la carte breakfast £14. Dinner £32. (Underground: South Kensington)

THE ARCH LONDON, 50 Great Cumberland Place, W1H 7FD. Tel 020 7724 4700, www.thearchlondon. com. On a pleasingly quiet street near busy Marble Arch, this colourful modern hotel is liked for its 'excellent' restaurant, 'unfailingly helpful' staff and 'well-thought-through details'. It is owned by the Bejerano family. A sympathetic conversion of seven Georgian town houses and two mews homes, 'it has an intimate feel for its size'. Stylish, 'comprehensively equipped' bedrooms have hand-printed wallpaper, original sash windows and the latest technology; modern dishes are served in the informal open-plan brasserie. 'We received superb service and splendid food every evening,

from a small but comprehensive menu.'
Bar, brasserie, library (afternoon tea,
cocktails), champagne salon; gym.
Free Wi-Fi. Background music. Valet
parking. Children and dogs welcomed.
82 bedrooms (2 suitable for disabled). Per
room from £250. Breakfast £18.50–£21.50.
Dinner £54. (Underground: Marble Arch)
25% **DISCOUNT VOUCHERS**

BERMONDSEY SQUARE HOTEL,
Bermondsey Square, Tower Bridge
Road, SE1 3UN. Tel 020 7378 2450,
www.bermondseysquarehotel.co.uk.
On the square in a 'happening' area, this
modern, privately owned hotel has a lively
interior. 'Reasonably sized' bedrooms
have a wet room and 'a comfortable bed
with plenty of pillows and cushions';
some rooms have views of the Shard.
GB Grill & Bar serves a short menu of
'uncomplicated' British food all day;
there are tables and chairs outside for
alfresco dining. The continental breakfast
has yogurts, 'reasonable' coffee, a 'good'
fruit salad. No alcohol is served; guests
may bring their own alcoholic drinks for
consumption in the room. City bike hire
adjacent; well placed for Borough Market
and walks across Tower Bridge. Business
functions. Lift. Free Wi-Fi. Background
music. In-house tailor service. Children
and dogs welcomed (boutique dog beds).
80 bedrooms (5 suites; family rooms;
4 suitable for disabled). Room only
from £114. Continental breakfast £9.95.
(Underground: Bermondsey, Tower Hill)

THE BULL & THE HIDE, 4 Devonshire
Row, EC2M 4RH. Tel 020 7655 4805,
www.thebullandthehide.com. On a
narrow, pedestrianised street in the busy
City of London, this refurbished modern
inn stands on a site that was once a Tudor

dwelling, and subsequently a tavern. It is
part of Richard Balfour-Lynn's Cunning
Plan Pub Company; James Minnis is the
manager. Guests check in at the copper-
fronted bar in the lively pub; upstairs, sleek
bedrooms have metallic finish, glossy fabrics,
and a bathroom with underfloor heating;
some early-morning street noise. A well-
stocked pantry has complimentary coffee
and tea. Refined modern dishes are served
in the elegant Hide restaurant; classic pub
food is available in the bar throughout the
day. Breakfast in the pub includes a selection
of egg and bacon butties. Bar, restaurant
(closed Sat lunch, Sun). Private dining. Free
Wi-Fi and local telephone calls. Background
music. 7 bedrooms. Room only from
£180. Breakfast £7.95. Dinner £35. Closed
Christmas. (Underground: Liverpool Street)

CHARLOTTE STREET HOTEL, 15–17
Charlotte Street, W1T 1RJ. Tel 020
7806 2000, www.firmdalehotels.com. In
Fitzrovia, this stylish hotel pays homage
to the Bloomsbury group, with flashes
of artistic exuberance, and original
paintings by Vanessa Bell, Duncan
Grant, Roger Fry and other famous
British artists of the period. Part of Tim
and Kit Kemp's Firmdale group, it has
the feel of a private home. Bedrooms are
decorated with cheery prints and fabrics;
each has a writing desk, a flat-screen
TV, an iPod dock, and a handsome
bathroom in granite and oak. The staff
are 'attentive, pleasant and helpful' in
the 'bright' open-plan restaurant, which
serves food all day; a room-service
menu is also available. Children are well
provided with books and board games,
DVDs, mini bathrobes, a welcome
gift, milk and cookies at bedtime. A
small cinema in the basement screens
current films and classics on Sunday

evenings. Within walking distance of the West End theatres. Drawing room, library, Oscar bar, restaurant. 3 private dining/meeting rooms; 75-seat screening room; gym. Ramp. Free Wi-Fi. No background music. Civil wedding licence. Children (cot, high chair, special cutlery, babysitting) and small dogs (by arrangement) welcomed. 52 bedrooms (family rooms; some suitable for disabled). Room only from £264. Breakfast £18–£30. Dinner £25–£34. (Underground: Goodge Street, Tottenham Court Road)

CITIZENM, 20 Lavington Street, SE1 0NZ. Tel 020 3519 1680, www.citizenm.com. Close to Tate Modern, this contemporary hotel represents 'excellent value for money'. It is part of an international chain of stylish budget hotels that cater for 'mobile citizens'. Service is minimalist: guests check themselves in and show themselves to their room; staff, when needed, are 'friendly and helpful'. 'Spotlessly clean' modular bedrooms have a large bed against a floor-to-ceiling window, a television (free movies on demand), a fridge, a shower room; lighting, room temperature, window blinds and TV are controlled via a touch-screen tablet. Filled with modern art, Vitra furniture and Apple iMacs, the vast lobby and open-plan bar and canteen serve as working and lounging space. Breakfast has 'divine', freshly squeezed clementine juice and 'probably the best breakfast coffee I can remember'. Open-plan lobby/bar/deli/work stations/seating areas. Meeting rooms. Lift. Free Wi-Fi. Children welcomed. 192 bedrooms (12 suitable for disabled). Room only £109–£229. Breakfast from £12.50.

Registered 'Citizens' receive the best available rate and a complimentary drink on arrival. (Underground: London Bridge, Southwark)

THE CONNAUGHT, Carlos Place, W1K 2AL. Tel 020 7499 7070, www.the-connaught.co.uk. On a peaceful corner in Mayfair, this revamped and restored late-Victorian luxury hotel retains many of its lavish period features, and a commitment to the standards of a bygone era. Part of the Maybourne Hotel Group, it is managed by Nathalie Seiler-Hayez. A grand staircase leads to the newly refurbished, classically styled bedrooms; sleeker, more modern rooms are in the new wing. Decorated in soft colours, they have Italian bedlinen, cashmere blankets and state-of-the-art technology; a marble bathroom. Many have views across the London skyline. In the elegant wood-panelled restaurant, Hélène Darroze has two Michelin stars for her fine French cooking (excellent vegetarian options); less formal meals, and afternoon tea, are taken in Espelette brasserie. 2 bars, 2 restaurants. Art Deco-style ballroom. Swimming pool; fitness centre. Spa (treatments). Moon Garden. Room service; butler service. Free Wi-Fi. Background music. Children welcomed (games, treats, amenities, bathrobes and slippers; baby monitors; babysitting by arrangement). 119 bedrooms (30 in new wing; some suitable for disabled). Room only from £480. Breakfast £29. (Underground: Bond Street)

COUNTY HALL PREMIER INN, Belvedere Road, SE1 7PB. Tel 0871 527 8648, www.premierinn.com. Steps away from many London landmarks, this good-value hotel occupies the historic Portland stone County Hall building on the banks of the Thames. Sea Life London Aquarium and the London Dungeon are in the same building; the attractions of the South Bank are five minutes' walk away. The simply furnished bedrooms have a desk, tea- and coffee-making facilities, a basic bathroom; double-glazing minimises street noise. Self-service check-in. Busy at breakfast. Lobby, bar, Thyme restaurant; lift. Conferences. Wi-Fi (first half-hour free; subsequently £3 per 24 hours or £10 per 7 days). Background music. Children welcomed. 314 bedrooms (some suitable for disabled). Room only from £169. Meal deal (dinner and breakfast) £22.99 per person. (Underground: Waterloo)

Covent Garden Hotel, 10 Monmouth Street, WC2H 9HB. Tel 020 7806 1000, www.firmdalehotels.com. In the heart of Covent Garden, this characterful hotel (part of Tim and Kit Kemp's Firmdale group) has a theatrical air, with bright colours and clashing patterns. 'Distinctive', individually decorated bedrooms have an oversized bedhead; many have views of London's rooftops. Connecting rooms are available for families and groups. The wood-panelled drawing room and library have fresh flowers and a stone fireplace with a log-burning fire. A basement screening room hosts Saturday movie nights. Modern menus in Brasserie Max are also available for room service; breakfasts (extra charge) have a vast choice. Drawing room, library (honesty bar), restaurant. Meeting room; screening room; gym. Free Wi-Fi. No background music. Children (amenities, treats and activities) and small dogs (by arrangement) welcomed. Ramp. 58 bedrooms. Room only from £282. Breakfast £25. Dinner £25. (Underground: Covent Garden, Leicester Square)

Dorset Square Hotel, 39–40 Dorset Square, NW1 6QN. Tel 020 7723 7874, www.firmdalehotels.com. Overlooking a leafy garden square (the original site of Thomas Lord's first cricket ground), this Regency town house is decorated with a lively mix of colours, patterns and textiles. It is part of the Firmdale group owned by Tim and Kit Kemp. Individually styled bedrooms have a flat-screen TV and iPod docking station; many have garden views; some can be small. Afternoon tea, and drinks from the honesty bar are taken in the high-ceilinged ground-floor drawing room; English and Mediterranean-inspired brasserie dishes are served in the Potting Shed, a popular basement bar and restaurant. Children are welcomed with their own treats, toiletries and entertainment. Drawing room, brasserie. Lift. Ramps. Free Wi-Fi. No background music. Room service. DVD library. Civil wedding licence. Dogs welcomed, by arrangement. 38 bedrooms (1 suitable for disabled; 2 ideal for a family). Room only from £198. Continental breakfast buffet £10.50. (Underground: Marylebone)

Dukes London, 35 St James's Place, SW1A 1NY. Tel 020 7491 4840, www.dukeshotel.com. Members of the aristocracy once frequented this discreet town house hotel close to Clarence House and Buckingham Palace; today, it continues to be an intimate luxury hotel with peaceful bedrooms and suites, and a well-regarded restaurant serving modern British menus. Each bedroom has a marble bathroom; superior rooms also have a large wardrobe and extra seating. Once frequented by Ian Fleming who created James Bond, the legendary Dukes bar is renowned for its martinis. In Restaurant Thirty Six, chef Nigel Mendham cooks refined British dishes, including early dinner menus and Sunday brunches; afternoon tea is taken in the drawing room or conservatory. Hampers can be supplied for picnics in nearby Green Park, together with blankets, shrugs and a hot water bottle. Drawing room, Dukes bar, champagne lounge; conservatory, courtyard. Health club (steam room, gym, beauty treatments). Cognac and cigar garden. 24-hour room service. Civil wedding licence; function facilities. Free Wi-Fi. Background music. Children welcomed (treats and amenities). 90 bedrooms, 15 suites (1 suitable for disabled). Per room B&B from £330. Dinner £48. (Underground: Green Park)

41, 41 Buckingham Palace Road, SW1W 0PS. Tel 020 7300 0041, www.41hotel.com. There is a private club atmosphere at this discreet luxury hotel close to Buckingham Palace. On the fifth floor of a historic building (also home to sister hotel The Rubens at the Palace), it is part of the Red Carnation group. In public rooms of mahogany panelling and polished brass, guests are royally greeted with a glass of champagne by attentive staff; later, they are sent off with apples and bottles of water on departure. Decorated in a black-and-white theme, modern bedrooms have magazines, books, season-appropriate bathrobes; a plate of home-made treats is provided. Complimentary afternoon tea and canapés are taken in the lounge; guests are invited to 'plunder the pantry' and help themselves to light meals and snacks each evening until late. An extensive breakfast is served until 1 pm on Sundays. Room, and butler service. Free Wi-Fi. Background music. Business functions. Children and dogs welcomed. 30 bedrooms and suites. Per room B&B from £326. (Underground: Victoria)

GREAT NORTHERN HOTEL, Pancras Road, N1C 4TB. Tel 020 3388 0800, www.gnhlondon.com. 'Very well done.' Steps from the Eurostar terminus, in the regenerated King's Cross neighbourhood, this grand Victorian railway hotel has been transformed into an elegant luxury hotel with glamorous public spaces and sleek, modern bedrooms. It is managed by Jules Arlett. Designed in 1851 by master builder Lewis Cubitt (famous for King's Cross railway station), the dramatic, curving brick building has 'spacious' bedrooms reminiscent of railway carriage sleepers; each has a high ceiling, bespoke furniture, tall windows and good soundproofing; some rooms have dark walnut wood-panelled walls and vintage-style bathrooms. Guests help themselves to coffee, tea, biscuits, sweets and home-made cake in a pantry on each floor; there are also books, newspapers and magazines to borrow. Open all day, Mark Sargeant's lively Plum + Spilt Milk restaurant has 'excellent' food and service; an Art Deco bar provides light bites and cocktails. The hotel opens directly on to the Western concourse of King's Cross station; the Eurostar terminal at

St Pancras International is a few yards from the front door. 3 bars, restaurant, Kiosk food stall. Free Wi-Fi. Background music. Lift. 91 bedrooms (some suitable for disabled). Per room B&B from £208. Dinner £45. (Underground: King's Cross St Pancras, Euston)

HAM YARD HOTEL, 1 Ham Yard, W1D 7DT. Tel 020 3642 2000, www. firmdalehotels.com. The latest addition to Tim and Kit Kemp's Firmdale group, this large, modern hotel close to Piccadilly Circus wraps around a tree-filled courtyard whose grand centrepiece is an impressive bronze sculpture by the artist Tony Cragg. Kit Kemp has decorated the building in the eclectic, colourful style she is known for. The remarkable public spaces include a well-stocked library and, in the basement, a 1950s-style bowling alley. The roof terrace has upholstered seating and sweeping views over the city skyline; its garden is lush with apple and pear trees, and salads, herbs and vegetables grown for the restaurant's contemporary British menus. Large bedrooms have floor-to-ceiling windows overlooking the city or the leafy courtyard; each has a handsome bathroom in granite and oak. There is much choice at breakfast (charged separately), including an interesting selection of smoothies and freshly squeezed juices. Drawing room, library; theatre, bowling alley. Soholistic spa, gym. Lift. Rooftop terrace and garden. Free Wi-Fi. No background music. Valet parking (charge). Children welcomed (amenities, treats, entertainment). 91 rooms (6 suitable for disabled). Room only from £380. Cooked breakfast from £6. (Underground: Piccadilly Circus)

HAYMARKET HOTEL, 1 Suffolk Place, SW1Y 4HX. Tel 020 7470 4000, www. haymarkethotel.com. 'Beautifully furnished', this stylish hotel, part of Tim and Kit Kemp's Firmdale Hotels group, occupies three John Nash-designed buildings in lively Theatreland. It is managed by Lisa Brooklyn-Fuhres. Public rooms and bedrooms have spirited prints, striking sculptures, contemporary art and Kit Kemp's distinctive mix of antique and modern furnishings. Robin Reed, the chef, serves bistro food in the informal restaurant; drinks and small plates are taken in the chic cocktail bar. The 'stunning' indoor swimming pool has dramatic lighting and a pewter poolside bar. Lift. Conservatory, library, bar, Brumus restaurant. Indoor swimming pool, gym. Free Wi-Fi. No background music. Civil wedding licence. Children (amenities, treats and entertainment) and dogs (by arrangement) welcomed. 50 bedrooms (2 suites; 5-bedroom town house). Room only from £336. Breakfast £18.50–£28. (Underground: Green Park, Piccadilly)

THE HOXTON HOLBORN, 199–206 High Holborn, WC1V 7BD. Tel 020 7661 3000, www.thehoxton.com/london/ holborn. Close to Covent Garden, Bloomsbury and the Strand, this youthful modern hotel has enlivened a former office building with good-value accommodation and a number of buzzy eating and drinking spots. It is a sister hotel to The Hoxton Shoreditch (see next entry). Cleverly designed bedrooms come in four categories: Shoebox, Snug, Cosy and Roomy; with a Roberts radio and old Penguin Classics, they have a stylish retro feel. Each has tea- and coffee-making facilities, a mini fridge with fresh milk and bottled water, and an interesting guide to local attractions; guests also have an hour's worth of free local and international phone calls. A breakfast bag of orange juice, a banana and a yogurt and granola pot is left on the door handle in the morning. The street-level Hubbard & Bell restaurant is a Brooklyn-style grill; Chicken Shop, in the basement, has spit-roasted meats; coffee, cakes, pastries and sandwiches are taken in the Holborn Grind. Complimentary newspapers in the lobby. Meeting/function rooms. Nail salon. Free Wi-Fi. Background music; live DJ nights. Children welcomed. 174 bedrooms (some suitable for disabled). Per room B&B from £69. (Underground: Holborn)

THE HOXTON SHOREDITCH, 81 Great Eastern Street, EC2A 3HU. Tel 020 7550 1000, www.hoxtonhotels.com. In a lively part of town, this 'intensely stylish' hotel is liked for its good-value bedrooms and animated atmosphere. The 'enormous' lobby has exposed brick walls, stone fireplaces and leather armchairs; upstairs, 'well-equipped' bedrooms have a 'decent' large bed, 'proper' hangers, 'good lighting'; a 'splendid' bathroom. The 'excellent' Hoxton Grill serves an American-influenced menu all day; meals may be taken in the 'huge' brasserie or the covered garden courtyard. The 'buzzy' bar, popular with locals, is open till late. The room rate includes an hour's worth of free phone calls, and a breakfast bag (granola pot, banana, orange juice) delivered to the room each morning. Weekly music and art events. Lounge (background music) and outdoor space (interior courtyard). Lift. Meeting

rooms; shop. Free Wi-Fi. Children welcomed. 208 rooms (11 suitable for disabled). Per room B&B from £99. (Underground: Old Street)

H10 LONDON WATERLOO, 284–302 Waterloo Road, SE1 8RQ. Tel 020 7928 4062, www.hotelh10londonwaterloo. com. In an asymmetric, purpose-built block, this good-value Spanish chain hotel is on busy Waterloo Road. Service is 'highly organised and friendly'; guests are offered a complimentary glass of cava on arrival. Public rooms are decorated in sleek, contemporary style, with striking photographic murals, and have 'a good selection' of newspapers and magazines. There are large windows in the bright bedrooms (some compact; double glazing makes traffic noise 'bearable'); top-floor city-view rooms have the best, panoramic views. Mediterranean dishes are served in the modern restaurant; the Waterloo Sky bar, on the eighth floor, has fantastic views over the city. A wide choice at breakfast. The South Bank is 15 mins' walk away. Lounge, 2 bars, Three O Two restaurant. Beauty centre (gym, sauna, hydromassage shower; treatments); meeting rooms; function facilities. Free Wi-Fi. 177 bedrooms (some suitable for disabled). Per room B&B £195–£372. Dinner from £30. (Underground: Waterloo, Lambeth North)

INDIGO, 16 London Street, W2 1HL. Tel 020 7706 4444, www.ihg.com/ hotelindigo. Conveniently located for Paddington station and the express trains to Heathrow, this modern hotel (part of the InterContinental Hotels Group) is in converted town houses opposite a small garden square. A glass staircase leads to colourful bedrooms (some small), equipped with an espresso machine and complimentary soft drinks; bathrooms are compact, with a spa-inspired shower. Street-facing rooms may have some noise (earplugs provided). Lounge/lobby, bar, brasserie; terrace. Fitness studio. Free Wi-Fi. Background music. Children welcomed. 64 bedrooms (some with private balcony or terrace; 2 suitable for disabled). Per room B&B from £246. (Underground: Paddington)

KNIGHTSBRIDGE HOTEL, 10 Beaufort Gardens, SW3 1PT. Tel 020 7584 6300, www.firmdalehotels.com. On a quiet, tree-lined street minutes from Hyde Park, this handsome town house hotel (part of Tim and Kit Kemp's Firmdale group) is within walking distance of Knightsbridge's cafés, bars and restaurants. Two cosy sitting areas, each with a working fireplace, are filled with original British art, ceramics and specially designed fabrics; bright, colourful bedrooms are individually designed. Most rooms have views of Beaufort Gardens or the city skyline. There is no restaurant, but cocktails and a room-service menu are available all day in the sitting rooms or bedroom. Families are welcomed; the children's afternoon tea has jellies and milkshakes. In-room massage and beauty treatments can be arranged. A short walk to the museums of South Kensington. Drawing room, library, bar. Free Wi-Fi. Room service. Civil wedding licence. No background music. Children (amenities, books, board games, DVDs, treats) and small dogs (by arrangement) welcomed. 44 bedrooms. Room only from £234. À la carte breakfast £3.50–£14.50. (Underground: Knightsbridge)

THE MAIN HOUSE, 6 Colville Road, W11 2BP. Tel 020 7221 9691, www.themainhouse.co.uk. There are period features, antique furnishings and an airy, uncluttered feel at Caroline Main's elegant Victorian house, on a quiet street off Portobello Road. B&B accommodation is in spacious suites that each occupy an entire floor; they are well equipped with purified water, guides and maps, umbrellas, adaptor plugs, an ironing board and a fridge. A complimentary newspaper and morning coffee or tea are brought to the room or served on the balcony; an organic continental or full English breakfast is also available. Guests receive special day rates at the nearby BodyWorksWest health club, and discounts at the neighbourhood deli and artisan baker. Roof terrace. Free Wi-Fi. No background music. DVD library. Reasonable rates for chauffeur service to airports. 3 bedrooms. Room only from £120 (min. 3-night stay). (Underground: Notting Hill Gate)

THE MONTAGUE ON THE GARDENS, 15 Montague Street, WC1B 5BJ. Tel 020 7637 1001, www.montaguehotel.com. 'In an exceptional location' across the street from the British Museum, this 'well-run' town house hotel (Red Carnation Hotels) occupies a Georgian terrace overlooking peaceful gardens. 'We had a wonderful stay.' It is managed by Dirk Crokaert, with 'friendly, helpful' staff. Public rooms are lavishly decorated with draped curtains, crystal chandeliers, graphic floral prints. With gilded mirrors and hand-crafted furniture, the 'very comfortable', well-equipped bedrooms can be equally flamboyant. Children are welcomed with games, DVDs, their own bathrobe and slippers. In the informal Blue Door Bistro, chef Martin Halls serves a seasonal menu; alfresco meals are taken on the Garden Grill terrace in summer. Breakfasts are 'good'. Classic/contemporary background music in public areas; pianist in Terrace bar in evening except Sun. Lounge, bar, 2 conservatories; terrace. Fitness suite. Designated outdoor smoking area. Civil wedding licence. Free Wi-Fi. Children, and dogs (special treats) welcomed. 100 rooms and suites (1 suitable for disabled). Per room B&B single from £232, double from £254. Dinner £37. (Underground: Russell Square)

THE NADLER KENSINGTON, 25 Courtfield Gardens, SW5 0PG. Tel 020 7244 2255, www.thenadler.com. Near the museums of South Kensington, this modern hotel occupies a white stucco town house on a leafy residential square. Part of the Nadler Hotels group (see also The Nadler Liverpool, Shortlist entry), it aims to provide 'affordable luxury' for style-conscious budget travellers. Compact, studio-style bedrooms, including many good-value single rooms, are simply furnished; each has a mini kitchen (microwave, fridge, sink, cutlery) and individually controlled heating and air conditioning. Larger rooms with a sofa bed are suitable for a family. There is no restaurant or bar, but guests receive discounts at local eating spots; a continental breakfast (£8.50) may be delivered to the room, by arrangement. Reception lobby (background music). Music library, games. Access to local Fitness First gym. Free Wi-Fi. Children welcomed. 65 bedrooms (some with bunk bed; 1 suitable for disabled). Room only

from £138. (Underground: Earl's Court, Gloucester Road)

THE PILOT, 68 River Way, SE10 0BE. Tel 020 8858 5910, pilotgreenwich.co.uk. Accessible by Tube, boat and cable car, this jauntily decorated North Greenwich pub-with-rooms is in a fine 1800s building. It is managed by Eduardo Labaronnie for Fuller's Brewery. Stylish bedrooms come in three categories, each with a media hub, radio and Nespresso machine; the snug Captain's Cabin, decorated in nautical style, has wood panelling and a porthole window. Modern dishes, pub classics, roast lunches and a daily-changing choice of fresh fish are served in the airy dining room or outside in the sunken garden. Popular for events at the O2 Arena nearby; the Royal Observatory, the National Maritime Museum, ExCeL London and London City Airport are all close by. Bar (award-winning ales), dining area; private dining room; garden, terrace. Free Wi-Fi. Background music. Parking. 10 bedrooms. Per room B&B from £126. Dinner £27. (Underground: North Greenwich)

QBIC HOTEL, 42 Adler Street, E1 1EE. Tel 020 3021 3300, london.qbichotels.com. In a lively neighbourhood known for its curry houses and young creatives, this funky modern hotel has stylish, no-frills rooms, high-spec technology and a buzzy atmosphere. The enormous, open-plan lobby/seating area, open to non-residents, has mismatched furnishings and plenty of space in which to work, socialise or eat throughout the day; complimentary teas and coffees are available on floors 1–4. Pod-like, pre-fabricated bedrooms come in three categories: Smart (which has no window), Standard and Fun; each has a large bed with an organic wool mattress, a TV, mood lighting, British and European plug sockets, and a compact power-shower room. Lifts. Children welcomed (connecting rooms, baby cots). No background music. Free Wi-Fi. Close to Brick Lane. Cycle tours. 171 rooms (18 suitable for disabled). Room only from £69. Continental breakfast buffet £7.50. (Underground: Aldgate East, Whitechapel, Liverpool Street)

THE ROYAL PARK HOTEL, 3 Westbourne Terrace, W2 3UL. Tel 020 7479 6600, www.theroyalpark.com. 'We really like this hotel.' Antique furniture and original oil paintings add a 'gracious' feel to this elegant hotel, in a conversion of three Grade II listed Georgian town houses on a tree-lined avenue. There is a 'comfortable and homely' atmosphere; staff are 'extremely nice'. Bedrooms have a handmade bed, a desk, a dining table, an easy chair; bathrobes and slippers in a 'spacious' limestone shower- or bathroom. Most have views over the city's rooftops or a private mews. A set menu of European dishes is served in Kiyan restaurant; private dining and afternoon teas are available. Breakfast, which can be taken in the room, is 'excellent'. Bar, restaurant. Garden; terrace. Lift. Business/function facilities. Room service. Free Wi-Fi. Limousine service. Children welcomed. 48 bedrooms. Per room B&B (including welcome drink) from £208. Dinner £22.95. (Underground: Paddington, Lancaster Gate)

ST JAMES'S HOTEL AND CLUB, 7–8 Park Place, SW1A 1LS. Tel 020 7316 1600, www.stjameshotelandclub.com. Close to Green Park, this luxury hotel (Althoff Hotels) has marble pillars, Murano glass chandeliers, rich fabrics and original artwork, including a collection of antique portraits. The Victorian building has sumptuous bedrooms, each with a glamorous bathroom; some rooms have their own balcony with views over the city's rooftops. In Seven Park Place, the boldly decorated restaurant, chef William Drabble has a Michelin star for his modern French cooking. Light lunches and pre- and post-theatre suppers are taken in William's Bar & Bistro; traditional afternoon tea is served in the elegant lounge. Lounge, bar, bistro, restaurant (closed Sun, Mon). 4 private dining rooms. Free Wi-Fi. Background music. Children welcomed (dedicated kids' concierge; cot £36; extra bed £60). 60 bedrooms (10 suites; 2 on ground floor). Room only from £267. Breakfast £24. Dinner £61. (Underground: Green Park)

ST PAUL'S HOTEL, 153 Hammersmith Road, W14 0QL. Tel 020 8846 9119, www.stpaulhotel.co.uk. Beside a small park, a former boys' school has been transformed into this smart, modern hotel. It was built in 1884 by Alfred Waterhouse, who designed the Natural History Museum; with its detailed terracotta brickwork and Romanesque style, it bears a pleasing resemblance to the handsome monument. John Georgy is the manager. Sleek bedrooms have a sitting area and a marble bathroom; some have an original fireplace. The tranquil Melody restaurant overlooking the garden serves European cuisine; champagne afternoon teas are available. Bar, restaurant (open to non-residents); garden. Lift. Room service. Free Wi-Fi. Background music. Wedding/

business facilities. Limited parking (reservation necessary). Children welcomed (extra bed). 35 bedrooms (1 suitable for disabled). Room only from £212. Breakfast £9.50. Dinner £50. (Underground: Hammersmith, Kensington Olympia, Barons Court)

THE SANCTUARY HOUSE, 33 Tothill Street, SW1H 9LA. Tel 020 7799 4044, www.sanctuaryhousehotel. co.uk. Westminster Abbey, the Houses of Parliament and St James's Park are all within easy reach of this updated Victorian ale-and-pie house, on one of the most ancient streets in Westminster. It is managed by Solanily Yepes for Fuller's Brewery. Home-made pies, traditional pub grub and sharing platters are served in the wood-lined bar; upstairs, there are 'very comfortable' modern bedrooms (some can be snug). They have a desk, tea- and coffee-making facilities and air conditioning; superior rooms also have bathrobes and take-home slippers. Lobby with seating, bar, restaurant. Lift. Room service. Free Wi-Fi. Background music. Children welcomed. 34 bedrooms (some suitable for disabled). Room only from £180. Breakfast £12.95. Dinner £30. (Underground: St James's Park)

SLOANE SQUARE HOTEL, 7–12 Sloane Square, SW1W 8EG. Tel 020 7896 9988, www.sloanesquarehotel.co.uk. On a fashionable square, this 'very pleasant' hotel is well located for the shops and restaurants of Chelsea and Knightsbridge. Visitors were 'impressed by the clever design and smart fixtures' of the peaceful bedrooms (some are small); each has views of the lively square or, at the rear of the building, a

historic church. French-inspired dishes are served all day in Côte brasserie, downstairs, at street level. Breakfast has 'good cooked dishes'. Cadogan Hall and the Royal Court Theatre are nearby. Côte brasserie (background music), bar. Meeting rooms. Lift. Free Wi-Fi and local and national phone calls. Parking (charge). Children welcomed. 102 bedrooms (some interconnecting). Room only from £188. Full English breakfast £7.75. (Underground: Sloane Square)

SOFITEL LONDON ST JAMES, 6 Waterloo Place, SW1Y 4AN . Tel 020 7747 2210, www.sofitel.com. 'We have taken to staying here whenever we are in London.' In a 'wonderful' location just off Pall Mall, this large hotel (part of French group Sofitel) is in a handsome neoclassical building with an alluring, glitzy interior. It is managed by Nicolas Pesty, with mainly French staff who address guests in French as a default. 'Exceptionally comfortable' bedrooms (some are small) have a desk, minibar, bottled water, tea- and coffee-making facilities; bathrooms have luxury toiletries. Afternoon tea and champagne are taken in the elegant and popular Rose Lounge (live harp music); 'excellent' French and British dishes are served in Le Balcon brasserie. The breakfast buffet is 'delicious'. Lounge, bar, restaurant. Spa (treatments); gym. Business facilities. Free Wi-Fi. Room service. Background music. Valet parking. Children welcomed (babysitting on request). 183 rooms (1 suitable for disabled; some interconnecting). Room only from £415. Breakfast £25. (Underground: Charing Cross, Piccadilly Circus)

THE SOHO HOTEL, 4 Richmond Mews, off Dean Street, W1D 3DH. Tel 020 7559 3000, www.firmdalehotels. com. Fernando Botero's ten-foot-high sculpture of a bronze cat greets guests in the lobby of this glamorous hotel, part of Tim and Kit Kemp's Firmdale collection. It is on a quiet street in an area packed with restaurants, bars, cafés, theatres and nightlife; leafy Soho Square is close by. The drawing room and library have a large French fireplace, fresh flowers and modern art. Elegant bedrooms – decorated with a riot of prints, colours and patterns – have floor-to-ceiling windows and a luxurious bathroom. Children are welcomed with books and board games, DVDs, a mini bathrobe, milk and cookies at bedtime. A small cinema hosts regular Sunday afternoon film events including lunch, tea or dinner. Drawing room (honesty bar), library, bar, Refuel restaurant; 4 private dining rooms. Lift. Gym; beauty treatment rooms. 2 screening rooms; DVD library. Free Wi-Fi. Background music. Civil wedding licence. Ramp. Children (high chair, special cutlery, cot, extra bed; babysitting) and small dogs (by arrangement) welcomed. 91 bedrooms and suites (4 suitable for disabled). Also 4 apartments. Room only from £294. Breakfast £19.50–£32. Set dinner £20. (Underground: Leicester Square)

SOUTH PLACE HOTEL, 3 South Place, EC2M 2AF. Tel 020 3503 0000, www. southplacehotel.com. Style-conscious and sophisticated, this modern luxury hotel was designed by Terence Conran for restaurant group D&D London. Madelon Boom is the manager. Lively public spaces have quirky furnishings and original artwork; bedrooms have floor-to-ceiling windows (electric blackout blinds), ample storage space, and a minibar filled with British treats. Tony Fleming is the executive chef at the top-floor Angler restaurant (closed Sat lunch and Sun; Christmas period), which has a Michelin star for its British seafood dishes; an adjoining roof terrace has a barbecue. Bistro food is available all day at 3 South Place bar and grill. The extensive breakfast selection, served until 11 am, has healthy options, a butty menu, porridge served with London honey. 3 bars, 2 restaurants, Le Chiffre residents' lounge and games room (books, magazines, games, turntable, cocktails); roof terrace; 'secret' garden. Gym; steam, sauna, treatment room. 5 private dining and meeting rooms. Civil wedding licence. Free Wi-Fi. Background music (live DJ Fri and Sat nights in bars). Children (cot; interconnecting rooms) and small/medium-size dogs welcomed. 80 bedrooms, studios and suites (4 suitable for disabled). Per room B&B £176–£465. Dinner £25–£54. (Underground: Liverpool Street, Moorgate)

THE STAFFORD, 16–18 St James's Place, SW1A 1NJ. Tel 020 7493 0111, www.thestaffordhotel.co.uk. In a peaceful setting just off Piccadilly, this sophisticated hotel, in three converted town houses, has a long and intriguing history weaving together a nanny to Queen Victoria's children, several troops of foreign servicemen, and a heroine of the French Resistance. Bedrooms are in the main house, Mews suites and converted stables across the courtyard; each is individually styled. In the elegant Lyttelton restaurant, chef Carlos Martinez cooks modern dishes at lunch and dinner; afternoon tea is taken in the lounge or the characterful American Bar. Plenty of choice at breakfast, including smoked fish dishes. Regular wine tasting events and dinners in the historic wine cellars. Lounge, bar, restaurant; lift. Courtyard. No background music. Children welcomed. Civil wedding licence; function facilities. Parking (charge). 105 bedrooms (11 in Carriage House; 26 in Mews; 1 suitable for disabled). Per room B&B (excluding VAT) from £355. (Underground: Green Park)

Ten Manchester Street,
10 Manchester Street, W1U 4DG. Tel 020 7317 5900, www.tenmanchesterstreethotel.com. In a red-brick Edwardian building just off charming Marylebone High Street, this discreet hotel (City & Country Hotels) has 'comfortable', individually designed bedrooms; four open on to a private terrace with seating, music and heaters. Modern Italian menus are served in Dieci restaurant; snacks are available all day in the cosy, L-shaped bar. Service is attentive and helpful. Cigar smokers are well provided for with a walk-in humidor, cigar-tasting room and all-weather smoking terrace. Regent's Park is 10 minutes' walk away. Lounge/bar (background music). Free Wi-Fi. Children welcomed. 24-hour room service; chauffeur service. 44 bedrooms (9 suites). Per room B&B £165–£375. Dinner £45. (Underground: Baker Street, Bond Street, Marylebone)

Threadneedles, 5 Threadneedle Street,
EC2R 8AY. Tel 020 7657 8080, www.hotelthreadneedles.co.uk. Close to the Bank of England, this luxury hotel (part of Marriott's Autograph Collection) is in a converted Victorian banking hall with marble floors, walnut panelling, ornate pillars, and a glorious hand-painted stained-glass dome over the reception lobby. 'Beautifully decorated' with rich fabrics and wood furnishings, modern bedrooms have a small sitting area and 'every amenity'. The room rate includes a daily newspaper, shoe shine and a day pass to a local gym. Chef Marco Pierre White opened Wheeler's Oyster Bar & Grill Room in 2015, serving steaks and fish dishes; the lounge has sandwiches and light meals on Saturdays. Peaceful at weekends. Lounge, bar, restaurant (closed Sat, Sun and bank holidays). Lift. 3 meeting rooms; conferences. Free Wi-Fi. Background music. Children welcomed. 74 bedrooms (1 suitable for disabled). Room only from £199. Breakfast £22.50. (Underground: Bank, Liverpool Street)

Town Hall Hotel & Apartments,
Patriot Square, E2 9NF. Tel 020 7871 0460, www.townhallhotel.com. In an animated spot in east London, this trendy, modern hotel occupies a sympathetically refurbished Grade II listed Edwardian building that was once the Bethnal Green town hall. It has stylish rooms and 'friendly, helpful' staff. 'We would definitely stay there again.' The ornate moulded ceilings, stately staircases and marble pillars have been restored; spacious, individually styled bedrooms have vintage furniture and sheepskin rugs. 'Our large, airy apartment had an excellent kitchen; a modern bathroom with lots of storage space; large, opening windows.' The light-filled Corner Room serves a short menu

of modern dishes; chef Lee Westcott cooks five- and seven-course dinner menus in the well-regarded Typing Room restaurant. A room-service menu is available 24 hours a day. Free shuttle bus to Liverpool Street and Bank on weekday mornings. Parking can be difficult. Bar, 2 restaurants. 'Gorgeous' indoor swimming pool, gym (open 6 am to midnight). Lift. Free Wi-Fi. Background music. Civil wedding licence/function facilities. Children welcomed. 98 bedrooms and studios (4 suitable for disabled). Room only from £173. Breakfast from £15. (Underground: Bethnal Green)

ENGLAND

ALDEBURGH Suffolk
Map 2:C6

DUNAN HOUSE, 41 Park Road, IP15 5EN. Tel 01728 452486, www. dunanhouse.co.uk. Simon Farr, an artist, and Ann Lee, a potter, have enlivened their Victorian home with vibrant colours and their own eye-catching artwork. On a wooded private road, the B&B is close to the beach and the high street. Spacious bedrooms have garden or river views; a family room on the top floor has a smaller connecting room with a single bed. Communal breakfasts include freshly laid eggs from resident hens, served on Ann Lee's pottery. Ten minutes' walk from the town centre; a footpath beyond the front gate leads to the marshes and the river. ½-acre garden. Free Wi-Fi. No background music. Parking. Children welcomed. 3 bedrooms (1 family room). Per room B&B £75 single, £85 double. 2-night min. stay preferred. Closed Christmas.

ALFRISTON East Sussex
Map 2:E4

WINGROVE HOUSE, High Street, BN26 5TD. Tel 01323 870276, www. wingrovehousealfriston.com. Guests are pleased to return to Nick Denyer's welcoming restaurant-with-rooms, in a 19th-century colonial-style house fronted by an elegant veranda. Friendly and 'relaxed', staff willingly supply maps and local information. 'Top-quality' modern European dinners, served in the candlelit restaurant, are cooked by Matthew Comben, who sources ingredients from local farms and the South Downs. 'Lunch was as good as ever.' The stylish bedrooms are 'perfection'; two on the first floor have a veranda; all have views of the village and surrounding countryside. Breakfast has fruit salad, croissants, home-made jams. Lounge/bar (extensive gin menu), restaurant (background music; closed Sun eve in winter; special diets catered for). Free Wi-Fi. Children welcomed. 7 bedrooms (2 with access to balcony). Per room B&B £100–£200. Dinner £25–£29.

ALKHAM Kent
Map 2:D5

THE MARQUIS AT ALKHAM, Alkham Valley Road, CT15 7DF. Tel 01304 873410, www.themarquisatalkham. co.uk. In the countryside, close to Dover and the Channel Tunnel, this contemporary restaurant-with-rooms is in a 200-year-old inn overlooked by the 12th-century St Anthony's church. It is managed by David Harris for Bespoke Hotels. Smartly decorated, it has exposed brickwork, wooden floors, up-to-date fabrics and furnishings. Bedrooms have a 'large, comfortable' bed, underfloor heating

and views of the Alkham valley. In the restaurant, Andrew King, the new chef, uses seasonal Kentish produce on his modern British menus. Breakfast has an extensive buffet with seasonal fruits, cured meats, fish and cheese; hot dishes cooked to order. The building is on a busy road 4 miles W of Dover; rooms at the back are quietest. Lounge/bar, restaurant (closed Mon lunch); small garden. Free Wi-Fi. Classical background music. Civil wedding licence. 10 bedrooms (1 suitable for disabled; 3 rooms in 2 cottages, 3 mins' drive away). Per room B&B from £99, D,B&B from £159.
25% DISCOUNT VOUCHERS

ALLERFORD Somerset
Map 1:B5
CROSS LANE HOUSE, TA24 8HW. Tel 01643 863276, www.crosslanehouse. com. 'We have found another home from home.' In a pretty village below the Selworthy Woods, 'dedicated' owners Max Lawrence and Andrew Stinson run their restaurant-with-rooms by the packhorse bridge over the village brook. The beautifully restored medieval farmhouse has crooked floors, low ceilings and panelled walls. In the rustic dining room, lunch and dinner menus use home-grown produce from the kitchen garden. During the summer months, alfresco meals are taken in the ancient linhay across a cobbled courtyard; tasting menu weekends are held throughout the year. Immaculately presented bedrooms blend period and contemporary furnishing. They have designer fabrics and a window seat; fruit, home-made biscuits and a Nespresso machine are provided. 'Breakfast had the lot.' Afternoon tea

and picnic hampers available. The owners are 'a mine of information' on local walks and places to visit, and proffer parting gifts for the onward journey. Lounge/bar (wood burner), dining room (candlelit at night; background music; closed Sun and Mon). 1-acre garden. Free Wi-Fi. Parking. Children over 14, and dogs (£8 per night, including biscuits, food and water bowl) welcomed. 4 bedrooms. Per room B&B from £125, D,B&B from £175.

APPLEDORE Devon
Map 1:B4
THE SEAGATE, The Quay, EX39 1QS. Tel 01237 472589, www.theseagate. co.uk. On the quay of a small fishing village, this white-painted 17th-century inn overlooks the Torridge estuary. It is managed by Phil and Jan Hills. Extensively refurbished, it retains an inviting atmosphere: 'muddy boots and dogs' are welcomed. Simply furnished bedrooms (some beamed) have tea- and coffee-making facilities, a modern bathroom; a family room has a bunk bed for children. Chef Neil Timothy cooks daily fish specials at dinner; weekend barbecues are held throughout the summer months. Two terraces have tables and seating, and views across the estuary. Breakfast has local yogurts, fresh fruit and a good selection of cooked dishes. Open-plan restaurant/bar (local ales); 2 terraces, walled garden. 'Easy listening' background music. Free Wi-Fi. Parking. Children and dogs welcomed. 2 miles from Bideford. 10 bedrooms. Per room B&B single £55, double from £80. 2-night min. stay at weekends preferred. Dinner £24.

ARMSCOTE Warwickshire
Map 3:D6

THE FUZZY DUCK, Ilmington Road,
CV37 8DD. Tel 01608 682635, www.
fuzzyduckarmscote.com. In a small
village eight miles south of Stratford-
upon-Avon, this 18th-century coaching
inn has 'a comfortable, home-from-home
feel, with a sophisticated edge'. It has been
stylishly refurbished by owners Tania
and Adrian Slater, the sister-and-brother
team behind beauty products company
Baylis and Harding. Distinctive flagstone
floors, exposed beams and original
fireplaces have been retained; bedrooms
(some small) have luxury linens, woollen
bed-throws, complimentary goodies. A
large room with an extra loft bed above
the bathroom is suitable for a family. A
double-aspect fireplace separates the main
restaurant from a cosy private dining area;
in both spaces, traditional pub favourites
are given a contemporary twist by chef
Joe Adams. Bar, restaurant (closed Sun
eve and Mon). 1-acre garden. Free Wi-Fi.
Background music. Children (special
menu; dressing-up box) and dogs (doggy
welcome pack; home-made dog biscuits
and snacks in the bar) welcomed. Hunter
boots and guide books available to borrow.
4 bedrooms. Per room B&B from £120.
Dinner £30.

ARNSIDE Cumbria
Map 4: inset C2

NUMBER 43, The Promenade, LA5 0AA.
Tel 01524 762761, www.no43.org.uk.
Lesley Hornsby's modern B&B is in a
peaceful row of Victorian hillside villas
on the seafront promenade. Overlooking
the Kent estuary, it has exceptional views
of the surrounding fells; trains can be
seen crossing the picturesque Arnside
viaduct. The elegant, spacious lounge has
window seats, sofas, books, magazines
and an honesty bar. Bedrooms have plenty
of pillows and cushions, ample storage
space, a hospitality tray with freshly
ground coffee and home-made biscuits.
Two suites overlooking the South Lakes
landscape have binoculars for watching
wildlife. Alfresco drinks may be taken on
terraces at the front and back. Breakfast
is generous: home-made compotes,
home-roasted granola, locally caught and
smoked haddock. Light suppers (meat,
cheese and smoked fish platters) available;
summer barbecue packs by arrangement.
Lounge, dining room; garden; patio. Free
Wi-Fi. Background music. Children over
5 welcomed. 6 bedrooms. Per room B&B
£100–£185.

BAINBRIDGE North Yorkshire
Map 4:C3

YOREBRIDGE HOUSE, Leyburn,
DL8 3EE. Tel 01969 652060, www.
yorebridgehouse.co.uk. By the River
Ure, Charlotte and David Reilly's small
hotel and restaurant occupy a Victorian
stone-built school outside a pretty
village with stunning views of the Dales.
The former schoolmaster's house stands
opposite the courtyard. Individually
styled bedrooms have been designed
with the owners' favourite places in
mind: Mougins, the French room, is
decorated in creams, whites and gold,
with chandeliers and carved furniture;
Greenwich is a New York-style loft
suite with a large leather settee and two
freestanding baths. Six rooms have a
private terrace with an outdoor hot tub.
In the candlelit restaurant, chef Dan
Shotton's modern menus use produce
from many local suppliers. Lounge, bar,
restaurant (open to non-residents). Free
Wi-Fi (in public areas). Background

music. Civil wedding licence. Children, and dogs (in 2 rooms) welcomed. 2-acre grounds. 12 bedrooms (4 in schoolhouse; 2 in village, 5 mins' walk; ground-floor rooms suitable for disabled). Per room B&B £200–£285, D,B&B £310–£395.

BARNSLEY Gloucestershire
Map 3:E6

THE VILLAGE PUB, GL7 5EF. Tel 01285 740421, www.thevillagepub.co.uk. In a pretty Cotswold village, four miles from Cirencester, this chic, rustic restaurant-with-rooms is under the same ownership as Calcot Manor, Tetbury, and Barnsley House, up the street (see main entries). Pub guests have complimentary access to the famous gardens designed by the late horticulturalist Rosemary Verey. Cosy bedrooms have a separate entrance from the pub; some have exposed beams or sloping ceilings, others a four-poster bed. (Road-facing rooms may have traffic noise.) Daniel Craythorne is the new chef; his modern pub menus, which use plenty of fruit and vegetables from Barnsley House's kitchen garden, include 'a considerable range of fish dishes'. English farmhouse breakfasts; home-made jams and home-baked bread. Bar, restaurant. Free Wi-Fi. Background music. Children (cot, high chair) and dogs welcomed. 6 bedrooms. Per room B&B from £145. Dinner £30.

BATH Somerset
Map 2:D1

ABBEY HOTEL, 1 North Parade, BA1 1LF. Tel 01225 461603, www. abbeyhotelbath.co.uk. In a 'very convenient setting', within walking distance of the Abbey and the Roman Baths, Christa and Ian Taylor have refurbished this large hotel with style. The light and airy public areas are decorated with an eclectic collection of artworks; a terrace on the wide pavement is open seasonally for alfresco meals, drinks and afternoon tea. Colourful bedrooms range in size; many have views over Parade Gardens towards Pulteney Bridge. The informal Allium Restaurant (Chris Staines is the chef) and lively cocktail bar are popular with locals. Lounge, bar, restaurant. Lift. Free Wi-Fi. Background music. Civil wedding licence. Children, and dogs (charge) welcomed. 60 bedrooms (some on ground floor; 7 family rooms). Per person B&B from £100.

AQUAE SULIS, 174–176 Newbridge Road, BA1 3LE. Tel 01225 420061, www. aquaesulishotel.co.uk. David and Jane Carnegie's traditional guest house, in an Edwardian building two miles west of the centre, is a pleasant 30-minute stroll along the river, or a short bus ride into town; there is easy parking for visitors arriving by car. The simply furnished, well-equipped bedrooms (Freeview TV, iPod docking station) are named after personalities associated with Bath, and have a modern bathroom. Ana-Maria Mandra is the manager; French and Spanish are spoken. Lounge (bar), dining room (evening snack menu); patio/garden with tables and chairs. Free Wi-Fi. Background music. Courtesy car to and from Bath Spa railway and bus station. Private parking, and unrestricted parking on street. Children welcomed (over-3s £20). 14 bedrooms (2 on ground floor; 2 single; 1 in annexe with separate entrance). Per room B&B single £55–£89, double £69–£140. 2-night min. stay at weekends. Closed Christmas.

BRINDLEYS, 14 Pulteney Gardens, BA2 4HG. Tel 01225 310444, www.brindleysbath.co.uk. In a peaceful residential area, this 'attractive' Victorian villa is within walking distance of the city centre. It is owned by Michael and Sarah Jones, and run by David Roberts and Laura Warington, who are helpful with local information. White-painted furniture, pretty fabrics and fresh flowers create a contemporary French look in the bedrooms; some rooms have views over the city. The 'very smart and bright' breakfast room overlooks the 'well-kept' front garden; breakfast choices are listed on a blackboard menu. Lounge, breakfast room. Small garden. Free Wi-Fi. No background music. Complimentary on-street parking permits. 6 bedrooms (some are small). Per room B&B £100–£185. 2-night min. stay at weekends preferred. Closed Christmas.

DORIAN HOUSE, 1 Upper Oldfield Park, BA2 3JX. Tel 01225 426336, www.dorianhouse.co.uk. Up the hill from the city centre, this modern B&B has 'fabulous' views over the Royal Crescent. It is owned by Timothy Hugh, a cellist; Robert and Lize Briers are the managers. The Victorian stone house is filled with Asian antiques and contemporary art. Named after composers (Gershwin, Ravel, Rossini, etc), the smart bedrooms have bathrobes and a marble bathroom. Breakfast has fruit, granola, freshly baked croissants; a choice of cooked dishes. 10 mins' walk from the centre. Lounge (open fire), conservatory breakfast room/music library; classical background music. Free Wi-Fi. Small, hilly garden. Parking. Children welcomed. 13

bedrooms (1 on ground floor). Per room B&B £109–£175.

GRAYS, 9 Upper Oldfield Park, BA2 3JX. Tel 01225 403020, www.graysbath.co.uk. A short downhill walk to the centre, this charming B&B is in a large Victorian villa with good views over Bath. It is under the same ownership as Brindleys (see left). Light, bright rooms, painted in soft colours, have chic French-style furniture; many have city or garden views; some in the attic may be snug. The sunny breakfast room has cereals, yogurts, fruit, compotes and preserves; hot dishes (vegetarian option available) are cooked to order. 15 mins' walk to the centre. Lounge, breakfast room; small garden. Free Wi-Fi. No background music. Parking. 12 bedrooms. Per room B&B £105–£200. 2-night min. stay at weekends preferred. Closed Christmas.

HARINGTON'S HOTEL, 8–10 Queen Street, BA1 1HE. Tel 01225 461728, www.haringtonshotel.co.uk. In a listed Georgian building on a cobbled side street, Melissa and Peter O'Sullivan's stylish small hotel is within walking distance of many of the city's attractions. The brightly decorated bedrooms are on three floors (no lift; help with luggage is offered); each is well equipped with a flat-screen TV, DAB radio, desk fan/heater, tea- and coffee-making facilities. The coffee lounge and bar are open until midnight; drinks can be taken in the outdoor hot tub. Breakfast has a buffet with fruit, yogurt, pastries, boiled eggs; cooked dishes include smoked kippers and buttermilk pancakes. Lounge, breakfast room, café/bar ('easy listening' background music); small conference room. Free Wi-Fi. Small courtyard;

hot tub (£7.50 per person per hour). Secure reserved parking nearby (£11 for 24 hrs). Children over 12 welcomed. 13 bedrooms, plus self-catering town house and apartments. Per room B&B from £99. 2-night min. stay on some weekends. Closed 23–26 Dec.
25% DISCOUNT VOUCHERS

THE KENNARD, 11 Henrietta Street, BA2 6LL. Tel 01225 310472, www. kennard.co.uk. In a 'superb location' just across Pulteney Bridge, this long-established hotel is 'clearly in safe hands' under its 'delightful' new owners, Natalie and Guy Woods. The 18th-century town house has an Italianate aura, with chandeliers, mirrors and small, elegant seating areas in the entrance hall; some superior bedrooms have a high ceiling, fine plasterwork and a canopied bed. Bedrooms are gradually being refurbished in plainer style. Breakfast, 'surely unbeatable for quality', is served in the original Georgian kitchen, on tables set with fine linen and china. There is a lovely formal garden. 2 sitting areas, breakfast room; courtyard. Free Wi-Fi. No background music. Drivers are given a free parking permit. 12 bedrooms (2 on ground floor; 2 share a bathroom; 6 flights of stairs). Per person B&B £89–£170. 2-night min. stay at weekends preferred. Closed Christmas.

PARADISE HOUSE, 86–88 Holloway, BA2 4PX. Tel 01225 317723, www.paradise-house.co.uk. There are panoramic views across the city from this elegantly furnished, honey-coloured Georgian mansion standing in award-winning walled gardens. It is owned by David and Annie Lanz. B&B accommodation is in well-equipped bedrooms, which range from period to modern in style; each has bathrobes and a modern bathroom with a power shower. Some have a four-poster bed. In the evening, drinks are served in the drawing room, which has floor-to-ceiling windows overlooking the garden and Bath. Extensive choice at breakfast, which may be taken in the bedroom. 15 mins' downhill walk in to town. Drawing room, breakfast room. 1-acre garden. Free Wi-Fi. No background music. Parking. Children welcomed (cot). 11 bedrooms (4 on ground floor; family suite; 3 in annexe). Per room B&B £75–£200. 2-night min. stay at weekends. Closed Christmas.

THREE ABBEY GREEN, 3 Abbey Green, BA1 1NW. Tel 01225 428558, www. threeabbeygreen.com. Nici and Alan Jones run their 'very comfortable' B&B in a Grade II listed town house on a quiet square in the centre of the city. Handsome bedrooms retain original features such as wood panelling and a fireplace; they are furnished with antiques. 'Our room had a good bed; a lovely big bath.' Breakfast has plenty of choice, 'all freshly cooked and promptly served'. Friendly and efficient, the hosts offer visitors information about the city. Close to the Abbey, the Roman Baths and the Pump Rooms. Dining room (background radio). Free Wi-Fi (computer and printer available). Children welcomed. 10 bedrooms (3 in adjoining building; 2 on ground floor suitable for disabled; plus 1-bedroom apartment). Per room B&B £90–£220. 2-night min. stay at weekends. Closed Christmas.

VILLA MAGDALA, Henrietta Road, BA2 6LX. Tel 01225 466329, www. villamagdala.co.uk. Overlooking

Henrietta Park, John and Amanda Willmott's refurbished Victorian villa has a pleasing modern interior decorated with interesting prints and wallpapers. Guests are offered complimentary refreshments on arrival. Three categories of bedroom (Good, Better and Best) vary in size and aspect; each has a hospitality tray with biscuits. Tea and coffee are served throughout the day; alfresco drinks may be taken on the sunny terrace overloooking the park; breakfast includes a glass of Buck's Fizz. Dining room; garden (deck chairs); terrace. Free Wi-Fi. Classical background music. On-site parking. Children (in some rooms; cot; extra bed £45 per night) welcomed. 20 bedrooms. Per room B&B £140–£190. Closed Christmas.

BELPER Derbyshire
Map 2:A2

DANNAH FARM, Bowmans Lane, Shottle, DE56 2DR. Tel 01773 550273, www. dannah.co.uk. Joan and Martin Slack's B&B stands in extensive gardens on a 150-acre working farm, on a ridge in the Derbyshire Dales. The individually styled bedrooms overlook the garden and beautiful surrounding countryside; many have an indulgent bathroom with a roll-top or double spa bath. A spa cabin (available for exclusive use) houses a Finnish sauna and a double steam shower; an outdoor hot tub sits on a large secluded terrace. Cooked farmhouse breakfasts include award-winning black pudding, locally made sausages and eggs from free-range hens; supper platters with home-baked bread and home-made puddings are served in the room. Vegetarians catered for. 2 sitting rooms, dining room; meeting room. Licensed. Free

Wi-Fi. No background music. Large walled garden; arbour; medieval moat. Parking. 2 miles from town. Children (£25 per night) and dogs (in Chatsworth suite, £5 per night) welcomed. 8 bedrooms (4 in adjoining converted barn; 3 on ground floor). Per room B&B £185–£295. Supper platter £16.95. 2-night min. stay on Fri, Sat. Closed Christmas.

BERWICK East Sussex
Map 2:E4

GREEN OAK BARN, The English Wine Centre, BN26 5QS. Tel 01323 870164, www.englishwine.co.uk. In landscaped gardens, Christine and Colin Munday's wine centre includes a well-regarded restaurant, 'comfortable' accommodation and a shop with more than 140 varieties of English wines. 'Smart' bedrooms are in Green Oak Lodge, a reconstructed traditional Sussex barn; the large communal space on the ground floor has sofas, a bar and a baby grand piano. In the thatched Flint Barn nearby, unusual English wines can be sampled by the glass to accompany the 'short, interesting' seasonal menus devised by Austin Gould; alfresco meals may be taken in the courtyard in summer. Close to the South Downs national park; 5 miles from Glyndebourne. Bar/lounge, restaurant (open lunch Wed–Sun, dinner Fri, Sat); weddings/functions in 17th-century country barn (civil wedding licence). Free Wi-Fi. No background music. Lift; ramps. Garden with water features. Wine shop; tutored wine tastings. Children welcomed. 5 bedrooms (1 suitable for disabled). Per room B&B £120–£170. Closed Christmas.
25% DISCOUNT VOUCHERS

BEXHILL-ON-SEA East Sussex
Map 2:E4

COAST, 58 Sea Road, TN40 1JP. Tel
01424 225260, www.coastbexhill.co.uk.
'A delight.' In a coastal town reputed
to be the birthplace of British motor
racing, Piero and Lucia Mazzoni run
their 'lovely' B&B in an Edwardian
villa close to the seafront. 'Impeccably
decorated and furnished' bedrooms,
each with a seating area, are bright
and modern; they are equipped with
tea- and coffee-making facilities,
bottled water and biscuits. 'Warm
and friendly', the hosts provide a
good choice of hot dishes at breakfast,
including pancakes with crème fraîche,
fresh fruit and maple syrup, as well as
vegetarian dishes, served in a sunny
room. 'We plan to escape there again.'
Convenient for shops, restaurants and
the station. Lounge, breakfast room
(soft background music). Secure bicycle
storage. Free Wi-Fi. Children over 5
welcomed. 3 bedrooms. Per room B&B
£79–£105. Closed Christmas, New Year.

BIBURY Gloucestershire
Map 3:E6

THE SWAN, GL7 5NW. Tel 01285
740695, www.cotswold-inns-hotels.
co.uk. In a little village once described
by William Morris as 'the most beautiful
village in England', this 17th-century
former coaching inn (Cotswold Inns and
Hotels) is in a picturesque setting beside
the River Coln. It has been refurbished
in country house style by owners Pamela
and Michael Horton; Quentin Fisher is
the manager. Most of the individually
designed, well-equipped bedrooms
overlook the river; four cottage suites,
a short walk from the inn, have their
own garden. Modern European cuisine

is served in the brasserie; in summer,
doors open on to a courtyard for alfresco
dining. Lift. Lounge, bar (wood-
burning stove), brasserie. Free Wi-Fi.
Background music. ½-acre garden. Civil
wedding licence; functions. Children,
and dogs (in some bedrooms) welcomed.
Trout fishing can be arranged. 22
bedrooms (4 in garden cottages, 1 with
hot tub). Per room B&B from £170,
D,B&B from £229.

BISHOP'S CASTLE Shropshire
Map 3:C4

CASTLE HOTEL, Market Square,
SY9 5BN. Tel 01588 638403, www.
thecastlehotelbishopscastle.co.uk.
On the site of the ancient castle
bailey, Henry and Rebecca Hunter's
refurbished hotel has commanding
views over the 'smart', historic market
town and the surrounding Shropshire
hills. It is co-owned with Henry
Hunter's parents, who own Pen-y-
Dyffryn, Oswestry (see main entry).
The 300-year-old listed building has
beams, and sloping floors and ceilings.
Reached via a fine Georgian staircase,
individually designed bedrooms vary in
size and style. Chef Steve Bruce's bistro
food is served in the casual bar areas
or, more formally, in the 'handsome'
panelled restaurant; special fresh fish
menus are added on Thursday and
Friday. The large enclosed garden has
a terrace with a pergola for alfresco
dining. Free Wi-Fi. Walkers and cyclists
welcomed; bicycle storage. Children
and well-behaved dogs welcomed.
No background music. In-room spa
treatments. 3 bars (local ales; open fires;
traditional pub games), dining room;
garden with fish pond, patio and terrace.
Parking. 12 bedrooms (2 family rooms).

Per room B&B £95–£150, D,B&B
£150–£205. Closed Christmas.
25% DISCOUNT VOUCHERS

BISHOP'S TACHBROOK
Warwickshire
Map 3:D6
MALLORY COURT, Harbury Lane, CV33
9QB. Tel 01926 330214, www.mallory.
co.uk. Standing in 'extensive' landscaped
grounds with a pond and a formal
Old English rose garden, this 'elegant'
manor house (Relais & Châteaux) is
well situated for Warwick Castle and
Stratford-upon-Avon. Sarah Baker is the
long-serving manager; staff are 'helpful,
pleasant and attentive'. 'Comfortable'
bedrooms are divided between the main
house and the adjacent Knight's Suite;
the best have views over the gardens. In
the oak-panelled restaurant, chef Paul
Foster serves daily-changing modern
menus using vegetables and soft fruits
from the kitchen garden. Informal meals
are served in the Art Deco brasserie in
the grounds; a jazz evening is held here
every Thursday. 'Excellent' full English
breakfast. Ramp, lift. 2 lounges, brasserie,
restaurant. Background music. Free
Wi-Fi. Terrace (alfresco snacks). Outdoor
swimming pool, tennis court, croquet.
Civil wedding licence; function facilities.
Children welcomed. 31 bedrooms (11 in
Knight's Suite, 2 suitable for disabled). Per
room B&B from £159, D,B&B from £254.
Set dinner £47.50.
25% DISCOUNT VOUCHERS

BLACKBURN Lancashire
Map 4:D3
MILLSTONE AT MELLOR, Church Lane,
Mellor, BB2 7JR. Tel 01254 813333,
www.millstonehotel.co.uk. In a pretty
Ribble Valley village, this stone-built

former coaching inn (Thwaites Inns
of Character) is run by chef/patron
Anson Bolton and his wife, Sarah. The
country-style bedrooms have fluffy
bathrobes, tea- and coffee-making
facilities and home-made biscuits. In
the wood-panelled restaurant, Anson
Bolton cooks seasonal Lancashire dishes,
including daily specials, using much
local produce. Breakfast has a buffet of
fresh fruit, yogurts and freshly baked
croissants; cooked dishes include a
smoked haddock omelette and a full
Lancashire grill. Residents' lounge (log
fire), bar, restaurant (open to non-
residents); terrace (alfresco dining).
Free Wi-Fi. Background radio at
breakfast. Parking. Children welcomed.
23 bedrooms (6 in courtyard; 2 suitable
for disabled). Per room B&B single
£56–£100, double £62–£120. Dinner £30.

BLACKPOOL Lancashire
Map 4:D2
NUMBER ONE ST LUKE'S, 1 St Luke's
Road, FY4 2EL. Tel 01253 343901,
www.numberoneblackpool.com.
In the residential South Shore area,
Mark and Claire Smith's stylish B&B
is in a detached 1930s Art Deco house
with a large conservatory overlooking
the garden. Individually decorated
bedrooms have a king-size bed; up-to-
date gadgetry includes a large plasma
TV, PlayStation2 and remote-controlled
lighting. Bathrooms have a whirlpool
bath. Breakfast has a full Blackpool,
among other, lighter options; special
diets are catered for. Conservatory;
garden (hot tub); putting green. Free
Wi-Fi. No background music. Parking.
2 miles from town centre; 5-min.
walk to the promenade and Blackpool
Pleasure Beach. Children over 4

welcomed. 3 bedrooms. Per person B&B from £50.

NUMBER ONE SOUTH BEACH, 4 Harrowside West, FY4 1NW. Tel 01253 343900, www.numberonesouthbeach. com. Overlooking South Beach Promenade, this 'very comfortable' modern hotel is owned by 'excellent hosts' Janet and Graham Oxley and Claire and Mark Smith (see Number One St Luke's, preceding entry). The colourful bedrooms are 'well equipped' with 'lovely beds and bedlinens'; some have a balcony with sea views. There is plenty of choice at breakfast. 'We could not have stayed at a better establishment.' Lift. Lounge, bar, restaurant; background music; pool table; meeting/conference facilities. Free Wi-Fi. Garden with putting green. Parking. Children over 5 welcomed. 14 bedrooms (disabled facilities). Per room B&B £139–£175. Dinner £30. 2-night min. stay at weekends in high season.

RAFFLES HOTEL & TEA ROOM, 73–77 Hornby Road, FY1 4QJ. Tel 01253 294713, www.raffleshotelblackpool. co.uk. Home-made cakes are served at teatime in Graham Poole and Ian Balmforth's small hotel and traditional English tea room in this flower-bedecked, bay-fronted house. It is close to the Winter Gardens and the promenade. Traditionally furnished bedrooms are homely, with a TV and a hospitality tray; in the evening, Ian Balmforth cooks good-value three-course set dinners. Local bacon and sausages at breakfast. Lounge, bar, breakfast room, tea room (closed Mon, and midweek out of season). Free Wi-Fi. Classical background music.

Parking. Children welcomed; dogs by arrangement (own bedding required). 17 bedrooms, plus 4 apartment suites (2 ground-floor rooms). Per person B&B from £38. Dinner (set menu) from £9.95. Closed Christmas.

BORROWDALE Cumbria
Map 4: inset C2
LEATHES HEAD HOTEL, CA12 5UY. Tel 01768 777247, www.leatheshead. co.uk. There are spectacular views towards Skiddaw from this country hotel in secluded grounds in the Borrowdale valley. Jamie Adamson is the 'enthusiastic' manager; staff are 'friendly and helpful'. Bedrooms in the Edwardian house are a blend of old-style elegance and modern comfort. Some bathrooms have a whirlpool spa bath and walk-in monsoon shower. All rooms have 'magnificent' views of the surrounding countryside or the hotel grounds. Daniel Hopkins's fine-dining menus use locally grown and home-reared Cumbrian produce, including Herdwick lamb, local cheeses and Keswick brewery ale. Lounge, bar, dining room, drying room; conservatory. 3-acre grounds. Free Wi-Fi. Background music. Dogs allowed in 1 room (£7.50 per day). 3 miles from Keswick. 11 bedrooms (1 on ground floor). Per room B&B £110–£203, D,B&B £150–£260. 2-night min. stay preferred. Closed Dec–4 Mar.

BOURNEMOUTH Dorset
Map 2:E2
THE GREEN HOUSE, 4 Grove Road, BH1 3AX. Tel 01202 498900, www. thegreenhousehotel.com. Close to the seafront and town centre, this handsomely restored Grade II

listed Victorian villa is run with a commitment to sustainability and environmental awareness. There are beehives on the roof, and an ecological energy system; the chic, modern interior has been decorated with natural and organic materials, eco paints, and furniture made from storm-felled trees. Olivia O'Sullivan is the manager. Smart bedrooms have a stylish bathroom with a walk-in shower; some can be small. Chef Andy Hilton uses much local and organic produce in his unfussy modern menus; alfresco meals may be taken on the lawn in warm weather. Bar, Arbor restaurant. Background music. Children welcomed (special menu, cot). Free Wi-Fi. Lift. Civil wedding licence. Parking. 32 bedrooms (1 suitable for disabled; 5 master doubles have an open-plan bathroom). Per room B&B from £129, D,B&B from £179.

URBAN BEACH, 23 Argyll Road, BH5 1EB. Tel 01202 301509, www. urbanbeach.co.uk. There is a laid-back, friendly vibe at this small, contemporary hotel a short walk from Boscombe beach. Owner Mark Cribb runs it with manager Helen McCombie and helpful staff. Individually decorated bedrooms, including two snug singles, vary in size and aspect; some are large enough to accommodate a family. The bar has a large cocktail list; the buzzy bistro serves local, seasonal produce and home-baked bread. Packed lunches available. Hotel guests have priority booking at sister restaurant Urban Reef on the beach. Bar/bistro; covered seating deck. DVD and iTunes library. Free Wi-Fi. Background music. Wellies, umbrellas, universal phone charger available on request. 1 mile E of town

centre. Complimentary use of local gym. Children welcomed (special menu; cot, baby bath, extra bed, monitor, high chair; toys, activities). 12 bedrooms. Per room B&B single £72, double £145–£180. Dinner £35. 2-night min. stay at weekends.
25% DISCOUNT VOUCHERS

BOWNESS-ON-WINDERMERE
Cumbria
Map 4: inset C2
LINDETH HOWE, Lindeth Drive, LA23 3JF. Tel 01539 445759, www. lindeth-howe.co.uk. In extensive gardens with sloping lawns, ponds and woodland, this Victorian country house overlooking Lake Windermere was once owned by Beatrix Potter. She spent family holidays and wrote some of her books here. Most of the 'well-appointed' bedrooms have views over the lake or gardens; some are large enough to accommodate a family. In the candlelit dining room, Adrian Fenon, the new chef, cooks English dishes with a French influence; good vegetarian options might include beetroot and spring onion risotto, pickled shimeji mushrooms, crisp leeks. There are board games and books in the sitting room; drinks and afternoon tea may be taken on the sun terrace. Ramps, sitting room, library, lounge bar, restaurant ('relaxing' background music, pianist on Sat evenings). Free Wi-Fi. Civil wedding licence. Sun terrace; indoor swimming pool, sauna, fitness room, treatment room. 5-acre grounds. Electric bicycles for hire. Children welcomed (no under-7s in restaurant at night; children's high tea, babysitting available). Dogs allowed in some rooms. 34 bedrooms (2 on ground floor suitable for disabled).

Per room B&B from £140, D,B&B from £210. Tasting menu £65, à la carte £35–£55. Closed 2–16 Jan.
25% DISCOUNT VOUCHERS

BRANSCOMBE Devon
Map 1:C5

THE MASON'S ARMS, EX12 3DJ. Tel 01297 680300, www.masonsarms.co.uk. There are low-beamed ceilings, timber frames, slate floors and a log fire at this 14th-century pub-with-rooms, once a cider house and a row of cottages, in a 'delightful' village close to the shingle beach. 'Comfortably furnished' bedrooms are in the main building and thatched cottages in the garden; most have antique furnishings and many original features. The cosy bar, popular with locals, has real ales; in the restaurant, 'outstanding' fish dishes cooked by Lee Villiers, the chef, are particularly recommended. 'A very good example of the all-too-rare village inn.' Ten minutes down a field path to the sea. 'Well placed for visiting other south coast resorts.' Bar, restaurant; garden with outdoor seating. Free Wi-Fi (in main bar only). No background music. Children, and dogs (in some cottages, £10 per night) welcomed. 27 bedrooms (14 in cottages, some suitable for disabled). Per room B&B £95–£195. Dinner £35.

BRIGHTON East Sussex
Map 2:E4

DRAKES, 43–44 Marine Parade, BN2 1PE. Tel 01273 696934, www.drakesofbrighton.com. Close to the pier, this modern hotel occupies two Regency town houses on the seafront. It is owned by Andy Shearer; Richard Hayes manages, with 'courteous,

helpful' staff. Bedrooms vary in size: some can be small. Most have views of the water; 'if you feel adventurous', four attic rooms have a large balcony accessed by climbing out the window. 'We enjoyed the atmosphere in the bar.' In the 'smart' basement restaurant, chef Andrew MacKenzie serves 'some seriously good cooking', including interesting vegetarian options. Lounge/bar, restaurant, meeting room. Free Wi-Fi. Civil wedding licence. Background music. Children welcomed. Limited on-site parking. 20 bedrooms. Room only £120–£360. Breakfast £6–£12.50, set dinner £32.50–£60.

FIVE, 5 New Steine, BN2 1PB. Tel 01273 686547, www.fivehotel.com. A stone's throw from the seafront, Caroline and Simon Heath's homely B&B is in a Regency town house within easy reach of shops and restaurants, the conference centre and universities. Well-equipped modern bedrooms (some are snug) are decorated with local artwork and photography; many face the sea or overlook the garden square. A continental breakfast hamper containing pastries, muffins, cereals, yogurts, fruit and juice is delivered to the bedroom at a time to suit guests. The friendly hosts have much local knowledge to share. Good-value single room. Free Wi-Fi. No background music. DVD library. Bicycle storage. Children over 5 welcomed. 9 bedrooms. Per person B&B from £45 (2-night min. stay on weekends).

PASKINS, 18–19 Charlotte Street, BN2 1AG. Tel 01273 601203, www.paskins.co.uk. 'Met my needs perfectly.' Friendly hosts Susan and Roger Marlowe run their characterful Art Deco B&B in two Grade II listed 19th-century houses near the seafront in Kemp Town. Bedrooms are immaculate and 'comfortable', though some can be small. 'Delicious' organic breakfasts are sourced from local farms and have 'unusual options'; vegetarian and vegan guests are well catered for with home-made meat-free sausages and fritters. Lounge, breakfast room. Free Wi-Fi. No background music. Children, and dogs (by arrangement) welcomed. 19 bedrooms. Per person B&B £50–£75.

A ROOM WITH A VIEW, 41 Marine Parade, BN2 1PE. Tel 01273 682885, www.aroomwithaviewbrighton.com. Stephen Bull's 'immaculately presented' guest house, in a Grade II listed Georgian building in Kemp Town, has 'cheerful, friendly' staff and 'lovely' views over the seafront and the Brighton Wheel. Decorated in soft, neutral tones, the modern bedrooms are light and airy. An attic room, though small, was 'delightful, clean and well thought out'. 'It had a comfy bed, coffee- and tea-making kit with biscuits, fluffy dressing gowns, spare slippers, ear plugs in the bedside drawer – almost like being in a hotel.' A guest this year found the heating, which is turned on at the management's discretion, 'a niggle'. The 'excellent' breakfast menu includes a 'highly recommended' double eggs Benedict. Some steep stairs. 'Metres from the beach; a few minutes' walk to the Lanes, restaurants and shops.' Lounge (gentle background music), breakfast room. Free Wi-Fi. 'Tight but helpful' parking. 9 bedrooms. Per room B&B £115–£250.

BUCKFASTLEIGH Devon
Map 1:D4
KILBURY MANOR, Colston Road, TQ11 0LN. Tel 01364 644079, www.kilburymanor.co.uk. Deep in the countryside, down a single-track lane, Julia and Martin Blundell's 'tastefully furnished' B&B is in a renovated 17th-century longhouse. Standing in four-acre grounds, it has direct access, through a meadow, to the River Dart. Comfortable, spacious bedrooms have a fireplace, quality fabrics and furnishings, and bathrobes; hospitality trays are supplied with tea, coffee, hot chocolate and locally bottled water. Two rooms, in the converted barn across the courtyard, have their own entrance. Extensive breakfasts include Julia Blundell's home-made compotes, marmalade and conserves; special dietary needs are catered for. 'Outstandingly kind', the hosts give helpful advice on local eating places. Plenty of seating in the peaceful garden and courtyard. One mile from town; the South Devon Railway runs behind the house. Dining room (wood-burning stove). Free Wi-Fi. No background music. Bicycle and canoe storage. Children over 8 welcomed. Resident dogs, Dillon and Buster. 4 bedrooms (2 in converted stone barn; plus one 1-bedroom cottage). Per room B&B £79–£95.

BUDLEIGH SALTERTON Devon
Map 1:D5
ROSEHILL ROOMS AND COOKERY, 30 West Hill, EX9 6BU. Tel 01395 444031, www.rosehillroomsandcookery.co.uk. Close to the beach, the Coastal Path and the centre of town, Willi and Sharon Rehbock's immaculate B&B is in a Grade II listed Victorian house set in peaceful gardens. Spacious bedrooms

have large windows, a sofa, home-made cakes or biscuits. Communal breakfasts are plentiful. A large veranda overlooks the garden, with distant views to the sea. In winter months, Willi Rehbock, a professional chef, hosts cookery classes and demonstrations on bread-making, seafood, Mediterranean cuisine, etc. Dining room. Free Wi-Fi. No background music. 4 bedrooms. Per room B&B £105–£135. 2-night min. stay.

BURFORD Oxfordshire
Map 2:C2

BAY TREE HOTEL, Sheep Street, OX18 4LW. Tel 01993 822791, www.cotswold-inns-hotels.co.uk. Just off the high street, this 'lovely old building', with wisteria winding up its honey-coloured walls, has been welcoming visitors for more than 400 years. It is part of Michael and Pamela Horton's small Cotswold Inns and Hotels group. It has a galleried staircase, oak-panelled rooms, an inglenook fireplace, tapestries and flagstone floors; upstairs, bedrooms are individually designed in country style with fine, often antique, furniture. Award-winning modern British food is served in the elegant restaurant overlooking the patio and rose garden. Library, bar, Bay Tree restaurant; patio (alfresco dining). Free Wi-Fi. No background music. Walled garden; croquet. Civil wedding licence; function facilities. Children and dogs welcomed. 21 bedrooms (2 adjoining garden rooms on ground floor). Per room B&B from £190, D,B&B from £245.

BURWASH East Sussex
Map 2:E4

PELHAM HALL, High Street, TN19 7ES. Tel 01435 882335, pelhamhall.co.uk.

Within the Sussex Weald, an area of outstanding natural beauty, this restored 14th-century hall house has been turned into an elegant B&B by owner Matthew Fox. The house is eclectically furnished with luxurious fabrics and antiques; there are books, interesting pottery and porcelain, and an ancient fireplace in the library. The bedrooms are individually styled: Phoenix, on the ground floor, has French doors opening on to a private patio overlooking the garden; Bantam, in the oldest part of the house, has a stunning beamed ceiling; Labrador is arranged over three levels, with a private entrance and sitting area overlooking the Weald. Matthew Fox, a native New Yorker, cooks American-style pancakes, Latin-style baked eggs or a full English for breakfast; vegetarian options are available. Close to Bateman's and Great Dixter; pubs and restaurants within easy reach. Reception room, library/bar, dining room. Patio (alfresco breakfasts); garden. Free Wi-Fi. No background music. Children over 11 welcomed. 3 bedrooms. Per room £115–£135. No credit cards accepted. 2-night min. stay preferred. Closed Christmas, New Year.

BUXTON Derbyshire
Map 3:A6

HARTINGTON HALL, Hall Bank, SK17 0AT. Tel 01298 84223, www.yha.org.uk/hostel/hartington. In 'immaculate' grounds close to the village centre, this 'lovely old building' is run as an upmarket youth hostel by the YHA. It offers 'amazing value'. Period features (mullioned windows, oak panelling) and log fires make a handsome backdrop for basic accommodation in the main house; more rooms are available in the coach house and barn. Walks and cycle routes from the front door; packed lunches provided. 2 lounges, bar, restaurant (home-cooked, hearty English fare; local ingredients). Games room; self-catering kitchen; drying room; meeting rooms. Free Wi-Fi (YHA members, in public rooms only). Background music. Extensive grounds: beer garden, pet area. Civil wedding licence. Parking. 20 mins' drive from Buxton. Children welcomed (adventure playground, giant Connect 4). 35 bedrooms (19 en suite; 10 in barn annexe, 5 in coach house; 1 suitable for disabled). Room only from £19. Breakfast £5.25, dinner from £11.95.

CAMBRIDGE Cambridgeshire
Map 2:B4

HOTEL FELIX, Whitehouse Lane, Huntingdon Road, CB3 0LX. Tel 01223 277977, www.hotelfelix.co.uk. In large landscaped gardens on the edge of the city, this smart, contemporary hotel is in a late-Victorian villa with modern extensions. The staff are 'welcoming, attentive, well trained and efficient'; Shara Ross is the manager. Public rooms have displays of modern art; there are regular exhibitions of local artists' works. Bedrooms are divided between the original house and more recently added wings. Individually decorated, they have a 'great' bed and a bathroom with underfloor heating. In the restaurant overlooking the south-facing terrace and garden, chef Jose Graziosi serves modern dishes with an Italian twist. Informal meals and afternoon tea are taken in the Orangery and the bar, or on the pretty terrace during the summer months. Small lounge, bar, Graffiti restaurant; Orangery. Room service. Civil wedding and partnership licence; function facilities. Free Wi-Fi. Background music. 4-acre garden, terrace (alfresco dining). Lift to first floor. Parking. 2 miles E of city. Children (special menu; cot; extra bed £20) and dogs (charge upon departure) welcomed. 52 bedrooms (family rooms; 4 suitable for disabled). Per room B&B (continental) from £212, D,B&B from £272. Full English breakfast £7.95. Set menu £33.

THE VARSITY HOTEL & SPA, 24 Thompson's Lane, off Bridge Street, CB5 8AQ. Tel 01223 306030, www. thevarsityhotel.co.uk. Guests rave about the 'wonderful' views from this 'very convenient' hotel on the River Cam. The modern bedrooms (some small) have large windows and a bathroom with underfloor heating; some superior rooms have extra seating and a four-poster super-king-size bed. Room service is available all day. The rooftop terrace is open in season for alfresco drinks and evening barbecues. Next door, in a restored 17th-century warehouse on the quayside, the River Bar grill is particularly liked for its steaks. 'Plenty of choice' at breakfast. Complimentary walking tours every Sat. Roof terrace (in season; open to non-residents); Glassworks health club and spa (spa bath overlooking the River Cam); lift; gym. Free Wi-Fi. Background music in restaurant. Civil wedding licence; conference facilities. Valet parking service (parking charge); local car parks. Children welcomed. 48 bedrooms (3 suitable for disabled). Per room B&B (continental) from £140.

CANTERBURY Kent
Map 2:D5
CANTERBURY CATHEDRAL LODGE, The Precincts, CT1 2EH. Tel 01227 865350, www.canterburycathedrallodge. org. Guests have private access to the cathedral precincts from this 'very special' purpose-built hotel and conference centre in the grounds of the UNESCO-designated World Heritage site. 'I couldn't resist sitting on the window seat and just staring at the magnificence.' Modern, 'very comfortably furnished' courtyard bedrooms, decorated in ecclesiastic red or purple, overlook lawns and gardens, or have views of the cathedral; they are equipped with tea- and coffee-making facilities and a TV. Some 'no-frills' rooms are on the second floor of the adjacent Burgate annexe (no lift, no views). Breakfast, taken in the Refectory restaurant, was 'memorable'; there is alfresco seating on the terrace in the summer months. Guests have free entry into the cathedral, and may walk through the grounds after the public have left at the end of the day. No evening meals are served, but many restaurants are within walking distance. 'I was highly satisfied.' Library, breakfast room; Campanile Garden. Meeting/function facilities. Lift. Limited parking (pre-booking required). Free Wi-Fi. No background music. 35 bedrooms (1 suitable for disabled). Per room B&B £90–135.

CHADDESLEY CORBETT
Worcestershire
Map 3:C5
BROCKENCOTE HALL, DY10 4PY. Tel 01562 777876, www.brockencotehall. com. 'A wonderful battery recharger.'

Up a sweeping drive, past a 'serene' lake and grazing sheep, this 'very elegant' country house hotel (Eden Hotel Collection) has 'pleasantly large' bedrooms, 'terrific' dinners and 'charming' staff. It is managed by Dean Gunston. Plushly decorated bedrooms have a modern bathroom; all have views of the estate. Slippers are laid out at turn-down; in the morning, a newsletter with the day's weather forecast is delivered to the room. Chef Adam Brown serves 'very good' modern menus in Chaddesley restaurant (open to non-residents); informal meals and afternoon tea are taken in the high-ceilinged bar and lounge. Library, conservatory/lounge, restaurant; 2 private dining rooms. Civil wedding licence. Free Wi-Fi. Light jazz and classical background music. 72-acre grounds; 3 miles SE of Kidderminster. Children welcomed. 21 bedrooms (some suitable for disabled). Per room B&B single £115–£345, double £135–£435. D,B&B £130–£205 per person (min. 2-night stay). Set dinners £42.95–£59.95, tasting menu £75.

CHARMOUTH Dorset
Map1:C6
THE ABBOTS HOUSE, The Street, DT6 6QF. Tel 01297 560339, www. abbotshouse.co.uk. Close to the centre, and a five-minute walk from the beach, Sheila and Nick Gilbey's small, characterful B&B is run with 'amazing' attention to detail. The carefully restored house dates back to the 16th century: it has oak-panelled walls, an ornate beamed ceiling, flagstone floors and dainty bedrooms; bathrooms have a double-ended bath and flat-screen TV. Breakfast has home-baked bread

and home-made jams and marmalade, which are available for purchase. Lounge, garden room, garden (model railway). DVD library. Free Wi-Fi. Background music at breakfast. 4 bedrooms (plus 1-bedroom self-contained cottage in the garden). Per room B&B £110–£150 (2-night min. stay). Closed 16 Dec–10 Jan.

CHATTON Northumberland
Map 4:A3

CHATTON PARK HOUSE, New Road, NE66 5RA. Tel 01668 215507, www. chattonpark.com. Husband-and-wife team Paul and Michelle Mattinson are the 'most welcoming' hosts at this B&B, in an imposing Georgian house on a peaceful country estate on the edge of Northumberland national park. 'It exceeded our expectations.' Spacious, well-equipped bedrooms are named after local towns or villages, and furnished in period style. 'Superlative' breakfasts, with much local produce, are ordered in advance. The Mattinsons help with bookings at local pubs and restaurants. 'Huge' sitting room, cosy bar, breakfast room. Free Wi-Fi; weak mobile telephone signal. No background music. Parking. 4-acre grounds; grass tennis courts (May–Sept). ½ mile from Chatton; Alnwick, Bamburgh and Holy Island are close by. 4 bedrooms (plus 2-bedroom self-catering stone lodge with private garden). Per person B&B from £50. Closed Jan.

CHELTENHAM Gloucestershire
Map 3:D5

BEAUMONT HOUSE, 56 Shurdington Road, GL53 0JE. Tel 01242 223311, www.bhhotel.co.uk. 'A thoroughly enjoyable experience.' Fan and Alan Bishop's 'excellent' guest house is in a former Victorian merchant's home in large, well-tended gardens. Well-appointed bedrooms vary considerably in size; two are themed (Out of Africa and Out of Asia); all have a 'comfortable' bed, tea- and coffee-making facilities and biscuits. The spacious lounge has an honesty bar and complimentary hot drinks; a 'limited but changing' menu is available in the evenings (Mon–Thurs, 5.30 pm–8 pm). In the dining room overlooking the flower garden, breakfast includes smoked fish, local sausages and American-style pancakes; breakfast in bed can be arranged. The shops and restaurants of Montpellier Arcade are 25 mins' walk away. Lounge, dining room (background music), conservatory. Free Wi-Fi. Parking. Children welcomed (cot; £30 per night charge). 16 bedrooms (2 family suites). Per room B&B single £75–£220, double £109–£275.

BUTLERS, Western Road, GL50 3RN. Tel 01242 570771, www.butlers-hotel. co.uk. On a quiet street, an easy stroll to the town centre, 'friendly and helpful' owners Robert Davies and Guy Hunter have embellished this former gentleman's residence with butler memorabilia such as candlestick telephones, old hats and photographs. The 'comfortable' lounge has newspapers, books, games and stationery. 'Well-appointed' bedrooms, named after famous butlers in literature and film (Jeeves, Hudson, Brabinger, etc), have a radio, hospitality tray, and ironing and pressing facilities. A 'good' breakfast is taken in a high-ceilinged room overlooking the pretty walled garden. 10 mins' walk to the bus and railway stations. Drawing room, dining room (quiet radio in the morning); ¼-acre garden. Free Wi-Fi. Parking. 9 bedrooms. Per room B&B £75–£120. 2-night min. stay during weekends and festivals.

THE CHELTENHAM TOWNHOUSE, 12–14 Pittville Lawn, GL52 2BD. Tel 01242 221922, www.cheltenhamtownhouse. com. There are modern, airy rooms and a relaxing atmosphere at Adam and Jayne Lillywhite's peaceful B&B, in a renovated Regency house five minutes' walk from the centre. It is managed by Nathaniel Leitch. The comfortable lounge has fresh flowers and newspapers, an open fire in cool weather; drinks may be taken on the sun deck on warm days. Individually designed bedrooms vary in size, from a compact 'economy' rooms to studio apartments with a kitchen and additional sofa bed. Good breakfasts. Two bicycles and helmets available to borrow. Convenient for the Pittville Pump Room and the racecourse. Lounge (honesty bar; help-yourself fruit bowl), breakfast room; sun deck. DVD library. Free Wi-Fi. No background music. Lift. Parking (limited on-site; permits supplied for street). Children welcomed (family rooms; cot, extra bed, high chair, milk warming). 26 bedrooms (some family), plus 5 studio apartments (4 in annexe), one 2-bed suite. Per room B&B £73–£150.

HANOVER HOUSE, 65 St George's Road, GL50 3DU. Tel 01242 541297, www. hanoverhouse.org. In the centre of town, Veronica and James McIntosh-Ritchie's 'beautiful' Italianate home is filled with fresh flowers, pictures,

'interesting objects' and a 'splendidly varied selection of books'. Spacious, colourful bedrooms in the Grade II listed Victorian town house have lots of home comforts; beds have an electric blanket in wintertime. A civilised breakfast, served on blue-and-white china, is taken in the Aga-equipped kitchen or the Victorian dining room overlooking the walled garden; there are home-made bread and preserves, and locally sourced produce. Drawing room (open fire in winter), breakfast room; walled garden. Parking. Free Wi-Fi. Classical background music. Resident dog. Children over 12 welcomed. 4 bedrooms (1 with separate bathroom; robes provided). Per room B&B from £110. Closed 19 Dec–31 Jan.

No. 131, 131 The Promenade, GL50 1NW. Tel 01242 822939, www.no131. com. There is 'a nice atmosphere' at this handsomely restored Grade II* Georgian villa on the historic promenade. It is owned by Sam and Georgina Pearman; Stephen Wadcock is the manager. Individually decorated with original artwork, the 'very comfortable' bedrooms are well equipped with tea-making facilities, a Nespresso machine, interesting minibar snacks and a hot-water bottle; 'a great bed'. The glamorous Crazy Eights bar is popular with locals, who come for the cocktails and sharing plates; in the restaurant, chef Michael Bedford's menus focus on seafood and prime cuts cooked in the wood-fired Josper oven. Afternoon tea has home-made sausage rolls and Victoria sponge cake. The Pearmans also own the Wheatsheaf, Northleach (see main entry). Drawing room, lounge, games room, bar, restaurant. Terrace (alfresco dining). Private dining rooms. Free Wi-Fi. Background music. 'Very convenient' parking. Children welcomed. 11 bedrooms. Per room B&B (continental) £150–£220. Dinner £38.

NO. 38 THE PARK, 38 Evesham Road, GL52 2AH. Tel 01242 822929, www. no38thepark.com. Guests receive the keys to this modern B&B in a stylishly refurbished Georgian town house overlooking Pitville Park. It is owned by Sam and Georgina Pearman, who also own No. 131 (see previous entry). Bedrooms are individually styled with original artwork and a mix of vintage and modern furniture; some, entered via a shared doorway, are ideal for a family. Each room has the latest technology: an iPod docking station, a flat-screen TV with a pre-loaded library of movies. No evening meals are served, but sister restaurant The Tavern is a ten-minute walk away. The breakfast buffet has cereals, pastries, fruit, cold cuts and juices; cooked dishes cost extra. On the A435 towards Evesham (front windows are double glazed). Drawing room, open-plan dining area, private dining room. Small courtyard garden. Free Wi-Fi. Background music. Limited parking. Children welcomed. 13 bedrooms. Per room B&B (continental) £120–£180.

CHESTER Cheshire
Map 3:A4

THE CHESTER GROSVENOR, Eastgate, CH1 1LT. Tel 01244 324024, www. chestergrosvenor.com. Close to the cathedral and the Eastgate Clock, this large, luxurious hotel 'could not be more centrally placed'. It is managed by Bespoke Hotels for the Duke of Westminster. 'Well-appointed, spotless' bedrooms are traditionally styled; they have an 'outstandingly comfortable' bed with 'quality' linens; robes, slippers and 'excellent' large towels in the marble bathroom. No tea- or coffee-making facilities in the room, but 'I rang and it was only minutes before a member of staff arrived with lovely china cups, teapots, biscuits and fresh milk'. There are several dining options: the 'smart' Michelin-starred restaurant, Simon Radley at The Chester Grosvenor, is 'an experience not to be missed'. 'Service and food are great' in the 'attractive' Brasserie. Afternoon tea and light meals are served in the Arkle bar and lounge. 'Everything we ordered was fresh and tasty' at breakfast. Lift. Ramps. Drawing room, gallery lounge, private dining room. Civil wedding licence; function facilities. Spa (crystal steam room, herb sauna, themed shower, ice fountain; 5 treatment rooms). Free Wi-Fi. Background music. Valet parking service; multi-storey car park at rear of hotel. Children welcomed (special menu; interconnecting family rooms; no under-12s in restaurant). 80 bedrooms and suites (1 suitable for disabled). Per room B&B (continental) from £175, D,B&B from £210 in brasserie, from £290 in restaurant. Set menus (in restaurant) £75 or £99.

EDGAR HOUSE, 22 City Walls, CH1 1SB. Tel 01244 347007, www.edgarhouse. co.uk. On the River Dee, this peacefully located 19th-century villa leads directly on to the walkway of the ancient city walls. Tim Mills and Michael Stephen, the owners, have given it a glamorous feel, with bespoke furniture, glittering chandeliers and designer wallpaper; quirky touches include an eclectic collection of art, and an honesty bar housed in a refurbished telephone box. Spacious bedrooms have a super-king-size bed and a sofa. Bathrooms have a rain shower and underfloor heating; four have a freestanding bath. Some rooms have a private balcony overlooking the river. On Friday and Saturday evenings, chef Neil Griffiths serves modern English and French dishes in the library dining room or the riverside garden. Breakfast has freshly squeezed juice, local honeys, 'properly toasted' teacakes. 2 lounges, restaurant (closed Mon and Tues, except bank holidays; open to non-residents); garden. Parking. Free Wi-Fi. Background music. Children over 14 welcomed. 7 bedrooms. Per room B&B £179–£289, D,B&B £249–£359. Closed New Year's Eve, Jan (2- to 3-night Christmas breaks available).

ODDFELLOWS, 20 Lower Bridge Street, CH1 1RS. Tel 01244 345454, www.oddfellowschester.com. Oddfellows by name and odd in decor. Close to the shops and cafés of the Rows, this listed neoclassical mansion is said to be a former meeting place for the altruistic Independent Order of Odd Fellows. Beyond its Georgian facade, there are topsy-turvy lamps, typewriters and oversized nature scenes on the panelled walls. Very individually styled bedrooms are in the main house and the new annexe at the bottom of the garden; some have a sloping ceiling, others a circular bed; one has twin roll-top baths. Drinks may be taken in the Secret Garden (artificial grass, fire pits, heated private booths) or the flamboyant lounge bar. In the Garden restaurant, chefs Steven Tuke and Simon Radley (of the Chester Grosvenor, see Shortlist, previous page) serve a modern menu with a Mediterranean slant. A light breakfast bag (croissant, natural yogurt, fresh orange juice and fruit) is delivered to the bedroom in the morning. Lobby, bar, restaurant, conservatory; garden. Private dining room and terrace. Free Wi-Fi. Background music. Children welcomed (cot, extra bed £30 per night). 18 bedrooms (14 in annexe; 1 suitable for disabled). Per room B&B from £162, D,B&B from £222. Closed Christmas Day.

CHEWTON MENDIP Somerset
Map 2:D1

THE POST HOUSE, BA3 4NS. Tel 01761 241704, www.theposthousebandb.co.uk. In a village close to the cathedral city of Wells, 'excellent hostess' Karen Price offers stylish B&B accommodation in her renovated Grade II listed former post office and bakery. Charming and spacious, the rustic, French-style bedrooms have muted colours and wild flowers; a supply of home-made biscuits is topped up every day. The Old Bakery, 'a luxurious space', is equipped for self-catering; it has a stone fireplace and its own secluded courtyard. Breakfast has fresh fruit salad, home-baked bread, locally sourced bacon and sausages. Bath, Cheddar Gorge, Tyntesfield, Longleat and Wookey Hole are all within easy reach. Sitting room, dining room (no background music); Mediterranean-style courtyard; small garden. Free Wi-Fi. Parking. Resident dog, Monty. 2 bedrooms (plus 1 self-catering cottage). Per room B&B £90–£140. 2-night min. stay at weekends.

CHICHESTER West Sussex
Map 2:E3

CROUCHERS, Birdham Road, PO20 7EH. Tel 01243 784995, www.crouchers countryhotel.com. In open countryside where pheasants can be seen roaming the fields, Lloyd van Rooyen's much-extended hotel is set in 'refreshing greenery' close to West Wittering beach. Simply furnished bedrooms are divided between the main house and the converted coach house, barn and stable; several have a private patio. The hotel is on the main road between Chichester and the Witterings; there may be some traffic noise; rear rooms are quietest. Modern dishes are served in the oak-beamed restaurant; drinks and casual lunches may be taken in the wine bar. 3 miles S of the town centre. Lounge, bar, restaurant (classical background music; open to non-residents); courtyard; 2-acre garden. Civil wedding licence; function facilities. Free Wi-Fi. Parking. Children welcomed (family rooms). 26 bedrooms (23 in coach house, barn and stables; 10 with patio; 2 suitable for disabled). Per room B&B £144–£165, D,B&B £189–£210. Set dinner £25.50.

ROOKS HILL, Lavant Road, PO18 0BQ. Tel 01243 528400, www.rookshill.co.uk. New owner Erling Sorensen runs this smart B&B in a Grade II listed former farmhouse in a little village at the foot of the South Downs. Bedrooms have feather pillows, crisp linens, a hospitality tray with hot chocolate; bathrooms have a power shower; double glazing keeps out noise from the road. In an oak-beamed room opening on to a wisteria-clad patio, breakfast has local produce, and fruit and vegetables from the garden. No evening meals are served, but there is a choice of nearby restaurants, including the recommended Earl of March pub, opposite. Goodwood is within easy reach. Drawing room, breakfast room. Free Wi-Fi. Classical background music. Parking. 4 miles N of city centre. 3 bedrooms (1 suitable for disabled; plus two 1-bedroom apartments). Per room B&B £120–£175.

CHIDDINGFOLD Surrey
Map 2:D3

THE CROWN INN, The Green, Petworth Road, GU8 4TX. Tel 01428 682255, www.thecrownchiddingfold.com. With stained-glass windows, medieval walls and 'passageways a bit like a rabbit warren', Daniel and Hannah Hall's restored 14th-century inn, on a corner of the village green, exudes a 'genuine', old-fashioned atmosphere. Marcus Tapping is the manager. Characterful bedrooms (some with a four-poster bed) have ancient oak beams, sloping floor and handsome antique furnishings; up-to-date technology includes a flat-screen TV and an iPod dock/digital clock radio. Traditional dishes are served in the 'superb' oak-panelled restaurant; 'all was delicious'. The bars, popular with locals, have a barbecue and wood-burning pizza oven in summer. Plenty of choice at breakfast. 2 bars (Crown and Half Crown with open fire; monthly quiz night), restaurant (background jazz/radio; special diets catered for); 2 small courtyard gardens for alfresco dining; private dining room. Free Wi-Fi. Children welcomed (special menu; children's play area). 8 bedrooms (front ones hear traffic). Per room B&B single £85–£100, double £110–£200. Dinner £25–£30.

CHILGROVE West Sussex
Map 2:E3
THE WHITE HORSE, 1 High Street,
PO18 9HX. Tel 01243 519444, www.
thewhitehorse.co.uk. 'Simply lovely',
this 18th-century staging post inn,
in the foothills of the South Downs,
has been renovated in contemporary
rustic style. Niki Burr is the 'charming'
manager. Bedrooms have a modern
four-poster bed; there are steamer
trunks, sheepskin rugs and wool throws.
Two rooms have a private patio with a
hot tub. All open on to a courtyard with
wonderful views of the Downs. In the
'welcoming' bar and stylish restaurant
(banquette seating, cosy booths covered
in yak skin), chef Rob Armstrong
serves 'simple but satisfying' pub food,
including trout from nearby rivers.
Bar, restaurant, private dining room. 2
patios; garden. Function facilities. Free
Wi-Fi. Soft background music. Croquet.
Parking. Helipad. Children (cot, no
bedding supplied; charge for extra bed)
and dogs (£15 per stay) welcomed. 15
bedrooms (all on ground floor; 2 in main
building, 13 in rear annexe; 2 suitable
for a family). 10 mins' drive from
Chichester. Per room B&B £90–£220.
Dinner £28.50.

CLEY-NEXT-THE-SEA Norfolk
Map 2:A5
CLEY WINDMILL, The Quay, NR25 7RP.
Tel 01263 740209, www.cleywindmill.
co.uk. Overlooking the salt marshes
and the sea, this characterful B&B and
restaurant occupies an 18th-century
grinding mill standing among the
reed beds by the River Glaven. It is
managed by Simon Whatling for the
owners, Julian and Carolyn Godlee.
There are sofas, antiques and an open

fire in the circular sitting room at
the base of the mill. Upstairs, and in
converted buildings in the courtyard,
charming, country-style bedrooms
are individually decorated. 'Only for
the adventurous', the top-floor Wheel
Room, accessed via a steep ladder, has
a different panoramic view out of each
of its four windows. In the candlelit
dining room, part of the original
granary, chefs Emma Wedderburn
and Jimmi Cubitt produce daily-
changing three-course menus which
are served communally. Locally
smoked kippers and haddock may be
pre-ordered from the village smokery
for breakfast. Sitting room, restaurant
(background music; open to non-
residents); ¼-acre garden. Free Wi-Fi.
Civil wedding licence. Children
welcomed in some rooms (early supper
by arrangement). 9 bedrooms (3 in
converted boathouse and granary).
Per room B&B £159–£219, D,B&B
£217–£277. Set menu £32.50. 2-night
min. stay on Fri and Sat nights.

COLWALL Worcestershire
Map 3:D5
COLWALL PARK, Walwyn Road WR13
6QG. Tel 01684 540000, www.colwall.
com. With 'a charm all of its own', this
black-and-white Edwardian building
stands in lovely landscaped gardens
in a peaceful village on the flank of
the Malvern Hills. Originally built to
serve the now-defunct Colwall Park
racecourse, it is now a country house
hotel. A programme of refurbishment is
under way after a change of ownership
in June 2014; Laura Fish is the general
manager. Rooms vary in size, and are
individually decorated in chic, simple,
style; a family suite has a separate

bedroom for children. Spacious public areas include an attractive modern bar. Chef Eugine Andreas cooks modern British dishes using local, seasonal produce; bread rolls are freshly baked each morning. Light meals are available in the bar, which has real ales. Through the large garden, paths lead directly to the hills, via a railway footbridge. 2 lounges (1 with TV), library, bar, restaurant, ballroom. 1-acre garden. Free Wi-Fi. Background music. Wedding/conference facilities. Children welcomed (cot, extra bed £35 per night). 22 bedrooms. B&B £85–£125. Dinner £25.

CONSTANTINE Cornwall
Map 1:E2

TRENGILLY WARTHA, Nancenoy, TR11 5RP. Tel 01326 340332, www.trengilly. co.uk. 'Down the narrowest of Cornish lanes', Will and Lisa Lea's family-friendly pub-with-rooms is in a wooded valley close to the Helford River. The lively bar, 'well stocked with interesting real ales and ciders', is popular with locals. In the restaurant, long-serving chef Nick Tyler uses locally sourced produce, perhaps mussels, in his classic menus. Bedrooms are simply furnished in country style, and have views over the large, lush garden or the village; each has tea- and coffee-making facilities and biscuits. The award-winning breakfast includes a full Cornish with local sausages. Bar (quiz nights, live music Sun night), restaurant; private dining room; games room; conservatory. Terrace (alfresco dining), garden (sheltered pond). Free Wi-Fi. Children and dogs welcomed. 11 bedrooms (2 in garden annexe). Per room B&B £84–£106.

CONSTANTINE BAY Cornwall
Map 1:D2

TREGLOS HOTEL, Beach Road, PL28 8JH. Tel 01841 520727, www. tregloshotel.com. 'How nice to come back to this lovely hotel.' In landscaped gardens, overlooking the white sandy beach of Constantine Bay, the Barlow family has owned this traditional hotel for 50 years. Popular with families, it is run with staff who are 'very helpful, and anxious to please'. Many of the 'well-appointed, comfortable' bedrooms have fine sea views; some have a balcony. Chef Gavin Hill's 'imaginative' daily-changing menus are served in the award-winning restaurant. 2 lounges, bar, conservatory, restaurant (smart/ casual attire after 7 pm); children's den, snooker room; indoor swimming pool; spa treatments. 1-acre grounds; sunken garden. Lift. Ramps. Free Wi-Fi (variable signal). Background music (optional). Children (special menus) and dogs (in some rooms) welcomed. Parking. 3 miles W of Padstow. 42 bedrooms (1 on ground floor; 2 suitable for disabled; plus self-catering apartments in grounds). Per person B&B from £75, D,B&B from £95. 2-night min. stay during some periods. Closed Nov–Mar.

25% DISCOUNT VOUCHERS

CORNWORTHY Devon
Map 1:D4

KERSWELL FARMHOUSE, Furze Cross, TQ9 7HH. Tel 01803 732013, www.kerswellfarmhouse.co.uk. In magnificent Dartmoor countryside, this 400-year-old longhouse has been lavishly renovated in rustic modern style by owners Nichola and Graham Hawkins. It has English oak fittings, a mix of antique and modern furnishing, and displays of original work by British artists. Homely, country-style bedrooms have a large bed, fresh flowers and individually controlled underfloor heating. One, in a converted barn, has a sitting room and a private terrace and garden. Breakfast is served in the old farmhouse dining room or in the conservatory overlooking rolling countryside; there is a good choice of cooked dishes, including a toasted club sandwich. Works of ceramicists, glassmakers, painters and photographers are exhibited in the former milking parlour. Gallery sitting room (honesty bar, including wines from a local vineyard), dining room, garden dining room. DVDs, books. 14-acre grounds; woodland and riverside walks from the house; kayaking (1 kayak available to loan). Free Wi-Fi. No background music. Parking. 5 miles from Totnes. 5 bedrooms (2 in adjacent barn; 1 on ground floor). Per room B&B £110–£140. Credit cards not accepted. Closed Christmas, New Year.

CORSE LAWN Gloucestershire
Map 3:D5

CORSE LAWN HOUSE, GL19 4LZ. Tel 01452 780771, www.corselawn.com. 'A relaxing and pleasant stay.' In the Severn valley, this small hotel and restaurant is run with 'old-school values' by Baba Hine with her son, Giles. It is fronted by a large ornamental pond (originally a coach wash into which a driver could steer and turn a stagecoach and four horses). Inside the 'lovely' Grade II listed Queen Anne building, there are cheering open fires and antiques in the drawing rooms. Spacious bedrooms, decorated in country house

style, are supplied with a generous bowl of fresh fruit, 'excellent' biscuits, loose tea, ground coffee, fresh milk. Old-style bathrooms have 'superb', large towelling gowns. The chef, Martin Kinahan, serves 'very good, well-presented' French and English dishes in the salmon-pink dining room; snacks are available in the new snug bar. 6 miles W of Tewkesbury. 2 sitting rooms, bar, bistro, restaurant. Free Wi-Fi. No background music. Civil wedding licence; function facilities. 12-acre grounds (gardens, croquet lawn, all-weather tennis court); heated indoor swimming pool. Children and dogs welcomed. 18 bedrooms. Per room B&B from £170, D,B&B from £215. Closed 24–26 Dec.

25% DISCOUNT VOUCHERS

CORSHAM Wiltshire
Map 2:D1

THE METHUEN ARMS, 2 High Street, SN13 0HB. Tel 01249 717060, www.themethuenarms.com. A popular hub for locals, this handsomely restored Georgian coaching inn is in a market town eight miles from Bath. It is run as a restaurant-with-rooms by owners Martin and Debbie Still, who have updated the interior with a modern rustic look. Intimate dining areas have elm floorboards, ancient beams, exposed stone walls and log fires; tasteful, well-equipped bedrooms are individually decorated in heritage colours. Food is available throughout the day: chef Piero Boi cooks robust modern British dishes with an Italian influence. Lounge, 2 bars (West Country ales, Somerset cider brandy); private dining room. Large garden; courtyard (alfresco dining). Boules piste. Free Wi-Fi. No background music. Parking. Children welcomed (special menu). 14 bedrooms (1 in annexe; family room). Per person B&B £90–£175, D,B&B from £125. Closed Christmas Day.

COVENTRY Warwickshire
Map 3:C6

BARNACLE HALL, Shilton Lane, CV7 9LH. Tel 02476 612629, www. barnaclehall.co.uk. A welcoming refuge, Rose Grindal's rural B&B is in a Grade II listed 16th-century farmhouse five miles from the city centre. Full of nooks and crannies, the house has oak beams, polished wood and an inglenook fireplace with a wood-burning stove. Simply decorated, the large, comfortable bedrooms have fresh flowers. Tasty breakfasts have lots of choice; guests needing to make an early start are served from 7 am. Easy access from the motorway. Sitting room, dining room; garden, patio. Free Wi-Fi (in 2 rooms). No background music. Children welcomed. 3 bedrooms. Per person B&B single £45–£55, double £75–£85. Credit cards not accepted. Closed Christmas, New Year.

COVERACK Cornwall
Map 1:E2

THE BAY HOTEL, North Corner, TR12 6TF. Tel 01326 280464, www. thebayhotel.co.uk. 'Friendly and pleasant', Ric and Gina House and their daughter, Zoë, run their 'comfortable' hotel in a 'very personal way'. The white-painted building is in the centre of a pretty fishing village, above a wide bay on the Lizard Peninsula; the lounge and many of the bedrooms have panoramic views across the water. In the candlelit restaurant, Ric House uses Cornish produce, and fresh fish

landed in the bay for his 'very good' cooking. Full Cornish breakfasts. Lawned gardens on two levels lead to the beach; a coastal path starts at the foot of the drive. Lounge, bar/restaurant (soft background music), conservatory, large sun terrace; garden. Free Wi-Fi in public areas; no mobile phone signal; no telephone in the bedrooms. Background music (between 7 pm and 9 pm). Parking. Children over 8 by arrangement; small to medium dogs accepted. 14 bedrooms (1 on ground floor suitable for disabled). Per person B&B £55–£125, D,B&B £85–£145. Closed 5 Nov–end Feb.

CRAYKE North Yorkshire
Map 4:D4

THE DURHAM OX, Westway, YO61 4TE. Tel 01347 821506, www.thedurhamox. com. There are exposed beams, carved wood panelling and an inglenook fireplace in this characterful 300-year-old country pub-with-rooms, which has been owned by the Ibbotson family for more than 15 years. Andy Eaton-Carr is the manager. Bedrooms are in the main building or renovated farm cottages; a spacious studio, over the pub, has sofas, a kitchen, an honesty bar and a private balcony with views across the Vale of York. Meals are taken in the flagstone-floored dining room, a traditional bar or the Burns Bar, an all-weather garden room; Matthew Meek, the chef, cooks modern British pub classics and a blackboard menu of daily specials. Walks from the door; walking guides available. 3 bars, restaurant, private dining room. 1-acre grounds. Function facilities. Free Wi-Fi. Background music. Parking. Convenient for Park and Ride into York. Children (special menu, high chairs) and dogs (in some public areas) welcomed. 6 bedrooms (1 suite, accessed via external stairs; 5 in converted farm cottages; 2 on ground floor), plus 3-bedroom self-catering cottage in village. Per room B&B from £120. Dinner £28.

CROSTHWAITE Cumbria
Map 4: inset C2
THE PUNCH BOWL INN, Lyth Valley, Kendal, LA8 8HR. Tel 01539 568237, www.the-punchbowl.co.uk. Close to Lake Windermere, this 'fantastic' 300-year-old inn is liked for its 'comfortable' country-style bedrooms and 'extraordinary' cooking. It is owned by Richard Rose. Individually designed bedrooms, many with views over the unspoilt Lyth valley, have a Roberts radio; bathrooms have underfloor heating and a freestanding roll-top bath. Morning tea or coffee is 'swiftly' brought to the room on request; a cream tea is offered every afternoon. In the 'lovely' restaurant, chef Scott Fairweather's menu 'featured great imagination': 'We enjoyed some of the best food we have had in a long time, in particular a delicate, delicious venison tartare; a flavourful guinea fowl breast was served with an earthy, unctuous wild mushroom tagliatelle.' 2 bars, restaurant (background jazz); 2 terraces. Civil wedding licence; conference facilities. Free Wi-Fi (in bar only). Parking. Children welcomed. 9 bedrooms. Per room B&B £105–£305.

DARLINGTON Co. Durham
Map 4:C4
HEADLAM HALL, nr Gainford, DL2 3HA. Tel 01325 730238, www. headlamhall.co.uk. Surrounded by vast farmland, this handsome 17th-century country house in beautiful walled gardens is 'a very pleasant place to stay'. The Robinson family owners run it with long-serving, 'enthusiastic' staff; housekeeping is 'excellent'. It has a Jacobean hall, stone walls, huge fireplaces and traditional furnishing; many bedrooms have antiques, and work by local artists. Modern British dishes, using produce from the kitchen garden, are served in the panelled dining room, the airy Orangery and the spa brasserie. Private dining is also available. In a hamlet 8 miles W of Darlington. 3 lounges, bar, brasserie ('easy listening'/jazz background music). Free Wi-Fi. Lift. Civil wedding licence; function facilities. Spa (14 by 6-metre indoor pool; outdoor hydrotherapy pool, sauna, gym; treatment rooms). Terraces; 4-acre garden: lake, ornamental canal; tennis, 9-hole golf course, croquet. Parking. Children, and dogs (in mews rooms only) welcomed. 39 bedrooms (6 in mews, 9 in coach house, 7 in spa; 2 suitable for disabled). Per person B&B from £65, D,B&B from £99. Closed Christmas.
25% DISCOUNT VOUCHERS

HOUNDGATE TOWNHOUSE, 11 Houndgate, DL1 5RF. Tel 01325 486011, www.houndgatetownhouse.co.uk. 'Very nicely done.' On the western edge of the market town, Natalie Cooper's small guest house and restaurant are in a meticulously restored 18th-century town house. The quirky interior pays homage to the building and the town's past with witty wallpaper and bespoke furniture; specially commissioned artefacts and sculptures include an impressive chandelier. Smart bedrooms are

individually decorated; the best have a huge four-poster bed and a freestanding bath. Bistro menus are served in the restaurant at lunch and dinner; meals may be taken in the terraced courtyard in good weather. Breakfast, with home-made granola, French toast and a choice of egg dishes, is served until noon every day; afternoon tea has home-baked breads and cakes. Lounge, bar, Eleven restaurant (Saturday brunch, traditional Sunday lunch). Courtyard. Room service. Lift. Free Wi-Fi. Background music. Paid parking. Children welcomed (special menu, high chair, cot). Complimentary access to local indoor pool across the road. 8 bedrooms (1 suitable for disabled). Per room B&B from £90, D,B&B from £129.
25% DISCOUNT VOUCHERS

DARTMOUTH Devon
Map 1:D4

BROWNS HOTEL, 27–29 Victoria Road, TQ6 9RT. Tel 01803 832572, www. brownshoteldartmouth.co.uk. Clare and James Brown's informal hotel is in a 200-year-old town house within easy walking distance of the waterfront. Modern bedrooms vary in size and style; each has space to sit. Food and wine events (open to the public) are occasionally organised in the sleek, open-plan wine bar and shop; when the bar is closed, guests are offered complimentary pre- and post-dinner drinks. Tapas and light, Mediterranean-influenced meals are available during the day; sharing platters on Friday and Saturday evenings. Lounge, bar (complimentary tapas on Fri eve), restaurant (closed Sun–Thurs). Free Wi-Fi. Soft background jazz. Parking permits supplied. Children welcomed.

8 bedrooms. Per room B&B £90–£225. Dinner £30. 2-night min. stay in peak season. Closed Christmas, Jan.

STRETE BARTON HOUSE, Totnes Road TQ6 0RU. Tel 01803 770364, www. stretebarton.co.uk. Close to the South West Coastal Path, this 16th-century manor house has panoramic views across the bay, from Start Point lighthouse to the mouth of the River Dart. Owners Stuart Litster and Kevin Hooper have decorated it in a contemporary style with an Eastern flavour; bedrooms have silks, Buddha carvings and bold prints. Guests take tea and home-made cake beside a roaring fire in winter; on warm days they sit on the terrace overlooking the sea. Seasonal fruit and local farm yogurts are served at breakfast. 5 miles SW of Dartmouth. Sitting room, breakfast room. Garden. Free Wi-Fi. No background music. In-room massages/spa treatments, by arrangement. Children over 8, and dogs (in cottage suite) welcomed. 6 bedrooms (1 in cottage annexe). Per person B&B from £52.50. 2-night min. stay preferred in peak season.

DOVER Kent
Map 2:D5

WALLETT'S COURT, Westcliffe, St Margaret's-at-Cliffe, CT15 6EW. Tel 01304 852424, www.walletts courthotelspa.com. In a pretty hamlet near St Margaret's Bay, the Oakley family's quirky hotel has a broad choice of accommodation, and plenty to occupy young guests. There are spacious traditional rooms in the white-painted Jacobean manor house; snug stable-block rooms overlooking the gardens and wild flower meadows;

high-ceilinged Kentish barn suites; and a hut, a woodcutter's cabin, a bathing wagon and luxury tipis, all with outdoor fire pits, spread out in the extensive landscaped gardens. In the oak-beamed restaurant, Chris Oakley and Michael Fowler, the new chef, use home-grown and foraged produce alongside locally landed fish and St Margaret's Bay lobster; Chef's Table tasting menus may be arranged for parties of four or more. Breakfast, served 'at a leisurely pace', has eggs from resident hens, and locally sourced bacon and sausages. 10 mins' drive from the port and cruise terminal. Lounge, bar, library, conservatory, Oakley & Fowler restaurant (background music; open to non-residents). Free Wi-Fi in main house. 12-metre indoor swimming pool with Endless Pools swim trainer and hydrotherapy massage; sauna, steam room, fitness studio, indoor hot tub, treatment cabins, relaxation room; tennis courts, badminton, croquet lawn, boules court; golf pitching range, jogging trail, tree house; sun terraces. Civil wedding licence; functions. Children (baby-listening devices; high teas; £20 per child for an extra bed) and dogs welcomed. 17 bedrooms (13 in barns, stables and cottages; plus 2 tipis in grounds). Per room B&B from £135, D,B&B from £215. 2-night min. stay July, Aug preferred. Closed Christmas. **25% DISCOUNT VOUCHERS**

DULVERTON Somerset
Map 1:B5

THREE ACRES COUNTRY HOUSE, Ellersdown Lane, TA22 9AR. Tel 01398 323730, www.threeacresexmoor.co.uk. On the southern edge of Exmoor national park, Julie and Edward

Christian's B&B stands in secluded grounds, with stunning hillside views over the small farming village of Brushford. The 1930s house is 'peaceful, comfortable and beautifully furnished'. Airy bedrooms have a large bed, a fridge, a silent-tick alarm clock; a ground-floor room has a small south-facing terrace and its own front door. West Country produce is served at breakfast, with home-made fruit compotes using berries from the garden. Light suppers (soups, pâtés, sandwiches) can be arranged. Country pursuits; picnic hampers available. 2 miles S of Dulverton. Bar (local beer, cider, wine, spirits), sitting room (log fire), dining room; sun terrace. 2-acre grounds. Free Wi-Fi. No background music. Ideal for shooting parties, family celebrations, and fishing and walking groups, the house is also available for exclusive use. Children welcomed (cot, high chair; toys; play equipment in garden). 6 bedrooms (1 on ground floor; family suite). Per person B&B £45–£60. 2-night min. stay preferred. Open for exclusive use only at Christmas, New Year.

DUNWICH Suffolk
Map 2:B6

THE SHIP AT DUNWICH, St James Street, IP17 3DT. Tel 01728 648219, www.shipatdunwich.co.uk. 'Unspoilt and unpretentious', this old inn is in an 'atmospheric' village that was the main town in East Anglia until the sea destroyed the medieval port. It is close to the beach and the RSPB reserve at Minsmere. Owned by the small Agellus Hotels group, which specialises in providing accommodation in interesting old buildings, it has a warren of public rooms with original wooden and stone floors. The bedrooms are in the main house and converted outbuildings, some reached by an outside staircase. Dogs are 'warmly' welcomed and may join their owners at meals in the bar, conservatory and breakfast room (but not the dining room). A lengthy menu has pub favourites and traditional English puddings. There is a covered courtyard and a beer garden. Breakfast has a help-yourself buffet and a range of cooked dishes whose ingredients are locally sourced. Free Wi-Fi. No background music. Children and dogs welcomed. 15 bedrooms (4 on ground floor in converted stables; 1 suitable for disabled). Per room B&B £112.50–£135. Dinner £24.

25% DISCOUNT VOUCHERS

EAST WITTON North Yorkshire
Map 4:C4

THE BLUE LION, DL8 4SN. Tel 01969 624273, www.thebluelion.co.uk. Homely and comforting, Paul and Helen Klein's old stone coaching inn, in a Yorkshire Dales village, has roaring fires, flagstone floors, sturdy settles, old prints on the walls. Country-style bedrooms in the original building may be snug; larger rooms with modern furnishings are across the courtyard in the converted stables; many have views across the surrounding countryside. In the rustic restaurant (candlelit at night), chef Steven Carr's blackboard menus include robust dishes using meat from local farms. 2 bars (real ales), restaurant. Private dining room. 2-acre garden; beer garden. No Wi-Fi. No background music. Parking. Children (over-2s £15.00 per night) and dogs (in some rooms) welcomed. 15 bedrooms (9 in courtyard annexe). Per person B&B from £47, D,B&B from £67.50.

EASTBOURNE East Sussex
Map 2:E4

THE GRAND HOTEL, King Edwards Parade, BN21 4EQ. Tel 01323 412345, www.grandeastbourne.com. Returning guests like the 'old-fashioned in the best sense' feel and 'unfailingly helpful staff' at this 'impeccable' traditional hotel, a majestic Victorian building on the seafront. Many of the 'genteel' bedrooms have sea views. 'We were upgraded to a very spacious and comfortable suite – admirable in every way.' The monthly gathering of the Palm Court quartet at teatime is 'an event worth going to'; live band at weekends. 2 lounges, bar, Mirabelle (closed Sun, Mon) and Garden restaurants; 'nice' terrace. Civil wedding licence; conference/function facilities. Free Wi-Fi. No background music. Health spa; 'lovely' heated indoor and outdoor swimming pools. 2-acre garden. Parking. Children (Junior Crew club, family dining, crèche) and dogs welcomed. 152 bedrooms (1 suitable for disabled). Per room B&B £145–£395. Dinner £50.

OCKLYNGE MANOR, Mill Road, BN21 2PG. Tel 01323 734121, www.ocklyngemanor.co.uk. Close to the seafront, this pink Georgian mansion stands in stunning gardens with an 18th-century gazebo, an ancient oak and plenty of places to sit. It was once the home of children's book illustrator Mabel Lucie Attwell; today, it is a small B&B run by Wendy and David Dugdill. The traditionally styled bedrooms have tea- and coffee-making facilities and views over the garden; organic breakfasts have home-made bread and marmalade. A short walk from the town centre. Free Wi-Fi.

No background music. 1¼ miles from seafront. Parking. 3 bedrooms (1 with private shower room). Per person B&B from £50. 2-night min. stay at weekends.

EASTON GREY Wiltshire
Map 3:E5
WHATLEY MANOR, SN16 0RB. Tel 01666 822 888, www.whatleymanor.com. 'The approach is most impressive' to this luxury hotel and spa (Relais & Châteaux). It stands in 'gorgeous', extensive grounds with woodland, wild flower meadows and secluded arbours. It is owned by Alix Landolt and her son, Christian; Gurval Durand is the manager. Well-equipped bedrooms in the 18th-century manor house have original artwork, and a mix of antique and modern furniture. 'Our beautiful, spacious superior room overlooked the kitchen garden. We had a large bed, a huge wardrobe with excellent hangers, a coffee table, a sofa in the bay window.' Martin Burge, the chef, has two Michelin stars for his modern cooking; in the Dining Room restaurant, his tasting menus include good vegetarian options. 'Delicious' informal meals are taken in the 'very pleasant' Swiss-style brasserie or, in good weather, on its garden terrace. 'Well-executed' breakfasts have a 'very good' buffet. Close to Highgrove House and Malmesbury Abbey. 3 lounges, 2 bars, brasserie, restaurant. Cinema. Gym, spa (hydrotherapy pool, mud chamber, salt scrub shower, Iyashi Dome). Free Wi-Fi. Civil wedding licence; conference facilities. 'Ambient' background music. 12-acre garden. Bicycles available to borrow. Children over 12, and dogs (in some rooms; treats and toys provided; £30 per night) welcomed. 23 bedrooms

and suites. Per room B&B from £315. Set dinners £110 or £175. À la carte (brasserie) £32.

EDINGTON Wiltshire
Map 2:D1
THE THREE DAGGERS, 47 Westbury Road, BA13 4PG. Tel 01380 830 940, www.threedaggers.co.uk. 'We were impressed.' On the outskirts of a village near the Uffington White Horse, this popular pub has been remodelled to include 'well-thought-through' accommodation, a characterful bar and restaurant serving 'unpretentious and tasty' food, and an on-site micro-brewery and farm shop. Managed by Robin Brown, it is 'staffed by some lovely people'. Decorated in modern rustic style, 'comfortable' bedrooms have their own entrance in an adjoining building. They share a 'splendidly equipped' sitting room with a squashy sofa, wood-burning stove, honesty bar and fridge (orange juice, bottled water and fresh milk provided). Guests choose between a continental breakfast in the lounge, and a more extensive one in the pub's conservatory. 'I particularly liked my eggy bread with local smoked back bacon.' Bar (draught beers), dining area; private dining room. Garden with picnic bench seating. Ramp. Free Wi-Fi. Background music. Children welcomed (special menu, colouring sets; adjacent public play area). 3 bedrooms. Per room B&B from £85. Dinner £25.

EGGESFORD Devon
Map 1:C4
THE FOX & HOUNDS, EX18 7JZ. Tel 01769 580345, www.foxandhoundshotel. co.uk. The Culverhouse family's 'lovely' hotel is a former Victorian coaching inn

on the banks of the River Taw; pheasants, owls, woodpeckers and siskins can be spotted in its large grounds. It is also home to the Devon School of Fly Fishing, and has two lakes and five miles along the river where guests may cast a line. Country-style bedrooms have antique furniture; some overlook the gardens, with views over the river to Heywood Forest. Alex Pallat, the chef, cooks 'a good choice' of traditional West Country food in the informal restaurant. In fine weather, drinks and afternoon tea may be taken on the terrace. Within North Devon's Biosphere Reserve, renowned for its conservation and beauty, Eggesford is on the Tarka Line between Exeter and Barnstaple. Lounge, bar (background music), dining room; terrace; health and beauty room (holistic treatments). Free Wi-Fi. Civil wedding licence; function facilities. 6-acre garden. Children (cots, high chairs, monitors; babysitting; special menus) and well-behaved dogs (by arrangement; £10 per night) welcomed. 20 bedrooms (3 on ground floor; 1 suitable for disabled); plus 1 luxury self-catering tree house. Per room B&B single from £67, double from £112; D,B&B single from £97, double from £172.
25% DISCOUNT VOUCHERS

EGTON BRIDGE North Yorkshire
Map 4:C5
BROOM HOUSE, Broom House Lane, YO21 1XD. Tel 01947 895279, www. broom-house.co.uk. 'Excellent hosts' Georgina and Michael Curnow run their small B&B in a restored Victorian farmhouse in the North York Moors national park. In a tranquil country garden setting, the house has wonderful views over the Esk valley, and makes a good base for walking, mountain biking or salmon and trout fishing. In the older part of the building and a modern extension, immaculate, 'very comfortable' bedrooms vary in size; the self-contained cottage suite has a large lounge and a private patio. Locally sourced and freshly cooked breakfasts include smoked haddock, Whitby kipper and home-made jams and fruit smoothies. Pubs serving food are a short stroll away, along the banks of the River Esk. Lounge, breakfast room. Free Wi-Fi. Background music. Children welcomed. 2 miles W of village. 7 bedrooms (1 family room). Per room B&B £90–£150. Closed Dec–Feb.

ELTERWATER Cumbria
Map 4: inset C2
THE ELTERMERE INN, LA22 9HY. Tel 015394 37207, www.eltermere.co.uk. Guests are offered tea and cake on arrival at Mark and Ruth Jones's country hotel in a small Lakeland village overlooking Elter Water. Cosy and welcoming, it is run as a family affair: daughter Aimee is manager; son Edward is chef. Elegant bedrooms vary in size; many have a window seat for admiring lake or fell views. A log fire burns in the 'beautiful' stone fireplace in the beamed bar; Edward Jones's modern European dishes and daily specials may be taken here, or while admiring the panoramic views from the smart restaurant. 'The food was really excellent. Nicely served and presented.' The large gardens have access to the lake; guests may use the hotel's private jetty for fishing. Walks from the front door. 2 lounges, bar, restaurant; terrace. 3-acre garden. Free Wi-Fi (in public areas). Contemporary background music. Complimentary leisure passes

for the spa at the Langdale Hotel (pool, hot tub, steam room; 10 mins' walk). 2 miles from Grasmere. 12 bedrooms. Per room B&B £140–£275. Dinner £30–£40. Closed Christmas.

ELTON Cambridgeshire
Map 2:B4
THE CROWN INN, PE8 6RQ. Tel 01832 280 232, www.thecrowninn.org. 'Thoroughly recommended.' Near the green in a pretty village, a noble horse chestnut tree marks the entrance of chef/patron Marcus Lamb's thatch-roofed 16th-century country inn. 'Good', wholesome pub favourites and Sunday lunches use produce from local suppliers; a table d'hôte menu is served on Saturday nights. 'Well-equipped modern rooms', some above the pub, have tea- and coffee-making facilities, fresh milk and bottled water; two, across the courtyard, have French windows opening on to a private garden. Breakfast hampers may be delivered to the room. Bar (local ales, open fire), snug, restaurant. Free Wi-Fi. Background music. Parking. Children welcomed (special menu). 8 miles SW of Peterborough. 8 bedrooms (2 on ground floor). Per room B&B £65–£160.

EVERSHOT Dorset
Map 1:C6
THE ACORN INN, 28 Fore Street, DT2 0JW. Tel 01935 83228, www.acorn-inn.co.uk. In a pretty Dorset village, this welcoming 16th-century stone inn (Red Carnation Hotels) is said to have provided inspiration for the Sow and Acorn pub in Thomas Hardy's novel Tess of the d'Urbervilles. Run in a relaxed way by Jack MacKenzie and his wife, Alex, it has beams, stone floors, log fires

and 'a good atmosphere'. Smart bedrooms, each named after a Thomas Hardy theme, have tea- and coffee-making facilities, bottles of still and sparkling water, luxury toiletries in a modern bathroom. Two rooms may be connected to accommodate a family. There are deep leather seats in the Hardy bar, 'a local pub for faithful regulars'; chef Guy Horley's hearty dishes are served in the restaurant. Dorset breakfasts are 'good'. Guests may use the spa swimming pool, sauna and gym of sister hotel Summer Lodge, opposite (£15 charge). 'We would return.' Lounge, 2 bars (over 100 single malts; 39 wines by the glass), restaurant; skittle alley; small beer garden. Free Wi-Fi. No background music. Children (cots, extra beds, baby changer, high chairs, children's menu) and dogs (£10 charge; treats) welcomed. 10 bedrooms. Per room B&B £99–£205, D,B&B £159–£265.

EXETER Devon
Map 1:C5
THE MAGDALEN CHAPTER, Magdalen Street, EX2 4HY. Tel 01392 590257, www.themagdalenchapter.com. The original marble floors and gold-lettered visitor notices have been preserved at the former West of England Eye Hospital, today a smart city-centre hotel (Chapter Hotels) with a stylish interior. Fiona Moores is the manager. Sleek, modern bedrooms (single rooms available) are decorated with original works of art; they have a Nespresso coffee machine and a complimentary minibar. There are a number of places to sit and relax: drinks and snacks are taken in the light-filled lounge; afternoon tea may be served in the serene library; the intimate bar has seasonal cocktail menus. 'Dinner was very good' in the

circus tent-like restaurant which leads to the terrace and walled garden. Lounge, bar, library, dining room. Free Wi-Fi. Background music. 1-acre garden. Indoor/outdoor swimming pool with wood-burning stove. Spa; treatments (open to non-residents); gym. Limited parking. Children welcomed (special menu, indoor and outdoor games). 59 bedrooms (some interconnecting; 2 suitable for disabled). Per room B&B from £150. Dinner £30.

25% DISCOUNT VOUCHERS

SOUTHERNHAY HOUSE, 36 Southernhay East, EX1 1NX. Tel 01392 435324, www.southernhayhouse.com. In a central location minutes from the cathedral, this Grade II* listed Georgian mansion has been turned into a town house hotel by Deborah Clark and Anthony Orchard, who also own Burgh Island Hotel, Bigbury-on-Sea (see main entry). It has flamboyant bedrooms, a lively cocktail bar and a small restaurant serving Mediterranean-influenced food; simple bar menus are available throughout the day. Drinks can be taken on the ironwork veranda overlooking the garden. Individually decorated with prints and antiques, bedrooms have a handmade bed, a large TV, a radio and an iPod docking station; two have a free-standing roll-top bath in the room; others have toilet and shower behind glass doors. There are fruits, compotes, yogurts and freshly baked pastries at breakfast; cooked dishes include a stack of pancakes with streaky bacon and maple butter. 'Insider' city guides available. Bar, dining room; private dining room. Garden; terrace. Free Wi-Fi. Background music. Civil wedding licence. Limited on-site parking; secure,

paid parking nearby. 10 bedrooms. Per room B&B £150–£240. Dinner £30.

FALMOUTH Cornwall
Map 1:E2

THE ROSEMARY, 22 Gyllyngvase Terrace, TR11 4DL. Tel 01326 314669, www. therosemary.co.uk. Close to the beach, Lynda and Malcolm Cook's 'beautifully furnished' B&B is 'spot on for comfort, cleanliness and attention to detail'. The peaceful Edwardian town house has 'well-appointed' bedrooms; most have 'fantastic' sea views. 'Good-quality' Cornish breakfasts (dietary requirements catered for); cream teas. Lounge, dining room, bar; south-facing garden, sun deck. Free Wi-Fi. No background music. Children (travel cot £10; extra bed £25; high chair) and dogs (not in high season) welcomed. 10 mins' walk to town. 8 bedrooms (two 2-bedroom suites, ideal for a family). Per room B&B single £50–£70, double £79–£157. Closed mid-Nov–Feb.

FOLKESTONE Kent
Map 2:E5

ROCKSALT, 4–5 Fish Market, CT19 6AA. Tel 01303 212070, www.rocksaltfolkestone.co.uk. 'Modish and imaginative', Mark Sargeant's well-regarded restaurant (co-owned with Josh de Haan) is a striking dark-timber-and-glass building cantilevered over Folkestone's fishing harbour. It has limewashed oak flooring, curved banquettes and floor-to-ceiling windows with views out to sea; a wide-ranging menu includes home-cured and smoked fish dishes cooked by Simon Oakley. The lively bar above serves cocktails and light bites. Across a cobbled street, accommodation is in a converted old building on a narrow passageway; snug, comfortable rooms have exposed brick walls, an antique bed and a wet room. Continental breakfast hampers are delivered to the room. Bar, restaurant (last orders by 5 pm in winter); terrace. Free Wi-Fi. No background music. Children welcomed. On-street parking. 4 bedrooms (1 family room). Per room B&B from £85. Dinner £25–£35.

FONTMELL MAGNA Dorset
Map 2:E1

THE FONTMELL, SP7 0PA. Tel 01747 811441, thefontmell.com. The village stream flows between the bar and dining room of this quirkily renovated roadside inn. Popular with locals, the bar has beer from local breweries and a weekly changing guest ale. In the smart dining room lined with books and wine bottles, imaginative dishes and comfort food are cooked by chef/manager Tom Shaw. On weekend evenings in summer, pizzas are cooked in two wood-fired ovens in the garden. Upstairs, comfortable bedrooms are prettily decorated and have tea- and coffee-making facilities; the best room, Mallyshag, has a super-king-size bed, a large sofa and a roll-top bath on a wooden dais. Bar, restaurant. Large garden. Free Wi-Fi. Background music. Children (special menu; cot, extra bed) and dogs (in 1 room) welcomed. 4 miles from Shaftesbury. 6 bedrooms. Per room B&B £75–£155. Dinner £25–£30.

GATWICK West Sussex
Map 2:D4

LANGSHOTT MANOR, Ladbroke Road, Langshott, Horley, RH6 9LN. Tel 01293 786680, www.langshottmanor. com. There are exposed beams and feature fireplaces in this 'beautiful' Elizabethan timber-framed manor house in 'peaceful', well-kept grounds close to Gatwick airport. It is part of the small Alexander Hotels group; Katie Savage is the manager; the staff are 'first rate'. Many of the smartly decorated bedrooms have an antique bathtub or a four-poster bed; all have tea- and coffee-making facilities, robes and slippers. Some superior rooms also have a private patio garden. Phil Dixon, the chef, serves modern European dishes, including a seven-course tasting menu, in the Mulberry restaurant overlooking the gardens; lighter meals and afternoon tea are taken in the lounges. Full English breakfasts have local pork and apple sausages; porridge may be served with a dash of whisky. 2 lounges (background music), bar, restaurant; terrace (alfresco dining). Civil wedding licence; conference facilities. Free Wi-Fi. 3-acre garden; medieval moat. Children welcomed. 22 bedrooms (15 in mews, a short walk across the hotel grounds). Per room B&B from £119, D,B&B from £198. Dinner £49.50, tasting menu £70.

GILSLAND Cumbria
Map 4:B3

THE HILL ON THE WALL, Brampton, CA8 7DA. Tel 01697 747214, www. hillonthewall.co.uk. In an outstanding hilltop location, Elaine Packer's 'magnificent' Grade II listed home, a fortified 'bastle' farmhouse built in 1595, overlooks Hadrian's Wall near Birdoswald. B&B guests receive an 'excellent' welcome, with tea and home-made cake beside a roaring fire in the drawing room. 'Elegant' bedrooms are supplied with thoughtful items. Locally sourced Northumbrian breakfasts, ordered the night before, are 'delicious'.

Walkers and cyclists welcomed; packed lunches available (£6). Lounge (library, wood-burning stove), breakfast room; terrace; 1-acre garden. No Wi-Fi. No background music. Parking; secure bicycle storage. 3 bedrooms. Per person B&B £45. Credit cards not accepted. Closed Nov–Mar.

WILLOWFORD FARM, CA8 7AA. Tel 01697 747962, www.willowford.co.uk. In the Irthing valley, Liam McNulty and Lauren Harrison's 100-acre organic farm is right on one of the longest, best preserved stretches of Hadrian's Wall, running along the National Trail between Gilsland village and Birdoswald Roman fort; the remains of a bridge and two turrets can still be seen. B&B accommodation is in a converted byre, where homely, energy-efficient bedrooms have exposed wooden beams, slate floor and antique furniture; bathrooms have underfloor heating and a waterfall shower. Evening meals can be taken at the Samson Inn in the village (under the same management; lifts offered); lamb from the farm appears on the menus. Packed lunches available (£6). Plenty of places for guests to walk, picnic and sit. Lounge/breakfast room. Free Wi-Fi (in public areas). No background music. Children welcomed (family rooms); well-behaved dogs by arrangement (chickens and sheep on farm). Resident dog. 1 mile W of Gilsland. 5 bedrooms (all on ground floor). Per person B&B £35–£45. Dinner £18. Closed Nov–Feb.

GRAFFHAM West Sussex
Map 2:E3

WILLOW BARNS, GU28 0NT. Tel 01798 867493, www.willowbarns.co.uk. On the edge of a village five miles from Petworth, this 'stylish' B&B is in a 'stunning, quiet location' in the South Downs national park. It is owned by Amanda and William Godman, who had it built in 2010 using traditional methods in flint and brick. Pretty bedrooms are set around a serene courtyard; all have fresh flowers, sweet treats, a 'gorgeous' bathroom and wonderful views of the countryside. The Godmans also own the adjacent pub, The White Horse, where a varied menu uses meat and fruit from their farm; ice cream is home made. Cyclists and riders welcomed; many footpaths and bridleways nearby. Turnout for visiting horses, by arrangement (midweek only). Clay-pigeon shooting can be organised. Sitting room with log fire in the pub (restaurant closed Sun); large courtyard garden with grassed area, and garden. Free Wi-Fi in pub. No background music. Parking. 6 bedrooms (all on ground floor). Per room B&B from £110 (2-night min. stay at peak weekends). Dinner £26.

GRANGE-IN-BORROWDALE
Cumbria
Map 4: inset C2

BORROWDALE GATES, CA12 5UQ. Tel 017687 77204, www.borrowdale-gates. com. At the head of Derwentwater, the Harrison family's Lakeland hotel is an extended country house standing in peaceful wooded grounds. Most of the comfortable bedrooms have a balcony or window seat to take in the views of the Borrowdale valley and fells; several have patio doors leading to the garden. Chef Christopher Standhaven serves 'superb' contemporary menus in the elegant dining room that overlooks the surrounding scenery. Plenty of choice at breakfast, including smoked fish and a full Cumberland. Open-plan bar, dining room and lounge (log fire), reading room; terrace (alfresco drinks). Lift. Free Wi-Fi. No background music. Wedding facilities. Walking and climbing routes from the door; a local bus runs nearby. Children (£25 per night) and dogs (in 4 rooms; £7 per night) welcomed. 2-acre grounds. 25 bedrooms (10 on ground floor; 1 suitable for disabled). Per person B&B from £78, D,B&B from £108. Closed Jan.

GRANGE-OVER-SANDS Cumbria
Map 4: inset C2

CLARE HOUSE, Park Road, LA11 7HQ. Tel 01539 533026, www.clarehousehotel. co.uk. Returning guests appreciate the 'great welcome', spacious bedrooms and 'outstanding' dinners at the Read family's traditional hotel, in a 'delightful' setting in well-maintained gardens. There are log fires in the elegant sitting rooms; most of the bedrooms in the Victorian house have 'wonderful' views over Morecambe Bay. Morning coffee and afternoon tea may be taken in the lounges or the garden; a five-course dinner cooked by Andrew Read and Mark Johnston is served between 6.30 pm and 7.30 pm. 2 lounges, dining room (open to non-residents). Ramps. Free Wi-Fi. No background music. ¾-acre grounds (croquet, loungers, tables and benches). Mile-long promenade at the bottom of the garden (bowling green, tennis courts, putting green; easy access to ornamental gardens). Parking. Children welcomed. 18 bedrooms (1 on ground floor suitable for disabled). Per person B&B £73–£78, D,B&B £93–£98. Closed mid-Dec–mid-Mar.

25% DISCOUNT VOUCHERS

GRASSINGTON North Yorkshire
Map 4:D3

GRASSINGTON HOUSE, 5 The Square, BD23 5AQ. Tel 01756 752406, www. grassingtonhousehotel.co.uk. 'We were pleased with it in every way.' John and Sue Rudden's small hotel overlooks the cobbled square of this Yorkshire market town. The limestone Georgian house has a contemporary interior and glamorous bedrooms, some with views over the town's ancient rooftops. 'Very enjoyable', classic English food is served in the smart restaurant and the fireside bar; alfresco meals may be taken on the terrace in good weather. The Ruddens's rare-breed pigs provide the restaurant with bacon, sausages and plenty of crackling. Lounge, bar, No. 5 restaurant; terrace. Civil wedding licence; functions. Free Wi-Fi. Background music. Children welcomed (travel cot, extra bed). Cookery master classes. Horse riding, cycle hire, fly fishing and shooting can be arranged. Parking. 9 bedrooms. Per room B&B £120–£140, D,B&B £195–£230. Closed Christmas Day.

GREAT LANGDALE Cumbria
Map 4: inset C2

THE OLD DUNGEON GHYLL, LA22 9JY. Tel 01539 437272, www.odg.co.uk. At the head of the Great Langdale valley, fell walkers and climbers have been welcomed at this popular inn for more than 300 years. It is run by Jane and Neil Walmsley for the National Trust. Simple, country-style bedrooms have floral curtains and a brass bedstead; most have views of the surrounding fells. The residents' lounge provides home-baked treats with morning coffee and afternoon tea; the lively Hikers' Bar, in the old cow stalls, has real ales, a wide selection of malt whiskies and occasional open-mic nights. No television; patchy mobile reception. Walking routes and packed lunches available. Residents' bar and lounge, dining room, public Hikers' Bar; live music on first Wed of every month. No background music. Free Wi-Fi (in some rooms and public areas). Drying room. Children (special rates) and dogs (£5 per night) welcomed. 1-acre garden. 12 bedrooms. Per person B&B from £58, D,B&B from £78. 2-night min. stay at weekends. Closed 1 week at Christmas.

GURNARD Isle of Wight
Map 2:E2

THE LITTLE GLOSTER, 31 Marsh Road, PO31 8JQ. Tel 01983 200299, www. thelittlegloster.com. Chef/patron Ben Cooke and his wife, Holly, run their charming restaurant-with-rooms by the water's edge, on a little bay just west of Cowes. The much-praised restaurant has Scandinavian-inspired dishes using Isle of Wight produce, such as Bembridge crab and crayfish, and locally farmed meat. In a separate wing, with its own entrance, coastal-themed bedrooms have binoculars for the superb sea views. Breakfast, served until 11 am on weekends, has plenty of choice, including 'super' juices, home-made marmalade, home-cured gravadlax, and eggs all ways. Bar, restaurant (closed Sun, Mon; plus Tues in winter; background music); functions. Free Wi-Fi. Garden; croquet lawn. Children welcomed (over 2s £30 per night). 5 mins' drive from Cowes. 3 bedrooms (in adjoining building). Per room B&B £100–£230. Dinner £40. Closed 21 Dec–12 Feb.

HALIFAX West Yorkshire
Map 4:D3

SHIBDEN MILL INN, Shibden Mill Fold, HX3 7UL. Tel 01422 365840, www. shibdenmillinn.com. 'The staff really care' at Simon and Caitlin Heaton's 'very attractive' 17th-century country inn, opposite a mill stream in the Shibden valley. Glen Pearson is the manager. 'Great' bedrooms, some with archways and a soaring ceiling, have 'individual style'; they are equipped with bathrobes and modern amenities. In the characterful restaurant, chef Darren Parkinson serves seasonal Yorkshire fare. The 'bustling' oak-beamed bar has an open fire and a selection of cask ales, including Shibden Mill's own brew. 'Lovely breakfasts.' 2 miles NE of Halifax. Bar, restaurant; private dining room; patio (alfresco dining). DVD library. Small conference facilities. Free Wi-Fi. Background music. Parking. Children welcomed (special menu). 11 bedrooms. Per room B&B from £100, D,B&B from £182. Closed Christmas, New Year.

HARROGATE North Yorkshire
Map 4:D4

THE BIJOU, 17 Ripon Road, HG1 2JL. Tel 01423 567974, www.thebijou.co.uk. Stephen and Gill Watson's good-value B&B is in a Victorian villa within easy walking distance of the town centre and the railway station. The sitting room has a wood-burning stove. Cosy bedrooms (some small; those at the back are quietest) have bathrobes and a hospitality tray with water, sweets and biscuits. The refurbished coach house at the rear of the building has two bedrooms and two bathrooms, ideal for a family or small group. Breakfasts are 'excellent'. Some steep stairs. Lounge (afternoon teas; honesty bar; computer), breakfast room. Free Wi-Fi. Background music. Front garden with fountain and seating. Parking. Children (cot, extra bed, high chair; board games) and small dogs (in coach house only) welcomed. 10 bedrooms (2 in coach house; 1 on ground floor). Per room B&B single £64–£74, double £84–£114. Discounts for 3-night stays from Fri to Sun.

HASTINGS East Sussex
Map 2:E5

THE LAINDONS, 23 High Street, TN34 3EY. Tel 01424 437710, www. thelaindons.com. Sara and Jon Young run their modern B&B and coffee shop in a Grade II listed Georgian building on the historic high street of Hastings Old Town. Spacious, high-ceilinged bedrooms, each with a tiled fireplace, have been updated with Scandinavian simplicity in blue, white and grey tones, with decorative nautical features. Beds are locally handmade using recycled wood. Cakes, biscuits and freshly ground coffee are provided for each night's stay. Home-made granola, muesli and bread, together with produce from local suppliers, are served at breakfast in the first-floor conservatory overlooking the town and surrounding hills. The lounge has an open fire, books and a help-yourself area for hot drinks; an honesty larder has bottled water, soft drinks and snacks. Open to the public, the Coffee Bar and Roastery has an extensive coffee menu, using beans roasted on the premises by Jon Young; resident guests receive a discount. 5 mins' walk to the beach. Lounge, conservatory/breakfast room (gentle soul, jazz background music); coffee bar. Free Wi-Fi. Overnight parking permits supplied. Children over

10 welcomed. 5 bedrooms. Per room B&B £115–£130. Closed 21 Dec–20 Jan.

THE OLD RECTORY, Harold Road, TN35 5ND. Tel 01424 422410, www. theoldrectoryhastings.co.uk. On the edge of Hastings Old Town, a short stroll from the seafront, this 18th-century rectory has a modern country house interior and a lovely walled garden with a pond and a paved terrace. Owned by Lionel Copley, it is a sister property to Swan House, a ten-minute walk away (see main entry). Tracey-Anne Cook and Helen Styles are the managers. Each of the smart, stylish bedrooms has been distinctively decorated with an opulent chandelier, trompe l'oeil touches or vintage wallpaper and furniture; one has a secret door; three overlook the garden. In the elegant lounge, a fire blazes in an enormous hearth on cold days. Breakfast has home-made sausages, home-cured bacon and home-baked bread; kippers, haddock and smoked salmon are from the local fishery. 2 lounges (newspapers, magazines; honesty bar), breakfast room; walled garden with terrace and seating. Civil wedding licence. Free Wi-Fi and local telephone calls. DVD library. Background music. Limited parking (5 cars); permits are provided for local car parks. 8 bedrooms (one 2-bedroom, 2-bathroom suite). Per room B&B from £99. Closed 1 week at Christmas, 2 weeks Jan.
25% DISCOUNT VOUCHERS

HATCH BEAUCHAMP Somerset
Map 1:C6

FARTHINGS, Village Road, TA3 6SG. Tel 01823 480664, www.farthingshotel. co.uk. In a quiet village, this small country hotel and restaurant is in a white-painted Georgian house with ironwork balustrades, bays and shuttered windows. It is owned by John Seeger. The lounge has crackling log fires in winter; bedrooms are individually decorated with antique furniture. Two rooms on the ground floor have direct access to the gardens. Extensive orchards in the grounds produce figs, cherries, medlars and sweet chestnuts for the kitchen; in the 'intimate' dining rooms, chef Shaun Barnes uses home-reared meat, home-cured gravadlax and home-grown salad for his traditional menus. Lounge, bar, 3 dining rooms; patio. 3-acre grounds (walled garden; orchards, roses; peacocks, chickens, pigs). Civil wedding licence. Wi-Fi (£5 for 24 hours). Classical background music in bar, restaurant. 4 miles S of Taunton. Children, and 'well-behaved' dogs (£8 charge) welcomed. Resident dogs. 12 bedrooms (2 on ground floor), plus 1-bed cottage. Per room B&B from £99, D,B&B from £150. **25% DISCOUNT VOUCHERS**

HEACHAM Norfolk
Map 2:A4
HEACHAM HOUSE, 18 Staithe Road, PE31 7ED. Tel 01485 579529, www.heachamhouse.com. Rebecca and Rob Bradley's beautifully presented Victorian house is in an area famed for its miles of sandy beaches, salt marshes and sunset views. B&B guests are welcomed with tea and home-made cake on arrival; walkers and cyclists are provided with drying and secure storage. Immaculate bedrooms have fresh flowers. The varied breakfast menu includes home-baked bread, home-made preserves, award-winning sausages, and muffins served with crème fraîche and fruit compote. The Bradleys are helpful

with suggestions on restaurants and places of interest. Lounge with log burner, breakfast room. Free Wi-Fi. No background music. Small front garden overlooking the village duck pond. Parking; bicycle storage. 3 bedrooms. Per room B&B single £50–£65, double £85–£95. Credit cards not accepted. Closed Christmas, New Year.

HELMSLEY North Yorkshire
Map 4:C4
No54, 54 Bondgate, YO62 5EZ. Tel 01439 771533, www.no54.co.uk. Lizzie Rohan's welcoming B&B is in a house formed from two cottages in a York stone terrace, half a mile from the market square. Near the North York Moors national park, it makes 'a very good base' for exploring the 'wonderful' surrounding countryside. The main building has flagstone floors and open fires. Pretty bedrooms ('quiet and well equipped') are set around a sunny, flowery courtyard. Tea and home-baked cake are offered on arrival. An 'excellent' breakfast, served at a communal table, includes locally smoked kippers, freshly baked muffins, and eggs from free-range hens just down the road. Dining room with comfortable seating. Garden with lawn and raised vegetable beds. Free Wi-Fi. No background music. Children over 11 welcomed. Resident dog. Picnics available. 3 rooms (on ground floor, in courtyard). Per person B&B £50. Closed Christmas, New Year.

HERTFORD Hertfordshire
Map 2:C4
NUMBER ONE PORT HILL, 1 Port Hill, SG14 1PJ. Tel 01992 587350, www.numberoneporthill.co.uk. Well placed

for visiting the town, Annie Rowley's B&B is in a Grade II listed Georgian town house mentioned in the Pevsner architectural guide to Hertfordshire. It is filled with chandeliers, huge mirrors, vintage glassware, sculptures and fresh flowers. Up the mahogany staircase, guests retire to the drawing room for a drink of home-made sloe gin or vin d'orange. On the top floor, bedrooms have extras such as bathrobes and slippers, an electric fan and reading material; treats include Belgian hot chocolate, biscuits, pretzels and toffees. An accommodating hostess, Annie Rowley serves organic breakfasts, taken at a communal table or in the pretty garden; home-cooked dinners may be ordered in advance. Drawing room; walled courtyard garden. Free Wi-Fi. No background music. Resident Labrador, Presley. Limited street parking. 3 bedrooms. Per room B&B £105–£130. Dinner £40. Closed Christmas, New Year.
25% DISCOUNT VOUCHERS

HEXHAM Northumberland
Map 4:B3
BARRASFORD ARMS, Barrasford, NE48 4AA. Tel 01434 681237, www.barrasfordarms.co.uk. There is a 'relaxed, pleasant' atmosphere at this 'very attractive old pub' in a quiet village near Hadrian's Wall. Popular with locals, the 'welcoming' bar has an open fire and hand-pulled ales. In the 'smart' dining room, chef/patron Tony Binks cooks traditional English dishes with a French twist, using locally sourced ingredients (local lamb, Cumbrian chicken, Shields plaice). Some of the understated bedrooms are suitable for a family. 'A good base for walking and enjoying the great outdoors'; salmon fishing on the North Tyne river can be arranged. Regular quoits tournaments, hunt meets, darts finals and vegetable competitions. Bar, 2 dining rooms; private dining. Background music in bar and restaurant. Free Wi-Fi. Parking. Children welcomed (family rooms). 7 bedrooms. Per room B&B single £67, double/family £87–£105. Dinner from £25.

THE HERMITAGE, Swinburne, NE48 4DG. Tel 01434 681248, www. thehermitagebedandbreakfast.co.uk. In a 'charming setting' at the end of a long drive, Katie and Simon Stewart's 'beautiful' stone-built house is 'very traditional, but just lovely'. There is 'a true country house atmosphere': the home is furnished with antiques; 'very comfortable' bedrooms have fresh flowers. A welcoming tea with home-baked cake is served on the terrace or in front of a roaring log fire; the hosts are happy to help with restaurant bookings, and advise on circular walks on Hadrian's Wall nearby. 'Excellent breakfasts.' Drawing rooms, breakfast room; 2-acre grounds: terrace, tennis. Free Wi-Fi. No background music. Babes in arms and children over 7 welcomed. Resident dogs. 7 miles N of Corbridge (ask for directions). 3 bedrooms (no TV). Per room B&B £90 (credit cards not accepted). Closed Nov–Feb.

HOOK Hampshire
Map 2:D3
TYLNEY HALL, Ridge Lane, RG27 9AZ. Tel 01256 764881, www.tylneyhall.co.uk. 'We all felt special.' In 'lovely, peaceful' countryside, this privately owned Grade II listed Victorian mansion (Pride of Britain Hotels) has 'fantastic

grounds and facilities' and 'excellent' staff. There is a 'friendly, intimate' feel: 'Everyone knows your name and says hello.' Bedrooms are traditionally decorated, with period furniture; a family room with a large sitting area had 'comfortable' beds. Golf carts ('swift at all times') are available to ferry guests from the main house to cottage rooms in the grounds. There is much to keep young guests entertained: games, exploration trails, a treasure hunt; food is provided so children may feed the hotel's ducks. 'My two active boys were made to feel very welcome.' Stephen Hine, the chef, cooks 'very good', formal meals, including 'a delicious soufflé', in the wood-panelled Oak Room restaurant. Afternoon tea, sandwiches and light snacks are taken in the lounge or on the terrace. Breakfast is 'excellent'. 2 lounges, bar, restaurant; private dining rooms. Spa (sauna, treatment rooms, indoor and outdoor pools, gym). Civil wedding licence. Conference/function facilities. Free Wi-Fi. No background music. Room service. 66-acre grounds ('huge' lawn, gardens, parkland; walking and jogging trails; tennis, croquet, cricket, mountain bicycles to borrow). Children (goody bags), and dogs (in some rooms) welcomed. 112 bedrooms (some in cottages in the grounds; some suitable for disabled). Per room B&B from £250.

HOPE Derbyshire
Map 3:A6
LOSEHILL HOUSE, Losehill Lane, Edale Road, S33 6AF. Tel 01433 621219, www.losehillhouse.co.uk. 'Absolutely brilliant from start to finish.' In a 'beautiful' hillside setting, this spa hotel has footpath access to the Peak District

national park; it has 'amazing' views over the Hope valley. It is run by Paul and Kathryn Roden with 'attentive, polite' staff. Modern bedrooms in the Arts and Crafts house are well equipped with bathrobes, slippers, locally produced biscuits; a complimentary newspaper is provided. Pre-dinner drinks and canapés are taken in the lounge and bar. In the restaurant, chef Darren Goodwin serves 'excellent' modern regional dishes. Breakfast is 'superb'. Drawing room, bar, restaurant. Lift. Civil wedding licence; function/conferences; exclusive use. Free Wi-Fi. Background music. 1-acre garden; terrace. Spa (indoor swimming pool, outdoor hot tub, treatment rooms; open to non-residents). Children, and dogs (in 2 rooms) welcomed. Parking. 23 bedrooms (4 with external entrance). Per room B&B single from £160, double from £195. Dinner £39.50. 2-night min. stay on weekends.

HUDDERSFIELD West Yorkshire
Map 4:E3
THE THREE ACRES INN & RESTAURANT, Roydhouse HD8 8LR. Tel 01484 602606, www.3acres.com. There are 'tremendous views to all sides' from this old roadside drovers' inn set in rolling Pennine countryside. It is owned by Brian Orme, Neil Truelove and Neil's son, Tom; Terence Mackinder is the manager. Simply decorated bedrooms (some small) are divided between the main building and adjacent cottages in the garden; each has tea- and coffee-making facilities. In the restaurant, chef Tom Davies serves 'trencher portions' of English comfort food with international influences; Sunday lunches are popular. 5 miles from the town centre (busy

morning traffic); close to the Yorkshire Sculpture Park and National Mining Museum. Bar, restaurant; ramp. Civil wedding licence; small function/private dining facilities. Free Wi-Fi. Background music. Terraced garden; decked dining terrace. Well-behaved children welcomed. 17 bedrooms (1 suitable for disabled; 8 in adjacent cottages). Per room B&B single from £50, double £80–£150. Dinner £50. Closed Christmas, New Year's Eve day.

ILMINGTON Warwickshire
Map 3:D6

THE HOWARD ARMS, Lower Green, CV36 4LT. Tel 01608 682226, www.howardarms.com. A log fire burns in the hearth at this easy-going 400-year-old Cotswold stone inn on the village green. Country-style bedrooms are upstairs in the main building; rooms in the garden wing are more modern. All have tea- and coffee-making facilities and shortbread biscuits. The popular pub and restaurant has flagstoned floors and blackboard menus of comfort food, sharing platters and a fish of the day. Breakfast, with home-made muesli, Cotswold honey, and milk and eggs from the local farm, is 'particularly good'. Good walks from the village. Snug, bar, dining room ('easy listening' background music); patio/garden (alfresco dining). Free Wi-Fi. Parking. Children welcomed. 8 bedrooms (5 through separate door under covered walkway). Per room B&B £96–£150. Dinner £30.

ILSINGTON Devon
Map 1:D4

ILSINGTON COUNTRY HOUSE, nr Newton Abbot, TQ13 9RR. Tel 01364 661452, www.ilsington.co.uk. The Hassell family's 'delightful' hotel, in a stunning location high in Dartmoor national park, is 'worth finding, though off the beaten track'. Bedrooms, traditionally furnished, have 'lovely' moorland views all around; they are equipped with tea- and coffee-making facilities and bottled water. The sleek spa, newly refurbished, has a hydrotherapy pool, sauna, steam room and fitness suite. In the dining room, chef Mike O'Donnell's 'simple but delicious' modern British and European menus focus on local produce. Bistro food and snacks are taken in the Blue Tiger Inn (popular with locals; staff are 'pleasant and courteous'). 2 lounges, bar, restaurant, pub, conservatory. Spa. Lift. Ramps. Civil wedding licence; conference facilities. Free Wi-Fi. Background music. 5-acre grounds (croquet). Children (special menu; PlayStation; garden games) and dogs (in ground floor rooms; £8 per night) welcomed. 25 bedrooms (8 on ground floor; family suites). Per room B&B from £125, D,B&B from £190.

IRONBRIDGE Shropshire
Map 2:A1

THE LIBRARY HOUSE, 11 Severn Bank, TF8 7AN. Tel 01952 432299, www.libraryhouse.com. Once the village library, this 'beautifully decorated' Grade II listed Georgian guest house, by a bridge over the River Severn, has been sensitively restored by owners Tim and Sarah Davis. The sitting room has comfortable seating, a wood-burning stove and the original library shelves. Bedrooms, named after writers, are well equipped with a hospitality tray, TV and DVD player and cotton waffle dressing gowns. Well placed for visiting the World Heritage Site of Ironbridge Gorge and its museums. Sitting room, breakfast room. Mature garden; courtyard. Free Wi-Fi. No background music. Parking passes supplied for local car parks. Restaurants and pubs nearby. 3 miles from Telford. Children by arrangement. Resident dog. 4 bedrooms (1 with private terrace). Per person B&B £75–£110.

25% DISCOUNT VOUCHERS

KESWICK Cumbria
Map 4: inset C2

DALEGARTH HOUSE, Portinscale, CA12 5RQ. Tel 01768 772817, www. dalegarth-house.co.uk. In a quiet, rural setting high above Derwentwater, Craig and Clare Dalton are the attentive and easy-going hosts at this traditionally furnished Edwardian house. Bedrooms are comfortable and modern; most have stunning lake and fell views. Daily changing home-cooked dinners – 'A taste of the Lakes' – are served at 7 pm. Special dietary requirements are catered for by prior request. Cumbrian breakfasts. Walkers can access the fells straight from the front door; the Daltons readily share their knowledge of routes and local information. Background radio at breakfast; classical/'easy listening' music at dinner. Lounge, bar, dining room. Free Wi-Fi. Garden. Parking. In a village 1 mile W of Keswick. Children over 12 welcomed. 10 bedrooms (2 on ground floor in annexe). Per person B&B from £44, D,B&B from £64. Closed Dec–Feb.

25% DISCOUNT VOUCHERS

LYZZICK HALL, Underskiddaw, CA12 4PY. Tel 01768 772277, www. lyzzickhall.co.uk. 'Thoroughly recommended.' On the lower slopes of Skiddaw, the Fernandez and Lake families run their country hotel amid the 'stunning' scenery of Catbells and the Borrowdale valley. Most bedrooms have 'glorious' views towards the Lakeland fells. Lounges have comfortable seating and log fires; a spacious, sunny orangery leads directly to the garden. Returning guests praise the 'food, presentation and service' in the elegant dining room, where chef Ian Mackay cooks 'excellent' traditional and modern British dishes. An inventive seven-course tasting menu is also available. 'Plenty of choice at breakfast.' 2 lounges, orangery, bar, restaurant (open to non-residents). Free Wi-Fi. Background music. Indoor swimming pool; sauna; whirlpool bath. 4-acre landscaped grounds. 2 miles N of Keswick. Children welcomed. 30 bedrooms (1 on ground floor). Per person B&B from £76, D,B&B from £100. Closed Christmas, Jan.

KINGSBRIDGE Devon
Map 1:D4

THURLESTONE HOTEL, Thurlestone, TQ7 3NN. Tel 01548 560382, www. thurlestone.co.uk. Five minutes' walk from the sea, this 'very good', family-friendly hotel (Pride of Britain Hotels) is in large subtropical gardens with plenty of activities for young guests. It has been owned by the Grose family since 1896; 'staff are first class'. Extensive facilities include sun terraces, croquet lawns, sports facilities and a spa. Children are well provided for, with a games library, a playroom, family badminton courts, and a children's club during the school holidays. Many of the well-equipped bedrooms have 'wonderful' sea views; 'housekeeping is of the highest standard'. Guests have many eating and drinking options to choose from: formal meals are served in the restaurant with views to Thurlestone Bay; the terrace bar has crab sandwiches and seafood platters; real ales are quaffed in the 16th-century village pub; cream teas are taken in the garden in fine weather. 'All the food was excellent.' 4 miles SW of Kingsbridge. Lounges, bar, Margaret Amelia restaurant (open to non-residents; Hugh Miller cooks); lift. Outdoor Rock Pool eating area (teas, lunches, snacks, dinners); terrace; The Village Inn pub. Civil wedding licence; functions. Spa (indoor swimming pool, laconium, fitness studio, speciality showers; treatments); outdoor heated swimming pool (May–Sept); tennis, squash, badminton, croquet, 9-hole golf course; children's club in school holidays. Free Wi-Fi. No background music. Children, and dogs (in some rooms; £8 per night) welcomed. 65 bedrooms (2 suitable for disabled; some with balcony, sea views). Per room B&B £225–£460 (2-night min. stay). Dinner £39.50.

KNARESBOROUGH North Yorkshire
Map 4:D4
NEWTON HOUSE, 5–7 York Place, HG5 0AD. Tel 01423 863539, www.newtonhouseyorkshire.com. In the centre of this charming market town, Denise Carter provides B&B accommodation in her elegantly furnished 300-year-old town house, which is said to have been built with stones from Knaresborough Castle nearby. Spacious bedrooms are traditionally styled; they have books, magazines, bottled water, and tea- and coffee-making facilities. Organic breakfasts are highly praised; the menu includes poached haddock, eggs Benedict, and porridge with whisky-

soaked sultanas. Sitting room (honesty bar, books, magazines, newspapers). Free Wi-Fi. Classic FM at breakfast. Small courtyard garden and 'wildlife' area with bird feeders. Parking. 4 miles from Harrogate. Children (cot, high chair, books, games and toys) and dogs (in 2 rooms with outside access; home-made treats) welcomed. 12 bedrooms; 2 on ground floor, suitable for disabled; 3 in converted stables). Per room B&B single £60, double £105–£125.
25% DISCOUNT VOUCHERS

KNUTSFORD Cheshire
Map 4:E3
BELLE EPOQUE, 60 King Street, WA16 6DT. Tel 01565 633060, www.thebelleepoque.com. In the centre of a 'delightful' town, this brasserie-with-rooms is filled with an eclectic mix of marble pillars, gilded figurines, Art Nouveau fireplaces and Venetian glass mosaic floors. It has been owned by the Mooney family for more than three decades; Paul Holland is the manager. Overlooking the walled courtyard, the spacious bedrooms are modern in style. In the restaurant, Kevin Lynn, the new chef, cooks classic and modern French-influenced dishes using local and regional produce. Popular for weddings. The Mooney family also owns the Victorian-style Rose and Crown pub next door. Convenient for Tatton Park. Lounge/bar, restaurant (closed Sun), private dining rooms; roof garden (alfresco dining). Free Wi-Fi. Civil wedding licence. Background music. 7 bedrooms. Per room B&B (continental on weekdays) single £95, double £110–£115. Dinner £35.
25% DISCOUNT VOUCHERS

LANCASTER Lancashire
Map 4:D2

THE ASHTON, Well House, LA1 3JJ. Tel 01524 684600, www.theashtonlancaster. com. Self-confessed 'hyper critical' fellow hoteliers rated hospitality, breakfast and accommodation 'superb' at this elegant, modern B&B run by James Gray, a former TV and film set designer. Impeccably styled inside, the sandstone Georgian house stands in its own well-maintained grounds, near Williamson Park and the university. Guests are greeted with drinks and a home-baked treat; much local information is provided. Ordered in advance, supper platters of locally sourced meat, fish and cheese, with chutneys and home-baked bread, can be taken in the dining room or bedroom. Generous breakfasts include eggs from the house's free-range hens. The Forest of Bowland, an area of outstanding natural beauty, is within easy reach. Lounge, dining room (occasional background music); 1-acre garden. Free Wi-Fi. Parking. Children (no under-7s at weekend) and medium-sized dogs (in 1 room) welcomed. 1 mile E of city centre. 5 bedrooms (1 on ground floor; some overlook the garden and park). Per room B&B £100–£175. Closed Christmas, New Year.

GREENBANK FARMHOUSE, Abbeystead, LA2 9BA. Tel 01524 792063, www. greenbankfarmhouse.co.uk. In a peaceful rural spot, Sally Tait's 'homely' B&B is in a Victorian stone-built house on a former cheese-making farm. It is 'a haven for birdwatchers' – curlews, swifts, herons, pheasants and partridges are among the many birds that have been spotted. Country-style bedrooms have a spacious bathroom and panoramic views of the fells, greaves and gills from which the rooms take their name. Breakfast has local produce, eggs from the garden hens, and 'delicious' home-baked bread. 8 miles from the city. Dining room; ½-acre lawned garden. Free Wi-Fi. No background music. Parking. 4 bedrooms (1, on ground floor, in annexe). Per person B&B single £40, double £60 (credit cards not accepted).

LAVENHAM Suffolk
Map 2:C5

THE SWAN, High Street, CO10 9QA. Tel 01787 247477, www. theswanatlavenham.co.uk. Formed from three timber-framed 15th-century buildings in this medieval village, this refurbished hotel has oak-beamed rooms, open fires and an impressive period dining room with a minstrels' gallery. It is part of the small Suffolk-based TA Hotel Collection. Bedrooms are individually furnished in country-house style; each is equipped with bathrobes, bottled water and tea- and coffee-making facilities. Characterful suites with a separate lounge have period features such as an inglenook fireplace and mullioned windows. Guests have a choice of places to eat: the Airmen's bar has light bites; the 'bright, modern' brasserie overlooks the quiet garden; chef Justin Kett cooks classic British dishes in the Gallery restaurant (no children under 10). Afternoon tea is popular. The new Weavers' House Spa opened in spring 2015. Lounge, bar, brasserie, restaurant. Courtyard; small garden. Spa (treatment rooms, hot stone sauna, steam room, outdoor hydrotherapy pool, garden terrace). Free

Wi-Fi. Occasional background music. Civil wedding licence; private dining/function facilities. Children (early suppers), and dogs (in some rooms) welcomed. 45 bedrooms (some suitable for disabled). Per room B&B £155–£360.

LEEK Staffordshire
Map 2:A2

THE THREE HORSESHOES, Buxton Road, Blackshaw Moor, ST13 8TW. Tel 01538 300296, www.3shoesinn.co.uk. On the edge of the Peak District national park, with views over the Roaches and the surrounding countryside, this extended old stone inn has been owned and run by the Kirk family for 35 years. Bedrooms vary in size and decor; all have tea- and coffee-making facilities; superior garden rooms have a private patio with an outdoor hot tub. There are low-beamed ceilings, dark oak furnishings and real ales in the popular traditional pub and carvery; modern British dishes with a Thai influence are served in the brasserie. The Mill Wheel spa opened in spring 2015. Generous breakfasts. Bar, 2 restaurants, 7 dining areas; patio (alfresco dining); garden; rooftop terrace. Free Wi-Fi. Background music. Lift. Civil wedding licence; conference facilities. Spa (sauna, steam baths, beauty treatments, outdoor heated hydrotherapy pool, garden). Parking. Children welcomed (outdoor play area). 2 miles N of town. 26 bedrooms. Per room B&B £130–£260, D,B&B £180–£280.50.

LEICESTER Leicestershire
Map 2:B3

THE BELMONT, De Montfort Street, LE1 7GR. Tel 01162 544773, www.belmonthotel.co.uk. In a 'brilliant' location on leafy New Walk, this large town hotel, formed from a row of Victorian residences, is within easy reach of the city and the station; it has useful on-site parking. It has been owned by the Bowie family for four generations, with continual refurbishment. Individually decorated in a mix of traditional and contemporary styles, bedrooms have a large, comfortable bed. Guests have a choice of places to eat and drink: the stylish Windows on New Walk restaurant serves modern British food with continental flourishes (special diets catered for); Jamie's Bar has snacks, light bites, coffees and cocktails; pre-dinner drinks can be taken in Will's Bar or the adjacent conservatory. A 'grab and go' menu is available at breakfast and lunch. Lounge/bar, bar/conservatory, restaurant (open to non-residents; closed Sun eve). Free Wi-Fi. Background music. Lift. Civil wedding licence; function facilities. Parking. Children welcomed. 75 bedrooms (3 family rooms; 1 suitable for disabled). Per room B&B single from £59, double from £79. Dinner £28–£35.

HOTEL MAIYANGO, 13–21 St Nicholas Place, LE1 4LD. Tel 01162 518898, www.maiyango.com. In a 150-year-old former shoe factory near the centre, this contemporary hotel has been decorated throughout with bespoke wood furnishings and commissioned artwork. It is owned by Aatin Anadkat. Spacious bedrooms have a large bed and a chic bathroom; they are well equipped with organic tea and coffee, fresh milk, a snack tray and a DVD library. The Glass Bar, overlooking Jubilee Square, has floor-to-ceiling windows and a wrap-around terrace with fantastic views over the city. In the informal restaurant (lanterns, cushions, booths made of uneven wooden slats), new chef Salvatore Tassari cooks modern international dishes using locally sourced ingredients. The Maiyango Kitchen Deli around the corner serves 'convenience restaurant food', available to take away. Bar, cocktail lounge, restaurant (closed lunchtime Sun–Tues); terrace. Free Wi-Fi. Lift. Background music. 24-hour room service menu. Bar, restaurant; terrace. Function facilities. Paid public parking nearby; 15 mins' walk to train station. Cooking and cocktail classes. 14 bedrooms (1 suitable for disabled). Per person B&B from £89, D,B&B from £119. Closed Christmas, New Year.

25% DISCOUNT VOUCHERS

LINCOLN Lincolnshire
Map 4:E5

THE CASTLE, Westgate, LN1 3AS. Tel 01522 538801, www.castlehotel.net. The staff are 'extremely pleasant and welcoming' at this smartly refurbished hotel, built on the site of Lincoln's Roman Forum, in the historic Bailgate area. 'We were well looked after.' 'Comfortable', modern bedrooms (some small) have views of the castle walls or the medieval cathedral; those in the 250-year-old Coach House are all on the ground floor. Chef Mark Cheseldine serves 'good, beautifully presented' modern European dishes, perhaps a 'superb' cullen skink and smoked haddock terrine, in the 'charming' panelled restaurant; lighter meals are taken in the bar. Good breakfasts. 2 small lounges, bar (a popular local), Reform restaurant (evenings only; background music). Free

Wi-Fi. Massage and beauty treatments. Wedding/function facilities. Parking. Children welcomed. 18 bedrooms (some in attic, some in courtyard; 1 suitable for disabled); plus 1 apartment, and Castle Cottage (available for self-catering). Per room B&B single £90–£130, double £110–£150; D,B&B single £120–£165, double £170–£220. Set dinner £28.95 (Sun–Fri) or £32.95 (Sat).

LIVERPOOL Merseyside
Map 4:E2

HARD DAYS NIGHT, Central Buildings, North John Street, L2 6RR. Tel 01512 361964, www.harddaysnighthotel.com. Beatles fans come together at this hotel inspired by the Fab Four. Close to the Cavern Club, the grand Grade II listed building is fronted by marble columns; inside, its interior is packed with original paintings, statues and photographs, as well as artful references to the iconic group; Beatles music is played throughout. Modern bedrooms are individually designed, with a monsoon shower in the bathroom; some rooms have a private balcony. Michael Dewey is the manager. Lounge (live music on Fri and Sat nights), Bar Four cocktail bar, brasserie, Blakes restaurant (open to non-residents; closed Sun, Mon; 2- and 3-course menus; chef Paul Jobling cooks modern British food); art gallery. Lift. Free Wi-Fi. Background music. Civil wedding licence; function facilities. Beatles tours can be arranged. 110 bedrooms (1 suitable for disabled). B&B from £125. Dinner £15–£45. Closed Christmas.

HOPE STREET HOTEL, 40 Hope Street, L1 9DA. Tel 0151 709 3000, www. hopestreethotel.co.uk. 'A real find.'

In the cultural quarter, opposite the Philharmonic Hall, this handsome modern hotel is 'bookended' by the city's two cathedrals, and surrounded by theatres and universities. 'Very pleasant and tastefully decorated', it is in a former Victorian coach factory, and has exposed brick walls, old beams, solid birch and oak floors and minimalist bedrooms, some with 'fantastic' views of the river, the cathedral or the city skyline. Mary Colston is the manager. Chef David Critchley cooks 'delicious' modern international dishes for The London Carriage Works restaurant; the residents' lounge has cocktails, sandwiches and sharing plates. Tea and coffee are brought to the table at breakfast; a good variety of hot dishes is cooked to order. 'We look forward to returning.' Lounge, bar, restaurant; lift; gym, treatment rooms. Private dining. Free Wi-Fi. Background music. 24-hour room service. Civil wedding licence; functions. Limited parking nearby (£10 charge). Children (special menu) and dogs (£15 per night) welcomed. 89 bedrooms (some interconnecting; 2 suitable for disabled). Per room B&B from £114, D,B&B from £164.

THE NADLER LIVERPOOL, 29 Seel Street, L1 4AU. Tel 0151 705 2626, www.thenadler.com. The stylish, good-value rooms at this 'practical and efficient' hotel in the lively Rope Walks area are ideal for 'a simple, short stay'. The hotel is a sister to the Nadler Kensington, London (see Shortlist). Each of the smart, modern bedrooms has a well-equipped mini kitchen with tea, coffee, a microwave, a fridge, crockery and cutlery; for families or larger groups, the Secret Garden suite, spread out over two levels, has bathrobes, slippers and a private garden area. There is no bar or restaurant, but a continental breakfast can be ordered in advance; guests are offered a complimentary Nespresso coffee in the lounge. Discounts at local restaurants, bars and clubs. 30 mins' of free local and national landline calls per day. Free Wi-Fi. Lounge, meeting room. Background music. Lift. Vending machines. Parking discounts. Children welcomed. 106 bedrooms (some suitable for disabled). Room only from £49 (single), double from £59. Breakfast £6–£8.50.

2 BLACKBURNE TERRACE, 2 Blackburne Terrace, L8 7PJ. Tel 01517 024840, www.2blackburneterrace.com. On a hill close to the city's two cathedrals, Sarah and Glenn Whitter (a former teacher and a musician) have added striking interior design features to their Grade II listed town house in the Georgian quarter. The house is arty and colourful throughout, with a mix of modern furnishings, antiques and references to the building's architectural past. Sophisticated, spacious bedrooms (some with a freestanding bath) have a large TV, wireless sound system, luxurious bedding, bathrobes and slippers; a well-stocked hospitality tray includes speciality tea and coffee, sloe gin and treats. Lavish breakfasts are taken around a communal table set with silver cutlery, porcelain and crystal. Guests can relax in a south-facing walled garden in the summer months. Drawing room/library, breakfast room. Free Wi-Fi (in room). No background music. Children over 10 welcomed. Small walled garden. Parking. 4 bedrooms. Per room B&B £160–£220.

LOOE Cornwall
Map 1:D3
TRELASKE HOTEL & RESTAURANT,
Polperro Road, PL13 2JS. Tel 01503
262159, www.trelaske.co.uk. In a
tranquil location, Hazel Billington and
Ross Lewin's 'exceptional' small hotel
has 'lovely' views over the gardens to
rolling moorland beyond; there are
wonderful coastal and woodland walks
from the doorstep. Inside, 'spacious'
modern bedrooms, each with a balcony
or patio, have ample storage and seating
space. 'Warm and welcoming', Hazel
Billington adds 'extra touches that make
a stay special'; Ross Lewin ('a genius in
the kitchen') reinvents classic British
dishes using freshly caught fish, Cornish-
reared meat, and fruit, vegetables and
herbs from the hotel's polytunnels for his
award-winning, daily-changing menus.
'The service and food are outstanding.' 2
lounges, bar/conservatory (background
radio/music); terrace (summer barbecues).
4-acre grounds. 2 miles from Looe; 2
miles from Polperro. Free Wi-Fi (in main
house only). Function facilities. Parking.
Children welcomed (no under-4s in
restaurant). Dogs allowed in 2 bedrooms
(£7.50 per night). 7 bedrooms (4 ground-
floor garden rooms in building adjacent
to main house). Per room B&B £110–£120,
D,B&B £150–£180. Closed Nov–Mar.

LUDLOW Shropshire
Map 3:C4
HOPTON HOUSE, Hopton Heath,
SY7 0QD. Tel 01547 530885, www.
shropshirebreakfast.co.uk. Surrounded
by 'beautiful' Shropshire countryside,
Karen Thorne's 'fabulous' B&B, in
a former granary, is a 'wonderful
and welcoming hideaway'. Spacious,
well-equipped bedrooms have a large
bed, comfortable seating and double- or
triple-aspect windows; the Paddock
Room has a balcony. A 'brilliant' hostess,
Karen Thorne provides 'delicious'
home-made lemon drizzle cake and
biscuits in the room; supper platters of
local cheese, smoked salmon and a deli
selection are available by arrangement;
BYO wine (glasses and corkscrews
supplied). Resident hens supply the eggs
for the 'phenomenal' breakfasts, ordered
the night before. Dining room ('gentle'
background music); garden. Dogs
welcomed, by arrangement; resident dogs.
Free Wi-Fi. 3 miles from nearest village;
10 miles W of Ludlow. 3 bedrooms (2 in
building across the drive). Per room B&B
£115–£130. Closed Christmas.

SHROPSHIRE HILLS, Aston Munslow,
SY7 9ER. Tel 01584 841565, www.
shropshirehillsbedandbreakfast.co.uk.
An excellent base for walking the
Shropshire Way, Chris and Linda
Baker's B&B is in a conservation village
in an area of outstanding natural beauty
on the slopes of Wenlock Edge. The
welcoming hosts offer complimentary
cake and refreshments to arriving
guests. The bedrooms in the modern
house are furnished to a very high
standard; they have a separate entrance,
comfortable seating, a silent fridge
and home-made cakes, and overlook
beautiful countryside or the garden;
three alpacas graze in the paddock
beyond. Breakfast has apple juice,
home-made jams and compotes made
from fruit in the garden, tomatoes from
the greenhouse, eggs from the Bakers'
own chickens, and local produce.
There is a boot room and changing
and drying for walkers and cyclists.
Lounge/dining room; terrace with table

and chairs; 2-acre garden. Free Wi-Fi. No background music. 7 miles NE of Ludlow. 3 bedrooms. Per room B&B £95–£118. Closed Nov–Apr.

LUPTON Cumbria
Map 4: inset C2

THE PLOUGH, Cow Brow, LA6 1PJ. Tel 01539 567700, www.theploughatlupton. co.uk. In a tiny hamlet close to Kirkby Lonsdale, this smartly refurbished 18th-century coaching inn is 'an attractive place to eat and stay'. It is owned by Paul Spencer; Susannah Harris and Holly Duffy are the managers. Public rooms have oak beams, antique furniture, comfortable sofas and wood-burning stoves; the restaurant serves refined pub food. Upstairs, country-style bedrooms vary in size and decor: Bellingham has an adjoining sitting room; Hutton, a family suite, has superb views over Farleton Knott. Lounge, bar, restaurant; terrace; garden. Free Wi-Fi (signal variable). Background music. Civil wedding licence. Parking. Children, and dogs (in 1 room only) welcomed. 6 bedrooms (family room). Per room B&B from £150. Dinner £28.

LYNMOUTH Devon
Map 1:B4

SHELLEY'S, 8 Watersmeet Road, E35 6EP. Tel 01598 753219, www. shelleyshotel.co.uk. There are fine views over Lynmouth Bay from this 18th-century house which takes its name from Percy Bysshe Shelley, who brought his child bride, Harriet, here in 1812 for their honeymoon. Today, it is an informal B&B run by hands-on owners Jane Becker and Richard Briden. Pristine bedrooms have views of the sea and the river; some have a private balcony. Generous breakfasts ('kippers are always on the menu') are taken in the conservatory, overlooking the bay. Short walk to the harbour. Lounge, bar, conservatory breakfast room. Courtyard garden. Free Wi-Fi. No background music. Children over 12 welcomed. 11 bedrooms (1 on ground floor). Per room B&B £85–£125. 2-night min. booking preferred. Closed Dec–Mar.

LYTHAM Lancashire
Map 4:D2

THE ROOMS, 35 Church Road, FY8 5LL. Tel 01253 736000, www. theroomslytham.com. In a resort town on the Fylde coast, Jackie and Andy Baker's modern B&B is within walking distance of shops, restaurants and the sea. 'Beautifully fitted' bedrooms are equipped with up-to-date technology (digital radio, iPod docking station, flat-screen TV); stylish wet rooms, one with a bathtub, have underfloor heating. Served in the walled garden in good weather, breakfast has home-made smoothies and locally baked bread; a 'large' choice of cooked dishes includes local sausages, smoked haddock fish cakes, pancakes, waffles, and eggs Benedict, Arlington or Florentine. Buck's Fizz is available at weekends. Andy Baker is 'a helpful host' with much local knowledge. Breakfast room (background TV). Decked garden. Free Wi-Fi. Children welcomed. 5 bedrooms ('lots of stairs'), plus 2-bed serviced apartment. Per room B&B single £95–£125, double £125–£160.

MALVERN Worcestershire
Map 3:D5

THE OLD RECTORY, Cradley, WR13 5LQ. Tel 01886 880109, www. oldrectorycradley.com. At the foot of the Malvern hills, Claire Dawkins and John Miller's Georgian house, next to St James the Great Church, is 'a special place; we were made to feel welcome'. The drawing room has a large chess set and an open fire in cool weather. Elegant B&B accommodation is in well-appointed rooms with antiques, original art and fresh flowers. A monthly-changing dinner menu uses much home-grown produce and plenty of ingredients from local suppliers. Breakfast has bread from the local baker; jams and marmalade are home made. Good walks from the door; lifts are offered to and from the Malvern hills. Packed lunches available. Drawing room, 'well-stocked' library, morning room, dining room. 1-acre garden; croquet, boules. Free Wi-Fi. No background music. Parking. Weddings. Well-behaved children (cot) and dogs welcomed. 5 bedrooms. Per person B&B from £70. Dinner £38.50.

MANCHESTER
Map 4:E3

DIDSBURY HOUSE, Didsbury Park, Didsbury Village, M20 5LJ. Tel 0161 448 2200, www.didsburyhouse.co.uk. Within easy reach of the airport and the city centre, this stylish modern hotel (part of the Eclectic Hotel Collection; see Eleven Didsbury Park, below) occupies a Victorian villa in a leafy suburb. The sitting rooms have books, fresh flowers and deep sofas; alfresco drinks may be taken on the walled terrace (heated in cool weather). 'Pleasant' bedrooms are individually styled with prints and feature wallpaper; many have a freestanding roll-top bath. Breakfast is served until noon on weekends. Reached by a 'quick train'

from East Didsbury; otherwise, 'a cab ride from the centre late at night'. 'Good walks' in the botanic gardens, nearby. 2 lounges, bar, breakfast room; meeting room; gym; walled terrace with water feature. Free Wi-Fi. 'Chill-out' background music. Exclusive use for weddings/functions. Children welcomed. 27 bedrooms. Room only £144–£264. Breakfast £14–£16.

ELEVEN DIDSBURY PARK, 11 Didsbury Park, Didsbury Village, M20 5LH. Tel 0161 448 7711, www.elevendidsbury park.com. In a peaceful suburb near the city centre, this contemporary hotel, in a stylishly refurbished Victorian town house, has a log fire in the sitting room, and a walled garden with loungers, a hammock and a croquet set. Elegant bedrooms range in size from snug Classic rooms with an en suite walk-in monsoon shower to a lofty Veranda suite with French doors leading to a private balcony. There is no restaurant, but a deli menu, which can be taken anywhere in the hotel, has sandwiches and steaks. Convenient for the airport (ten mins' drive). 2 lounge/ bars (background music); veranda; large walled garden. Free Wi-Fi. Gym; treatment room. Conference facilities. Parking. Children and dogs welcomed. 20 bedrooms (1, on ground floor, suitable for disabled). Per room B&B from £110.

MARAZION Cornwall
Map 1:E1

GODOLPHIN ARMS, West End, TR17 0EN. Tel 01736 888510, www. godolphinarms.co.uk. In a 'superb' location overlooking St Michael's Mount, this extensively refurbished beachside inn has attractive modern bedrooms, an airy terrace restaurant and far-reaching views over Mount's Bay. It is owned by James and Mary St Levan; Robin and Angela Collyns are the managers. Light-filled, 'well-planned' bedrooms are decorated with local artwork; they are equipped with coffee-making facilities, bathrobes and an iPod dock/radio; some have a balcony. A glass-and-zinc dining area opens out on to a balcony upstairs and a terrace below, with direct access to the beach; on cold days, there are comfy sofas and chairs beside a wood-burning stove. Chef Bernie Powling's 'good' cooking uses many local specialities, including Cornish sausages and shellfish from Newlyn Harbour. It is served throughout the day by 'young, friendly, obliging and efficient' staff. Gig bar, bar, split-level dining area; 2 terraces. Buckets, spades and fishing nets available to borrow. Free Wi-Fi. 'Easy listening' background music. Wedding/function facilities. Parking. Children (cot; extra bed £25 per night) and dogs (in some rooms) welcomed. 4 miles E of Penzance. 10 bedrooms (2 suites with adjoining rooms, suitable for a family). Per room B&B £95–£240. Dinner £25.

MARCHAM Oxfordshire
Map 2:C2
B&B RAFTERS, Abingdon Road, OX13 6NU. Tel 01865 391298, www.bnb-rafters.co.uk. Sigrid Grawert, a welcoming host, runs her B&B in a half-timbered house on the edge of a village eight miles south of Oxford. Pretty bedrooms have fresh flowers, tea- and coffee-making facilities and chilled water; bathrooms are modern. Breakfast, taken at a communal table, includes freshly squeezed orange juice, home-baked bread, and home-made jams and marmalades; whisky porridge and eggs Benedict are specialities. Vegetarian and special diets can be catered for. Lounge, breakfast room; lawned front garden. Free Wi-Fi. No background music. Parking. 4 bedrooms. Per person B&B £60–£150. Closed Christmas, New Year.

MARGATE Kent
Map 2:D5
THE READING ROOMS, 31 Hawley Square, CT9 1PH. Tel 01843 225166, www.thereadingroomsmargate.co.uk. With distressed walls, polished wooden floors, original shutters and antiques, there is an air of 'dilapidated grandeur' at this upmarket B&B in a stylishly restored Georgian town house minutes from the seafront. It is owned by Louise Oldfield and Liam Nabb. Each of the three expansive bedrooms occupies an entire floor; overlooking the tree-lined square, they have vintage hues, a super-king-size bed, and a freestanding roll-top bath in the 'stunning' bathroom. Breakfast is 'beautifully served' in the bedroom, at a table by the huge window. The Old Town and the Turner Contemporary art gallery are nearby. Parking vouchers available. Free Wi-Fi. No background music. 3 bedrooms. Per room B&B £160–£180. 2-night min. stay on weekends and bank holidays.

MARTINHOE Devon
Map 1:B4
HEDDON'S GATE HOTEL, EX31 4PZ. Tel 01598 763481, www.heddonsgatehotel.co.uk. In a 'magical setting' in the Heddon valley, Mark and Pat Cowell's small hotel is surrounded by gardens

and woodland. It is approached by a long private road owned by the National Trust. The former Victorian hunting lodge has been sympathetically extended and restored with period details intact; there is a country house ambience throughout. Named after trees, most of the 'spacious, comfortable' bedrooms are in the original building, accessed by a dog-legged staircase; three, in a new wing above the dining room, are more contemporary. Most have 'spectacular views' across the valley. In the elegant dining room, daily-changing three-course dinners, followed by coffee and chocolates, are 'excellent value'. Complimentary afternoon tea and coffee are taken on the terrace or in the large lounge with a wood-burning stove. Lounge, bar, TV room, library, breakfast/dining room. Terrace; 3-acre grounds. 'Stunning' circular walks. Free Wi-Fi (in public areas). No mobile phone signal; guests may use the landline free of charge. No background music. Children (extra bed £15 per night) and dogs (£10 per stay) welcomed. 1 mile from the sea. 11 bedrooms (1 family room; 3 in new wing). Per room B&B £110–£130, D,B&B £130–£190. Closed Dec, Jan (open for groups only).

MATLOCK Derbyshire
Map 3:A6

MANOR FARM, Dethick, DE4 5GG. Tel 01629 534302, www.manorfarmdethick. co.uk. 'Welcoming and friendly' hosts Gilly and Simon Groom run their 'excellent' B&B in this historic Grade II* listed stone house on an 'attractive' sheep farm. There is a peaceful rural ambience inside and out: the farmhouse is in a tranquil hamlet with a church and plenty of winding lanes. Within the house's stone walls, cosy, country-style bedrooms are full of character, with beams, buttresses and corbels. Fresh local ingredients and home-grown produce are served at breakfast, on a large refectory table in the original Tudor kitchen; all diets are catered for. Chatsworth House, Hardwick Hall and Haddon Hall are within easy reach. Sitting rooms (TV, games), breakfast room. Free Wi-Fi. No background music. Drying facilities. 1-acre grounds. Parking; bicycle/motorcycle storage. Children over 5 welcomed. 2 miles E of Matlock; collection from railway/bus station can be arranged. 4 bedrooms (1, on ground floor, suitable for disabled). Per room B&B £85–£95. 2-night min. stay on Sat, Apr–Oct.

MATLOCK BATH Derbyshire
Map 3:B6

HODGKINSON'S HOTEL, 150 South Parade, DE4 3NR. Tel 01629 582170, www.hodgkinsons-hotel.co.uk. Chris and Zoë Hipwell run their 'very special' hotel in a Grade II listed town house in the centre. It has a quirky Victorian interior, with a tiled entrance hall, ornate glasswork, an original wood-and-glass bar, and an old-fashioned cash register. Adventurous guests may explore the hotel's cellars, which were used by Job Hodgkinson, the Victorian-era homeowner, to store his own locally brewed beer. Some of the traditionally furnished bedrooms have river views; the best has a four-poster bed and a roll-top bathtub. In the restaurant, chef Leigh Matthews serves 'excellent' two- and three-course menus of modern British dishes. There is plenty of choice at breakfast, including kedgeree, breakfast butties and yogurt pots served with local honey. A large terraced garden overlooks the village rooftops, with views of the granite cliffs and the River Derwent beyond. 'There are excellent, challenging walks from the door, providing superb views of the valley.' Sitting room, bar, restaurant (open to non-residents; closed Sun eve). Garden. Free Wi-Fi. Background music/radio. Limited on-site parking; additional parking nearby. Children (extra cot/bed £10) and dogs (by arrangement, £10 per night) welcomed. 8 bedrooms. Per room B&B £50–£145, D,B&B £76–£197. Closed Christmas.

MELTON MOWBRAY Leicestershire
Map 2:A3
SYSONBY KNOLL, Asfordby Road, LE13 0HP. Tel 01664 563563, www.sysonby.com. Less than a mile from the town centre, this traditional hotel and restaurant, in an extended, brick-built Edwardian house, has 'fine' views of the gardens and the River Eye. It has been owned by the same family since 1965; at the helm today are 'friendly and flexible' hosts Jenny and Gavin Howling, who run it with Richard Booth. Vicky Wilkin is the manager. Bedrooms vary in size; some are large enough for a family. 'Impeccable' meals, cooked by Sue Meakin, have 'more-than-generous servings, including the local Stilton cheese'. Complimentary fishing for guests (tackle available to borrow). Good walks nearby. Lounge, bar, restaurant (background music). Free Wi-Fi. 4½-acre gardens and meadow. Parking. Children (cot, extra bed) and dogs (in some rooms; £5 per stay) welcomed. Resident dog. 30 bedrooms (some on ground floor; some in neighbouring

annexe; family rooms; ramp). Per room B&B from £84.50, D,B&B from £103. Closed Christmas, New Year.

MEVAGISSEY Cornwall
Map 1:D2
TREVALSA COURT, School Hill, PL26 6TH. Tel 01726 842468, www.trevalsa-hotel.co.uk. In a 'stunningly beautiful' location, Susan and John Gladwin's 'superb' cliff-top hotel is in an Arts and Crafts house in subtropical gardens leading to the Coastal Path; a steep staircase takes guests to a secluded sandy beach. Most of the individually styled, 'very well furnished' bedrooms have 'spectacular' sea views; there are books and games in the sitting room, and a roaring fire in cold weather. Drinks can be taken on a terrace overlooking the sea. Chef Adam Cawood sources local produce for his 'exceptionally good food', served in the oak-panelled dining room (light jazz background music). Staff are 'friendly, helpful and well trained'. Lounge, bar, restaurant; 2-acre garden (summer house). Free Wi-Fi. Children (cot; extra bed £15 per night) and dogs (under supervision) welcomed. 10 mins' downhill walk to village. 15 bedrooms (3 on ground floor; family suite accessed from outside). Per person B&B from £70, D,B&B from £95. Closed end Nov–12 Feb.
25% DISCOUNT VOUCHERS

MIDHURST West Sussex
Map 2:E3
THE CHURCH HOUSE, Church Hill, GU29 9NX. Tel 01730 812990, www.churchhousemidhurst.com. In the centre of the market town, guests are greeted with tea and home-made cake

at Fina Jurado's B&B, in a spacious, elegant home formed from four cottages dating back to the 13th century. The house has beams, wide-planked wooden floors, antique furniture, and a large open-plan sitting room with a blazing fire in the hearth. A modern glass staircase leads to stylishly rustic bedrooms. The hospitable owner, who originates from Spain, serves breakfast at a huge oak table, at a time to suit guests; jams and marmalades are home made. Private dinner parties can be arranged. Sitting room/dining room, conservatory with TV. Garden. Free Wi-Fi. No background music. Children welcomed. 5 bedrooms (1 on ground floor). Per room B&B £140–£160. Closed Christmas, New Year.

MILLOM Cumbria
Map 4: inset C2

Broadgate House, Broadgate, Thwaites, LA18 5JZ. Tel 01229 716295, www.broadgate-house.co.uk. Within the Lake District national park, Diana Lewthwaite's peaceful guest house is surrounded by colourful gardens; there are panoramic views across the Duddon estuary. The fine Georgian house, which has been in the Lewthwaite family for almost 200 years, has grand public rooms with antique furniture, sumptuous fabrics and an original fireplace; spacious bedrooms have a separate bathroom with a throne loo and freestanding bath. The two-acre grounds are designed as a series of 'garden rooms', with a walled garden, terraces, a croquet lawn and an 'oasis' with a palm tree. Sitting room (wood-burning stove), dining room, breakfast room. No Wi-Fi. No background music. 4 miles from town; beaches

nearby. 5 bedrooms (all with private bathroom). Per room B&B single £55, double £95. Dinner (by arrangement) £25. No credit cards accepted. Closed 1–27 Dec.

MISTLEY Essex
Map 2:C5

The Mistley Thorn, High Street, CO11 1HE. Tel 01206 392821, www.mistleythorn.co.uk. A good base for exploring Constable country, this congenial restaurant-with-rooms is in a former 18th-century coaching inn, in a historic coastal village on the River Stour. It is run by chef/proprietor Sherri Singleton and her husband, David McKay. Thoughtfully equipped bedrooms (some with traffic noise) have dressing gowns, luxury toiletries and home-made biscuits; four have views down the Stour estuary. 'Unpretentious' menus focus on seafood; local beef, chicken and interesting vegetarian and vegan dishes are also available. The restaurant is popular with locals at Sunday lunch. Sherri Singleton also holds cookery workshops at the Mistley Kitchen next door (special room rates for those attending). Bar, restaurant (background jazz); ramp. Outdoor seating. Free Wi-Fi. Children (special menu, cot) and small/medium dogs (in 3 rooms; £5 per night charge) welcomed. 11 bedrooms (3 in annexe). Per room B&B £85–£145, D,B&B £95–£195.

MORETON-IN-MARSH
Gloucestershire
Map 3:D6

The Old School, Little Compton, GL56 0SL. Tel 01608 674588, www.theoldschoolbedandbreakfast.com. A huge monkey puzzle tree in the front garden of this former Victorian schoolhouse is a local landmark. Inside the refurbished stone building, Wendy Veale, a food writer and stylist, provides homely B&B accommodation. The one-time assembly hall is now a spacious open-plan sitting/dining room; the beamed drawing room upstairs has a log burner, books and a large church-style window. Decorated in country style, the pretty bedrooms have fresh flowers, bathrobes, a super-king-size bed. Wendy Veale prepares light suppers and four-course dinners by arrangement. Breakfast, taken communally at a long oak table, has freshly ground coffee, local honey, and eggs from the house's own chickens. Vaulted drawing room, dining room (BYO bottle at dinner); boot room. Free Wi-Fi (computer available). No background music. Garden (pergolas, patios, fish pond, orchard; bantam hens; pet rabbits, cat). 4 bedrooms (1 on ground floor). Per person B&B from £60. 2-night min. stay at weekends. Dinner £32.

MULLION Cornwall
Map 1:E2
POLURRIAN BAY HOTEL, Polurrian Road, TR12 7EN. Tel 01326 240421, www.polurrianhotel.com. On a clifftop above a sandy bay on the Lizard peninsula, this imposing Edwardian building has been stylishly revamped into a modern hotel, with 'excellent' diversions for all ages. Part of Nigel Chapman's Luxury Family Hotels group, it is managed by Yvonne Colgan. 'Well-appointed, comfortable' bedrooms have stunning views of the coastline; some are interconnecting; many others have plenty of space for an extra bed or cot. In 12 acres of landscaped gardens, facilities for children and their parents include indoor and (seasonal) outdoor swimming pools, a hot tub, a gym and a spa (treatments); tennis courts, a sports field; an adventure playground. There are books and board games, cream teas and cocktails, a games room and a cinema. 'Freshly cooked and plentiful' food is available throughout the day. 6 lounges, dining room (background music), cinema; terrace. The Den (nursery for children 3 months–8 years old); the Blue Room (older children; video games, pool, table football). Lift. Free Wi-Fi. Civil wedding licence; functions. Children (special menu; baby equipment) and dogs (in some rooms; £15 per night) welcomed. 41 bedrooms (some on ground floor, 1 suitable for disabled). Per room B&B £200–£460, D,B&B £260–£520. 2-night min. stay in peak season.

NEWBY BRIDGE Cumbria
Map 4: inset C2
THE SWAN HOTEL & SPA, The Colonnade LA12 8NB. Tel 015395 31681, www.swanhotel.com. On the banks of the River Leven, at the southern tip of Lake Windermere, this family-friendly 17th-century coaching inn has pretty, modern bedrooms, elegant lounges and a popular local pub. It is owned by the Bardsley family. Bedrooms overlook the garden or river; family suites of interconnecting rooms have toys, books and video games. Chef Claire Asbury serves a cheery menu, mixing pub classics and more modern dishes, in the rustic Swan Inn and the smart River Room restaurant. There is plenty of choice at breakfast, including vegetarian options. Sheltered moorings; popular

with boating visitors. Fell Foot park, on the shores of Lake Windermere, is nearby. Sitting room, library, Swan Inn 'pub', River Room restaurant, breakfast room; terrace. Free Wi-Fi. Background music. Spa (treatments), indoor pool, hot tub, sauna, steam room; gym. Civil wedding licence; function facilities. 10-acre grounds. Parking; mooring. Children welcomed (adventure playground, nature trail, milk and cookies before bed). 51 bedrooms (some interconnecting, some suitable for disabled). Per room B&B from £99. 2-night min. stay on bank holiday weekends. Dinner £30.

NEWENT Gloucestershire
Map 3:D5
THREE CHOIRS VINEYARDS, GL18 1LS. Tel 01531 890223, www.three-choirs-vineyards.co.uk. On a working vineyard and winery (one of the largest in Britain), this restaurant-with-rooms has 70 acres of cultivated vines to explore. Guided tours take in the history and processes of wine-making, with opportunities to taste the results. Bedrooms are in a single-storey block beside the restaurant; each has French doors opening on to a small private patio. Five hundred yards from the main building, three rooms are in lodges among the vines, overlooking a string of ponds (continental breakfast hampers are delivered to these rooms). Local produce accompanies the wines in the popular restaurant, which has a large log-burning stove and views over the vine-clad valley. Barbecues are cooked on the terrace in fine weather. Lounge, restaurant, wine shop. Free Wi-Fi (in public areas). No background music. Wedding facilities. 2 miles N of Newent. 11 bedrooms (all on ground floor; 1 suitable for disabled). Per room B&B from £140, D,B&B from £199. Closed Christmas, 1–15 Jan.

NEWQUAY Cornwall
Map 1:D2
THE HEADLAND HOTEL, Headland Road, TR7 1EW. Tel 01637 872211, www.headlandhotel.co.uk. A short stroll from the beach, the Armstrong family's large, red brick Victorian hotel has spectacular views over Fistral Bay. There are several categories of bedroom, most with coastal views; the best have a private balcony. Families are warmly welcomed: there is plenty of outdoor diversion for young guests, including a surf school on the beach below; games, DVDs, buckets and spades are available to borrow. The elegant restaurant uses much locally sourced produce, such as Newquay lobster; informal meals are taken on the terrace overlooking the beach. Lounges, bar, 2 restaurants (background music; alfresco dining); veranda. Free Wi-Fi. 10-acre grounds. Table tennis; 2 heated swimming pools (indoor and outdoor); croquet; 3 tennis courts; putting, boules; on-site surf school. Spa (swimming pool, Cornish salt steam room, sauna, aromatherapy showers, hot tub; gym; lounge). Civil wedding licence; conference/event facilities. Children (bunk beds; entertainment) and dogs (£20 per night charge) welcomed. 96 bedrooms (12 suites; 1 room suitable for disabled), plus 39 self-catering cottages in the grounds. Per room B&B £95–£395.

LEWINNICK LODGE, Pentire Headland, TR7 1QD. Tel 01637 878117, www.lewinnicklodge.co.uk. Pete and Jacqui

Fair's stylish restaurant-with-rooms is on the edge of a rocky headland, with stunning coastline or promontory vistas. Dan Trotter is the manager. Decorated in soothing coastal hues, the well-equipped, modern bedrooms have a large bed, local artwork and home-made biscuits; bathrooms, some with a view, have a power shower and slipper bath. In the open-plan restaurant and bar, Rich Humphries, the chef, uses Cornish produce, fish and seafood for his daily-changing specials; floor-to-ceiling windows open on to a large decked terrace jutting over the sea. Good walks from the door; Fistral Beach is nearby. Bar, restaurant (open to non-residents); occasional 'gentle' background music/radio. Free Wi-Fi. In-room treatments. Lift. Parking. 2½ miles from town centre. Children (extra bed on request; 20% charge for 3- to 11-year-olds) welcomed; dogs (in some rooms, £15 per night) by arrangement. 11 bedrooms (some suitable for disabled; 1 family suite). Per room B&B £135–£230. Dinner £25.

NORTHALLERTON North Yorkshire
Map 4:C4
CLEVELAND TONTINE, Staddlebridge, DL6 3JB. Tel 01609 882671, www.theclevelandtontine.co.uk. 'A complete surprise inside – modern, comfortable, quirky.' At the foot of the North York Moors, this Grade II listed, stone-built Victorian house was a resting place for weary travellers and mail coaches on the Sunderland-to-London route in the early 1800s. It has been dramatically transformed by the owners, Charles and Angela Tompkins; Stephane Leyreloup is the manager. The small hotel is

colourfully decorated throughout, with Art Deco flourishes; sophisticated, air-conditioned bedrooms have eye-catching wallpaper, a stylish bed, and a bathroom (two are up stairs) with underfloor heating, bathrobes and slippers. Informal dining is in the intimate, candlelit bistro with its original vaulted ceiling and stone fireplace, or in the conservatory, which leads directly to the gardens. Chef James Cooper cooks classic French dishes with local ingredients and an English twist. Yorkshire breakfasts. 'A great night's stay.' Close to the A19. Lounge, morning room, bar, bistro. Free Wi-Fi. Background jazz. Private dining. Room service. Functions. Parking. Children welcomed (special menu; extra bed £20). 7 bedrooms. Per room B&B single from £115, double £130–£190. Dinner £35.

NORWICH Norfolk
Map 2:B5
NORFOLK MEAD, Church Loke, Coltishall, NR12 7DN. Tel 01603 737531, www.norfolkmead.co.uk. 'The welcome was lovely.' James Holliday and Anna Duttson's Georgian house is in a little village outside Norwich, in a 'near-perfect' position, with pretty gardens stretching down to the River Bure. The smart, modern bedrooms are individually designed. Chantilly has a balcony and 'beautiful views of the grounds and the river'. More spacious rooms in Sweet Chestnut cottage and Crab Apple summer house accommodate families, dogs and parties. In the restaurant overlooking the garden and river, Anna Duttson serves modern British menus inspired by locally sourced produce. Breakfast

is 'very good' and includes home-made cereals, fruit compotes, 'perfectly cooked scrambled eggs'. Afternoon tea and drinks with aperitifs may be taken in the walled garden in fine weather. Lounge, bar, snug, restaurant; background music; private dining. Free Wi-Fi. Walled garden; fishing lake (swans, geese); off-river mooring. Civil wedding licence. Small conference/wedding facilities. Day boating trips arranged. Children (cot, extra bed) and dogs (in 3 rooms; £15 per night charge) welcomed. 7 miles NE of Norwich. 13 bedrooms (some in cottage and summer house). Per room B&B £130–£185. Dinner £28–£35.

OUNDLE Northamptonshire
Map 2:B3

Lower Farm, Main Street, PE8 5PU. Tel 01832 273220, www.lower-farm.co.uk. Arranged around a central courtyard, 'excellent' B&B accommodation has been created from a former milking parlour and old stables on the Marriott family's small arable farm. It is situated at one end of a pretty village. The Nene Way footpath runs through the farm; there are plenty of tracks and cycleways to explore. Caroline Marriott is the 'friendly and accommodating hostess'; husband Robert and his brother John manage the farm. Copious farmhouse breakfasts include a steak-and-eggs special. Breakfast room (background radio/CDs); courtyard garden with seating. Free Wi-Fi (limited); no mobile telephone signal. Parking. Children, and dogs (in 2 rooms) welcomed. 3 miles from Oundle. 10 bedrooms (on ground floor; family rooms; 1 suitable for disabled). Per person B&B £45.
25% DISCOUNT VOUCHERS

OXFORD Oxfordshire
Map 2:C2

The Bell at Hampton Poyle, 11 Oxford Road, Hampton Poyle, OX5 2QD. Tel 01865 376242, www.thebelloxford.co.uk. In a small village near Oxford, this welcoming roadside pub dates in part from the mid-1700s. It has beams, flagstone floors, cosy snugs and a large log fire. It is owned by George Dailey and Robert Brooks; Suzy Minichova is the manager. Simply decorated bedrooms have plenty of natural light; bathrooms have a walk-in monsoon shower or roll-top bath. In the restaurant, chef Nick Anderson's menus use locally sourced meats and grilled fish and shellfish; pizzas are cooked in a wood-fired oven. 2 bars (background music), library (private parties), restaurant; terrace. Free Wi-Fi. Wedding/function facilities. Parking. Children over 10, and dogs welcomed. 4 miles N of Oxford. 9 bedrooms (1 on ground floor). Per room B&B (continental) single £95–£130, double £120–£155. Dinner £35 (£10 set menu Mon–Thurs, 6–7.30 pm).

Burlington House, 374 Banbury Road, OX2 7PP. Tel 01865 513513, www.burlington-hotel-oxford.co.uk. Guests praise the breakfasts at this 'cheerfully decorated' B&B, in a refurbished Victorian merchant's house in a suburb north of Summertown. There is freshly ground coffee, home-made granola and yogurt, and 'excellent' home-baked bread; a speciality is the marmalade omelette. Nes Saini is the 'extremely efficient' manager. Modern bedrooms are divided between the main house and the Japanese courtyard; some are snug; all have a refreshment tray with home-made biscuits. 15 minutes outside the city; frequent buses into the centre. Sitting room, breakfast room; small Japanese garden. Free Wi-Fi. No background music. Limited parking. Children over 12 welcomed. 12 bedrooms (4 on ground floor; 2 in courtyard). Per room B&B £70–£139. Closed 20 Dec–5 Jan.

Vanbrugh House Hotel, 20–24 St Michael's Street, OX1 2EB. Tel 01865 244622, www.vanbrughhousehotel. co.uk. On a quiet side street near the Oxford Union, this impeccable B&B is spread over two buildings dating from the 17th and 18th centuries. David Robinson is the manager. Handsome bedrooms are individually styled along three themes – Georgian, Eclectic and Arts and Crafts. Each has a fireplace, hand-crafted furniture, a media hub, and a minibar with fresh milk and complimentary drinks and snacks. The Vicarage Suite and Nicholas Hawksmoor Room have a private garden and terrace area. Breakfast is taken in the basement restaurant or on the sunken terrace with its 'secret' garden. Set lunches are served until 2 pm (2 courses £9.95; 3 courses £12.95). Breakfast room; small terrace. Free Wi-Fi. Background music. Park and Ride recommended. Children welcomed. 22 bedrooms (1 suitable for disabled). Per room B&B from £136. 2-night min. stay at weekend.

PENRITH Cumbria
Map 4: inset C2
Tebay Services Hotel, nr Orton, CA10 3SB. Tel 01539 624351, www. tebayserviceshotel.com. 'We really liked this out-of-the-ordinary motorway

hotel.' With 'superb' views of the fells, this deep-pitched building (reminiscent of mountain architecture) is just off the M6, between junctions 38 and 39, yet it lies in a peaceful area. Formerly known as the Westmorland Hotel, it is owned by the Dunning family, whose farm is nearby; beef and lamb from the farm feature in the restaurant's 'well-cooked' rustic British dishes. Bedrooms have handmade shortbread biscuits and cafetière coffee; bathrooms have locally made organic toiletries. There are cosy seats and, in winter, a roaring fire in the lounge; light meals and snacks are available here all day. 'We were impressed that they provide both feather and synthetic pillows, and linen table napkins at breakfast.' Part of the Tebay Motorway Services site; an on-site farm shop sells food from local producers. Lounge, bar (log fires), dining room. Free Wi-Fi. No background music. Civil wedding licence; function/ conference facilities. Children, and dogs (in some rooms; £10 per night, including bowls and treats) welcomed. 50 bedrooms (some family rooms with bunk bed; 1 suitable for disabled). Per room B&B £65–£118. Dinner £28.

PENZANCE Cornwall
Map 1:E1
Artist Residence, 20 Chapel Street, TR18 4AW. Tel 01736 365664, www. artistresidence.co.uk. Quirky and bright inside, this Grade II listed 17th-century Georgian house is on a narrow street in the historic heart of Penzance. Owners Justin Salisbury and Charlotte Newey have added a creative touch to bedrooms and apartment. They are decorated in vintage style, with reclaimed furniture and limited-edition prints; 'artist' rooms

have eye-catching murals painted by local artists. Jason Clark manages, with a friendly team. A varied breakfast of local produce is taken in the newly refurbished dining room on the ground floor; in the rustic Cornish Barn, chef Gareth Spencer's dinners use Cornish produce. 5 mins' walk from the railway station. Lounge/breakfast room. Small courtyard garden. No background music. Free Wi-Fi. Children (cots) and dogs (in some rooms) welcomed. 18 bedrooms (family rooms; 5 self-contained apartments next door). Per room B&B £75–£145.

PRESTON Lancashire
Map 4:D2
Barton Grange Hotel, 746–768 Garstang Road, PR3 5AA. Tel 01772 862551, www.bartongrangehotel.co.uk. The Topping family have run their hotel in this old manor house, once the country home of a cotton mill owner, for 65 years. Daniel Rich is the manager. Modern bedrooms, many recently refurbished and decorated with lively colours, are in the main house and a cottage in the grounds. They are well equipped with a coffee machine, minibar, trouser press and iron. In the Walled Garden bistro, chef Steve Hodson's menu has a mix of traditional and modern dishes. Drinks are taken in the oak-panelled lounge, with a fire in winter. Buffet breakfasts; a 'grab and go' breakfast bag is available to take away, by arrangement. Lounge, snug, bistro/wine bar; private dining. Lift. Free Wi-Fi. 'Easy listening' background music. Leisure centre ('nice' indoor swimming pool, sauna, gym). Pool/bar billiards. Civil wedding licence; conferences. Parking. Children welcomed. Barton Grange Garden Centre, in the same ownership, is near. A few mins' drive from the M6; 6 miles from the city centre. 51 bedrooms (8 in the Garden House in the grounds; 1 suitable for disabled; family rooms). Per person B&B from £81, D,B&B from £96.

RICHMOND North Yorkshire
Map 4:C3
Easby Hall, DL10 7EU. Tel 01748 826066, www.easbyhall.com. In a tranquil setting above the ruins of Easby Abbey, John and Karen Clarke's family home is in an impressive stone-built Georgian country house, with luxurious B&B suites in a separate wing. Surrounded by beautiful gardens (including an organic vegetable garden), the house is an easy, traffic-free stroll to Richmond, along the banks of the River Swale. Romantic bedrooms have plush designer fabrics, vintage furniture, a mini fridge, and a log burner or open fire. Bathrooms are glamorous and spacious. Afternoon tea is taken in a large drawing room with an open fire and a grand piano. Breakfast, served at a time to suit guests, has a wide selection of home-made preserves, compotes, smoothies and fruit, as well as local bacon, and eggs from the house's free-range hens. Drawing room, dining room. Gardens. Free Wi-Fi. No background music. Children, well-behaved dogs, and horses (paddocks, loose boxes, stables) welcomed. 3 bedrooms (1, on ground floor, has easy access for disabled guests), plus 2-bedroom self-catering cottage. Per room B&B single £150, double £180. Dinner £40–£60. Credit cards not accepted.

ROMSEY Hampshire
Map 2:E2
THE WHITE HORSE, 19 Market Place,
SO51 8ZJ. Tel 01794 512431, www.
thewhitehorseromsey.co.uk. In the
centre of town, this medieval coaching
inn has been 'smartly refurbished'
in modern style. There are exposed
timbers, panelled corridors and witty
hunting-scene wallpapers. The Tudor
lounge – a 'cosy and appealing' setting
for afternoon tea – has board games,
newspapers, and a cheery stove in
the hearth. Attractive bedrooms
are individually decorated; some
interconnect to accommodate a family.
Opening on to a courtyard, the brasserie
is 'a lovely place to eat – restful but
interesting'. New chef Nick O'Halloran
cooks modern European food. Lounge,
2 bars, brasserie; courtyard (alfresco
dining). Beauty treatments in the
Saddlery. Civil wedding licence;
function facilities. Free Wi-Fi.
Background music. Room service. Pay-
and-display parking. Children (special
menu, cot, extra bed) and dogs (£10 per
night) welcomed. 31 bedrooms (5 in
Coach House across the courtyard). Per
room B&B from £110. Dinner £30.

RYE East Sussex
Map 2:E5
THE GEORGE IN RYE, 98 High Street,
TN31 7JT. Tel 01797 222114, www.
thegeorgeinrye.com. One of Rye's oldest
coaching inns (established around 1575)
has been renovated with great style by
the owners, Alex and Katie Clarke. On
the high street, it consists of a series of
interconnecting buildings surrounding
a central courtyard. 'Well-appointed,
comfortable' bedrooms are individually
decorated with designer fabrics and
wallpaper and singular furniture; there
may be a slipper chair here, a collection
of Penguin Classics there; many have
a copper or zinc bath. Earplugs are
provided to counter the early-morning
seagulls. In the handsome George
Grill restaurant, the menu is 'rich in
seafood', including fish from Rye bay;
much is cooked on a wood charcoal
grill. 'Good' breakfasts. Guest lounge,
bar (log fire), restaurant, decked
courtyard garden (alfresco meals). Civil
wedding licence; function facilities
(in the original Regency ballroom,
with large bay windows, chandeliers
and a minstrels' gallery). Free Wi-Fi.
'Ambient' background music. Children
(cot, extra bed; £20 per night) welcomed.
34 bedrooms (10 across a courtyard). Per
room B&B £135–£325. Dinner £30.

THE HOPE ANCHOR, Watchbell
Street, TN31 7HA. Tel 01797 222216,
www.thehopeanchor.co.uk. A once-
upon-a-time smugglers' refuge,
and a watering hole for sailors and
shipbuilders past, this white-painted,
family-owned hotel stands at the end
of a cobbled street. It has good views
across the quayside, Romney Marsh
and Camber Castle, to the sea beyond.
Managed by Christopher George, it
is run with 'pleasant' staff. Most of
the 'comfortable', simply furnished
bedrooms have panoramic views; all are
equipped with tea- and coffee-making
facilities, a clock radio, a TV and
slippers. In the spacious, modern dining
room, chef Kevin Santer serves 'well-
cooked' traditional English dishes using
fish, meat and produce from Rye and
surrounding areas. Lounge, bar (snack
menu), dining room; room service. Free
Wi-Fi. Background music. Weddings.

Parking permits supplied. Children (special menu; cot, monitor, high chair; over-5s £30 per night) and dogs (in some rooms) welcomed. 16 bedrooms (1 in roof annexe; 2 apartments, 1 on ground floor with patio; 1 cottage). Per room B&B from £115, D,B&B from £160. 2-night min. stay on bank holidays.

THE SHIP INN, The Strand, TN31 7DB. Tel 01797 222233, www.theshipinnrye. co.uk. A 'charming hodgepodge of a pub', this 16th-century building was once used as a warehouse to store contraband seized from smugglers. It is owned by Karen Northcote; Theo Bekker is the manager. The easy-going inn, 'in a good position' in the town, has uneven wooden floors, exposed beams (some low), mismatched furniture and quirky retro decorations; bedrooms are cheerfully styled. Chef John Tomlinson's cooking 'goes well beyond pub grub', with seasonal specials, fish from Rye bay ('you can taste how fresh it is'), and bread from a local artisan baker. 'Breakfast is taken seriously.' Close to Rye Harbour Nature Reserve and Camber Sands. Lounge (board games, books, DVDs), bar, snug (with fire), restaurant; terrace with seating. Function facilities. No Wi-Fi. Background music. Pay-and-display parking. Children (extra bed £10 per night) and dogs (£10 per night) welcomed. 10 bedrooms. Per room B&B £110–£125. 2-night min. stay on Sat. Dinner £27.

ST IVES Cornwall
Map 1:D1
BLUE HAYES, Trelyon Avenue, TR26 2AD. Tel 01736 797129, www.bluehayes. co.uk. Owned by Malcolm Herring, this small hotel is in a 1920s house high above Porthminster Point. There is a

homely, restful ambience: guests are encouraged to relax on squashy sofas in the sitting room, or outside in the palm-fringed garden. Decorated in chic coastal style, bedrooms have sea views; some have a balcony, roof terrace or patio. In good weather, breakfast, cream teas and snacks can be taken on the balustraded terrace, which has stunning views over the harbour and bay. A gate from the small garden leads directly to the beach (5 mins' walk) or to the harbour, half a mile away. 2 lounges, bar, dining room (light, Mediterranean-style suppers; Nicola Martin is chef); terrace. Free Wi-Fi. No background music. Room service. Small functions. Parking. Children over 10 welcomed. 6 bedrooms. Per room B&B single £120–£140, double £180–£260. Supper from £12. Closed Nov–Feb.

HEADLAND HOUSE, Headland Road, TR26 2NS. Tel 01736 796647, www. headlandhousehotel.co.uk. There are panoramic views of the sandy beach and turquoise waters of Carbis Bay from Mark and Fenella Thomas's B&B. The three-storey Edwardian house has bright bedrooms decorated in maritime stripes or colonial hues; Heligan has its own secluded garden with a table and chairs. Guests relax in the snug, which has board games, magazines and books and a fully stocked bar. With lawn seating, a decked terrace and hammock, there is plenty of space for alfresco lounging. Breakfast, with organic and local produce, has plenty of options; a continental breakfast bag is available for guests who need to make an early start. Complimentary afternoon tea and cake. Lounge, conservatory dining room; large front garden; terrace. Free

Wi-Fi. No background music. Parking. Beach 600 yards; 1½ miles from St Ives. 7 bedrooms. Per room B&B £95–£160. Closed Nov–Feb.

No1 St Ives, 1 Fern Glen, TR26 1QP. Tel 01736 799047, www.no1stives.co.uk. Anna Bray and Simon Talbot's impeccable B&B is in a stone-built house, a short downhill walk from the town and the Tate gallery. Hot drinks and biscuits are replenished daily in the well-decorated, modern bedrooms; two rooms have distant ocean views towards Godrevy Lighthouse. There is much to choose from at breakfast, including pancakes, omelettes and natural smoked Cornish haddock, served communally at a large wooden table. Sitting room, dining room (background jazz); small back garden; terrace. Free Wi-Fi. 4 bedrooms. Parking. Children over 12 welcomed. Per room B&B £109–£145. Closed Christmas.

Trevose Harbour House, 22 The Warren, TR26 2EA. Tel 01736 793267, www.trevosehouse.co.uk. In the historic centre, between the Porthminster and Harbour beaches, this 'very chic, beautifully appointed' B&B is in a whitewashed terraced house. It is run by Angela and Olivier Noverraz, 'a lovely, sophisticated young couple', with welcoming staff. Blue-and-white bedrooms 'echo the colours of surf and sky' and are furnished with vintage pieces and the latest gadgetry; each has a large bed, a hospitality tray and organic toiletries. The cosy snug has newspapers, books, magazines, an open fire and an honesty bar; the sunny terrace overlooks the pretty streets of the Warren. There are organic yogurts, muesli and granola and home-made preserves at breakfast; picnic hampers are available. Snug, breakfast room; terrace. In-room treatments on request. Free Wi-Fi. Background music. Limited parking close by. Children over 12 welcomed. 6 bedrooms (1 in annexe behind the house). Per room B&B from £140. Closed mid-Dec–early Mar.

SALCOMBE Devon
Map 1:E4
South Sands, Bolt Head, TQ8 8LL. Tel 01548 845 900, www.southsands. com. There is a breezy, maritime feel at this 'relaxed and informal' family-friendly hotel on the beach in South Sands bay. Public spaces are 'beautifully designed'; 'it was a pleasure to walk up the light wood circular staircase, with its contrasting banded treads'. Named after sailing boats, bedrooms are decorated in coastal colours; some have large windows with views of the beach and sea. The beachside restaurant has painted wicker chairs and a wooden floor (it can be noisy); fish and seafood appear on the modern menu. Lounge, bar, restaurant (background music); terrace. Free Wi-Fi. Civil wedding licence. Parking. Electric bicycles to borrow. Children and dogs (in some bedrooms; £12.50 per night; Oct–May) welcomed. Beaches and coastal paths. 27 bedrooms (5 beach suites; ground-floor rooms). Per room B&B from £190, D,B&B from £240. 2-night min. stay on weekend preferred.

SALISBURY Wiltshire
Map 2:D2
Leena's Guest House, 50 Castle Road, SP1 3RL. Tel 01722 335419, www.leenasguesthouse.co.uk. A short riverside walk from the city centre and cathedral, the Street family has been welcoming B&B guests for more than

30 years. The comfortable Edwardian house has good-value, traditionally decorated bedrooms; a family room sleeps three. Gary Street, an accommodating host, cooks 'excellent' breakfasts, with plenty of choice; organic raspberries and redcurrants from the garden are available in season. Guests in need of a snack may help themselves to the regularly replenished fruit bowl. 15 mins' walk to centre. Lounge, breakfast room; garden. Free Wi-Fi. No background music. Parking. Children welcomed. 6 bedrooms (1 on ground floor). Per room B&B single from £56, double from £72. Credit cards not accepted.

SPIRE HOUSE, 84 Exeter Street, SP1 2SE. Tel 01722 339213, www.salisbury-bedandbreakfast.com. Lois and John Faulkner run their small, 'very nice' B&B in this Grade II listed 18th-century town house, a ten-minute walk from the cathedral. They give 'a helpful and friendly welcome', and offer ready advice on restaurants, pubs and places to visit in the city. 'Lovely' bedrooms ('no chintz!') are 'pleasant to be in'; two overlook the quiet walled garden; all have biscuits and fresh fruit. 'Good and plentiful' breakfasts have lots of choice. Breakfast room; garden. Free Wi-Fi. No background music. Parking opposite. Children over 10 welcomed. 4 bedrooms. Room only from £90. Breakfast £5. Closed Christmas.

SCARBOROUGH North Yorkshire
Map 4:C5
PHOENIX COURT, 8–9 Rutland Terrace, YO12 7JB. Tel 01723 501150, www.hotel-phoenix.co.uk. Walkers are warmly welcomed at this environmentally friendly guest house in two Victorian houses overlooking North Bay and the beach. Owners Alison and Bryan Edwards provide hikers with drying facilities, route information, and packed lunches with home-baked rolls and cakes (£6 per person). Founts of local knowledge, they can also suggest 14 days of activities that can be carried out via public transport. Many of the simply furnished bedrooms have sea views; two can accommodate a family. Breakfast has home-baked bread, home-made jams and marmalade, and much Yorkshire produce, including locally smoked kippers and sausages from local farms. A continental breakfast may be taken in the bedroom. Vegetarian and vegan options available. Special breaks can be organised for theatregoers, including tickets for the Stephen Joseph theatre. 10 mins' walk from the town centre. Lounge, bar area, breakfast room (background radio). Ramp. Free Wi-Fi. Parking. Children welcomed (£5 per night charge for child over 2 in own travel cot). 13 bedrooms (9 with sea views; 1 on ground floor; 2 family rooms). Per room B&B single £36–£40, double £50–£64. Closed Nov–Jan, except New Year.
25% DISCOUNT VOUCHERS

SEDLESCOMBE East Sussex
Map 2:E4
KESTER HOUSE, The Street, TN33 0QB. Tel 01424 870035, www.kesterhouse.co.uk. In a conservation village within the High Weald, a designated area of outstanding natural beauty, Derek and Monique Wright run their small B&B in this 16th-century listed house. The rooms are full of historic features: guests can choose the soaring oak beams and four-poster bed in Armada, or the cosy, country feel of Brede; Tithe Barn has its

own sitting room and quirky reminders of its original use. Varied breakfasts, ordered the night before, include freshly baked bread, muffins and home-made jams; packed lunches are available. On Sundays, indulgent afternoon teas are served in the sitting rooms by an open fire. 2 sitting rooms, dining room; licensed bar; small walled garden. Free Wi-Fi (in public areas). No background music. Holistic therapies, massage, health and beauty treatments can be booked. 7 miles N of Hastings. 3 bedrooms. Per room B&B single £50–£85, double £80–£110. Closed Christmas, New Year.

SETTLE North Yorkshire
Map 4:D3

SETTLE LODGE, Duke St, BD24 9AS. Tel 01729 823258, www.settlelodge.co.uk. There are far-reaching views of the surrounding fells from this substantial Victorian residence, a five-minute walk from the town centre and train station. Amanda and Eduardo Martinez are the hospitable owners, who greet guests with tea and home-made cake on arrival. They are also happy to provide maps and information, and make suggestions on where to eat in the town. B&B accommodation is in 'spacious' bedrooms, each with lovely views. Breakfasts are 'delicious, with generous portions'. An ideal base for exploring the Dales; walkers are welcomed. Sitting room, dining room. Garden; terrace. Free Wi-Fi. Parking. 7 bedrooms. Per room B&B £70–£95.

SHANKLIN Isle of Wight
Map 2:E2

RYLSTONE MANOR, Rylstone Gardens, Popham Road, PO37 6RG. Tel 01983 862806, www.rylstone-manor.co.uk.

Within easy reach of the town, Mike and Carole Hailston's 'delightfully relaxing' small hotel is in a public park on a cliff above Sandown Bay, with steps going down to the shore. The house was built in 1863 as a gentleman's residence, with Gothic, Tudor and Georgian influences, and has 'wonderful' sea views from the garden. There are heavy fabrics, books and ornaments in the green-walled lounge; basket chairs in a Victorian covered patio. Traditional, country house-style bedrooms on the first floor have antique furniture; they vary in size. In the dining room, with its ornate chandelier and matching wall lights, Mike Hailston serves a short menu of modern and classic dishes based on seasonal availability. 'The fish was perfect every night.' The secluded private garden is 'a pleasant place to sip wine on a summer afternoon'. Drawing room, bar lounge, dining room; terrace. Free Wi-Fi. Optional background music. ¼-acre garden in 4-acre public gardens; direct access to sand/shingle beach. 9 bedrooms. Per person B&B from £67.50, D,B&B from £96.50. 2-night min. stay in peak season. Closed mid-Nov–early Feb.
25% DISCOUNT VOUCHERS

SHEFFIELD South Yorkshire
Map 4:E4

LEOPOLD HOTEL, 2 Leopold Street, Leopold Square, S1 2GZ. Tel 01142 524000, www.leopoldhotelsheffield.com. In a sympathetically converted Grade II listed building that once housed a boys' grammar school, this modern hotel (part of Small Luxury Hotels of the World) is on a lively public square with cafés and restaurants. It is well located for shops, theatres, the cathedral and the station. Arched doorways, school photos and memorabilia and ranks of coat pegs echo the building's history. Sleek, modern bedrooms have top-of-the-class technology (iPod docking station, digital radio, flat-screen TV). A small gym was recently added. Breakfast is served until 10.30 am on the weekend; meals and drinks may be taken on the terrace facing bustling Leopold Square. Lounge bar, dining room; terrace. Free Wi-Fi. Background music. 24-hour room service; private dining rooms. Lift. Fitness suite. Civil wedding licence; conference/function facilities. Parking discounts in public car park nearby (£7 per 24 hours). Children welcomed. 90 bedrooms (6 suitable for disabled). Room only from £90. Breakfast £12.95.

SHERBORNE Dorset
Map 2:E1

THE EASTBURY HOTEL, Long Street, DT9 3BY. Tel 01935 813131, www. theeastburyhotel.co.uk. A 'lovely', large walled garden with a lawn, pathways, nooks and crannies sits behind Paul and Nicola King's 'very pleasant' hotel, off the main streets of this fine Dorset town. 'Very comfortable' bedrooms are traditional or modern in style; some overlook the courtyard; one has a private garden. Chef Matt Street cooks a seven-course tasting menu with salads and herbs from the garden; alfresco meals may be taken on the terrace in good weather. Drawing room, lounge, bar, library, conservatory restaurant (background music); terrace; garden. Free Wi-Fi. Wedding/function facilities; private dining. Golf breaks. Children (special meals by request; cots £8.50; extra beds £20) and dogs (£10 per night) welcomed. 23 bedrooms (3 with external access; 1 suitable for disabled). Per room B&B single from £80, double from £150. Tasting menu £55.
25% DISCOUNT VOUCHERS

THE KINGS ARMS, North Street, Charlton Horethorne, DT9 4NL. Tel 01963 220281, www.thekingsarms.co.uk. Behind the stately facade of this Edwardian building, chef/patron Sarah Lethbridge and her husband, Anthony, have created a modern country pub with smart accommodation and a well-regarded restaurant. Colourful, individually styled bedrooms have a marble wet room; some have views of the croquet lawn. Downstairs, public rooms are decorated with local art and sculpture; a log-burning stove separates a cosy seating area from the slate- and wood-floored bar. Sarah Lethbridge's modern dishes, many cooked in a Josper charcoal oven, are served in the restaurant, which has large doors opening on to a terrace with views of the countryside. Lift. Lounge, snug, bar, restaurant. Free Wi-Fi. No background music. Terrace; garden; croquet. Functions; shooting parties. Free use of sports centre in Sherborne (4 miles); discounts at Sherborne Golf Club; clay-pigeon shooting can be arranged. Parking. Children welcomed (special menu). 10 bedrooms (1 suitable for disabled; 3 accessible by lift). Per room B&B from £135, interconnecting family room £250. Dinner £35.

SHREWSBURY Shropshire
Map 3:B4

CHATFORD HOUSE, Chatford, SY3 0AY. Tel 01743 718301, www.chatfordhouse. co.uk. Christine and Rupert Farmer's Grade II listed 18th-century farmhouse, surrounded by organic farmland, is 'first class all round'. The Farmers rear hens, ducks, geese, sheep and cattle on their smallholding; guests are welcome to visit the animals and explore the pretty garden and orchard. Tea and home-made cake are served on arrival; simple, country cottage-style bedrooms have fresh flowers, magazines and a hospitality tray. All rooms overlook the garden and the Wrekin. Aga-cooked breakfasts use eggs from the resident hens; there are also home-made jams and compotes and local honey. Close to the Shropshire Way. 5 miles S of Shrewsbury; within walking distance of Lyth Hill. Sitting room, breakfast room (open fire). Free Wi-Fi. No background music. Garden; orchard. Parking. Children welcomed (high chair, cot). 3 bedrooms. Per room B&B single from £50, double from £70. Credit cards not accepted.

GROVE FARM HOUSE, Condover, SY5 7BH. Tel 01743 718544, www. grovefarmhouse.com. In a peaceful setting, Liz Farrow's B&B is in a three-storey Georgian house on the edge of a small village; there are many walks to be had through beautiful parkland and wooded areas. Modern, country-style bedrooms have a DVD/CD player, bathrobes, home-made biscuits, and flowers from the garden; local guidebooks are available to borrow. Breakfast has locally produced meat, eggs from home-reared chickens, and home-made blueberry muffins. Complimentary tea and cake are offered to guests arriving in the afternoon; a full English tea (scones with cream and jam, and a selection of cakes and biscuits) is available by arrangement (£5.50). Liz Farrow happily makes recommendations for dinner

at local restaurants. Lounge, dining room; ½-acre garden. Free Wi-Fi. No background music. Parking. 6 miles S of Shrewsbury. Children welcomed. 4 bedrooms, plus 2 self-catering suites with log burner and private courtyard. Per room B&B £90. 2-night min. stay May–Sept. Closed Christmas, New Year. **25% DISCOUNT VOUCHERS**

THE INN AT GRINSHILL, High Street, Grinshill, SY4 3BL. Tel 01939 220410, www.theinnatgrinshill.co.uk. 'Excellent hosts' Victoria and Kevin Brazier run their 18th-century country inn in the lee of Grinshill, a site of special scientific interest. In the restaurant and conservatory, Arron Christopher, the new chef, serves seasonal, local fare; bistro meals are taken in the popular wood-panelled bar, which has books, games, comfy sofas and an open fire. Bedrooms are understated and 'charming', with a stylish bathroom. From the front door, walkers can explore part of the Shropshire Way through sandstone quarries; a map is provided. 2 bars, restaurant (closed Sun, Mon and Tues evenings; optional background music/ radio). Free Wi-Fi. Rose garden with fountain. Functions. Parking. Children welcomed. 7 miles N of Shrewsbury. 6 bedrooms. Per room B&B single £89.50, double £119.50. D,B&B £79.50 per person (based on 2 people sharing). **25% DISCOUNT VOUCHERS**

LION AND PHEASANT, 50 Wyle Cop, SY1 1XJ. Tel 01743 770345, www. lionandpheasant.co.uk. 'A pleasant place to stay', this former coaching inn is on one of the oldest streets in town, by the English Bridge. It is owned by Dorothy Chidlow; Jim Littler manages, with 'caring' staff. The inn has been modernised with 'a simple but sure touch'. A warren of smartly styled, beamed corridors leads to the 'well-furnished and -equipped' bedrooms (some overlooking the river; some snug). Double glazing and earplugs help dampen early-morning traffic noise; rooms at the back of the hotel are quietest. Innovative à la carte menus and Sunday lunches are served in several dining areas, from the bar (oak floors, wide benches) to the inglenook room (flagstone floors, open fire) to the split-level restaurant (cosy, with bare tables); David Martin is head chef. 'Handy for the town centre.' 3 bars, restaurant, function room; garden terrace (alfresco dining). Room service. Free Wi-Fi. Background music. Children welcomed (extra bed £15 per night). Narrow entrance to car park. 22 bedrooms. Per room B&B from £104, D,B&B from £165. 2-night min. stay preferred.

THE SILVERTON, 9–10 Frankwell, SY3 8JY. Tel 01743 248000, www. thesilverton.co.uk. Within easy walking distance of the riverside, town centre and Theatre Severn, this restaurant-with-rooms is in a refurbished former dairy near the Welsh Bridge. It is owned by Doug Blackmore, a local restaurateur. Modern bedrooms, named after Shropshire hills, have tea- and coffee-making facilities, a digital radio, TV and iPod dock; some have views of the river or historic Tudor buildings. 'Excellent' breakfasts include smoked mackerel, egg dishes and a full English. Lunch, afternoon tea, dinner and pre-theatre menus are served. On a main road; front-facing rooms are supplied with ear plugs to counteract any traffic noise. Bar, restaurant. Lift. Terrace. Free Wi-Fi. Background music; live music every Fri and Sat night.

Valet parking. Children welcomed. 7 bedrooms (1 suitable for disabled; some interconnecting). Per room B&B £75–£135. Dinner £30.

SIDLESHAM West Sussex
Map 2:E3
THE CRAB & LOBSTER, Mill Lane, PO20 7NB. Tel 01243 641233, www. crab-lobster.co.uk. In a peaceful situation on the banks of the Pagham Harbour nature reserve, this 350-year-old inn has been renovated in spare, modern style by structural engineer-turned-hotelier Sam Bakose and his wife, Janet. Sophie Harwood is the manager. Comfortable bedrooms are decorated in soft pastels; one room under the eaves has low ceilings and a large bathroom with views over the sea and fields; binoculars are provided. Clyde Hollett, the chef, cooks fresh local fish, crab and lobster to 'a very high standard'; breakfast has honey from Sidlesham bees. Bar, restaurant (background jazz); terrace; garden. Free Wi-Fi. Children welcomed (£30 per night). 4 miles S of Chichester. 6 bedrooms (2 in adjoining cottage). Per room B&B £160–£280. Dinner £36. 2-night min. stay on weekends.

SIDMOUTH Devon
Map 1:D5
VICTORIA HOTEL, The Esplanade, EX10 8RY. Tel 01395 512651, www. victoriahotel.co.uk. 'A very comfortable hotel – old-fashioned in the best sense of the word.' Overlooking the bay, this large, traditional hotel (Brend Hotels) in five acres of landscaped grounds has many returning visitors. Most of the 'immaculate' bedrooms are south facing; some have a balcony; a turn-down

service is provided each evening. There is plenty of space to relax in the lounges or out in the 'delightful' garden; more active guests have access to a tennis court and an 18-hole golf course. Men are asked to wear a jacket and tie at dinner in the Jubilee restaurant, which has live musical accompaniment, and dinner dances on Saturday nights. 'The food is interesting, but unfussy.' Sun lounge, lounge bar, restaurant; outdoor and indoor swimming pools; tennis court, snooker, putting. Spa, sauna, treatments. Room service. Free Wi-Fi. Background music. Gift shop. Parking. Children welcomed. 65 bedrooms (3 poolside suites). Room only £215–£330. Breakfast from £18. 2-night min. stay.

SISSINGHURST Kent
Map 2:D5

THE MILK HOUSE, The Street, TN17 2JG. Tel 01580 720200, www. themilkhouse.co.uk. In a village renowned for its gardens, this laid-back, popular pub is 'attractive both inside and out'. The former 16th-century hall house, which retains its timber beams and Tudor fireplace, has been refurbished by Dane and Sarah Allchorne in 'simple, fresh, elegant' style, with creamy colours throughout. Contemporary, light-filled bedrooms (Byre, Buttery, Churn and Dairy) have scenic views of the village and surrounding orchards. Dane Allchorne, 'a very competent cook', serves Sunday roasts, classic pub fare and a seasonal dining menu; an all-day 'grazing menu' is also available; pizzas are cooked in a wood-fired oven on the terrace. The bar stocks cask ales from Kentish breweries and a wide selection of wines from local vineyards. Generous breakfasts.

Sissinghurst Castle Garden is half a mile's walk away. Bar, restaurant ('easy listening' background music); private dining. Sun terrace (alfresco dining). Free Wi-Fi. Parking. Children (special menu, outdoor play area) and dogs welcomed. 4 bedrooms (1 family room). Per room B&B from £100. Dinner £35. 2-night min. stay at weekends.

SISSINGHURST CASTLE FARMHOUSE, nr Cranbrook, TN17 2AB. Tel 01580 720992, www.sissinghurstcastlefarm house.com. Sue and Frazer Thompson's elegant B&B is in a Victorian farmhouse filled with pictures, fresh flowers, and a mix of contemporary and period furniture. Restored by the National Trust, it is on the Sissinghurst estate, near the entrance to the castle and gardens; guests have access to the estate grounds. The Thompsons serve complimentary tea and home-made cake to arriving guests; individually designed bedrooms have breathtaking views of ancient woodland, fields, gardens or the castle's Elizabethan tower. There is home-made marmalade at breakfast; hot dishes are cooked to order. Sitting room (books, magazines), dining room; meeting room; small functions. Lift. Free Wi-Fi. No background music. Garden. Children welcomed. Resident dog. 7 bedrooms (1 with easy-access wet room). Per room B&B £130–£190. 2-night min. stay on weekends, Easter–Sept. Closed Jan, Feb.

SNETTISHAM Norfolk
Map 2:A4

THE ROSE & CROWN, Old Church Road, PE31 7LX. Tel 01485 541382, www.roseandcrownsnettisham.co.uk. 'Comfortable, with delicious food',

Jeannette and Anthony Goodrich's quintessential English inn is a whitewashed 14th-century building in the village centre, opposite a cricket pitch. It has low beams, leaning walls, twisting passages and cosy corners. 'Charming', modern bedrooms have fresh milk and home-made biscuits on a hospitality tray. Adjoining the lounge, a garden room has comfortable seating and a large open fire. In the bars and dining rooms, chef Jamie Clarke serves traditional pub favourites and more adventurous dishes, using produce from local suppliers. Lounge (background music), 3 bars, 3 dining areas. Large, sunny walled garden. Ramps. Beaches nearby. Children (high chair, colouring sets; cot £10 per night; play galleon climbing frame) and 'well-behaved' dogs welcomed. 16 bedrooms (2 on ground floor; 2 suitable for disabled). Per room B&B single £80–£110, double £100–£125. 2-night min. stay July, Aug and bank holidays. Dinner £27.

SOMERTON Somerset
Map 1:C6

THE WHITE HART, Market Place, TA11 7LX. Tel 01458 272273, www. whitehartsomerton.com. In a historic town on the edge of the Somerset Levels, this 16th-century pub stands near a church on an attractive market square. It has been revamped with flair by the Draco Pub Company, owners of The Swan, Wedmore (see Shortlist entry). Natalie Zvonek-Little is the manager. Exposed stone walls, wooden floors and patchwork tiling create a contemporary rustic look throughout. Refurbished bedrooms, with a wide bed and quirky features, are well stocked with freshly ground coffee and luxury toiletries. Three front rooms overlook the square and the 13th-century church of St Michael and All Angels; three rooms at the rear have views of the courtyard or garden. Chef Tom Blake (formerly of the River Cottage Canteen) supports West Country suppliers in his 'fresh, simple' dishes – 'a model of what local and organic food should be'. Fish is smoked on site in a wood-fired oven; bread, jams, chutneys, cakes and ice creams are all home made. Bar (local brews, newspapers, open fires), conservatory restaurant (closed Sun eve; 3 dining areas); large garden and courtyard. Ramps. Free Wi-Fi. Background music. Children (special menu; cot; extra bed £20) and dogs (in some rooms, by arrangement) welcomed. 8 bedrooms. Per room B&B £85–£130, D,B&B from £165.

SOUTH MOLTON Devon
Map 1:C4

ASHLEY HOUSE, 3 Paradise Lawn, EX36 3DJ. Tel 01769 573444, www. ashleyhousebedandbreakfast.com. In a handsomely restored former gentleman's residence, Nicky Robbins runs her small B&B with much attention to detail. The brick-built Victorian villa in the town centre has an interesting history, and features on the official South Molton Heritage Trail. A blue plaque is dedicated to Samuel Widgery, who served as Lord Chief Justice of England from 1971 to 1980. High-ceilinged bedrooms, in an adjoining annexe, have been elegantly furnished with antiques, contemporary pieces, and original photography and artwork depicting the local area. Fresh milk, coffee and a selection of teas are provided. Devonshire breakfasts include home-made preserves, eggs from resident hens, fruit and vegetables from the garden, and locally sourced bacon and sausages. Walkers and cyclists are welcomed. Breakfast/sitting room (wood-burning stove; classical background music). Free Wi-Fi. Large garden. Resident dog. Parking. 3 bedrooms. Per person B&B £75–£105. Credit cards not accepted.

SOUTHAMPTON Hampshire
Map 2:E2

WOODLANDS LODGE HOTEL, Bartley Road, SO40 7GN. Tel 02380 292257, www.woodlands-lodge.co.uk. In a semi-rural setting, Imogene and Robert Anglaret's dog-friendly hotel has direct access into the New Forest from the garden. 'It's not grand, but the bedrooms and sitting rooms are comfortable, the food is good, and the staff could not be more helpful.' Most of the country-style bedrooms have views over the gardens and woodland; each is equipped with tea- and coffee-making facilities and hot chocolate. In Hunters restaurant, dinner, served between 6.30 pm and 8.30 pm, uses fruit and vegetables from the walled kitchen garden; free-range chickens provide the eggs. Afternoon tea and an all-day snack menu may be taken in the conservatory and lounge or in the bedroom. 1 mile from Ashurst village (train station). Lounge, bar, conservatory, restaurant. 3-acre garden. Free Wi-Fi (in public areas). 'Easy listening' background music in the evening; Radio 2 during the day (optional). Civil wedding licence; business facilities. Children (cot, extra bed) and dogs (in some rooms) welcomed. 15 mins' drive from Southampton. 17 bedrooms (2 with garden access; 1 suitable for disabled). Per room B&B from £79, D,B&B from £129.

SOUTHPORT Merseyside
Map 4:E2

THE VINCENT, 98 Lord Street, PR8 1JR. Tel 01704 883800, www.thevincenthotel. com. Within walking distance of the promenade and the King's Gardens, this large, fashionable hotel was transformed from a former cinema by local restaurateur Paul Adams. Beyond the striking glass facade, the chic, modern interior has a buzzing bar and café. Some of the plush, sophisticated bedrooms have an adjoining lounge and balcony. Andrew Carter, the chef, serves sushi and other international dishes in the V-Café, which is open till late. Bar, café; members' bar; background music. Free Wi-Fi. Spa; gym; beauty treatments. Civil wedding licence; functions. Valet parking. Children welcomed. 59 bedrooms (3 suitable for disabled; some interconnecting). Per room B&B from £143. Dinner £35.

STAMFORD Lincolnshire
Map 2:B3

THE BULL AND SWAN AT BURGHLEY, High Street, St Martins, PE9 2LJ. Tel 01780 766412, www.thebullandswan. co.uk. The alleged meeting place of the Honourable Order of Little Bedlam, a riotous 17th-century gentlemen's drinking club, this refurbished old coaching inn today hosts quirky bedrooms and a popular bistro. It is managed by James Chadwick for Hillbrooke Hotels. Attractive bedrooms, given the pseudonyms of Little Bedlam members, have crisp linen and smart fabrics; two are spacious enough to accommodate a family. In the dining rooms, new chef Phil Kent cooks modern pub grub using produce from local suppliers; Sunday roasts and a special menu for early diners are available. The town centre is a short stroll across the river; Burghley House can be reached via a cross-country walk. Bar; 3 dining areas. Free Wi-Fi. Background music. Courtyard garden with seating. Parking (narrow entrance). Children (£20 per night; special menu) and dogs (in 3 rooms; dog bed, bowls, special treats, room-service menu) welcomed. 9 bedrooms. Per room B&B from £120, D,B&B from £170.

STOWMARKET Suffolk
Map 2:C5
BAYS FARM, Earl Stonham, IP14 5HU. Tel 01449 711286, www.baysfarm suffolk.co.uk. 'Tastefully modernised', Stephanie and Richard Challinor's welcoming B&B is a 17th-century farmhouse surrounded by lovely countryside, on the outskirts of a peaceful village. The extensive, award-winning grounds (included in the National Gardens Scheme) have an orchard, a wild flower garden, and vegetable and fruit gardens, as well as plenty of comfortable seating. Guests may relax in the pavilion, which has its own heating, lighting and iPod docking station. Overlooking the gardens, the Hayloft suite is in a converted building with a balcony. New this year, a shepherd's hut in the grounds provides quirky accommodation: overlooking the newly landscaped moat, it has a king-size bed, up-to-date gadgetry, an oversized shower and a wood burner. A communal breakfast is served in the former dairy, the oldest part of the house, at a time to suit guests. Bread, marmalade and jams are home made. A farmhouse

supper and snacks are available; licensed. Drawing room (open fire), dining room (background music). Free Wi-Fi. 4-acre garden. Resident dog. 4 miles E of Stowmarket. 5 bedrooms (1 in adjacent building, 1 in shepherd's hut). Per room B&B £75–£120.

STRATFORD-UPON-AVON
Warwickshire
Map 3:D6
CHURCH STREET TOWNHOUSE, 16 Church Street, CV37 6HB. Tel 01789 262222, www.churchstreettownhouse. com. Opposite the grammar school that William Shakespeare attended, this 400-year-old, Grade II listed building combines characterful low ceilings and beams with comfortable, modern bedrooms, a bustling all-day bistro and a lively bar. It is managed by David Mackinnon for the City Pub Company. Rooms vary in size, but all have a large bed, TV/DVD player, iPod dock and period features. Complimentary port, champagne, fresh milk and nibbles are provided. Heavy drapes, armchairs, and a candelabra on each table give the restaurant a theatrical intimacy; chef Andrew Taylor's modern dishes include a pre-theatre menu. 2 bars (live piano music), restaurant (Sunday roasts). Free Wi-Fi. No background music. Parking can be arranged. A short walk from the Royal Shakespeare Theatre. 12 bedrooms (1 suitable for disabled). Per room B&B from £110, D,B&B from £150. 2-night min. stay at weekends. Closed Christmas Day.

WHITE SAILS, 85 Evesham Road, CV37 9BE. Tel 01789 550469, www.white-sails.co.uk. 'High standards' and lots of little extras are provided by owners Tim and Denise Perkin, at their comfortable B&B on the outskirts of Stratford. Guests help themselves to complimentary coffee, sherry and home-made treats in the lounge. Bedrooms are supplied with bathrobes, a DAB radio/iPod docking station, and a silent fridge with a supply of chilled water and fresh milk. Lounge, dining room. No background music. Free Wi-Fi. Garden with summer house. Bicycle storage. 1 mile W of centre (on a bus route). Within walking distance of Anne Hathaway's cottage and gardens. 4 bedrooms. Per room B&B £105–£132 (2-night min. stay preferred at weekends). Closed Christmas, New Year.

TEIGNMOUTH Devon
Map 1:D5

THOMAS LUNY HOUSE, Teign Street, TQ14 8EG. Tel 01626 772976, www. thomas-luny-house.co.uk. Approached via a walled courtyard set back from the street, John and Alison Allan's B&B is a short walk from the town and quay. The Allans are 'very pleasant, attentive' hosts, who serve complimentary tea or coffee with home-made cake in the spacious drawing room each afternoon. Books, magazines and fresh flowers in the traditionally decorated bedrooms are appreciated; bathrooms are spotless. An 'excellent variety' is served at breakfast; a daily newspaper is provided. 2 lounges, breakfast room; small garden. Free Wi-Fi. No background music. Parking. 4 bedrooms. Per person B&B £44–£80.

TETBURY Gloucestershire
Map 3:E5

OAK HOUSE No.1, The Chipping, GL8 8EU. Tel 01666 505741, www. oakhouseno1.com. Sumptuously furnished, this fine Georgian house is run as a small, luxury B&B by interior designer and art collector Gary Kennedy, with Nicola MacWilliam. Strikingly decorated public rooms are filled with antiques, paintings, photographs and intriguing artefacts. Individually styled suites range from the Cavalier, which has its own library sitting room, to the eclectic Prince's Suite and more modern Garden View Suite. They each have cashmere throws and a silver tea set. A complimentary afternoon tea is served at a time to suit guests. Sitting room, dining room. Free Wi-Fi. Background jazz. Walled garden. Luxury picnic hampers. Beauty treatments. Concierge service. Wellington boots and thick socks supplied for walkers wanting to explore the countryside. Babies, and children over 11, welcomed. 3 suites. Per suite B&B £345–£495.

THE ROYAL OAK, Cirencester Road, GL8 8EY. Tel 01666 500021, theroyaloaktetbury.co.uk. Husband-and-wife team Chris York and Kate Lewis have added retro features to complement the original character of this 18th-century Cotswold stone inn near the centre. Its lively bar is popular with locals; guests may choose their favourite tunes on a jukebox. In the raftered restaurant upstairs, chef Richard Simms serves modern bistro food, using organic produce; an interesting vegan menu is available. In a separate building opposite the pub, contemporary, rustic bedrooms open on to the courtyard; the best, the Oak Lodge mezzanine suite, has leather armchairs and a wood burner. The spacious garden has a boules pitch and space for alfresco dining. From May to September, casual food is served from a vintage Airstream trailer on the terrace.

Bar (real ales), restaurant (closed Sun eve). Garden. Free Wi-Fi. Background music; monthly live music sessions. Children (special menu; games; garden; not after 8 pm in restaurant) and dogs (in ground-floor rooms; £10 per night) welcomed. 6 bedrooms (1 suitable for disabled). Per room B&B £95–£160. Dinner £25.

THORPE MARKET Norfolk
Map 2:A5

THE GUNTON ARMS, Cromer Road, NR11 8TZ. Tel 01263 832010, www. theguntonarms.co.uk. 'An interesting place to stay', this sophisticated yet 'relaxed' pub-with-rooms is an old, red-gabled inn on the edge of a deer park. It is owned by art dealer Ivor Braka; the 'vibrant' interior is filled with artwork ranging from Stubbs engravings to a neon sign by Tracey Emin. Simone Baker is the manager. Within flint walls, public areas have stone-flagged floors, roaring fires, mounted antlers on wood-panelled walls. 'Lovely' bedrooms have handmade wallpaper, Turkish rugs and antique furniture. One visitor's room had 'plenty of storage' and good lighting; 'a double washbasin and a huge retro bathtub in the bathroom'. No television in the bedrooms; instead, a Roberts radio 'in colours to match the decor'. Each of the two lounges has a TV. Guests may help themselves to juice, tea and coffee in a downstairs pantry. In the Elk dining room – 'like a medieval banqueting hall' – Stuart Tattersall, the chef, cooks potatoes and 'chunks of meat' (steaks, ribs of beef, Barnsley chops, sausages, etc) on a grill set over a huge open fire; bread is fresh from the oven. 5 miles from Cromer. 2 lounges, bar, restaurant (closed Sun). Free Wi-Fi. Background music.

Children (cot; extra bed £15 per night) and dogs (£15 per night) welcomed. Per room B&B £95–£185 (2-night min. stay at weekends). Dinner from £35. Closed Christmas.

THURNHAM Kent
Map 2:D4

THURNHAM KEEP, Castle Hill, ME14 3LE. Tel 01622 734149, www. thurnhamkeep.co.uk. Amanda Lane extends a friendly welcome, with tea and freshly made scones, to B&B guests arriving at her childhood home, a 'very impressive' Edwardian house on the North Downs. At the end of a long drive, it stands in extensive grounds, with views over the Weald of Kent. 'Beautiful' bedrooms are traditionally furnished; two have a huge, original Edwardian bath. Communal breakfasts include home-made jams, honey from the garden's bees, and eggs from resident free-range hens. Supper is available, by arrangement; plenty of pubs nearby. Oak-panelled sitting room (wood-burning stove), conservatory, dining room; terrace (alfresco breakfasts); snooker room (in the old chapel). Free Wi-Fi. Background music (weekend eves only; 'easy listening'/ classical/jazz). 7-acre terraced garden: heated outdoor swimming pool (June–early Sept); pond; kitchen garden; dovecote; summer house; tennis, croquet. Parking. 3 bedrooms. Per room B&B £130–£160.

TISBURY Wiltshire
Map 2:D1

THE COMPASSES INN, Lower Chicksgrove, SP3 6NB. Tel 01722 714318, www.thecompassesinn.com. 'In the middle of nowhere', this medieval

English country inn has a thatched roof, low ceilings, huge beams, a crackling log fire, and plenty of nooks and crannies. Owned by Susie and Alan Stoneham, it is in an area of outstanding natural beauty, and makes a good base for country walks and visits to Longleat, Stonehenge and Wilton House. In the main bar and adjacent dining room, Dan Cousins and Ian Chalmers, the chefs, cook traditional pub grub based on local produce in season; there is an extensive wine list. Simply furnished, country-style bedrooms are accessed separately from the pub; each has a hospitality tray and a modern bathroom. Bar, dining room. Free Wi-Fi. No background music. Front and rear gardens. Small functions. Children (special menu; DVDs, games, toys; colouring sets; baby monitor, babysitting) and dogs welcomed. 4 bedrooms, plus adjacent 2-bed cottage. Per person B&B £85–£90 (2-night min. stay on summer and bank holiday weekends). Dinner from £25. Closed Christmas.

TITCHWELL Norfolk
Map 2:A5

BRIARFIELDS, Main Road, PE31 8BB. Tel 01485 210742, www.briarfieldshotel norfolk.co.uk. With breathtaking views over marshland and the sea, this family-friendly, flint-built hotel on the north Norfolk coast is popular with walkers, birdwatchers and dog owners. It is managed by Bradley Williams. There are many spots in which to relax: the lounge has books, magazines and games; drinks and afternoon tea may be taken in front of the fire in the beamed snug; a sunny courtyard has a fish pond for quiet contemplation; the decked terrace overlooks the children's play area. Spacious, modern bedrooms are neatly decorated; some have views over the RSPB reserve. Chef Richard Bargewell's dishes are based on local and home-smoked produce; throughout the summer months, the popular Seafood Bar has freshly caught crabs, prawns and oysters from along the coast. The Royal West Norfolk Golf Club is 5 mins' drive away. 3 lounges; 5-acre garden. Free Wi-Fi. 'Easy listening' background music. Children (special menu; cot £10 per night; board games; play area; 11–16s £35 per night) and dogs welcomed. 23 bedrooms (20 around the courtyard; 3 family rooms; 1 suitable for disabled). Per room B&B £75–£180, D,B&B £100–£230 (2-night min. stay in summer).

TOLLARD ROYAL Wiltshire
Map 2:E1

KING JOHN INN, SP5 5PS. Tel 01725 516207, www.kingjohninn.co.uk. In a pretty village on the edge of Cranborne Chase, this roadside pub was rescued from dereliction by owners Alex and Gretchen Boon, and updated in modern country style. The Victorian building has an open-plan bar and dining area with large black-and-white photographs; a snug has comfy sofas by an open fire. Chef Simon Trepess catches fish, bakes bread, makes his own cheese and uses local game for his daily-changing menus. Alfresco dining is in the terraced garden; on fine days, there may be barbecues, served in the Victorian-inspired pavilion. Five smart, well-designed bedrooms are accessed via a steep, narrow staircase; three are in the converted coach house opposite. Fresh orange juice, 'proper' toast and 'perfectly cooked' hot dishes at breakfast. Bar, restaurant; wine shop. Garden (outdoor functions; music licence). Free Wi-Fi. 6 miles W of Shaftesbury. Parking. Dogs welcomed. 8 bedrooms (some on ground floor; plus 2/3-bed self-catering cottage). Per room B&B single from £90, double from £160. Dinner from £20.

TORQUAY Devon
Map 1:D5
THE 25, 25 Avenue Road, TQ2 5LB. Tel 01803 297517, www.the25.uk. Experienced hoteliers Andy and Julian Banner-Price have turned their attention to this B&B, renamed it and refurbished it with panache. Formerly the Glenross, the Edwardian villa stands behind Torre Abbey. It is a pleasant ten-minute walk through picturesque gardens to the sea front; the main harbour, with shops, restaurants, bars and a theatre, is close by. Guests arriving in the afternoon are greeted with tea and home-made cake in the elegant drawing room. Colourful bedrooms are well equipped with home-made biscuits, bathrobes and slippers, a silent fridge with fresh milk and bottled water, and an Apple TV with on-demand movies. Breakfast has hot chocolate, fruit smoothie shots, fruit salad and home-made yogurt and granola; toast and hot dishes are served at table. Drawing room, dining room ('easy listening' background music). Patio. Free Wi-Fi. Computer for guests' use. Parking. Children over 13 welcomed; dogs (in some rooms, £10 per night) accepted. Resident dog, Patsy. 6 bedrooms. Per room B&B £79–£149. Closed Christmas, New Year.
25% DISCOUNT VOUCHERS

TOTNES Devon
Map 1:D4
ROYAL SEVEN STARS, The Plains, TQ9 5DD. Tel 01803 862125, www.royalsevenstars.co.uk. 'A very good stay.' Steps from the River Dart, in the centre of this bohemian town, Anne and Nigel Way's hotel occupies an 'interesting' 17th-century coaching inn with an imposing original facade and a cobbled front terrace. Inside, there is a bright, modern interior and a lively atmosphere: it is a popular events venue, and its restaurant and bars are well patronised by local residents. 'The staff were all very helpful and interested.' 'Very good and comfortable' bedrooms vary in size and decor; the largest have a spa bath in the bathroom. Light bar meals are available all day; brasserie dinners are served in the refurbished former stables at the end of the courtyard. Lounge, 2 bars (log fires in winter), TQ9 brasserie and grill ('easy listening' background music), champagne bar; terrace (alfresco meals); balcony. Free Wi-Fi. Civil wedding licence; business functions; ballroom. Parking. Children and dogs welcomed. 21 bedrooms (quietest rooms at back). Per room B&B single £91–£122, double £125–£135. Dinner from £30.

TRESCO Isles of Scilly
Map 1: inset C1
NEW INN, TR24 0QQ. Tel 01720 422849, www.tresco.co.uk. A hub of the community, this friendly pub, in a peaceful position near the beach and harbour, is the only one on Robert Dorrien-Smith's private, car-free island. 'The welcome was very good.' Decorated with nautical memorabilia, the informal bars and restaurant are

popular with visitors to the timeshare cottages on the island; music, beer and cider festivals are held. Accommodation is 'basic, clean and comfortable'. Along with traditional pub favourites, menus feature crab claws, potted shrimps, fish stew, and other local delicacies such as Cornish pork and Tresco partridge sausage roll. Residents' lounge, 2 bars (background music), pavilion, restaurant, patio (alfresco eating); garden. Outdoor heated swimming pool. Children welcomed. 16 bedrooms (some with terrace, some with sea views). Per person B&B £55–£120. Dinner from £44.

TROUTBECK Cumbria
Map 4: inset C2
BROADOAKS, Bridge Lane, LA23 1LA. Tel 01539 445566, www.broadoaks countryhouse.co.uk. In extensive landscaped grounds with views towards Windermere, Tracey Robinson and Joanna Harbottle's 'beautiful, very welcoming' hotel is in a 'stunning' 19th-century country house built of stone and slate. 'Gorgeous' bedrooms (some compact) are individually styled with bold wallpaper and antique furniture; some have leaded windows or a roll-top bath. Canapés are taken in the music room before dinner. In Oaks brasserie, chef Sharon Elders combines 'excellent' modern French dishes with Cumbrian favourites, using much local produce; vegetarian options are available. Afternoon tea is served in the new orangery. Music room (vintage Bechstein piano; log fire), bar, restaurant, orangerie. Free Wi-Fi. 1930s background music. 8-acre grounds; stream. Civil wedding licence. Popular as a wedding venue. Free membership at nearby spa. 19 bedrooms (some

on ground floor; 5 in coach house; 3 detached garden suites, 5 mins' walk from house). 2 miles N of Windermere. Children, and dogs (in some rooms; £25 per night) welcomed. Resident cockapoo, Molly. Per room B&B from £120, D,B&B from £169.
25% DISCOUNT VOUCHERS

TUNBRIDGE WELLS Kent
Map 2:D4
HOTEL DU VIN TUNBRIDGE WELLS, Crescent Road, TN1 2LY. Tel 08447 489266, www.hotelduvin.com. 'An excellent choice, within walking distance of the historic Pantiles.' Period details mix with smart, modern rooms in this outpost of the du Vin group. It occupies an 18th-century Grade II listed sandstone mansion facing Calverley Park. Some of the bedrooms overlook the park; all have air conditioning and a well-stocked minibar. Reliable bistro dishes are served in the informal dining room (paintings, period fireplaces, reclaimed dark wood floorboards); alfresco meals may be taken on the garden terrace. Afternoon tea; Sunday brunch. Bar, bistro, tea lounge; private dining room. Free Wi-Fi. No background music. Wedding/function facilities. 1-acre garden: terrace (alfresco dining); vineyard; boules. Close to the station. Limited parking. Children and dogs welcomed. 34 bedrooms (4 in annexe). Per room B&B £135–£195. Dinner from £36.

VENTNOR Isle of Wight
Map 2:E2
OCEAN VIEW HOUSE, 46 Zig Zag Road, PO38 1DD. Tel 01983 852729, www. oceanviewhouse.co.uk. Sarah Smith's 'gorgeous' B&B is in a Victorian villa at the top of a steep hill, with 'beautiful

views' over Ventnor. It is 'a wonderful place' where guests in search of 'privacy and relaxation' are well catered for: they have a separate entrance, and can come and go as they please. Two of the neat, modern bedrooms have a balcony with panoramic sea views; the other two have access to a small area of garden with sun loungers. Each room has a dining area, and is equipped with wine glasses and a corkscrew, plates and cutlery for picnics and takeaway meals. A 'delicious' breakfast may be served in the room. Books and games are available to borrow; the terraced garden has hammocks and decked areas with sunshades and cushions. The town and beach are a short downhill stroll away (guests returning on foot catch their breath on a bench halfway, or take a bus or taxi back up). Picnic hampers available (from £8). Free Wi-Fi. No background music. Garden. 'Plenty' of free street parking. 1 mile N of town centre. 4 bedrooms. Per person B&B £75–£95. 2-night min. stay preferred.

THE ROYAL HOTEL, Belgrave Road, PO38 1JJ. Tel 01983 852186, www.royalhoteliow.co.uk. Close to the seafront and town centre, this traditional seaside hotel is 'all the better' for its 'olde-worlde charm'. It is owned by William Bailey, and managed by Philip Wilson with 'very friendly and helpful' staff. Gracious, country house-style bedrooms are well appointed with silks, velvets and toile de Jouy fabrics; the best have views over the gardens and Ventnor Bay. In the elegant Appuldurcombe restaurant (closed for lunch Oct–June, except Sun), chef Steven Harris's award-winning seasonal menus are 'absolutely excellent'. Lunch and afternoon tea can be taken in the colonial-style conservatory; picnic hampers are enjoyed on the Riviera Terrace, with its glorious panoramic views. Lounge, bar, restaurant, conservatory; terrace. Lift to some rooms. Ramp. Background music; resident pianist during peak-season weekends. Free Wi-Fi in public areas. Civil wedding licence; function rooms. 2-acre subtropical grounds: heated outdoor swimming pool (May–Sept). In-room massages and beauty treatments. Sandy beach nearby (hilly walk). Parking. Children (baby listening; children's high tea; 3–8s £35 per day; 9–15s £50 per day) and dogs (£25 per day) welcomed. 52 bedrooms (1 suitable for disabled). Per room B&B £190–£290, D,B&B £260–£360. 2-night min. stay at peak weekends. Closed 2 weeks in Jan. **25% DISCOUNT VOUCHERS**

WALLINGTON Northumberland Map 4:B3

SHIELDHALL, NE61 4AQ. Tel 01830 540387, www.shieldhallguesthouse.co.uk. Celia and Stephen Robinson Gay run their welcoming B&B with their daughter, Sarah, and son-in-law, John. Overlooking the National Trust's Wallington estate, their stone-built house has a beautiful setting amid gardens and parkland, with a stream, woodland and natural meadow; it was once owned by the family of Capability Brown. The converted farmstead has been decorated with antiques, original art, and furniture handcrafted by Stephen and his sons. Traditionally furnished bedrooms open on to a central courtyard; each has fresh flowers and light refreshments. Celia Robinson Gay serves Aga-cooked four-course dinners by arrangement, using home-grown vegetables and eggs from her own hens. Library, 'secret' bar, dining room. 10-acre grounds. Free Wi-Fi. No background music. Children over 12 welcomed. 4 bedrooms (all on ground floor). Per person B&B from £40, D,B&B from £70. Closed Christmas, New Year.

WARTLING East Sussex
Map 2:E4
WARTLING PLACE, Herstmonceux, nr Hailsham, BN27 1RY. Tel 01323 832590, www.wartlingplace.co.uk. 'We were very pleased with the rooms, the atmosphere, the garden and the breakfast.' Visitors to nearby Glyndebourne were 'delighted' by Rowena and Barry Gittoes's tastefully furnished B&B in a Grade II listed former rectory. The Georgian building is opposite a church and a pub in a tiny village mentioned in the Domesday Book. It stands in landscaped gardens filled with subtropical plants and shrubs, on the edge of the Pevensey Levels nature reserve. Inside, there are interesting prints and pictures on the walls, and comfortable seating in the large lounge. Well-appointed bedrooms have bathrobes, 'real' coffee and Fairtrade tea, a digital radio, an iPod dock; DVDs are available to borrow. Breakfast is served at a long mahogany table or can be taken in the bedroom. An evening meal or a late supper is available, by arrangement. Rowena Gittoes is 'full of helpful advice'. Drawing room, dining room (honesty bar, CD player). Free Wi-Fi. No background music. 3-acre garden. Parking. Children welcomed. 3 miles N of Pevensey. 4 bedrooms (plus 2-bedroom self-catering cottage; suitable

for disabled). Per room B&B from £130 (2 people sharing). Dinner £35.

WARWICK Warwickshire
Map 3:C6
PARK COTTAGE, 113 West Street, CV34 6AH. Tel 01926 410319, www. parkcottagewarwick.co.uk. At the entrance to Warwick Castle, Janet and Stuart Baldry's 'good-value' B&B is in a 15th-century Grade II listed black-and-white timber-framed building. It has oak beams, sloping floors and plenty of history: the breakfast room, with its original sandstone floor, once served as the castle dairy. Most of the spacious, comfortable bedrooms are up a steep, narrow staircase; one has a 300-year-old four-poster bed, another has a bathroom with a king-size spa bath. A ground-floor room has doors opening on to the pretty patio garden. An antique Welsh dresser is laid with cereals, yogurts, fruit and juices at breakfast; cafetière coffee or a pot of Yorkshire tea is served at table; a generous full English is 'perfectly cooked'. The owners' thoughtful gestures are appreciated: 'Chocolate mints were left in reception for us when we returned after an evening out with friends.' On the A429 into town; the racecourse is nearby. Reception/sitting area, breakfast room; small garden (patio, tables and seating). Free Wi-Fi. No background music. Parking. Children welcomed. 8 bedrooms (2 on ground floor; 2 family rooms). Per room B&B single £55–£75, double £77.50–£90. Closed Christmas, New Year.

WATCHET Somerset
Map 1:B5
SWAIN HOUSE, 48 Swain Street, TA23 0AG. Tel 01984 631038, www.swain-house.com. In the centre

of a charming harbour town, Jason and Annie Robinson's chic B&B was remodelled from an 18th-century town house and shop. Decorated in modern industrial grey, white and stone colours throughout, it has slate floors, a cosy lounge with a silver velvet sofa, and a hefty wood dining table where praiseworthy breakfasts (including vegetarian options) are served. Upstairs, well-thought-out bedrooms have a large bed and a mural based on an Old Master painting; bathrooms have bathrobes, a roll-top slipper bath and a large walk-in shower. A light charcuterie board supper (£12) may be provided; lunchtime picnic hampers with a rug can be supplied; three-course dinners for exclusive-use stays. 7 miles from Dunster Castle. Lounge, dining room. Free Wi-Fi. No background music. 4 bedrooms. Per room B&B £135. Closed Christmas.

WATERGATE BAY Cornwall
Map 1:D2

WATERGATE BAY, On the beach, TR8 4AA. Tel 01637 860543, www. watergatebay.co.uk. On a spectacular two-mile stretch of sandy beach on the north Cornish coast, Will Ashworth's large, extended hotel has plenty of outdoor activities for families, water-sports enthusiasts and the less adventurous. The leisure complex, Swim Club, has a 25-metre ocean-view infinity pool, hot tub, fitness studio and treatment rooms (open to day members). A boardwalk leads to the beach. The on-site Extreme Academy specialises in tuition for surfing, kitesurfing, wave skiing, stand-up paddlesurf and handplaning; equipment is available for hire. Inspired by the coast, contemporary bedrooms have dark wood flooring, bright colours and stripy

fabrics; many face the sea. There are several eating options: Zacry's specialises in modern American cuisine; the Living Space has sharing platters and seasonal salads to accompany the stunning coastal views; menus at the Beach Hut feature steaks, burgers and shellfish. Mark Williams is the manager. Lounge/bar, 3 restaurants; terrace, sun deck. Free Wi-Fi. Background music. Indoor/outdoor pool. Surf school: waterskiing, etc. Children, and dogs (in some rooms; £15 per night) welcomed. 69 bedrooms (family suites; 2 suitable for disabled). Per room B&B from £145, D,B&B from £195.

WEDMORE Somerset
Map 1:B6

THE SWAN, Cheddar Road, BS28 4EQ. Tel 01934 710337, www. theswanwedmore.com. 'We will visit again.' In a pretty village, this popular pub-with-rooms has 'well-appointed', modern bedrooms, and a 'lovely informal atmosphere' in the bustling bar and restaurant, where snacks, drinks and home-made cake are served all day. It is owned by the Draco Pub Company, which also runs The White Hart, Somerton (see Shortlist entry). Bedrooms have vintage features, a 'comfortable' super-king-size bed and 'super' toiletries; the hospitality tray has freshly ground coffee with a cafetière, and a stash of old-fashioned sweets. On the second floor, the peaceful new Loft room has beams, a claw-footed bath and a wet room with a power shower. There are newspapers, fires and local ales in the pub; Pimm's and home-made lemonade in summer. In the informal restaurant, chef Tom Blake (formerly of the River Cottage Canteen) cooks 'very good', unfussy dishes using free-range, organic and Somerset produce in season, and locally reared meat; alfresco dining on the patio. Breakfast 'is a real treat', with home-cured bacon and freshly baked bread; it is served till 11 am. Bar (wood-burning stove; bar snacks), restaurant (closed Sun eve). Terrace; garden (wood-fired oven and barbecue). Free Wi-Fi. DVD library. Background music. Civil wedding licence. Functions. Parking. Children (cot; extra bed £20) and dogs (not in restaurant) welomed. 6 miles from Wells, Cheddar. 7 bedrooms. Per room B&B £85–£125.

WESTBROOK Herefordshire
Map 3:D4

WESTBROOK COURT B&B, HR3 5SY. Tel 01497 831752, www.westbrookcourt bandb.co.uk. In tranquil grounds with views over the Wye valley, Kari Morgan, an interior designer, and her husband, Chris, have transformed a former stable into stylish accommodation for B&B guests. The Morgans live in their 'rambling' 17th-century farmhouse in the grounds. The modern annexe, which opens on to a landscaped courtyard, has spacious, light-filled suites with a lounge area and a private terraced deck angled to catch the sun. Four suites have a mezzanine bedroom overlooking Merbach Hill; one, with a sofa bed, can accommodate a family. On the weekend, communal breakfasts, with home-baked bread, home-made jam, local meats, and eggs from the garden hens, are taken in the Morgans' cheery farmhouse kitchen; during the week, a generous breakfast hamper (pastries, smoked salmon, freshly boiled eggs, fruit, yogurt pots) is brought to the bedroom. Free Wi-Fi. No background music. Children welcomed (cot: linen

not provided; extra bed £15 per night). In secluded 5-acre grounds. 3 miles E of Hay-on-Wye. 5 bedrooms (1 family room; 1 suitable for disabled). Per room B&B £85–£100. Credit cards not accepted.

WESTON-SUPER-MARE Somerset
Map 1:B6

BEACHLANDS HOTEL, 17 Uphill Road North, BS23 4NG. Tel 01934 621401, www.beachlandshotel.com. At the southern end of Weston Bay, this family-friendly hotel overlooks sand dunes and a golf course; a sandy beach is close by. Charles Porter is the hands-on owner. Comfortable, simply furnished bedrooms have tea- and coffee-making facilities; some have a veranda opening on to the secluded garden. A daily-changing menu of traditional fare is served in the restaurant which has garden views; special diets are catered for. 4 lounges, bar, restaurant; private dining; background music. Free Wi-Fi. 10-metre indoor swimming pool, sauna. Garden. Civil wedding licence; functions/conferences. Parking. Children welcomed (baby-listening service; high tea; swimming lessons by arrangement). Golf packages. 20 bedrooms (some on ground floor; some family rooms; 1 suitable for disabled). Per room B&B single from £67, double £133.75–£144.25.

WHEATHILL Shropshire
Map 3:C5

THE OLD RECTORY, WV16 6QT. Tel 01746 787209, www.theoldrectory wheathill.com. In beautiful Shropshire countryside, Izzy Barnard's charming B&B is in a handsome Georgian house. It stands in extensive gardens where free-range chickens and ducks strut across the lawn. Guests like the many delightful touches: home-made scones or cake on arrival, wild flowers throughout the house, knitted cosies on the boiled eggs at breakfast. The drawing room has family photographs, sofas, and a roaring fire in cold weather. Comfortable bedrooms have books and plenty of treats (a decanter of sherry; home-made biscuits or flapjacks tied with a ribbon). A candlelit three-course dinner may be requested in advance (BYO bottle); light supper trays are available. Breakfast has jams and compotes from home-grown summer fruit, local sausages and home-cured bacon, and freshly squeezed orange juice. On a bridleway amid acres of riding country (guides and route cards to borrow); horses (£20 per night) welcomed. Drawing room, dining room; sauna (in cellar). Boot room. Loose boxes; tack room. No Wi-Fi. No background music. In-room treatments by arrangement. Children, and dogs (£10 per night in boot room) by arrangement. Resident dogs and cat. 7-acre gardens (ancient cedar tree). 7 miles E of Ludlow. 3 bedrooms. Per room B&B single from £70, double £85–£125. Dinner £35.

WHITSTABLE Kent
Map 2:D5

THE CRESCENT TURNER HOTEL, Wraik Hill, CT5 3BY. Tel 01227 263506, crescentturner.co.uk. On a hill outside the town, this red brick hotel (Bespoke Hotels) is set in large gardens with wide views of the Kent coast. It is named after JMW Turner who painted in the area; prints of his works are displayed. Toni Spasovski is the manager. The modern, rustic lounge has squashy sofas and a wood-burning stove; the spacious terrace looks over the garden to the sea. Bedrooms are individually designed, with glitzy touches such as a mirrored bedside table, an animal-print throw or an ornate mirror; many rooms have views across the coast or surrounding countryside. In the restaurant, chef Mark Kember, a Whitstable native, cooks modern British dishes using locally sourced produce; oysters (plain or with a chilli and mango salsa) feature on the menu. A beach hut on Whitstable beach is available to reserve (from £100 per day): it has a kitchen, a lounge and three canoes. Lounge, restaurant (open to non-residents), function room. Civil wedding licence. Free Wi-Fi. Soft instrumental background music. 3-acre garden; terrace; gazebo. 'A short drive' or a 30-minute stroll to the town. Children welcomed. Parking. 17 bedrooms. Per room £75–£195. Dinner £30–£40.

WILMSLOW Cheshire
Map 4:E3

KINGSLEY LODGE, 10 Hough Lane, SK9 2LQ. Tel 01625 441794, www. kingsleylodge.com. Jeremy Levy and Cliff Thomson's discreet, luxurious B&B is in a remodelled 1950s Arts and Crafts house in a peaceful residential area within easy walking distance of the town centre. Handcrafted antiques sit comfortably with more modern pieces; elegant bedrooms have fresh flowers, scented candles and original works of art. There are ponds, a pine wood, a formal parterre, and a seating deck with a water cascade, in the large, landscaped garden. Lounge (honesty bar), breakfast room; 2-acre garden; patio. Free Wi-Fi (in public areas). DVD library. No background music. Parking. Children welcomed. Close to Manchester airport. 6 bedrooms. Per room B&B from £110.

WILTON Wiltshire
Map 2:D2

THE PEMBROKE ARMS, Minster Street, SP2 0BH. Tel 01722 743328, www.pembrokearms.co.uk. Opposite the entrance to Wilton House, seat of the earls of Pembroke, this extensively refurbished Georgian building is once again run by Ido and Alison Davids who were at the reins from 2000 to 2012. Jon Russell is the manager. Bedrooms are colourfully decorated, with quirky touches; one, with an extra daybed, can accommodate a family. Drinks and nibbles are taken in the bar; the informal restaurant ('no tailcoats, starch or presumption') has plenty of vegan and vegetarian options. 3 miles W of Salisbury. Lounge (wood-burning fire), bar, restaurant. Large garden. Free Wi-Fi. No background music. Weddings/functions. Shooting parties. Children welcomed. Parking. 15-mins' drive to Stonehenge. 9 bedrooms. Per room B&B £75–£200, D,B&B £100–£200. Closed Christmas.

WINCHESTER Hampshire
Map 2:D2

HANNAH'S, 16a Parchment Street, SO23 8AZ. Tel 01962 840623, hannahsbedandbreakfast.co.uk. Once a stable, then a dance hall, Hannah McIntyre's small B&B, in a quiet mews off the high street, has been winsomely refurbished to include modern country-style bedrooms, a book-filled library with an open fire, and a spacious, beamed breakfast room with fresh flowers and a grand piano. Open from Thursday to Sunday, it is ideal for a long weekend stay. Guests are welcomed with an afternoon tea of freshly baked scones, cakes and biscuits. Pretty bedrooms have a super-king-size bed, space to sit, and a bathtub big enough for two. Breakfast has home-made jams and granola, specially blended teas and coffees, and bacon and sausages from Hampshire farmers. Breakfast room, library (honesty bar); terrace with seating. Free Wi-Fi. No background music. Resident cat, Leyla. Children over 12 welcomed. 3 bedrooms. Per room B&B £185–£205. Closed Mon–Wed; week before Christmas–1st weekend Feb.

THE OLD VINE, 8 Great Minster Street, SO23 9HA. Tel 01962 854616, www.oldvinewinchester.com. 'Perfectly situated' for both spiritual sustenance and shopping therapy, Ashton Gray's small, design-conscious hotel is in a Grade II listed 18th-century inn opposite the cathedral green. Elegant, well-furnished bedrooms have designer fabrics and wallpapers, and a mix of antique and modern furniture; water, soft drinks and a Nespresso machine are supplied. A top-floor suite has views of the cathedral. Hampshire produce features on the menu in the oak-beamed restaurant, where an open fire burns in cool weather. The bar has real ales, a small, flower-filled patio and a bright conservatory. Bar ('easy listening' background music), restaurant. Free Wi-Fi. Children welcomed (cot; £40 per night; no under-6s in restaurant and bar). Permits supplied for on-street parking. 6 bedrooms (1 family room, a 2-bed self-contained apartment with garage, in annexe). Per room B&B £130–£220, D,B&B (Mon–Thurs) £170–£210. Closed Christmas Day.

THE WYKEHAM ARMS, 75 Kingsgate Street, SO23 9PE. Tel 01962 853834, www.wykehamarmswinchester.co.uk. Between the cathedral and the college, this 18th-century former coaching inn has open log fires, and characterful nooks and crannies embellished with pictures, ale mugs and memorabilia. It is managed by Jon Howard for Fuller's, and run with enthusiastic, friendly staff. Well-equipped bedrooms, some with a four-poster bed, are reached via a narrow staircase; others are in a 16th-century building opposite. Old school desks feature as dining tables in the wood-panelled restaurant; chef Gavin Sinden's modern British dishes and pub classics, cooked using Hampshire ingredients, are served here. Bar (local ales), restaurant, 2 function rooms; small patio with seating. No background music. Free Wi-Fi (in public areas). Children over 12, and dogs (in 2 bedrooms; not in restaurant; £15 per night charge) welcomed. Parking. 14 bedrooms (7 in annexe). Per person B&B £64.50–£72. Dinner £20–£35.
25% DISCOUNT VOUCHERS

WINDERMERE Cumbria
Map 4: inset C2
CEDAR MANOR, Ambleside Road, LA23 1AX. Tel 01539 443192, www.cedarmanor.co.uk. Named after the 200-year-old cedar tree in the walled gardens, Caroline and Jonathan Kaye's handsomely appointed 19th-century house is within easy reach of the lake and village. 'Warm and sincere', the Kayes delight in sharing local knowledge of the Lake District. Bedrooms, some sumptuously refurbished, have a large bed, bathrobes, tea- and coffee-making facilities and a fridge with fresh milk. A suite in the coach house has a lounge with a Juliet balcony, an entertainment system and a luxurious bathroom. In the elegant restaurant, Roger Pergl-Wilson's 'superb' modern British cooking focuses on seasonal, locally sourced produce: menus include a list of suppliers. Breakfast has home-made jams and marmalade, locally smoked haddock, award-winning sausages. 2 lounges, dining room (light background music during meals). Free Wi-Fi. Small garden with lawn and patio seating. Bicycle storage; electric bike hire. Small weddings. 7 miles from town. 10 bedrooms (1 suite in coach house). Per room B&B £135–£385, D,B&B £214–£464 (2-night min. stay at weekends preferred). Closed 14–27 Dec, 4–21 Jan.

WOODBRIDGE Suffolk
Map 2:C5
THE CROWN, The Thoroughfare, IP12 1AD. Tel 01394 384242, www.thecrownatwoodbridge.co.uk. In a thriving market town near the Deben estuary, this white-painted 16th-century coaching inn is smartly decorated with Nantucket overtones; a wooden sailing skiff hangs from the ceiling in the chic, glass-roofed bar. It is run by Garth Wray for the Suffolk-based TA Hotel Collection. Bright bedrooms are styled in neutral tones and shades of grey; modern lighting is 'excellent throughout'; bathrooms have underfloor heating. Local residents come for chef Luke Bailey's 'seasonal, fresh and tasty' brasserie-style food; meals are served in two bustling, informal dining rooms, at a communal table in the bar, or on sofas in front of the fire. Fixed-price dinners available. Bar (cocktails, Suffolk brews), 4 dining areas; courtyard garden.

Private dining. Spa breaks. Free Wi-Fi. Background music; monthly jazz evenings. Parking. Children welcomed (£20 per night). 10 bedrooms. Per room B&B from £100, D,B&B from £160.

WOODSTOCK Oxfordshire
Map 2:C2

THE FEATHERS, 16–20 Market Street, OX20 1SX. Tel 01993 812291, www.feathers.co.uk. There is 'a good atmosphere' at this town house hotel in a row of buildings in the centre of a 'handsome' market town on the edge of the Blenheim estate. Dominic Bishop manages for Premier Cru Hotels. Traditional features are offset with modern colours and bold wallpapers. Most of the bedrooms (there are five categories) are reached by a series of winding staircases – 'an intimate experience'. 'Our high-ceilinged room was of a good size, with an enormous sleigh bed, a desk and table, an armchair and adequate storage; the superb bathroom had excellent lighting and underfloor heating.' There are no tea- or coffee-making facilities in the room, but guests may order a tea tray, or take complimentary afternoon tea and morning coffee in the lounge. In the restaurant, tables are 'smartly laid' for 'sophisticated dinners'; informal meals are served in the bar. Study, Courtyard gin bar (more than 280 gins), restaurant (closed Sun, Mon night). Free Wi-Fi. Background music. Functions. Picnic hampers. Free long-term parking within walking distance. Children, and dogs (in some rooms) welcomed. 21 bedrooms (5 in adjacent town house; 1 suitable for disabled; 1 suite has a private steam room). Per room B&B from £199, D,B&B from £279.

WORCESTER Worcestershire
Map 3:C5

THE MANOR COACH HOUSE, Hindlip Lane, Hindlip, WR3 8SJ. Tel 01905 456457, www.manorcoachhouse.co.uk. In a semi-rural location two miles from the city centre, Terry and Sylvia Smith have renovated outbuildings next to their fine 1780s house to create 'top-notch' B&B accommodation. The simply furnished bedrooms have private access from the courtyard, and are equipped with bathrobes, a hospitality tray, a small fridge and a clock radio; fresh milk is available on request. One room has a kitchenette. Generous, locally sourced breakfasts include a fresh fruit salad; they may be taken in the garden ('a bird-lover's paradise') in fine weather. A good base for walking the Worcester and Birmingham canal. Afternoon tea. Breakfast room. 1-acre garden; courtyard with table and seating. Free Wi-Fi. No background music. Parking. 5 bedrooms (in private courtyard; 2 family rooms; 1 suitable for disabled). Per room B&B single £59, double £85. Closed Christmas, New Year.
25% DISCOUNT VOUCHERS

WROXTON Oxfordshire
Map 3:D6

WROXTON HOUSE HOTEL, Silver Street, OX15 6QB. Tel 01295 730777, www.wroxtonhousehotel.com. Guests this year were 'very impressed' by this 'exquisite' thatched-roof manor house on the edge of a picturesque village close to Banbury. It is ably run as a Best Western hotel by the Smith family; Sean Wilson is the manager. Dating back to 1649, it has many original features (inglenook fireplace, oak beams) and characterful refurbished bedrooms. In the award-winning restaurant, chef

Steve Mason-Tocker serves 'extensive and imaginative' daily-changing contemporary menus. A 'superb' breakfast has home-made jams and marmalade; 'perfectly spreadable room-temperature butter'. Open-plan lounge, bar, 1649 restaurant; terrace. Free Wi-Fi. Background music. 2 private function rooms. Civil wedding licence. Parking. 3 miles NW of Banbury. Children welcomed. 32 bedrooms (7 on ground floor; 3 in adjoining cottage). Per room B&B single £79–£115, double £109–£145. Dinner £33. 2-night min. stay at weekends.

25% DISCOUNT VOUCHERS

YORK North Yorkshire
Map 4:D4

BAR CONVENT, 17 Blossom Street, YO24 1AQ. Tel 01904 643238, www. bar-convent.org.uk. By the historic city walls at Micklegate Bar, a five-minute walk to the centre, this unusual place to stay is in England's oldest active convent (founded in 1686). The Grade I listed Georgian building houses a 'magnificent' glass-roofed entrance hall, an 18th-century domed chapel, and a library full of antique Catholic texts. Rooms in the spotless guest house are spacious and restful, with a well-stocked hospitality tray. James Foster is the manager. In a tranquil garden, the café is open for breakfast, morning coffee, lunch and afternoon tea. As the Guide went to press, the building was undergoing refurbishment to become a living heritage centre; part of the renovations includes the creation of a multimedia exhibition recounting the history of the convent. Sitting room; licensed café. Meeting rooms; museum; shop; chapel (Catholic weddings); function facilities. Lift to 1st and 2nd floors. Free Wi-Fi. No background music. ¼-acre garden. Children welcomed. 20 bedrooms (16 en suite; 4 others, on 3rd floor, share a bathroom; 3 family rooms). Per room B&B (continental) from £37. Dinner from £17. Closed Christmas–late Jan.

THE BLOOMSBURY, 127 Clifton, YO30 6BL. Tel 01904 634031, www. bloomsburyhotel.co.uk. 'We had a great stay.' In a leafy neighbourhood close to Clifton Green, Steve and Tricia Townsley are 'exceptionally friendly, efficient and helpful' hosts, who greet guests to their Victorian home with tea and biscuits. B&B accommodation is in 'spotless', well-lit bedrooms, which have recently been refurbished; each room has tea- and coffee-making facilities, a TV and a radio alarm clock. 'Good' breakfasts include home-made preserves and 'lovely' bacon and sausages; dietary requirements are catered for, by arrangement. The city centre is reached via a scenic river walk (15 mins) or a short bus ride; on-site parking is a 'bonus'. Sitting room, dining room (optional background music); terrace; flowery courtyard; 'secret garden'. Free Wi-Fi. Parking. Within a mile of the city. Children welcomed (no special facilities). Resident dog, Harvey. 6 bedrooms (1 on ground floor). Per person B&B £37.50–£43 (2 people sharing); 2-night min. stay on Sat. Credit cards not accepted. Closed mid-Dec–mid-Jan.

25% DISCOUNT VOUCHERS

THE GRANGE, 1 Clifton, YO30 6AA. Tel 01904 644744, www.grangehotel.co.uk. Vivien and Jeremy Cassel's family-friendly hotel is in a Grade II listed Regency town house a short walk from the city walls and the Minster. Jackie

Millan is the manager. Individually decorated bedrooms have a selection of teas and infusions; there are bottles of mineral water and fresh milk in a fridge. Some rooms may be small; a suite has a spacious sitting area with a sofa, armchairs, books and a fireplace. Guests have a choice of places to eat: modern English cuisine is served in The Ivy restaurant; in the original brick-vaulted cellars, the informal brasserie has comfort food, grilled meats and salads. Lounge, 2 bars, restaurant (dinners only Mon–Sat; Sun lunch; closed Sun eve), brasserie (live music every other Fri night; closed Sun lunch). Free Wi-Fi. Background music. Room service. Ramps. Civil wedding licence; function facilities. Limited parking. Children (high chair, children's cutlery, baby bath, cot, extra bed; books, family games, jigsaws, colouring sheets) and dogs (by arrangement, £20 charge) welcomed. 36 bedrooms (6 on ground floor). Per room B&B £120–£320. Dinner from £34.

MOUNT ROYALE, 117/119 The Mount, YO24 1GU. Tel 01904 628856, www. mountroyale.co.uk. 'Away from the bustle of the city', this traditional hotel has been owned by the Oxtoby family for more than 45 years; it is run with long-serving staff who 'take a genuine interest in their guests'. Near the racecourse and Micklegate Bar, the hotel is formed from two Grade II listed William IV houses. Although it is on a busy road, there is a relaxing ambience within: 'the antique-filled entrance hall has a calming atmosphere'; the two-acre garden is 'an oasis of peace'. Traditionally furnished bedrooms have cafetière coffee and tea-making facilities; four garden suites have a veranda that opens on to the mature gardens. Chef Russell Johnson serves 'Yorkshire portions' of French-influenced English food in Oxo's on the Mount restaurant. Lounge, bar, restaurant. 5 Senses spa. Wedding/ function facilities. Free Wi-Fi. No background music. Garden (outdoor hot tub, heated outdoor swimming pool (open May–Sept), Scandinavian log cabin with sauna and steam room). 15 mins' walk to town centre. Children (£20 per night) and dogs welcomed. 24 bedrooms (some on ground floor). Per room B&B £135–£265. Dinner £40.

SCOTLAND

ABERDEEN
Map 5:C3
ATHOLL HOTEL, 54 King's Gate, AB15 4YN. Tel 01224 323505, www. atholl-aberdeen.co.uk. In a residential neighbourhood, within easy reach of the city centre, this privately owned hotel is in a dignified Victorian Gothic revival building. It has pleasing accommodation, friendly staff and traditional Scottish cuisine. Gordon Sinclair is the manager. Refurbished bedrooms have plaid bedcovers and cushions and every comfort; some rooms are large enough to accommodate a family. A frequent bus goes to and from the centre; the airport is a 15-minute drive away. Lounge, bar, restaurant; patio. Free Wi-Fi. Background music. Weddings/functions. Lift to first floor. Parking. 1½ miles W of the city centre. Children welcomed (£10 per night). 34 bedrooms (2 suitable for disabled). Per room B&B single £70–£155, double £85–£170. Dinner £27.

APPLECROSS Highland
Map 5:C1
APPLECROSS INN, Shore Street, IV54
8LR. Tel 01520 744262, www.applecross.
uk.com. Visitors flock to this white-
painted inn, in a remote location on the
shores of the Applecross peninsula, for
the warm welcome, the fresh seafood
and the breathtaking views of the isles
of Skye and Raasay. It has been owned
by Judith Fish since 1989; Carolyn
Littlewood manages, with a team of
friendly staff. The lively bar has a
stuffed otter, a wood-burning stove
and a large selection of malt whiskies.
In the small dining room, chef Robbie
Macrae's daily-changing menus,
displayed on blackboards, include plenty
of garden produce, and fish and shellfish
from Applecross Bay. Simple bedrooms
are clean and comfortable, with sea
views; there may be some noise from
the pub. Cyclists, walkers, kayakers and
campers are welcomed. Bar (draft ales)/
dining area, dining room. Beer garden
on the shore. Bicycle storage. Free Wi-
Fi. No background music. Children
(cot, extra bed, high chair; over-5s £10
per night) and dogs (in some rooms;
£10 per stay) welcomed. 7 bedrooms (1
on ground floor for assisted access). Per
person B&B £65. Dinner £35. Closed for
accommodation 20 Dec–5 Jan.

ARINAGOUR Argyll and Bute
Map 5:C1
COLL HOTEL, Isle of Coll, PA78 6SZ. Tel
01879 230334, www.collhotel.com. In the
only village on the small Hebridean Isle
of Coll, notable for its Dark Sky status,
Kevin and Julie Oliphant run their small
hotel with their daughter, Laura. Standing
in large gardens, with views across a
lovely bay, it is a lively community hub:

locals and visitors are drawn to the cosy
bars, and to the Gannet restaurant where
Julie Oliphant and chef Graham Griffiths
cook uncomplicated dishes specialising in
island produce and local fish and seafood.
Guests are welcomed with tea or coffee
and home-made shortbread on arrival;
simply furnished bedrooms, most with
spectacular views across the bay to the
Treshnish Isles and Mull, have a book on
birds and a glow-in-the-dark skyscope.
No light pollution; astronomy workshops
in the autumn and winter months.
Complimentary pick-up from and return
to the ferry pier. Lounge, 2 bars (darts,
pool table, open fires), 2 restaurants. Free
Wi-Fi. No background music. Garden
(decking, plenty of seating; pétanque).
Bicycles and helmets available to borrow.
Helipad. Children welcomed (special
menu). 1 mile from the ferry pier; 3-hour
ferry journey from Oban. 6 bedrooms.
Per room B&B single £55–£65, double
£120–£150. Dinner £25–£30. House parties
only at Christmas and New Year.

ARISAIG Highland
Map 5:C1
THE OLD LIBRARY LODGE AND
RESTAURANT, PH39 4NH. Tel 01687
450651, www.oldlibrary.co.uk. 'In a
beautiful spot' on the waterfront of the
old village, this informal restaurant-
with-rooms, in converted 200-year-old
stables, looks across Loch nan Ceall to
the Inner Hebrides. It is surrounded
by stunning Highland scenery. Owners
Mags and Allan Ritchie took over
in February 2014. Simple bedrooms
are 'fine and comfortable'; four, in
an extension at the rear, have a little
balcony with a table and chairs,
overlooking the small terraced garden.
'Our room at the front of the hotel

had a wonderful view across the bay, with sight of the Small Isles Rum and Eigg.' Dinner is 'excellent': 'lovely' and 'very well presented'. 'I would go back tomorrow for another of those wonderful chocolate fondants served with home-made Drambuie ice cream.' 'Appetising' breakfasts include Scottish choices, with black pudding and haggis. 10 mins' drive from the ferry to and from the Isle of Skye. Residents' lounge, restaurant. Free Wi-Fi. Traditional background music. Terraced garden. Children and dogs welcomed. Per person B&B from £60. Closed Jan.

AUCHENCAIRN Dumfries and Galloway
Map 5:E2

HAZLEFIELD HOUSE, DG7 1RF. Tel 01556 640597, www.hazlefieldhouse. co.uk. Amid lawns and wooded grounds, Moyra and Rod Davidson's white-painted Georgian house is peacefully located in rolling Galloway farmland, with uninterrupted views across the Solway Firth. There is 'a real sense of warmth and welcome' at the homely B&B: large bedrooms have thoughtful touches, such as a hot water bottle. Home-cooked dinners, based on local and home-grown produce, are available on request (except Wed; BYO alcohol – no corkage charge). An 'ample and beautifully arranged' breakfast includes home-made marmalade, and honey from hives in the garden. Sitting room/study (log burner), dining room. Free Wi-Fi. No background music. Drying and storage facilities. Ramp. Parking. Dogs (in kennels only, by arrangement) welcomed. 3 bedrooms (1 on ground floor, suitable for disabled). Per room B&B single £55, double £80–£90.

BALLYGRANT Argyll and Bute
Map 5:D1

KILMENY COUNTRY HOUSE, PA45 7QW. Tel 01496 840668, www.kilmeny.co.uk. Margaret and Blair Rozga's 'absolutely faultless' B&B is in a handsomely furnished 19th-century house standing in a 300-acre expanse of farmland, with 'spectacular views' over the Islay countryside. Warm, welcoming hosts, the Rozgas greet guests with tea and home-baked cakes on arrival. Country house-style bedrooms are furnished with antiques; two, on the ground floor, have French doors leading to a small, sheltered garden. A suite has its own entrance, a kitchen and an extra-large bathroom with twin basins, a slipper bath and a walk-in shower. Breakfast, with home-baked bread and cakes, is praised. 10 mins' drive to Port Askaig, for the ferry to the Isle of Jura. Drawing room, dining room, sun lounge; ½-acre garden. Free Wi-Fi. No background music. ½ mile S of Ballygrant. Children over 6 welcomed. 5 bedrooms (2 on ground floor). Per room B&B from £148. Credit cards not accepted. Closed Nov–Feb.

BRAE Shetland
Map 5: inset A2

BUSTA HOUSE, ZE2 9QN. Tel 01806 522506, www.bustahouse.com. In a beautiful setting on the sheltered shore of Busta Voe, this characterful small hotel has parts dating back to 1588. It has a quirky layout, creaky floors, lots of stairs, an open peat fire and a friendly ghost. It is owned and run by Joe and Veronica Rocks with warmly welcoming staff. Traditionally furnished bedrooms, named after islands around the coast of mainland

Shetland, overlook the gardens or the harbour. Generous portions at dinner; informal meals are taken in the lounges. The bar has an extensive selection of malt whiskies. 2 lounges, bar/dining area, Pitcairn restaurant (background music). Free Wi-Fi; computer available. Garden. Weddings. Children welcomed. 22 bedrooms. Per room B&B £115–£170. Dinner from £35. Closed from 20 Dec for 2 weeks.

BRAEMAR Aberdeenshire
Map 5:C2

CALLATER LODGE, 9 Glenshee Road, AB35 5YQ. Tel 01339 741275, www. callaterlodge.co.uk. Built with local granite, this renovated Victorian shooting lodge is a caber's toss from the centre of a town famed for its Highland Games. In the Cairngorms national park, it is 'a good base for hill-walkers and explorers of Royal Deeside'. Scotland's largest ski resort, Glenshee, is ten minutes' drive away; there are golf courses in the area. Consummate hosts Julian and Katy Fennema (a former economist and a musician) provide substantial packed lunches of sandwiches, home-baked goodies, fruit and a flask of tea. In the evenings, guests can relax by a cosy wood-burner with a local beer, a glass of wine, or one of more than 20 malt whiskies. Comfortable, simply furnished bedrooms have daily treats, such as 'the most delicious home-made, sugary, orangey sponge cake with pistachios and berries – a nice, personal touch'; one room has a four-poster bed and a sofa. An 'extremely good' breakfast includes sausages and bacon from the local butcher, salmon from Loch Fyne, eggs from resident hens, freshly cooked

tattie scones and home-made preserves. Ordered in advance, a light supper is available until 8.30 pm each evening; a set three-course menu is served once a week during the summer season. Sitting room (wood-burning stove), dining room. Drying room. Licensed. Free Wi-Fi. No background music. 1-acre grounds (mature Scots pine trees, red squirrels, free-range hens). Resident dogs. Braemar Gathering (Sept); skiing (9 miles S of Braemar); golf. Children welcomed. 6 bedrooms (1 family room). Per person B&B from £40. Dinner £25. Closed Christmas.

BRIDGEND Argyll and Bute
Map 5:D1

BRIDGEND HOTEL, PA44 7PJ. Tel 01496 810212, www.bridgend-hotel.com. Guests like the homely atmosphere at this small hotel in a peaceful village close to most of the island's distilleries. It is managed by Lorna McKechnie for the Islay Estates Company. Surrounded by greenery, the house has been refurbished in simple, modern style; tastefully decorated bedrooms have a hospitality tray with Islay tablet fudge, and locally made toiletries. There are plenty of places to eat, drink and relax: the garden-view restaurant serves traditional Scottish cuisine; Katie's Bar has pub-style dishes, Islay ales and a wood-burning stove; tea, coffee and home-baking may be taken beside a log fire in the tartan-carpeted Strath Lounge. The hotel has complimentary access to bank fishing, and preferential rates for boats on Islay Estate's trout-fishing lochs. Popular with shooting parties. Walkers and cyclists are welcomed; drying room. Lounge, bar, restaurant. Garden; terrace. Weddings.

Free Wi-Fi. Traditional background music. Children (cot, high chair; extra bed £20 per night) and well-behaved dogs welcomed. Parking. 11 bedrooms (1 family room with bunk bed). Per room B&B from £130, D,B&B from £170. Closed Feb.

BRODICK North Ayrshire
Map 5:E1
AUCHRANNIE HOUSE HOTEL, Auchrannie Road KA27 8BZ. Tel 01770 302234, www.auchrannie.co.uk. Standing in 'lovely' landscaped gardens, the Johnston family's child-friendly resort on the Isle of Arran is 'a very special holiday experience'. Among the many diversions are three restaurants and two leisure clubs; the two hotels include this 19th-century country house, which has modern bedrooms and 'plush lounges to relax in'. Richard Small is the manager. A contemporary bar/brasserie serves informal meals all day; Brambles has grills and West Coast seafood; the seasonal (Mar–Oct) eighteen69 conservatory restaurant serves an extensive menu of Scottish-themed tapas. A complimentary bus service operates between the resort and the ferry terminal. Bar, 3 restaurants; spa (20-metre indoor pool, steam room, spa bath; gym). Free Wi-Fi. Background music. Parking. 5 miles from town. Children (special menu; play barn, external play and picnic area, children's pool, library) and dogs (in some rooms) welcomed. Civil wedding licence; function facilities. 115 bedrooms (including accommodation in the modern spa resort; some suitable for disabled; also 30 self-catering lodges). Per room B&B from £89, D,B&B from £119.

BRUICHLADDICH Argyll and Bute
Map 5:D1
LOCH GORM HOUSE, PA49 7UN. Tel 01496 850139, www.lochgormhouse.com. On the northern shore of Islay, Fiona Doyle's 'gorgeous' stone-built house has stunning sea views over Loch Indaal and across to the island of Jura. 'Sumptuously furnished', the house has 'magnificent' flower arrangements (the 'great' hostess is an accomplished florist); pretty bedrooms have a 'beautiful' bathroom. Guests relax in the peaceful garden in the summer months; in winter, drinks are taken by the fire. Generous breakfasts are 'delicious'. Sandy beaches, historic sites and good walks are all close by; wellies, coats and beach towels are provided; drying facilities. Free Wi-Fi. No background music. Children welcomed. Drawing room, dining room. Garden. 3 bedrooms. Per room B&B from £95. Closed Jan, Feb.

CUMNOCK East Ayrshire
Map 5:E2
DUMFRIES HOUSE LODGE, Dumfries House Estate, KA18 2NJ. Tel 01290 429920, www.dumfrieshouselodge. com. 'The highlight of our Scottish trip.' 'Beautifully furnished', this 18th-century factor's house has been turned into a 'luxurious' guest house with cosy lounge areas and bedrooms filled with antiques. On the edge of the 2,000-acre Dumfries House estate, it is minutes from the historic house built by Robert Adam, in the mid-1750s, for the Earl of Dumfries; Kathleen McLeod manages for the Prince's Trust. There are open log fires in the lounge and snug study. Traditional, country house-style bedrooms, some with their own private access and entrance, are decorated with period prints and

pictures. 'We were encouraged to treat the place as our country home.' Private tours of Dumfries House can be booked (£25). Lounge, study, breakfast room; private function room. Free Wi-Fi. No background music. 22 bedrooms (some in courtyard; some suitable for disabled; plus 2 self-catering cottages). Per room B&B £70–£145. Closed Christmas.

DALKEITH Midlothian
Map 5:D2
THE SUN INN, Lothianbridge, EH22 4TR. Tel 0131 663 2456, www.thesuninnedinburgh.co.uk. Within easy reach of Edinburgh city centre, the Minto family's 'down-to-earth' gastropub-with-rooms stands in five acres of wooded grounds close to the banks of the River Esk. The 'busy' dining room serves 'very good' modern interpretations of pub classics using much Scottish produce; the covered courtyard has barbecues and spritzers in the summer. Stylish bedrooms in the handsomely refurbished former coaching inn have a Roberts radio, DVDs and home-made biscuits; one wood-panelled room has a copper bath big enough for two at the foot of a handcrafted four-poster bed; quietest rooms face away from the street. Bar, restaurant (background music); garden. Free Wi-Fi. Parking. Children welcomed (special menu). 7 miles from Edinburgh. 5 bedrooms (1 suite). Per room B&B from £95. Dinner £30. Closed 26 Dec and 1 Jan.

DERVAIG Argyll and Bute
Map 5:D1
KILLORAN HOUSE, PA75 6QR. Tel 01688 400362, www.killoranhouse.co.uk. Set into a hillside, with panoramic views over Loch Cuin and this village on the Isle of Mull, Janette and Ian McKilligan's purpose-built guest house is in 'a wonderful location'. Spacious bedrooms, all on the first floor, have tea- and coffee-making facilities and home-baked treats; a study has books, maps and plenty of local information. Pre-dinner drinks may be taken in the lounge or on the balcony overlooking the surrounding countryside; binoculars are provided for guests eager to spot red deer on the hill opposite, or eagles in flight. Ian McKilligan's 'imaginative and well-executed' daily-changing set dinners are served in the dining room at 7.30 pm (background music). Lounge, study, dining room. Free Wi-Fi. 2 acres of garden/woodland. Parking. 1½ miles SW of Dervaig on the Calgary road. Children over 12 welcomed. 5 bedrooms. Per person B&B from £60, D,B&B from £85. Closed Nov–Feb.

DORNOCH Highland
Map 5:B2
2 QUAIL, Castle Street, IV25 3SN. Tel 01862 811811, www.2quail.com. Close to the cathedral and the Royal Dornoch Golf Club, golf enthusiasts Michael and Kerensa Carr run this 'very pleasant, comfortable and quiet' B&B in their mellow stone house. 'Pleasant, helpful and chatty', Kerensa Carr, a picture framer and restorer, is a welcoming host; golfing visitors can sample Michael Carr's cooking at the club, where he is executive chef. The house is traditionally decorated with tartan carpets and family antiques; a book-lined lounge has a wood-burning stove for cool months. Well-proportioned bedrooms have tea- and coffee-making facilities and a

radio alarm clock; a power shower in the bathroom. A 'delicious' breakfast is served at an agreed time from 7 am ('for those with early tee times'). Beautiful stretches of sandy beaches are a short distance away. Lounge/library, dining room. Licensed. Free Wi-Fi. Occasional background music. 'Babes in arms' and children over 8 welcomed. 3 bedrooms, plus 3-bedroom self-catering cottage nearby. Per room B&B from £80. Closed Christmas, 2 weeks in late Feb/early Mar.

DULNAIN BRIDGE Highland
Map 5:C2

MUCKRACH COUNTRY HOUSE HOTEL, PH26 3LY. Tel 01479 851227, www.muckrach.com. Surrounded by ten acres of pastureland, within the Cairngorms national park, this Victorian shooting lodge has sprung back to life after exuberant refurbishment by the Cowap family. Traditional features such as wood-panelled walls and wood-block flooring have been carefully restored; local artwork, and bright, modern furnishings with Scottish flourishes have been added. Glamorous, heather-toned bedrooms have a crystal chandelier, textured wallpaper and plaid fabrics; they are equipped with bathrobes, bottled water, a hospitality tray and the latest gadgetry (smart TV, iPod dock, ceiling speakers). Chef Rayner Muller's 'home-style cooking with a twist' is served in the conservatory restaurant which has views over the garden to the mountains beyond. Light meals, snacks and afternoon tea are available all day in the coffee shop. Local brews and more than 100 whiskies are served in the bar. Lounge, library, bar, restaurant (open to non-residents), coffee shop; drying room. Meeting room. Private dining

room. Garden; terraced patio. Free Wi-Fi. Background music. Children welcomed. 5 miles from Grantown-on-Spey. Fishing nearby. 11 bedrooms. Per room £149–£225. Dinner £35.

DUNDEE
Map 5:D3

DUNTRUNE HOUSE, Main Wing, Duntrune, DD4 0PJ. Tel 01382 350239, www.duntrunehouse.co.uk. In extensive gardens with woodland walks and beautiful scenery, Olwyn and Barrie Jack's restored 19th-century manor house has a welcoming, home-away-from-home atmosphere. Tranquil B&B accommodation is in traditionally furnished bedrooms equipped with bathrobes, organic toiletries and a well-considered hospitality tray; all have views over the grounds to Fife and beyond (deer and buzzard are often sighted). Breakfast is taken communally; there is good variety, including home-made muesli and jams, local honey, and fresh garden fruit in season. Sitting room, dining room; 8-acre garden. Free Wi-Fi. No background music. Laundry. Parking. Children welcomed. Retreat breaks (yoga, Bellyfit; sauna and beauty treatments) nearby. 3 bedrooms (1 on ground floor; plus a self-catering flat). Per person B&B from £45. 2-night min. stay. Closed Nov–Mar.

EDINBANE Highland
Map 5:C1

GRESHORNISH HOUSE, IV51 9PN. Tel 01470 582266, www.greshornishhouse.com. 'An outstanding hotel in an idyllic location.' In secluded grounds that once belonged to the local laird, this elegant white-painted Georgian house (with Victorian additions) is beside a loch in a remote corner of Skye. Neil and Rosemary Colquhoun are the owners. There is an easy-going country house feel throughout: the drawing room has squashy sofas and a log fire; guests are invited to play chess, snooker or two-piano duets in the billiard room. Bedrooms, named after Scottish islands, have 'gorgeous' views of the loch or the garden. Rosemary Colquhoun, 'a very capable cook', offers guests a choice of a light dinner or a set menu, served in the candlelit dining room. 'Food and accommodation are both excellent.' Drawing room, bar, conservatory, dining room (non-residents welcome, closed Mon), billiard room. Free Wi-Fi (limited). No background music. 10-acre grounds (tennis court, croquet lawn). Parking. Children welcomed; dogs by arrangement (£10 per night). 17 miles NW of Portree. 6 bedrooms (plus 2 attic rooms). Per person B&B £65–£95. Dinner £30–£45. 2-night min. stay. Closed early Nov–mid-Mar.

25% DISCOUNT VOUCHERS

EDINBURGH
Map 5:D2

THE BALMORAL, 1 Princes Street, EH2 2EQ. Tel 0131 556 2414, www. roccofortehotels.com/the-balmoral-hotel/. Once one of the great railway hotels, this grand Victorian building in the centre of the city is today a luxury enterprise (Rocco Forte Hotels). Franck Arnold is the manager. The hotel's clock, an iconic feature of the city skyline, has been set three minutes fast since 1902, to ensure that a train will never be missed. Guests are greeted by a kilted doorman. Inside the elegant hotel, there is a wide choice of eating, drinking and lounging areas. Many of the understated modern bedrooms have views of Edinburgh Castle and the Old Town. Under the direction of chef Jeff Bland, the Michelin-starred restaurant, Number One, has a blend of modern Scottish and French cuisine; the lively Hadrian's brasserie is ideal for informal eating. Afternoon tea is taken under the glass dome and Venetian chandelier of the Palm Court; the whisky bar has tweed sofas and more than 400 malts, blends and vintages. Drawing room, 3 bars, restaurant, brasserie. Free Wi-Fi. No background music. 15-metre indoor pool. Spa (treatment rooms, sauna, gym, exercise studio). Room service; 24-hour concierge. Civil wedding licence; conferences. Valet parking. Children welcomed (special menus, amenities). 188 bedrooms (3 suitable for disabled; 20 suites). Per room B&B £252–£790. Dinner £68–£75.

BROOKS HOTEL EDINBURGH, 70–72 Grove Street, EH3 8AP. Tel 0131 228 2323, www.brooksedinburgh.com. In the west end of the city, close to the Edinburgh International Conference Centre, this 1840s stone building has been restyled inside with a mix of vintage and contemporary furnishings. It is owned by Andrew and Carla Brooks (see also Brooks Guesthouse, Bristol, main entry). Half-panelled bedrooms vary in size, and are decorated with designer wallpaper in pastel shades; well equipped, they have an iPod docking station and a DVD player (a selection of DVDs is available to hire at reception). The lounge has magazines, newspapers, classic leather seating and a chandelier; an open fire burns in the winter. Scottish breakfasts include haggis and tattie scones. No evening meals; room service menu. Lounge (honesty bar; jazz/contemporary background music), breakfast room; private dining room. Free Wi-Fi. Courtyard garden. Small conferences. Paid parking nearby (£12 per day). Children welcomed (cots; high chairs; extra bed £20). 46 bedrooms (some in annexe; 1 suitable for disabled). Per room B&B from £79. Closed Christmas.

CITYROOMZ EDINBURGH, 25–33 Shandwick Place EH2 4RG. Tel 0131 229 6871, cityroomz.com. Fifteen minutes' walk from Haymarket station, and close to all the city's major attractions, this no-frills hotel is liked for its central location and cheerful, modern decor. Bedrooms are comfortably furnished and fully equipped with toiletries, and tea- and coffee-making facilities; they have blackout curtains or blinds, an iron and ironing board, and a laptop safe. Bathrooms have the option of a bath or shower. A continental breakfast buffet is available in the bright dining room; a breakfast bag with coffee and pastries can be taken away or eaten in the bedroom. In the evening, guests may use the dining area for a takeaway meal (crockery and cutlery provided). Discounts for parking at Castle Terrace car park, close by. Good value for families. Dining room. Lift. Free Wi-Fi. Background music. Children welcomed. 45 rooms (9 family rooms with bunk bed). Per room £75–£120. Breakfast £7.95.

94DR, 94 Dalkeith Road, EH16 5AF. Tel 0131 662 9265, www.94dr.com. Paul Lightfoot and John MacEwan run this modern B&B in their restored Victorian town house. Considerate hosts, they readily assist with restaurant, theatre and concert bookings, car hire and guided tours. Sleek bedrooms (Couture, Bespoke or Tailored) have a mix of contemporary and traditional furniture and modern Scottish artwork. Front-facing rooms have panoramic views of the Salisbury Crags and Arthur's Seat; those at the back look over the walled gardens towards the Pentland hills. In the new orangery, Paul Lightfoot, a trained chef, serves organic breakfasts, including a daily special; breakfast boxes can be brought to the room. 10 mins by bus from the centre; bicycles are available to borrow. Lounge (honesty bar; soft jazz, classical, contemporary Scottish background music), drawing room, breakfast room. Free Wi-Fi. Walled garden. Children welcomed (books, DVDs, games, Xbox). Resident labradoodle, Molli. Pop-up dining event twice a month. 6 bedrooms (1 interconnecting family room). Per room B&B £100–£220 (based on 2 people staying). 2-night min. stay on Sat in high season. Closed Christmas, 2 weeks Jan.

PRESTONFIELD, Priestfield Road, EH16 5UT. Tel 0131 225 7800, www. prestonfield.com. In 20 acres of private grounds at the foot of Arthur's Seat, this opulently decorated, baroque house is 'an orgy for the eyes and senses'. It has gilded furniture, swags, velvets and brocades, lavish flower arrangements, leather-panelled rooms and black-kilted staff. Owned by James Thomson (see also The Witchery by the Castle, Edinburgh, Shortlist entry), it is managed by Alan McGuiggan. Seductive bedrooms, each with views over parkland, are furnished with antiques and a remarkable bed; guests are welcomed with a bottle of chilled champagne. Scottish cuisine is served in the glamorous Rhubarb restaurant; afternoon tea is taken by a log fire, on the terrace or in a 'Gothic' tea house. 2 drawing rooms, salon, whisky bar; 4 private dining rooms. Free Wi-Fi. Background music. Terraces, tea house. Lift. Civil wedding licence; function facilities. Parking (reserved parking for disabled). Children (high chair; babysitting by arrangement) and dogs welcomed. 23 bedrooms (5 suites; 1 suitable for disabled). Per room B&B from £325, D,B&B from £395.

THE RUTLAND HOTEL, 1–3 Rutland Street, EH1 2AE. Tel 0131 229 3402, www.therutlandhotel.com. Steps from the top of Princes Street, this stylish, modern hotel is discreetly hidden in a 19th-century building that was once the home of Sir Joseph Lister, a pioneer of antiseptic medicine. It is owned by Nic Wood; Murray Ward is the manager. The contemporary interior has a touch of baroque, with rich fabrics here and ornate mirrors there. Colourful, well-equipped bedrooms have bathrobes, a daily newspaper, a fully stocked minibar, filter coffee and unusual teas; home-baked muffins are offered on arrival. There is a choice of places to eat: the buzzy Huxley Bar, with large windows for people-watching, serves burgers, hotdogs and small plates; overlooking the castle, the handsome Kyloe restaurant specialises in prime steaks, as well as seafood and vegetarian dishes. Outfitted with working gin stills, the basement is home to the Edinburgh Gin Distillery. Tours and classes are held during the day; in the evenings (Tues–Sun, 5 pm until late), it operates as Heads and Tales, a popular bar and gin emporium with cocktails and small bites. 2 bars, restaurant (open to non-residents); private function room. Lift. Free Wi-Fi. Background music. Discounted parking at Castle Terrace car park, nearby. Children welcomed (special menu; iPad in restaurant). 11 bedrooms (plus 5 serviced apartments in adjacent buildings). Per room B&B from £120, D,B&B from £180. Closed Christmas Day.

THE SCOTSMAN, 20 North Bridge, EH1 1TR. Tel 0131 556 5565, www.thescotsmanhotel.com. There are stunning views across the city from this 'stylish and tasteful' hotel on the historic North Bridge. Formerly the offices of the Scotsman newspaper, the iconic building has been carefully renovated to preserve its original architectural features. The printing rooms are now a 20,000-square-foot state-of-the-art spa; the editorial offices have been transformed into luxurious suites and individually designed bedrooms, many featuring oak panelling, ornate metalwork and an ornamental fireplace. The North Bridge Brasserie retains the marble staircase and towering balcony of the former advertising sales floor. Extensive breakfasts. Drawing room, breakfast room, bar/brasserie; lift, ramps. Free Wi-Fi. No background music. Private cinema; health spa (20-metre swimming pool, sauna, gym, treatment rooms; juice bar, café). Civil wedding licence; function/conference facilities. Children welcomed. 69 bedrooms (2 suitable for disabled). Per room from £349.

SOUTHSIDE GUEST HOUSE, 8 Newington Road, EH9 1QS. Tel 0131 668 4422, www.southsideguesthouse.co.uk. Franco and Lynne Galgani's welcoming B&B is in a Victorian terraced house close to the Meadows and Holyrood

Park, and within easy walking distance of restaurants, pubs and shops; a bus stop is nearby. Colourful, modern bedrooms have comfortable seating and pampering extras; two rooms have a four-poster bed and an espresso machine. Guests are offered a whisky nightcap. Comprehensive breakfasts include a daily special, vegetarian options and Buck's Fizz. Breakfast room (light classical background music). Free Wi-Fi. Limited parking. Children over 8 welcomed. 8 bedrooms. Per room B&B from £90 (2-night min. stay preferred). Closed Christmas, New Year; Jan.

TIGERLILY, 125 George Street, EH2 4JN. Tel 0131 225 5005, www.tigerlilyedinburgh.co.uk. Behind its Georgian exterior, this stylish hotel in New Town is decorated with a sense of fun: it is filled with spirited prints, pink hues and shiny surfaces. It is on a street popular for shopping and nights out; its two opulent, lively bars (mirrored walls, chandeliers, an extensive cocktail list) are popular with locals. Spacious bedrooms are equipped with a plasma-screen TV, a pre-loaded iPod and an extensive DVD library; a black-painted room in the eaves has a fireplace, and a wicker chair hanging from the ceiling. In the busy restaurant, the modern menu includes steaks and sharing platters. 2 bars (resident DJs), restaurant (background music); lift. Free Wi-Fi. Children welcomed (cot; babysitting by arrangement). 33 bedrooms (some smoking). Per room B&B from £195. Dinner £37.

21212, 3 Royal Terrace, EH7 5AB. Tel 0131 523 1030, www.21212restaurant.co.uk. Paul Kitching and Katie O'Brien's award-winning restaurant-with-rooms is at the end of a Georgian terrace, five minutes' walk from the centre. Paul Kitching has a Michelin star for his creative cooking; diners can watch him and his team of seven chefs at work in the open kitchen. The enterprise is spread over four floors of the listed town house. Pre- and post-dinner drinks may be taken in the glamorous first-floor drawing room, whose oversized windows give good views across Royal Terrace and its gardens to the Firth of Forth and beyond. On the upper floors, large, sleek bedrooms have an ample seating area and plenty of storage; rooms at the front have views over the city; those at the rear overlook the gardens. Drawing room, restaurant (closed Sun, Mon); private dining rooms. Free Wi-Fi. No background music. 4 bedrooms. Per room B&B £150–£325. Dinner £49. Closed Christmas, New Year; 2 weeks Jan; 1 week Sept.

THE WITCHERY BY THE CASTLE, Castlehill, EH1 2NF. Tel 0131 225 5613, www.thewitchery.com. By the gates of Edinburgh Castle, overlooking the Royal Mile, this theatrical restaurant-with-suites occupies two 16th- and 17th-century buildings with dramatic candlelit rooms, secret doors, and plenty of nooks and crannies. It is owned by James Thomson (see Prestonfield, Edinburgh, Shortlist entry); Jacquie Sutherland is the manager. Sumptuous, Gothic-style bedrooms are decorated with antique velvet drapes and gold-laced brocade; the Turret Suite has a tapestry-lined entrance, a collection of stags' antlers, an oak-panelled bathroom and exceptional views over the city's rooftops. A bottle of champagne is presented on arrival; in the morning, a breakfast hamper is delivered to the room. Prime Scottish produce is served in the atmospheric restaurants, The Witchery and The Secret Garden (background music); Douglas Roberts is chef. Terrace. Free Wi-Fi. 9 suites. Per room B&B £325–£395. Dinner £55.

FORT WILLIAM Highland
Map 5:C1

THE LIME TREE, Achintore Road, PH33 6RQ. Tel 01397 701806, www.limetreefortwilliam.co.uk. 'Well designed and decorated', this former manse near the town centre has been converted into a small hotel, restaurant and modern art gallery. David Wilson, the owner, is a visual artist; his 'exciting' work is displayed, along with that of other artists, throughout the hotel and exhibition space. Most of the modern rustic bedrooms have lovely views overlooking Loch Linnhe and the hills beyond; the cosy lounges have open fires. In the well-regarded restaurant, Andrew Cook, the new chef, serves modern European food with a Scottish slant. 3 lounges (a map room has books and guides), restaurant (jazz/Scottish background music); gallery; garden with seating area. Free Wi-Fi. Drying room; bicycle storage. Children, and supervised dogs (charge) welcomed. Resident dog. 9 bedrooms (1 family room; some in modern extension). Per room B&B from £90. Dinner £29.95.

GLASGOW
Map 5:D2

BLYTHSWOOD SQUARE HOTEL, 11 Blythswood Square, G2 4AD. Tel 0141 248 8888, www.blythswoodsquare.com. 'World-class cool.' Occupying the former headquarters of the Royal Scottish Automobile Club, this 'imposing' building on a 'splendid' garden square has been transformed into a 'comfortable and glamorous place to stay'. Part of the Town House Collection, it is managed by Murray Thomson. The hotel's sweeping staircase, original marble floors and pillars and dramatic spaces are offset with modern furnishings; opulent bathrooms give the bedrooms 'a real touch of luxury'. The restaurant and lively cocktail bar are 'busy all day and evening'; champagne afternoon teas are served in the salon. 'Great' breakfasts. 10 mins' walk to Buchanan Street. Salon, 3 bars, restaurant; private screening room. Free Wi-Fi. No background music. Lift. Spa (2 relaxation pools, treatment rooms, rasul mud chamber, relaxing lounge, café). Civil wedding licence. Valet parking (from £27.50 for 24 hours). Children (special menu, cot, sofa beds, extra bed; 6–12s £30 per night) and dogs (in some bedrooms; £30) welcomed. 100 bedrooms (some suitable for disabled). Per room B&B from £130, D,B&B from £174.

15GLASGOW, 15 Woodside Place, G3 7QL. Tel 0141 332 1263, www.15glasgow.com. Shane and Laura McKenzie's town house B&B, in a Victorian terrace in a peaceful location at the west end of the city, is within walking distance of many major attractions; the University of Glasgow and museums are close by. The McKenzies' award-winning restoration has retained original fireplaces, intricate cornicing, wooden shutters, stained glass and oak panelling. Pared-down, modern bedrooms are spacious and comfortable, with tall windows, high ceiling, mood lighting and a super-king-size bed; Tunnock's teacakes are a welcome gesture. Breakfast is brought to the room at an arranged time. Guests are given a key to the private gardens across the road. Lounge; garden. Free Wi-Fi. Parking. Children welcomed (extra bed £20). 5 bedrooms. Per room B&B £99–£175. 3-night min. stay for advance bookings. Closed Christmas, New Year.

GLENDEVON Perth and Kinross
Map 5:D2

THE TORMAUKIN HOTEL, FK14 7JY. Tel 01259 781252, www.tormaukinhotel. co.uk. In peaceful Perthshire countryside, David and Lesley Morby's refurbished 18th-century drovers' inn has easy access to fly fishing sites and the Glendevon Reservoir Walks. Public rooms have open fires and a welcoming atmosphere; simply furnished bedrooms retain many original features, such as old beams and a fireplace. Two rooms, in chalets on a slope behind the main house, have a terrace and outdoor seating. Chef David McAskill's weekly-changing menus feature Scottish cuisine using ingredients from local suppliers; meals may be taken on the patio in good weather. Lounge, bar, restaurant, conservatory; patio. Private dining room. Free Wi-Fi. Background music. Parking. Children (cot) and dogs (£10 charge) welcomed. Fishing. 6 miles from Gleneagles. 13 bedrooms (some on ground floor; 4 in adjoining stables block, 2 in chalets). Per room B&B from £50, D,B&B from £100. Closed Christmas.

GRANTOWN-ON-SPEY Highland
Map 5:C2

THE DULAIG, Seafield Avenue, PH26 3JF. Tel 01479 872065, www.thedulaig.com. 'It was everything we could have hoped for,

and more.' In a rural position, Carol and Gordon Bulloch's 'gorgeous' B&B is in an Edwardian house, a ten-minute walk from town. It is 'utterly luxurious' inside: Arts and Crafts antiques have been mixed with contemporary furniture throughout. 'Small and thoughtful' touches include freshly baked treats left daily by the 'cake fairy' in the spacious, elegant bedrooms. Extensive Scottish breakfasts include haggis, home-made potato scones, and eggs from the Bullochs' brood of free-range Black Rock hens; porridge is served with heather honey, cream and whisky. Packed lunches available. 'The gardens are spectacular, and even include tame wildlife.' Drawing room, dining room (optional background music), veranda; secluded 1½-acre garden (pond, summer house). Free Wi-Fi; computer available. Parking (garage for motorbikes and bicycles). 3 bedrooms. Per person B&B £80–£87.50. Closed Christmas, New Year.

GULLANE East Lothian
Map 5:D3

GREYWALLS, Muirfield, EH31 2EG. Tel 01620 842144, www.greywalls.co.uk. On the edge of Muirfield golf course, with nine other fine courses nearby, this elegant hotel (Relais & Châteaux) is ideally placed for golfers. It is managed by Duncan Fraser. The crescent-shaped stone house was designed by Sir Edwin Lutyens; its interior remains faithful to the Edwardian period. Individually styled bedrooms have antique furnishings; most rooms have views towards the Firth of Forth, or over the gardens and farmland to the Lammermuir Hills. Chef Mark Sadler's French-inspired country cooking is served in Chez Roux restaurant; snacks and lighter meals are taken in the bar and lounge. Delightful walled gardens (attributed to Gertrude Jekyll) have secluded seating, arches, 'rooms' and vistas; the grounds have plenty of space for tennis, croquet or a game of putting. Bar/lounge, drawing room, library, conservatory, Chez Roux restaurant (open to non-residents). Free Wi-Fi. No background music. Treatments. 4-acre garden. 15 mins' walk to sea. Weddings/functions. Children, and dogs (in 5 lodges only) welcomed. 23 bedrooms (4 on ground floor; some in lodges nearby). Per room B&B single £110–£315, double £230–£335. Dinner £30–£45.

INNERLEITHEN Scottish Borders
Map 5:E2

CADDON VIEW, 14 Pirn Road, EH44 6HH. Tel 01896 830208, www.caddonview.co.uk. In beautiful countryside on the edge of a small Borders town, this handsome Victorian house, set in mature grounds, is ideally located for walking, fishing, cycling and golf. It is run as a guest house and licensed restaurant by Stephen and Lisa Davies. There is a country house atmosphere inside: the cosy drawing room has a log fire, books, guides, magazines and games; tea and home-baked cake are served to arriving guests. Some bedrooms are 'very small'; they have pretty floral wallpaper, while some are more simply decorated. Five nights a week, Stephen Davies serves two- and three-course Scottish menus in the candlelit dining room; game such as venison, duck or partridge is served in season. The restaurant is closed for dinner on Sundays and Mondays; room snacks are available. Drawing room, dining room (background music). Free Wi-Fi. ½-acre garden. Picnics available.

Storage for bicycles and fishing gear. Parking. Dogs (in 1 bedroom, by arrangement; £5 per night charge) welcomed. 8 bedrooms. Per room B&B £55–£110, D,B&B £77–£164.

INVERNESS Highland
Map 5:C2

MOYNESS HOUSE, 6 Bruce Gardens, IV3 5EN. Tel 01463 233836, www.moyness.co.uk. 'Very handy for the town centre', this restored B&B is in a Victorian villa on a quiet residential street. Formerly the home of Scottish Renaissance author Neil M Gunn, it has 'comfortable', individually styled bedrooms named after Gunn's works. Scottish breakfasts include eggs from the garden hens. Wilma and John Martin, the new owners, are helpful with advice on restaurants and activities in the area. Sitting room, dining room; ½-acre garden. Free Wi-Fi. No background music. Parking. Children welcomed (high chair, cot, extra bed). 6 bedrooms (1 family room). Per room B&B £73–£110. Closed Christmas.

TRAFFORD BANK GUEST HOUSE,
96 Fairfield Road, IV3 5LL. Tel 01463 241414, www.traffordbankguesthouse.co.uk. 'The whole experience is top quality.' Interior designer Lorraine Pun has furnished her bay-windowed, sandstone Victorian house with an attractive mix of antique and contemporary pieces, including interesting sculptures in the mature garden. B&B accommodation is in large bedrooms, each with a hospitality tray, a fridge and a Nespresso machine; all rooms are well equipped with up-to-date technology (flat-screen TV, DVD and CD player, iPod dock) and helpful

amenities (ironing board, hairdryer, hair straightener). With home-made scones and oatcakes, breakfast, ordered the evening before, 'hits all the right buttons'. Joggers and walkers appreciate the closeness to the Caledonian Canal. 10 mins' walk from the centre. 2 lounges, conservatory; garden. Free Wi-Fi. No background music. 5 bedrooms. Per room B&B £94–£132. Closed Dec, Jan.

KELSO Scottish Borders
Map 5:E3

THE CROSS KEYS, 36–37 The Square, TD5 7HL. Tel 01573 223303, www. cross-keys-hotel.co.uk. Well placed for walks along the River Tweed, this 'friendly, relaxing' 18th-century coaching inn is on the busy square of a historic Borders town. Owned by the Ballantyne family, the hotel has been managed for more than two decades by the 'delightful' Becattelli family. Bedrooms vary in size and shape; interconnecting family rooms, with a shared bathroom, are available. In the Oak Room restaurant, new chef Paul Sellers cooks hearty modern Scottish and continental dishes; good vegetarian choices. Popular with groups. Lounge, Saddlers bar, 2 restaurants (closed Mon lunchtime); ballroom. Free Wi-Fi. Background music. Lift. Ramp. Conference facilities. Parking. Children welcomed (£15 charge); special menu. 26 bedrooms (some family rooms, some suitable for disabled). Per room B&B from £79, D,B&B from £99.

KILMARTIN Argyll and Bute
Map 5:D1

DUNCHRAIGAIG HOUSE, Lochgilphead, PA31 8RG. Tel 01546 510396, www. dunchraigaig.co.uk. Opposite a group

of standing stones, in an area rich in prehistoric sites, this B&B is run by Cameron Bruce and Lynn Jones. The hosts are 'a delightful couple' who provide a wealth of useful information on the area, including the best picnic spots. 'Relaxing' bedrooms, all on the first floor, have a 'sparkling' bathroom; rooms at the front have views of the standing stones; those at the back, overlooking the burn and woodland, are ideal for spotting deer and the 'resident' pine marten (a past star of Springwatch). Breakfast includes home-made marmalade, jam from garden fruit, and eggs from the resident hens; muffins or rolls are baked daily. 'Interesting' walks; packed lunches (£5). Cupcake-decorating workshops. Lounge (books, games, information), dining room; ½-acre garden. Free Wi-Fi. No background music. Parking. 1 mile S of village, 7 miles N of Lochgilphead. Children over 12 welcomed. 5 bedrooms (1 room accessed via external stairs). Per person B&B £35–£50. Credit cards not accepted. Closed Dec–Feb.
25% DISCOUNT VOUCHERS

KINCLAVEN Perth and Kinross
Map 5:D2

BALLATHIE HOUSE, PH41 4QN. Tel 01250 883268, www.ballathiehousehotel. com. Approached up a long wooded drive, the Milligan family's 'impressive' 19th-century house is in 'fabulous' grounds on the west bank of the River Tay. A 'marvellous' Scottish country house hotel, it has a long-standing association with salmon fishing; display cabinets in the public rooms showcase 'monster' fishing trophies. Andrew Seal is the manager. There is a traditional grandeur in the public areas (sporting prints, open

fires); bedrooms have period features
and views of the river or surrounding
countryside. In the restaurant, chef Scott
Scorer's menus have trout and salmon
from local rivers, locally reared meat and
home-grown herbs. Bar lunches, Sunday
lunch; afternoon teas. Drawing room, bar,
restaurant; private dining rooms. Free
Wi-Fi. No background music. Weddings/
functions. 900-acre estate: golf, fishing,
shooting, sled-dog racing by arrangement.
Children, and dogs (£20 charge) welcomed.
50 bedrooms (16 in riverside building
reached via a lit garden pathway; 12 in
Sportsman's Lodge). Per person B&B from
£120; in Sportsman's Lodge, per person
B&B from £70.

KIPPEN Stirlingshire
Map 5:D2

THE CROSS KEYS, Main Street,
FK8 3DN. Tel 01786 870293 , www.
kippencrosskeys.com. In a small village
close to the Trossachs national park, this
unpretentious 300-year-old inn attracts
a lively gathering of locals, walkers,
families and dogs. It is owned by Debby
McGregor and Brian Horsburgh. One
of Scotland's oldest inns, it has a rustic
bar with low lintels, flagstone floors,
and cosy fires in winter; there is a wide
selection of malts and blended whiskies,
and real ales made in a nearby brewery.
In the dining room, chef Liam Davies
serves tasty Scottish fare using local
lamb, and sausages, haggis and black
pudding made by the butcher across the
road; there is a terrace and a spacious
enclosed garden for alfresco eating.
Simple, modern bedrooms have crisp
white linen, a TV and a small selection
of DVDs; underfloor heating in the
bathroom. A hospitality tray is not
provided. Bar, dining areas; beer garden,
terrace. Free Wi-Fi. Background music.
Civil wedding licence. Children (£10 per
night for extra bed) and dogs (£10 per
night) welcomed. 10 miles W of Stirling.
3 bedrooms. Per room B&B £70–£90.
Closed Christmas, New Year.

LOCHINVER Highland
Map 5:B1

INVER LODGE HOTEL, Iolaire Road,
IV27 4LU. Tel 01571 844496, www.
inverlodge.com. On a hillside above
the harbour, this purpose-built luxury
hotel is surrounded by countryside
and wildlife; bedrooms have gorgeous
views of the bay or the mountains.
It has a relaxing atmosphere, and an
understated decor in tones of earth and
heather, with plaid fabrics. The foyer
lounge has comfortable sofas, a roaring
log fire and picture windows. Hearty,
daily-changing menus are served in
Chez Roux, the restaurant. Walkers,
climbers and birdwatchers have much
diversion; stalking on local estates can
be arranged; for anglers, the hotel has
boats on four lochs, some of which have
sea trout and salmon. Lounge, bar,
restaurant. Free Wi-Fi. No background
music. Snooker table; sauna; massages
and treatments available. ½-acre
grounds. Children (extra bed for over-8s
£50) and dogs welcomed. 21 bedrooms
(11 on ground floor; 1 suitable for
disabled). Per room B&B single from
£150, double from £225. D,B&B from
£177.50 per person. Closed Nov–Mar.

LOCHRANZA North Ayrshire
Map 5:D1

APPLE LODGE, KA27 8HJ. Tel 01770
830229, www.applelodgearran.co.uk.
Surrounded by dramatic countryside
where deer and eagles are often sighted,

Jeannie and John Boyd's small guest house is in a white-painted Edwardian manse near the ferry to the Kintyre peninsula. Peaceful and welcoming, the home is filled with ornaments, paintings and antique furniture. Each bedroom, named after an apple variety, has home-made biscuits and a collection of books and local information; the Apple Cottage, a self-contained suite with a sitting room and kitchen, has French doors opening on to the garden. Enjoyable three-course, no-choice dinner menus (not Tues, or in July, Aug; no licence, BYO) use locally sourced ingredients; breakfasts are 'hearty'. Lounge, dining room; ¼-acre mature garden. Free Wi-Fi. No background music. Parking. 4 bedrooms (1 on ground floor). Per person B&B £39–£45, D,B&B from £64. 3-night min. stay. Closed mid-Dec–mid-Jan.

MELROSE Scottish Borders
Map 5:E3
BURT'S, Market Square, TD6 9PL. Tel 01896 822285, www.burtshotel.co.uk. In a lovely Borders town on the banks of the River Tweed, the Henderson family has been running this 'excellent' small hotel in a listed 18th-century building for 44 years. The Hendersons also own The Townhouse, across the square (see next entry). Comfortable, 'immaculate' bedrooms (some may be small) are decorated with tartan cushions and blankets; each room has a radio alarm clock and tea- and coffee-making facilities. The restaurant specialises in local game and fish; the bar has a dedicated whisky menu and 'good' beer. For anglers and other outdoorsy guests, many rural pastimes – walking, cycling, stalking, game shooting – are available

on the doorstep. 2 lounges, bistro bar, restaurant (closed for lunch Mon–Fri); ¼-acre garden. Free Wi-Fi. Background music. Parking. Weddings/functions. Children (no under-8s in restaurant) and dogs (in some rooms) welcomed. 20 bedrooms (some recently refurbished). Per room B&B from £65, D,B&B from £90. Closed Christmas; 3–10 Jan.

THE TOWNHOUSE, Market Square, TD6 9PQ. Tel 01896 822645, www. thetownhousemelrose.co.uk. In the town centre, this smart, modern hotel is a sister to Burt's, across the market square (see previous entry). It is owned by the Henderson family, and run with 'extremely pleasant and helpful staff'. Well-appointed bedrooms vary in size; one is large enough to accommodate a family. Chef Johnny Streets cooks informal meals in the brasserie; the elegant restaurant has chef's specials (perhaps rolled shoulder of border venison, black pudding gnocchi, parsley root purée) and tasting menus. 'Excellent' breakfasts. Good walking nearby. Brasserie, restaurant, conservatory, patio/decked area; ramps. Free Wi-Fi. Background music. Weddings/functions. Parking. Children welcomed. 11 bedrooms (1 family room). Per room B&B from £132, D,B&B from £184 (2-night min. stay). Closed Christmas, 12–20 Jan.

MOFFAT Dumfries and Galloway
Map 5:E2
HARTFELL HOUSE & THE LIMETREE RESTAURANT, Hartfell Crescent, DG10 9AL. Tel 01683 220153, www. hartfellhouse.co.uk. 'We were delighted to find Hartfell House.' Robert Ash's guest house and restaurant are in a listed

stone-built Victorian house, in a rural setting overlooking the surrounding hills. Traditionally decorated public rooms retain some original features, including ornate cornices and woodwork; bedrooms have a Memory foam mattress, Scottish biscuits and fine toiletries. In the restaurant, which is popular with locals, chef Matt Seddon's modern Scottish dishes are cooked to a 'high standard'. Breakfast has freshly ground coffee, home-baked bread and home-made preserves. 'Highly recommended, and very good value for money.' 5 mins' walk from the town centre. Lounge, dining room (classical background music; closed Sun, Mon); garden. Free Wi-Fi. Bicycle storage; parking. Children welcomed (high chair, cot). 7 bedrooms (plus self-catering cottage in the grounds). Per person B&B £32.50–£37.50, D,B&B £57.50–£66.50. Closed Christmas.

NAIRN Highland
Map 5:C2

SUNNY BRAE, Marine Road, IV12 4EA. Tel 01667 452309, www.sunnybraehotel. com. Overlooking the green and the promenade of this seaside town, this 'good-value' small hotel has been extended to provide a glass-fronted lounge that enjoys 'the panorama of the sea'. It has been run by the Bochel family for 19 years; son John is now in charge, with his wife, Rachel Philipsen, as manager. Well-equipped bedrooms are decorated in 'light, cheerful' colours; four face the sea; others overlook the garden, which has a hedged lawn and flowerbeds. In the bright dining room, John Bochel's 'homely and competently prepared' Scottish dishes have an international influence; there

is an extensive wine list and a selection of 100 malt whiskies to choose from. Good variety at breakfast. 'A pleasing stay.' Lounge, bar, dining room ('easy listening' background music); terrace; ½-acre garden. Ramp. Free Wi-Fi. Parking. Children welcomed (cot). 8 bedrooms (1 suitable for disabled). Per room B&B £85–£170. Dinner £30. Closed Nov–Jan.

OBAN Argyll and Bute
Map 5:D1

GREYSTONES, 1 Dalriach Road, PA34 5EQ. Tel 01631 358653, www. greystonesoban.co.uk. Mark and Suzanne McPhillips run their modern B&B in this Scottish baronial mansion on a short, steep slope overlooking the bay and across to the Isle of Mull. It has been thoughtfully decorated: period features such as stained-glass windows, moulded ceilings and a fine wooden staircase are paired with understated furnishings and contemporary art. Most of the minimalist bedrooms have sea views; the chic bathrooms are spacious. In the turreted dining room, breakfast has interesting choices, including kedgeree, a spinach and Parmesan frittata, and porridge with a splash of whisky. Helpful hosts, the McPhillipses provide itineraries for day trips to Mull, Iona, Inveraray, Kerrara and Lismore. Library, dining room; ½-acre garden. Free Wi-Fi. No background music. Parking. 5 bedrooms. Per room B&B £120–£165. Closed Christmas, New Year.

PEAT INN Fife
Map 5:D3

THE PEAT INN, Cupar, KY15 5LH. Tel 01334 840206, www.thepeatinn.co.uk. Chef/patron Geoffrey Smeddle and his wife, Katherine, run their well-regarded restaurant-with-rooms in 'beautifully kept' grounds, in a peaceful hamlet six miles from St Andrews. An open fire burns in the reception lounge of the 18th-century former coaching inn; in the elegant dining rooms, Geoffrey Smeddle has a Michelin star for his 'excellent and very professional' modern Scottish dishes. In the adjoining Residence, individually designed suites have a separate living room with views over the garden and countryside. A 'good' continental breakfast is brought to the room. Lounge, restaurant (background music). Garden. Children welcomed. 8 suites (in annexe; 7 split-level, 1 with no stairs). Per room B&B £195–£205, D,B&B from £295 (includes tasting menu). Dinner £45–£65. Closed Sun, Mon; Christmas; 1–8 Jan.

PEEBLES Scottish Borders
Map 5:E2

HORSESHOE INN, Eddleston, EH45 8QP. Tel 01721 730225, www.horseshoeinn. co.uk. In the heart of the Scottish Borders, this sophisticated restaurant-with-rooms occupies the former inn of a tiny village a few miles north of Peebles. Mark Slaney is the manager. Comfortable accommodation is in a converted Victorian schoolhouse across a rear courtyard; despite their 'modest' size, rooms are well equipped, with bathrobes, organic toiletries, fresh fruit, home-made cake, bottled water and a tea- and coffee-making tray with fresh milk. Pre-dinner drinks are served in the cosy lounge (flagstone floor, deep sofas, wood-burning stove); in the elegant restaurant, chef Alistair Craig's modern British menus use 60-day-aged beef from nearby farms, and vegetables and herbs from the kitchen garden. Breakfast has local honey and home-made jams and marmalade.

Excellent walks from the front door. Lounge, restaurant; private dining room; small kitchen garden. No Wi-Fi. Background music. Parking. Children (no under-5s in restaurant) and well-behaved dogs (in some rooms; £10 per night) welcomed. 8 bedrooms. Per room B&B £140–£165, D,B&B £180–£200. Closed Mon, Tues; 2 weeks Jan, 2 weeks July.

PERTH Perth and Kinross
Map 5:D2

THE PARKLANDS, 2 St Leonard's Bank, PH2 8EB. Tel 01738 622451, www. theparklandshotel.com. A short walk from the town centre, this Victorian stone-built house stands in lovely terraced gardens overlooking South Inch Park. Penny and Scott Edwards, the owners, have refurbished it with a bright, contemporary interior. Colourful, modern bedrooms are equipped with a smart TV and DAB radio/iPod dock; tea- and coffee-making facilities are provided. In the two restaurants, executive chef Graeme Pallister focuses on seasonal, regional cuisine. 63@Parklands (open Thurs–Mon) has fine-dining set menus; the more informal No. 1 The Bank Bistro has à la carte and grill dishes. Lounge, bar, 2 restaurants; private dining room; terrace (alfresco dining); garden leading to park. Free Wi-Fi. No background music. Weddings/functions. Parking. Children and dogs welcomed. 15 bedrooms (4 on ground floor; 1 family room). Per person B&B from £55, D,B&B from £80. Closed 25 Dec–5 Jan.
25% DISCOUNT VOUCHERS

SUNBANK HOUSE, 50 Dundee Road, PH2 7BA. Tel 01738 624882, www. sunbankhouse.com. Overlooking the

River Tay and the city, this traditionally furnished hotel is in a Victorian house in large landscaped gardens on the outskirts of town. Within easy walking distance of shops, restaurants and bars, it is run in a friendly fashion by Remigio and Georgina Zane. 'Remo' Zane cooks uncomplicated à la carte dinners, often with an Italian influence (booking is advised); sandwiches and snacks are served until late in the lounge. Bedrooms are spacious and comfortable; those at the back are quietest. Plentiful breakfasts have lots of choice; packed lunches and picnics are available on request. Lounge/bar, restaurant (light background music); terrace; ½-acre garden. Free Wi-Fi. Weddings/functions. Parking. Children and dogs welcomed. Parking. ½ mile NE of town centre. 9 bedrooms (some on ground floor; 2 suitable for disabled; 2 family rooms). Per person B&B from £50, D,B&B from £70. Closed Christmas, 5 Jan–5 Feb.

PITLOCHRY Perth and Kinross
Map 5:D2

EAST HAUGH HOUSE, by Pitlochry, PH16 5TE. Tel 01796 473121, www. easthaugh.co.uk. The McGown family's friendly small hotel is in a turreted stone house set in two acres of gardens in a village near Pitlochry. Outdoorsy visitors may fish for salmon and trout on the River Tay (the fishing lodge has a barbecue and cooking facilities); stalking and shooting on nearby estates is regularly arranged. Decorated in tartan and toile de Jouy, comfortable bedrooms (some may be small) have home-baked shortbread and fresh milk; one has a fireplace and a four-poster bed. In the restaurant and cosy bar, chef/proprietor Neil McGown's menus feature fish and game in season.

Lounge, bar, restaurant (background jazz); patio; ramps. Free Wi-Fi. Large grounds; river beat. Civil wedding licence; function/conference facilities. Parking. Children welcomed; dogs by arrangement. 1 mile S of town centre. 13 bedrooms (1 suitable for disabled; 5 in a converted 'bothy' adjacent to the hotel), plus 2 self-catering cottages. Per room B&B from £79, D,B&B from £129. Closed Christmas.

PINE TREES, Strathview Terrace, PH16 5QR. Tel 01796 472121, www. pinetreeshotel.co.uk. A short walk from town, Valerie and Robert Kerr's 'beautiful' Victorian hillside mansion is set in spacious grounds where roe deer and red squirrels roam amid the pine trees. 'Warm and welcoming' public areas have cosy seating, half-panelled walls and an open log fire. 'Very comfortable' bedrooms are traditionally furnished. Overlooking the gardens, the restaurant serves 'excellent' Scottish-influenced dishes cooked by Cristian Cojocaru; special diets are catered for. 2 lounges, bar, restaurant; soft background music in the evenings. Free Wi-Fi (in lounge only). 7-acre grounds. Parking. Children (in Coach House; cot, extra bed) and dogs (charge) welcomed. ¼ mile N of town. 29 bedrooms (3 in annexe, 6 in Coach House; 7 on ground floor). Per person B&B £52–£72, D,B&B £72–£92.

PORT APPIN Argyll and Bute
Map 5:D1

THE PIERHOUSE, PA38 4DE. Tel 01631 730302, www.pierhousehotel.co.uk. In an idyllic spot on the shores of Loch Linnhe, this 'pretty little building' lies at the end of a single-track road. It has spectacular views to the Isle of Lismore and the mountains beyond. Formerly the 19th-century pier master's residence, it is today an informal hotel and restaurant owned and run by Nick and Nikki Horne. Bright, breezy bedrooms are in a modern, purpose-built block; many have views over the loch to the islands of Lismore and Shuna. 'We had the most comfortable bed, with wonderful pillows; we could hear the gentle lap of the waves just outside the window.' Huge picture windows in the restaurant overlook the original pier and the local fishermen bringing in their catch; fittingly, chef Laura Milne's 'very good' menus specialise in local fish and shellfish, including mussels and langoustines from the loch, and lobsters and crabs caught at the end of the pier. An outdoor terrace leads directly to the shore. Lounge, Ferry bar (wood-burning stove), snug, restaurant; private dining room; terrace. Free Wi-Fi. Celtic and 'easy listening' background music. Sauna; treatments available. Civil wedding licence. Yacht moorings for visitors. Mountain bike hire. Parking. Children (special menu; high chair, rollaway bed) and dogs (in some rooms) welcomed. 20 miles N of Oban. 12 bedrooms (3 family rooms). Per room B&B £90–£225. Dinner £35–£40. Closed Christmas.

ST ANDREWS Fife
Map 5:D3
RUFFLETS, Strathkinness Low Road, KY16 9TX. Tel 01334 472594, www. rufflets.co.uk. Guests receive 'a warm and helpful welcome' at this family-owned hotel in a 1920s turreted mansion that was built for the widow of a Dundee jute baron. It is managed by Stephen Owen with 'excellent'

staff. The 'comfortable' building has 'touches of luxury': antique furnishings mix with contemporary fabrics and wallpaper; the drawing room and lounge have open fires. Individually styled bedrooms are spread across the main house, and a lodge and gatehouse in the 'beautiful' ten-acre grounds; two characterful rooms have extra seating space in the turret. Chef Grant MacNicol makes use of locally sourced produce, supplemented by home-grown vegetables and fruits, for his daily-changing modern Scottish menus, served in the Terrace restaurant; bread, pastas, ice creams and sorbets are all home made. Drawing room, library, bar, restaurant. Free Wi-Fi. No background music. 10-acre grounds. Civil wedding licence; function facilities. Children (£20) and dogs (in some rooms) welcomed. 1½ miles W of town. 24 bedrooms (3 in gatehouse; 2 in lodge; 2 family rooms; 1 suitable for disabled), plus 3 self-catering cottages in gardens. Per room B&B from £175, D,B&B from £235. Closed 2 weeks Jan.

SANQUHAR Dumfries and Galloway
Map 5:E2
BLACKADDIE HOUSE, Blackaddie Road, DG4 6JJ. Tel 01659 50270, www. blackaddiehotel.co.uk. 'A special place to eat.' Overlooking the River Nith and fields, this 'quiet, small' hotel, in a 'beautiful' 16th-century stone-built manse, is owned by chef/patron Ian McAndrew and his wife, Jane. Traditionally furnished bedrooms have views of the gardens or the hills of Dumfries and Galloway; bathrooms have a spa bath and a monsoon shower. Adjacent to the hotel, the River Suite ('very peaceful and private') has its

own patio, with a magnificent view of the river. Ian McAndrew, who has received a Michelin star for his past cooking, uses much local produce in his 'really outstanding' fine-dining and eight-course tasting menus. The Scottish breakfasts 'suit all tastes and appetites'. 'We enjoyed a memorable and satisfying visit.' On the edge of the village. Bar, library, breakfast/function room, conservatory; 2-acre grounds. Free Wi-Fi (on ground floor and in some rooms only). 'Easy listening' background music. Weddings/functions. Good riverbank walks; cycling. Cookery school; fishing, shooting and photography breaks. Parking. Children (extra bed £20 per night) and dogs (in some rooms) welcomed. 7 bedrooms (1 suite), plus two 2-bedroom self-catering cottages. Per room B&B single £85, double £120–£210, D,B&B single £140, double £195–£310.

SCOURIE Highland
Map 5:B2

EDDRACHILLES HOTEL, Badcall Bay, IV27 4TH. Tel 01971 502080, www. eddrachilles.com. In 'lovely, extensive grounds along the seashore', Isabelle and Richard Flannery's relaxing hotel is in an 18th-century manse at the head of Badcall Bay. Simple, traditionally furnished bedrooms are well equipped with tea- and coffee-making facilities and useful amenities (iron, trouser press, hairdryer). In the conservatory overlooking the garden and the bay, Isabelle Flannery's 'very good', French-inspired cooking focuses on seafood from the bay, fish from Kinlochbervie, and Lochinver and Highland meat; charcuterie is from a smokehouse in the grounds. Special diets are catered for.

'Knowledgeable' hosts, the Flannerys provide 'excellent details on local attractions and walks'. Lounge/bar, breakfast room, restaurant (extensive wine list; open to non-residents), bar (over 150 single malt whiskies). Classical background music. Free Wi-Fi (in public areas); computer available. 4-acre garden. Parking. Children welcomed (cot; high tea at 6 pm for under-6s). 11 bedrooms (some on ground floor; 3 suitable for a family). Per person B&B £55, D,B&B £74. Closed Oct–Mar.

SKEABOST BRIDGE Highland
Map 5:C1

THE SPOONS, 75 Aird Bernisdale, IV51 9NU. Tel 01470 532217, www. thespoonsonskye.com. 'Words cannot describe how beautiful the location is.' In a quiet Isle of Skye hamlet half a mile from the main road, Marie and Ian Lewis run their B&B on a working croft overlooking Loch Snizort. 'Wonderful hosts', they have stylishly decorated the house with original works by local artists. Bedrooms, which mix antique and modern furnishings, have cashmere and sheepskin throws, a DVD/CD player and a Nespresso coffee machine. There are freshly baked treats at afternoon tea. 'Delicious', lavish breakfasts include smoked fish, home-baked bread, wild flower honey from the Lewises' bees, and eggs from resident hens. Good walks from the door. Sitting room (wood-burning stove), dining room. Ramps. Free Wi-Fi. No background music. Children over 14 welcomed. 8-acre grounds (sheep, ducks, geese). Per room B&B £120–£165. 2-night min. stay preferred. Closed Nov–mid-Mar.

SLEAT Highland
Map 5:C1

DUISDALE HOUSE, IV43 8QW. Tel
01471 833202, www.duisdale.com. In
extensive gardens and woodland on
the Isle of Skye overlooking the Sound
of Sleat, Anne Gracie and Ken Gunn
have fashioned a small, hospitable hotel
from a former Victorian hunting lodge;
they also own Toravaig House nearby
(see main entry). Modern bedrooms
are decorated with bold prints and
swirling wallpaper; some overlook the
gardens or loch; others have views of
the Highlands beyond. Traditional
dishes, using seasonal produce from
Skye and the Highlands, are served
in the restaurant; the Chart Room is a
relaxing place for pre-dinner drinks and
casual dining. Afternoon tea is taken by
the log fire in the lounge or outside on
the south-facing deck. From April to
September, guests may book days out on
the hotel's luxury yacht, with lunch and
champagne included (whales, dolphins,
seals and seabirds optional). Lounge,
bar, restaurant, conservatory. Free
Wi-Fi. Background music. Weddings.
Parking. 35-acre grounds (10-person
garden hot tub). Children welcomed.
18 bedrooms (2 family rooms; 1 garden
suite suitable for disabled). Per room
B&B £210–£338. Dinner £45.

SPEAN BRIDGE Highland
Map 5:C2

SMIDDY HOUSE, Roy Bridge Road,
PH34 4EU. Tel 01397 712335, www.
smiddyhouse.com. Robert Bryson and
Glen Russell's 'beautifully decorated'
restaurant-with-rooms is in a village on
the scenic West Highland rail route. It is
well situated for trips to the mountains
or lochs, or for travellers en route to
the Isle of Skye. Guests receive 'a warm
welcome', with a light afternoon tea in the
garden room; those who arrive later in
the evening find sherry and home-made
shortbread in the bedroom. Decorated in
calming shades, snug bedrooms are 'very
comfortable'; they have bottled water,
tea- and coffee-making facilities and lots
of toiletries. Russell's, the award-winning
restaurant, makes good use of shellfish
from the islands and organic salads from
the Isle of Skye; 'excellent' vegetarian
options are available. Good variety at
breakfast. Garden room, restaurant
(booking essential; closed Sun pm, Mon,
Tues Nov–Mar). Free Wi-Fi. Classical
background music. Parking. Golf,
mountain bike trails nearby. 4 bedrooms
(plus self-catering accommodation in
adjacent building, The Old Smiddy).
9 miles N of Fort William. Per room
B&B £90–£120, D,B&B £165–£185.
Closed Christmas.

STIRLING
Map 5:D2

POWIS HOUSE, FK9 5PS. Tel 01786
460231, www.powishouse.co.uk.
Beneath the Ochil hills, this listed
Georgian mansion is set in secluded nine-
acre grounds of woodland and pasture.
It has been carefully restored by Jane and
Colin Kilgour. Bedrooms have a Georgian
fireplace, polished flooring and handmade
Harris Tweed curtains and bed throws;
a bowl of fresh fruit is provided. Ample
breakfasts, served in the sun-filled dining
room, include eggs from the Kilgours'
hens. Lounge (open fire, board games,
DVDs), dining room. Free Wi-Fi. No
background music. Terrace; garden
(ha-ha; listed shafted stone sundial).
Parking. Children welcomed (over-2s £10
per night). 2 miles E of town. 3 bedrooms

(plus 2 gypsy caravans and a shepherd's hut in the grounds). Per room B&B single £65, double £100. Closed Nov–Feb.

Victoria Square, 12 Victoria Square, FK8 2QZ. Tel 01786 473920, www.victoriasquareguesthouse.com. 'We were very impressed.' A short walk from the castle, Kari and Phillip Couser's guest house is in a 'lovely' double-fronted Victorian building, on a peaceful, tree-lined square in the King's Park conservation area. Arriving guests are welcomed with complimentary refreshments in the comfortable lounge, which has floor-to-ceiling windows, period features and a notable decorative ceiling. A fine staircase with ironwork balustrades leads to six of the elegantly furnished bedrooms; all are spacious with a seating area and a mini-fridge; bathrooms have bathrobes and underfloor heating. The breakfast buffet has juices, fruit, yogurt, pastries and cereals; cooked dishes include pancakes with home-made fruit compote, and poached eggs with haggis. ½ mile to city centre and Stirling Castle. Lounge, breakfast room. Free Wi-Fi. No background music. Garden. Parking. Children over 12 welcomed. 7 bedrooms (1 on ground floor). B&B per room £70–£140. Closed Christmas.

STRACHUR Argyll and Bute
Map 5:D1
The Creggans Inn, PA27 8BX. Tel 01369 860279, www.creggans-inn.co.uk. Gill and Archie MacLellan's 'smoothly run', 'extremely welcoming' hotel is liked for 'the enjoyable food, the real ales and the fantastic lochside situation'. The white-painted inn has simply decorated, pretty bedrooms (many with loch views);

the popular bistro and restaurant have 'breathtaking' views over Loch Fyne to Kintyre. 'Like an old friend, reliable and comfortable.' Two moorings are available to guests arriving by boat; sea rods, for fishing from the pier, are available to borrow. 2 lounges, bar/bistro, restaurant. Free Wi-Fi. No background music. 1-acre garden. Weddings/functions. Children and dogs welcomed. Resident dogs, Hector and Boo. Unsuitable for disabled. 1 hour from Glasgow. 14 bedrooms. Per person B&B £50–£95, D,B&B £80–£130. Closed Christmas.

SWINTON Scottish Borders
Map 5:E3
The Wheatsheaf, Main Street, TD11 3JJ. Tel 01890 860257, www.wheatsheaf-swinton.co.uk. Opposite the village green, Chris and Jan Winson's cosy, stone-built roadside inn has comfortable, country-style accommodation and an award-winning restaurant, popular with locals and visitors alike. Impeccable bedrooms are light and airy, with a bath or shower room; home-made shortbread is provided. The tartan-walled lounge/bar has armchairs, pews and, in winter, an open fire. In the restaurant, new chef Peter Carr's seasonal cooking includes much fish and seafood from nearby Eyemouth. Tasting menus, with wine pairings, are available. Extensive wine cellar; large collection of single malt whiskies. Lounge/bar, 3 dining areas; small beer garden. Ramp. Free Wi-Fi. 'Easy listening' background music. Functions. Children (cot; extra bed £20 per night) and dogs (in 2 rooms and Myrtle Cottage) welcomed. 12 bedrooms (1 cottage room, 20 yds from main house; 1 suitable for disabled). Per person B&B £89–£159. Dinner £34. **25% DISCOUNT VOUCHERS**

TARBERT Argyll and Bute
Map 5:D1
WEST LOCH HOTEL, Campbeltown Road (A83), PA29 6YF. Tel 01880 820283, www.westlochhotel.com. At the top of the Kintyre peninsula, Andrew and Rosaline Ryan run their welcoming hotel and restaurant in this white-painted 18th-century coaching inn overlooking the loch from which it takes its name. Many of the simply furnished bedrooms have lovely views across the water. The beamed bar has a fireplace and more than 60 whiskies. In the rustic restaurant, chef Ross Payne's seasonal Scottish menus feature local fish and game. Close to the ferries for Islay, Arran and Gigha. 2 lounges, bar, restaurant. Function room. Free Wi-Fi. Background jazz. Parking. Children, and dogs (not in restaurant; £4.50 per night) welcomed. 1 mile from village. 8 bedrooms. Per room B&B single from £59.50, double from £89.50. Dinner £24.

TARBERT Western Isles
Map 5:B1
HOTEL HEBRIDES, Pier Road, HS3 3DG. Tel 01859 502364, www.hotel-hebrides. com. Beside the harbour, Angus and Chirsty Macleod's modern hotel on the Isle of Harris is a convenient base for touring the Western Isles; boat trips can be arranged to St Kilda and other islands. The 'boxy' building is 'adroit and stylish' inside. Visitors and locals throng the lively bar for drinks and light meals; local seafood is served in the Pierhouse restaurant. Bedrooms are bright and well equipped, though 'smallish'; board games and DVDs are available to borrow. Mote bar, restaurant. Free Wi-Fi. Traditional Scottish background music. Small

conferences. Parking. Near the 'spectacular' white sandy beach at Luskentyre Bay. Children welcomed (special menu). 21 bedrooms. Per person B&B from £75. Dinner £30. Closed Christmas, New Year.

TAYNUILT Argyll and Bute
Map 5:D1
ROINEABHAL COUNTRY HOUSE, Kilchrenan, PA35 1HD. Tel 01866 833207, www.roineabhal.com. Homely and welcoming, Roger and Maria Soep's peaceful country guest house is beside a tumbling stream in the wild glens of Argyll, close to Loch Awe. It is well placed for visits to Inveraray, Glencoe, Fort William and Kintyre; from the nearby port of Oban, ferries offer transport to Skye, Mull, Iona and the outer islands. Individually styled bedrooms, all with good views, have fresh flowers and shortbread. Breakfast includes locally smoked kippers, porridge and home-made bread; light supper platters of smoked fish, venison, cheese and oatcakes are available, by arrangement (£25). Lounge, dining room, covered veranda; 1½-acre garden. Free Wi-Fi. No background music. Ramp. Children (over-3s half price) and well-behaved dogs (must have own bedding) welcomed; resident dog. 18 miles E of Oban. 3 bedrooms (1 on ground floor, suitable for disabled). Per person B&B from £55. 2-night min. stays preferred. Closed Dec–Easter.

TOBERMORY Argyll and Bute
Map 5:D1
GLENGORM CASTLE, PA75 6QE. Tel 01688 302321, www.glengormcastle. co.uk. High on a cliff, this fairytale building with turrets and towers

(completed in 1863) is peacefully situated on a 5,000-acre estate where owners Tom and Marjorie Nelson raise Highland cattle and sheep. Walking routes and maps are available for guests to explore the expanse of heather, forest and rugged coastline; there are astounding views over the Sound of Mull to the Western Isles beyond. Books, board games and complimentary whisky are enjoyed by the open fires inside. Spacious, country-style bedrooms and bathrooms overlook the sea or the front lawns. Satisfying Scottish breakfasts are taken communally at a large oak table. Main hall, library, dining room; coffee shop; farm shop. Free Wi-Fi (in main hall). No background music. Packed lunches available. Fishing; guided walks. Children (cot; extra bed £15) and dogs welcomed; resident spaniels. 5 miles from Tobermory. 5 bedrooms (plus 6 self-catering cottages). Per room B&B £135–£215. Coffee-shop meals until 4 pm. Closed Christmas, New Year, Jan–Feb.

TONGUE Highland
Map 5:B2
THE TONGUE HOTEL, IV27 4XD. Tel 01847 611206, www.tonguehotel.co.uk. 'Wonderfully remote', Lorraine and David Hook's small hotel is in a sleepy coastal village in 'a spectacular area' beneath Ben Loyal; there are plenty of opportunities for bird- and otter-watching, hill climbing, fishing and stalking. 'It is a homely and characterful place; traditional decor, dark furniture and tartan fabrics suit the hunting lodge atmosphere.' Staff are 'friendly and helpful'. Bedrooms in the former Victorian sporting lodge have sweets, a decanter of sherry, and views of the sea or countryside; many also retain an old fireplace or a marble washstand. Simple Scottish fare is served in the restaurant, beside a cosy fire. Ordered the night before, breakfast has home-made compotes, granola and muesli, and porridge with cream and heather honey ('whisky available to add'). Lounge, bar, restaurant; therapy room. Free Wi-Fi (in public areas only). Background music. Weddings. Children welcomed (6–13s £20). 19 bedrooms. Per person B&B from £45, D,B&B from £82. Closed Oct–Easter.

TORRIDON Highland
Map 5:C1
THE TORRIDON, Annat IV22 2EY. Tel 01445 700300, www.thetorridon.com. 'A fabulous stay.' In a 'wildly beautiful' location, Rohaise and Daniel Rose-Bristow's 'atmospheric' luxury hotel is at the end of a single-track road, on a wooded estate beside a vast sea loch. The former shooting lodge has 'lovely' reception rooms with big open fireplaces, leather sofas, moulded plaster ceilings and panelling. 'Very comfortable', well-equipped bedrooms vary in size and style; the best have views of the loch (the rest overlook the mountains or grounds). Chef David Barnett's French-inspired five-course table d'hôte menus are based on Scottish produce including grouse, fish and seafood and moorland venison; herbs, vegetables and fruit are from the kitchen garden. The informal, family-friendly Torridon Inn is also on the estate. 'Wonderful' porridge at breakfast has demerara sugar, cream and whisky. Complimentary activities range from gorge scrambling and archery to 'excellent' guided walks at sunrise and sunset. Drawing room, whisky bar (more than 350 malts), dining room (classical background music). Free Wi-Fi. Weddings. 58 acres of parkland;

walled garden. Children (2–10s £40) welcomed. 10 miles SW of Kinlochewe. 18 bedrooms (1 on ground floor, suitable for disabled; 1 deluxe suite in adjacent cottage; dogs allowed). Per room B&B £235–£360. Dinner £60. Closed Jan, Mon–Wed Nov–Mar.

UIG Western Isles
Map 5:B1
Auberge Carnish, 5 Carnish, HS2 9EX. Tel 01851 672459, www.aubergecarnish. co.uk. On a working croft above Uig Sands on the Isle of Lewis, Richard and Jo-Ann Leparoux's purpose-built beachside guest house has 'stunning' views of the sea and the white sand beach. The lounge has a wood-burning stove, and doors leading to a decked terrace for alfresco coffees and aperitifs. Styled in calming natural shades, modern bedrooms, each with window seating, are decorated with original work by local artists. In the restaurant overlooking the bay, Richard Leparoux uses seasonal island ingredients (fish and shellfish, venison and lamb) in his French-Scottish dishes. Breakfast has home-baked bread and home-made marmalade. Trips and day cruises to St Kilda. Dining room (open to non-residents), lounge, patio. Free Wi-Fi. No background music. 4 bedrooms (1 suitable for disabled; plus 1-bedroom self-catering cottage). Per room B&B from £130. Dinner £29.50–£35.50. Closed mid-Nov–mid-Mar.

ULLAPOOL Highland
Map 5:B2
The Sheiling, Garve Road, IV26 2SX. Tel 01854 612947, www.thesheilingullapool.co.uk. In a 'good' location beside Loch Broom, Iain and Lesley MacDonald's comfortable, modern B&B is in lovely gardens with stunning views over the bay and the mountains beyond. Large bedrooms have complimentary sherry and sweets; two rooms have views of the loch. An open fire burns in the lounge where guests are provided with books, games, magazines and newspapers. 'Wonderful' Highland breakfasts, served in a bright room overlooking the loch, have local sausages, and porridge with honey and cream. The town centre is 10 mins' walk away; 5 mins' walk to the ferry for the Hebrides. Sitting room, dining room; Sportsman's Lodge (guest laundry, drying room; sauna, shower; bicycle store). Free Wi-Fi. No background music. 1-acre garden; lochside patio; fishing permits. Parking. Children (cot with bedding £10 per night) and dogs (by prior arrangement, in downstairs rooms; £10 per night) welcomed. 6 bedrooms (2 on ground floor). Per room B&B £75–£87.50.
25% DISCOUNT VOUCHERS

WALES

ABERGELE Conwy
Map 3:A3
The Kinmel Arms, St George, LL22 9BP. Tel 01745 832207, www.thekinmelarms.co.uk. 'A delightful and relaxed hideaway', Lynn Cunnah-Watson and Tim Watson's refurbished inn is in a secluded hamlet in the Elwy valley. The handsome sandstone building has mullioned windows, and a modern interior 'finished to a high standard'; Tim Watson's own artwork decorates the walls. 'Beautifully appointed' bedrooms, each with a large bed, have French

windows that open on to a decked balcony or a patio. Popular with locals, the bar has real ales and Welsh ciders, and a large choice of wines by the glass. The conservatory restaurant (Chad Hughes is chef) champions seasonal produce, and local fish and meat, for brasserie-style lunches and dinners. A generous continental breakfast, with home-baked bread, pastries, meats, cheeses, yogurt and fruit compote, is taken in the room. Good walks; golf nearby. Bar (wood-burning stove), restaurant (closed Sun, Mon). Free Wi-Fi. No background music. Small rear garden; seating area at front. Parking. 4 bedrooms (2 on ground floor). Per room B&B £115–£175, D,B&B from £195. Closed Christmas, New Year.

AMROTH Pembrokeshire
Map 3:D2

MELLIEHA GUEST HOUSE, SA67 8NA. Tel 01834 811581, www.mellieha.co.uk. 'Friendly, professional' hosts, Julia and Stuart Adams run their peaceful, 'ranch-style' B&B in a small seaside village at the start of the Pembrokeshire Coastal Path. 'Delicate touches make it stand out from the competition.' Guests are offered tea and a 'generous' portion of home-made cake on arrival. Neat, bright bedrooms (one with a balcony, another a private terrace) have views over the garden to the sea; each is equipped with thoughtful extras such as bathrobes and a torch. 'Properly cooked' breakfasts have Welsh choices, such as laver bread and cockles. Easy access to the beach; pubs, restaurants and shops nearby. Lounge, dining room. Free Wi-Fi. No background music. 1-acre garden with pond. Parking. 2 miles E of Saundersfoot. Children over 12

welcomed. 5 bedrooms. Per room B&B £80–£95. Closed Christmas, New Year.

BRECON Powys
Map 3:D3

THE COACH HOUSE, 12 Orchard Street, LD3 8AN. Tel 07974 328437, www. coachhousebrecon.wales. A short walk from the centre, this modern, 'beautifully decorated' B&B is run by friendly owners Tony Morris-Davies and Marc Pearce-Hopkins. Narrow stairs in the former Georgian coaching inn lead to 'comfortable' bedrooms, each equipped with bottled water and tea- and coffee-making facilities; a spacious new mini suite has a separate seating area. 'Very good' breakfasts, chosen from 'the longest breakfast menu I've ever seen', are cooked by Tony Morris-Davies; 'the variations on Welsh rarebit are gorgeous'. In fine weather, guests can relax with a drink in the 'pleasant' garden. The hosts happily share their knowledge of walks and the local area; they offer a drop-off service to a walking point (subject to availability). Packed lunches and evening snacks available. Sitting area, breakfast room, drying room. Licensed. Free Wi-Fi. Classical and Welsh harp background music. Garden. Secure bicycle storage. 6 bedrooms. Per room B&B £80–£160. Credit cards not accepted.

CAERNARFON Gwynedd
Map 3:A2

PLAS DINAS COUNTRY HOUSE, Bontnewydd, LL54 7YF. Tel 01286 830214, www.plasdinas.co.uk. 'We had a memorable experience.' Once the country home of the Armstrong-Jones family, this 'lovely' 17th-century Grade II listed building, standing in 15-acre grounds, is packed with history. Owners Neil Baines and Marco-David Soares have filled the sumptuously decorated rooms with antiques, portraits and memorabilia. Bedrooms are individually styled with vintage and modern pieces; all have a hospitality tray with ground coffee, hot chocolate, home-made biscuits and a selection of teas. Guests take drinks in front of a log fire in winter, on the terrace in warm weather. A daily-changing four-course set menu, cooked by Marco-David Soares, includes locally sourced Welsh cheeses. 'Breakfast was great.' Drawing room, restaurant (closed Sun, Mon); private dining room (huge inglenook fireplace). Free Wi-Fi. Background music. Civil wedding licence. Parking. Children over 14 welcomed. Well-behaved dogs welcomed in 2 rooms, by arrangement (£10 per night charge); resident dogs, Malta and Blue. 2 miles from Caernarfon. 9 bedrooms (1 on ground floor). Per room B&B £99–£249 (2-night min. stay at weekends). Dinner £35. Closed Christmas.

CARDIFF
Map 3:E4

CATHEDRAL 73, 73 Cathedral Road. CF11 9HE. Tel 02920 235005, cathedral73.com. Guests like the personal touch at Nigel John's stylishly converted Victorian town house on a leafy thoroughfare within easy walking distance of many of the city's attractions. A butler and a personal chef are available; 'Mrs Bramley', a vintage yellow Rolls-Royce, may be used to transport guests to their destination. Modern bedrooms have good lighting, a large bed, tea- and coffee-making facilities, a fridge with fresh milk; three apartments have a kitchen and living room. There is a turn-down service in the evening. An elegant space, Tea at 73 has light lunches, and afternoon tea with home-made cakes. Evenings, from Thursday to Saturday, it operates as a wine bar (live piano music). A large paved smoking area behind the building has parasols and plenty of seating. Sitting room, orangery, bar/tea room. Free Wi-Fi. Background music. Civil wedding licence. Children welcomed. Limited parking. ½ mile from city centre. 12 bedrooms (1 on ground floor; plus 3 apartment suites, 1 in coach house behind the hotel). Per room B&B from £150. Dinner £30. **25% DISCOUNT VOUCHERS**

JOLYON'S AT NO. 10, 10 Cathedral Road, CF11 9LJ. Tel 029 2009 1900, www.jolyons10.com. Occupying a Victorian villa in the Pontcanna area, Jolyon Joseph's relaxed hotel is behind Sophia Gardens and within walking distance of the city centre. The decoration is bright and eclectic throughout: gold-painted armchairs, crystal chandeliers, swathes of leopard print, grand walnut wardrobes, tasselled four-poster beds. A Welsh-themed menu is served in the enveloping Cwtch Mawr (Big Cuddle) restaurant, which has plush seating, a grand bar and a cosy fire; Robbie Aherne is chef. Lounge/bar, restaurant; terrace. Lift. Free Wi-Fi. Background music. Conferences/ functions. Limited parking (pre-booking required). 21 bedrooms (1 suitable for disabled). Contact hotel for prices. Closed Christmas Day. **25% DISCOUNT VOUCHERS**

CARDIGAN Ceredigion
Map 3:D2

CAEMORGAN MANSION, Caemorgan Road, SA43 1QU. Tel 01239 613297, www.caemorgan.com. In a peaceful location just beyond the town, David and Beverley Harrison-Wood have remodelled this stately house and transformed it into a 'startlingly good', modern guest house and restaurant. It is run along green lines, with water recycling, eco-friendly toiletries, a biomass boiler for hot water and heating, and solar photovoltaic panels to support electricity usage. Spacious bedrooms have a 'superb' bed and high-quality linens, towels and bathrobes, and are supplied with home-made biscuits and a coffee/tea/hot chocolate machine; DVDs and books are available to borrow. In the elegant dining room, with its wood-burning stove, David Harrison-Wood cooks 'outstanding' modern European food. Breakfasts are 'another delight'. Indulgent afternoon teas. Lounge/bar, restaurant (background music; open to non-residents). 2-acre grounds (lawns, gardens, paddocks). Free Wi-Fi. Wedding/function facilities. Parking. Secure bicycle storage. ½ mile N of town centre; beaches within easy reach. 5 bedrooms. Per room B&B from £114. Dinner £28. Closed Christmas.

COLWYN BAY Conwy
Map 3:A3

ELLINGHAM HOUSE, 1 Woodland Park West, LL29 7DR. Tel 01492 533345, www.ellinghamhouse.com. A short walk from the town and the sea, Ian Davies and Chris Jennings's traditionally furnished B&B is peacefully located in a leafy conservation area. There is a relaxed, informal atmosphere; friendly and welcoming, the owners readily share local knowledge and recommendations. Spacious bedrooms in the late Victorian villa are well equipped with bathrobes, biscuits and fruit; a 'wonderful' bathroom. Wholesome breakfasts are taken in an elegant room with period features. Lounge (DVD library), dining room. Lawned garden with seating. Free Wi-Fi. No background music. Parking. Children welcomed (high chair, cot, extra bed £20 per night); dogs by arrangement (£5 per night). 5 bedrooms. Per room B&B £82–£110. Closed Dec, Jan; open at Christmas and New Year.

CONWY Conwy
Map 3:A3

CASTLE HOTEL, High Street, LL32 8DB. Tel 01492 582800, www.castlewales. co.uk. Five minutes from the medieval Conwy Castle, a World Heritage Site, this old coaching inn stands on the site of a Cistercian abbey; parts of the building, once two hostelries, date back to the 1400s. It is run by the Lavin family as an atmospheric hotel and restaurant. The quirky interior has characterful nooks, crannies and creaky floors; public rooms are furnished with antiques, and paintings by Victorian artist John Dawson Watson. Bedrooms vary in size; some have castle views. In the restaurant, chefs Andrew Nelson and Leigh Marshall showcase local seafood, and Welsh produce from artisan suppliers. Bar, lounge, Dawson's restaurant. Treatment room. Free Wi-Fi. Background music. Courtyard garden (alfresco dining). Parking (narrow entrance). Children (special meals; 6–13s £20 per night) and dogs (bed 'and other bits' provided; £10 per night) welcomed. 27 bedrooms (1 with 16th-century four-poster bed; some on ground floor). Per person B&B £65–£135, D,B&B from £90.

COWBRIDGE Vale of Glamorgan
Map 3:E3

THE BEAR, 63 High Street, CF71 7AF. Tel 01446 774814, www.bearhotel.com. Well liked by locals, this historic coaching inn has a relaxed, welcoming atmosphere: visitors come for the real ales at the bar, and the 'satisfying' dishes cooked by chef Richard Bowles; traditional Sunday roasts are popular. Sian Bradley is the manager. Individually decorated bedrooms are bright and cheerful; some have a beamed ceiling, four-poster bed or chandelier. There is a choice of places to eat: Cellars restaurant, with its stone-vaulted ceiling; the informal Teddies Grill Bar; the lounge, by a fire; and alfresco in the courtyard. 20 mins' drive from Cardiff; a local bus service goes straight to the city centre. Complimentary access to Cowbridge Leisure Centre, a short stroll from the hotel. Lounge, 2 bars, restaurant. Free Wi-Fi. Background music. Civil wedding licence; conference facilities. Parking. Bicycle hire. Children welcomed. 33 bedrooms (some in annexe; plus 1- and 2- bedroom apartments a short walk away). Per room B&B from £113. Dinner £25–£30.

CWMBACH Powys
Map 3:C3

THE DRAWING ROOM, LD2 3RT. Tel 01982 552493, www.the-drawing-room. co.uk. On a quiet country road, this intimate restaurant-with-rooms is run by Colin and Melanie Dawson in a Georgian stone-built house. The sitting room has fresh flowers, comfortable seating and an open fire. Bedrooms are finely furnished, though snug; bathrooms have underfloor heating. In the open-plan kitchen, the Dawsons' seasonal dishes use fruit and vegetables from the kitchen garden, along with prime Welsh Black beef and lamb from local farms. Guests are expected to dine in. Indulgent breakfasts have fresh fruit, home-made muesli and scrambled eggs with home-cured salmon. Lounge, restaurant (open to non-residents). Small garden. Free Wi-Fi. Background music. Exclusive-use cookery weekends. Children over 12 welcomed. 3 bedrooms. Per room D,B&B £205–£230. 3 miles N of Builth Wells, on the old A470. Closed Christmas, New Year.

DOLGELLAU Gwynedd
Map 3:B3

FFYNNON, Love Lane, LL40 1RR. Tel 01341 421774, www.ffynnontownhouse. com. In a small market town within the Snowdonia national park, Debra Harris and Steven Holt run their comfortable B&B in this handsomely refurbished Gothic Victorian rectory. Period features, such as an Adam fireplace and stained-glass windows, have been retained; in the lounge, an old gramophone chest filled with local beers and snacks serves as an honesty bar. Overlooking the garden and surrounding valley, well-equipped bedrooms have modern touches (flat-screen TV, iPod dock, CD/DVD player); bathrooms have a walk-in drench shower and large bathtub. Plenty of local produce at breakfast, including Glamorgan sausages and Welsh pancakes. Lounge (contemporary background music; card and board games), dining room, butler's pantry

(room-service menu); drying room. Free Wi-Fi. ½-acre garden: patio; outdoor hot tub. Small functions. Parking. Children welcomed (high chair, cot, extra bed; £25 per night); dogs allowed (they sleep and eat in a dedicated room; allowed in guest lounge). Steps and level changes; steep, narrow approach. 3 mins' walk to town. 6 bedrooms. Per room B&B £150–£210. 2-night min. stay at weekends. Closed Christmas.
25% DISCOUNT VOUCHERS

HAY-ON-WYE Powys
Map 3:D4
THE BEAR, 2 Bear Street, HR3 5AN. Tel 01497 821302, www.thebearhay.com. In a former 16th-century coaching inn, David Gibbon's B&B is steps away from the world-renowned bookshops, galleries and attractions of this small border town. Decorated in a smart, eclectic style, bedrooms have old beams and vintage furniture offset by quirky artwork and modern accessories. Well supplied with books, the sitting room has a comfortable sofa in front of a wood-fired stove. Breakfasts include home-made fruit salads and compotes, and locally baked bread. Sitting/dining room; walled patio. Free Wi-Fi in public rooms. No background music. Children welcomed. Small car park. Walking, canoeing, fishing nearby. 3 bedrooms. Per room B&B £75–£95 (£25 additional charge during Festival). Credit cards not accepted. Closed Christmas, New Year.

LLANDUDNO Conwy
Map 3:A3
ESCAPE, 48 Church Walks, LL30 2HL. Tel 01492 877776, www.escapebandb. co.uk. Near sandy beaches and the promenade, Sam Nayar and Gaenor Loftus run their design-conscious B&B in a white-stucco Victorian villa. Beyond the traditional facade, there is a cool, urban interior: contemporary and vintage furnishings and fabrics are set against a backdrop of oak panelling, stained glass and period fireplaces. Staff are welcoming and friendly. Modern bedrooms are imaginatively designed: one has a floating bed, another a coastal look with deckchair stripes; the Loft, set over three levels, has a wall-mounted fireplace, and a body-dryer in the shower room. Up-to-date technology in the rooms includes a flat-screen TV, Blu-ray player and iPod docking station; guests may borrow from a DVD library. Welsh breakfasts are praised. Lounge, breakfast room; honesty bar. Garden. Free Wi-Fi. No background music. Limited parking. Children over 10 welcomed. 9 bedrooms. Per room B&B £95–£149. Closed Christmas.

LLANDYRNOG Denbighshire
Map 3:A4
PENTRE MAWR, Pentre Mawr, LL16 4LA. Tel 01824 790732, www.pentremawrcountryhouse.co.uk. 'Beautifully kept', this 400-year-old farmstead has 'excellent' accommodation spread out between the main house and unusual 'glamping' options in the extensive grounds. Bre and Graham Carrington-Sykes are the owners. Welcoming hosts, they make 'great' home-cooked dinners on Friday and Saturday evenings; bread, cakes and other treats are baked daily. Spacious, country house-style bedrooms in the old farmhouse have antiques and a large spa bath; modern cottage suites, next door, have a private terrace with a hot tub; canvas safari lodges in the grounds

('Shetland ponies will give you a feel for the wild') have upmarket touches such as a sofa and hot tub. A communal hot tub has recently been added next to the swimming pool. 2 sitting rooms, dining room, conservatory; gallery for parties/functions. Free Wi-Fi (in main house). Organ background music. 2-acre grounds: walled garden; solar-heated saltwater swimming pool; hot tub. Tennis; croquet. Dogs welcomed; resident dogs. Shetland ponies; husky experience; falconry demonstrations are 'a highly recommended adventure'. Weddings. Golf buggy lifts for the mobility-impaired. Children over 12 welcomed. 12 bedrooms (3 in main house; 3 suites in cottage; 6 safari lodges). 5 miles from Denbigh. Per room B&B from £180, D,B&B from £230. Closed Christmas.

LLANGAFFO Isle of Anglesey
Map 3:A2

THE OUTBUILDINGS, Bodowyr Farm, LL60 6NH. Tel 01248 430132, www.theoutbuildings.co.uk. Down winding country lanes, Judith 'Bun' Matthews's restaurant-with-rooms is 'very different, and very much enjoyed'. Set in tranquil farmland, the converted barn and granary have glorious views to Snowdonia and the mountains of the Lleyn peninsula. Quirkily named bedrooms (Pink Spotty Jug, Button's Room, etc) are decorated in lively style, and have a radio and iPod dock. In the garden, The Pink Hut is a cosy shepherd's hut with a small wood-burning stove and 'full mod cons'. Tea and home-made cake are offered on arrival. Chef François Bernier cooks 'excellent' set menus using foraged wild ingredients and fresh local produce ('François will chat with the butcher and fishermen before choosing his menus'); guests are consulted on their preferences. Breakfast

is served communally at a long table in the farmhouse kitchen; afternoon tea is taken by a log fire in the sitting room, or outside on the terrace. 2 sitting rooms, restaurant (open to non-residents). Holistic treatment studio. Garden, with seating. Tennis court (racquets and balls available to borrow). Free Wi-Fi. Background music (optional). Civil wedding licence/function facilities. Private dining. Parking. Children over 9, and well-behaved dogs (in 1 room; surrounding farmland has livestock) welcomed; resident dog. 15 mins' drive from the bridge to Anglesey; 25 mins' to the ferry terminal at Holyhead; Llanddwyn beach is close by. 5 bedrooms (1 on ground floor; 1 in garden). Per room B&B £90; Pink Hut £75. Dinner £35.

LLANGOLLEN Denbighshire
Map 3:B4

GALES, 18 Bridge Street, LL20 8PF. Tel 01978 860089, www.galesofllangollen.co.uk. Richard Gale opened his wine bar in the centre of town in 1977; the family-run enterprise eventually expanded to include this quirky hotel and popular restaurant. Pip Gale is the manager. Individually decorated bedrooms are divided between the main Georgian town house and an older timber-framed building opposite; many retain the building's original features; some are large enough to accommodate a family. There is a lively atmosphere in the informal, wood-panelled restaurant, where chef Daniel Gaskin's seasonal dishes are praised; an extensive wine list has many wines available by the glass. Bar/restaurant (closed Sun), wine shop; patio. Free Wi-Fi. Background music. Conferences. Parking. Children welcomed (6–15s £10 per night). 15 bedrooms (1 suitable for disabled; 7 in adjoining building). Per room B&B (continental) from £100. Cooked breakfast £10; dinner £25. Closed Christmas–New Year.

MANORHAUS LLANGOLLEN, Hill Street, LL20 8EU. Tel 01978 860775, www.manorhausllangollen.com. In the centre of town, this stylish restaurant-with-rooms occupies a handsomely renovated Victorian town house with a smart black-and-white facade. Christopher Frost and Gavin Harris are the owners. Through the brilliant vermilion door, modern bedrooms on the first and second floors are well equipped with armchairs, a desk and a beverage-making cabinet; many have views of the town and the medieval Castell Dinas Brân. A weekly-changing dinner menu is served in the informal restaurant; seasonal cocktails, wine and local beers are taken in the contemporary bar and lounge. Lounge, bar, restaurant (closed Mon/Tues); small terrace; rooftop hot tub. Free Wi-Fi (in public areas). Background jazz. Parking permits supplied. Children over 12, and small dogs (in 2 rooms, by arrangement; £10 per night; bed, blanket, bowl, doggy treats provided) welcomed. 6 bedrooms. Per room B&B £110–£190, D,B&B £129–£249.
25% DISCOUNT VOUCHERS

LLANWRTYD WELLS Powys
Map 3:D3
LASSWADE COUNTRY HOUSE, Station Road, LD5 4RW. Tel 01591 610515, www.lasswadehotel.co.uk. 'We were impressed.' Roger and Emma Stevens run their welcoming hotel and restaurant in this large Edwardian house, in a semi-rural location on the edge of the UK's smallest town. Traditionally furnished bedrooms have 'superb' views of the surrounding countryside; all are equipped with refreshments and organic toiletries; no telephone. Roger Stevens cooks 'exceptional' daily-changing menus with a Mediterranean influence; vegetarian and special diets are catered for, by arrangement. The large sitting room has reading materials, comfortable seating and a log fire. Hearty breakfasts are served in the conservatory. Incentives are offered to guests who arrive by public transport. Drawing room, restaurant (pre-booking essential), conservatory; function room. Free Wi-Fi. No background music. Small garden; patio. Parking. Children (high teas on request; no under-8s in restaurant) and dogs (by arrangement) welcomed. 8 bedrooms. Per room B&B £90–£120, D,B&B £160–£200. Closed Christmas Day.
25% DISCOUNT VOUCHERS

MONTGOMERY Powys
Map 3:C4
THE CHECKERS, Broad Street, SY15 6PN. Tel 01686 669822, www.thecheckersmontgomery.co.uk. There are smartly rustic bedrooms and much-admired meals at this 'charming' restaurant-with-rooms, overlooking the town square of a laid-back border town. It is owned by sisters Kathryn and Sarah Francis, and Sarah's husband, Stéphane Borie; together, they have 'tastefully updated' the old coaching inn. Modern bedrooms (some with low ceiling and doorway) are cosy, and equipped with a large bed, home-made biscuits and the latest gadgetry; some bathrooms have a freestanding bath. In the pleasant restaurant, Stéphane Borie has a Michelin star for his classic French dishes; a seven-course tasting menu, to

be taken by the whole table, is available. Breakfast has local sausages and bacon, and home-made brioche toast. 'Epic' walks from the front door. Lounge/bar, restaurant (closed Sun, Mon); small terrace. Free Wi-Fi (signal variable). No background music. Chef's masterclasses. Children welcomed, by arrangement; no under-8s in restaurant in the evening. 5 bedrooms (1 accessed via the roof terrace). Offa's Dyke is 1 mile away. Per room B&B £135–£180. Dinner from £50, tasting menu £75. Closed Christmas; 2 weeks in Jan; 1 week in late summer.

MUMBLES Swansea
Map 3:E3

PATRICKS WITH ROOMS, 638 Mumbles Road, SA3 4EA. Tel 01792 360199, www.patrickswithrooms.com. On the seafront of a pretty village near Swansea, this long-established restaurant-with-rooms is run by two husband-and-wife teams, Sally and Dean Fuller and Catherine and Patrick Walsh, with 'knowledgeable and accommodating' staff. 'Comfortable' bedrooms are decorated in bright colours; all have views of the sea. In the popular restaurant, Patrick Walsh and Dean Fuller, the chefs, serve a monthly-changing menu using much home-grown and Welsh produce. Children are made very welcome, with toys, books, DVDs, skateboards, and plenty of pasta on request; interconnecting rooms are ideal for a family. Cooked to order, breakfast has kedgeree, a full English, and a full Welsh with cockles and laver bread. Lounge/bar, restaurant. Free Wi-Fi. Background music. Gym. Greenhouse. Lift. Civil wedding licence; meeting room. On-street parking (can be difficult at peak times). Children welcomed (high chair, cot, baby monitors, DVDs; playground across the road). 16 bedrooms (1 suitable for disabled; 6 in converted boathouse). Per room B&B £115–£185. Dinner £30.

NARBERTH Pembrokeshire
Map 3:D2

CANASTON OAKS, Canaston Bridge, SA67 8DE. Tel 01437 541254, www.canastonoaks.co.uk. Surrounded by woodland and river walks, the Lewis family's 'very good' B&B is in converted barns designed and built by Pembrokeshire craftsmen. Homely bedrooms are equipped with dressing gowns and slippers, a fridge with milk and water, and up-to-date gadgetry (flat-screen TV, DVD player, iPod docking station); thoughtful extras, including candles and a sewing kit, are provided. Three rooms are on the first floor of a newly constructed lodge, with sweeping countryside views. Light lunches and afternoon teas are served in a number of dining areas, including the new Oak Lodge Tea Rooms; there is plenty of space for alfresco drinks. Dining rooms, tea room. Free Wi-Fi. Parking. Children welcomed (cot, high chair, extra bed). 10 bedrooms (7, on ground floor, in courtyard; 3 in Lodge; 2 suitable for disabled; 1 family room). 3 miles W of Narberth. Per room B&B from £90.
25% DISCOUNT VOUCHERS

NEWPORT Pembrokeshire
Map 3:D1

Y GARTH, Cae Tabor, SA42 0XR. Tel 01348 811777, www.bedandbreakfast-pembrokeshire.co.uk. Joyce Evans, a welcoming hostess, offers complimentary afternoon tea to guests arriving at her 'faultless' B&B. Situated between Newport and Fishguard, the house is popular with walkers: the Pembrokeshire Coastal Path is a ten-minute walk away, and there are a number of beaches nearby. Decorated with bold wallpapers and plush fabrics, bedrooms have fresh flowers, chocolates and a mini fridge; all have distant views of the sea or open countryside. Generous Pembrokeshire breakfasts are ordered the evening before. Convenient for the ferry to Rosslare. Lounge, breakfast room (background music); patio with seating. Free Wi-Fi. Parking. 3 bedrooms. Per room B&B £90–£105. Closed Christmas.

NEWTOWN Powys
Map 3:C4

THE FOREST COUNTRY GUEST HOUSE, Gilfach Lane, SY16 4DW. Tel 01686 621821, www.bedandbreakfastnewtown. co.uk. In undulating countryside in the Vale of Kerry, Paul and Michelle Martin's family-friendly B&B is in a Victorian country house, three miles outside the town. Elegantly furnished in period style, it has been updated along eco-friendly lines, to include a biomass heating system and solar panels. Peaceful bedrooms have views of the large, colourful garden. Breakfasts include locally sourced, organic produce and eggs from the Martins' free-range hens. Well located for exploring the Marches area of Mid Wales. Drawing room (books, games, piano), dining room; kitchenette with fridge, microwave. Free Wi-Fi. No background music. Games room (pool, table football, table tennis); toy box. 4-acre garden; play area with swings, house and large timber fort; tennis. 3 miles SE

of Newtown (train and bus stations). Secure bicycle storage. Children (travel cot, high chair, extra bed) and dogs (in kennels) welcomed. Resident dog and cat; chickens and sheep. 1 mile from Kerry village. 5 bedrooms (plus 4 holiday cottages in outbuildings). Per room B&B £80–£120. Closed Christmas, New Year (except cottages).

SAUNDERSFOOT Pembrokeshire
Map 3:D2

ST BRIDES SPA HOTEL, St Brides Hill, SA69 9NH. Tel 01834 812 304, www.stbridesspahotel.com. 'We had a good stay.' High above Carmarthen Bay, this relaxed, modern hotel, on the Coastal Path, has 'very good views' of the harbour and up the coast. It is run by Andrew and Lindsey Evans. Light, breezy bedrooms have a chic maritime theme; most have a sea view and a balcony. 'Excellent' dinners are served in the Cliff restaurant or the less formal Gallery bar; for alfresco meals, a large decked terrace 'would have a "wow" factor on a summer's day'. There are 'good' spa facilities; B&B guests receive a complimentary 90-minute session in the thermal suite and hydro pool, and unlimited access to the fitness suite. Sister eateries, The Mermaid and The Marina, are down by the harbour. Bar, sitting area, restaurant. Lift. Spa (steam room, salt room, rock sauna, adventure shower, ice fountain, hydro pool with sea views). Gallery of contemporary Welsh art. Free Wi-Fi. Background music. Parking. Children welcomed (special menu). Functions. 34 bedrooms (1 suitable for disabled), plus six 2-bedroom apartments (pets allowed in some apartments). Per room B&B £160–£310; apartments from £250.

SKENFRITH Monmouthshire
Map 3:D4

THE BELL AT SKENFRITH, NP7 8UH. Tel 01600 750235, thebellatskenfrith. co.uk. In a lovely setting by a bridge over the River Monnow, this refurbished 17th-century coaching inn is 'very much recommended'. Sarah Hudson and Richard Ireton are the new owners. The revitalised bar areas have flagstone floors, solid beams and an inglenook fireplace; the sitting room has an open fire and comfortable sofas. Appealing bedrooms, named after brown trout fishing flies, have traditional Welsh wool blankets; hospitality trays include freshly ground coffee, fresh milk, traditional and herbal teas, and home-made biscuits. In the restaurant, chef Marc Montgomery bases his seasonal menus on the vegetables, fruit and herbs grown in the kitchen garden behind the hotel. Walkers are welcomed: seven routes across farmland and along river banks start and finish at the front door; maps are provided. Picnic hampers available. Sitting room, bar, restaurant. Function facilities. Free Wi-Fi. No background music. Large garden (member of the National Gardens Scheme) and meadow; terrace. Children (special menu; no under-8s in restaurant in evening) and dogs welcomed. Regular events (wine tastings, bridge evenings, etc); canoeing, fishing, golf and horseriding nearby. 11 bedrooms (1 duplex). Per room B&B from £110, D,B&B from £150.

CHANNEL ISLANDS

ST MARTIN Guernsey
Map 1: inset E5

BELLA LUCE HOTEL, La Fosse, GY4 6EB. Tel 01481 238764, www.bellalucehotel. com. Above Moulin Huet Bay, a spot favoured by Renoir in his paintings, the Wheadon family's beautifully restored manor house (Small Luxury Hotels of the World) sits in lush walled gardens. The interior is understated and elegant; calming bedrooms have magazines, bathrobes and slippers; some have a modern four-poster bed. Overlooking the courtyard garden, the award-winning restaurant has exposed stone walls, and candles and log fires at night; in summer, French windows open on to a sunny terrace for alfresco dining. Chef Sebastian Orzechowski's modern European dishes focus on local seafood, with herbs from the kitchen garden; 'uncomplicated' food is served in the intimate bar. Snug, bar, Bella Bistro restaurant, cellar lounge (tasting room; extensive wine list, cigars, whiskies, gin still). Free Wi-Fi. Background jazz. 3-acre garden; courtyard (alfresco dining). Outdoor swimming pool (heated in summer; loungers, sofas), spa. Civil wedding licence; function facilities. 2 miles to St Peter Port; rock beach 5 mins' walk. Victor Hugo's house is nearby. Trips to Herm and Sark can be arranged. Parking. Children welcomed (special menu). 23 bedrooms (2 on ground floor; some family rooms). Per room B&B £135–£240. Dinner from £25. Closed Jan, Feb.

ST PETER PORT Guernsey
Map 1: inset E5

LA COLLINETTE HOTEL, St Jacques, GY1 1SN. Tel 01481 710331, www. lacollinette.com. A short walk from the seafront and centre, this welcoming hotel has been run by the Chambers family for more than 50 years; it attracts many returning guests. Cyril Fortier is the much-loved manager. The white-painted house, decked with window boxes, has bright, modern rooms; most overlook the grounds, with distant views of Guernsey to the north. In the grounds, self-catering cottages and apartments have a terrace or balcony overlooking the gardens. Boats to Sark and Herm leave from the pretty harbour nearby. Lounge, bar, restaurant (brasserie menu; seafood and local produce); background music. Free Wi-Fi. DVD library. Conferences. 1-acre garden; heated outdoor swimming pool; gym; massages. Children welcomed (teddy bear gift; baby-listening, high chair, cots, extra bed; children's menu; children's pool; play area). 23 bedrooms (plus 15 self-catering cottages and apartments). Per person B&B from £50, D,B&B from £70.

25% DISCOUNT VOUCHERS

THE DUKE OF RICHMOND, Cambridge Park, GY1 1UY. Tel 01481 726221, www. dukeofrichmond.com. Overlooking Cambridge Park, this large, family-friendly hotel (part of the Red Carnation Hotel Collection) has fine views over the town to the neighbouring islands of Herm and Sark beyond; day trips can be arranged. Andrew Chantrell is the manager. Public rooms have been lavishly styled: the residents' lounge, decorated in a striking black-and-white theme, has antiques and an ornate brass fireplace; the glamorous Leopard bar and restaurant mix graphic stripes with animal-print fabrics. Elegant, air-conditioned bedrooms are equipped with bottled water and tea- and coffee-making facilities; the best rooms have a balcony with sea views. An evening newspaper is delivered at turn-down. Children are well provided for with

card and board games, a toy basket, DVDs, bathtime treats, robes and slippers; they may decorate their own cupcake with the chef. The heated outdoor swimming pool and the terrace have stunning views over Candie Gardens. Lounge, bar, restaurant; terrace. Free Wi-Fi. Background music. Room service. Swimming pool. Wedding/function facilities. Children, and dogs (in 2 rooms; not in restaurant) welcomed. 73 bedrooms (1 penthouse suite). Per room B&B £148–£408, D,B&B £183–£443.

IRELAND

ARDMORE Co. Waterford
Map 6:D5
THE CLIFF HOUSE, Middle Road. Tel 353 024 87 800, www.thecliffhousehotel. com. In glass, steel and slate, this modern luxury hotel (Relais & Châteaux) is in a dramatic position on a cliff above Ardmore Bay; there are uninterrupted views over the water from every bedroom. It is owned by Barry O'Callaghan, who also owns The Cliff Townhouse, Dublin (see Shortlist entry); Adriaan Bartels is the manager. Bright, contemporary bedrooms mix historic furnishings with an original work by an Irish artisan; the best have a private balcony or terrace from which guests can try to spot dolphins and Minke whales in the bay. In the House restaurant, chef Martijn Kajuiter has a Michelin star for his modern Irish cooking; the stylish bar has sandwiches, steaks and seafood dishes (alfresco dining in summer). Walks from the front door; rock fishing nearby (fishing equipment available to borrow); golf tee box in the garden, aiming for a

floating pontoon in the bay. Library, bar, restaurant (closed Sun, Mon, except bank holidays). Terrace. Private dining room. Lift. Spa (sauna, steam room; treatments, therapies); 15-metre indoor infinity pool; gym. Natural rock pool. Table tennis. Free Wi-Fi. Background music. Wedding facilities. Valet parking; 2 moorings for yachts. Children (welcome pack, playroom, children's menu) and dogs (heated kennels) welcomed. 39 bedrooms (2 suitable for disabled; plus self-catering cottage). Per room B&B €190–€280, D,B&B €330–€420. Closed Christmas.

BALLINTOY Co. Antrim
Map 6:A6

WHITEPARK HOUSE, 150 Whitepark Road, BT54 6NH. Tel 028 2073 1482, www.whiteparkhouse.com. 'The attention to detail and comfort is exemplary' at Bob and Siobhan Isles's B&B, in a crenellated 18th-century house above the spectacular sandy beach of Whitepark Bay. 'We were entertained royally.' The characterful house is decorated with art, artefacts and souvenirs from the owners' travels around the world. Tea and home-baked goodies are served every afternoon in the 'delightful' lounge. Bedrooms, with bathrobes and a hot-water bottle, have views of the lovely garden or the sea; bathrooms are large. Warm and welcoming, the hosts are happy to advise on restaurants and places to visit. Full Irish breakfasts (vegetarians catered for). Sitting room (peat fire), conservatory. 1-acre garden. Free Wi-Fi. No background music. Children over 10 welcomed. 2 miles W of town; 4 miles E of the Giant's Causeway. 4 bedrooms. Per room B&B £80–£120. Closed Christmas Day.

BALLYGALLY Co. Antrim
Map 6:B6

BALLYGALLY CASTLE, Coast Road, BT40 2QZ. Tel 028 2858 1066, www.hastingshotels.com/ballygally-castle. 'A surprisingly pleasant experience.' In 'an extremely scenic' area on the Causeway coastal route, this 17th-century castle (with later additions) is in 'well-kept' grounds overlooking the beach. The hotel is managed by Norman McBride for Hastings Hotels. Well-appointed bedrooms have an iPod dock and tea- and coffee-making facilities; deluxe rooms in the new wing have wide-reaching views over the bay to the Scottish coastline beyond. Characterful rooms in the tower are accessed by a stone spiral staircase; they have thick walls, sash windows and exposed wooden rafters. Modern bistro dishes are served in the Garden restaurant. An 'excellent' breakfast is taken in a 'pretty, well-lit' room with a view of the grounds. 'I was mightily impressed to find that you could have not only honey with your porridge but also a glug of Bushmills whiskey.' 2 lounges. Free Wi-Fi. 'Easy listening' background music. 1½-acre gardens. Children welcomed (charge for over-4s). 10 mins' drive from the Larne ferry terminal. Wedding/function facilities. 54 bedrooms (some suitable for disabled). Per room B&B from £110, D,B&B from £130.

BALLYVAUGHAN Co. Clare
Map 6:C4

GREGANS CASTLE HOTEL, Gragan East. Tel 00 353 65 707 7005, www.gregans.ie. 'Really lovely.' Simon Haden and Frederieke McMurray's 'magical' 18th-century country house stands in tranquil grounds with spectacular views across the Burren to Galway Bay. Public rooms have antiques, sofas and jugs of garden flowers; bedrooms, decorated with elegant fabrics and original artwork, have seats for admiring the views. Some rooms have direct access to the garden; four suites have a private sitting room. Chef David Hurley serves 'creative' modern Irish and European dishes; an early dinner for children is available by arrangement. Donkeys, ducks and a pony roam the extensive grounds. Drawing room, bar (background jazz, classical music), restaurant (closed Sun, Wed; dinner is served in the bar). Free Wi-Fi. 15-acre grounds: ornamental pool; croquet. No TV. Weddings. 5 km S of Ballyvaughan. Children (no under-5s in dining room at night) and dogs (in some bedrooms) welcomed. 21 bedrooms (7 on ground floor; 1 suitable for disabled). Per room B&B €225–€265, D,B&B €325–€380. Closed early Nov–mid-Feb.

BELFAST
Map 6:B6
THE OLD RECTORY, 148 Malone Road, BT9 5LH. Tel 028 9066 7882, www.anoldrectory.co.uk. Close to the centre and the university, Mary Callan's homely guest house is in a 19th-century rectory. A friendly place, it has many thoughtful touches: the drawing room has games, and books on Irish history, architecture and culture; comfortable bedrooms have books, magazines and biscuits. During the cooler months, guests are offered a complimentary hot whiskey in the evening. Award-winning breakfasts have lots of choice, including Irish smoked salmon, and porridge with cream, honey and Irish Mist liqueur; raspberry jam, whiskey marmalade, and soda and wheaten breads are all home

made. A small supper menu is available Mon–Fri. 1¾ miles to city centre. 10 mins' walk to Lagan Meadows (river walks). Drawing room. Garden. Free Wi-Fi. No background music. Parking. Children welcomed. 6 bedrooms (1 on ground floor). Per person B&B £46–£56. Credit cards not accepted. Closed mid-Jul–mid-Aug; Christmas, New Year.

RAVENHILL HOUSE, 690 Ravenhill Road, BT6 0BZ. Tel 028 9020 7444, www.ravenhillhouse.com. Within easy walking distance of shops, pubs, restaurants and a park, Olive and Roger Nicholson's welcoming B&B is in a restored Victorian house two miles from the centre. Guests are greeted with tea, coffee and biscuits beside an open fire in the sitting room, which is well stocked with local-interest books and maps; the Nicholsons share tips about the city. Bedrooms, decorated with stylish floral fabrics, have locally handcrafted furniture. Breakfasts include home-made marmalade and freshly baked Irish wheaten bread and sourdough; good vegetarian options. Sitting room, dining room; small garden. Free Wi-Fi. Occasional background radio; Radio 3 at breakfast. Street parking. Children welcomed (high chair, cot). 7 bedrooms (1 on ground floor). Per room B&B £60–£110. Closed Dec, Jan.

BUSHMILLS Co. Antrim
Map 6:A6
BUSHMILLS INN, 9 Dunluce Road, BT57 8QG. Tel 028 2073 3000, www.bushmillsinn.com. In a town at the heart of Northern Ireland's Causeway Coast, this higgledy-piggledy old coaching inn and adjoining mill house are hospitably run by Alan Dunlop, with friendly staff.

Alan Walls is the manager. Dating in part from the 17th century, it has a grand staircase, a 'secret' library, and a web of interconnecting snugs with peat fires, oil lamps and ancient wooden booths. Many of the spacious bedrooms have views over the River Bush; split-level suites have a large lounge and shower room downstairs, with a sleeping area and another bathroom above. Traditional Irish music is performed in the Gas bar, which is lit by the original gas lights; movies are screened on Thursday nights. In the restaurant overlooking the garden courtyard, chef Donna Thompson serves traditional Irish cuisine with a modern twist. Drawing room, restaurant, gallery, oak-beamed loft; patio; 2-acre garden. Lift. Free Wi-Fi. Background music. Conferences; 30-seat cinema; treatment room. Parking. Children welcomed (family rooms; cots). 2 miles from the Giant's Causeway. 41 bedrooms (some on ground floor; spacious ones in mill house, smaller ones in inn; some suitable for disabled). Per room B&B £128–£398. Dinner from £37.50. Closed for accommodation at Christmas.

CALLAN Co. Kilkenny
Map 6:D5

BALLAGHTOBIN COUNTRY HOUSE, Ballaghtobin. Tel 00 353 56 772 5227, www.ballaghtobin.com. Catherine and Mickey Gabbett's 18th-century ancestral home stands on a site where 14 generations of the Gabbett family have lived. In a remote situation, it is in informal gardens within a 500-acre farm producing cereals, blackcurrants and Christmas trees (wood chips power the boiler for heating and hot water). Country house-style bedrooms are decorated in soothing colours and furnished with paintings and antiques;

generous breakfasts are served at a large table in the dining room. Drawing room, dining room, study, conservatory. Free Wi-Fi. No background music. Tennis, croquet, clock golf. Children (50% reduction), and dogs welcomed. Parking. 4 km E of Callan; 30 mins' drive to Kilkenny. 3 bedrooms. Per person B&B €50. Credit cards not accepted. Closed Nov–Feb.

CASTLEBALDWIN Co. Sligo
Map 6:B5

CROMLEACH LODGE, Lough Arrow. Tel 00 353 71 916 5155, www.cromleach. com. Surrounded by 'beautiful' Sligo scenery, Moira and Christy Tighe's spa hotel has 'superb' views over Lough Arrow. Spacious, traditionally decorated bedrooms in the main house have loch views. More modern rooms, some with a private balcony, are in a purpose-built block accessed via enclosed walkways (some rooms are 'a considerable distance' from the public areas). Modern Irish dishes are served in Moira's restaurant, overlooking the lough and mountains; the bar has sandwiches and light meals. Keen walkers, the hosts are happy to advise on the best routes for varying abilities. Lounge, bar, restaurant; spa (sauna, steam room, outdoor hot tub; treatment rooms). Ramps. Free Wi-Fi (in public rooms). Background music. 30-acre grounds: forest walks, private access to Lough Arrow (fishing, boating, surfing), hill climbing. Barbecue area. Wedding/function facilities. Good walks from the front door; packed lunches available. Children and dogs welcomed (dog-grooming parlour). 4 km from Castlebaldwin. 30 bedrooms (1 suitable for disabled). Per room B&B from €65,

D,B&B from €130. Open May–Sept, 'mostly weekends' Oct–Apr.

COBH Co. Cork
Map 6:D5

KNOCKEVEN HOUSE, Rushbrooke. Tel 00 353 21 481 1778, www. knockevenhouse.com. Just outside the historic seaport town, Pam Mulhaire's B&B is in a double-fronted Victorian house in well-kept gardens; displays of magnolias, azaleas and camellias in season can be seen from the spacious bedrooms. The gracious hostess welcomes guests with hot drinks and delicious home-made scones in the comfortable drawing room. Richly furnished bedrooms have a high ceiling and large windows; bathrobes are provided. Generous breakfasts, with seasonal fruits, preserves and home-baked breads, are taken at a large mahogany table. Drawing room, dining room. 2-acre grounds. Free Wi-Fi. Background music. Children welcomed. 1 mile W of town; 3 mins' drive from Rushbrooke railway station. Titanic Trail and Museum, Cobh Heritage Centre, Lusitania Monument close by. 4 bedrooms. Per person B&B from €50. Closed Christmas.

DONEGAL Co. Donegal
Map 6:B5

HARVEY'S POINT, Lough Eske. Tel 00 353 74 972 2208, www.harveyspoint. com. On the shores of Lough Eske, this traditional hotel has been owned by the Gysling family since 1989. Spacious bedrooms have views of the surrounding landscape; lakeshore suites, accessed via a separate entrance, have their own terrace overlooking the water. Fresh milk, fruit and biscuits are delivered to all rooms daily. Finishing touches were being put to the newly refurbished lodge, on a hill behind the hotel, as the Guide went to press; with a patio and two lounges, it is destined for guests travelling in a large group. A turf fire burns in the cosy bar; in the restaurant overlooking the lake, Chris McMenamin, the chef, serves a four-course menu with amuse-bouche. Activity breaks (fishing, canoeing, golf, walks, archery) available. Lounge, drawing room, bar (turf fire), restaurant (closed Sun–Tues, Nov–Mar), ballroom (resident pianist; Irish/classical background music). Summertime cabaret dinners June–Oct. Free Wi-Fi. Beauty treatments; massage. Lift; ramps. Wedding/conference facilities. 20-acre grounds. Children (babysitting, early supper) and dogs (in some bedrooms) welcomed; stabling and grazing for horses. 4 miles from town. 64 bedrooms and suites (some suitable for disabled), plus The Lodge for group bookings. Per person B&B from €150, D,B&B from €190. 2-night min. stay at weekends. Set dinner €55.

DUBLIN
Map 6:C6

ARIEL HOUSE, 50–54 Lansdowne Road. Tel 00 353 1 668 5512, www. ariel-house.net. In the leafy Ballsbridge neighbourhood, the McKeown family's B&B occupies three refurbished Victorian town houses with many period features, such as ornate stained glass and the original bay windows. A 'light, spacious' lounge is a 'comfortable' place for afternoon tea. Bedrooms are divided between the main house and a modern wing; all have views of the garden. Breakfast, with home-made granola, and jam, cheese and sausages from local suppliers, is 'served with some flair'. Convenient for the Aviva

Stadium and Ballsbridge village. Drawing room, dining room; garden. Free Wi-Fi. Limited parking. Children welcomed. 37 bedrooms (some with a four-poster bed). Per room B&B from €130. Closed 19 Dec–8 Jan.

THE CLIFF TOWNHOUSE, 22 St Stephen's Green. Tel 00 353 1 638 3939, www.theclifftownhouse.com. Opposite St Stephen's Green, this handsome Georgian house was once home to one of the oldest private members' clubs in Ireland. Now a stylish town hotel and popular seafood and oyster restaurant, it is run by owner Barry O'Callaghan; Siobhan Ryan is the manager. The hotel is decorated in pleasing heritage shades, and furnished with a mix of antique and modern pieces. On the third and fourth floors, bedrooms have reproduction period prints and Donegal tweed blankets; some of the marble bathrooms have a quirky hip bath and vintage fittings. Most deluxe rooms overlook the green. In the elegant restaurant (high ceiling, leather booths), chef Sean Smith's menus specialise in hearty salads and local seafood, including Galway oysters and native lobster. Bar, restaurant (pre- and post-theatre service); private dining room. Free Wi-Fi. No background music. Wedding/function facilities. Reduced rates at St Stephen's Green car park, nearby. Children welcomed. 9 bedrooms. Per room B&B from €150. Dinner €28–€70. Closed Christmas Day.

THE MERRION, 21–24 Upper Merrion Street. Tel 353 1 603 0600, www.merrionhotel.com. 'Thoroughly recommended.' A conversion of four extensively restored Georgian town houses, this large luxury hotel is in an excellent location 'both for business and for sightseeing'. Peter MacCann is the manager. Spacious public rooms have chandeliers and peat fires; afternoon tea is served in the elegant drawing room. Gracious bedrooms and suites have armchairs, a desk and a fully stocked minibar; the best have views over the 18th-century classical gardens. Guests have a choice of places to eat: the stylish Restaurant Patrick Guilbaud has two Michelin stars for its innovative fine dining (four-course degustation menus, Tues–Fri); modern Irish dishes are served in the Cellar restaurant; informal gastropub meals are taken in the Cellar bar, formerly the building's 18th-century wine vaults. There are secluded places to sit in the lovely gardens; guests may dine alfresco in the summer. The hotel is home to Ireland's most important private collection of 19th- and 20th-century Irish and European art; a tour of the collection can be arranged with a guide from the National Gallery. Drawing room, 2 bars, 2 restaurants. Spa (steam room, treatment rooms, 16-metre indoor swimming pool); gym. ¾-acre grounds; garden terrace. Wedding/function facilities. Free Wi-Fi. No background music. Valet parking (€20 per night). Children welcomed (cot, extra bed; babysitting; junior room service menu). 142 rooms (some in garden wing; some suitable for disabled). Room only €187–€417; suite from €514. Breakfast €24–€29. Dinner (in Cellar restaurant) from €32.

WATERLOO HOUSE, 8–10 Waterloo Road. Tel 00 353 1 660 1888, www.waterloohouse.ie. Guests praise the 'helpful' service at Evelyn Corcoran's comfortable B&B, in a 'very central' location close to the city centre, parks and many public transport connections. Traditionally furnished bedrooms (some compact) have tea- and coffee-making facilities; those facing the garden are quietest. Served in the dining room or adjoining conservatory, breakfast has home-made traditional Irish soda bread, fresh fruit and a choice of cooked dishes, including a 'catch of the day'. Lounge (classical background music), dining room, conservatory; garden. Free Wi-Fi. Lift; ramp. Parking. Children welcomed. 19 bedrooms (some family rooms; some suitable for disabled). Per room B&B single €99–€109, double €139–€155.

DUNFANAGHY Co. Donegal
Map 6:A5

THE MILL, Figart. Tel 00 353 74 913 6985, www.themillrestaurant.com. On the outskirts of a small resort town along the Wild Atlantic Way, this converted 19th-century flax mill overlooking a 'lovely' lake is run as a friendly restaurant-with-rooms by Susan and Derek Alcorn. Simply furnished with antiques, the homely bedrooms are well equipped with tea- and coffee-making facilities, bottled water, wine and home-made oatmeal cookies. Dinner orders are taken in the conservatory overlooking the lake, or in the drawing room, which has an open fire on cool evenings. In the split-level restaurant, Derek Alcorn serves modern, seasonal menus with an emphasis on local seafood and shellfish. 'Excellent' breakfasts have smoked fish, award-winning sausages and home-made potato bread; vegetarian options are available. Drawing room, restaurant (dinner served 7 pm–9 pm,

Tues–Sun; popular with non-residents; booking advisable), conservatory. Free Wi-Fi. Background music. Garden. Children welcomed. ½ mile W of town. 6 bedrooms. Per person B&B €48–€60. Dinner €42.50. Closed Jan–mid-Mar.

GALWAY Co. Galway
Map 6:C5

THE G HOTEL, Wellpark. Tel 00 353 91 865200, www.theghotel.ie. On the edge of Lough Atalia, this glamorous modern hotel (part of the Edward Hotels group) is within easy reach of the city centre and the airport. Designed by Philip Treacy, it has dramatic light installations, mirrored walls, and vibrantly decorated public rooms filled with a mix of antique and contemporary furniture. Bedrooms, styled in calmer shades, overlook the city or the bamboo garden; some are roomy enough for a family. There are a number of eating options: the clubby restaurant has European-inspired dishes and Irish steaks; lighter menus and afternoon tea are taken in the lounges. Cocktail bar, 3 lounges, Gigi's restaurant; spa (indoor swimming pool, sauna, steam room, treatments); gym; bamboo Zen garden. Free Wi-Fi. Background music. Lift. Wedding/function facilities. Parking. Children welcomed (milk and cookies on arrival, DVD and games library; babysitting). 101 rooms (some suitable for disabled). Per room B&B €140–€430. Dinner €29.50–€48.

GLASHABEG Co. Kerry
Map 6:D4

GORMAN'S CLIFFTOP HOUSE. Tel 00 353 66 915 5162, www. gormans-clifftophouse.com. In a 'splendid location', Síle and Vincent

Gorman's welcoming guest house and restaurant are on the Dingle Way walking trail at the western edge of the peninsula, where their families have fished and farmed for seven generations. Comfortable public rooms have books and board games; on cool days, the 'friendly, helpful' hosts provide a pot of tea by an open turf fire. Spacious, modern bedrooms, each with a seating area, have stunning sea or mountain views; all are well equipped with books, a DVD player, and tea- and coffee-making facilities. The restaurant's huge picture windows have sunset views of Smerwick Harbour and out over the Atlantic Ocean. 'Very good' dinners, cooked by Vincent Gorman, use local produce, and organically grown vegetables and fruit from the garden and polytunnel. Breakfast has home-baked bread, organic compotes and yogurt, home-made muesli, granola and jams; a good variety of hot dishes. Lounge, library, restaurant (closed Sun; lighter meals available for staying guests). Free Wi-Fi. Classical and traditional Irish background music. 2-acre garden, bogland and cliff. Children welcomed. Resident dog, Molly. 12.5 km W of Dingle. 8 bedrooms (1 family room). Per room B&B €110–€150. Closed Nov–Feb. **25% DISCOUNT VOUCHERS**

GLASLOUGH Co. Monaghan
Map 6:B6

CASTLE LESLIE. Tel 00 353 47 88100, www.castleleslie.com. In 1,000 acres of rolling countryside, ancient woods and lakes, this 'excellent' luxury hotel remains in the hands of the Leslie family who founded the estate in the 1660s. It is managed by Brian Baldwin. Individually designed bedrooms are spread out between the castle, the lodge, and mews and cottages (available for self-catering) on the estate. Furnished in sumptuous country house style, castle rooms have antiques and old paintings; there is much interesting family history to explore. Near the main gate, the stone-built lodge has been sympathetically restored and extended to accommodate more modern bedrooms; it is the social hub of the estate, with a light, spacious restaurant, a traditional pub, nooks, crannies, books and board games. In Snaffles restaurant, chef Andrew Bradley's modern menus use much local produce. Breakfast has plenty of choice, including buttermilk pancakes, grilled Irish kippers, and a full Irish with black and white pudding. Drawing rooms, bar, breakfast room, restaurant; conservatory, billiard room, library, cinema. Free Wi-Fi. Background music in Lodge only. Spa (7 treatment rooms, relaxation area; outdoor hot tub). Wedding facilities. Equestrian centre; fishing, boating, kayaking, clay-pigeon shooting, falconry, walking trails, picnics; hot-air balloon rides. Children (cots; special menu; €40 per night charge) and dogs (in Old Stable Mews rooms, or overnight in stables in the Equestrian Centre) welcomed. 6 miles from Monaghan. 121 bedrooms (29 in the Lodge, some suitable for disabled; 11 in old stable mews; 12 in cottages with self-catering facilities). Per person B&B from €62, D,B&B from €97. Closed 24–27 Dec.

INIS MEÁIN Co. Galway
Map 6:C4

INIS MEÁIN RESTAURANT AND SUITES. Tel 00 353 86 826 6026, www.inismein. com. On the most remote of the three Aran Islands (a stronghold of Irish culture), this 'stunning' modern stone-and-glass building was designed to blend into the native terraced stone fields; there are panoramic views to Galway Bay and the mountains of Connemara. It is run as a restaurant-with-suites by chef/patron Ruairí de Blacam and his wife, Marie-Thérèse, who offer a 'gentle and warm' welcome. Based on a philosophy of elemental eating, Ruairí de Blacam's four-course menus use hyper-local ingredients (lobster and crab caught by island fishermen from traditional currachs; vegetables fertilised by island seaweed); cooked simply, each dish consists of just two elements, to let the natural flavours shine. Minimalist suites are decorated in muted colours, with wooden floors and furnishings designed by the owners; each has a large bed, a living space, vast floor-to-ceiling windows and an outdoor seating area. Guests are provided with packed lunches, maps and nature guides, bicycles, fishing rods, binoculars and swimming towels, all included in the rates. A breakfast box is delivered to the suite. 45-min. ferry from Ros a' Mhíl; 7-min. flight from Connemara airport. Restaurant/lounge (dinner served at 8 pm; closed Sun nights). 3-acre grounds. Free Wi-Fi. No background music. Children accepted, by arrangement. 5 suites. Per person B&B from €82, D,B&B from €130. 2-night min. stay. Closed Oct–Mar.

KANTURK Co. Cork
Map 6:D5
GLENLOHANE HOUSE. Tel 00 353 29 50014, www.glenlohane.com. Acres of landscaped gardens, meadows and fields surround this handsome 18th-century country house which has belonged to the Sharp Bolster family for seven generations. Desmond and Melanie Sharp Bolster and their son, Gordon, delight in sharing the interesting history of their home, which is filled with heirlooms and family memorabilia; guests are encouraged to enjoy the house, large walled garden and terraced lawns 'as if staying with friends'. Tastefully furnished bedrooms are spacious and light; the red-walled library has comfortable seating, and an open fire in the evenings. Three-course dinners (by arrangement) are taken with the family. Drawing room, library, dining room. 250-acre gardens and parkland (chickens, fantail pigeons, sheep, horses). Free Wi-Fi. No background music. 1½ miles E of town; plenty of pubs and restaurants. The Sharp Bolsters are a family of motorcycle enthusiasts; weeklong tours in classic cars and motorcycles and high-performance BMW motorcycles can be arranged. Resident cat and dogs. 3 bedrooms (plus 2-bedroom self-catering cottage nearby, suitable for disabled). Per person B&B €65. Dinner €36.

KENMARE Co. Kerry
Map 6:D4
BROOK LANE HOTEL. Tel 00 353 64 664 2077, www.brooklanehotel.com. An ideal base for exploring the Ring of Kerry and the Ring of Beara, this small hotel is in a pretty heritage town on the bay. Owners Una and Dermot Brennan and well-informed staff offer helpful suggestions on routes and places to visit. Bedrooms are well equipped, with an alarm clock, a yoga mat, bathrobes and slippers; a morning newspaper is provided. Tea, coffee and a cake of the day are served in the lobby. Modern Irish dishes, using

locally sourced ingredients, are served in the bistro; Nigel Higgins is chef. A sister restaurant, No. 35, is a 15-minute walk away. Extensive Irish breakfasts. Library, bar/restaurant; courtyard, small garden. Free Wi-Fi (in public areas). Background music. Lift. Wedding/conference facilities. Golf, walking, cycling. Parking. Children welcomed. 20 bedrooms (1 suitable for disabled), plus 2-bedroom apartment. Per room B&B €120–€260. Dinner €35. Closed Christmas.

SHEEN FALLS LODGE. Tel 00 353 64 6641600, www.sheenfallslodge.ie. Across the suspension bridge from the heritage town, this 17th-century fishing lodge stands in extensive grounds with woodlands and riverside walks, and spectacular views over Kenmare Bay, the McGuillicuddy Reeks and the Sheen waterfalls. It has had much investment and improvement since it was bought in 2013 by the Palladian Hotels group, whose chairman is Nigel Chapman; today, it is a luxury hotel (Relais & Châteaux) with newly refurbished bedrooms, a collection of thatched cottages and villas, and a well-regarded restaurant serving modern Irish menus. There are many public spaces in which to relax: the bar has an extensive list of Irish whiskeys; informal meals may be taken in the Restaurant Lounge and Sun Lounge; children are 'happily catered for'. On the Wild Atlantic Way. 2 lounges, cocktail bar, bar/bistro, The Falls restaurant, private dining room; terrace (alfresco dining). Spa (sauna, steam room, treatment room, beauty and holistic therapies); indoor heated pool. Wine cellar (tours by arrangement). Live piano and traditional Irish folk background music. Wedding/function facilities. Free Wi-Fi. 300-acre grounds (tennis, horse riding,

falconry, clay pigeon shooting; woodlands, riverside walks, 19th-century plantation); salmon and trout fishing on private stretch of river. Bicycles to borrow. Children, and dogs (in heated stables) welcomed. 66 rooms (1 suitable for disabled; 11 suites), plus 5 villas available for self catering. Per room B&B €170–€750. Dinner €49 or €65.

KILKENNY Co. Kilkenny
Map 6:D5
ROSQUIL HOUSE, Castlecomer Road. Tel 00 353 56 772 1419, www.rosquilhouse. com. Phil and Rhoda Nolan's 'pleasing' B&B is liked for its good-value bedrooms and praiseworthy breakfasts. The simply furnished rooms are equipped with a tea tray and thoughtful extras (hairdryer, iron, etc); the lounge has books and large sofas. Welcoming hosts, the Nolans readily recommend restaurants and places to visit. There is much choice at breakfast: granola, fruit compotes, organic yogurt, hams, local cheeses; bread, cakes and scones are all home made. A 20-minute walk from the 'interesting' town. Lounge, patio; small garden. Free Wi-Fi. No background music. Close to Kilkenny Golf Club. Children and dogs welcomed. Resident dog. 7 bedrooms (1 suitable for disabled), plus The Mews self-catering apartment. Per person B&B from €35.

KILLARNEY Co. Kerry
Map 6:D4
THE BREHON, Muckross Road. Tel 00 353 64 663 0700, www.thebrehon.com. Guests praise the 'fantastic attention to detail' at the O'Donahue family's large spa hotel next to Killarney national park. Modern bedrooms have tea- and coffee-making facilities, bottled water, bathrobes and slippers; room service is available all

day. In Danú restaurant, chef Chad Byrne serves traditional dishes with a modern twist; informal meals and snacks may be taken in the bar. Families are welcomed: young guests have access to the children's club at sister hotel The Gleneagle, next door; family-friendly facilities there include a large swimming pool, a pitch-and-putt course and a children's play centre. Lounge, bar, restaurant; private dining room; playroom. Spa (12-metre indoor Vitality pool, crystal steam room, herb sauna, tropical showers, ice fountain, kubel dusche, spa bath; fitness centre; Thai-style massages and treatments). Free Wi-Fi. Background music. Lift. Wedding/function facilities. ½ mile from town centre; INEC is close by. Parking. Children welcomed. 123 bedrooms (family suites). Per room B&B €99–€299. Dinner €41.

THE DUNLOE, Beaufort. Tel 00353 64 6644111, www.thedunloe.com. On an extensive private estate with gardens and farmland, this 'magical' luxury hotel is surrounded by stunning scenery overlooking the Gap of Dunloe; guests can explore the ruins of the 12th-century Dunloe Castle. It is managed by Jason Clifford, who 'simply thinks of everything'. Contemporary bedrooms have bathrobes, slippers, a sumptuous bathroom; most have a balcony or terrace with views over the gardens and surrounding countryside. Family rooms were refurbished in 2015. Children are made very welcome: their many activities and diversions include pony riding, indoor tennis, a playground and a games room; movie nights and a kids' club are organised in the summer. There is complimentary fishing on the River Laune; the kitchen will prepare and cook guests' catch for their dinner. 3 lounges, bar, Garden café, Oak restaurant; terrace. 64-acre grounds. Free Wi-Fi. Background music. 24-metre heated indoor pool; sauna, steam room; treatment rooms; gym; tennis courts. Wedding/function facilities. Children, and dogs (in some rooms; kennels available) welcomed. 15 mins' drive from town. 102 bedrooms (some interconnecting; 1 suitable for disabled). Per room B&B from €180, D,B&B €140–€165 per person. Closed early Oct–mid-Apr.

KINSALE Co. Cork
Map 6:D5
THE OLD PRESBYTERY, 43 Cork Street. Tel 00 353 21 477 2027, www.oldpres.com. On a quiet street in the centre of this historic port and fishing town, Philip and Noreen McEvoy's B&B is in a rambling, 200-year-old house that was once the residence of the parish priests. The home is packed with fascinating memorabilia; bedrooms have antiques and a brass or cast-iron bed. Some superior rooms have a balcony. Obliging hosts, the McEvoys provide complimentary hot drinks and snacks, and cheese and wine in the afternoon. Substantial breakfasts, using organic produce, are well cooked by Philip McEvoy, a professional chef; vegetarian options are available. Sitting room, dining room; patio. Free Wi-Fi. Classical/Irish background music. Parking. Children welcomed. 9 bedrooms (3 suites; 2 self-catering). Per room B&B €90–€180. Closed Nov–mid-Feb.

LAHINCH Co. Clare
Map 6:C4
MOY HOUSE. Tel 00 353 65 708 2800, www.moyhouse.com. In extensive grounds with mature woodland and a

river, this white-painted 19th-century country house has spectacular views over Lahinch Bay; guests have direct access to the stony beach. Caroline Enright is the manager. Bedrooms are individually decorated; a modern suite has a private conservatory, and an original well in the bathroom. Guests help themselves from the honesty bar in the drawing room; in the candlelit conservatory restaurant overlooking the ocean, chef Matthew Strefford serves daily-changing five-course menus using home-grown produce and locally landed seafood. Praiseworthy breakfasts include home-made bread and granola. Drawing room (open fire), library, restaurant (closed Sun, Mon in low season). Free Wi-Fi; computer provided. Drying room. 15-acre grounds. 2 miles outside Lahinch; golf course nearby. Children welcomed. No background music. 9 bedrooms. Per room B&B €117.50–€270. Dinner €60. Closed Nov–Mar.

LISNASKEA Co. Fermanagh
Map 6:B5

WATERMILL LODGE, Kilmore Quay South, BT92 0DT. Tel 028 6772 4369, www.watermillrestaurantfermanagh. com. Surrounded by 'fabulous scenery' on the shore of Lough Erne between Lisnaskea and Derrylin, Valerie Smyth and Pascal Brissaud run their restaurant-with-rooms in this pretty thatched house. In the smartly rustic restaurant, Pascal Brissaud, the chef, cooks with local produce, fish from the lough, and vegetables and herbs from the garden; his 'delicious' food has a Gallic slant. Comfortable bedrooms in an adjacent building have access to a little patio with a table and chairs; there are views of the lough from the doorstep. 'Superb' breakfasts have fresh croissants and baguettes. Traditional Irish Sunday roasts. Bar, restaurant (background music). Free Wi-Fi. Wedding facilities. Fishing breaks; lodge and boat can be arranged. Children (special menus) and small dogs welcomed. 8 bedrooms. Per room B&B single £59, double £76. Dinner £25.95.
25% DISCOUNT VOUCHERS

MAGHERAFELT Co. Londonderry
Map 6:B6

LAUREL VILLA TOWNHOUSE, 60 Church Street, BT45 6AW. Tel 028 7930 1459, www.laurel-villa.com. For fans of Seamus Heaney, Eugene and Gerardine Kielt's elegant B&B is a literary cornucopia. A rich collection of the poet's memorabilia is on display; Eugene Kielt, a Blue Badge guide, arranges poetry readings and tours of 'Heaney country'. The large garden has mature trees and a poetry trail; comfortable bedrooms are named after great Ulster poets. A breakfast of fresh fruit salad and an Ulster fry is served in the panelled dining room; Gerardine Kielt's afternoon teas, with home-baked cakes and scones, are highly praised. The owners hold a large collection of local genealogical and historical materials, and provide an ancestry-tracing service for guests who wish to trace their Northern Irish roots. 2 lounges, dining room; patio. In the centre of town. Free Wi-Fi. No background music. Children welcomed. Parking. 4 bedrooms. Per person B&B single £60–£70, double £40–£45. Closed Christmas, New Year.

MOYARD Co. Galway
Map 6:C4

CROCNARAW COUNTRY HOUSE. Tel 00 353 95 41068, www.crocnaraw.ie. In 20 acres of wooded gardens and meadows,

close to Ballinakill Bay in Connemara, Lucy Fretwell's genteel Georgian guest house is filled with fresh flowers and plenty of character. Traditionally furnished bedrooms are 'full of light'; one bathroom has an old-fashioned claw-footed bath. 'A terrific hostess', Lucy Fretwell serves afternoon tea with home-made scones and strawberry jam by a peat fire in the drawing room. Generous breakfasts include home-made Irish bread, and produce from the kitchen garden and orchard. Fully licensed. Private parties with a chef can be arranged. Fishing, angling, pony trekking, golf nearby. Dining room, drawing room, snug; gardens (donkeys), orchard. Free Wi-Fi. No background music. Children (over 6 months) welcomed. 2 miles from Letterfrack. 4 bedrooms. Per person B&B €55. Closed Nov–mid-May.
25% DISCOUNT VOUCHERS

NEWPORT Co. Mayo
Map 6:B4
NEWPORT HOUSE. Tel 00 353 98 41222, www.newporthouse.ie. Overlooking the estuary, this grand Georgian country house is a magnet for fisherfolk, who come to cast their rod on the Newport river. It is owned by Kieran Thompson; Catherine Flynn is the 'chatty and helpful' manager. Traditionally decorated public rooms are filled with intricate mouldings, oil paintings, bronzes and statuary; the high-ceilinged drawing rooms have bookcases, 'lived-in' sofas and an open fire. In the dining room overlooking the gardens and the river, John Gavin's 'meticulously presented' six-course menus include produce from the fishery, garden and farm, home-smoked salmon and 'delicious' home-baked bread. Sitting

room, bar, dining room, restaurant, billiard/TV room, table tennis room. 15-acre grounds; walled garden. Free Wi-Fi (in public areas and some bedrooms). No background music. Children, and dogs (in courtyard bedrooms) welcomed. In a village 7 miles N of Westport. 16 bedrooms (5 in courtyard; 2 on ground floor). Per person B&B €105–€152, D,B&B €170–€217. Closed Nov–late Mar; Christmas, New Year.
25% DISCOUNT VOUCHERS

NEWTOWNARDS Co. Down
Map 6:B6
BEECH HILL COUNTRY HOUSE, 23 Ballymoney Road, BT23 4TG. Tel 028 9042 5892, www.beech-hill.net. In a rural setting close to Belfast, Victoria Brann's Georgian-style house stands in beautiful 15-acre grounds, with a large pond, waterfalls and a working water wheel. It is ideally placed for Belfast City Airport and the ferries. The stunning entrance hall, painted a vivid red, has a chandelier and fresh flowers; elsewhere, the B&B is imaginatively decorated with interesting antiques and period pieces. Bedrooms are spacious, and have panoramic views over the North Down countryside. Extensive breakfasts use locally sourced produce. Drawing room, dining room, conservatory. Free Wi-Fi. No background music. Dogs welcomed. Parking. 4 miles from town. 3 bedrooms (all on ground floor; plus The Colonel's Lodge, available for self-catering). Per person B&B £60.

RAMELTON Co. Donegal
Map 6:B5
FREWIN, Rectory Road. Tel 00 353 74 915 1246, www.frewinhouse.com. Regina and Thomas Coyle's restored Victorian rectory stands in mature

wooded grounds on the outskirts of a historic Georgian port. 'Charming' hosts, they greet B&B guests with afternoon tea, served by a big open fire in the cosy library. Decorated 'with flair', the family home has stained-glass windows, an elegant staircase and antiques; country house-style bedrooms are spacious (with a compact bathroom). Taken communally, breakfast is praised; candlelit dinners are served, by arrangement. Sitting room, library, dining room; 2-acre garden. Free Wi-Fi. No background music. Children welcomed. 4 bedrooms (plus 1-bedroom cottage in the grounds). Per person B&B €60–€80. Dinner €45–€50. Closed Dec–Feb.

RATHNEW Co. Wicklow
Map 6:C6

HUNTER'S HOTEL, Newrath Bridge. Tel 00 353 404 40106, www.hunters.ie. In large grounds on the banks of the River Vartry, this former coaching inn is said to be the oldest remaining inn in Ireland; it retains all the charms of a bygone age. Traditionally decorated, it has been in the same family for five generations; today, brothers Richard and Tom Gelletlie are at the helm. Bedrooms have antiques, prints and creaking floorboards; many overlook the beautiful gardens. In the half-panelled dining room, Martin Barry, the chef, serves set lunch and dinner menus using freshly picked garden produce. Afternoon tea and drinks may be taken in the garden in fine weather. Lounge, bar, restaurant; conference room; garden. Free Wi-Fi. No background music. Children, and dogs (by arrangement) welcomed. Golf, tennis, riding, sea, sandy beach, fishing nearby. 16 bedrooms (1 on ground floor). Per

person B&B from €65, D,B&B from €95. Closed Christmas.

RECESS Co. Galway
Map 6:C4

LOUGH INAGH LODGE, Inagh Valley. Tel 00 353 95 34706, www.loughinagh lodgehotel.ie. In a 'spectacular' position on the shores of Lough Inagh, this 'lovely, peaceful' 19th-century fishing lodge has been owned by the O'Connor family since 1989. Dominic O'Morain is the long-serving manager. Morning coffee and afternoon tea are taken in public rooms filled with antiques, old photographs and interesting knick-knacks; open log fires burn in cool weather. Traditionally furnished, the spacious bedrooms have views over the water and the surrounding mountains. In the dining room, chef Julie Worley's country menus specialise in seafood and wild game (local suppliers are prioritised); a bar menu is also available. Good walks, fishing. Sitting room, bar, library, dining room. Free Wi-Fi. No background music. 10-acre grounds. Wedding facilities. Children and dogs welcomed. 13 bedrooms (4 on ground floor). Per room B&B from €169, D,B&B from €269. Set menus €44. Closed Christmas–Feb.

STRANGFORD Co. Down
Map 6:B6

THE CUAN, 6–10 The Square, BT30 7ND. Tel 028 4488 1222, www. thecuan.com. Personable hosts Peter and Caroline McErlean have run their guest house on the main square of this conservation village on the shores of Strangford Lough for 25 years. The 200-year-old inn has comfortable, simply furnished bedrooms and a popular local pub; the restaurant specialises in traditional roasts and locally sourced seafood, including langoustines freshly caught from the lough. 2 lounges, bar, restaurant (traditional background music). Wedding/function facilities. Free Wi-Fi. Live music events in the summer. Children welcomed. 9 bedrooms (1 suitable for disabled), plus 1 self-catering cottage. Per person B&B £42.50–£65, D,B&B £58–£80.

THOMASTOWN Co. Kilkenny
Map 6:D5

BALLYDUFF HOUSE. Tel 00 353 56 775 8488, www.ballyduffhouse.ie. In a 'fabulous situation' amid farmland and gardens on the banks of the River Nore, thoughtful host Brede Thomas runs her B&B with 'real style and friendliness'. The Georgian house has oil paintings, fresh flowers, a book-lined library, and open fires in the public rooms. Pretty, country-style bedrooms are furnished with antiques. 'Delicious' full Irish breakfasts are taken in the elegant dining room overlooking the river. Drawing room, library, dining room. Free Wi-Fi. No background music. Fishing, canoeing. 1 hour from Dublin. Children welcomed; pets allowed by arrangement. 6 bedrooms. Per person B&B €50.

WATERFORD Co. Waterford
Map 6:D5

FOXMOUNT COUNTRY HOUSE, Passage East Road. Tel 00 353 51 874308, www. foxmountcountryhouse.com. There are family photographs, log fires and a warm, welcoming ambience at Margaret and David Kent's B&B, a 17th-century house standing amid lush, well-kept gardens on a working dairy farm. Homely, traditionally furnished bedrooms each have a private bathroom; a spacious room is suitable for a family. Tea and home-made scones are taken by an open fire in the drawing room; guests are welcome to bring their own wine and aperitifs. Breakfast is praised: home-baked bread, eggs from the farm, compotes and preserves made from home-grown fruit. Dining room, drawing room. 4-acre grounds. Free Wi-Fi. No background music. Children welcomed; dogs stay in kennels in the grounds. 2 miles S of the city. 4 bedrooms. Per person B&B €50–€60. Closed mid-Sept–mid-Mar.

WATERVILLE Co. Kerry
Map 6:D4

BUTLER ARMS. Tel 00 353 66 947 4144, www.butlerarms.com. Overlooking the Atlantic Ocean, this 'friendly' hotel is in a little village on the Wild Atlantic Way. Owned by the Huggard family since 1915, 'it is a well-run place; the management are highly visible at all times'. 'Straightforward' bedrooms are 'simple, clean and unfussy'; most have views towards Ballinskelligs Bay. 'Excellent' fish and seafood and locally sourced meat are served in the restaurant; light meals and sharing platters are taken in the 'lively' Fishermen's Bar, popular with locals. Irish breakfasts. Good walks; bicycles for hire; fishing, shooting, horse riding and surfing can be arranged. Golf nearby. Lounge, bar, restaurant; garden. Free Wi-Fi. Background music. Wedding/function facilities. Parking. Children (family rooms) and dogs welcomed. 36 bedrooms. Per person B&B €60–€90. Closed Nov–Mar.
25% DISCOUNT VOUCHERS

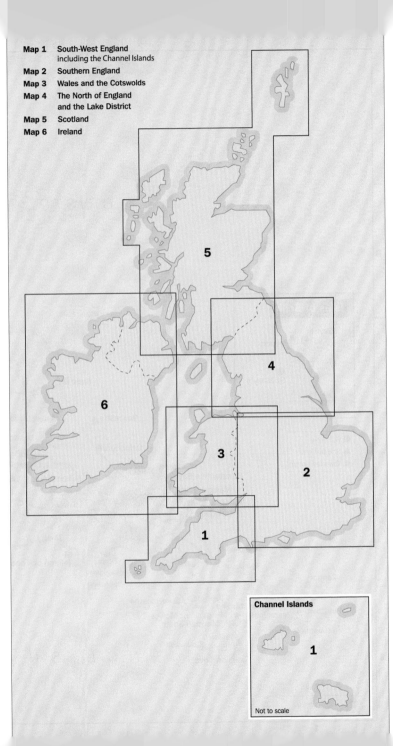

Map 1 South-West England
        including the Channel Islands
Map 2 Southern England
Map 3 Wales and the Cotswolds
Map 4 The North of England
        and the Lake District
Map 5 Scotland
Map 6 Ireland

Channel Islands

Not to scale

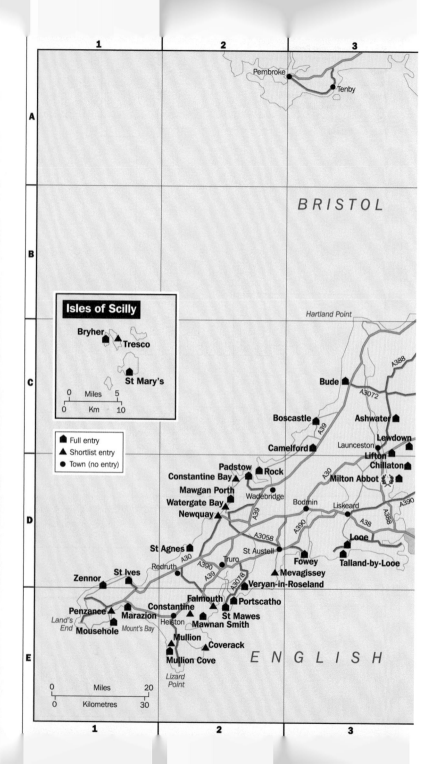

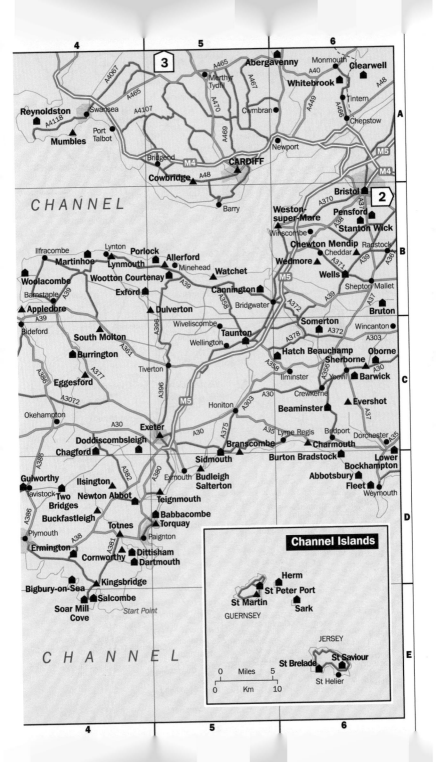

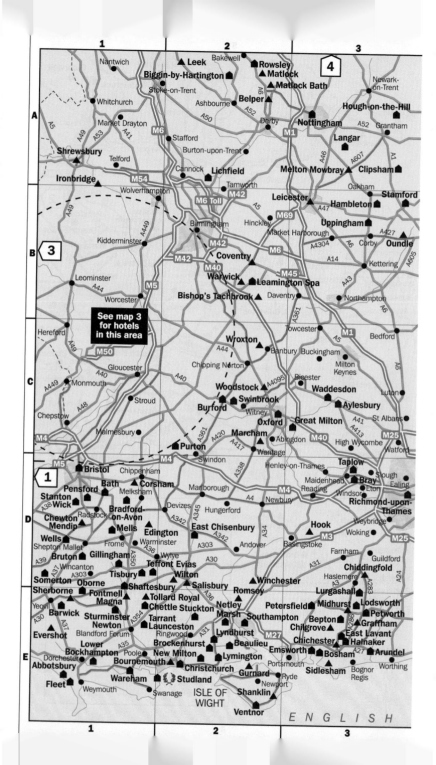

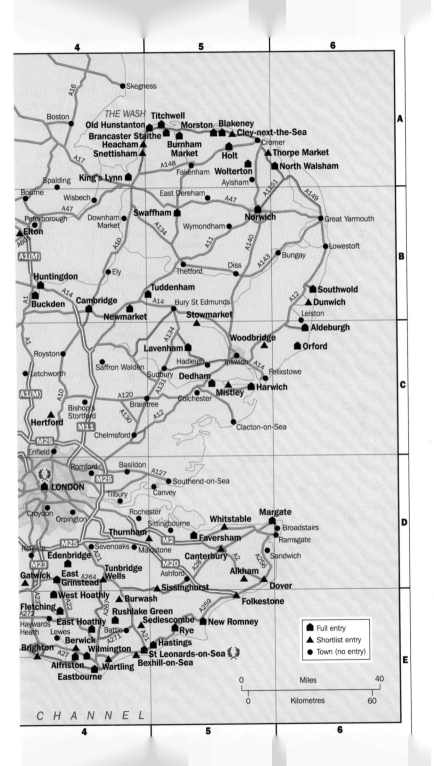

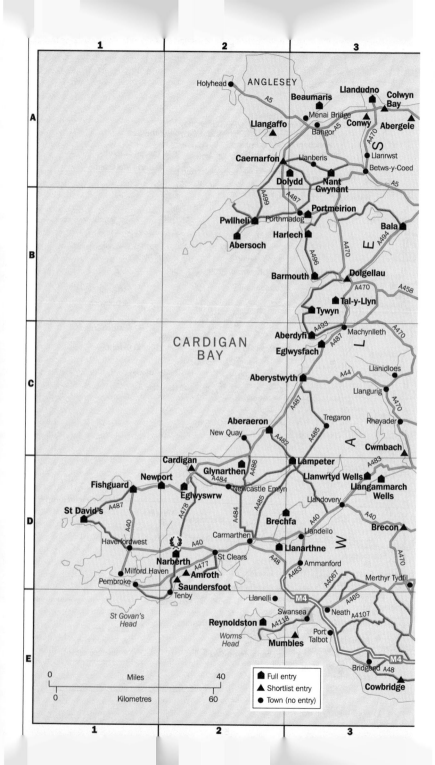

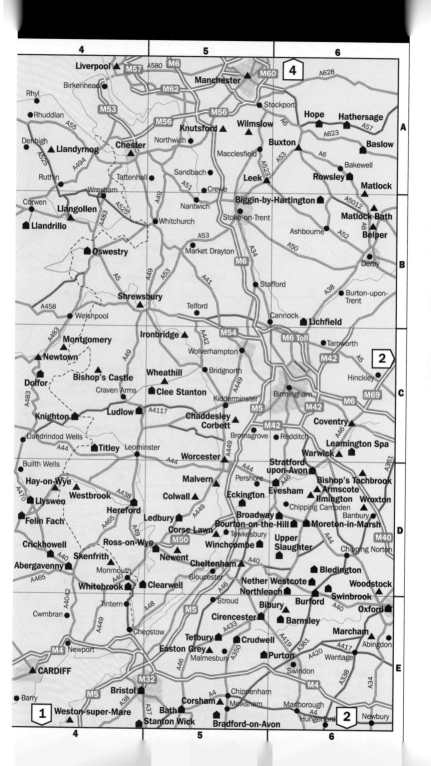

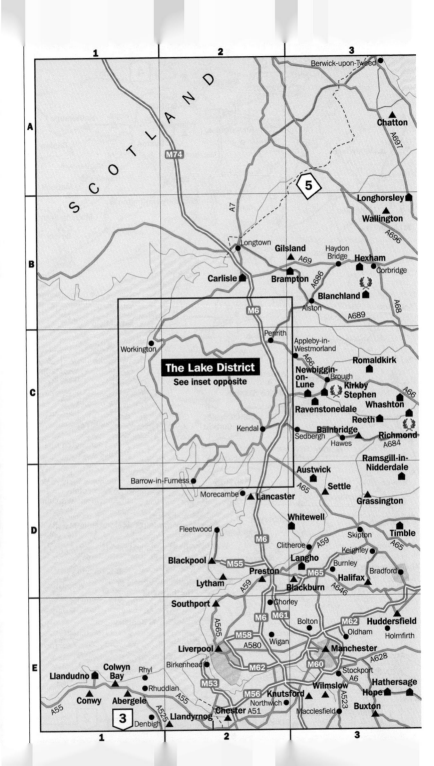

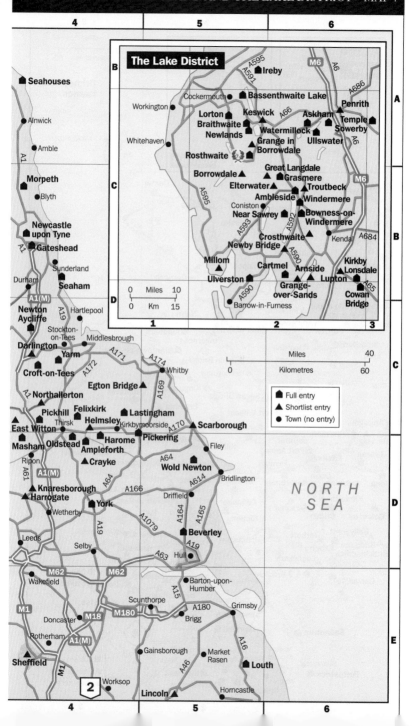

The Lake District

Ireby
Cockermouth
Bassenthwaite Lake
Workington
Penrith
Lorton
Keswick
Askham
Temple
Sowerby
Braithwaite
Watermillock
Newlands
Ullswater
Whitehaven
Grange in
Borrowdale
Rosthwaite
Great Langdale
Borrowdale
Grasmere
Elterwater
Troutbeck
Ambleside
Windermere
Coniston
Bowness-on-
Near Sawrey
Windermere
Crosthwaite
Newby Bridge
Kendal
Millom
Cartmel
Arnside
Kirkby
Lonsdale
Ulverston
Grange-
Lupton
over-Sands
Cowan
Bridge
Barrow-in-Furness

0 Miles 10
0 Km 15

Seahouses
Alnwick
Amble
Morpeth
Blyth
Newcastle
upon Tyne
Gateshead
Sunderland
Durham
Seaham
Newton
Hartlepool
Aycliffe
Stockton-
on-Tees
Darlington
Middlesbrough
Yarm
Whitby
Croft-on-Tees
Egton Bridge
Northallerton
Pickhill
Felixkirk
Lastingham
Helmsley
Scarborough
Thirsk
Kirkbymoorside
East Witton
Harome
Pickering
Masham
Oldstead
Filey
Ripon
Ampleforth
Crayke
Wold Newton
Bridlington
Knaresborough
Driffield
Harrogate
York
Wetherby
Beverley
Leeds
Selby
Hull
Wakefield
Barton-upon-
Humber
Scunthorpe
Grimsby
M1
Doncaster
Brigg
Rotherham
Sheffield
Gainsborough
Market
Rasen
Louth
Worksop
Lincoln
Horncastle

Miles 40
0
Kilometres 60

■ Full entry
▲ Shortlist entry
● Town (no entry)

NORTH
SEA

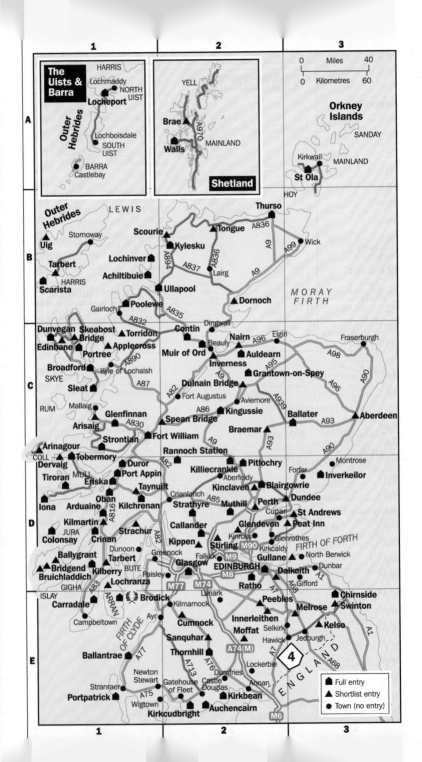

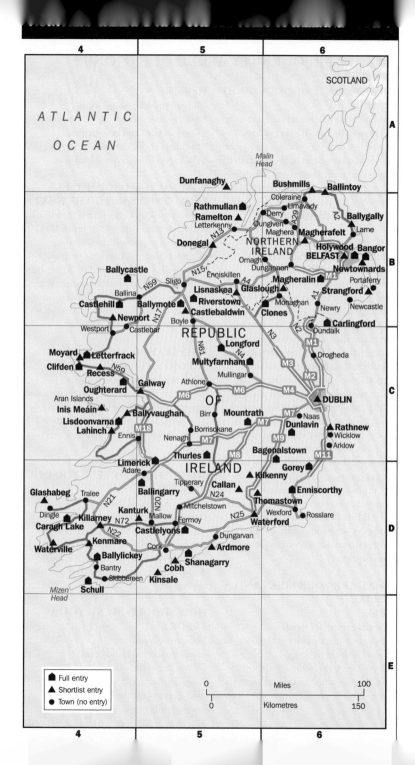

FREQUENTLY ASKED QUESTIONS

HOW DO YOU CHOOSE A GOOD HOTEL?

The hotels we like are relaxed, unstuffy and personally run. We do not have a specific template: our choices vary greatly in style and size. Most of the hotels in the Guide are family owned and family run. These are places where the needs and comfort of the guest are put ahead of the convenience of the management.

YOU ARE A HOTEL GUIDE – WHY DO YOU INCLUDE SO MANY PUBS AND B&BS?

Attitudes and expectations have changed considerably since the Guide was founded in the 1970s. Today's guests expect more informality, less deference. There has been a noticeable rise in the standards of food and accommodation in pubs and restaurants. This is demonstrated by the number of such places suggested to us by our readers. While pubs may have a more relaxed attitude than some traditional hotels, we ensure that only those that maintain high standards of service are included in our selections. The best B&Bs have always combined a high standard of accommodation with excellent value for money. Expect the bedrooms in a pub or B&B listed in the Guide to be well equipped, with thoughtful extras. B&B owners invariably know how to serve a good breakfast.

WHAT ARE YOUR LIKES AND DISLIKES?

We like

* Flexible times for meals.
* Two decent armchairs in the bedroom.
* Good bedside lighting.
* Proper hangers in the wardrobe.
* Fresh milk with the tea tray in the room.

We dislike

* Intrusive background music.
* Stuffy dress codes.
* Bossy notices and house rules.
* Hidden service charges.
* Packaged fruit juices at breakfast.

WHY DO YOU DROP HOTELS FROM ONE YEAR TO THE NEXT?

Readers are quick to tell us if they think standards have slipped at a hotel. If the evidence is overwhelming, we drop the hotel from the Guide or perhaps downgrade it to the Shortlist. Sometimes we send inspectors just to be sure. When a hotel is sold, we look for reports since the new owners took over, otherwise we inspect or omit it.

WHY DO YOU ASK FOR 'MORE REPORTS, PLEASE'?

When we have not heard about a hotel for several years, we ask readers for more reports. Sometimes readers returning to a favourite hotel may not send a fresh report. Readers often respond to our request.

WHAT SHOULD I TELL YOU IN A REPORT?

How you enjoyed your stay. We welcome reports of any length. We want to know what you think about the welcome, the service, the building and the facilities. Even a short report can tell us a great deal about the owners, the staff and the atmosphere.

HOW SHOULD I SEND YOU A REPORT?

You can email us at editor@goodhotelguide.com. Or you can write to us at the address given on the report form opposite, or send a report via the GHG's website: www.goodhotelguide.com.

Please send your reports to:

The Good Hotel Guide, Freepost PAM 2931, London W11 4BR

NOTE: No stamps needed in the UK.

Letters/report forms posted outside the UK should be addressed to:

The Good Hotel Guide, 50 Addison Avenue, London W11 4QP, England, and stamped normally.

Unless asked not to, we assume that we may publish your name. If you would like more report forms please tick ☐ Alternatively, you can either photostat this form or submit a review on our website: www.goodhotelguide.com

NAME OF HOTEL: _____

ADDRESS: _____

_____

Date of most recent visit: _____ Duration of stay: _____

☐ New recommendation ☐ Comment on existing entry

Report:

I am not connected directly or indirectly with the management or proprietors

Signed: _____

Name: (CAPITALS PLEASE) _____

Address: _____

_____

Email address: _____

INDEX OF HOTELS BY COUNTY
(S) indicates a Shortlist entry

ALPHABETICAL LIST OF HOTELS
(S) indicates a Shortlist entry